The
WESTERN EXPERIENCE
VOLUME I
To 1715

FOURTH EDITION

PHYSIOGRAPHY OF EUROPE

▨ Areas Below Sea Level

0   100   200   300   400 Miles

NORWEGIAN SEA

ICELAND

SCANDINAVIAN PENINSULA

KIOLEN MOUNTAINS

GULF OF BOTHNIA

FINNISH LAKE REGION

SHETLAND I.

ORKNEY I.

HEBRIDES

Oslo

Dal R.

ÅLAND I.

Helsinki

GULF OF FINLAND

L. Peipus

ATLANTIC OCEAN

BRITISH ISLES

GRAMPIANS

SCOTTISH LOWLANDS

Edinburgh

NORTH SEA

Skagerrak

Kattegat

L. Vänern

L. Vättern

Stockholm

GOTLAND I.

ÖLAND

BALTIC SEA

Riga

Dvina R.

JUTLAND PENINSULA

Copenhagen

IRELAND

IRISH CENTRAL PLAIN

Dublin

IRISH SEA

PENNINE CHAIN

THE WASH

HELIGOLAND

FRISIAN I.

Gdansk (Danzig)

Masurian Lakes

Niemen R.

St. George's Channel

MIDLAND PLAIN

Amsterdam

IJsselmeer

Elbe R.

NORTH GERMAN PLAIN

Berlin

Warta R.

Warsaw

Vistula R.

Bug R.

Bristol Channel

Thames R.

London

Maas R.

Rhine R.

Weser R.

Neisse R.

Oder R.

PR MAR

SCILLY I.

Strait of Dover

Schuldt R.

HARZ MTS.

ERZ MTS.

SUDETEN MTS.

LAND'S END

ENGLISH CHANNEL

CHANNEL I.

ARDENNES

Main R.

Prague

BOHEMIAN PLAIN

USHANT I.

BRITTANY PENINSULA

Paris

Marne R.

Meuse R.

Moselle R.

VOSGES MTS.

BLACK FOREST

Danube R.

BOHEMIAN FOREST

CAR

Seine R.

Loire R.

Inn R.

Vienna

BAY OF BISCAY

Vienne R.

Saône R.

JURA MTS.

Constance

Budapest

L. Balaton

Tisza R.

Drave R.

PLAIN OF HUNGARY

TRANSYLVANIA

CAPE FINISTERRE

Bordeaux

PLAIN OF FRANCE

Garonne R.

MASSIF CENTRAL

Lyons

Mt. Blanc

Geneva

SAVOY

Trieste

ISTRIA

Save R.

Belgrade

IRON GATE PLAI WALL

CANTABRIAN MTS.

PYRENEES

PO R.

PLAIN OF LOMBARDY

DINARIC ALPS

DALMATIAN I.

Sofia

IBERIAN PENINSULA

Douro R.

SPANISH

GUADARRAMA

Madrid

Ebro R.

LIGURIAN SEA

Arno R.

APENNINES

ADRIATIC SEA

BALKAN PENINSULA

Mt. Olympus

Lisbon

Tagus R.

PLATEAU

CORSICA

ELBA

Rome

Tiber R.

ITALIAN PENINSULA

Mt. Vesuvius

CORFU

PINDUS

Guadiana R.

SIERRA MORENA

Guadalquivir R.

BALEARIC I.

MINORCA

MAJORCA

SARDINIA

TYRRHENIAN SEA

IONIAN I.

Athens

SIERRA NEVADA

IVIZA

MOREAN PENINSULA

CAPE TRAFALGAR

Strait of Gibraltar

Gibraltar

Mt. Etna

SICILY

Strait of Messina

IONIAN SEA

Algiers

Tunis

PANTELLERIA

Fez

LITTLE ATLAS MOUNTAINS

MALTA

MEDITERRANEAN SEA

ATLAS MOUNTAINS

SAHARAN ATLAS MOUNTAINS

GREAT ATLAS MOUNTAINS

Tripoli

GULF OF SIDRA

LIBY

ALGERIAN SAHARA

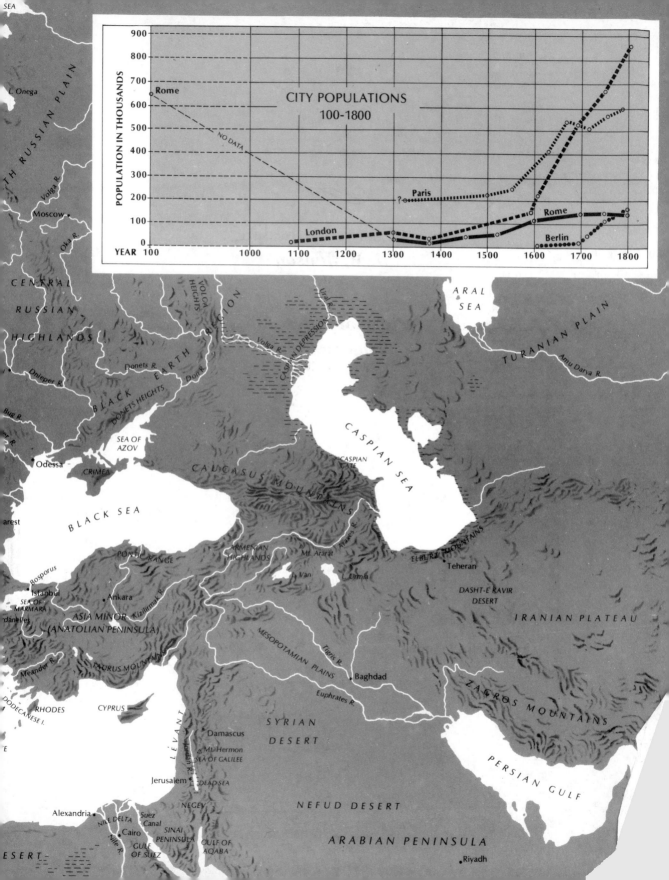

CITY POPULATIONS
100-1800

POPULATION IN THOUSANDS

Rome

NO DATA

Paris

London

Rome

Berlin

YEAR 100 1000 1100 1200 1300 1400 1500 1600 1700 1800

Art Essays by the late
H. W. Janson

Advisory Editor:
Eugene Rice
Columbia University

The
WESTERN EXPERIENCE

VOLUME I
To 1715

Mortimer Chambers
University of California, Los Angeles

Raymond Grew
University of Michigan

David Herlihy
Brown University

Theodore K. Rabb
Princeton University

Isser Woloch
Columbia University

FOURTH EDITION

Alfred A. Knopf   New York

THIS IS A BORZOI BOOK
PUBLISHED BY ALFRED A. KNOPF, INC.

Fourth Edition
987654321

Library of Congress Cataloging-in-Publication Data

The Western experience.

    Includes bibliographies and index.
    Contents: vol. 1. To 1715—vol. 2. Since 1600.
    1. Civilization—History. 2. Civilization,
Occidental—History. I. Chambers, Mortimer.
II. Rice, Eugene F.
CB59.W38 1987   909   86–27629
ISBN 0-394-36432-5 (v. 1)
ISBN 0-394-36434-1 (v. 2)

Cover Illustration: Roman city, Dougga, Tunisia. Mark
Antman/The Image Works.

Maps were executed by Jean Tremblay and Vantage Art,
Inc.
Map consultant D. W. Meinig

Manufactured in the United States of America

Introduction

Everyone uses history, and all of us use it in many ways. We use it to define who we are and to connect our personal experience with the history of the groups we belong to and with the history of a particular region, nation, and culture. Both individually and collectively we use the past to explain our hopes and ambitions and to justify our fears and conflicts. The Charter of the United Nations, like the American Declaration of Independence, is based on a view of history. When workers strike or armies march, they cite the lessons of their history. Because history is so important to us psychologically and intellectually, historical understanding is always shifting and often controversial. Indeed, the process of historical understanding is in itself circular: We are shaped by values, interests, and customs that (like our churches, universities, and political parties) have been formed by past experience. At the same time, the way we look at the past and what we see there—the questions we ask and the problems we pose—arise out of current concerns. Today we are likely to ask what industrialization did to the environment; in the 1950s scholars more often asked about the conditions that led to economic growth; a generation earlier the central question was how workers had gained a larger share of industrial wealth. Conservatives were more likely to study industrialization's effects on community and values, liberals to explore its relation to political freedom and education. Similarly, whether the undying interest in ancient Rome focused on civic virtue in the Republic, on Roman law, on the strength of the Roman Empire, or on its decline, the interest usually reflected some pressing issues of the historian's own era.

The circularity helps to keep the study of history alive, stimulating new interest and fresh research. We, who have been formed by the past, ask of history questions from our own time in order to learn more about both past and present. Some questions must be asked repeatedly, some issues arise again and again; but much of this knowledge is cumulative, for while asking new questions, historians integrate the answers learned from previous studies, and historical knowledge grows. History is not merely a subjective exercise in which all opinions are equally valid. No matter what motivated a particular historical question, the answer to it stands until overturned by better evidence. We now know more about the past than ever before and understand it as the historical figures whom we study could not. Unlike them, we know how their history came out; we can apply methods they did not have, and often we have evidence they never saw. This knowledge and the ways of interpreting it are the collective achievement of thousands of historians.

We also use history for pleasure—as a cultivated entertainment. The biographies of great men and women, dramatic accounts of important events, colorful tales of earlier times can be fascinating in themselves; and in enjoying them we share a pleasure felt by those who lived before us and by thousands of our contemporaries, thereby rooting ourselves more deeply in our common culture. In general the deeper our understanding of an historical era the richer our response to its art and thought is likely to be. That is not the least of the reasons for studying history. The historically well-educated person is like a privileged tourist, who can turn from the inspiring prospect of a great cathedral to the bustle of a simple village market or from the organization of a city to a single painting, able to see in each the achievements of particular eras, the expression of specific social and political arrangements, and the formation of a tradition still alive in our own time.

We also use history to discover about human behavior by discovering its variety, its similarities, and its limitations in different times and circumstances. In what kind of God or gods did people believe? What customs and institutions sustained those beliefs? How did people obtain food and protect human life? What tasks in each society were assigned to men and to women, to young and old, rich and poor? Did formal beliefs, economic activities, established institutions, and social classes sustain each other or did they conflict? Can we estimate for any particular moment the countervailing pressures for change and for continuity? These types of questions concern all the social sciences, and all of them make use of historical examples in seeking answers. Historians, however, tend to emphasize how in a specific place at a particular moment the various aspects of social life were interrelated.

Readers of the fourth edition of *The Western Experience* will find themselves using this book in all these ways: to learn history as a subject in itself, to enrich their culture, and to test their ideas of social behavior; but they will also want to bear in mind how the authors selected what history to include. The very concept of a Western civilization is itself the result of history. The Greeks gave the names east and west to those points on the horizon where the sun rises and sets. Because the Persian Empire and India lay to their east, the Greeks were the first "westerners," their continent, Europe, was considered the west and Asia the east. The distinction between Western civilization and others—ethnocentric, often arbitrary, and frequently exaggerated—continued even as that civilization changed and expanded with the Roman Empire, Christianity, and the European conquest of the New World. The view that this is one civilization with America tied more closely to ancient Greece than Greece is to Egypt or Spain to Islam can be easily challenged in every respect save the conscious tradition that has shaped our culture.

The Western Experience, then, honors that tradition and gives primary attention to a small part of the world. That focus provides the opportunity to observe the processes of change and continuity over a long period of time. It includes important examples of city and of rural life; of empires and monarchies and republics; of life before and after industrialization; of societies in which labor was organized through markets, serfdom, and slavery; of cultures little concerned with science and of ones that used changing scientific knowledge; of non-Christian religions and of all the major forms of Christianity in action. All these types can be found in many other civilizations, but in a single civilization they can be seen evolving, influencing, and borrowing from each other.

Far more is known about Western history than can be put into a single book. Each paragraph is therefore, in some sense, a synthesis of scores (and sometimes more) of valuable books that have treated these same topics in greater depth. This new edition thus incorporates much new research that has modified views held only a few years ago, particularly in the greater awareness of women's roles, of the lives of ordinary people, of the lasting structural arrangements by which society is organized, of social conflicts often ignored and subtle changes easily overlooked.

At the same time one of the important aspects of the Western tradition is a general sense that certain great thinkers and artists, certain leaders, certain movements and events have been particularly important. That importance may lie in the trends they epitomize, the changes they brought, the influence they have exercised or the inspiration they provide. Whatever its basis, this tradition of Western history is generally acknowledged here, helping to determine the information included. For a long time historians emphasized politics as the activity that summarized a whole society and determined its course, a view reinforced by emphasis on the development of the national state; and that familiar perspective with its convenient chronological framework is generally maintained in this account.

But this book also reflects the influence of a distinctive kind of historical writing, commonly called "social history," which has greatly affected historical understanding in the past twenty years or so. Neither the name nor the impulse behind it is altogether new. As early as the eighteenth century many historians (of whom Voltaire was one) called for a history that was more than chronology, more than an account of kings and battles. In the nineteenth century even while historical studies paid dominant attention to past politics, diplomacy, and war (taking the evidence primarily from official documents found in state archives), there were important and systematic efforts to encompass the history of intellectual and cultural trends, of law and constitutions, of religion, and of the economy.

Social history, as a field of study, emerged as one among these efforts at broader coverage. For some it was primarily the history of the working class, often narrowed to be the history of labor movements. For others it was the history of daily life— daily life in ancient Rome or Renaissance Florence or old New York as reflected in styles of dress, housing, diet, and so on. This "pots and pans history" was the sort of history featured in historical museums and popular magazines. Appealing in its concreteness, it tended (like the collections of interesting objects that it resembled) not to have any theoretical or interpretative point to make.

Modern social history is an approach to history that pays attention to society in all its aspects (including institutions, culture, all social groups, economic ties, daily life, demography, and climate).

It has come to be distinguished by a certain point of view, particular methods and unusual sources, and a characteristic style. The point of view seeks to compensate for the fact that most historical writing has been about the tiny minority of the powerful, rich, and educated (who, after all, left behind the fullest and most accessible records of their activities). The new social history aims to be as mindful of popular culture as it is of formal or official culture, as interested in the family as it is in the state, in living conditions as it is in political theory. Social history tries to recover as much as it can of the experience of ordinary people, to look at the society from the bottom up as well as from the top down.

In method the new social history borrows theories, terminologies, and techniques from the social sciences—especially anthropology, sociology, economics, and political science. Thus social historians use models of "development," "modernization," and "cultural diffusion"; and they employ typologies of social stratification and family structure. They make sophisticated use of techniques developed by statisticians, demographers, behavioral scientists (especially survey researchers), and economists. Characteristically, such methods include a great deal of quantification, and social historians tend to be eager to count and ready to use computers whenever sufficient data can be uncovered. Careful sampling, statistical techniques, and computer analysis when combined with hard work and a new awareness have recently made it possible to discover information previously thought unobtainable about every period of the past. New interests and new techniques have in fact greatly expanded the range of useful historical sources, for important information can be gleaned from anything that records the pulse of human life: coins; pots and lamps; fiscal records and price lists; parish records of births, deaths, and marriages; weather reports and crop records; travel accounts and private letters; minutes of meetings and petitions; police and journalists' reports; and personal diaries. The social history written with these concerns, sources, and formal methods tends to be analytical rather than narrative in structure.

The authors of this book have been active in these new approaches, and they are thus particularly aware of some of the difficulties they raise for a general textbook. Those mainstays of historical organization, clear chronology and periodization, have been made more complex. The periodization of history based on the rise and fall of dynasties, the formation of states, and on the duration of wars and revolutions usually does not fit the periodization most appropriate for changes in culture and ideas, economic production, or science and technology. Historical surveys have therefore frequently been organized topically as well as chronologically, with special chapters on economic or intellectual developments. But the history of ordinary life, especially in the period before industrialization, moves on a still different scale. A history of social processes that tend to move at a glacial pace, it often lacks sharp chronology. A history of structures more than events, it tends to be organized around problems rather than the biographies of individuals or the story of a nation.

In *The Western Experience* an effort has been made to combine the approaches and needs just discussed. The tradition of the introductory course in European history (and our cultural tradition as well) is recognized by keeping the book's chapters essentially chronological in sequence, sometimes using groups of chapters to cover a particular period of Western history. At the same time each chapter is presented as an interpretative essay, introducing a set of historical problems important to the understanding of the period treated. The "facts" that follow include the events and figures that all interpretations must take into account—the famous names and dates that are an important part of our historical lore—but the "facts" also include basic information about social organization, about modes of production and of exchange, and about cultural activity that are crucial to understanding the way of life of a particular society. All this information—much of it narrative after all, some of it good stories and accounts of dramatic events—is used to explore the problems on which a particular chapter focuses. There is also explicit attention to the kind of evidence on which these interpretations rest and the controversies that accompany them.

An innovation in this edition is the inclusion, between chapters, of short essays on experiences of daily life. This provides space for presenting in its concrete and colorful detail some of the fabric of ordinary life, space that would be inappropriate in the main body of the text which must be controlled by the logic of coherent interpretation on a large scale and by the importance of the essential information a textbook should provide. The topics of these essays have been chosen to illustrate themes significant for various periods of Western history, but the essays have another purpose as well. Professional historians think concretely even when arguing abstractly. They read discussions of the factors that led to the crusades or to industrialization having in mind a picture of what people wore and where they lived, of what preachers said, how wars were fought, and how goods were made. Descriptions of the experience of daily life should help students to remember that the analysis of history, like the narrative of events rests on the details of what real people really did and thought at a particular time in history.

Many of the users of earlier editions of this book have contributed to changes in the fourth edition.

Professors have pointed to passages that could be clearer, emphases that might be reconsidered, and sometimes to errors to be corrected. The timelines in each chapter have been expanded and improved because students requested it. Historians, determined that history should not be conceived as a string of dates, are likely to be uncomfortable with chronological tables. They tend to emphasize events rather than interpretation and political "facts" rather than cultural ideas or economic and social trends. The timelines produced for this edition seek to overcome these limitations; and, for students who have read a chapter thoughtfully and imaginatively, the timelines should provide a useful review of major points as well as events and a helpful sense of the larger chronological framework.

The readers of this text, then, can use the book as an introduction to historical method and will find within it a framework to which they can attach whatever else they know about Western society, a framework on which in the future they can build a richer appreciation of Western culture. History is essentially an integrative enterprise in which long-term trends and specific moments, social structure and the actions of particular individuals can all be brought together in the understanding of a given society. Readers should find some of their preconceptions—about the past, about how societies are organized, and about how people behave—severely challenged. Some will want to compare the response to historical problems in different societies and across time (for history is essentially a comparative mode of thought). Others will want to compare other civilizations as they ask themselves what qualities have characterized the Western world.

A college course is not the only way to build a personal culture. Nor is history the only path to integrated knowledge. Western history is not the only history one should know, or an introductory survey necessarily the best way to learn it. Still, as readers consider and then challenge interpretations offered in this text, they will exercise critical and analytical skills. They can begin to erode parochialism that views only the present as important, to acknowledge the greatness of their Western heritage and the value of familiarity with it, and to recognize the injustice, cruelty, and failures it includes. To be able to do these things is to experience the study of history as one of the vital intellectual activities by which we come to know who and where we are.

Acknowledgments

We wish to thank the following reviewers and users for their helpful suggestions for *The Western Experience:* Catherine Albanese, Wright State University; Thomas M. Bader, California State University-Northridge; B. D. Bargar, University of South Carolina; Edward E. Barry, Montana State University; Iris Berger, State University of New York-Albany; Charles R. Berry, Wright State University; Stephen Blum, Montgomery County Community College, PA; Jack Bournazian; Elspeth Brown, Hamilton College, NY; Paul Chardoul, Grand Rapids Junior College; Craig A. Czarnecki, Baltimore, MD; Ronnie M. Day, Eastern Tennessee State University; Bradley H. Dowden, California State University-Sacramento; Veron Egger, Georgia Southern College; Elfriede Engel, Lansing Community College, MI; R. Finucane, Georgia Southern College; Willard C. Frank, Jr., Old Dominion University, VA; Ellen G. Friedman, Boston College; James Friguglietti, Eastern Michigan College; Robert Gottfried, Rutgers University; Katherine J. Gribble, Highline Community College, WA; Drew Harrington, Western Kentucky University; Neil M. Heyman, San Diego State University; Deborah L. Jones, Lexington, KY; Nannerl O. Keohane, Stanford University; Donald P. King, Whitman College, WA; William J. King, Wright State University; Gordon Lauren, University of Montana; Phoebe Lundy, Boise State University; Vesta F. Manning, University of Arizona, Tucson; Julius Milmeister, Pittsburgh, PA; Frederick I. Murphy, Western Kentucky University; Linda J. Piper, The University of Georgia-Athens; Carl Pletsch, Chapel Hill, NC; Ronald A. Rebholz, Stanford University; John F. Robertson, Central Michigan University; Louisa Sarasohn, Oregon State College; Judy Sealander, Wright State University; Ezel Kural Shaw, California State University, Northridge; Alan Spetter, Wright State University; Richard E. Sullivan, Michigan State University; George Taylor, University of North Carolina-Chapel Hill; Armstrong Starkey, Adelphi University, NY; Richard Weigel, Western Kentucky University; Robert H. Welborn, Clayton State College; Michael J. Witt, FSC, Christian Brothers College, TN; and Richard M. Wunderli, University of Colorado.

Contents

Art Essays

Maps

The
WESTERN EXPERIENCE
VOLUME I
To 1715

FOURTH EDITION

LAND AND SOCIETY THROUGH THE AGES
A Cartographic Essay

MICHAEL P. CONZEN
University of Chicago

To accompany *The Western Experience, Third Edition,* by Mortimer Chambers, Raymond Grew, David Herlihy, Theodore K. Rabb, and Isser Woloch.

Maps were executed by David Lindroth.

INTRODUCTION

The history of Western civilization—indeed of any civilization—can be thought of as a kind of dialogue between society and nature. In this dialogue, men and women make a complicated series of choices within the limits imposed by nature. The results of these decisions, the way a society actually *looks* in its habitat, is called its cultural landscape. In a way, then, the history of European civilization is a rich succession of layers of cultural landscape, each showing the ways human beings have tried to occupy and use space during different historical periods. This essay highlights some of the main patterns of cultural landscape that have characterized the Western experience.

Maps that show the spatial distribution of characteristic human activities can communicate much about the relationship between social organization and environmental space. A careful reading of the following maps can lead to a deeper understanding of this complex and ever-changing relationship.

THE CLASSICAL WORLD: THE CITY-STATE

A singular achievement of Greek civilization was the city-state. This institution had a firm geographical basis as well as a political and philosophical significance. The topography of the Greek peninsula was clearly influential in the emergence of this form of government. Essentially, the city-state represented a rational effort to organize populations scattered among coastal and river basins of uncertain fertility and separated by rocky mountain ridges.

Geographic Origins of the City-State

Between Minoan and Mycenaean times, the "polis" developed from a castle stronghold, situated on a hilltop and presiding over a territory of dispersed rural villages, into a more recognizably urban settlement with civilian housing and public spaces. Mycenae illustrates this growth well (Map A-1). Early but elaborate burials testify to the site's central importance for the surrounding region (see text pp. 37–

MYCENAE

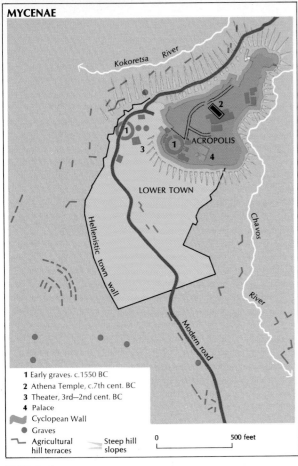

Kokoretsa River

ACROPOLIS

LOWER TOWN

Hellenistic town wall

Chavos River

Modern road

1 Early graves, c.1550 BC
2 Athena Temple, c.7th cent. BC
3 Theater, 3rd–2nd cent. BC
4 Palace
〰 Cyclopean Wall
● Graves
〜 Agricultural hill terraces   〜 Steep hill slopes

0   500 feet

MAP A–1

SPARTA AND ITS POLIS TERRITORY

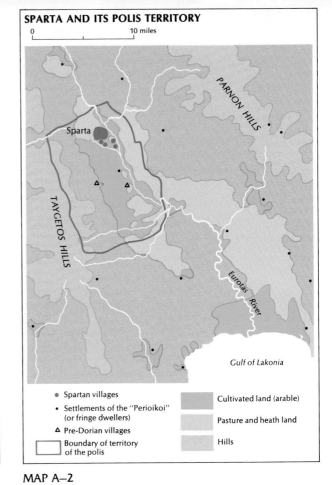

0   10 miles

PARNON HILLS

Sparta

TAYGETOS HILLS

Eurotas River

Gulf of Lakonia

● Spartan villages
· Settlements of the "Perioikoi" (or fringe dwellers)
△ Pre-Dorian villages
▢ Boundary of territory of the polis

▨ Cultivated land (arable)
▨ Pasture and heath land
▨ Hills

MAP A–2

MAP A–4

POLIS DIFFUSION THROUGHOUT THE MEDITERRANEAN WORLD, 250 B.C.–A.D. 400

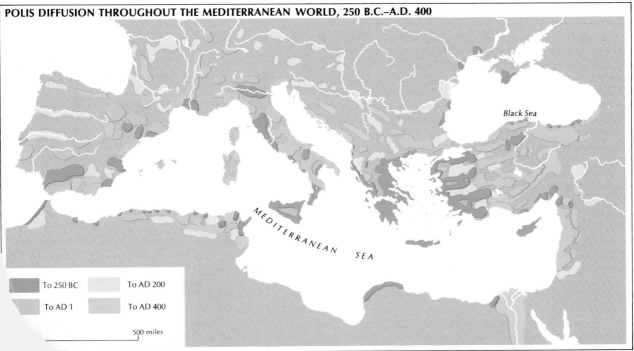

Black Sea

MEDITERRANEAN SEA

▨ To 250 BC   ▨ To AD 200
▨ To AD 1   ▨ To AD 400

500 miles

BOEOTIA
The Regional Scale of City States
and Federations, c.395 BC
Named cities belonged to
the Boeotian Federation

0   10 miles

Gulf of Euboia

Orchomenos

Thebes

Thespiai

Gulf of Corinth

Plataiai

— Regional boundaries
--- Individual polis boundaries
■ Major cities
○ Early (Mycenaean)
  settlement only
● Settlement since
  Mycenaean times
• Later settlement

MAP A–3

required direct citizen participation in politics. The
area shown in the Boeotia map (A-3) is no larger
than that of metropolitan Chicago.

Urbanization in the Roman Empire

Greek overseas settlement spread the concept of the
polis throughout the Mediterranean, as later the idea
of a city with a politically related territory penetrated
every part of the Roman Empire (Map A-4). In
practice this form of settlement had to be adjusted
to local environments, and many areas of Europe
were too sparsely populated to justify such Roman
"coloniae." But the seed of an urbanized civilization,
the polis, was nevertheless implanted throughout
Europe.

The City and Agriculture in the Roman Empire

In addition to establishing the continental road system (Map 4.3, p. 113), town networks, and frontier
defense lines, the Romans expanded local economies

MAP A–5

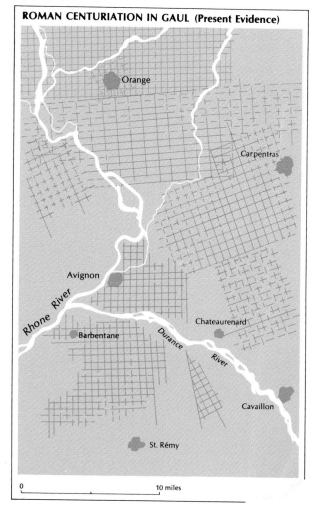

ROMAN CENTURIATION IN GAUL (Present Evidence)

Orange

Carpentras

Avignon

Rhone River

Chateaurenard

Barbentane

Durance River

Cavaillon

St. Rémy

0   10 miles

41). The hilltop between the two rivers acquired
stout defenses, a palace complex, temples, and housing. Hill terraces, evidence of Greek efforts to grow
food for the town, indicate the close relationship
between the town, its food supply, and the surrounding district. Gradually this fortified hilltop settlement, or "acropolis," became physically more
complex as Mycenaean political power and trade
grew; a lower town developed adjacent to the fortress site, also surrounded by a military defense wall.

Such a "town," however, was merely the functional center of a territory that might include hundreds of square miles. For instance, Sparta in its early
stages of development occupied a small but strategic
portion of the Eurotas Valley over which it had
primary control (Map A-2). This territory included
much of the available cultivated land in the region.
Consequently, villages beyond the borders of the
polis territory were tied to Sparta by special economic and political bonds (see pp. 52–53).

The Network of City-States

City-states formed a loose regional network, usually
without strong domination by any one state. The
polis might expand or contract, or change its shape
as a result of political alliances (such as the Boeotian
Federation) and the fortunes of war. But the natural
environment itself had much to do with the way the
polis developed. In fact, the marginal fertility of the
habitat meant that the polis had to be small. This,
in turn, made possible Greek "democracy," which

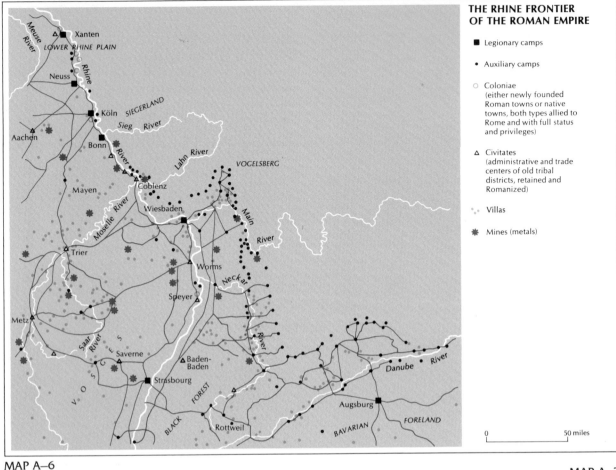

MAP A–6

MAP A–7

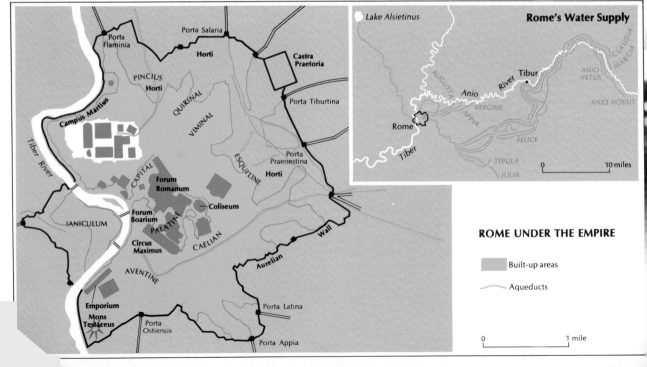

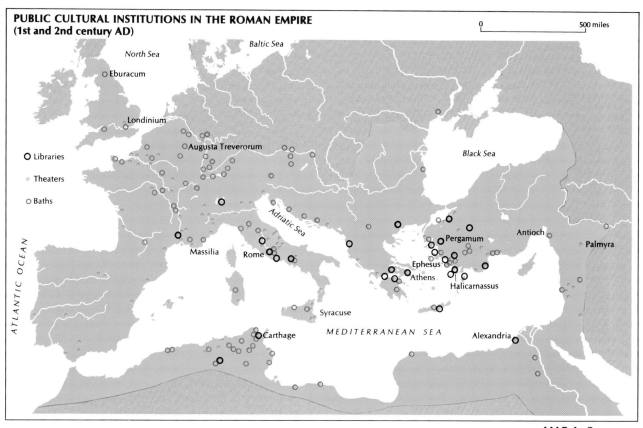

PUBLIC CULTURAL INSTITUTIONS IN THE ROMAN EMPIRE
(1st and 2nd century AD)

0   500 miles

North Sea

Baltic Sea

Eburacum

Londinium

Augusta Treverorum

Black Sea

○ Libraries

· Theaters

○ Baths

Adriatic Sea

Pergamum

Antioch

Palmyra

Massilia

Rome

Ephesus

Athens

Halicarnassus

ATLANTIC OCEAN

Syracuse

MEDITERRANEAN SEA

Alexandria

Carthage

MAP A–8

through agricultural colonization. Whether reorganizing native farming or clearing tracts of wilderness, they surveyed large areas of arable land into a grid system of fields (a process called centuriation). Traces of this grid system are occasionally visible in present-day landscapes. The Roman sense of order is well illustrated in the grid pattern around the French town of Avignon (Map A-5). Even so, because of environmental and administrative needs the overall grid pattern was irregular.

At regional levels, Roman economic organization was strongly affected by both nature and the demands of imperial defense. In what is now central Germany, agricultural villas worked the lighter alluvial soils found in or near river valleys. Where necessary, roads were cut through dense forests to link vital frontier outposts with mining centers and the cities, such as Augsburg and Trier (Map A-6), that served as administrative centers. Not only did these imperial frontier regions define the edge of the civilized world for the Romans, but, with their natural resources, they contributed directly to the might of Rome.

The Urban Culture of the Roman Empire:
The Metropolis

Rome, begun as a union of several villages situated on neighboring hills, grew into a sprawling metropolis as it became the center of an empire (Map A-7). Repeated urban renewal cleared ground for vast ceremonial complexes of temples, public squares, market buildings, theaters, and circuses. Outside these complexes were neighborhoods of crowded buildings and irregular streets, a vibrant mixture of residences and craft shops. Aqueducts brought a vast water supply to the congested city, symbolizing Rome's dependence on outside resources for its survival and growth.

Provincial Towns of the Roman Empire

In its provincial towns Rome built theaters, libraries, and public baths in an attempt to spread a higher culture throughout the Empire (Map A-8). Here, again, the Greek legacy is apparent. For instance, because of a long tradition of intellectual attainment there were many more libraries in Greece than anywhere else in the Empire.

THE ECONOMY OF THE MIDDLE AGES

Economic Life and the Monasteries

The Church played a major role in the political, economic, and social life of Europe after the decline of the Roman Empire. By the height of the Middle Ages monastic orders had proliferated throughout Europe, establishing centers of learning, extending charity, and undertaking agrarian colonization without regard for political boundaries. The Cistercians, a Benedictine reform order devoted to simple living, emerged in northeast France in the twelfth century and quickly grew as the early monasteries expanded their activities by founding daughter houses (Map A-9). Through these daughter houses, the Cistercians spread a common tradition of land colonization in agriculturally marginal areas. At many sites sacred relics drew pilgrims from far and wide. Other religious activities, however, were more regional and centralized. One site, the abbey at Einsiedeln, Switzerland, not surprisingly attracted more visitors from northern regions than from the more mountainous south. Yet the overall pattern of pilgrimage coincided reasonably well with what was later to become the broad transcontinental trade corridor between northern Italy and the North Sea.

Rural Settlement

During the Middle Ages differences in local environments and cultural traditions produced a wide variety of rural settlement forms. Common to many regions was the open-field village shown in the Swedish example (Map A-10). The irregular area of cultivable land was divided into narrow strip plots, and most farmers had fragmented holdings. The pasturelands and woodland of the village, however, were not divided and were used by all farmers.

Clearing the Land

Rural settlement expanded greatly in medieval times as large forest tracts between major river valleys were cleared and villages, like Otterstorpaby (see Map A-10), grew up. Occasionally the reverse happened as populations were decimated by war, famine, or disease. Many cleared areas near the Weser, for example, were lost to readvancing forests between 1290 and 1430, in the aftermath of the Black Death (Map A-11).

The Growth of Towns

Relative political stability and a consolidating agrarian base provided the groundwork for improved trade and growth of towns (see Map A-11). This

MAP A–9

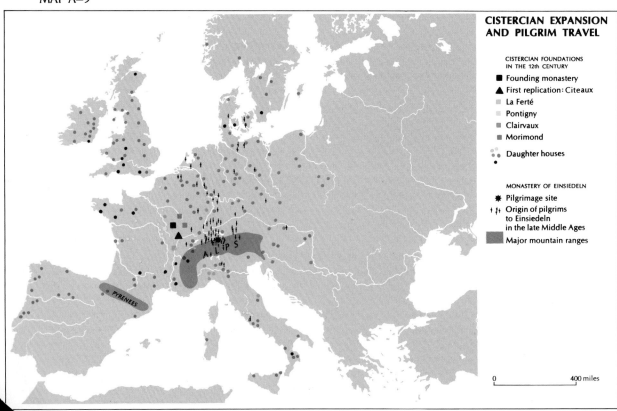

CISTERCIAN EXPANSION AND PILGRIM TRAVEL

CISTERCIAN FOUNDATIONS
IN THE 12th CENTURY
- ■ Founding monastery
- ▲ First replication: Citeaux
- ▪ La Ferté
- ▪ Pontigny
- ▪ Clairvaux
- ▪ Morimond

- Daughter houses

MONASTERY OF EINSIEDELN
- ✳ Pilgrimage site
- ꜜꜜ Origin of pilgrims to Einsiedeln in the late Middle Ages
- Major mountain ranges

0   400 miles

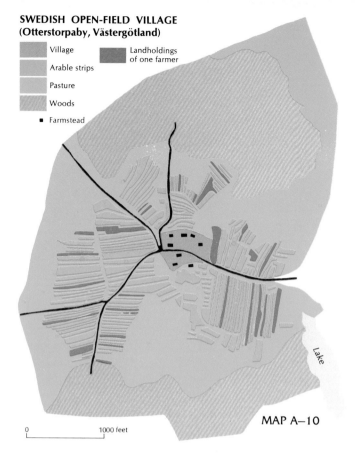

SWEDISH OPEN-FIELD VILLAGE
(Otterstorpaby, Västergötland)

- Village
- Arable strips
- Pasture
- Woods
- Landholdings of one farmer
- ■ Farmstead

Lake

0   1000 feet

MAP A–10

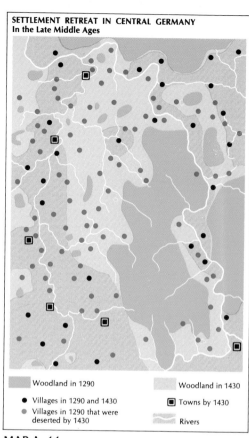

SETTLEMENT RETREAT IN CENTRAL GERMANY
In the Late Middle Ages

- Woodland in 1290
- Woodland in 1430
- ● Villages in 1290 and 1430
- ● Villages in 1290 that were deserted by 1430
- ☐ Towns by 1430
- Rivers

MAP A–11

MAP A–12

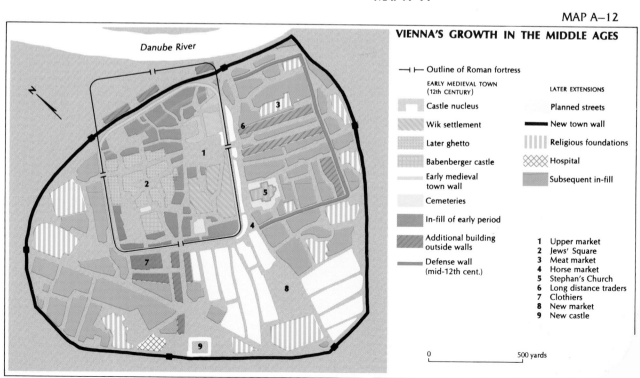

VIENNA'S GROWTH IN THE MIDDLE AGES

⊢⊣ Outline of Roman fortress

EARLY MEDIEVAL TOWN (12th CENTURY)

- Castle nucleus
- Wik settlement
- Later ghetto
- Babenberger castle
- Early medieval town wall
- Cemeteries
- In-fill of early period
- Additional building outside walls
- Defense wall (mid-12th cent.)

LATER EXTENSIONS

- Planned streets
- New town wall
- Religious foundations
- Hospital
- Subsequent in-fill

1 Upper market
2 Jews' Square
3 Meat market
4 Horse market
5 Stephan's Church
6 Long distance traders
7 Clothiers
8 New market
9 New castle

Danube River

N

0   500 yards

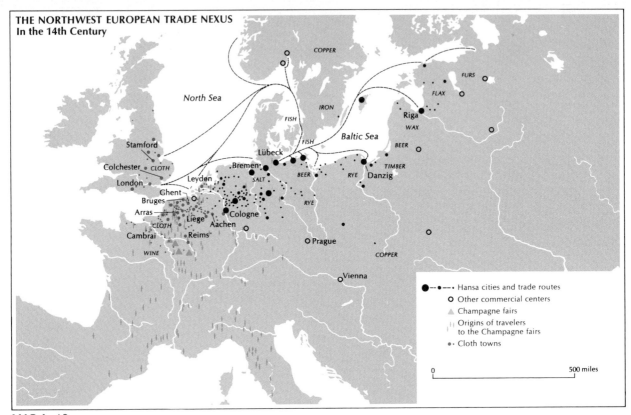

THE NORTHWEST EUROPEAN TRADE NEXUS
In the 14th Century

North Sea

COPPER

FURS

FLAX

IRON

Riga

WAX

FISH

Stamford

Colchester *CLOTH*

London

Leyden

Ghent

Bruges

Arras

Cambrai

WINE

Reims

CLOTH

Liège

Aachen

Cologne

Bremen

Lübeck

SALT

FISH

BEER

RYE

RYE

BEER

TIMBER

Danzig

Baltic Sea

BEER

Prague

COPPER

Vienna

● –•– – Hansa cities and trade routes
○ Other commercial centers
▲ Champagne fairs
||| Origins of travelers to the Champagne fairs
• Cloth towns

0 _____ 500 miles

MAP A–13

MAP A–14

MAP A–15

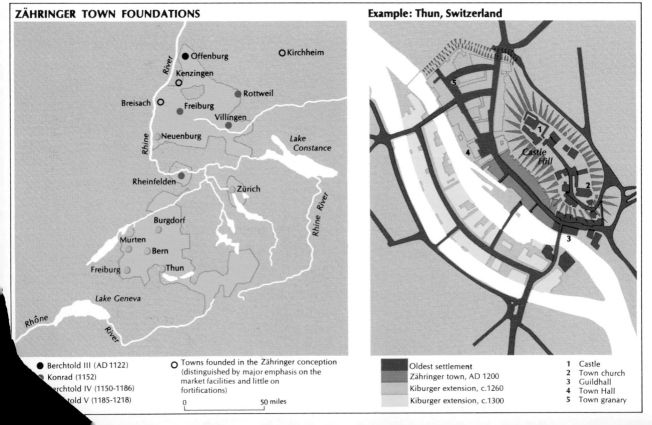

ZÄHRINGER TOWN FOUNDATIONS

River

○ Kirchheim

● Offenburg

○ Kenzingen

● Rottweil

Breisach ○

● Freiburg

Villingen ●

Rhine

Neuenburg ○

Lake Constance

Rheinfelden ●

Zürich ○

Rhine River

Burgdorf ○

Murten ○

Bern ○

Freiburg ○

Thun ○

Lake Geneva

Rhône River

● Berchtold III (AD 1122)
○ Konrad (1152)
● Berchtold IV (1150–1186)
○ Berchtold V (1185–1218)

○ Towns founded in the Zähringer conception (distinguished by major emphasis on the market facilities and little on fortifications)

0 _____ 50 miles

Example: Thun, Switzerland

Castle Hill

1
2
3
4
5

■ Oldest settlement
■ Zähringer town, AD 1200
■ Kiburger extension, c.1260
■ Kiburger extension, c.1300

1 Castle
2 Town church
3 Guildhall
4 Town Hall
5 Town granary

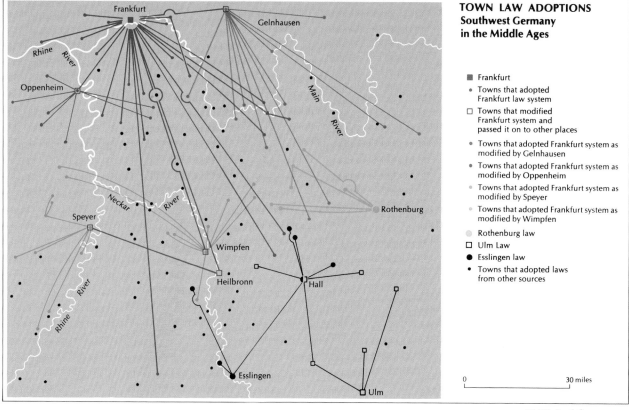

TOWN LAW ADOPTIONS
Southwest Germany
in the Middle Ages

■ Frankfurt
• Towns that adopted Frankfurt law system
□ Towns that modified Frankfurt system and passed it on to other places
• Towns that adopted Frankfurt system as modified by Gelnhausen
• Towns that adopted Frankfurt system as modified by Oppenheim
• Towns that adopted Frankfurt system as modified by Speyer
• Towns that adopted Frankfurt system as modified by Wimpfen
○ Rothenburg law
□ Ulm Law
● Esslingen law
• Towns that adopted laws from other sources

0   30 miles

was a slow process, as shown in the case of Vienna (Map A-12), which grew from about 12,000 to 20,000 between A.D. 1200 and 1300. On the site of an earlier Roman fortress at this important Danube River crossing point, a castle was built and a traders' district (Wik) sprang up, surrounded by a town wall (subsequently obliterated by later development). Jewish merchants gathered here, but were forced to live in a settlement outside the city walls, thus being denied the rights of municipal citizenship. Later, other merchant quarters (not necessarily Jewish) and craft districts were established outside the old walls, joined by several newly founded monasteries. There was enough room to lay out "planned" streets to the south of the old town, and a new, enlarged wall was built to enclose the whole settlement, which by then included a new and larger castle. During this period of growth and change, three of the four gates of the Roman fortress were still used as part of the medieval street system.

Trade Routes

The prosperity of towns such as Vienna was made possible through a combination of local and long-distance trade. The axis of trade between the Mediterranean and the Low Countries was anchored at one end around the North Sea, the site of Europe's major clothmaking region (Map A-13). Lying between the Rhine and Seine rivers, this area was supported in part by wool supplies from England and from the Ardennes Hills just south of Liège and Aachen. The robustness of medieval trade was reflected in the great international trade fairs of the Champagne district, where individual merchants gathered from all over Europe. Conversely, competition, uncertain markets, and security problems in the North Sea and Baltic regions produced closed trade associations such as the Hanseatic League of north German cities, which sought to monopolize the northern market (see p. 358).

Colonization

Some regions of Europe were comparatively late in being drawn into international trade or even in acquiring towns of local significance. One example of commercial town founding was the colonization of Eastern Europe by German subjects (see Map 8.1, p. 242); another example, on a smaller scale, is pro-

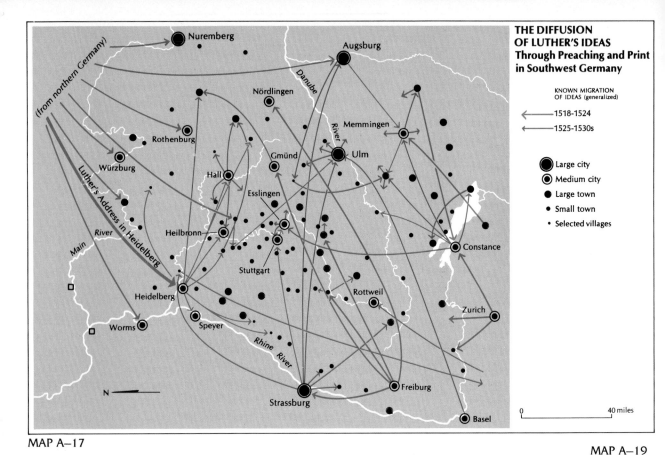

MAP A–17

THE DIFFUSION OF LUTHER'S IDEAS
Through Preaching and Print in Southwest Germany

KNOWN MIGRATION OF IDEAS (generalized)

← 1518–1524
← 1525–1530s

● Large city
◉ Medium city
● Large town
• Small town
· Selected villages

Nuremberg
Augsburg
Nördlingen
Memmingen
Rothenburg
Ulm
Würzburg
Gmünd
Hall
Esslingen
Heilbronn
Constance
Stuttgart
Rottweil
Heidelberg
Zurich
Worms
Speyer
Freiburg
Strassburg
Basel

(from northern Germany)
Luther's Address in Heidelberg
Main River
Rhine River
Danube River

N

0   40 miles

MAP A–19

FINANCING TRADE:
The Fuggers and Medici Banks

SCOTLAND
IRELAND
ENGLAND
SWEDEN
DENMARK
Danzig
POLAND
London
Bruges
Antwerp
(BURGUNDY)
Leipzig
Breslau
Cologne
Frankfurt
Cracow
Nuremburg
FRANCE
HOLY ROMAN EMPIRE
Augsburg
Hall
Salzburg
BURGUNDY
Innsbruck
HUNGARY
Lyon
Geneva
Venice
Milan
Avignon
VENICE
OTTOMAN EMPIRE
Marseilles
Florence
PORTUGAL
SPAIN
Rome
Naples
Lisbon
Madrid
Seville
(SPAIN)

MEDICI BANK (1429–1494)
▣ Main headquarters
▪ Branch headquarters
• Wholesale depots and manufactories
⚒ Mines
— Medici trade routes

FUGGER BANK (1485–1525)
▣ Main headquarters
● Major wholesaling centers
· Minor wholesaling centers
⚒ Mines
△ Metal foundries
— Fugger trade routes

— Other major trade routes

0   300 miles

vided by the mosaic fiefdom of the counts of Zähringen, knit together from sparsely settled political territories in the Upper Rhine region and central Switzerland (Map A-14).

New Towns

Often new castles, built to control particular areas, stimulated local market and craft activities that gave rise to a new set of towns. Thun was one of these towns (Map A-15). Until 1200 it consisted of a single street tucked between the castle and the river, a pattern typical of European villages, still common even today in Austria and Romania. In the next fifty years Thun extended to the northwest, where the street pattern could branch out and there was room for a marketplace. Further expansion spilled onto the island in the river as the next most logical defensive location.

The Spread of Urban Forms

Founding new towns involved more than choosing a site. Laws for local government had to be worked out. Since one attraction of towns was their departure from feudal ties, their founders often adopted the municipal laws and codification of rights of existing towns, either because the same overlord ruled both the new and the old towns or because settlers

from the older town had helped establish the new. This pattern of town law diffusion, characteristic of towns in southwest Germany, illustrates how urban legal "families" evolved (Map A-16).

THE EARLY MODERN ERA

Reformation: Preaching

The fifteenth and sixteenth centuries witnessed major changes both in the climate of ideas and in the means of communicating them across long distances. It was, in fact, during these centuries that explorers boldly extended European knowledge of the world (Map 13.1, p. 416). Of equal significance was Luther's challenge to Church orthodoxy, which rapidly transformed the religious map of northern Europe. Luther's public appearances and the subsequent movements inspired by his example disseminated the new doctrines among the generally larger towns of southwest Germany (Map A-17). In printed form, Luther's ideas swept over Germany without regard for town size. Ideas spread as readily from small towns to large towns as from large to small, although many large towns became the centers from which new ideas radiated.

MAP A–18

THE SPREAD OF PRINTING and Traditional Language Areas, 1455-1500

- To 1470
- 1471-1480
- 1481-1490
- 1491-1500

Color areas distinguish traditional language areas

0   200 miles

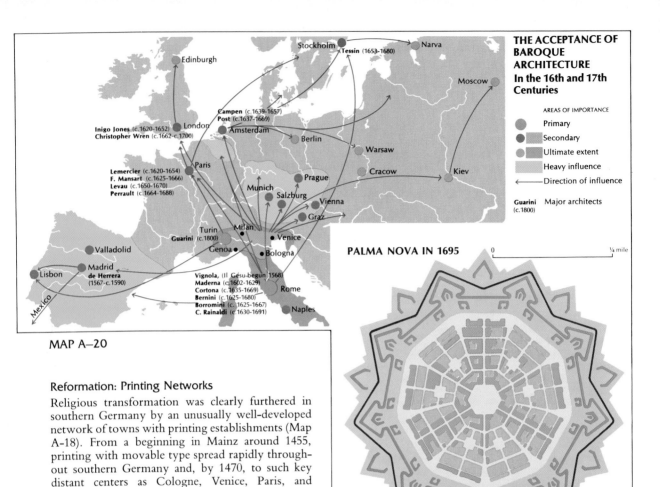

THE ACCEPTANCE OF BAROQUE ARCHITECTURE In the 16th and 17th Centuries

AREAS OF IMPORTANCE
- ⬤ Primary
- ◼ Secondary
- ⬤◼ Ultimate extent
- Heavy influence
- ← Direction of influence
- Guarini (c.1800) Major architects

Stockholm Tessin (1653–1680) Narva
Edinburgh
Moscow
Campen (c.1639–1657) Post (c.1637–1669)
Inigo Jones (c.1620–1652) London Amsterdam Berlin
Christopher Wren (c.1662–c.1700)
Warsaw
Lemercier (c.1620–1654) Paris Prague Cracow Kiev
F. Mansart (c.1625–1666) Munich
Levau (c.1650–1670) Salzburg
Perrault (c.1664–1688) Vienna
Graz
Turin Milan
Guarini (c.1800) Venice
Genoa Bologna
Valladolid
Lisbon Madrid Rome
de Herrera Vignola, (Il Gesù begun 1568)
(1567–c.1590) Maderna (c.1602–1629)
Mexico Cortona (c.1635–1669) Naples
Bernini (c.1625–1680)
Borromini (c.1625–1667)
C. Rainaldi (c.1630–1691)

MAP A–20

PALMA NOVA IN 1695

0   ¼ mile

- —— Defense walls
- —— Main ditch
- Remaining defense system (or berms)
- Town buildings

MAP A–21

Reformation: Printing Networks

Religious transformation was clearly furthered in southern Germany by an unusually well-developed network of towns with printing establishments (Map A-18). From a beginning in Mainz around 1455, printing with movable type spread rapidly throughout southern Germany and, by 1470, to such key distant centers as Cologne, Venice, Paris, and Utrecht. During the next thirty years the further adoption of movable type created dense printing networks in northern Italy, Germany, and the Low Countries—areas long accustomed to outside influences through their mercantile traditions (see pp. 379–381).

The Spread of Renaissance Ideas: Mercantile Ties

Traditions of trade were being modified by new capitalist developments. The wealthiest merchants became bankers to monarchs and supervised vast trading systems. The Fugger family of Augsburg (see p. 422) and the Medici Bank in Italy (see p. 361) created wholesale trading empires, complete with their own warehouses, mines, foundries, trading posts, and fleets that stretched from Danzig to Lisbon (Map A-19).

The Spread of Renaissance Ideas: Style

The cultural dynamism of Italy continued long after the Renaissance. Baroque art, architecture, and town planning in the seventeenth century originated from the same centers and spread across the continent along similar paths, reflecting the influences of trading ties, dynastic connections, and the tastes of rulers (Map A-20). In this case Rome's preeminence first influenced southern Germany and Paris, and later Spain and Stockholm. Paris in turn influenced the cultural climate of London and Stockholm, as London then spread the prevailing ideas of the time to Edinburgh.

The Spread of Renaissance Ideas: The Town

The principles of town planning had meanwhile been revolutionized by the invention of firearms, and town fortifications grew to gigantic proportions. Vast earthworks of mounds, ditches, and berms (flat, grassy open spaces) were constructed outside the town walls so that the town itself was beyond the range of any attacker's cannon. Palma Nova, near Venice, provides a splendid example of new-town construction in which modern concepts of street geometry were combined with defense requirements (Map A-21). As with medieval town extensions or new foundations, walls were built to enclose areas large enough to allow for later building. But by the seventeenth century urban growth had so far outdistanced the provisions of an earlier time that many farmers were displaced as towns expanded into the countryside. In many large towns later expansion occurred completely beyond the earthworks.

THE INDUSTRIAL ERA

Enclosure and Demographic Changes

The greatest transformation of the cultural landscape in modern times, perhaps most conspicuous in the massive shifts of populations from countryside to city, has been associated with the new industrialism. But forces were at work in the preindustrial countryside that paved the way for these demographic changes. An agricultural revolution that was well advanced by the eighteenth century modernized many farming practices and considerably altered the look of the land (see pp. 674–676). A key element of this revolution was the enclosure of traditional open-field village lands to form large fenced fields owned by individuals. This process had taken hold

MAP A–22

ENCLOSURE OF COMMON FIELD, 1700-1800

ENCLOSED BY 1700
Over 70%
50-70%
Enclosed by Act before 1801

0   100 miles

MAP A–24

OPEN AND CLOSED VILLAGES IN NOTTINGHAMSHIRE, 1848

Worksop
Retford
Mansfield
Farnsfield
Southwell
Newark
Ilkeston
Nottingham
Bingham
Trent River

• Open village
• Closed village
— Daily movement of laborers

0   5 miles

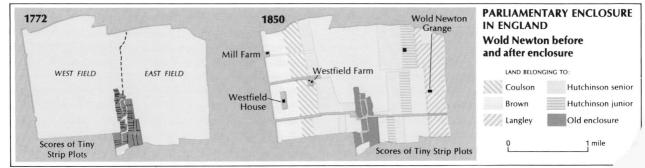

1772
WEST FIELD   EAST FIELD
Scores of Tiny Strip Plots

1850
Wold Newton Grange
Mill Farm
Westfield Farm
Westfield House
Scores of Tiny Strip Plots

MAP A–23

PARLIAMENTARY ENCLOSURE IN ENGLAND

Wold Newton before and after enclosure

LAND BELONGING TO:
Coulson   Hutchinson senior
Brown   Hutchinson junior
Langley   Old enclosure

0   1 mile

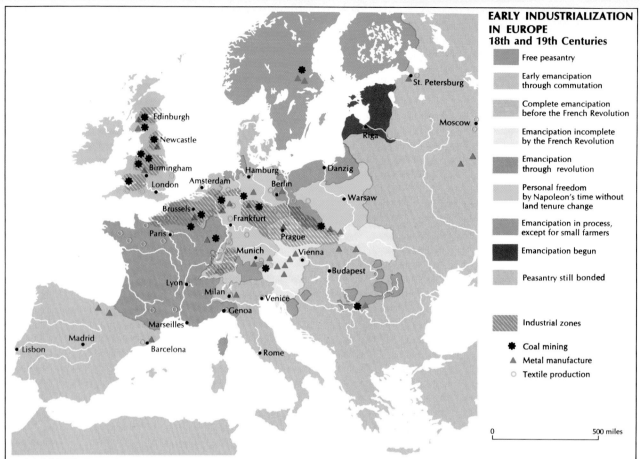

EARLY INDUSTRIALIZATION IN EUROPE
18th and 19th Centuries

- Free peasantry
- Early emancipation through commutation
- Complete emancipation before the French Revolution
- Emancipation incomplete by the French Revolution
- Emancipation through revolution
- Personal freedom by Napoleon's time without land tenure change
- Emancipation in process, except for small farmers
- Emancipation begun
- Peasantry still bonded

- Industrial zones
- ✳ Coal mining
- ▲ Metal manufacture
- ○ Textile production

0   500 miles

MAP A–25

MAP A–26

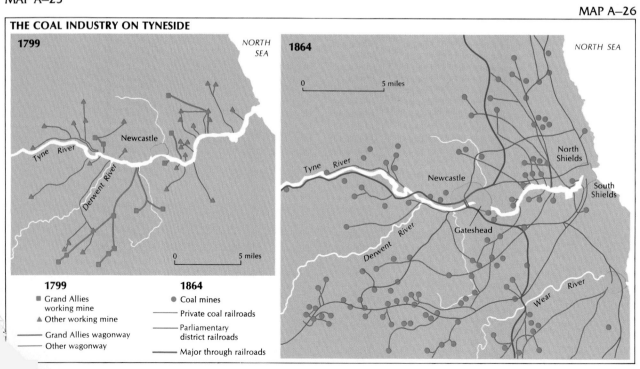

THE COAL INDUSTRY ON TYNESIDE

1799
NORTH SEA

Tyne River
Newcastle
Derwent River

0   5 miles

1864

0   5 miles

NORTH SEA

Tyne River
Newcastle
Derwent River
Gateshead
North Shields
South Shields
Wear River

1799
- ■ Grand Allies working mine
- ▲ Other working mine
- ▬ Grand Allies wagonway
- — Other wagonway

1864
- ● Coal mines
- — Private coal railroads
- — Parliamentary district railroads
- ▬ Major through railroads

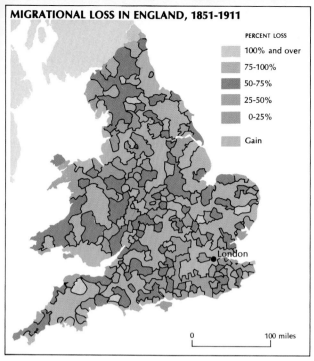

MIGRATIONAL LOSS IN ENGLAND, 1851-1911

PERCENT LOSS
- 100% and over
- 75-100%
- 50-75%
- 25-50%
- 0-25%
- Gain

London

0   100 miles

MAP A–27

in England by 1700, and parliamentary action enforced it in the following century. Very few areas were left untouched (Map A-22). The example of Wold Newton illustrates the change on a local scale as two large open fields, which in 1772 contained scores of narrow strip plots (compare with Map A-10), were consolidated into a handful of individual holdings consisting of a few large fields (Map A-23).

Village Work

Change was not smooth, however, and one consequence of the piecemeal reorganization of land tenure in England was that labor opportunities varied from one farming community to another. In "closed" villages, where and ownership was concentrated in only a few hands, farm labor became inflexible. Village laborers that could not be absorbed locally thus had to commute to nearby "open" villages, where diverse ownership created a more fluid labor market (Map A-24). Since farm laborers journeyed to work on foot, most commuted to neighboring villages. In Nottinghamshire, by the middle of the nineteenth century, more than half the villages could be classified as "closed"; two-thirds of these exported some labor to at least one neighboring settlement and in many cases to several villages at a time. Such inter-village migration was a symptom of broader problems of rural employment in a world of tenurial reorganization, farm mechanization, and the increasing lure of industrial job opportunities.

Free Labor

England was the first European country to industrialize intensively, but the agrarian groundwork for this was being laid in many parts of the continent. Emancipation of the peasantry (see pp. 792–794) has long been regarded as a necessary prelude to industrialization, and the progress made toward this goal as early as 1812 clearly indicated which countries would follow Britain's lead (Map A-25).

Coal and Iron

By the nineteenth century industrial regions had emerged primarily where coal and iron ore could be brought together cheaply. When such locations had been major centers of trade since medieval times, old cities, such as those in Belgium and southern Germany and Newcastle or Bristol in England, flourished again. In other cases, coalfield industrialism and the rapid spread of railroads combined to bring entirely new settlement complexes into existence, as happened in the Ruhr valley and the British west midlands (see p. 783).

A region that gained major new impetus from the steam era was Tyneside in northeast England. Newcastle had exported coal to London for domestic use since Roman times. By 1799 the general demand for coal had produced a dense network of wagonways for delivering coal down the valley to the Tyne River (Map A-26). Typical of some early industrial concerns, one-third of the mines were owned by an oligopoly known as the "Grand Allies." Mines multiplied as the demand for coal to fuel steam engines increased. Railroad lines proliferated. Many railroads were simply laid along the former wagon roads, but a clear distinction developed about which railroads handled coal, which handled other freight, and which carried passengers. By the twentieth century, many mines had been exhausted or had become uneconomical to operate and were closed, leaving many railroad lines abandoned in this compact coalfield.

The Move to Cities

The growth of old and new industrial centers was made possible by a heavy immigration of people from rural areas and traditional small towns. Since industrialization was not ubiquitous, the patterns of population movement were geographically biased (see p. 794). Census statistics for the years between 1851 and 1911, the period when Britain's industrial growth reached maturity, show the attraction of port cities and urban job opportunities (Map A-27). With few exceptions the areas that showed gains in population through migration were on or near coalfields. Greater London, continuing its historic role as Brit-

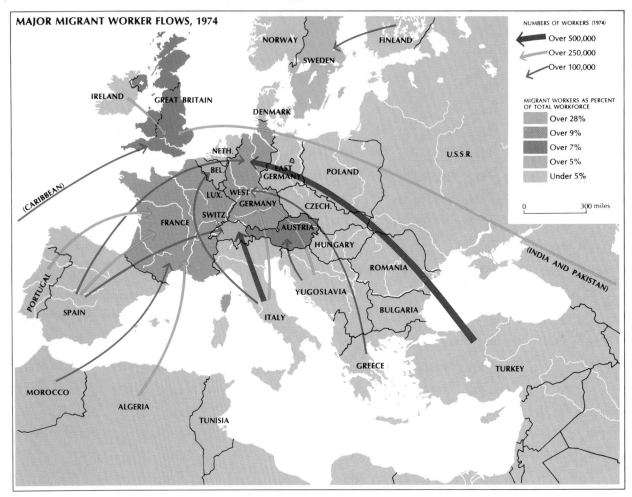

MAP A–28

Migration

During the nineteenth and twentieth centuries, expanding worldwide markets spurred industrial production, particularly in the oldest and most successful industrial countries. As a result, larger numbers of people have moved across greater distances more frequently than ever before. The drain of population ain's capital city, provided the chief exception. Areas of poor farming in Wales and northern England suffered drastic population losses. The result was a cultural landscape in which some regions were densely populated and others were almost deserted.

from rural regions, with restricted opportunities, to urban areas, with their myriad attractions, has been a constant, but the *scale* of movement has changed. Industrial growth has outstripped the locally available labor supply and has led to the phenomenon of temporary "guest workers," from less industrialized countries such as Turkey, Yugoslavia, and Greece, to industrial nations (Map A-28). The social and political consequences of these migrations have posed serious planning problems, particularly within the European Economic Community, and will strongly influence the diversity and cohesion of European society.

Chapter 1

The First Civilizations

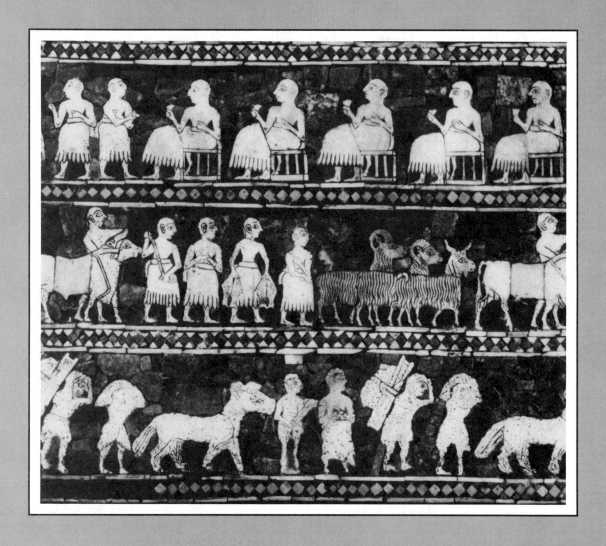

The subject of this book is the Western experience. By Western experience we mean the history of European civilization and its remoter origins in earlier civilizations located in Mesopotamia and around the Mediterranean.

Human beings began to abandon a nomadic existence and live in settled agricultural communities only about 10,000 years ago. The earliest farming villages so far identified appeared in the hills of Asia Minor. Some 5000 years later, settlements grew up along the banks of the Tigris, Euphrates, Nile, and Indus. The richer lands irrigated by these rivers supported many more people than could the highlands and did not require the effort of the whole population to guarantee a stable supply of food. This margin of freedom and leisure made possible a diversity of occupations, specialization of skills, and experiments in building, thought, law, government, and military organization. Permanence, complexity, and sophisticated social organization transformed the agricultural village into something we can recognize as urban, the form of habitation crucial for the development of civilization.

Expansion caused these early societies to develop still more complicated forms of political and social control. Powerful kingdoms and great empires, dotted with sizable cities, arose in Asia Minor and in Egypt. For a time, the Persian Empire united the entire Near East under its Great King. The achievement of literacy and a proliferation of written records, long-distance trade, the invention of increasingly ingenious tools, utensils, vehicles, and weapons, the development of monumental architecture and representative art, advances in medicine, astronomy, and mathematics document the change from primitive to civilized conditions.

The most distinctive contribution of the ancient Near East to the unity of the Western experience was religious: the monotheism of the Old Testament. Other kingdoms conquered territory (and lost it); Israel permanently conquered people's imaginations.

I. THE EARLIEST HUMANS

Perhaps our first task in thinking about historical chronology is to grasp the overwhelmingly long period that we must view as "ancient history." The astronomer Carl Sagan has reckoned that, if the entire history of the universe were plotted out over the span of one year, all that we usually think of as European history would have occurred within the last few minutes of the year. Yet it is this period on which we have by far the most evidence, and inevitably we must discuss it in greater detail than the millions of years that preceded it.

The earth may be about 4 to 6 billion years old. For more than half that time it lacked life entirely. The date for the origin of human beings is highly controversial. Recent genetic

2

research suggests that chimpanzees, gorillas, and human beings are biochemically virtually identical. The slight genetic differentiation, on which human civilization is based, may have occurred only about 5 million years ago. Another school of anthropologists, which lays greater stress on fossil patterns and skeletal development, would push the origin of human beings back to about 20 million years ago. The study of early humanity is changing more rapidly than any other field of history, for one newly found fragment of a skull can crucially support, or undermine, a theory of human development. Thus it is safest, for our purposes, to survey only the latest stages in the rise of humanity.

All human inhabitants of the world are members of the species Homo sapiens ("thinking human being"). Present evidence would date Homo sapiens to about 350,000 years ago. The immediate predecessor was Homo erectus, who may have emerged as long ago as 1,500,000 years. Back beyond Homo erectus in time is another area of controversy. Some scholars, notably Sir Louis Leakey and his school, would recognize an earlier species, Homo habilis (roughly "skilled human being"), who emerged in east Africa perhaps 1,800,000 years ago, but others would classify these fossil remains with those of Homo erectus. Further research may confirm a growing tendency to conclude that humanity originated in east Africa, but this is not yet fully demonstrable.

Human Beings as Food Gatherers

For the greatest part of their time on earth, human beings have had to struggle for some kind of control over their environment. By far the longest period has been that in which people got food by hunting and gathering; only recently has food production been practiced. It is hard to construct a portrait of society during the long period of gathering food, but one social division, that of gender, was automatically present. It may well be that women provided most of the food supply through gathering; this indeed is the pattern of many nonindustrial societies today—the woman in the family is sent off to search for firewood, even performing at the same time another task, that of nursing children. Thus, by maintaining a stable food supply, and obviously by caring for the new generation of gatherers, women may have been the dominant members in the economies of such gathering bands.

Division of labor by gender might also suggest that the men did most of the hunting and killing of animals, though this can hardly be proved. When a large animal was finally killed, it provided food and thus relief from gathering for several days. If such an achievement was mainly the work of men, it could have given them a kind of social dominance. The trapping and killing of an animal must have been less common than the daily gathering of food. If the model we are constructing is valid, the more specialized work of hunting and killing may have led to a more elite social position for men.

In most societies that we can describe, men have obtained roles as governors and leaders, while women have done the less visible work of maintaining the family. In a roaming, gathering society, such direction by males must have been connected with aggression and defense against aggression. One hunting band might have to turn aside the claims of another band to certain territory. In such clashes, we may also guess that men assumed the leading role; so a combination of assertiveness by males and acquiescence by females may have pointed toward social divisions based on gender.

The period of food gathering is often called the Old Stone Age, or Paleolithic Age, ranging from the beginning of human history down to about 10,000 B.C. The most striking documents we have from gathering societies are a series of cave paintings that survive at their finest in Lascaux in France and Altamira in Spain. These early attempts at artistic creation normally show wild animals, enemies of human beings and yet part of their essential support. The paintings may have a quasi-religious meaning, as symbolic attempts to gain power over the quarry; scars on the walls seem to show that people threw spears at the animals after painting them, as if thus to symbolize killing them.

Human Beings as Food Producers

About 10,000 B.C. occurred the most important single event in human history. People turned from hunting animals and gathering food to producing it from the earth. This event, the rise of agriculture, is often called the Neolithic Revolution. The word revolution usually implies a dramatic action taking place within a short time, which was in no way true of this one—yet revolution it was, for it made possible the maintenance of larger populations. Again, it gave continuity to human existence; it demanded and allowed long-term planning and the division of labor into new skills and departments. Those not needed in agriculture could engage in hunting (for this still had to accompany agriculture) weaving, pottery, metal work, and trade.

But *why* did this revolution take place, what caused people to turn from the gathering pattern that had lasted hundreds of thousands of years? Probably no single cause can provide the answer, but we cannot neglect the question. For millennia the glaciers, which had, long before, advanced from both polar regions, were shrinking back toward the poles. This enabled the animals that the glaciers had in fact driven into the arms and weapons of human beings to wander away again. To hunt and trap animals now demanded longer journeys in search of less common prey. There has been much debate on the role of population pressure. Some historians hold that increasing populations in the later (or "upper") Paleolithic Age made it desirable, even imperative, to develop new sources of food. Other historians have denied this: for them, a large increase in population became *possible* only after the revolution assured a steady and even increasing supply of the things that have sustained humanity in all later times— domesticated animals (sheep, pigs, cattle), vegetables, and grains (and one of their products, beer). Certainly the latter thesis is partly true, but so is the first: it must have been clear that a new supply of food would have to be found. Also, it is surely more agreeable to have a settled home, with areas for storage and permanent defenses against aggression, than to face constant danger and upheavals of a nomadic existence.

The revolution first occurred among the hills of what is now southern Turkey and northern Iraq, especially in the Zagros hills east of the Tigris River. But, again, why was *this* region the cradle of Near Eastern agriculture? Archaeologists have concluded that only here was there a sufficient supply of animals for domestication along with the vegetables and cereals needed. Archaeologists have found some settlements from as early as about 9000 B.C. These were unwalled and unfortified, and their people lived in simple huts. About 8000 the first somewhat larger villages appeared; the oldest appear to be Jericho and Jarmo. They were small settlements—Jarmo's population is estimated at about 150.

We cannot write a social history of any of these communities, but we can ask questions about social roles based on gender. It is possible that, while males in a group were hunting, women played a crucial part in the discovery and nurturing of early agriculture. In any case, women must now have had more work to do; the disposal of wastes must at least partly have

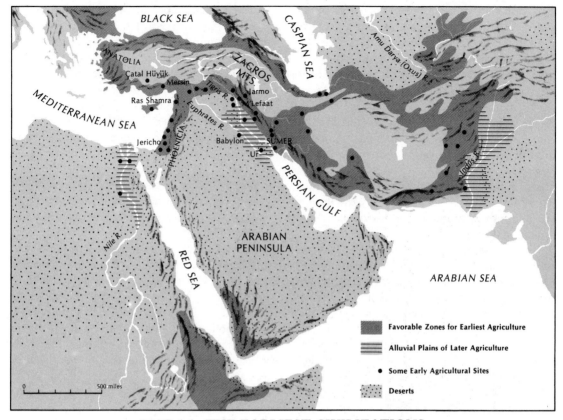

MAP 1.1. THE EARLIEST CIVILIZATIONS

fallen to them, along with much else in maintaining a community—activities that bands of hunters and gatherers could have ignored. By about 6500 pottery appeared in what is now Iran; this invention, in whose expansion women must have played a part, allowed the storage of food and sustained the population in periods when hunting and gathering would have been more difficult. The resulting expansion of families increased the importance—and the burdens—of the females.

The art of weaving existed in Anatolia, or modern Turkey, by about 6000, and we may assume that this craft was largely practiced by women. About this time people began to travel in crude rafts and in carts with wheels (this latter being, oddly enough, an invention never made by either the Aztecs or the Mayas). Potters were now learning to fashion their wares on the surface of a turning wheel, so that they could make in minutes what had previously taken days; and the pot, the raft, and the wheel combined to provide the means to transport grain and other goods. A trading economy thus began to emerge. Some archaeologists even hold that some cities were formed not for the sake of local agriculture but as trading centers.

The largest known food-producing village of early times is Çatal Hüyük (*sha-tal hoo-yook*). It lies in present-day Turkey, covers 32 acres, and contains twelve successive levels of buildings thought to range in date from 6500 to 5650. It is also the oldest known site with buildings constructed for exclusively religious purposes, and its remains preserve an unusually clear record of some early religious practices. As we might expect, early agriculturalists were much concerned with breeding and fertility; the ruins of Çatal Hüyük contain female statuettes, idols of unmistakable earth-mother types, with large buttocks and breasts, whose fertile bodies, it was hoped, would make the soil productive. These figures probably also signify the importance of human mothers, for the villages could remain and flourish only if women could produce and sustain the new generation. The emphasis on the importance of females and female deities has led some historians to deduce that matriarchy, the political domination of the society by women, existed among some early peoples, and that men had to overturn it in order to gain or regain mastery. It would be interesting if this were so, but there is no clear evidence that women exercised political rule.

So by stages there arose primitive agrarian communities with communal gods, domesticated animals, simple technologies and economies, and some regulation of social behavior. Yet we must bear in mind how painfully slow was the transition from nomadic hunters to food-producing villagers. And still another five thousand years separated the first agricultural villages from the first civilizations.

II. THE FIRST CIVILIZATIONS IN MESOPOTAMIA

Early Urban Societies

Mesopotamia is a rich alluvial plain created by deposits from the Tigris and Euphrates rivers. Historians have long recognized this area as the home of the first civilizations, which arose about 3000 B.C. The rise of civilization, as opposed to farming villages, was not really an abrupt beginning from point zero, but was part of a long development. Still, the presence of an urban culture, with more complex rules to govern behavior, political organizations, and more sophisticated divisions of labor, does seem to suggest a life different in substance from life in a farming village, and we may use the word civilization to denote these conditions.

Among other telling features of civilization is law, as distinct from simple customs; law is often recorded in detailed law codes, which tell us how rulers controlled their populations and often portray the nature of life in these early societies. Political organization—one of the major themes of this book—must become more complex. Cities are larger and therefore stronger than villages; they have the power to dominate the hinterland and even to enslave its population. Slavery itself allowed the enslavers more varied occupations by freeing them from some mundane requirements of mere existence. But when we speak of multiple occupations available in urban life, we are talking mainly (but not at all exclusively) about men. We have already tried to infer what occupations women may have performed in precivilized societies, but from the dawn of civilization until the most recent times women were assigned or withdrew to such duties as raising children, spinning, weaving, baking, and seeing to the home. This work was important, indeed imperative, for the growth of cities, but it led to women's being private and not public citizens—at many times disappearing from conventional history and historical documents.

The technology of cities developed further the arts of pottery, weaving, and domestication of animals, but a major step forward took place when workers discovered how to blend other metals with copper to fashion bronze, especially for weapons. At about the same time as the first cities, therefore, humanity also entered the Bronze Age, which started about 3000 B.C. and ended between 1200 and 1000.

Sumer

At the southern end of the long Mesopotamian plain were the first cities, in the area known as Sumer. This rich, highly inventive civilization is a paradox, for we do not yet know the ultimate origin of the Sumerians. The people themselves and their language appear to be unrelated to any other known people or language. The Sumerians evidently came down from the neighboring hills, attracted by the rich soil of the valley. To take advantage of the fertile land as well as to channel and control the periodic floods, they had to construct a complex system of canals for irrigation.

By about 3000 B.C. Sumer contained a dozen or more city-states, each independent of the others, worshiping its own patron deity and ruled by its own king. Jealousy among them led to constant fighting for power and land, but no single city could dominate the others permanently. Ur, the largest, covered about 150 acres and had a population of about 25,000—but perhaps 200,000 if we add those living in the suburbs and hinterland. The citizens of each city were divided into three classes: nobles and priests, commoners, and slaves—the first example of what we shall often meet, a recognized, legal division of people into social orders. The king was not considered divine; he held power only so long as he could command support from the more powerful priests and nobles.

At the center of a Sumerian city there usually stood a ziggurat—a terraced tower built of baked brick and culminating in a temple, probably for the patron god of the city. A ziggurat might be a stupendous structure: The wall surrounding one of them was some 36 feet thick. The Old Testament contains many echoes from Sumer, and it seems likely that the story of the Tower of Babel was ultimately based on the memory of a ziggurat.

The Sumerian family arranged marriages for its daughters (as families in a great many other societies have done) on receipt of a gift from the groom. Monogamy was the rule, and parents had complete power over their children, including the right to sell them as slaves. But even to mention this may give a wrong impression, for Sumerian records speak of families with affection. "The wife," says one document, "is a man's future; the son is a man's refuge; the daughter is a man's salvation." Women could hold property and do business, though, as we have said, they did not hold political office.

In Sumerian culture, theoretically the patron god owned the whole city; but in fact much of the land was private property, held in great part by princes and their families but also by private citizens. Most houses were of a single story, jammed into narrow streets, but some richer houses had two stories and an open court.

One of the Sumerians' chief contributions to civilization was the art of writing. The most important intellectual tool ever discovered, writing enables people to keep records, codify laws, and transmit knowledge, so that their achievements will not be lost. It is true that we know of some earlier attempts at writing, or at least at communication through symbols, but the Sumerians developed the art in an efficient form. Their language was pictographic: Each sign was originally a simplified picture of the article that the scribe had in mind. In time scribes reduced the complexity of the system by simplifying pictures and by combining several pictures into one. In this process of abstraction the meaning of a sign might change. For example, a crude picture of a star was simplified into four wedge-shaped marks and given the meaning "god" or "heaven."[1] Sumerian texts were written on clay tablets by pressing the end of a reed or bone stylus into the wet clay; the resulting wedge-shaped marks are *cuneiform* (Latin *cuneus*, "wedge"), a name used for all such scripts in whatever language they occur.

Decipherment of the many surviving Su-

---

[1] The Sumerian method of writing is described by S. N. Kramer in *The Sumerians,* pp. 302 ff.

merian clay tablets has revealed that Sumer had a developed mythology. People of the time speculated about the origin of the world, which they saw as having been created by a god. Moreover, the gods had established the standards by which people must live. One of their main deities, Enlil, was primarily a storm god who lived in heaven. Normally kind and fatherly, Enlil made the rich soil of Mesopotamia fertile and was even credited with designing the plow. At times, however, when Enlil had to carry out harsh decrees of the gods, he became terrifying. This alternation may reflect the uncertainty bred by the threat of floods that always hovered over Sumer. When the rivers overflowed and destroyed the crops, the gods had evidently withdrawn their favor, and the Sumerians rationalized this by assuming that they had somehow offended the gods' codes.

Some Sumerian myths passed into the traditions of other peoples. For example, one of the great Sumerian epics tells the story of the hero Gilgamesh. Amid his wanderings and adventures, he stands at the entrance to the underworld, talking with the spirit of a departed comrade; this foreshadows a scene in Homer's *Odyssey*, Book 11. Neither the Sumerian nor the Greek poem tries to make the world of the dead attractive; the concept of fulfillment after death was foreign to both cultures. Other Sumerian myths foreshadow the biblical accounts of eating from the tree of knowledge in Paradise and of the Flood that covered the earth. But we must recognize the differences between Sumerian myths and their remarkable parallels in the Bible. Uncertain conditions of life in Sumer led to considerable anxiety in Sumerian myths. The position of humanity was one of nearly complete dependence on the gods. Indeed, Sumerian myth taught that the gods had created people merely to provide slaves for themselves. In the Sumerian epic *The Creation of Man*, Marduk the creator says, "Let him be burdened with the toil of the gods, that they may freely breathe." The Hebrew scriptures,

Sumerian cuneiform tablet, *The Creation of Man*.
(Photo: The University of Pennsylvania)

by contrast, place more emphasis on the possible redemption of humanity through following God, who looks on human creatures in a stern but still loving, nurturing way.

A precious document in Sumerian texts is a reforming law code handed down by Urukagina of Lagash about 2350. Evidently the bureaucracy had been abusing the people. "Formerly the head shepherd seized the sheep. The man in charge of the fisheries seized the fisheries. . . . He who brought the dead man to the cemetery received seven pitchers of beer and 420 loaves of bread. . . . Urukagina banned the head shepherd from seizing the donkeys and sheep. . . . He who brought the dead to the cemetery received only three pitchers of beer and only 80 loaves of bread."[2]

Essential for the growth of Sumerian cities was trade, for despite the region's astonishing fertility it lacked good timber, good stone, and such important metals as gold, silver, and copper. Sumerians pioneered the art of building in baked brick, but to obtain other materials they had to export. One of their main trading partners was apparently the Indus Valley (or Harappan) civilization of Mohenjo Daro in India (this is itself a civilization of unknown origin that was destroyed by Indo-Aryan invaders some time between 1700 and 1500). The Sumerians could indeed export food, but this was heavy and perishable. They turned instead to manufactured goods, especially metal work, and became outstanding metal workers—because, it has been said, they had no metal of their own.

Perhaps to bolster their expertise in the essential art of trading, the Sumerians developed a precise system of mathematical notation. Their system was the "sexagesimal," in which the number 60 (Latin *sexaginta*, 60) is one of the main elements; this system has the advantage of including both 3 and 10 as factors. Sumerians had numbers for 1, 2, 3, 4, 5, and 10; then they leaped to 60, 600, 3600, and 36,000. One of the dramatic legacies of Mesopotamia to our world is this system: The foot has 12 inches, the day 24 hours, the minute and hour each 60 units, and the circle 360 degrees (and until recently the British had 12 pence to a shilling).

The Sumerians, though the first civilization, had a mental world that is like ours in many ways. Their gods were personal ones, not simply unknown forces. One was Ninhursag, "the exalted lady, the mother of all living things." The medical texts among the clay tablets rise above mere incantations and magic and contain true prescriptions, however primitive they may have been. A king, as we have seen, could boast of having established justice and honesty; and the family as the basic unit of social life emerges into historical light.

Sargon and the Revival of Ur

Wars among the Sumerian cities weakened them and prepared the way for the first great warlord of Western history: Sargon, of the region of Akkad, an area just north of Babylon. He ruled from 2371 to 2316[3] and conquered all Mesopotamia; his kingdom even reached the Mediterranean Sea. From Akkad his language is named Akkadian;[4] it is of the Semitic linguistic family—thus with Sargon we first meet the Semites. This family of languages in antiquity included Akkadian, Hebrew, and Canaanite; in our day the Semites are represented by Jews and by such speakers of Arabic as Syrians, Jordanians, and Arabs. Akkadian now replaced the Sumerian language, which passed out of use.

Sargon and his successors ruled from Akkad until about 2230, when invasion, and perhaps internal dissension, dissolved the Akkadian kingdom. The Sumerians now regained control of southern Mesopotamia and established the so-called Third Dynasty of Ur. The chief ruler of this period was Ur-Nammu (2113–2096). He established the first comprehensive law code (the "reform code" of Urukagina was directed

---

[2] Kramer, op. cit., pp. 317 f.

[3] Dates in early Near Eastern history are constantly being revised. For dates in this chapter we normally rely on the *Cambridge Ancient History,* 3rd ed. 1970.

[4] The Babylonian and Assyrian dialects are closely related. The term Akkadian is now used to refer to Assyro-Babylonian.

The "Standard of Ur," a trapezoidal object found in the Royal Cemetery, Ur; probably used in processions. The scenes portray a royal banquet, animals, and treasures belonging to the rulers. Early Dynastic period, ca. 2550 B.C. (Photo: The British Museum)

at specific abuses of the bureaucracy), which spelled out regulations and penalties for a broad range of offenses. He established honest weights and measures, a clear recognition of the importance of trade to the people of his state. The code is preserved in fragmentary form, but it is clear that he laid down fines in money rather than calling for strict physical retribution: "If a man has cut off the foot of another man . . . He shall pay ten shekels. . . . If a man has severed with a weapon

the bones of another man . . . He shall pay one mina of silver."

Ebla in Syria

The story of the early Near East is usually built around the cities and kingdoms of Mesopotamia, but a striking new element has entered the picture through the discovery of a large city, Ebla, near modern Aleppo in Syria. Excavations in the 1970s produced thousands of clay tablets, written in cuneiform in a Semitic language. They date from about 2500 B.C. Syria was formerly considered a land of nomads in the third millennium B.C., but Ebla is forcing a reconsideration of this concept, for it was a highly organized city with a population of about 260,000 (including all suburbs) and an unusual social structure.

Ebla was much less "Oriental" in social style than many other eastern states. There was no absolute monarch set on high: rather, the kings of Ebla appear to have been elected for seven-year terms. A succession of five kings spanning some 60 years (for re-election was possible) is known from the period of Ebla's flourishing; then Sargon boasted of having conquered Ebla, in the 2300s. Probably the city was reoccupied, for Sargon's grandson repeats the same boast.

The king's title was *en*, the queen's *maliktum*. It is notable that the queen of Ebla had great wealth and evident influence. Some tablets show goods being delivered to her rather than to the king, and she evidently played an important part in the economy by directing the spinning mills, where women worked and were paid in measures of barley. The queen also had an important political-religious duty, that of consecrating the king as he took office.

Within Ebla the basic medium of exchange was silver. The people traded widely in Syria, exporting food, metals, and especially textiles. They were organized into hundreds of small "villages," which were groups of 20 persons. There were 14 chief administrators who used the title *lugal*, normally the Mesopotamian word for king, but these men too were elected along with the king of Ebla.

The Eblaites recognized about 500 gods, who received offerings of sheep, bread, beer, oil, sometimes even the expensive donation of an ox. One of the chief male gods, perhaps the most important of all, was Dagan, who had a divine companion called *delatu*, "lady." His name often accompanies that of a city of which he was the patron god. The Eblaites filled out their vast pantheon by accepting gods from Sumer, whose Sumerian names they listed on tablets along with the Eblaite equivalents of their names. Priests not only were attendants in temples but sometimes traveled from city to city in a role perhaps like that of the prophets of Judaism.

It will take years to make a thorough analysis of the tablets from Ebla. Their great contribution has been to reveal a complex urban culture in northern Syria. Some features of its society, such as the elected kings, are highly unusual in Mesopotamia. In comparison with Sumer, where the local god owned the whole city, at least in religious theory, Ebla has even been called a "'lay" society—that is, one in which religion did not dominate society and the state. Some scholars have seen parallels between religious practices in Ebla and the Old Testament. For example, the syllable *Ya* in personal names may mean "deity," according to one interpretation, and this reminds us of the Hebrew YHWH, the name of the god of Israel (see p. 27). Whether or not this is confirmed by further study, Eblaite scribes preserved a striking creation myth, probably passed down from Sumer, that was to be echoed in the opening words of the Bible:

> Lord of heaven and earth, the earth was not, you created it; the light of day was

not, you created it; the morning light you had not yet made to exist.

The Babylonian Kingdom

The cities of southern Mesopotamia succumbed, toward the year 2000, to the rising power of a Semitic people called Amorites (in Akkadian, "Amurru"). These invaders destroyed Ur in 2006 and soon established their own capital at Babylon, within the region known as Babylonia. For about two centuries Babylonia was in turmoil as several dynasties in various cities competed for power. Finally, the sixth king of the dynasty in Babylon itself, the famous Hammurabi, succeeded in unifying Mesopotamia under his rule.

Hammurabi (1792–1750) is a towering figure, not only for his political genius but also for his skill in administration. His most famous legacy is the most significant of all documents down to this time, a cuneiform inscription, now in the Louvre Museum in Paris, recording a long series of legal judgments published under his name. The Code of Hammurabi, like the earlier one of Ur-Nammu, is not a complete constitution or system of law; rather, it is a compilation of those laws and decisions that he thought needed restating. The code begins with a long prologue, in proud Oriental style, proclaiming that Hammurabi has been chosen by Marduk, the patron god of Babylon, to declare these regulations and to fix penalties for those who disobey them. There follows a code of some 270 sections, much more carefully organized than any earlier one that we know.

Hammurabi laid stress on retribution and fair dealing, but at the same time the code shows that justice was not the same for all groups in his society. Most of the laws are addressed to free men and women, but there was evidently a second class of citizens, whom some translators call "villeins," others "commoners"; they were in some way dependent on the wholly free citizens. Below them were slaves. Hammurabi does indeed say, "If a man puts out the eye of a free man, they shall put out his eye; if he breaks the bone of a free man, they shall break his bone." But also, "If he puts out the eye of a free man's slave or breaks his bone, he shall pay half his price"—rather than putting out the offender's eye or breaking his bone.

We cannot, in a few lines, summarize this fascinating document, which regulates virtually every aspect of the relations between citizens. The penalties for crime were severe, to say the least. If a son struck his father, his hand was cut off; if a man broke into a house, he was put to death; anyone who looted a burning home was thrown into the fire. Among the most forward-looking provisions in the code were those regarding the family. Hammurabi was evidently aware of the vulnerable position of women and children in his society and took care to protect them against exploitation. If a man's wife became ill, he could marry another woman but must continue to support the first wife, who could, if she wished, move out and keep her dowry. Again, a widower could not seize his dead wife's dowry and spend it but must save it for her sons; and widows could keep the dowry they brought into the marriage. A man was banished if he committed incest with his daughter. Divorce was also allowed— a wife could divorce her husband for adultery, but only if she had been chaste; if not, she was thrown into the water.

Evidence from outside Babylonia itself also throws light on the genius of Hammurabi in building his dominion. For example, excavations at the Sumerian city of Mari have disclosed more than 20,000 cuneiform tablets, many of them preserving correspondence and administrative documents from the early second millennium. They show constant diplomatic activity, negotiations, the dispatching of troops throughout the area, and the exchange of ambassadors. One tablet reports that "there

is no king who is the strongest by himself. Ten or 15 follow Hammurabi, the same number follow Rim-Sin of Larsa" (1822–1763 B.C.), and so on. By skillful diplomacy, Hammurabi maintained a balance of power until, in the 1760s, he defeated his rivals one by one and made Babylon the strongest power in Mesopotamia.

Mesopotamian Culture

Hammurabi's subjects used all manner of commercial records (bills, letters of credit, and the like), and their knowledge of mathematics was amazing. They built on foundations laid by the Sumerians, using the sexagesimal system, with 60 as the base. They had multiplication tables, exponents, tables for computing interest, and textbooks with problems for solution.

The Mesopotamians also developed complex systems of astrology and astronomy. It is not certain which science inspired the other, but we have both astrological predictions and astronomic observations from the second millennium. In particular, there are a series of tablets recording the rising and setting of the planet Venus, perhaps in connection with the calendar. The Babylonian calendar used twelve lunar months and thus had but 354 days, but astronomers learned how to regularize it by adding a month at certain intervals.

Medicine and surgery are needed in any civilization. Babylonian medicine was often superstitious. Disease was supposedly the result of the intrusion of evil spirits, which could be driven out by chants and prayers; no ancient society had a conception of germs as a cause of disease. At times, however, diagnosis and treatment of disease were rational, and we have documents listing symptoms and the drugs available as cures. Surgery was a more practical art, and the Code of Hammurabi prescribed severe penalties for unsuccessful surgery: if a patient died, the surgeon's hand must be cut off. It seems unlikely that such regulations were actually enforced, but at least they show an attempt to protect society against malpractice.

III. EGYPTIAN SOCIETY

The Nile River

The basic element in the long history of Egyptian civilization is the Nile River. It rises from the lakes of central Africa as the White Nile and from the mountains of Ethiopia as the Blue Nile; these two branches meet at Khartoum and flow together northward to the delta, where at last the journey of 4000 miles ends at the Mediterranean Sea. Less than two inches of rain a year falls in the delta; rain is altogether unknown in much of Egypt. Most of the land is therefore uninhabitable. These geographic facts determined much of the character of the country. The people had to farm only along the banks of the river, where one can stand with one foot in the fertile mud and the other in the arid sand. The desert that locks the river in its valley usually protected Egypt from invasion.

One miracle stood between the Egyptians and starvation. The Nile swells each summer as the rains pour down and the snow melts on the mountains; it overflows its banks, reviving the land with fresh water and depositing a thick layer of alluvial soil for cultivation. The Egyptians would then plant their grain and often reap two harvests before winter. This yearly flood gave them a natural beginning for their year, and their 365-day calendar is the direct forerunner of the calendar now used throughout the Western world. In case the Nile failed to rise to its usual height, they developed an elaborate storage system for grain. Normally, Egypt could support more than its own population; Greeks, Romans, and others drew large

A detail of the relief on the stele of Hammurabi shows the king standing before Shamash, the sun god, receiving Hammurabi's laws for the Babylonians.
(Photo: Photographie Giraudon)

portions of their food supply from the wheat grown in Egypt.

The List of Kings

The basic source for Egyptian history is a list of the kings compiled by an Egyptian priest named Manetho, who wrote his history nearly 3000 years after the reign of the first kings. Manetho wrote in Greek in about 280 B.C., after Alexander's conquest, for the Macedonians who ruled Egypt. He divided the kings into thirty dynasties (later chronicles added a thirty-first). Modern scholars accept these divisions and have grouped the dynasties in this manner.

Archaic Period (Dynasties 1–2)	3100–2700
Old Kingdom (Dynasties 3–6)	2700–2200
Intermediate Period (Dynasties 7–10)	2200–2050
Middle Kingdom (Dynasties 11–12)	2050–1800
Intermediate Period (Dynasties 13–17)	1800–1570
New Kingdom (Dynasties 18–20)	1570–1085
Postempire (Dynasties 21–31)	1085– 332

The first Egyptians appear to have used a Hamitic language that was probably native to Africa. A later group of Semitic immigrants fused with the Hamites, but their precise background is unclear. Early Egypt was divided into two kingdoms, one in upper Egypt (the Nile Valley) and one in Lower Egypt (the delta). This distinction may reflect two different groups of people among the ancient Egyptians.

The Old Kingdom

Menes (also known as Narmer), who lived about 3000, unified Upper and Lower Egypt and established a capital at Memphis. By the time of the Old Kingdom, the land had been consolidated under the strong central power of the king, who enjoyed a supremacy that we can hardly imagine today. The king (he was not called "pharaoh" until the New Kingdom) was the owner of all Egypt and supposedly a god as well. As such he stood above the priests and was considered the only direct contact with the other gods. The whole economy was a royal monopoly; thus there was no word in Egyptian for "trader." Under the king was a hierarchy of officials, ranging from governors of prov-

The Pyramids of Giza.
(Photo: Elliott Erwitt, Magnum)

inces down through local mayors and tax collectors. Artisans, peasants, and slaves nourished the whole system.

The Old Kingdom reached its zenith in the Fourth Dynasty, when wealth and prosperity increased greatly. The rulers waged successful wars with Libya and the Sudan. Overseas trade with Byblos, on the coast of Palestine, produced cedar for houses, furniture, and sailing craft, and copper mines were operated in the Sinai Peninsula. The appropriate symbols of this period of greatness are the three immense pyramids built at Giza between 2600 and 2500, staggering feats of engineering that still dwarf any other monuments to individual people from any age. Building such a pyramid may well have been the chief activity of the king during his rule. These were built by Khufu (called Cheops by the Greeks), Khafre, and Menkure.

The priests, an important body within the ruling class, were a social force working to modify the king's supremacy. Yielding to the demands of the priests of Re, a sun-god, kings began to call themselves sons of Re, adding his name as a suffix to their own: Khafre, Neuserre, and so on. Re was also worshiped in temples that were sometimes larger than the pyramids of later kings.

The Middle Kingdom

Political division and rivalry lie close beneath the surface in any state. The Old Kingdom dissolved into a period of general anarchy known as the First Intermediate Period. The collapse of a strong central government seems to have been partly caused by growing independence enjoyed by some local nobles. Invasion into the delta by foreign peoples also played a part. But gradually the anarchy passed away, and kings of the Eleventh Dynasty, centered at the city of Thebes, reunited Egypt and supplied kings during the Middle Kingdom. A sign of Theban supremacy was the prominence of the god Amen, whose principal seat of worship was Thebes. He was merged with Re as Amen-Re and became the Egyptian national god. In his honor, rulers of the Middle Kingdom began the construction of the stupendous temple at Karnak, the largest ever erected to an ancient god. Rulers of the Twelfth Dynasty also took Amen into their names: four of them were named Amenemhet, an indication of the new respect paid to this god.

Rulers of the Middle Kingdom expanded Egyptian influence toward Palestine and Asia and also southward up the Nile (see Map 1.2). Sources tell of one military expedition into Palestine, but apparently the Egyptians did not dominate any part of this region through direct military occupation. Their influence was, rather, economic and cultural. It was different with the territory up the Nile, where the Egyptians pushed their frontier beyond the First Cataract and penetrated the area south of the Second Cataract.

Egyptian Culture

Religion

The king and the gods closely associated with him stood at the pinnacle of Egyptian religion. Numerous other gods occupied lesser positions in the pantheon. These others appeared in a variety of forms, often as animals, and in origin were probably deities of the villages up and down the Nile. Patron deities presided over many aspects of Egyptian civilization.

Unlike some other peoples, the Egyptians believed in a pleasant life after death. The general conception of the hereafter had men performing their usual tasks but with more success. The king, already a god, would become a greater god; viziers, priests, and administrators would hold more responsible positions. For everyone there would be pleasures such as boating and duck hunting.

The god who ruled over the dead was Osiris. In Egyptian mythology, each dead king became Osiris; by about 2000 this doctrine had been extended so that every deceased man became Osiris and thus lived on in the next world. Osiris himself had once been killed and dismembered but had been reassembled, and thus given new life, by his wife Isis.

In harmony with their view of survival, the Egyptians made careful preparations for the physical needs of the afterlife. To preserve their bodies after death they perfected the art of em-balming and making mummies of the dead. Statues sat in the tombs of kings as receptacles for their spirits in case their bodies should be destroyed.

The wish to provide housing for the dead led to the most renowned monuments of Egypt, the pyramids. The earliest tombs were much smaller than the massive pyramids already mentioned. They were low structures with flat tops called mastabas, built of brick and decorated with brick paneling; most scholars see in this method of building an influence

MAP 1.2. ANCIENT EGYPT

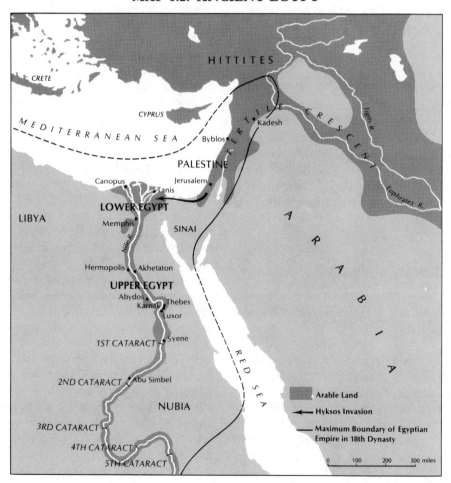

from Mesopotamia, where brick rather than stone was used.

Maat

The Egyptians recognized an abstract ethical quality called *maat*, which Egyptologists translate roughly as "right order" or "just state of things." *Maat* existed if everything was in the order that the gods had ordained. It was a kind of primeval, cosmic harmonizing force that arranged all created things in the right relationships. It is true that all ancient societies valued order and harmony—most of them had a monarchic system that naturally prized discipline—but the notion of *maat* seems to show a new way of reflecting on morality. When a society can give a name to the abstract idea of right order without having to attach it to a god, a subtler kind of thinking is taking place. Right order would, indeed, help to hold Egyptian society together. Thus *maat* illustrates another frequent use of religion: as a carefully crafted tool of politics in addition to expressing a people's feeling toward divine powers.

Art and Writing

Much of the surviving art of Egypt comes from the interior of tombs and is closely associated with Egyptian religion. Artists tried to represent scenes and pastimes familiar to the deceased: a king is shown defeating his enemies or in the company of his family; workers are shown building boats or tending fields. On the whole, the art is optimistic. Both inside and outside the tombs there were serene and imposing statues of the kings, often several identical ones located together, as if to emphasize by repetition the monumental strength of the rulers.

Egyptians developed a form of writing known as hieroglyphics ("sacred carvings"). The indispensable key to the Egyptian past was the Rosetta stone, discovered when Napoleon occupied part of Egypt at the end of the eighteenth century. This stone, now in the British Museum, contains a partly preserved hieroglyphic text along with translations in the cursive Egyptian script that evolved from hieroglyphics and also in Greek, a known language that offered a way of penetrating the other two. The decisive stage in decipherment came with the work of J. F. Champollion in 1822.

Like the cuneiform script of Mesopotamia, hieroglyphics began as pictorial signs. It is likely that the Sumerians influenced the Egyptians in the early stages, around 3000; but the pictures that the Egyptians developed were mostly original. Hieroglyphics sometimes use merely a picture of the object represented; for example, a small oval represents "mouth." But at some point the scribes decided to use the pictograms as phonetic signs; thus *ra* continued to mean "mouth" but was also used for the sound *r*. Fully developed hieroglyphics are therefore a combination of pictograms and phonetic signs.

The Egyptians made writing material from the papyrus plants that grow in abundance along the Nile. From papyrus comes our word *paper*. The reeds of the plant were placed crosswise in layers, then soaked, pressed, and dried to produce sheets and rolls. Because of the dry climate, thousands of papyri have survived in legible condition; most of these come from the later period when the Romans administered Egypt.

Literature

The rich variety of Egyptian literature illustrates the creativity of the early Egyptians and the liveliness of their culture. Their works often dealt, as did their art, with mythology and the afterlife, and their hymns to various deities, poems celebrating the king's victory over death, and stories about the gods reflect the serene Egyptian confidence in the beneficence of the gods. Various texts, collectively known

Top: The ceremonial palette of King Narmer is a symbolic representation of the unification of Upper and Lower Egypt. This side of the palette shows the king, wearing the white crown of Upper Egypt, smashing the head of an enemy. The god Horus, in the form of a falcon, holds a rope attached to a captive of Lower Egypt, a region symbolized by six papyrus plants.

Bottom: On this side of the palette King Narmer has completed his conquest of Lower Egypt and wears the red crown of that kingdom. He is reviewing the bodies of decapitated victims. The exotic beasts with necks intertwined may symbolize the unity of the two Egypts.
(Photo: Himer Fotoarchiv München)

as the Book of the Dead, provide charms and other methods of assuring a successful transition to the other world.

Success in this world appears as the central concern of another literary genre, appropriately known as "instructions" or "instructions in wisdom." These books, in which a wise man gives advice about how to get ahead in the world, reveal much about Egyptian social attitudes, especially the supreme position of the king; they counsel discretion and loyalty: "If you are a man of note sitting in the council of your lord, fix your heart upon what is good. Be silent—this is better than flowers. Speak only if you can unravel the difficulty . . . to speak is harder than any other work. . . . Bend your back to him that is over you, your superior in the king's administration. So will your house endure with its substance, and your pay be duly awarded. To resist him that is set in authority is evil."[5]

We also have scraps of Egyptian love poetry: "It is pleasant to go to the pond in order

---

[5] Adolf Erman, *The Ancient Egyptians: A Sourcebook of Their Writings* (1966), pp. 61–62 (language slightly modified).

to bathe in your presence, that I may let you see my beauty in my tunic of finest royal linen, when it is wet." And there are meditations, songs, ghost stories, and fables of all kinds. In fact, not until the Greeks did the ancient world have another literature with the richness and charm of that of Egypt.

Mathematics and Medicine

The Egyptians were the forerunners of the Greeks in applied science. The need for careful planting in the silt deposits of the Nile forced them to master the art of surveying, for an unusually rich overflow might wipe out the boundaries between plots of land, and when this happened the land had to be remeasured.

Medicine in Egypt depended largely on driving out demons from the body. The Egyptians believed that a separate god ruled over each organ and limb, and treatment consisted largely in finding the right chant to appease the appropriate deity and then delivering it in the right tone of voice. Sometimes the sorcerer simply threatened the demon by promising to invoke the aid of the gods if it did not depart at once.

But medicine was not based entirely on magic. One papyrus, a treatise on surgery, displays a more empirical approach to illness. It discusses some forty-eight medical problems, classified according to the various parts of the body. Whenever possible the author gives a diagnosis and suggests a treatment. A verdict is often given in one of three forms—"An ailment that I will treat," "An ailment with which I will contend," or "An ailment not to be treated"—probably according to whether the prognosis was favorable, uncertain, or unfavorable. This text is a witness to the birth of a kind of inquiry that transcends haphazard folk medicine. Such maturing and broadening of knowledge independent of magic characterizes the civilizing process throughout history.

The Invasion of the Hyksos

The prosperity and success of the Middle Kingdom declined in the late Twelfth and early Thirteenth Dynasties. The invasion by the so-called Hyksos, about 1720, ended the Middle Kingdom and led to the second intermediate period. Historians are still not certain who these invaders were, but they were probably a group of several western Asiatic peoples from Syria and Palestine. Manetho called them Hyksos, a name derived from that given their leaders, *Hikau-khoswet*, roughly "rulers of foreign lands."

The Hyksos controlled mainly the region of the delta. At about the time of their invasion, other tribes were overrunning Babylonia, and the activities of the Hyksos appear to have been part of a general disturbance in the Fertile Crescent that lasted from about 1750 to 1550. The Hyksos' invasion was a shock to Egyptian civilization, but it had some positive effects. The conquerers brought in the horse-drawn chariot as a vehicle in war and established the use of bronze rather than copper for weapons. They also stimulated the Egyptians to regroup and counterattack. By about 1570 Egyptian warriors from Thebes had driven the Hyksos from the delta and back into Asia Minor. The period following the expulsion is called the New Kingdom or the Egyptian Empire.

Hatshepsut and the New Kingdom

During the Eighteenth Dynasty the rulers from Thebes, now called "pharaohs," established the power of the central government over the nobles and organized Egypt into a military state. They enlarged their domain by encroaching on Asia Minor, where they encountered another large kingdom, that of the Hittites. These two kingdoms, the Egyptian and the Hittite, were the most powerful ones known down to their time, and also the last great kingdoms of the

Bronze Age, that period from about 3000 to 1000, when military supremacy rested on weapons fashioned of bronze.

Within this dynasty we meet the first, and greatest, woman ruler of ancient times, Hatshepsut. This brilliant, dynamic, and not wholly scrupulous woman was a daughter of Thutmose I. She married Thutmose II, the son of Thutmose I by another wife and thus her half brother. From 1512 to 1504, when Thutmose II died, they ruled jointly. Thutmose II meanwhile had a son, who was to become Thutmose III, by a harem girl. But Hatshepsut seized the post of regent for this child and in effect ruled as queen. Then in 1503 she had herself crowned king of Egypt, representing this as the divine will of the god Amen. She was aided in this *coup d'état*—it was nothing less—by her chief minister, Senenmut. It was an act of breathtaking audacity in a social system where men had held the supreme, absolute power of monarch. Perhaps to emphasize her right to rule as king, she had herself portrayed as a sphinx with a beard.

She undertook some military campaigns but evidently wanted to be remembered above all as a builder, the restorer of Egypt. "I have repaired what was destroyed [by the Hyksos], I have raised up what was in pieces ever since the Asiatics had been in the Delta, overthrowing what had been made." She turned to building her great temple tomb in the Valley of the Kings, the equal in majesty of any other building in Egypt. On its walls still stand inscriptions recording her career. She sent a large trading expedition to Punt, a territory to the south on the Red Sea, and proudly catalogued the goods Egypt received in the exchanges, including myrrh, wood, even baboons. One scene in her temple shows ships bringing granite obelisks (at 97 feet high, they are Egypt's tallest) to Karnak. She also resumed mining in the Sinai Peninsula.

Hatshepsut's ambition was not limited to her own lifetime, for she planned to pass the throne on to her daughter. But the girl died before Hatshepsut; her minister Senenmut also disappeared; finally in 1482 the queen died. In an act of rage against her long domination over him, Thutmose III had her name hacked and effaced from as many monuments as possible; the statues and tomb of Senenmut were also disfigured. Even her name was distorted and she is hardly to be recognized as "Amensis" in Manetho's list. But much of her temple, approached by a magnificent long entrance ramp, still stands.

Thutmose III, who ruled securely until 1450, became Egypt's most dynamic military statesman. He made 17 expeditions into Asia Minor and established the empire as far as the Euphrates River. His successors, exploiting these conquests, grew rich on the tribute paid by subject peoples such as the Israelites, many of whom became slaves in Egypt. With this economic power the Egyptians expanded their trade, honored the gods with more temples, and continued to work the mines in the Sinai.

Akhnaton's Religious Reform

After the conquests of Thutmose, a dramatic conflict of religions took place in the New Kingdom. This struggle arose from a contest between the pharaoh and certain priests and nobles. Each party strove to make its own god the supreme one. Thus the apparent religious battle—not for the last time in history—was, on a more realistic level, a political one. Although it was but one event during the centuries of the New Kingdom, its humanistic interest carries special fascination. Early in his reign King Amenhotep IV (1379–1362) began to oppose Amen-Re, for centuries the traditional god of Thebes, and sponsored the worship of the *aton,* the physical disk, or circle, of the sun. Supported by his wife, the exquisite Nefertiti, the pharaoh appears to have been trying to overcome the influence of priests and

Amenhotep IV-Akhnaton and his wife, Nefertiti, accompanied by one of their daughters, make offerings to Aton, the disk of the sun. Notice the hands on the ends of the sun's rays, reaching out to touch the king and his family.
(Photo: The Metropolitan Museum of Art, New York)

bureaucrats in Thebes. To advertise the new faith among his people, he changed his own name to Akhnaton, which may be translated as "he who serves Aton," and sent workers around Egypt to chisel off the name of Amen-Re from monuments. He moved his capital from Thebes to a completely new city called Akhetaton, "the horizon of Aton" (a village called El Amarna today), where he built a temple to Aton and lived rather like a pope serving his god. He composed a soaring hymn in praise of Aton, hailing him as the creator of the world—another account of creation that stands beside those of the Sumerians and the Israelites.

There is evidence that Akhnaton fought the worship of other gods, and some historians have gone so far as to call him the first monotheist. Such a conception is anachronistic and overlooks the real conditions of the worship of Aton. The royal family alone worshiped the god; the Egyptian people were expected to worship the pharaoh himself. Artistic scenes show priests and nobles in attitudes of reverence, but they are addressing their prayers to the pharaoh, not directly to Aton.

During the reign of Akhnaton even artistic traditions, unchanged for hundreds of years, underwent some reforms. Most portraits of Egyptian kings show them as handsome, massive creatures, but Akhnaton appears as a slender, aesthetic-looking man, with thin legs and a pot belly. This strain of realism could not have arisen without the king's approval.

Akhnaton fostered his new religion with passionate commitment, but in his zeal he neglected the kingdom. Princes took advantage of his inattention and, abandoning their loyalty to him, seized their independence. First in Syria and then in Palestine, Egyptian control was shaken loose. The Asiatic holdings fell away.

In the struggle between ideas, political authority is often ineffective. The more conservative priests, and probably most Egyptians, continued to worship Amen-Re, and the upheaval in religious and cultural life that Akhna-

ton had instigated came to an end with his death. The next pharaoh changed his name from Tutankhaton to Tutankhamen, thus indicating that Amen-Re, the older chief deity, was again in favor. The royal court moved back to Thebes, and the Theban priests of Amen-Re enjoyed their victory. The city named for Aton, Akhetaton, was first abandoned, then destroyed, and Akhnaton's name was savagely effaced from monuments and king lists. Indeed, he was now known as "the criminal of Akhetaton." The young king Tutankhamen, the heir of this quarrel, reigned for only seven years and was buried with dazzling splendor. His tomb, discovered in 1922, intact with all its treasures, has remained one of the most impressive finds in the history of Egyptology.

The New Kingdom emerged from its weakness in the Eighteenth Dynasty under the pharaoh Haremhab, who reestablished a strong central government and destroyed the final vestiges of the worship of Aton. The first pharaohs of the Nineteenth Dynasty continued the rebuilding. Seti captured portions of Syria and restored Egyptian power in Palestine. Ramses II had difficulty in maintaining Egyptian holdings. He fought a great, but inconclusive, battle with the Hittites in 1300, at Kadesh in Palestine. Conflict continued for years until the two kingdoms signed a peace treaty in 1284. The temporary peace that Ramses achieved allowed him to spend time and money on building projects. He renamed the city of Tanis in the delta for himself; and, according to tradition, he exacted forced labor from the Israelites in Egypt. At Karnak he completed an enormous hall of columns sacred to Amen-Re, who had now fully regained his old position. Even more impressive are the monuments that Ramses II built to himself. In front of the temple at Luxor, built by his predecessors, he constructed an entrance court, guarded by six colossal statues of himself. His supreme achievement as a builder is the temple that he had carved out of the rocky cliffs along the Nile at Abu Simbel. The building of the Aswan Dam by the modern Egyptians would have drowned the temple and its statues beneath the waters of an artificial lake; but an international group of engineers preserved Ramses' desire to be remembered for all time by cutting the outer monuments free and raising them above the level of the water.

A View of Egyptian Society

In antiquity, communication over navigable waterways in ships was greatly superior to overland transportation in animal-drawn carts. The Nile therefore imposed a natural administrative unity on Egypt. The kings secured their power through the help of ministers and advisers, especially the class of priests, while a complex bureaucracy carried out the routine work of government and saw to the royal monopoly over the economy. Slaves existed, but the economic difference between free citizens and slaves was not always vast; both classes worked the fields and labored on the pyramids. The ultimate economic basis for the regime was the peasants, whose lives changed little from one generation to another.

It was possible to enter and rise in the Egyptian hierarchy through education. The kings and their gods needed all manner of scribes, treasurers, and functionaries, and Egyptian children might learn the art of writing in a school run by a temple or a palace, even from a private teacher in a village. They studied normally from age 4 to age 16 and could then enter the army or the royal service. Scribes were also needed for the arts of medicine, architecture, and the priesthoods; most priests were men, but some priestesses are known.

Egyptian society was liberal in the scope given to women—more so, in fact, than Judaic or Greco-Roman societies. Women were not treated as the possessions of men, and we have no documents showing that they were ever sold as brides. Women could own and pass on property, as we see from a narrative of a certain Meten in the Fourth Dynasty: "His mother Nesbet gave him ten stadia of land; she wrote a deed to a house for his children." Again, a priest, Senenj, writes in the Sixth Dynasty to leave land to his wife Asenka "because I honor her so much in my heart." Women could appear as witnesses in court and could initiate action at law if anyone tried to take their land away. Officials were nearly always men, but women are sometimes found as scribes, even treasurers, something unknown in Greece and Rome. Among peasants, women toiled with men in agriculture and did most of the baking and spinning.

We must not overlook the turmoil within Egyptian history—the invasion of the Hyksos, wars in Asia, the vengeance taken on the memory of Hatshepsut and Akhnaton by their successors, the collapse of the New Kingdom and its conquest by Assyria, then by Persia. And yet there remains the awesome *permanence* of Egypt: No other state, in the nations we call Western, has ever survived so long. The Egyptians' faith must have aided them, for they solved religious questions with a fertile spirit of invention, finding gods everywhere—in the Nile, in the sun, in the king himself, who was often called Horus after one of the gods. On the whole, over the span of some thirty centuries, life flowed predictably, like the Nile, making severe demands but bringing the material for a well-earned reward.

IV. THE EARLY INDO-EUROPEANS

Most of the European languages—English, French, Greek, Latin, Russian, Spanish, and others—belong to the linguistic group that we call Indo-European; so do the languages of India, Pakistan, and Iran. Presumably, these languages descend from a mother tongue that we

Queen Hatshepsut of Egypt (1512–1482 B.C.),
history's first female ruler, pictured as a
sphinx, which was a divine animal. Surround-
ing her face are a lion's mane and a ceremo-
nial false beard.
(Photo: The Metropolitan Museum of Art, New York)

may call Indo-European, though we have no preserved writings in such a language. Speakers of Indo-European seem to have been clustered in southern Russia. Perhaps about 5000 B.C. they began a slow dispersion across Europe and parts of Asia. Some of them ultimately settled on the Indian subcontinent. Other groups of Indo-European peoples moved westward into Italy, Greece, central Europe, and Asia Minor.

The Hittite Kingdom

The Indo-Europeans who came to Asia Minor shattered the kingdom of Babylon established by Hammurabi and maintained by his dynasty (see p. 11). Among this group of peoples the Hittites were especially prominent. By about 1650 they established a capital at Hattusha (Bogazköy in modern Turkey). Excavations here have unearthed about 10,000 cuneiform tablets, the decipherment of which has made it possible to recover at least some of Hittite history.

The greatest early warrior of this nation, Murshili I (1595?–1520?), led armies south as far as Babylon, which he sacked about 1595, thus ending the kingdom once ruled by Hammurabi. Between 1400 and 1200 B.C. the Hittite kingdom reached its zenith. The reign of its most renowned king, Suppiluliumas (about 1380–1340), coincided with that of Akhnaton in Egypt; and the Hittites took advantage of the pharaoh's preoccupation with religious reform to tear away from Egypt the region of northern Syria. Under Ramses II, as we have seen, Egypt's unsuccessful attempt to regain this territory led, in 1284, to a treaty of non-aggression between the two nations. This modern-seeming document shows a growth in the techniques of diplomacy among ancient states.[6]

The Hittites shared various customs with other eastern states. They believed, for exam-

ple, that the king became a god after death. But they had other features that historians consider Indo-European. The whole army formed a kind of assembly, called the *pankus*, which acted as a court of law to punish criminals. Some think the *pankus* once chose the kings, but this power had passed away before our records begin, for it seems clear that kings had the right of inheritance. The queen retained her position even after the king's death, perhaps so that her religious duties should not be interrupted. The king was general, chief judge, and high priest, serving the many Hittite gods; most of these deities the Hittites adopted when they entered Asia Minor.

Power among the Hittites was in the hands of a limited number of families, who received grants of land and were bound to the king by oaths; this could be called a primitive feudal system (see p. 283). Like other societies in this era, the Hittites published law codes, which reveal that their society was patriarchal. Fathers gave their daughters in marriage, and (as also among the Greeks) a widow was normally married off to her father's next of kin. But women retained some rights of their own: For example, a free woman who married a slave remained free.

Close of the Bronze Age

The Hittite kingdom evidently collapsed because of the coming of iron. One of the commonest minerals on earth, iron had been known for many hundreds of years, but one of the tribes conquered by the Hittites had discovered a means of producing it in large quantities. Had the Hittites better exploited it to make weapons, they might have prolonged their rule.

Between 1250 and 1200 B.C. new waves of invaders from the north and east poured into Asia Minor, breaking up the Hittite kingdom. These peoples had learned the secret of working iron but they, unlike their more civilized Hittite

---

[6] Both the Hittite and Egyptian texts of this document are translated in James B. Pritchard (ed.), *Ancient, Near Eastern Texts Relating to the Old Testament* (1969), pp. 199–203.

contemporaries, promptly applied their knowledge to weaponry. As a result, they overcame the older and higher civilizations that still relied on bronze weapons. Between 1200 and 1000 B.C. the Bronze Age disappeared, to be replaced by an Iron Age, in which we still live.

The introduction of iron had profound social and political consequences for the development of civilization. Iron, more readily available than bronze, is not only harder but, most important for this discussion, was cheaper as well. As a result, more people came to own weapons, and Iron Age states grew militarily more formidable. As more of the population obtained weapons, there followed a partial shrinking of the distance between some socioeconomic groups in the society. Those who now served the state in the army began to claim some role in determining its policies, and the ruling elites had to open their ranks to the newcomers in order to maintain control over the masses.

The closing of the Bronze Age in the decades after 1200 marks a major turning point in the history of Near Eastern civilizations. Not only the Hittites but nearly every society in this part of the world experienced an upheaval at this time. The disturbances threatened, and in some places ended, various forms of political domination. But one society, more notable for its ideas than for its conquests, now began to emerge.

V. PALESTINE

The Hittites and their older neighbors shaped civilization in the ancient Near East, but the direct continuity of their influence stopped many centuries ago. The Israelites, however, provide a sharp contrast, for modern Jews feel an intimate kinship with their ancient ancestors. The modern state of Israel considers itself a child of the Israelite kingdom of antiquity, and

three of the great religions of the world—Judaism, Christianity, and Islam—descend from the Israelites' belief in a single, all-powerful god.

Canaanites and Phoenicians

Israelites did not create the first civilization in the region of Palestine. A group of Semitic tribes, the Canaanites, originally inhabited the area and established flourishing urban civilizations about the time of the Egyptian Old Kingdom. Among their cities were Jericho and Jerusalem. By about 1200 the Canaanites lost control of most of their domain and were forced into Phoenicia, a narrow region along the Mediterranean Sea.

The Canaanites in Phoenicia drew part of their culture from the Mesopotamian and Egyptian states nearby, but they were also innovators. Their outstanding contribution was a simplified alphabet with only about thirty characters that was later adopted by the Greeks and became the ancestor of Western alphabets.

The Phoenicians lacked the manpower to achieve an empire, but they influenced other cultures, especially through trade on both land and sea. Their commercial dynamism was unique in the ancient Near East. They established trading posts or colonies far from Palestine, the most famous of which was Carthage, a powerful city on the north coast of Africa that controlled parts of North Africa and Spain. Among the Phoenician articles of trade was a reddish dye that the ancients called purple; cloth dyed in this color became a luxury and has always remained a mark of royalty or eminence. The Phoenicians were also the first people to treat the art of war as a profession, and because of their sailing ability they were mercenaries in the Persian navy. They and other Canaanite peoples had thus developed a high urban civilization by the time the Israelites began their invasion of the Palestinian coast.

The Old Testament as a Historical Source

The Old Testament of the Bible provides a continuous record of how Israel viewed its past, but before historians can use the narratives and chronicles of the Scriptures as a source, they must determine the credibility of the documents. Scholars in the nineteenth century questioned whether the Old Testament contained unchallengeable, revealed truth. Archaeology in recent years has often confirmed the Bible, at least in questions of geography and topography, but literal accuracy is not, after all, the central issue. Religious traditions of any society, whether or not they are strictly verifiable, can provide historical information, just as law codes and king lists do.

The unique cultural contribution of the various writers in the Old Testament was to make creative use of familiar material, some of it descending from other Near Eastern peoples and some of it native to the Israelites themselves. These writers also demythologized much Canaanite literature. For example, the word *yam* meant "god of the sea" in prebiblical legends, but the Israelite chroniclers made this a nonmythical concept, "the sea." As they eliminated such deities, they concentrated on a single god and on our relationship to him. This great theme, varied in countless ways, fuses the Old Testament into a story about one god and the history of his chosen people. The Bible deals with real people and real times; it combines ethics, poetry, and history into the most influential book in the Western tradition.

The Old Testament was formed over many hundreds of years, starting perhaps in the twelfth century B.C. It probably assumed its present shape between A.D. 70 and 135. The long process of revision has left some interesting traces, such as parallel accounts of the same event. Chapters 1 and 2 of the Book of Genesis contain a classic example, for they offer two different views of the Creation, accounts that passed through oral tradition and were not reconciled when the text received its final polishing.

The Early Hebrews

Our knowledge of early Hebrew[7] society rests entirely on the traditions preserved in the Old Testament. There is no good reason to doubt the main lines of Biblical tradition. Beginning around 1900 B.C., tribes of nomads began to wander into Palestine from the east. Each one was led by a patriarch and they did not form a unified society. One such patriarch was Abraham, whose father came from a city called Ur (probably not the Sumerian Ur). Jacob, the grandson of Abraham, is said to have organized the growing nomadic people into twelve tribes under the leadership of his twelve sons. Jacob himself also took the name Israel (meaning "God strove" or "God ruled"). The people, which also called itself Israel, was therefore a tribal society, unlike the urban society of Sumer or the unified monarchy of Egypt.

Some Israelite tribes settled in Canaan. Others migrated to Egypt, where they were subjects under various pharaohs. Then, probably under Ramses II, the Israelites in Egypt left that land. At their head was a man with the Egyptian name of Moses. He crossed the Sinai Peninsula with them, about 1270, during the period of general unrest in the Near East.

Moses organized the tribes of Israel and some neighboring Canaanites into a confederation bound by a covenant to the god he named YHWH (by convention, we write this word Yahweh) and placed all the people in Yahweh's service. So far as we can tell, this was the first

---

[7] The term *Hebrew* should be restricted to the language and writings of this people. The word is probably related to *hapiru,* a term found in Egyptian sources; it means "caravaneer, wanderer, outsider" and is not an ethnic designation. The people known to us from the Old Testament called themselves "Israel" or "the sons of Israel," but before they took this designation we have little choice but to call them Hebrews.

time that the whole of Israel accepted one god. This tremendous moment is thus the birth of monotheism. But why did Israel accept one god, in contrast to the rest of the ancient world, where families of deities were the rule? We do not know, but we may guess that Moses saw the need to unify his people to enable them to regain their home in Palestine; and what could forge a stronger bond than having the whole people swear allegiance to a single god?

Moses proclaimed the new covenant between God and his people on Mount Sinai, in the pitiless wastes of the desert. According to the Book of Exodus, he received his instructions directly from Yahweh. These instructions, a document of the greatest historical interest, include the Ten Commandments, in which Yahweh issues the terse order, "Thou shalt have no other gods before me." The Old Testament shows that Israel at times did worship other gods and that prophets had to rebuke her time and again for lapsing from the true faith.

Early Israelite society was clearly father-dominated through the patriarchs and God, their supreme father. This assumption had an impact on the legal status of women. In the Commandments Moses assumes that a woman is the legal possession of her husband: "Thou shalt not covet thy neighbor's house, nor his wife, nor his servant, nor his ox, nor his ass." Marriage through purchase is assumed throughout the Old Testament, and a daughter might simply be given as a kind of salary: Jacob loved Rachel and served seven years to gain her (Gen. 29.20). The heroism of those women of the Bible who rose above this control—Ruth and Judith, for example—is all the greater. But the original restricted position of women continued in early Christianity. Paul commanded women to be silent in church; if they wished to learn something they should ask their men at home (I Cor. 14.34).

Moses also laid down a complex code of laws, only part of which has survived. It is clearly analogous to the earlier Mesopotamian and Hittite codes, but it differs from them in one basic aspect: it is a series of laws prescribing ethically right conduct. The historical reality of Moses and the fact that his laws are connected with the experience of a people have given the faith of Israel an immediacy to which Sumerian or Egyptian religion could hardly pretend.

The Israelite Monarchy

By a series of attacks on Canaanite cities and by convenants made with other tribes, the Israelites established themselves in Palestine. About 1230, they invaded Canaanite territory—a fertile, hilly refuge overlooking the Mediterranean. Biblical stories say that Joshua, the successor of Moses, led the tribes of Israel across the Jordan River and took the Canaanite city of Jericho by siege.

During the years of the conquest of Canaan, Israel still lacked a central government. A series of leaders (called "judges") appears in the Old Testament. These men managed to reunite the tribes in periods of crisis, but the tribes then habitually drifted apart. Ultimately, Israel developed a strong regime under a monarchy. According to the Bible, the people demanded a king, evidently wanting to imitate the practice of the Canaanites: "We will have a king over us; then we shall be like other nations, with a king to govern us, to lead us out to war and fight our battles" (1 Samuel 8.20). Saul became king about 1020 and then led Israel against the Philistines. His successor, David (1010?–960?), conquered Jerusalem and made it his capital. The entire nation now took the name Israel, and during this reign David extended the kingdom to its farthest boundaries.

Solomon, David's son and successor (960?–920?), was famed for his skillful administration and wisdom; he passed into Muslim literature as the clever and powerful Suleiman. He is the purported author of some books of the Bible—

Proverbs, Ecclesiastes, and the Song of Solomon—but it is clear that these works were composed considerably later.

Solomon ruled in a period when other Near Eastern powers were weak. He maintained peace by increasing the size of the standing army and equipping it with chariots; he also made a series of alliances with neighboring rulers who often sent him princesses in marriage as a token of good faith. These princesses, in a harem, provided political links to other important tribes. Thus a harem was actually a political device and was often used as such in the Near East.

Like all great kings of the period, Solomon was a builder. He left behind him the physical memorial that symbolized the faith of Israel through the centuries—the Temple in Jerusalem. But the temple could not compare in size with his magnificent palace and citadel. The tradition that the stables housed 12,000 horses gives some indication of its scale.

Solomon's autocratic rule and his extravagance caused resentment among his people, who were heavily taxed to pay for his palace and army. After his death his son was unable to control the kingdom, and it split into two parts. The northern half, based on the ancient town of Shechem, retained the name of Israel; the southern half was now called Judah and had its capital in Jerusalem. This division denied the people a chance for further political expansion and in fact led to the long period of tragedy that they were to suffer. The division was not only political, for the two kingdoms had distinct religious differences. Jeroboam I, the king of the northern kingdom, set up places of religion as rivals to Jerusalem and placed in the shrines a golden calf for the people to worship. This and other offenses against traditional religion are chronicled in the Books of Kings.

Weakened by internal quarrels, the northern kingdom of Israel was conquered in 722 by the Assyrians, who dispersed all its leaders into Assyrian territories. This scattered people became known in biblical lore as the ten lost tribes of Israel.

Judah was now the only Israelite kingdom, and from this point on the remaining Israelites are known as Jews. *Yehudim* was the name for those who settled around Jerusalem and from the Greek version of this name, *Ioudaioi,* was derived the English word "Jews." Judah fell in 586 to the Chaldean, or Neo-Babylonian, Kingdom. The captives were deported to Babylon—the so-called Babylonian captivity—but later in the same century were allowed to trickle back to Palestine. There were occasional revivals of an independent Jewish kingdom at other times, but in general the Jews became pawns of the various forces that ruled Palestine: Persians, Macedonians, Romans, Arabs, Turks. Only in our present time has a revived Jewish state—the republic of Israel, formed in 1948—taken its place among sovereign nations.

The Faith and the Prophets

The Jewish religion, like any institution tied to the fortunes of a people, changed and grew during more than a thousand years. One of the strongest forces that shaped it came from a few resolute social critics whose passionate conviction was sometimes close to fanaticism. These were the prophets—men of the people, tradesmen, preachers—who emerged in all periods of Israel's history. The most authoritative was Moses, and all successors looked back to him for guidance. They spoke one general message: Israel was becoming corrupt and only a rigid moral reform could save it. Worship of Yahweh had sometimes been blended with that of the gods, or Baalim, of the Canaanites. Luxury, promiscuity, and extravagance were weakening the discipline of Israelite society, a society built not only on belief but also on definite customs and behavior. But even as they denounced the prevalent wickedness, the prophets—men like Amos, Micah, Hosea, Jeremiah, Ezekiel, and the two Isaiahs—promised that God would forgive Israel if the people repented. God would prove his love to Israel by providing a Messiah. The word Messiah (Hebrew *mashiah*) means a person or even thing possessing a divine power or purpose; used of people, it came to mean one "anointed" by God to perform a special mission. From about 200 B.C. onward Jewish thought held that a king would some day appear, a descendant of David, who would deliver Israel from captivity and restore its power and glory on earth. The famous Dead Sea Scrolls, ranging in date from the second century B.C. through the first century A.D. (see Chapter 5), often speak of the awaited Messiah. Christians, too, developed their theory of a Messiah, who would return to rule on earth over all humanity: to them, the "anointed one" (in Greek, *ho christós*) is Jesus, but to Jews the hero is still unborn or unknown.

Another event that strengthened Judaism was the organization of the sacred writings. Ezra, whose work dates to about 445 B.C., is the prototype of a new kind of spiritual leader—the scribe and scholar. He collected and published the first five books of the Old Testament (the Pentateuch); later scholars collected the books of the prophets. The Temple in Jerusalem, destroyed during the Babylonian invasion, was rebuilt during the 500s and, in the absence of a free Jewish state, assumed even greater importance as the nucleus of the faith. It fell once more, in A.D. 70, this time to the Romans, who destroyed it. But part of the western wall of the outer court survived, and at this site, the "Wailing Wall," the Jews were permitted to weep and pray.

The Jewish Legacy

The Jews are the only society originating in the ancient Near East whose traditions have remained vital in modern times. For reasons that no one can fully explain, adversity has never broken the Jewish spirit, and over many centuries the Jews have persisted as a society even without an independent state. Their faith provided the most persuasive answer to the problem that also troubled their neighbors—the nature of the relationship between humanity and God. There was only one God; he was a jealous, vindictive God and, unlike the gods of the pagans, he was an exclusive and intolerant one. He judged severely, but was also prepared to forgive those who sincerely regretted wrong behavior. He created the world and stood outside the world; he had no association with the world of nature and never appeared as an animal or in any other form. Above all, he was a god for everyone, not just for nobles, priests, and kings. This simple but lofty conception of the divine, formed over the course of seven or eight centuries, drew its decisive impetus from the revelation granted to Moses, whose message was reinforced by the later prophets. To the Jews, history moves to and from three points—creation, revelation, and redemption. Moses stood at the central point, and only obedience to the laws that he transmitted can guarantee mankind's progress from revelation to final redemption.

Moses and the other prophets were not kings and could not force Jews to observe the law. The fact that ordinary men could influence the ethical behavior of a nation solely through their moral convictions anchored Judaism forever among the people. The Jewish religion is the experience of a people and the Bible is their record. Christianity, the religion of medieval and modern Europe, is a daughter of Judaism and has drawn upon the morality and ethics of the older faith. No matter how deep the wounds of persecution or how widely Jews were scattered in later times, nothing destroyed their loyalty to their traditions. They stand alone as the most influential culture of the ancient Near East.

VI. THE NEAR EASTERN EMPIRES

A series of general disruptions about 1200 left no state dominant for the next few centuries until the Assyrians began their conquests. They became the first people to accomplish a political unification of the entire Near East and thus formed the first true empire in history (see Map 1.3). The Persians, the next great imperialists of this region, built on foundations laid by the Assyrians and ruled with an administrative skill that only the Roman Empire would surpass in ancient times. They also developed a widely accepted religion, Zoroastrianism, some of whose doctrines persisted long after the Persian Empire disappeared.

The Assyrian State

The Assyrians were descended from Semitic nomads who had entered northern Mesopotamia about 2500 and founded the city of Ashur, named after their chief god. From this name comes the designation "Assyrian" for the people. Their language was a Semitic dialect closely resembling that of the Babylonians, and they wrote in the cuneiform script that had originated in Sumer and had remained in general use.

About 900 the Assyrians began their most important period of conquest and expansion. They became masters of the upper reaches of Mesopotamia, and their territory included Babylonia to the south, the cities of Palestine to the

MAP 1.3. FOUR ANCIENT STATES

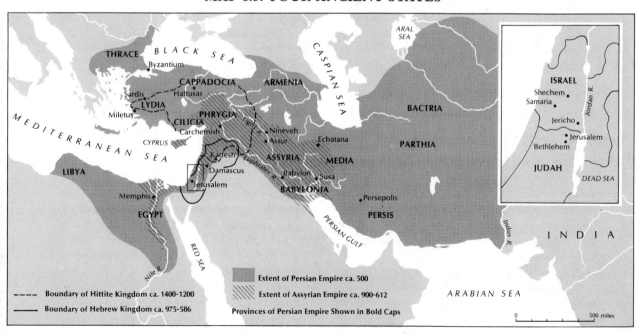

Boundary of Hittite Kingdom ca. 1400-1200
Boundary of Hebrew Kingdom ca. 975-586
Extent of Persian Empire ca. 500
Extent of Assyrian Empire ca. 900-612
Provinces of Persian Empire Shown in Bold Caps

west, and Egypt. By the late seventh century their empire embraced most of the Near East.

If any one concept could characterize Assyrian society it would be militarism. The army was especially dominant and efficient, and the Assyrians greatly extended the use of iron weapons. In administering their empire the Assyrians faced a greater challenge than any earlier state, for they had to absorb large kingdoms such as Egypt and Babylonia. They ruled with a degree of control unknown in any of the earlier conglomerates. In order to reflect the marked difference it is best to call the Assyrian domain the first empire and to designate those of earlier states as enlarged kingdoms.

The Assyrian kings exacted heavy payments of tribute as the price of leaving the conquered territories in peace. Some peoples, such as the inhabitants of Judah, escaped further burdens, but other, less independent peoples had to accept a vizier, or governor, serving the king. In some cases the imperial government deported subject peoples who might prove troublesome—for example, the inhabitants of Israel who were dispersed within the Assyrian Empire. Assyrian armies stationed in the provinces were a further guarantee of stability.

Language became another means of unifying the empire, for the Semitic language known as Aramaic was ultimately spoken everywhere in lands dominated by Assyria and became the common tongue of the Near East. In Palestine it was spoken by the Jews, including Jesus.

Among the brighter products of this harsh imperialism was Assyrian art. Much of the wealth extracted from the empire was spent on artistic glorifications of the king and his conquests. This art survives most notably in reliefs cut on the palace walls at Nineveh, the capital, and elsewhere.

The last important Assyrian king, Ashurbanipal (668–627) created a library of cuneiform texts, which have been translated in modern times. The largest single group of these texts concerns omens, divination, or observations of the stars, for Assyrian kings relied heavily on omens to guide their policy. Some scholars believe that this practice gave influence to the aristocratic priests of the state, whose interpretations of divine signs could sway the monarch's decisions.

It is hardly surprising that subject kingdoms within the Assyrian Empire watched for any chance to rebel. Finally, in 612, a combination of forces, led by Babylonians, captured Nineveh, and the Assyrians lost control of their empire.

The Chaldeans and the Medes

The Assyrian Empire gave way to two successor states: the Chaldean, or Neo-Babylonian, Kingdom and the Kingdom of the Medes.

The Chaldeans, the dominant tribe within the new kingdom based on Babylon, were the most learned astronomers of antiquity. They kept a minute record of eclipses, charted a plan of the heavens, and, most impressive of all, calculated the length of the year mathematically. Their discoveries were passed on to the Greeks and Romans and influenced all medieval and modern astronomy.

Babylon, the capital of the Chaldean Kingdom, was notorious as a center of luxury and wealth. Nebuchadnezzar (604–562), the most famous king of the Chaldean dynasty, built lavish temples to the gods and also constructed the terraced roof garden known as the Hanging Gardens, which was considered one of the Seven Wonders of the ancient world.

Media, the territory of the Indo-European Medes, was located east of Mesopotamia and became a coherent kingdom about 650. Among its subjects was another Indo-European group, the Persians. Media retained much of its prestige even after the Persians actually conquered it. Probably because Media was an older state than Persia, it was referred to first in official documents in which both states were named.

Assyrian reliefs often show kings with long curled beards and lofty headdresses as they receive prisoners or slaughter enemies, scenes closely related to historical events. In this relief the Israelite king Jehu prostrates himself before the Assyrians, to whom he paid tribute money in exchange for peace.
(Photo: The British Museum)

The Greeks used "Medes" as the term embracing both Medes and Persians, and called their decisive war with the Persians the Medic War.

The Persian Empire

It was the careful planning of Persia's resolute King Cyrus (559–530) that laid the basis for the Persian Empire. The Persians first extended their dominion by conquering the Medes, to their north, about 550. A few years later they expanded into western Asia Minor and confronted the recently formed kingdom of Lydia, whose ruler, Croesus, was famous as the richest man in the world, a reputation that may have derived partly from the fact that coins were invented by Lydia.[8]

Croesus, realizing that he would need allies against Persia, turned to the cities of Greece for help. Thus he involved European states for the first time in the affairs of the kingdoms of Asia Minor. Sparta agreed to join Croesus in war

---

[8] Ancient coins were lumps of precious metal stamped by the ruler to guarantee their weight and therefore their value. As coinage gradually replaced trade by bartering, it transformed methods of trade and strongly influenced Western civilization. Without acknowledged systems of trading in precious metal, the commerce of later antiquity and of the modern world would have been inconceivable.

against Persia, but Athens refused. Croesus also asked advice from the renowned oracle at Delphi, a shrine sacred to Apollo where the god supposedly spoke in prophecy through the mouth of a young girl. The shrewd Delphic priests gave Croesus a deliberately ambiguous reply: "If Croesus crosses the Halys River [the frontier between Lydia and Persia], he will destroy a mighty empire."

Croesus lost his ambitious campaign about 545 B.C. It was the Lydian Kingdom, not the Persian, that fell, and Cyrus took the Lydian capital, Sardis. This conquest brought the Persian Empire westward as far as the Aegean Sea, which separates Asia Minor from Greece. Now the stage was set for a direct clash between the vast empire of the Near East and the new culture of the Greeks, but this clash was not to come for another two generations.

To secure the southern flank of his growing empire, Cyrus led his forces against the Chaldeans and captured Babylon. Evidently, the inhabitants welcomed him, for they offered little resistance. Their judgment was sound; Cyrus treated the city with moderation, not sacking it as an Assyrian conqueror might have done. His wisdom is evident in his treatment of the Jews, whom he allowed to return to Jerusalem and rebuild their holy temple.

He did not live to make the third great conquest that enlarged the Persian Empire. His successor, Cambyses (529–522), conquered Egypt in 525, and the rich valley of the Nile remained under Persian rule until Alexander the Great captured it in 332 B.C. No Egyptian ruled independently over this ancient land again until A.D. 1952, when the government of Naguib and Nasser was established.

The most skillful administrator of the huge Persian Empire was Darius (521–486). He left behind a superb monument in Assyrian-Persian style, a description of his reign in a long inscription written, like the Rosetta Stone, in three languages (Old Persian, Akkadian, Elamite). It is carved, under a proud relief showing

Darius and some of his captives, high on the face of a rock at Behistun in Iran, and was first studied by the English scholar Rawlinson in the 1830s. In a series of paragraphs, each beginning "Saith Darius the King," he records his conquests, including that of Babylon, and the defeat and mutilation of his enemies. The tone and physical setting of this document assert and confirm the lofty position of the king.

Darius divided his empire into some twenty provinces, each ruled by a satrap ("protector of the realm"). The system worked successfully for the Persians because they had enough spies and civil servants to enable the king to keep close watch on his subordinates. The king was regarded as the supreme glory of the state, but the satraps had a high degree of independence; they dispensed justice, designed foreign policy, and were in charge of finance. Each one was responsible for an assigned amount of revenue from his province.

The Greek historian Herodotus mentions with admiration the Persian system of roads begun by Cyrus and perfected by Darius. A great highway ran across the empire from the capital at Susa westward to Sardis in Lydia, a distance of more than 1000 miles. The first long highway built anywhere, this road bound together the gigantic empire of the Persians.

Darius also built a lavish capital at the new city of Persepolis. The efficiency of his reign can be seen in his coinage, for he made creative use of this Lydian invention by issuing a famous series of gold coins called darics. He also installed a standard system of weights and measures for the empire.

Zoroastrianism

The prophet who formed Persian religion, Zoroaster (also known as Zarathustra), probably lived soon after 600 B.C. He taught that a supreme god, Ahura Mazda, created the world and directed the heavens and seasons. Beside him were the deities "Truth," "Righteous

Thought," "Devotion," and so on, whose ideals mankind should follow. But Ahura is opposed by Ahriman, a wholly evil spirit. Thus Zoroaster taught a dualist religion. After thousands of years, a day of judgment will see the triumph of good. Those who follow Ahura will gain Paradise; the rest will suffer in the realm of endless darkness.

Zoroaster's thought far outlasted the Persian Empire and strongly influenced other faiths. During the Roman Empire, this religion survived in the worship of Mithras, a Persian god who rivaled Jesus in popularity. The dualism of the Persian faith is reflected in Manicheanism, a sect of late antiquity, and in the beliefs of the Albigensians of southern France in the twelfth century.

Zoroaster lived at the same time as the Israelite prophets and the earliest Greek philosophers. Gautama, the Buddha, who founded the great Eastern religion of Buddhism, was active about 500 B.C.; and in distant China the philosopher Confucius was a precise contemporary of the Buddha. We shall not, in this book, study the thought of India and China, but it seems highly significant that people throughout the world felt, at about the same time, the need to restate their religious and moral creeds.

Vast is the catalogue of what Western civilization owes to the ancient Near East. First might come the art of writing, which spread outward from Sumer in the cuneiform style, appeared in hieroglyphics in Egypt, and was simplified into an alphabet in Canaan. There are monumental architecture and surveying, the latter especially necessary in Egypt; the methods of fortifying cities, military techniques, including casting weapons in bronze and, later, iron; the development of pottery; the art of trade, and the use of money and the Lydian invention, coins. In the intellectual world, there are the measurement of time, calendars, mathematics, lexicography, and a profound knowledge of astronomy. There is the organizing of society through proclaimed codes of law, early forms of diplomacy, and treaties. All these and more are the astonishing legacy of the first two or three thousand years of civilization.

Above all, perhaps, these early civilizations had various ways of looking at the two problems that will always most deeply concern people: their relationship to other human beings and their relationship to the forces that they consider divine or uncontrollable. Towering out of the great treasury of myths and tales about the gods is the monotheism of Israel, which is in turn the root of the three main Western religions—Judaism, Christianity, and Islam. The God of Israel, and none other, became the God of the Western world. But we are also close in spirit to the civilizations of Greece and Rome. To the legacy of the Near East they added a radical individualism and a passion for logical argument. Our politics and institutions also descend from Greco-Roman society. We shall therefore turn to the Mediterranean and the highly urbanized culture of Greece.

RECOMMENDED READING

Sources

Lichtheim, Miriam. *Ancient Egyptian Literature: A Book of Readings.* 1973–1980. 3 vols. Excellent gathering of original sources in modern translation.

Pritchard, James B. (ed.). *Ancient Near Eastern Texts Relating to the Old Testament.* 1969. A collection of translations from cuneiform and hieroglyphic texts, with brief commentaries, by eminent scholars.

Studies

Adams, Robert M. *The Evolution of Urban Society.* 1971. Contains chapters on both early Iraq and Mexico.

Albright, William Foxwell. *The Biblical Period from Abraham to Ezra.* 1963. A brief history of Israel by a giant in the field.

Cambridge Ancient History, The. 12 vols. Now being published in its third edition, the standard history of the ancient world; chapters by numerous scholars, with wide-ranging bibliographies.

Childe, V. Gordon. *What Happened in History.* 1985. Compact but profound analysis of history by a great anthropologist.

Dahlberg, Frances (ed.). *Woman, the Gatherer.* 1981. Studies of the economic and social roles of women in the earliest societies.

Emery, Walter B. *Archaic Egypt.* 1961.

Frankfort, Henri. *The Birth of Civilization in the Near East.* 1951. A comparison of early Mesopotamian and Egyptian history.

Gardiner, Sir Alan. *Egypt of the Pharaohs.* 1966. A detailed political narrative.

Hallo, William W., and William K. Simpson. *The Ancient Near East: A History.* 1971. American textbook survey of Mesopotamian-Egyptian history.

Kramer, Samuel Noah. *The Sumerians: Their History, Culture, and Character.* 1963. Full portrait of Sumerian society by a leading authority.

Laessøe, Jørgen. *People of Ancient Assyria: Their Inscriptions and Correspondence.* 1963.

Leakey, Richard. *The Making of Mankind.* 1981. By the son of Sir Louis Leakey, presenting a view different from that of the author's father.

Loewe, Raphael. *The Position of Women in Judaism.* 1966. Brief but exact discussion of the role of homemaker in Judaism.

Michalowski, Kazimierz. *Art of Ancient Egypt.* 1969.

Oates, Joan. *Babylon.* 1979. Survey for the nonspecialist.

Olmstead, A. T. *History of the Persian Empire.* 1948.

Pettinato, Giovanni. *The Archives of Ebla: An Empire Inscribed in Clay.* 1981. Detailed report on the newly found city.

Roux, Georges. *Ancient Iraq.* 1966. Detailed but readable survey of ancient Mesopotamia.

Sahlin, Marshall. *Stone Age Economics.* 1972. The life of earliest humanity.

Trigger, B. G. (ed.). *Ancient Egypt: A Social History.* 1983. Chapters by several historians.

Wilson, John A. *The Culture of Ancient Egypt.* 1956. Subtle treatment of cultural history of Egypt; superb for the history of ideas.

EXPERIENCES OF DAILY LIFE

Building a Pyramid

The Egyptian pyramids, especially the three located at Giza, now within Cairo, are the most famous monuments in all history. As one gazes up at them one cannot help asking how they were built. Ancient sources give us no satisfactory description of their building, and even today we cannot be certain of all the details, but the following suggested method combines proposals that have good support from experts.

First the builders selected land close to the Nile, so the stones to be used in the pyramid could be floated downriver from Upper Egypt to a point near the site. Next the land was cleared and leveled. The Egyptians' skill in preparing a level site is shown by the fact that the Great Pyramid, the one that has been most carefully measured and studied over the centuries, has sides of some 756 feet in length and yet slopes only one half inch from level. Next each corner of the square layout was oriented toward one cardinal point of the compass; this too was done with nearly perfect accuracy.

The "Step Pyramid" of Zoser (about 2650) was the first stone pyramid, but its sides rise in

Gustav Richter, Khufu Building his Pyramid. *This romanticized painting by a nineteenth-century artist attests to the special fascination the pyramids have cast on later eras.* (The Granger Collection)

steps rather than in a smooth face. The unseen interior of a true pyramid might look like this, but then the builders filled in the steps with casing stones that rose smoothly to the apex. The material for the core was limestone from Tura, near Giza, which the Egyptians could cut with sawing tools. When they needed granite for casing blocks, they quarried it up the Nile at Aswan, cutting it by driving wedges into the stone, then wetting them. As the wedges expanded they broke the rock loose (by this means they also quarried their tall obelisks).

The rocks then arrived by barge down the Nile. At the landing place workmen built a causeway or incline along which they dragged the blocks to the site. Men did all the hauling, since the Egyptians did not have draft animals. They pulled the blocks on sleds, which moved on beams or "sleepers"; these in turn were kept wet to reduce friction.

The core of the pyramid was built up of layers always diminishing in perimeter, but the most disputed question has been how the stones, weighing on average two and a half tons and sometimes as much as fifteen tons, were mounted to the needed level. Diodorus, a Greek historian of the first century B.C., states rightly that the Egyptians had no "machines," by which he must mean cranes or pulleys, and it is agreed that they used the simplest of methods. He further speaks of "mounds" on which they raised the stones, by which he must mean ramps—but how were they arranged? Some suggest a single ramp along (or perpendicular to) each face, but it has been objected that, as the pyramid rose, the ramps would have to be not only built up but also greatly extended at the base, to maintain the same rising slope; and this would have wasted time and manpower. More persuasive is the theory that there were ramps rising in a spiral around the pyramid, with at least one ramp for traffic returning

downward. Mortar, acting as a lubricant, helped in slipping the stones into place.

The pyramid thus approached its top as the platforms and slanted casing blocks were installed, while workers kept adding to the height of the ramps, which thus retained the same rise. Finally the capstone was set in place. The work of scraping, dressing, and smoothing the sides was done downward from the top. The Greek historian Herodotus says this and it seems right, for the ramps could then be demolished and removed at the same time. The Great Pyramid has lost its casing stones through plunder, but its neighbor, the pyramid of Chephren, retains a good sample of its casing near the top, which shows how a pyramid looked with its smooth sides complete.

The workers were mainly free citizens, not slaves, forced to work on the monuments at the pleasure of the king. Herodotus says that 100,000 men worked on the Great Pyramid, but this seems much exaggerated.

Many have deduced that a pyramid was a symbol of the rays of the sun shining downward and outward, as if to bless the king and Egypt. The harmonious architecture of the Great Pyramid has led to many mystical speculations, but, without losing ourselves in these, we may observe that, if the topmost stones were still in place, the height of the pyramid would be that of the radius of the circle that could be drawn around the base. The number of blocks in it has been estimated at 2.3 million; and it has been reckoned that, if these were cut into cubes one foot on a side, they could be continuously aligned to span two-thirds of the earth at the equator.

For more information, see I. E. S. Edwards, *The Pyramids,* 1960 (reprinted 1986); S. Clarke-R. Engelbach, *Ancient Egyptian Masonry,* 1930; Dows Dunham, in *Archaeology* 9 (1956) 159–65, with pictures of a modern model.

Chapter 2

The Foundations of Greek Civilization

Greek civilization influenced our own in a far more direct way than did that of the ancient Near East. This civilization in turn owed much to the topography of Greece. The land is broken by many narrow plains and valleys, and the thin soil offers a dramatic contrast to the fertile river-fed regions of Mesopotamia and Egypt. The Greeks turned to the sea for their wealth and became active traders and colonizers in the Mediterranean world.

At home, they lived within the pockets of habitable land in small, independent communities, or city-states. These cities were small enough to allow most Greeks to participate in government. They developed a new kind of urban life, in which citizens determined policy through argument and compromise in public assemblies. Over the years various kinds of self-government evolved that, for the most part, approached modern democracy. One notable exception, Sparta, chose a severe form of rule that restricted power to only a few.

The Greeks were highly creative. They were the first to write dramas, philosophical inquiries, and history; their poetry attained a depth and intensity never before known. Our ideas of beauty in literature and art have been formed largely by their achievement, and throughout modern history people have returned again and again to study and imitate Greek models.

Greece derived much from its neighbors: astronomy from Babylonia, an alphabet from Phoenicia, coinage from Lydia, decorative motifs from Crete. But the central legacy of Greece is its most daring invention—the art of self-government within small, intensely political communities.

I. EARLY GREECE (Ca. 3000–1100 B.C.)

The earliest inhabitants of Greece were not Greeks. We cannot yet identify them as belonging to any known ethnic group, but it seems probable that they came from Anatolia, or southwestern Turkey. Greek civilization began about 2000 B.C., when a group of Indo-Europeans, whose language had now become Greek, immigrated from the northern Balkans. A new culture slowly evolved, influenced in its early centuries by the more advanced civilization of Crete, the large island lying just south of the Aegean Sea. The history of Greece must, then, begin with Crete.

Cretan Civilization

The first inhabitants of Crete probably came from western Asia Minor well before 3000 B.C. In time, as the islanders mastered the sea, Crete became a thriving maritime power. Trade with the older civilizations of Egypt and Asia introduced new ideas and new skills. These, combined with the creative energy of the Cretans, produced a distinctive civilization.

We owe our knowledge of Cretan civilization to the work of the English archaeologist Sir Arthur Evans. In 1900 Evans began to excavate Knossos, the leading city of ancient Crete. There he uncovered a magnificent structure that he called the Palace of Minos, so naming it from the (perhaps) mythical king of Crete who appears in several Greek legends (hence the civilization of Crete is often called Minoan). Evans also established the usually accepted chronology for the history of Crete: Early Minoan (2600–2200), Middle Minoan (2200–1500), and Late Minoan (1500–1200).[1] He based his chronology on the residue of pottery found at Knossos, for different styles of pottery provide an accurate record of the successive stages of civilization at a site.

The Palace of Minos was built over several centuries from about 2000 onward. It was an extensive structure, with an impressive grand staircase and many wings, additions, and storage chambers. In designing some of its architectural features the Minoans displayed remarkable technical ability. The palace had a plumbing system with water running through fitted clay pipes, and the palace windows were covered with a form of glazed windowpane.

It was in the grace and beauty of their art that the Minoans achieved their greatest distinction. Minoan art bears witness to a civilization that valued elegance and style. The walls of the palace were decorated with frescoes showing jeweled ladies in elaborate gowns and graceful young men bearing cups and vases; paintings of gardens, birds, and animals express the Minoans' delight in nature. Minoan pottery often depicts marine themes: plants from the sea, flying fish, and lively renderings of the octopus. The gaiety and freedom of these designs are almost unique to Minoan artists.

[1] The system of Cretan chronology was established by Evans in his *The Palace of Minos* (1921–1936). Some scholars have attacked Evans' scheme. The most important difference is that they date the Linear B tablets to about 1200 rather than about 1400 (Evans). See, for example, L. R. Palmer, *Mycenaeans and Minoans* (1965).

The peaceful nature of Minoan civilization is suggested by the absence of fortifications at Knossos and at palaces excavated at other sites in Crete. Knossos was clearly the wealthiest of the Cretan cities and, judging from the size of its palace, was the center of a complex administration. Surviving records indicate that the king was served by an efficient bureaucracy. He probably acted as priest in religious ceremonies, for there is no evidence of a powerful priestly class like that of Egypt. Among the deities worshiped—and perhaps the chief one—was a bare-breasted goddess who was thought to rule over the world of nature.

Crete is well placed for communication within the Mediterranean and clearly had connections with Egypt. A statuette from the twelfth dynasty (about 1990 B.C.) was found at Knossos; this is an image of one User, who may have been an official representative or ambassador to the Cretan court. In Egypt, on the walls of the tomb of Senenmut, the vizier of Hatshepsut, are paintings of foreigners bringing in goods. Among them are men in obviously Cretan costume carrying Cretan pottery, perhaps items of trade or even tribute, during the 1500s.

Much of the wealth of Crete was generated by trade. The Greek historian Thucydides wrote that Minos was the first man to have a sea empire. We have no information about Minos from any sources close to his possible era, but there is a hint about the power of Minos in the legend of the Minotaur (the "Minos-bull"), the monster who lived in a labyrinth and devoured girls and boys sent to him as tribute. This legend, with Thucydides' evidence, suggests that the Greeks had a memory of a powerful ruler who dominated parts of the Aegean Sea. But any Cretan dominion overseas was not an empire in the modern sense, for Crete lacked the manpower to control it directly. At most, its dominion consisted of a group of trading posts distributing the products of Crete.

Minoan civilization reached its height be-

2600–508 B.C./TIMELINE

International and Military History	Political History
2600	
2200	
2000–1900 Greek speakers begin to settle in Greece	
1800	
	ca. 1700 Rise of monarchic–aristocratic regimes
ca. 1450 Greek influence in Knossos on Crete	
1400	
ca. 1380 Destruction of Knossos	
ca. 1250 Trojan War, destruction of Troy VII A	
1200–1100 Dorian invasion, attacks on Mycenaean towns	
1000	
750–600 Age of colonization by Greeks in Mediterranean and Black Sea	
ca. 730–716 Spartans conquer Messenia to west	ca. 700 Last kings disappear in Greek states
	ca. 650 First tyrants
	ca. 621 Legislation of Draco in Athens
600	
	ca. 575–570 Reforms of Solon in Athens
	561–528 Tyranny of Pisistratus in Athens
	508 Reforms of Cleisthenes

Social and Economic History	Cultural and Intellectual History
ca. 2600–ca. 2200 Early Minoan period on Crete	
ca. 2200–1500 Middle Minoan period	
1800	
ca. 1600–1100 Mycenaean Age	
ca. 1500–1200 Late Minoan period	
	ca. 1450–1400 Greek writing in Linear B, Knossos
1400	ca. 1350–1300 Walls and "tholos" tombs, Mycenae
	ca. 1200 Last known Linear B tablets, Pylos
	Return of illiteracy
Close of Bronze Age	
ca. 1100–800 Dark Age	
1000	
776 First Olympic games	ca. 800 Epic poems ascribed to Homer
750–600 Greek Renaissance	ca. 750 Adaptation of alphabet by Greeks
	ca. 700 Hesiod Black Figure pottery
	ca. 650 Archilochus
600	600 Sappho
	518 Birth of Pindar

This marble statuette of a goddess is a product of the Cycladic culture (so named from its home in the Cyclades Islands of Greece), which preceded the coming of the Greeks. Carved ca. 2800–2300 B.C., it represents the early emphasis on female rather than male gods. Neolithic art preferred abstraction to Palaeolithic realism and points the way toward later abstract thought. In our own century artists like Brancusi and Mondrian have returned to this type of noble, elegant simplicity.
(Photo: The British Museum)

tween 1550 and 1400 B.C., when Crete enjoyed its greatest influence in the Aegean world. Minoan pottery circulated widely, and there are several sites in the Aegean area named Minoa. Early mainland Greek art, architecture, and religion reveal Minoan influence. At least two Greek goddesses, Athena and Artemis, are believed to have been adopted from Crete.

Striking evidence of the Minoan-Greek interchange comes from Cretan writing on tablets that Evans and others discovered at Knossos. Most of the tablets fall into two classes, Linear A and Linear B. (Evans called them "linear" because the symbols are outlines rather than the detailed drawing found in hieroglyphics.) Both linear scripts are syllabic: each symbol represents a sound, such as *ko,* rather than a letter of an alphabet. Linear A, the older script, has not yet been deciphered; but in 1952 a British linguist and architect, Michael Ventris, showed that Linear B could be reconciled with an archaic form of classical Greek. The tablets he deciphered are inventories, rosters, and records of all kinds, listing foot stools, helmets, horses, vessels, seeds, and the like.

That these tablets were written in a form of Greek is highly significant, for it shows that Greeks were in Knossos during the period between 1450 and 1400 B.C., when the currently accepted chronology dates the Linear B tablets. While the Greeks were there, they learned to use the Cretan script in writing their own language. Another important clue suggests that there were Greeks on Crete. At this time the pottery made at Knossos changed in style; the painting became more regular and formalized. This change is probably due to Greek influence. There is evidence that they also introduced larger swords and the use of the horse both as a mount and with chariots. These changes at Knossos suggest that Greeks dominated the city not long before 1400, conceivably through outright military seizure.

About 1380, according to a widely accepted date, disaster engulfed Knossos and other Cretan cities; the stately palaces were burned or

Sea creatures were often used in the designs of Minoan pottery, and the octopus on this vase is an excellent example of the free-flowing style of Minoan artists.
(Photo: Himer Fotoarchiv München)

destroyed. There is continuing debate about what caused this catastrophe. A massive earthquake on the nearby island of Thera, about 1500, must have weakened Crete as well and may have assisted the Greeks in asserting their domination in the fifteenth century B.C.; perhaps the disaster ca. 1380 was connected with a quarrel or rebellion against Greek rule. In any event, the Greek city of Mycenae had now entered on a period of prosperity and power.

Mycenaean Civilization (Ca. 1600–1100 B.C.)

We have mentioned that Greeks first settled on the Greek mainland about 2000 B.C. (see p. 40).

Geography played a large part in the formation of their society, as it does in all civilizations. Mountain ranges divide Greece into many small valleys. The resulting pattern of settlement, so different from that of Egypt, encouraged the Greeks to develop independent political communities without the direction—or oppression—of a central ruler. The broken coastline, indented with countless small harbors, invited the people to become sailors, traders, and warriors at sea (see Map 2.1). By 1600 enterprises by sea had transformed a number of the independent Greek communities into wealthy, fortified states. Chief among them was Mycenae; therefore the years from 1600 to 1100 B.C. are often called the Mycenaean Age.

Two sets of graves found in the soil of Mycenae have given us a fascinating glimpse of the wealth and artistic accomplishments of this city. The graves in each were enclosed within a circular wall. The older set, tentatively dated between 1700 and 1600 B.C., was outside the walls that surround the citadel of Mycenae. Interred there were wealthy Greeks, perhaps from a royal family or clan. Alongside the bodies, the surviving relatives had deposited various offerings, for example, a golden rattle in a child's grave. The second set of graves, inside the citadel walls, far surpassed the older ones in wealth. These graves, dated between 1600 and 1500 B.C., were discovered in 1876 by one of the founders of Greek archaeology, Heinrich Schliemann, and are still among the wonders of archaeology. Their contents include such stunning luxuries as three masks of gold foil that were pressed on the faces of the dead and a complete burial suit of gold foil wrapped around a child, as well as swords, knives, daggers, and hundreds of gold ornaments. Bulls' heads in the graves indicate the influence of Crete on artists working in Greece.

The graves tell us little about the political or social history of Mycenae, but they do demonstrate its growing wealth in the sixteenth century. The city's king was probably its chief religious officer as well as commander of the

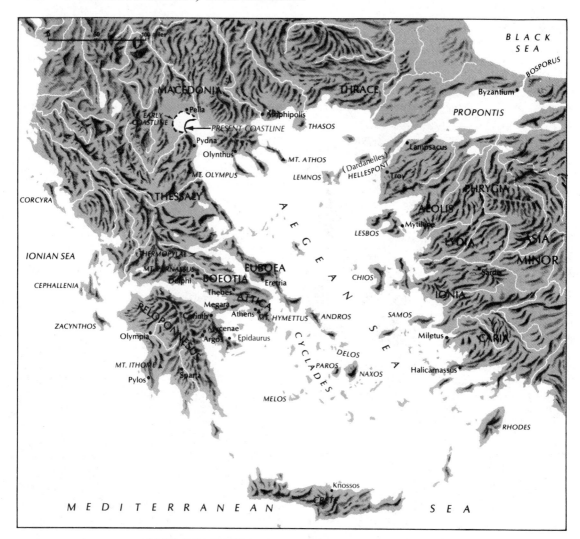

MAP 2.1. EARLY AND CLASSICAL GREECE

army. Elaborate fortifications and large numbers of swords and other weapons at Mycenae and other early Greek cities indicate that Greece was a more warlike society than Crete.

The economic organization of cities in the Mycenaean age resembled that of Oriental kingdoms in its centralized, "vertical" system. This is shown by the contents of Linear B tab-

lets, written in the same kind of early Greek that was used at Knossos, that have emerged from the soil at Mycenae, Thebes, and Pylos. The largest group, that from Pylos, can be dated soon after 1200 from the evidence of pottery fragments found with them. The tablets themselves are preserved only because they were baked in fire as these several cities were destroyed by invaders. All the tablets are rosters and inventories, cataloguing oil, seed, objects of metal, men, and women, all in the service of the palace bureaucracy.

Between 1400 and 1200, Mycenae reached the height of its prosperity and created the most imposing monuments in all Bronze Age Greece. Between 1350 and 1300 the stupendous walls around the citadel were built in their present form; it is significant that such defenses were apparently needed, as they were not (or at least none was built) on Crete. The mighty Gate of the Lionesses (or Lion Gate) was erected as an entrance to the city, and the most expensive Mycenaean tombs were built. These are the beehive-shaped, or *tholos*, tombs, large vaults with walled entranceways. The grandest and best preserved is the so-called Treasury of Atreus, conventionally named for the legendary father of King Agamemnon—but we do not really know which rulers were buried here. The high vaulted ceiling is still intact, and the somber cavern creates a breathtaking effect.

Each city of the Mycenaean period was probably independent under its own king. The only time these cities appear to have united was during the war against Troy, a prosperous city in Asia Minor near the Dardanelles. The origin of the Trojans is not yet clear, but some of their pottery suggest a close relationship to the Greeks. Apparently the Trojans were rich and offered a tempting prospect to pirates and looters. This was probably the real cause of the Trojan War, but ultimately Greeks explained the origins of the war by the romantic story in Homer's *Iliad* about the seduction by a Trojan of Helen, the wife of the king of Sparta. The excavation of Troy, begun by Schliemann at Hissarlik in Turkey, has disclosed several layers of building. One layer, called Troy VII A, was destroyed by an enemy about 1250. This evidence suggests that Homer's account of a successful Greek expedition against Troy contains some historical truth.

The war against Troy was the last feat of the Mycenaean Age. About 1300 or a little later, various marauders began to attack Greek ships and even mainland Greece. The identity of these warriors is still uncertain. Historians usually call them sea-peoples, and their homes were probably somewhere in Asia Minor. Whoever they were, they made trading by sea so dangerous that the export of Mycenaean pottery virtually ended. The raids by sea were temporarily destructive. But much more significant was a series of attacks by land, lasting roughly from 1200 to 1100. Near 1100, Mycenae itself was overrun and destroyed.

It is still not wholly clear who these land invaders were. Ancient Greek tradition spoke

Mycenaean gold funeral mask.
(Photo: Himer Fotoarchiv München)

The gravestone of a Greek warrior in archaic style, ca. 520 B.C. The warrior carries a shield bearing the head of the Gorgon, a mythical creature whose horrible face turned a beholder to stone. The goddess Athena is often portrayed wearing such a shield. Note the fleshy development of the legs. (Photo: The Metropolitan Museum of Art, New York. Samuel D. Lee Fund, 1942)

of the "return of the sons of Heracles," by which was meant the supposed return of Greeks speaking the Doric dialect of Greek to their ancestral home in the Peloponnese; the same traditions worked out a date for this event, which we can equate with about 1100 B.C. But we cannot accept such material from sagas without question, and this "Dorian in-

vasion" has been debated from the beginning of the modern study of Greek history. In an attempt to replace the traditional view, that the speakers of Doric Greek were roughly the last wave of Greeks to arrive in Greece, some historians have suggested that all the Greek dialects arrived more or less at once. Only later, they think, after a social revolution of some kind, did the speakers of non-Doric dialects in the Peloponnese take flight to other regions, thus allowing the Doric dialect to emerge in linguistic documents.

This is possible, but the traditional view can also be defended and seems preferable on balance. Mycenaean civilization suffered a series of shocks, and when we have evidence about Sparta and other sites in the Peloponnese we find many of them occupied by speakers of Doric Greek. Sparta in fact became the most important of the Dorian states after the Dorian invasion had run its course.

The period from 1100 to 800 B.C. is known as the Dark Age of Greece. Throughout the area there are signs of a sharp cultural decline. Some sites, formerly inhabited, were now abandoned. Pottery was much less elegant; burials were made without expensive ornaments; and the construction of massive buildings came to a halt. Even the art of writing in Linear B vanished. The palace-centered bureaucracies no longer existed, but of the political machinery that replaced them we know almost nothing.

Still, the cultural decline was not quite a cultural break. Farming, weaving, and other technological skills survived; pottery, though it was for a while much less gracious, revived and developed the so-called Geometric style. Nor was the Greek language submerged. Many Greeks, displaced from their homes, found safety by settling in other parts of Greece.

In a larger sense, the shattering of the monarchic pattern in the Mycenaean Age can be viewed as a liberating and constructive event. We cannot show that the kings and dynasties in Greece were dependent on or were imitating kings in the ancient Near East, but the two systems of monarchy resembled each other. If the Mycenaean kings had survived, mainland Greece might have developed as Anatolia did, with strong monarchies and priests who interpreted and refined religious thought in ways that would justify the divine right of kings. Self-government within Greek states might not

have emerged for centuries if it appeared at all. But the invasions of the twelfth century, in which the Dorians at least played a part, ended forever the domination of the palace-centered kings.

II. THE GREEK RENAISSANCE (Ca. 800–600 B.C.)

Epic Poetry

The so-called Dark Age following the collapse of the Mycenaean world was darker, for the modern historian, than the Christian Dark Age of Europe. But soon after 800 a spirit of optimism and adventure awakened the Greeks from their comparative lethargy. Greek literature now appears in the form of epic poetry (*epos,* "saga, narration"). Evidently the Greeks kept alive the memory of their glorious ancestors who had supposedly led the famous war against Troy. Poets chanted sagas about the personality and deeds of Agamemnon, Menelaus, Achilles, Odysseus, and other princes. We cannot be sure that these heroes ever existed, but to later Greeks they embodied the ideals of courage, honor, and nobility. As the sagas developed, they overlapped and multiplied; like streams they flowed together and became the epic poems ascribed to Homer, the *Iliad* and the *Odyssey.*

Each epic presents different aspects of heroic life. The *Iliad* is a portrait of a warrior aristocracy, in which greatness in combat is the highest virtue. The society is highly stratified; kings and nobles make policy and the lower classes have few rights, only duties. Women play no part in politics, but the portrait of wives and mothers is affectionate. Within this proud society, Homer concentrates on the headstrong warrior Achilles. He tells of his angry withdrawal from the siege of Troy when his honor is insulted through the seizure of his concubine; of his friend Patroclus fighting in his place and dying at the hands of Hector of Troy; and of Achilles' return to battle and his victory over Hector. The gods play a conspicuous part, now aiding one side, now the other; but the *Iliad* remains essentially a poem about human beings, a powerful study of men and women in conflict. The *Odyssey* celebrates the hero Odysseus, who triumphs through cleverness rather than sheer military prowess. After the fall of Troy he sets sail for his island, Ithaca, but the voyage takes 10 years (also the supposed length of the siege of Troy) and demands every kind of stratagem. When he does reach home, he and his son drive away a band of suitors to his faithful wife, Penelope; here too the portrait of a woman is remarkably noble and admiring.

The literary greatness of the Homeric epics requires no praise, but their genesis remains an insoluble problem. Neither ancient Greeks nor modern scholars have been able to prove when and where Homer lived, or whether the epics are the work of one man or of several. Various traditions about his birthplace point to Ionia, the area settled by Greeks on the western shore of Asia Minor. The story that he was blind seems to be a late invention. As to his work as an epic poet, some scholars forthrightly state that one man named Homeros created the whole of both the *Iliad* and the *Odyssey*. Admittedly, there is a difference in tone between the *Iliad*—the poem of force, as one critic has called it—and the gentler *Odyssey*. But those who think the epics are totally the work of one writer point out that Shakespeare wrote both tragedy and comedy, that his style and vocabulary changed as he matured, and that some critics keep trying, on flimsy grounds, to deny that Shakespeare wrote the plays attributed to him. Other readers of Homer, however, take a different view and detect multiple authorship in the epics; the works appear to be unified, but occasionally the seams show.

No solution to these problems will satisfy everyone, but we shall set forth what seems a tenable theory. From the Mycenaean era onward, a large number of poets in various parts of Greece sang and transmitted sagas about mythical heroes. All this poetry was composed and handed down in oral tradition. The nucleus of the *Iliad* may have been a saga about Achilles, a few thousand lines long. Perhaps, since Achilles supposedly came from central Greece (the area later called Thessaly), this particular saga was born there. If it had a title, it could have been "The Wrath of Achilles," for it was Achilles' anger that made him refuse to fight and indirectly brought death to his best friend, Patroclus. Around this possible nucleus, bards began to group other poems narrating the deeds of other Greek heroes and of their Trojan enemies. The greatly enlarged saga, now called the *Iliad* ("Tale of Ilium," another name for Troy), circulated in poetic tradition throughout Greece; but there was no strict, authorized version. Between 800 and 750 B.C. a poet of genius finally united the sagas and gave the story its present form and coherence. His name may have been Homeros.

We could analyze the composition of the *Odyssey* in a similar way. But did one man finally shape both epic traditions? On this point there is no decisive evidence. To some readers, the more civilized aura of the *Odyssey* suggests the hand of a different poet, but others reason that there is less demand for violence in this poem and see no difficulty in accepting both poems as the work of one man. The ancient Roman critic Longinus sought a solution by assuming that Homer composed the *Odyssey* in his old age; this theory, he thought, would account for its milder character.[2]

The Homeric epics remained the chief inspiration for Greek literature in all periods. Poets repeated the legends and wove variations on them. Historians and philosophers drew on

---

[2] See Longinus, *On the Sublime*, 9.11–15.

Homer for evidence or themes for debate. Plato, for example, severely criticized Homer's portraits of the gods: they were not pious and respectful enough to be used as literature in his ideal state, which he described in his *Republic*. Later Greek poets did not try to challenge Homer in long epic poems, but they did use epic meter and mythological subjects in a more delicate, restrained kind of poetry.

Homer's influence long outlasted classical Greek literature. Roman poets, Virgil particularly, wrote shorter epics inspired by Homer, and echoes of Homer are common in Chaucer, Shakespeare, and others.

Greek Religion

The *Iliad* and the *Odyssey* are more than great poetic narratives of heroic exploits; they also give us our first account of Greek religion. Most of the gods in the Greek pantheon appear in the two epics. Zeus had been the sky god of the first Greeks; his counterparts are Dyaus of early India, Jupiter in Rome, and Tiu in Norse myths. Some gods probably arrived from other cultures: Apollo, the sun god, from western Asia Minor; Aphrodite, goddess of love, from Cyprus; Athena, goddess of wisdom, and Artemis, goddess of forests and hills, from Crete.

What Homer did was to endow these gods with personality. Greek gods are not the remote, transcendent deities of Near Eastern religions. They intervene actively in human affairs, they assist their favorites, and they punish men and women who defy their will. Greek gods are anthropomorphic—that is, they are super-beings, differing from humans only in their physical perfection and immortality. Even Mount Olympus, their legendary dwelling place, is earthly, for it is an actual mountain in northern Greece.

The Greeks never developed a religious code of behavior as Israel did. Some acts, such as killing a parent or leaving a relative unburied, were considered wrong, as offending the general ethics of the world; and if people became too arrogant, Nemesis, a supernatural avenging force, would probably swoop down on them. But, on the whole, Greek religion had no spirit of evil and scarcely a demanding spirit of good.

The Greeks generally considered the gods potentially benevolent, but because an offended god might bring abrupt destruction, human beings had to appease the gods through appropriate offerings. The gods did not order people to obey or worship in any particular way, as did Yahweh, the god of Israel. A few ceremonies—such as the mysteries of Eleusis, which were sacred to Demeter, the goddess of fertility—did have complex rites, but on the whole people assumed that they could communicate with the gods through simple offerings and prayers. A remarkable feature of Greek religion was that there was never a priestly class; indeed, we scarcely know how priests were appointed. But *why* were the Greeks able to worship their deities without succumbing to the direction of a priestly hierarchy in their affairs? We do not know, but the reason may be connected to the political independence of the 600 to 700 individual Greek city-states. In the formative centuries of Greek culture there was no king, pharaoh, or emperor who could have installed a system of such powerful political-religious assistants.

Most gods were common to all Greeks, but each locality had its own patron. For instance, Athena was the protectress of Athens, but other gods also had temples there. Religion and the life of the city were intertwined, and the beautiful temples all over Greece were built by public decision, not at the orders of priests or viziers. And Greek drama emerged at the Dionysia, the Athenian festivals dedicated to the god of emotional religion, Dionysus.

The general acceptance of the various gods throughout Greece is a sign of the Panhellenic culture that arose during the Greek Renaissance. Another is the establishment of Panhellenic games in 776 B.C. This date is commonly agreed to mark the beginning of the "historic" period of Greek civilization. The first games took place every four years at Olympia, in the Peloponnese, and were held in honor of Zeus. Originally, the Olympics embraced only foot races and wrestling, but gradually they came to include horse and chariot races, boxing, javelin throwing, and other events. A victory brought an olive wreath, and lifelong glory as well. Modern athletes revived the Olympics in 1896, in Athens; though sometimes clouded by politics, they have remained the world's arena of supremacy in sports.

Other localities later founded games in imitation of the Olympics. One set was held at Delphi—the Pythian games, sacred to Apollo. Delphi was also the site of the famous oracle that Greeks consulted for advice on every sort of problem; this too is a symbol of growing Panhellenism. The god Apollo supposedly spoke through the mouth of a peasant girl whom the priests chose as the oracle. After first intoxicating herself by chewing laurel leaves, thus supposedly infusing herself with the presence of the god, she would babble in a state of frenzy. Two priests would present questions to her and then report her replies to the person seeking advice. The reply was often deliberately ambiguous; the duty of interpreting it rested with the inquirer. Delphi managed, as an exception, to blend religion with political importance. Many Greek states consulted the oracle before making war or sending out colonies and repaid the oracle with luxurious offerings. Though never more than a small village, Delphi was adorned with treasure houses built by the various Greek states to house their gifts, and many individuals also dedicated offerings to the god.

The Greeks took their gods seriously and were reluctant to act against what they considered the right interpretation of omens. They also created a rich mythology that passed on to

the Romans and inspired literature in later times.

Colonization (Ca. 750–550 B.C.)

During the Dark Age, for all its lack of dramatic activity, the population of Greece must have increased, with unfortunate consequences. Greece was relatively poor in agricultural resources, and by about 750 the population threatened to outgrow the local capacity to feed it. The problem of limited resources grew more and more acute: the struggle for survival caused social and economic conflict as people turned on each other. They solved this problem through foreign colonization. In effect, the mainland Greeks of the eighth and seventh centuries, instead of importing foodstuffs, exported their excess population. They colonized vigorously from about 750 to 600 and by the end of this period had spread over an enormous area, stretching from the northern, western, and southern shores of the Black Sea through Western Asia Minor and Greece proper, including the Aegean islands, to much of Sicily and southern Italy, then continuing west along both shores of the Mediterranean to Cyrene in Libya, to Marseilles, and to Spanish coastal sites. Wherever they went, the Greeks settled on the edge of the sea, never in the hinterland. Among their colonies are some of the great ports of modern Europe: Byzantium (today Istanbul), Naples, and Syracuse.

A colony became a wholly independent state, although the mother city might well expect some courtesies such as offerings during a religious festival. A classic quarrel arose, in the 430s B.C., between Corinth and one of her colonies on the island of Corcyra. Corinth complained that the colony did not show her enough respect, and ultimately the clash became one of the causes of the great Peloponnesian War (see Chapter 3).

This overseas expansion through colonization led to a revival of trade. The colonies supplied needed raw materials to the mainland Greeks, who in turn furnished them with manufactured goods. Trade brought prosperity to many of the Greeks cities and, even more important, the intangible benefits of contact with other peoples and other ideas.

The Alphabet

One of these intangible—and incalculable—benefits was the alphabet. By about 750 the Greeks began to trade with the Phoenicians, who were using a Semitic script called the alphabet (from the first two characters, *aleph,* which seems to mean "ox," and *beth,* "house"). The Greeks adapted this script to their own language. At some later time poets used the alphabet to preserve and improve texts of the Homeric poems, which had begun as oral literature.

Two versions of the alphabet developed. A Western version made its way to Cumae, a Greek town in Italy, and then to the Etruscans. They in turn passed it on to the Romans, who developed it into the alphabet that is now prevalent throughout the Western world and is being used more and more in such recently literate regions as Africa. Much later, many letters of the alphabet were used in an Eastern version, the Cyrillic form, the script for Russian and other Slavic languages. Thus large regions of the world use one or another derivative of the Phoenician alphabet in the form that the Greeks gave it.[3]

Archaic Literature

Homeric epics continued as the main inspiration during this new period of literacy, but

---

[3] The best study of the Greek alphabet is L. H. Jeffery's *The Local Scripts of Archaic Greece* (1961). She reviews the evidence for dating the adaptation of the alphabet to about 750.

poets adapted this legacy to express their own thoughts and feelings; Homer, by contrast, never speaks in the first person (except to invoke the Muses to inspire him). It is in the intense expression of the poet's own personality that Greek poetry is most different from literature of the ancient Near East—at least it is so in the samples we have.

The first major successor of Homer was Hesiod of Boeotia (in central Greece), whose *Works and Days* dates from around 700. The poem is a farmer's almanac that celebrates the pleasures of agriculture; the "days" of the title are the times of the year when one should plow and plant. Hesiod also tells the story of Pandora, the woman who opens the box of troubles that then fly into the world. Part of his poem is a bitter attack on the injustice of aristocratic landlords ("gift-devouring rulers") toward their peasants. In speaking up for the lower classes, Hesiod points to the general drift away from acquiescence in government by the elite class as it is seen in Homer. In his other poem, the *Theogony,* Hesiod tells of the ancestry and genealogy of the various gods. Part of his poem tells of the bloody rise of Zeus to supreme divine power. The god Cronus had castrated his father, Uranus, obtained the rule of the world, and killed his own children except Zeus, who escaped. Finally Zeus wins the battle with the demigods called Titans and himself becomes supreme. This struggle descends from similar sagas in Hittite tablets, in which gods kill and mutilate one another. But the difference in the Greek conception is that the supremacy of Zeus is not just another act of vengeance but fulfills the proper evolution of divine order.

About 650 we encounter poets who not only wrote in the stately hexameter of Homer and Hesiod but also experimented with other rhythms. Archilochus of Paros has left us many brief poems of brilliant vigor and audacity. He was a traveler, a man of action, and a mercenary soldier who died in battle. But his main stance is one of criticism of traditional forms of chivalry and supposedly aristocratic conduct (he boasts, for example, that he once threw away his shield to save his life; "never mind, I'll buy another one just as good"). In another poem, he calls on his heart to be brave: "My heart, my heart, worn by care, upright now! Face the enemy, don't give an inch!" His love poetry can be astonishingly frank. In a poem found in 1973 on a piece of papyrus wrapping a mummy, Archilochus tenderly yet passionately describes his seduction of a girl, including his sexual fulfillment at the end. He represents the movement toward total confession that runs through individual lyric poetry from him down through poets of today and tomorrow.

The most intense and subtle poet of her, and nearly of any, age was Sappho of Lesbos (about 600). She is also beyond doubt the hardest to interpret. Only one of her poems has survived complete, and one other nearly so; for the rest we rely on quotations in other writers and survivals on papyrus fragments. It may well be that medieval scholars did not copy manuscripts of her work because of her subject matter, with the result that her poetry has almost disappeared. Sappho was evidently a widow who maintained a school on Lesbos where elite young girls learned music, dance, poetry, and the art of elegant dress. They were preparing for marriage and Sappho hymns the beauty of the girls and the delights of love. The less important matter is the one most often discussed, whether Sappho herself, or the girls, was homosexual (this was allowed in ancient Greece); from such poetry as

> You have come, and done,
> And I was waiting for you
> To temper the red desire
> That burned my heart

physical love seems attested. In another poem, Sappho sees a young man near one of her girls; apparently in anguished envy, she writes,

> He seems to be a god, that man
> Facing you, who leans to be close,
> Smiles, and, alert and glad, listens
> To your mellow voice
>
> And quickens in love at your laughter
> That stings my breasts, jolts my heart
> If I dare the shock of a glance.
> I cannot speak,
>
> My tongue sticks to my dry mouth,
> Thin fire spreads beneath my skin,
> My eyes cannot see and my aching ears
> Roar in their labyrinths.
>
> Chill sweat slides down my body,
> I shake, I turn greener than grass,
> I am neither living nor dead and cry
> From the narrow between.
>
> But endure, even this grief of love.[4]

The more important matter is her poetry. Its exact analysis of feelings, its inventive images, its individuality all mark it as the product of a great writer of the highest originality.

Pindar of Thebes (518–438), the only important writer in the Doric dialect whose works have come down to us, is a glorious and difficult poet. We have four sets of his poems, which are choral odes written to celebrate victories of his patrons in the various Greek games. They were sung by choirs of boys at the homecoming banquets of the winners. Pindar's rhetoric and striking metaphors are brilliant, and his language is second to none in difficulty and complexity. His thought is deliberately traditional: he praises aristocracy, both personal and political, and urges his audience to follow the established rules of conduct. Since his patrons were members of the upper class, they probably wanted to hear such traditionalist views; however this may be, the world of the

---

[4] Translations by Guy Davenport, *Archilochos, Sappho, Alkman,* Berkeley-Los Angeles-London, 1980.

Greek elite could never have a more accomplished advocate.

Archaic Greek Art

In pottery, sculpture, and architecture the Greeks showed their ability to borrow motifs from other cultures and to transform them into something clearly Hellenic. This process reminds us how much European civilization owes to non-European peoples and how great is the role of cross-fertilization in cultural history.

Nearly all surviving examples of Greek painting come from vases, though some beautiful specimens of Greek wall painting are found in the Italian towns of Pompeii and Herculaneum. Pottery, along with most other products of high civilization, regressed to a nearly primitive state after the end of the Bronze Age. But by 850, the Greeks had developed the Geometric style, using various patterns and, later, stylized human figures. Then, about 725, as they came into more intimate contact with the East, such Eastern motifs as griffins, exotic animals, lions, and gods appear in the "Orientalizing" style.

The next stage of development, beginning about 700, is the Black Figure style of pottery, which is characterized by black designs on a background of natural orange clay. Over the next two centuries the Greeks brought vase painting to a height of creativity and elegance never seen before in the Western world.

Greek sculpture also drew on the kingdoms

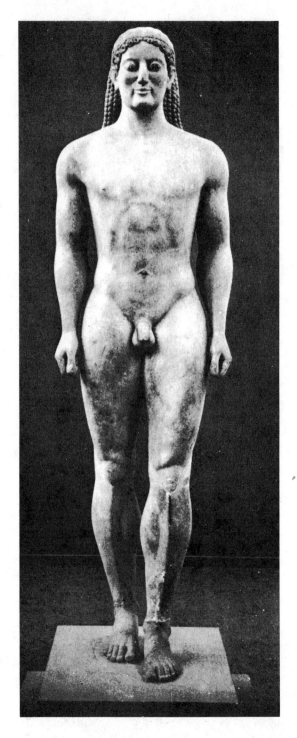

The kouros is characteristic of the rigid, formalized style of early Greek sculpture and clearly suggests the influences of Egypt and the Near East.
(Photo: Boudot-LaMotte)

of the Near East and Egypt for inspiration. The first type of freestanding marble statue was that of the *kouros,* a young man standing rigidly erect in the fashion of Egyptian statues, often with one foot extended. His female counterpart is called a *kore.*

The Greeks no longer spent their wealth and labor constructing palaces or immense tombs. Their buildings—temples, gymnasiums, and various other places of assembly—were to be enjoyed by all. Their most important architectural form was the temple, which appeared soon after 800. It was a simple rectangular structure with a sloping roof supported by columns; in the interior was a shrine, commonly containing a statue of the god to whom the temple was dedicated. Sacrifices were performed on altars outside the building, where the worshipers congregated. The oldest architectural style was the Doric order: the columns rested directly on the upper foundation, without any base, and were topped by a simple capital. At first the temples were made of wood, but later the Greeks—through their contacts with the Near East—acquired skill in working with stone. The temple, like the gymnasiums and theaters, was a civic building, a public expression of life in the polis.

III. THE POLIS

Government and Economic Life

For the social history of Western civilization, the most important event in the Greek Renaissance was the emergence, after 800, of the independent city-state, the *polis* (plural, *poleis*). In form, the polis was usually a central region, called the *astu,* often built around a citadel known as the *akrópolis* ("high city"). We must emphasize that there was considerable diversity among the seven hundred or more Greek poleis, and whatever generalizations we offer may not be true of every single one. Still, there are

Grecian bronze statuette of a woman holding an egg (490–480 B.C.), probably for a sacrifice. This figure, in the "severe" style (which follows the archaic style), begins to show motion and represents the transition from archaic motionlessness to the flowing, even violent, motion of Greek statuary in the late fifth and later centuries.
(Photo: Courtesy, The Walters Art Gallery)

some common features. In size, the poleis varied from a few hundred citizens to tens of thousands. Athens, the most populous, had from 35,000 to 45,000 adult male citizens during the middle of the fifth century. If to this we add the estimated number of women, children, slaves, and resident foreigners, the total population of Athens and her outlying villages in the region known as Attica was between 200,000 and 300,000. Sparta, by contrast, probably had an adult male population of no more than 12,000.

In the Greek states there was one overall social movement that seems common to all those we know anything about. This is the movement toward some kind of self-government by the male citizens. Indeed we may say that the problem that the Greek poleis faced and solved was how to integrate all citizens in a more or less harmonious state, how to consolidate everyone's energy toward building and supporting the city, rather than undergo self-destruction through permanent civil war between classes. We must not exaggerate, for not every state achieved democracy, control of affairs by the masses, but the general direction of politics was toward such a form.

But such social evolution is by no means inevitable in a state; it was not remotely approached in Egypt or Persia and, in fact, throughout history has been much less common than kingship or autocracy of various kinds. Why, then, did democracy (as we may call it) arise and survive in Greece? Perhaps no single answer would satisfy every historian, but the reason may resemble our explanation for the ability of Greek society to function without a priestly class. In a small state, which might be locked within a ring of hills, no monarch could long remain the remote, transcendent figure who ruled an Eastern kingdom. When we can first see the Greek states in history, they did have kings; the king also served as head of the army, at least in name, and probably as chief priest. As mainstays of his power he drew to

himself, in a kind of council, heads of clans or large families within his city. But by about 700, kings had vanished in nearly all poleis and had given way to land-owning oligarchies. Evidently the more influential citizens were no longer willing to submit to any kind of dynastic kingship. Sparta, the most conservative Greek state, was an exception and retained a system with two kings.

The upper classes—using the term loosely, we may call them aristocrats—must have governed through assemblies that, in origin, were the armed forces of the poleis. But as the population increased and poorer citizens became part of the armed forces, the ruling elites could no longer ignore their wishes. Aristotle, a clear-headed political philosopher, made it one of his principles that, as the number of citizens in a state increases, democracy will tend to arise. In the seventh and sixth centuries, legal codes defining citizens' rights were also published; such codes are further evidence that the populace was no longer willing to accept direction from its social betters.

Also within the seventh century we find the first popular leaders who united the masses behind them and challenged the rule of the aristocrats. These leaders installed themselves as "tyrants" (the Greek word *tyrannos* referred only to an autocrat who ruled without strict legal foundation, not necessarily to a cruel oppressor). The first known tyrant was Cypselus, who established a dynasty in Corinth in 657 B.C. The tyrants, though certainly no sponsors of democracy, helped to undermine the system in which birth within a noted family was a passport to leadership. Personal ability and military success became the main criteria; so in a way the tyrants laid the path to self-government in the poleis.

The poleis resembled one another enough to give us a general picture of economic conditions. The basic means of livelihood was agriculture. This remained true throughout Europe, despite revolutions and upheavals, until about two centuries ago. But in many areas of Greece the soil is thin and rocky, not suited to raising grain or pasturing animals. Therefore, at times farmers were threatened with a limited food supply.

It was the task of political leaders to discover new ways for Greeks to feed themselves. Some states, as we have seen, drained away part of their excess population through colonization. The colonies, in turn, became centers from which food could be returned to the Greek homeland; this happened especially through the Greek foundations on the north shore of the Black Sea, in south Russia (see Map A-4, in the Cartographic Essay). The Athenian reformer Solon found another solution. He turned the Athenians toward cultivation of olive trees (these were grown widely throughout Greece, as they are today). There was a ready market for olive oil and olives abroad, and in return the Greeks could import grain.

Greeks who could own land—and normally only citizens of the various poleis could do so—looked down on trading and manual labor as beneath their dignity. In fact, the general criticism of tradesmen and craftsmen probably hindered the Greeks from making progress in technology. Some cities on the sea—for example, Athens, Corinth, and Epidaurus—were centers of trade, but trade was often in the hands of resident aliens, not of citizens. We know that, of the 71 workers who were hired to construct the temple of Erechtheus in Athens, no fewer than 35 were foreigners; and we find slaves working on the Parthenon, paid the same as free men: one drachma a day, about the same wage paid to soldiers and sailors.

Industry was little more than household craft in Greece. One could increase productivity only be adding more hands, and a worker might have two or three slaves to help him in his work as potter, shoemaker, or stonecutter.

A few larger workshops are known: one shield maker had 120 slaves, and the father of the statesman Demosthenes owned about 50 and was considered fairly wealthy.

Greece differed from Rome in not using gangs of slaves in agriculture. The only industries in which slaves worked in large numbers were mining and stone quarrying. The Athenian general Nicias is said to have owned 1000 slaves that he rented out for such work. The Athenian silver mines, down the coast from Athens at Laurium, could absorb large numbers of workers, and the brilliant silver they yielded was a prime source of Athens' later wealth. In fact, a specially rich series of mines was opened here in 483 and helped to finance the Athenian fleet that fought in the Persian Wars (see p. 76). Conditions in mines were terrible. Slaves lay on their backs in narrow passages, chipping at the rock and choking in dust, and it is little wonder that we hear of widespread desertions whenever this was possible. Yet we do not read, in our sources, of rebellions by masses of slaves or of threats to the survival of any polis from slaves (Sparta is a notable exception, which we shall discuss later). Slaves were normally recruited from prisoners of war.

The development of an economy based on money was slow. Greece did not begin to use coins until nearly 600 B.C., and even then the smallest unit of coinage was usually a drachma, said to have been at that time the price of a sheep. The Greeks must have continued to use barter as their medium of exchange for some time after they adopted coinage from Lydia.

Taxation was haphazard in the poleis, for Greeks had little grasp of the mechanics of public finance. There was no permanent military treasury in the poleis until the 300s. In some ways this is surprising, since the cities were so often at war. Infantry soldiers were expected to arm themselves, but they did receive pay, and for this the state had to find money. When large amounts were needed for projects such as public buildings and maintenance of ships, the expenses were assigned to citizens judged capable of bearing the cost. This was only one of many services to the state that were imposed on the rich; others included paying for the training of the choruses in Greek dramas and seeing to the upkeep of gymnasiums for athletic training. Such contributions were called liturgies.

Life in the Polis

Greek city-states allowed their inhabitants more social mobility than did any Near Eastern kingdom, and they lacked the rigid divisions between citizens that form true social classes. Although some rich landed families had more influence than other citizens, and in that sense formed an aristocracy, there was no hereditary nobility. Moreover, the new wealth brought into prominence many men outside the ranks of the wellborn. It was legally possible for any citizen to make a reputation and eventually hold some kind of public office.

A polis was inhabited by citizens, foreign residents, and slaves. Roughly half these persons must have been women, but our sources are practically all written by men, and to deduce the place of women in Greek society is harder than to write the biography of some military hero. In our earliest source, Homer, women among the ruling class enjoyed considerable freedom and respect. Penelope, the wife of Odysseus, maintained his rule on Ithaca during his absence and was the model of wisdom and fidelity. In tragedy, Clytemnestra, Antigone, Medea, and others are independent and strong, if not always sympathetic, characters. Nor is it accidental that several of the most revered deities are women. Athena was respected for her warlike nature but was also the mother-figure to the Athenians, who held her in affection. And what deity has been portrayed in statuary more often than the goddess of love, Aphrodite?

Women did not normally own property. Marriages were arranged by families, and if the man of the house died the eldest son took over. If there were no sons, and the property fell to a daughter, she was married off to the nearest male relative; thus she "owned" the property only as a conveyer of it to a man. The purpose of this law was probably to maintain the property within the family or *oikos*.

Poorer women had to accept their condition and work as seamstresses, nurses, sellers in the market, even as prostitutes (these were normally slaves or foreigners). More elegant single women might become paid companions, *hetairai*, at men's social affairs; the most famous of all, Aspasia, married the statesman Pericles and bore him a son.

Greece was, then, a man's society, and women had less legal identity than they had had in some Near Eastern states. But the affection in which women—some women, at least, for we cannot express this statistically—were held is clear from the gracious burial reliefs from every polis. Typically, a woman is seated, members of her family stand nearby, and a son or her husband takes her hand in a quiet farewell.

Yet even in Homer it is clear that woman's primary duty is to remain at home weaving and managing the house, and so it remained. On the positive side, many women passed on to a slave much of the farming work that women in Greek villages still perform today. The myth that Greek women were always secluded in the home is easily exploded, but girls were kept sheltered from young men (this practice too survives in Greek villages), and when women of better class went out it was usually to some public event; shopping was mainly left to men. Differing pictures emerge of the education of women. A character in Xenophon's *Economicus* describes the education of a young wife as if he were training a docile animal, but since Athenian girls were often married at about 14 to a man 10 years or more older, the picture is less harsh than it might seem. The unusually liberated status of Spartan women (see page 61) may have had an effect on the philosopher Plato, who, like other conservatives, admired Spartan discipline. In his design for an ideal state, the *Republic,* he emphatically recommends that women should receive the same education as men.

Women (if not slaves or foreigners) were citizens of their state and had the protection of law, but they played no part in politics and did not vote. In harmony with these restrictions, our sources praise modesty and silence in women. The opposite kind of behavior is satirized by the comic playwright Aristophanes: in his *Ecclesiazousae* women hold an assembly, and in *Lysistrata* they go on a sex strike to press for an end to the Peloponnesian War. But as a comic writer he had the business of extracting the comic from any situation and his plays hardly demonstrate that Athenians disliked their wives and daughters.

Home life in the polis, even for the wealthy, was far less luxurious than that of an Egyptian noble or a lord within a palace in Crete. All dwellings were modest, and sanitation was primitive—though the Athenians managed to build a main drain under their market or agora. Fish, grain, and bread were staples of the diet; meat was usually reserved for festival days. The Greeks used olive oil extensively—as fat in cooking, as fuel for lamps, and even as a kind of soap. Breakfast, if taken at all, was a lump of bread dipped in olive oil. Sugar was unknown, and honey was the sweetening agent.

With few luxuries available, the Greeks could subsist on small incomes. In the fifth century, a skilled worker earned about a drachma a day. It has been estimated that 180 drachmas a year could support a married couple. It is clear that a Greek did not have to work unduly hard to make a living and that he had abundant free time. Given the seasonal nature of Greek farming, even the farmer had

several months a year when he had some leisure time.

This leisure time the Greek spent mainly in public places; it remains so today, as any visitor to Greece will observe. All life—religious, cultural, economic, and social—was centered in the town. The austerity of a Greek's home was balanced by the splendor of his public buildings. Life in a polis, for all citizens, was shared in many ways with all others. The cults of the polis were automatically the cults of every citizen, and a person who kept to himself was known as a private citizen, or *idiotes* (whence our word "idiot," a person who cannot communicate with others).

Sparta

There were hundreds of poleis in Greece, each legally separate from all others, thus forming independent states. We know little about the internal working of most of the poleis, and the ones we know best, Sparta and Athens, were not typical. All the same, their importance invites us to discuss them in detail.

Sparta, the leader of the Dorian states in the Peloponnese, achieved greatness by imposing on itself a rigid political system that made every citizen the unflinching servant of the state. At the cost of stifling artistic and literary development, it set the military standard for all other Greeks. Its militarism was the response to a problem common to Greek poleis: overpopulation. Instead of sending out colonies to relieve this pressure, Sparta conquered the people to the west, the Messenians, around 720. The territory of Messenia was divided among the Spartan warriors, providing each of them an allotment of land for subsistence. Spartan landowners then spent their lives in constant military training in order to maintain their control over the Messenians, who in turn worked the land for them.

Sparta also divided the population of its territory into strict classifications (see Map A–2 in the Cartographic Essay). Only those of demonstrably pure descent could be full Spartan citizens (called Spartiatai). Around Sparta were a number of villages, probably self-governing, whose members served in the army and were citizens of lower rank; these were the Perioikoi ("those who dwell around"). The bottom class were known as helots and were mostly the conquered Messenians. They had no rights whatever and were, in effect, slaves to the state; they were not privately owned and thus could not be bought and sold.

About 650 the Messenians rebelled. The revolt failed, and Sparta responded by making its army even more invincible and its constitution more rigid. This constitution, attributed to a legendary lawgiver named Lycurgus, dates from about 600. As finally evolved, the constitution established a government in which oligarchy, or the rule of a small number, was tempered with a measure of democracy. Sparta always retained two kings, a survival from prehistoric times. The ruling circle also included five *ephors* (overseers), elected annually by the citizens. Any Spartan could become a candidate for this office. The ephors acted as an executive body and also had great influence over Sparta's foreign policy. They initiated legislation, summoned the assembly and council, and wielded both police and judicial powers. The council of the elders, called the *gerousía,* was composed of twenty-eight men above sixty, who were chosen by the people for life. The assembly, the legislative body, comprised every male above thirty who could demonstrate that he was the child of full-fledged Spartan citizens. The assembly's powers were limited; the council brought before it the proposals for action, and the people voted yes or no. As a further safeguard against too much popular control, the leaders could dismiss the assembly if in their opinion it made the wrong decision. Thus the limited democracy of Sparta yielded to its ultimate faith in oligarchy.

In foreign affairs Sparta had tried to dominate other Peloponnesian states by outright conquest. When this policy failed, it sought strength through alliance rather than warfare. An interstate system arose, probably about 530, which Greeks called the "Spartans and their allies"; modern historians call it the Peloponnesian League. Sparta led but did not control the league, although if it refused to call the states to meet, no action could be taken. The league is one of the earliest examples of alliance in the Greek world and is a rare instance of the Greeks' transcending the normal exclusiveness of city-state politics.

The Spartan male dedicated most of his life to military service. Training started in boyhood. The Spartan warriors lived and ate together, and their military discipline approached sadism. As tests of their manhood, young men were required to go without food and shelter and received severe floggings, which sometimes proved fatal. Boys were taught to steal, and the crime lay in being caught.

Spartan women were admired by other Greeks for their beauty, but their life style was extraordinary. Marriage was usually preceded by abduction, usually indeed symbolic, but attesting to the warlike state the Spartans fashioned. Bridesmaids would then cut the girl's hair short. Dressed in a tunic, with no jewelry allowed, she then took part in male games. If a marriage was childless, a woman could bear a child by a man not her husband; we even have testimony that three or four men could share the same woman. This custom may have inspired Plato, in his *Republic*, to recommend that normal family ties be abolished in his ideal state: children should not even know who their parents were. These customs were meant to assure enough manpower for the army, but Aristotle (*Politics*, Book 2) lamented the permissive mores of Sparta. Women could own property in Sparta, and Aristotle also reports that they owned two-fifths of the territory.

Sparta was cut off from the other Greek

poleis by two mountain ranges, and this geographic isolation was deliberately reinforced by the state. The need for manpower at home made it difficult for Spartans to engage in international trade (we know of only one Spartan colony, the modern city of Taranto in Italy). Trade with others was further discouraged by the adoption of an intrinsically worthless iron currency. Perhaps because of this isolation and the rigors of military life, the Spartan's laconic way of speaking (so named from the plain of Laconia around Sparta) came to denote extreme terseness.

The isolation also cut the people off from new ideas that might have sparked creativity. The Spartans did not cultivate philosophic debate or historical writing. Though they did make fine pottery, at least until 525, the martial spirit of the society did not provide the right atmosphere for the general development of the arts.

Whatever we think of the principles of the Spartan regime, it was successful in preserving itself. The Spartan people, having to dominate a much larger population of potential enemies, chose to embrace rigid militarism. Yet the citizens were sovereign over the question of war or peace, and when they chose war, they were voting to put themselves in the field. To other Greeks, Sparta became a symbol of tenacity and strength. Plato approved of Spartan virility and lack of democratic follies; Aristotle and later philosophers praised Sparta for its mixed constitution, in which the kings represented the element of monarchy, the gerousía that of oligarchy, and the assembly that of democracy.

Athens

The city of Athens expanded its domain early in history until it controlled the whole plain of Attica, but it did not reduce the inhabitants of the other villages to a condition of servitude; thus it was free of the terrible problem that the Spartans created for themselves in having to restrain large numbers of angry subjects. Athens was a large polis with widespread trading interests, and its political currents were strong and turbulent. These are among the conditions that caused Athens to experiment again and again with its constitution; its political history is the most varied of all the city-states of Greece.

At one time Athens had a king as other poleis did. He was advised by a council of senior men, known as the Areopagus (the name is actually that of a hill in Athens, on which St. Paul was to preach). When the monarchy ended about 683, the king was replaced by three (later nine) archons, or administrators. At first the archons probably had to come from established families—the people whom we may loosely call the aristocracy. They were elected annually by the assembly of adult male citizens. After completing their year's term of office, the archons became permanent members of the Areopagus. Thus each year the Areopagus acquired nine new members with experience in high office, and eventually it numbered about 300 men. Since it was composed of senior men with permanent membership, the Areopagus was probably more influential than the board of archons in determining public policy.

Our first information about a major reform in Athens is dated around 621 when Draco, an otherwise unknown statesman, published or codified the law on homicide. That the law on homicide was now published for all to know was an important step forward for Athens. Draco's laws were later considered severe (such is the meaning of "draconian"); but they did establish a better judicial procedure than simply relying on the opinion of tribal elders. Among his other legal reforms, Draco apparently made a distinction between voluntary and involuntary homicide, which in itself was significant. Early societies often looked on any kind of homicide as defiling the community in the eyes of the gods.

About 600, when Sparta was revising its

state in the reform associated with Lycurgus, Athens was also dealing with a political crisis. The differing methods used by these states to solve their problems present an interesting contrast within the world of the poleis. Athens faced a serious agricultural crisis as her increasing population found it ever more difficult to feed itself from the available land. During lean years some farmers began to obtain additional food by pledging away a portion of the next year's crop. As they assigned more and more of their crops, they finally began to use the land itself as collateral. Some dispossessed peasants became tenant farmers, paying a portion of the crop (probably one-sixth) as their rent. If they defaulted on this rent, their creditors had the right to enslave them.

The resentment of the bankrupt peasants might have exploded into violent revolution had not the Athenians managed to solve the problem peacefully. Probably in the 570s they gave powers of arbitration to Solon, who had been archon in 594.[5] Aware that there was little hope that the poor farmers could ever repay their debts, Solon adopted a course of radical simplicity: he canceled all agricultural debts. At one stroke the enslaved men were free. As for the land they had earlier lost, it probably remained in the hands of its new owners. The important thing was that Solon had prevented civil war.

He also passed constitutional reforms. He divided all citizens into four classes based on their income from the land rather than on family background. Members of the three higher classes could hold public office. Those in the fourth class, common laborers and peasants, were probably half the population. They could

vote in the assembly; later, in the fifth century, they could sit on juries and serve in the council or steering committee (see p. 64). Solon's system for electing officials shows the importance of owning land in early Athens, for it apparently excluded all who did not own productive land, even traders and artisans. The historical significance of the new system was that it ended privileges based on birth. Men from newer families could work their way up economically and achieve positions of leadership, regardless of their family background.

Solon also seems to have created a court of appeal, the Heliaea, somehow drawn from the people at large, but our sources tell us little of how it worked. The best information about his work comes from surviving quotations from his poetry, and these show that he considered himself a moderate: "I gave the people just enough privilege, neither taking away nor adding anything." His chief contribution was recognizing the needs of the whole state; for the first time someone considered the common people as a group with justified grievances and took bold steps to solve them. We hear of no such arbitration in any ancient Near Eastern kingdom.

Solon's humane legislation did not end the agricultural crisis. Freeing the peasants from servitude was not the same as guaranteeing them enough to eat; hungry tenant farmers had become hungry free citizens, and the discontent remained. Pisistratus, an Athenian military leader supported by the poorer farmers from the hill country, saw his opportunity in this turmoil. In 561 he appeared in the city, displaying wounds that he had allegedly received from his enemies. His supporters demanded that the assembly give him a bodyguard. With the help of these club-bearers, as they were called, he seized the Acropolis and began to rule as a tyrant. Though he was driven from the city twice, he returned in 546 to seize authority decisively, and he ruled Athens from that year until his death in 528.

---

[5] That Solon was archon in 594 is fairly certain, and most scholars follow ancient tradition in dating his reforms in the same year. In all probability the assumed synchronism between his archonship and his reforms was an inference drawn in antiquity, and there is good reason to think that the reforms actually took place in the 570s: see C. Hignett, *A History of the Athenian Constitution* (1952), p. 316.

Pisistratus fits well the pattern of the Greek tyrant sketched earlier. Solon's failure to institute a distribution of land meant that Attica still suffered from her agricultural difficulties. Since Pisistratus had drawn some of his support from disgruntled farmers and workers, he now rewarded them with land grants from the confiscated estates of the wealthy landowning aristocrats who had opposed him. Responding to the changed conditions of the times, he sought to ameliorate the plight of the poor by further encouraging trade and industry. Under his aegis Athens became an important commercial center.

In order to turn men's loyalties away from their clan leaders and toward the new, larger unit he was attempting to create, Pisistratus initiated a splendid program of public works. He built a temple to Athena, the patron goddess of Athens, and in another part of the city he began a temple to Zeus, the largest of all Greek temples, not completed until about A.D. 120, when Athens was under the Roman Empire. He also established a yearly festival in Athens honoring the god Dionysus, and by encouraging dramatic contests at these festivals he opened the way for the development of Athenian tragedy in the next century.

The tyranny of Pisistratus, like some later ones, conferred many material benefits. Moreover, Pisistratus ruled by masking despotic realities in constitutional forms. For example, the archons were still elected by the assembly, though the candidates were almost certainly selected by the tyrant himself and had far less freedom of initiative than they would have had in a free society. The façade meant that Athenians grew accustomed to having some role in the choice of their magistrates, and this maintenance of democratic form made them receptive to real democracy when it finally came into existence at the end of the sixth century.

For some years after Pisistratus' death, in 528, his son Hippias ruled securely; but a conspiracy eventually frightened him into using terror as a means to keep peace. Some Athenians were forced into exile, among them Cleisthenes, the leader of a noted family. While in exile in Delphi, Cleisthenes and his supporters managed to enlist the help of the Spartans in a plan to drive the new tyrant from Athens. In 510 a Spartan army invaded Athens and exiled Hippias. Cleisthenes returned to his native city, determined to make himself the dominant Athenian politician.

Having observed how Pisistratus overcame all rivals by making the poor his supporters, Cleisthenes decided to use the same strategy. In 508 he proposed a scheme whereby the masses would participate more directly in running the state. Although Cleisthenes himself probably did not use the term, the Greeks eventually called this system *demokratia,* the rule of the demos or the entire body of citizens.[6]

Cleisthenes' aim in founding democracy was probably to secure his own supremacy and that of his associates rather than to further any special political theory. The basic reform was the creation of a Council of 500 (members). This council planned business for the public assembly and gradually surpassed the old Areopagus in political power. All male citizens above thirty could serve for one year, and the council was chosen afresh every year. In later times—or perhaps from the beginning—the members were chosen by drawing lots; this eliminated the influence of any special groups who might try to dominate the council. No man could serve more than twice: in this way political experience was shared by a great many citizens, even if this led to government by amateurs rather than professionals.

---

[6] Strangely (as we might think), the word *demokratia* was not always a favorable political term. It became such in Athens, but even there the historian Thucydides has Pericles say, in an oration, "Our system is called democracy; nevertheless, everyone is equal before the law"—that is, the masses have no advantage over the upper class, as one might fear in a system of mass sovereignty. Plato and Aristotle considered democracy a corrupt form of constitution.

The enforced rotation of service in the council was Cleisthenes' master stroke. There was a fair chance that every eligible Athenian would be chosen to serve on it once during his lifetime. With such a personal stake in democracy citizens would not conspire with those who wanted to abolish the system. The success of Cleisthenes' plan is evident from the remarkable tenacity of Athenian democracy, which endured for several centuries in its Cleisthenic form. It also administered domestic and foreign policies and controlled finance.

Cleisthenes also directed a radical revision of the Athenian social structure. He was evidently trying to break up the possible influence of regional groups. For political purposes he divided all Athenians into 10 tribes. The determining factor was the particular village, or *deme,* that a man lived in at the time of the reform. These villages, 139 in number, were grouped into 30 sets, called *trittyes* (the word means "thirds"). Three trittyes were grouped together to form a tribe, the 30 trittyes thus forming 10 tribes in all. A tribe included men dwelling in trittyes that were geographically separated from each other; thus no tribe came from a single region of Attica. This complex scheme assured that no local interests would dominate the opinions of a tribe. The Council of 500 included 50 men from each tribe and was thus meant to be a cross-section of all Athenian citizens.

Cleisthenes left the magistracies untouched. There were still nine archons, as before, and after their year in office they became permanent members of the Areopagus. The qualifications for office remained as they had been under Solon: only the upper two property-classes could be archons. We are not well informed about the judicial system at this time, but it seems that the archons conducted their own trials. Two ancient features of judicial procedure con-

The interesting procedure of ostracism was instituted in Athens about the time of Cleisthenes. Once a year the Athenians could vote for the man they considered most dangerous to the state by inscribing his name on *ostraka,* or scraps of pottery, such as those shown here. The one on the right bears the name of Themistocles. Six thousand votes in all had to be cast, and the "winner" went at once into exile for ten years. Themistocles was ostracized after the Persian Wars, when his influence had waned.
(Photo: American School of Classical Studies at Athens)

tinued. The Areopagus judged cases of homicide; and at times the people, or a section somehow formed into the Heliaea, acted as a court of appeal (this, as we saw, may have been a reform of Solon's).

The ultimate power in Cleisthenes' *demokratia* rested with the *demos,* the mass population, which met in the assembly. All adult male citizens, whether landowners or not, could attend and vote. The assembly passed laws, elected magistrates, voted for or against war, and accepted alliances with other states.

After the passing of his reforms in 508, Cleisthenes vanishes from our sources, but the Athenians continued to develop his system, especially through the use of drawing lots for office. In 487, for example, they began choosing their nine archons, from a preselected group of candidates, by this method. Later, in the fifth and fourth centuries, many other officials were so chosen, such as public auditors and managers of public land and mines. The officers chosen by lot, even the archons, surely lost some of their former prestige; but the political theory underlying allotment was that there were many men equally honest and capable of holding office in a democracy. Again, allotment elimi-

nated much of the quarrelsome rivalry over office. Also in 487 we hear for the first time of a man expelled from Athens for ten years by the colorful process of ostracism (Aristotle assigns this reform to Cleisthenes himself, but this remains controversial). In 457, by another extension of democracy, the third highest property-class was made eligible for the archonships.

Thus more and more citizens shared in running the state. By stages that we cannot trace precisely, the judicial system also came into the hands of the people. Trials were held (though never for homicide)[7] before juries numbering two hundred, five hundred, or more citizens—chosen by lot; and here even the lowest class could serve. Aristotle observed that "when the people gain control of the juries they are masters of the state." It is clear that the great majority of Athenians supported this constitution. This is shown by the abysmal failure of revolutions led by oligarchs. Intellectuals, such as Plato, deplored the power of the untaught masses, but the attachment of the people to their *demokratia* prevailed over all.

---

[7] The Areopagus retained jurisdiction over homicide.

The basic social organization of Greece was the independent city-state. These states existed in the hundreds and were not united by any central leadership or control. The civilization within these states surpassed anything in the Near Eastern kingdoms in diversity and richness of thought. Here political forms changed more rapidly than they did in Egypt or Mesopotamia. Aristocratic families gave way to tyrants as the dominant political element. The tyrants in turn awakened and represented the wish of the people themselves to manage their own affairs. Democracy, in varying degrees, became a common form of government. This was an extraordinary, and probably unpredictable, departure from the monarchies of the Near East and of Mycenaean Greece.

The establishment of self-government in Greek states reflects the willingness of Greek citizens to trust themselves in politics. Kings no longer held power through inheritance, and the people gave orders to themselves through elected officers. The Greeks believed that their own intelligence was capable of governing. This daring innovation, democracy, arose at about the same time as philosophic speculation. The universe was explained through conjectures derived from reason rather than through traditional, received myths. These political and intellectual discoveries had barely been made when the Greek states had to face their supreme challenge—an attack from the Persian Empire, the state that had unified the political heritage of the Near East.

RECOMMENDED READING

Sources

Herodotus. *The Histories.* Aubrey de Sélincourt (tr.). 1954.

Homer. *The Iliad.* Richmond Lattimore (tr.). 1951. An exact translation by a noted Greek scholar, himself a poet.

————. *The Odyssey.* Richmond Lattimore (tr.). 1968.

Studies

Andrewes, Antony. *The Greeks.* 1973. Chapters on Greek social and political life, not a continuous history.

Boardman, John. *Greek Art.* 1973.

Burkert, Walter. *Structure and History in Greek Mythology and Ritual.* 1980. By the most original and trenchant expert of our times.

Burn, A. R. *The Lyric Age of Greece.* 1960. History and literature in the archaic period.

Bury, J. B., and Russell Meiggs. *A History of Greece,* 4th ed. 1975. An old but still solid work for reference; emphasis on politics and wars.

Chadwick, John. *The Decipherment of Linear B,* 2nd ed. 1970. A study of the Cretan scripts, with notes on the method of decipherment.

————. *The Mycenaean World.* 1976. An attempt to reconstruct the society revealed in the clay tablets.

Desborough, V. R. d'A. *The Greek Dark Ages.* 1972. Based, as it must be, mainly on archaeology.

Finley, M. I. *The World of Odysseus.* 1979. The values, customs, and life style of society as portrayed in Homeric epic, by our leading social-economic historian.

————. *Atlas of Classical Archaeology.* 1977. The physical setting of the Greek world, with excellent brief commentary.

Guthrie, W. K. C. *The Greeks and their Gods.* 1968.

————. *A History of Greek Philosophy.* Vols. 1–4, 1962–1975. Brilliant, sensitive, elegant.

Hooker, J. T. *The Ancient Spartans.* 1980.

Hopper, R. J. *The Early Greeks.* 1976. Highly readable survey of ancient Greece to the beginning of the Classical period.

Jeffery, L. H. *Archaic Greece: City-States c. 700–500 B.C.* 1978. Mainly a close political narrative.

Murray, Oswyn. *Early Greece.* 1980. A brief, up-to-date survey.

Nilsson, Martin P. *The Mycenaean Origin of Greek Mythology.* 1972. An older classic study by the greatest historian of Greek religion.

Page, Denys L. *History and the Homeric Iliad.* 1959. On the long genesis of epic poetry and what the historian can learn from the documents.

Snodgrass, Anthony. *Archaic Greece: The Age of Experiment.* 1981.

Starr, Chester G. *The Economic and Social Growth of Early Greece, 800–500 B.C.* 1977. Brief, with references to sources.

Vermeule, Emily. *Greece in the Bronze Age.* 1972. Exact, comprehensive synthesis.

Warren, Peter. *The Aegean Civilizations.* 1975. On the Minoan-Mycenaean era, fully illustrated.

Yalouris, Nicolaos. *The Eternal Olympics.* 1979. History of the games, the Greek institution still alive today.

EXPERIENCES OF DAILY LIFE

The Greek Agora

Greek cities normally had a large open space, the *agorá*, that served as a civic center or main public square. The word comes from the verb *ageiro*, "gather"; thus the agora was the space where citizens gathered for public business or could even mean the assembly itself. This meaning is clear in the first mention of an agora, in Homer's *Iliad* (Book 18, line 497). Homer here describes a shield made for the Greek warrior Achilles, on which are engraved a number of scenes showing the social world of Homeric times. One scene shows a trial in progress: Elders of the state, acting as judges, sit in a "sacred circle" in the agora, where they hear rival claims in a homicide case. The agora was always a sacred place, or *temenos*.

In the other Homeric epic, the *Odyssey*, the hero Odysseus lands at the city of the Phaeá-cians and is invited to the agora to witness some games in honor of Poseidon. Games, too, were sacred: The greatest of all, the Olympics, were celebrated in honor of Zeus. This scene confirms the nature of the agora as a sacred center.

The agora that we know best is the huge one in the center of Athens, under the north slope of the Acropolis. The god originally worshiped in the sacred area was probably Dionysus, the deity of ecstatic religion based on the cult of fertility. From the sixth century B.C. at the latest the Athenians held games for Dionysus, which came to include choral contests; in these, men dressed like satyrs in goatskins danced around his altar and sang "goat songs." These choruses were the seeds of Athenian tragedies (*tragos*, "goat"). Even when the dramas moved to a permanent theater on the south

A nineteenth-century reconstruction of the Athenian Agora.
(The Granger Collection)

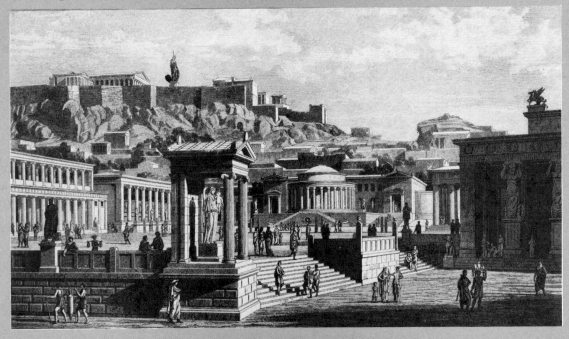

68

slope of the Acropolis (about 500), ceremonies dedicated to Dionysus still took place in the agora. Indeed, they could not have been wholly removed from that sacred area without offending the god.

With their easy acceptance of many gods at once, the Athenians built other shrines in the area. Zeus was given a stoa (the word usually means a long building with colonnades), about 430, to honor him as the savior of Athens during the Persian Wars. Nearby stood a temple to Apollo, father of the mythical Ion, from whom all Athenians were supposedly descended. To the west of these, on the hill called Kolonos Agoraios, is the well-preserved temple probably dedicated to Hephaestus about 450 (it is usually called, wrongly, the temple to Theseus, or Theseum). There were other shrines as well, and some gods honored in them obtained their own games. The Panathenaic games for Athena, immortalized on the famous frieze on the Parthenon, originally took place here, and the procession passed through the agora on the long Panathenaic Way. Along this street were also held chariot and torch races.

Since 1931 the Athenian agora has been excavated and studied by the American School of Classical Studies. The sacred area was marked off by large stone posts. One of these declares in Greek, "I am the boundary of the agora." Persons accused of serious crimes were forbidden to enter the agora, in order to keep out possible religious pollution. As Athenian democracy developed, the agora became its administrative center and was slowly converted into a large square through the addition of more public buildings. Most Greek agoras assumed a square or horseshoe shape, but the pattern varied according to the space and funds available. At Miletus, on the coast of Asia Minor, one side of the agora was bounded by a long stoa facing the sea.

The public assembly in Athens also moved from the agora, about 500, to the Pnyx, a large hill to the southwest. In the agora, the council of 500 that managed affairs of state had a meeting hall, with a nearby round building called the Tholos. For a period of 35 or 36 days, which was called a prytany, a group of 50 men from the council managed the business of the state and also dined and slept in the Tholos; then they turned the direction of affairs over to another group of 50. There were 10 such periods in a year, so all 500 members of the council had their turn at serving on the steering committee. To the north was the Royal Stoa, which housed the official copies of important laws such as those of Solon and Draco. Outside this stoa is a large rock, called simply "the stone," on which Athenian archons took their oath of office. Other documents were kept in the Metroön, or temple to the Mother (Greek *meter*) of the Gods; and hundreds of others were inscribed on walls or on free-standing marble blocks. Among many other buildings were other stoas; in these were offices, banks, law courts, and shops. The east side of the agora was brilliantly defined by a stoa 382 feet long, built by Attalus II, king of Pergamum (159–138), and rebuilt in the 1950s as an administrative center and museum for the agora.

In modern Greek *agorazo* means "I buy"; this points back right across the centuries to the everyday activities in the place—shopping, trading, selling. Some elite Athenians looked down on the common citizens who came here to buy groceries and clothing, to visit the barber, or to seek the modest pay (three obols, about half a day's regular wage) offered for jury duty. Yet Socrates and others argued philosophy here, and St. Paul preached Christianity. Ordinary people rubbed shoulders with archons and councilmen, who therefore could not remain on a higher level like the more remote authorities of an eastern kingdom. Civic life in the agora fostered conversation, debate, philosophic thought, and above all democracy. It provided the perfect cross-section of the citizen body. It remained an ancient site of worship but also became the mirror of Athenian history.

Chapter 3

Classical and Hellenistic Greece

At the beginning of the fifth century the mighty Persian Empire under Darius and Xerxes twice tried to conquer the small city-states of mainland Greece. Against all likelihood, in a series of military encounters that culminated in the famous battles at Plataea and Mycale in 479, a heavily outnumbered Greek hoplite army smashed the Persian invaders and drove them from Europe. The poleis of Greece, especially Sparta and Athens, had performed the miracle of routing the Persians. As the Persians withdrew from the Aegean, the crucial question became, Who should lead the Greeks? For the rest of the fifth century the inability of the Greeks to unite inspired a struggle for leadership that in 431 led to war. Almost all the poleis were drawn in eventually, forced to take sides as Sparta and Athens fought for hegemony. The war raged till 404, leaving the participants weak and demoralized. Thus it prepared the way for the conquest of Greece in the next century by the Macedonian king Philip II and his son Alexander the Great. These two monarchs then went on to conquer Egypt, Persia, and Asia Minor.

In the fifth and fourth centuries, the intellectual and artistic achievements of the Greeks reached their apex. Despite tumultuous political conditions—perhaps in some measure because of them—a sudden burst of creative energy occurred, concentrated in time and space to a degree that was then unprecedented and, some would argue, has never been duplicated. In these years lived the tragedians Aeschylus, Sophocles, and Euripides, and the comic poet Aristophanes; the historians Herodotus and Thucydides; the sculptors Phidias, Polyclitus, and Praxiteles; the philosophers Socrates, Plato, and Aristotle.

After the Macedonians had destroyed the autonomy of the polis, Greek culture took a decisive turning. During the last decades of the fourth century the Greeks, having lost the world of the independent polis, found the new, wider world of Alexander's empire. There followed a fascinating series of intellectual developments, including Stoicism and Epicureanism, that were to affect dramatically the future intellectual experience of the West.

I. THE CHALLENGE OF PERSIA

Invasions of Greece (490 and 480–479 B.C.)

By about 500, the Greek states had largely assumed some form of self-government. But now they had to face their supreme challenge: an attack from the colossal Persian Empire, which had recently unified the lands of the Near East. Among the territories controlled by King Darius of Persia (521–486) were the Greek cities on the western coast of Asia Minor. These Greeks rebelled against Persian control in 499—a prelude to the Persian Wars. This event is called the Ionian Revolt, after Ionia, the central portion of the shoreline. Sparta was asked to support the revolt but refused—according to Herodotus, because Persia was so far away. The Athenians did lend support, and for a time the revolt was successful, but it collapsed in 493.

Darius had no wish to leave the matter there. He now proposed to invade Greece itself, and one of the prime victims was to be Athens, the city that had dared to help the rebels. Darius probably also planned to conquer much or all of Greece; had he succeeded, he would have been the first ruler in history whose empire joined Asia and Europe. In pursuit of this aim,

MAP 3.1. THE PERSIAN WARS

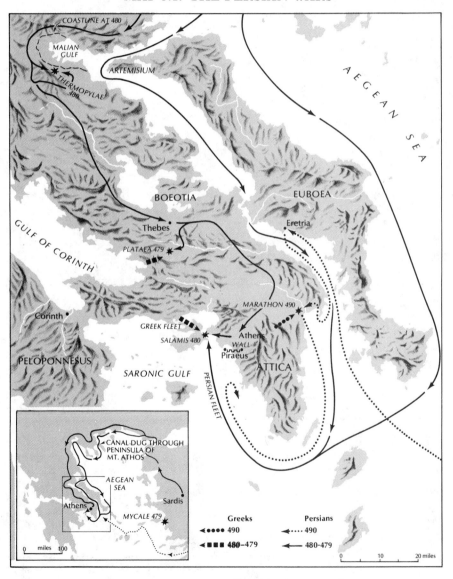

500–300 B.C./TIMELINE

International and Military History	Political History
500	
499–493 Ionian revolt	
490 First Persian War, Marathon	487 Athenians choose archons by allotment
	487? Ostracism introduced at Athens
480 Salamis	
479 Plataea	
478–477 Founding of Delian League	
460	
459–451 First Peloponnesian War	
450 End of Greek war against Persia	450–429 Supremacy of Pericles
446–445 Thirty years' peace between Athens, Sparta	
431–404 Peloponnesian War	
421 Inconclusive Peace of Nicias	
420	
415 Athenian expedition to Sicily	
405 Spartan victory at Aegospotami	403 Spartans impose oligarchy on Athens
380	
371 Thebes defeats Sparta at Leuctra	
359–336 Rule of Philip II of Macedon	
340	
338 Philip's victory at Chaeronea	
336–323 Reign of Alexander the Great	
331 Alexander's victory at Gaugamela	
323 Beginning of Hellenistic Age (323–30 B.C.)	
300	

500–300 B.C./TIMELINE

Social and Economic History	Cultural and Intellectual History

500

| | 496–406   Sophocles |

483   Athenians discover new veins of silver, Laurium
478–477   Athenian allies begin payment of tribute

c. 480–406   Euripides

469–399   Socrates

460

447–432 Parthenon, other buildings on Acropolis

458   *Oresteia* of Aeschylus
450–429   Age of Pericles

428–347   Plato
425   *Acharnians* of Aristophanes

420

399   Trial and conviction of Socrates
384–322   Aristotle, Demosthenes

380

341–270   Epicurus

340

335–263   Zeno, founder of Stoicism
335   Aristotle founds Lyceum in Athens

332–331   Alexandria founded in Egypt

300

c. 300   the *Elements* of Euclid

Darius sent a fleet across the Aegean Sea in 490 and confidently awaited news of the fall of Athens.

The Persians landed on the beach at Marathon, a village 26 miles north of Athens (see Map 3.1). There being no such thing as an army of all Greece, the Athenians sent out an army of about 9000 and Plataea, a small town in Boeotia, added 1000. The Greeks were commanded by Miltiades, a member of a great Athenian family. The Persian force was perhaps 20 to 25,000. Miltiades chose the moment to attack, and the Greeks charged, with most of their strength on the wings of their formation. They trapped most of the Persians in their center and won the battle decisively. The remainder of the Persian force sailed against Athens, but the Athenians marched back to the city in time to prevent the attack, and the Persians had no choice but to return to Asia. Herodotus reports that the Athenians lost 192 men, whose burial monument still stands at Marathon, and the Persians, about 6400. The victory was won by superior timing and discipline, aided by the heavy body armor of the Greeks.

Stung by this defeat, Darius began at once to prepare a second invasion, but he did not live to attempt it. The next king, Xerxes (486–465), took up the task, devoting four full years to preparing a huge force that would attack by land and sea. This time there would be no mistake.

Fortunately, an Athenian statesman now came to the fore—Themistocles, a shrewd political strategist. In 483 he had persuaded the Athenians to build a navy of 100 triremes, the classical Greek warship, with the proceeds of silver found in some new parts of the mines at Laurium (see p. 58), and since then more had been added. In this navy Themistocles saw the chance for Athenian survival. About the same time other Greek poleis began to fear annihilation from a Persian invasion—nothing less than the threat of foreign conquest could force the independent city-states to stand together.

Early in 480 some thirty states formed an alliance; Sparta, Athens, and Corinth were its most powerful members. The Spartans' traditions of discipline in war caused the allies to entrust to them the command on both land and sea—this even though the Spartans had failed to arrive in time to fight at Marathon because of the need to wait for a religious festival at home.

A few months later Xerxes began his march toward Greece. Historians estimate the strength of his force at about 60,000 men and 600 ships.[1] Whatever its exact size, this was the most grandiose invasion of Europe by sea until the Allied invasions of Sicily and Italy in 1943. The Persian infantry crossed into Europe on a pontoon bridge built across the Hellespont (the modern Dardanelles in Turkey) and soon arrived in Greece proper. In order to keep his army in close touch with his fleet, Xerxes had a canal cut through the isthmus joining Mount Athos to the mainland and passed his ships through it.

The Greeks decided to make a stand at Thermopylae in central Greece, a narrow defile that a few men could hold against a much larger force. About 5000 men from various states, including 300 Spartans under King Leonidas, took up their position in the pass, determined to hold it. When one Spartan was warned that the massive barrage of Persian arrows would block out the sun in the sky, he replied with Laconic wit, "Splendid news: if the Persians darken the sun, we'll be able to fight in the shade." The Greeks did hold the pass, to the frustration of Xerxes, who is said to have complained that he had "plenty of human beings but few real men." But a traitorous Greek led a Persian force through the hills to the rear of the Greeks, who thus had to fight, outnumbered, on two fronts. The position was hope-

---

[1] Herodotus, our source for the Persian Wars, was given fantastic reports and reckoned the total Persian force at more than 5 million men. The figure here is only an estimate.

less and the Greeks were killed nearly to the last man; King Leonidas of Sparta fell along with his countrymen.

At the same time, the Greek fleet had tried to hold off the Persian ships at Artemisium, at the north end of the island of Euboea. This battle was inconclusive, and the Persian navy continued its advance and waited off the coast of Attica. The Athenians abandoned Athens ahead of the Persian army, but there is much argument about the timing and planning of the evacuation. A Greek inscription, found in 1960, purports to be a copy of a resolution moved in the Athenian assembly by Themistocles himself. The decree orders that half the Athenian fleet should sail to Artemisium for the battle just mentioned, while the other half should lie in wait at the island of Salamis just off the coast of Athens; meanwhile the women and children should take refuge in other towns. The inscription is a superb specimen problem in the study of documents. Some historians accept it as an authentic source that compels us to correct the account given by our main historian, Herodotus, who says nothing of any such far-seeing plan. Others, though, find the document too good to be true and wonder whether the Athenians were really content to make Artemisium a half-hearted stand, and also whether Themistocles could have foreseen the coming battle at Salamis before Artemisium had even been fought. The stone itself was inscribed in the third century B.C., but this alone is not a conclusive argument against the authenticity of the document, since this copy may descend from a good historical tradition. But on the whole it seems safest to view the inscription as inauthentic, an attempt to tidy up the past, as it were. The version of events in Herodotus is to be preferred.

Greek Victory

In any case, Athens was largely abandoned, and the Persians marched across Attica and burned

CHRONOLOGY OF PERSIAN WARS

499, autumn: Greek cities of Ionia in Asia Minor revolt from Persian control.
498: Athens and Eretria take part in burning of Sardis in Persian Empire.
496: Persians besiege Miletus, leading city in the revolt.
494: Fall of Miletus.
493: End of Ionian revolt.
490, mid-August: Battle of Marathon near Athens, Persians defeated.
486, November: Death of King Darius of Persia.
484, spring–480, spring: King Xerxes prepares for new invasion of Greece.
480, spring: Persian army sets out from Sardis.
late August: Battles of Thermopylae and Artemisium.
late September: Battle of Salamis.
479, early August: Battle of Plataea.
mid-August: Battle of Mycale on coast of Asia Minor (according to Herodotus, fought on the same day as Plataea).

the city. In the nearly desperate situation, Themistocles devised an ingenious stratagem. He sent a slave to the Persian king with a false message: Themistocles wished him well and advised him to strike at once in order to prevent the demoralized Greeks from escaping; if he attacked quickly, he might win the decisive battle practically without a blow. Themistocles then persuaded the council of Greek commanders to follow his strategy.

The Persians were taken in by the ruse and sent their navy into the narrows between Athens and the island of Salamis. This put the Persian ships at a disadvantage. The Greek fleet, some 380 ships, rammed the Persians, thus shearing off and fouling their oars. At this point heavily armed Greek soldiers boarded the enemy's ships and fought as if on land. The Persian navy broke and retreated. On all sides the Greek victory was decisive as wrecks and remnants of the Persian ships drifted along the coast of Attica. Xerxes sailed back toward the Dardanelles with his shattered navy. A Persian king had gazed upon Europe for the last time.

Salamis is one of the most important battles in history. It inspired the Greeks to work toward the final expulsion of the Persians from Europe. Yet the Persian Wars were not over, for a Persian army remained in Greece. The reckoning with this force came in 479, at the village of Plataea. The Spartan general Pausanias directed the battle. Once more the Greek army utterly defeated the Persians; out of perhaps 50,000 Persians, only a few thousand survived the day.

From this point on the tide of Greek victory and liberation was irresistible. The Greeks won a further battle at Mycale on the shore of Asia Minor in 479. The Ionian Greeks proclaimed their freedom and thus completed the work of throwing off Persian control that they had begun twenty years earlier. The final reckoning with Persia did not come until Alexander the Great finally dissolved the empire. For the present, the Greek poleis had thrust back their most formidable enemy. If they had not done so and had become another satrapy of Persia, who can say whether Greek art, drama, philosophy, historical writing, and above all self-government would have emerged and been nourished—or how different Western civilization might have been?

II. THE SUPREMACY OF ATHENS

After the Persian Wars Athens was dominant in the Greek world for the next half-century. It headed a confederation of Greek states that gradually became an Athenian empire. With political leadership came commercial dominance; its trading activities spread throughout the Aegean and eastern Mediterranean. At home its democratic institutions were further strengthened as the citizens gained a full voice in all governmental affairs.

The Athenian Empire

The Greek victories over the Persians in 480 and 479 secured mainland Greece from further attacks, but the Athenians were determined to fight a war of pursuit against the Persians and their territory in Asia Minor. The Spartans joined briefly in this war, but their leader Pausanias alienated other Greeks with his arrogant manner and had to be recalled to Sparta in 478. The Spartans now reverted to their traditional policy of isolation and withdrew from further campaigning. The other Greek allies decided to form a permanent union to continue the war and met for this purpose on the island of Delos in the winter of 478–477. Here they founded a new alliance, the Delian League, under Athenian leadership. Each city-state was to have one vote in determining policy, and all agreed to make regular contributions of either money or manned ships for campaigns against Persia. Athens was assigned the command of the fleet.

The campaigns were successful. The Greeks liberated the cities in Asia Minor still held by the Persians and drove the Persian navy from the Aegean. Warfare between Greeks and Persians ended by about 450. During the intervening years Athens had initially acted with restraint in exercising its leadership over the other members of the league. Gradually, however, it began to extend its political influence, forcing some cities into the league against their will and refusing to allow others to withdraw. Athens intervened in the local politics of the member states, sometimes stationing garrisons or governors in the supposedly independent poleis. At other times Athens supported the local political faction that favored the domination of the masses; thus it sponsored the rule of governments that would tend to remain loyal to its leadership. Athenian dominance became manifest in 454, when the league agreed to transfer the common treasury from Delos to Athens. Henceforth, cash contributions to the league were actually payments of tribute to Athens: the alliance of equals had now become, in fact, an Athenian empire, even thought no such change was ever announced.

The Age of Pericles

Under the leadership of Pericles (490?–429), Athens enjoyed its greatest period. To the historian, Pericles is the best example of a familiar figure in Greek politics, an aristocrat from a wealthy family. Such a man may have political rivals in other aristocratic circles. In such contests, the common people are a powerful ally, and the aristocratic leader who can gain their support functions as a champion of the masses. Pericles offered benefits to the common people that had the effect of weakening the aristocracy as a whole. After his death the aristocracy lost control of Athenian politics. The historian Thucydides firmly pointed out that, as long as Pericles was in charge, "he controlled the masses, rather than letting them control him." He did this through the force of his character, his effective oratory, and his reputation for financial honesty. In Athenian history, Pisistratus and Cleisthenes are other prominent leaders who exploited the support of the common people. As we shall see in the history of Rome, Julius Caesar also fits this pattern. He, too, climbed to supreme power with the support of the masses and used them as his main weapon in overcoming rivals within the ruling elite.

Pericles first became prominent in the 460s, but his political dominance dates from the death of his older rival, Cimon, in 450. Cimon, the son of the Miltiades who directed the Athenian victory at Marathon in 490, believed in continuing the war against Persia and maintaining friendly relations with Sparta. Pericles' strategy was the exact opposite. He saw the Persian War as a quarrel of the past, and Sparta as the threat of the future. Most political leaders want to increase the power of their state, and Pericles

was no exception to this nearly universal law of history. The Athenian empire brought Athens prestige, wealth, and power, and Sparta was the only state that could threaten this system.

The only formal position Pericles held was that of general. The Athenians elected 10 generals every year. Since 487 they had chosen their archons by lot, and ambitious men no longer troubled to seek this office; the generalship was now far more important. From 443 to his death in 429, Pericles was general 15 years without a break.

Pericles proposed to the Athenians that they restore the damage done to their city in the Persian invasion of 480. On his initiative, the city undertook to rebuild the destroyed temples on the Acropolis. An architect of genius, Ictinus, designed the most nearly perfect of all Greek temples, the Parthenon, erected between 447 and 432. At the same time the Athenians built a magnificent gateway to the Acropolis. To fund these works they used money paid in by the allies to the treasury of the Delian League. Pericles' critics denounced this use of the allies' money as unscrupulous, but the people were in no mood to reject this project, on which many could make a living, and the Acropolis became Pericles' legacy.

Pericles also strengthened the Athenian empire through aggressive imperialism. When cities on the island of Euboea, just east of Athens (see Map 3.2), tried to rebel from the empire in 446, Pericles himself led an army that put the rebellion down. As a further measure of control, Athens took over one of the Euboean towns and sent out Athenians to live there. Pericles also strengthened the Athenian hold on the Dardanelles by installing settlers there; his purpose was to assure the Athenian grain supply, which came down through the straits from south Russia. And when the island of Samos and the city of Byzantium rebelled in 440, Pericles led the forces to Samos and assured that this revolt, too, was a failure.

The single most inspired architectural achievement of the Classical Age is the Athenian Acropolis, which dominated the surrounding city and could be seen from the marketplace below. Construction began in the sixth century, but the largest and most magnificent of its temples, the marble Parthenon dedicated to Athena, was built during the Age of Pericles.
(Photo: Alison Frantz)

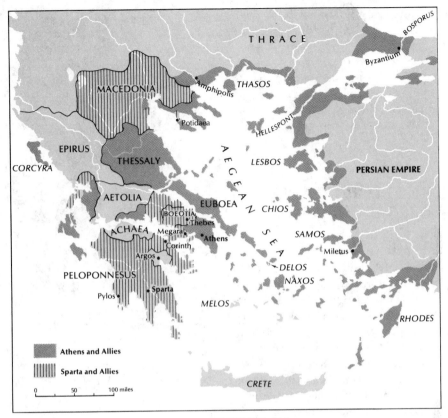

MAP 3.2. GREECE 431 B.C.

Pericles' lifetime coincided with the zenith of Athenian literature. Athenian drama, especially, reached its highest development in the plays of Sophocles (a personal friend of Pericles) and Euripides. Phidias, the sculptor who directed the making of the statue of Athena inside the Parthenon, was likewise Pericles' friend and received the commission for the statue through Pericles' building program. These artistic movements were already under way and would have developed in any case, but historians sometimes call the era from 450 to 429 the Age of Pericles in recognition of his remarkable statesmanship.

At this time the basis of Athenian military power became, more and more, the navy. This fact gave more importance to poorer citizens, who rowed in the fleet—just as, long before, the spread of iron weapons had made the armed warrior more of a political force. The constitution of Cleisthenes was still in operation. The assembly of all male citizens voted only on business brought before it by the Council of 500. As we have seen, the judicial system in the fifth century operated largely through juries numbering 200, 500, or even more citizens. There was no detailed body of civil or criminal law: juries had wide powers of interpretation, and there was normally no appeal from their decisions. Pericles instituted pay for jury duty in order to provide enough jurors to man the expanding system of courts. Critics of this judicial system saw it as too democratic, but it expressed the opinion of most Athenians—that the average citizen, through intelligence and dedication, could play a part in governing the city.

III. THE PELOPONNESIAN WAR (431–404 B.C.)

The War Years

Sparta, its allies, and some nonaligned states had long viewed the growth of the Athenian empire with suspicion, then with fear (see Map 3.2 for the alliances among Greek poleis). During the 450s there were several clashes between Athens and Sparta along with their respective allies (the so-called First Peloponnesian War), but fortunately they did not lead to a major war. As a further move toward détente, Athens and Sparta, again with their allies, signed a treaty of nonaggression in 446 that was supposed to be valid for 30 years. But in the 430s two events took place that convinced the Peloponnesian allies of Sparta that they must declare a preventive war on Athens.

First, in 435 a quarrel arose between Corinth, an ally of Sparta, and its neighbor-city, Corcyra (today the main city of the island of Corfu). The quarrel threatened to become a Panhellenic one when Corcyra appealed to Athens, in 433, to form an alliance. Despite the warning of Corinthian ambassadors that such an act would make war inevitable, the Athenians (surely influenced by Pericles, though the historian Thucydides does not say so) accepted the alliance with Corcyra. The combined naval power of the two poleis was easily the largest in Greece.

Second, also in 433 the Athenians demanded

This vase painting depicts the departure of a hoplite for war. Fully armed, he bids farewell to his wife and his father. The picture is a combination of military severity and tender family emotion. The vase is dated to the earliest years of the Peloponnesian War.
(Photo: Himer Fotoarchiv München)

that the town of Potidaea, in northern Greece, should demolish its defensive walls, send hostages to Athens, and banish its magistrates (these were Corinthian, for Potidaea too was a Corinthian colony). Though Potidaea was a member of the Athenian league, these demands infuriated the Corinthians. As for Potidaea, it refused to obey and the Athenians besieged the town. An assembly of the Peloponnesian League was convened, and the Corinthian embassy managed to convince Sparta and the other allies that war against Athens was the only solution. This war, known simply as the Peloponnesian War, was a major catastrophe for Greek politics. It did have the positive effect of breaking up the Athenian empire and liberating its subject states from Athenian control, but it was devastating to the population and morale of the poleis that fought one another. Its chief result was to make easier the Macedonian conquest of Greece. Both sides bore some responsibility for the outbreak of war, but the balance of blame must lie with Athens.

The war opposed two kinds of states. Sparta controlled no empire and relied on internal resources to maintain itself. Athens, the center of an empire, relied on its imperial system to provide grain for its people and tribute to pay for its navy. Sparta had the strongest army in Greece and Athens the strongest navy.

Fighting began in 431 but was inconclusive for several years. Sparta sought to break Athenian morale by invading Attica annually; its troops inflicted some damage and then departed in time for the Peloponnesian harvest. But the Athenians merely withdrew behind fortifications until the Spartans retreated. Pericles, still the leader of Athens, refused to allow the Athenian infantry to challenge Sparta on the field; instead, he launched sea-borne raids against various points in the Peloponnese. These raids left Sparta untouched and its infantry undefeated. Far more damaging than any offensive policy of Sparta was a serious plague (not yet identified with any known disease, despite many studies) that afflicted Athens in 430 and intermittently thereafter. The plague took thousands of lives within the crowded, unsanitary city; Thucydides the historian survived it and has left us a horrifying description of its effects. Unfortunately for Athens' effectiveness in the war, Pericles died of illness in 429.

In 425 both Athens and Sparta achieved certain successes, but the losses that both sides suffered in the next few years made all parties ready to end, or at least suspend, the war. A peace treaty was signed in 421 (the Peace of Nicias, named for the Athenian general who led the negotiations). At this point the poleis could have turned their backs on war, for both Athens and Sparta had shown their courage and neither had gained a dominant position. After

421 a few years of suspicious peace did in fact follow, but the issues that had caused the war had not been settled.

In 415 an occasion for renewed war arose. The people of Segesta, a polis in Sicily, appealed to Athens for help against another city on that island. The issue of war in Sicily was the subject of a crucial debate in Athens. The eloquence of Alcibiades, a talented young political leader of enormous ambition and—as it later turned out—few scruples, persuaded the Athenian assembly to raise a large fleet and sail to Sicily.

The original plan of aiding Segesta had to be deferred when Syracuse, the largest Sicilian city, entered the war against the Athenians. The Athenians now brought disaster on themselves by settling down to besiege Syracuse. Thucydides, who chronicled the war, makes it clear that a resolute attack might well have succeeded, but the Athenians failed to strike when they had a clear advantage. One event that blunted the Athenian attack was the loss of Alcibiades, one of the leaders of the expedition. He was recalled to Athens to stand trial on charges of violating the state's religion. Fearing that his political enemies would be able to secure his conviction, he defected to Sparta.

The Athenians finally lost a critical naval battle at Syracuse in 413 and had to retreat toward the interior of the island. During this desperate march the Syracusans and their allies cut the Athenians off and decimated them as they tried to cross a river. Those who survived this calamity surrendered and were kept in terrible conditions in a rock quarry at Syracuse; as Thucydides grimly says, "few out of many returned home."

The disaster in Sicily caused many defections among the members of the Delian League, but Sparta still could not strike the decisive blow, and the war dragged on inconclusively for eight more years; Sparta sought decisive help by enlisting the aid of Persia, promising it control over the cities in Asia Mi-

This bronze statuette of a Spartan soldier illustrates the helmet and draped garment worn during the time of the Peloponnesian War.
(Photo: Wadsworth Atheneum, Hartford)

nor that had freed themselves during the Persian Wars. In 405 a Spartan admiral captured the Athenian fleet on the shore of the Hellespont. Athens, no longer able to assure its food supply through the straits, had to surrender in desperate hunger in the next spring. It renounced contol over its empire and, as a guarantee for the future and a symbol of humiliation, had to demolish the defensive walls that reached from the city down to the coast of Attica. Sparta pronounced this event in April 404 as "the liberation of Greece."

Athens had lost its empire, most of its navy, and much of its trade; and it never recovered its former power. Though democracy was able to survive in Athens for long years afterward, the overall quality of political leadership had declined after the death of Pericles. Some ambitious leaders were demagogic, able to sway the assembly at will. On a number of occasions when the war appeared to be at an end, they could command support for rash ventures that ended in disaster, such as Alcibiades' expedition to Syracuse. Moreover, the war produced a number of atrocities by various parties.

Looking back at the long Peloponnesian War, we can see that it was fruitless for both sides. The Athenians lost their empire, which had brought in between 400 and 600 talents[1] a year in the form of tribute and had made them the most powerful polis in the history of the Greek people. Sparta, persuaded by its allies to go to war in 431, had removed the Athenian empire, but this empire was no threat whatever to Sparta's conservative life style in the mountains of the Peloponnese. The losses in manpower had been heavy, but Sparta could less easily sustain these losses, and in the fourth century it could put fewer and fewer troops in the field. Political leadership, too, had been decimated. The Athenians, for example, foolishly gave Alcibiades, their most competent general after Pericles, reasons to desert to

---

[1] A talent equalled 6000 drachmas, thus roughly 6000 days' pay for a skilled worker.

Sparta, and he harmed the Athenians greatly as a result.

Besides these losses, there was a failure of will, a spirit of pessimism and disillusion among Athenian intellectuals. Many of them thought uncontrolled democracy had led to social decline and military disaster. They contrasted the discipline of Sparta, the victor in the war, with the frequent chaos of Athenian democracy. Such ideas run through the work of Plato and other philosophers, who asked what had gone wrong with democracy and what system should replace it. History was preparing the answer.

IV. THE RISE OF MACEDONIA

The Era of Hegemonies

The beginning of the fourth century is usually called the "era of hegemonies," because first one polis and then another held the hegemony, or leadership, over a group of allies. Sparta, the winner in the Peloponnesian War, was the first state to establish hegemony, but Spartan traditions of isolation within the Peloponnesus did not make the Spartans good successors to the Athenians in international politics. Sparta established a puppet government of oligarchs in Athens, but within a few months popular opposition swept this group away; and soon Athens revived its naval league, though with fewer members than it had had in the fifth century.

The polis of Thebes became an important power, siding now with Athens, now with Sparta, in a series of never-ending quarrels. The quarrels themselves and their causes are too complicated to follow in detail, and no clear trend emerges except one of constant intrigue and war. During one of the struggles in these decades, the brilliant Theban general Epaminondas won a victory over Sparta in 371, exploding the belief, held with almost religious faith, that the Spartan infantry was invincible. Sparta continued to decline, partly through a

shortage of manpower; Aristotle informs us that Spartan armies in the field were now fewer than 1000 in size, rather than the 4000 or 5000 who had gone into battle during the wars of the fifth century.

The period of the hegemonies practically brought to a close the era of self-governing poleis. Constant struggles and internal weaknesses had made the system vulnerable. It was replaced by a reversion to monarchy, as the kingdom of Macedonia spread its influence over the Greek mainland.

The Monarchs of Macedonia

Macedonia (or Macedon) was an ancient, somewhat backward kingdom in northern Greece. Its emergence as a Hellenic power was due to a resourceful king, Philip II (359–336), whose

The head of Alexander the Great in heroic profile; the obverse of a silver coin issued by Lysimachus, one of Alexander's bodyguards, who after his master's death became king of Thrace.
(Photo: Courtesy, Museum of Fine Arts, Boston)

career has been unjustly overshadowed by the deeds of his son, Alexander the Great. With shrewd political skill Philip developed his kingdom, built up a powerful army, and planned a program of conquest.

Using both aggression and diplomacy, Philip added poleis and large territories to his kindgom and extended his control into central Greece. The great Athenian orator Demosthenes, in a series of fiery speeches ("Philippics"), called on his countrymen to recognize the danger and fight for Greek liberty. But by the time the Athenians responded, it was too late to halt the Macedonian advance. Philip won a decisive battle against Athens and several other poleis at Chaeronea in 338. All the city-states of southern Greece, except isolated Sparta, now lay at his disposal. He could have devastated many of them, including Athens, but his shrewd sense of tactics warned him not to do so. Therefore, he gathered the more important poleis, again excepting Sparta, into an obedient alliance called the League of Corinth. The league automatically recognized Philip as its leader and agreed to follow him in his next project, an invasion of Persia. But before he could open his Persian War, Philip was murdered in 336 by one of his officers. The killer, one Pausanias, apparently had a personal quarrel with the king. Some historians have wondered whether Philip's wife, a dynamic woman named Olympias, may have participated in a plot to put her son Alexander on the throne; or whether Alexander himself, who had the most to gain from Philip's death, was involved in a conspiracy against his father. Tempting as such speculations may be, the sources do not give them clear support.

The powerful empire built by Philip now passed to his son, Alexander III (336–323), and never has a young warrior prince made more productive use of his opportunities. During his brief reign Alexander created the largest empire the ancient world had known, and, more than any other man, he was responsible for the diffusion of Greek culture.

After he consolidated his rule in his Greek territory, Alexander began the invasion of the Persian Empire. The Persia that he attacked was a much weaker state than the one that conquered Croesus and Babylon or the one that Xerxes led against the Greeks in 480. Intrigue and disloyalty had weakened the administration of the empire. Moreover, the king, Darius III, had to rely on Greek mercenary soldiers as the disciplined element in the infantry, for native troops were mainly untrained serfs. These facts must be taken into account to understand Alexander's success, but in no way do they diminish his reputation as one of the supreme generals in history. His campaigns show physical courage, strategic cleverness, and superb leadership.

Alexander swept the Persians away from the coast of Asia Minor and in 332 drove them out of Egypt, a land they had held for two centuries. The Egyptians welcomed him as a liberator and recognized him as their pharaoh. In the next season Alexander fought Darius III at Gaugamela. A complete victory there opened the way for him to capture the rich cities of Susa and Persepolis.

From 331 onward Alexander met little opposition in Persia. Darius III was murdered by disloyal officers in 330, and Alexander assumed the title of king of Persia. The expedition had now achieved its professed aim; yet Alexander continued to make war. During the next few years he campaigned as far east as India, where he crossed the Indus River (see Map 3.3). Finally in 326 he began his march back. At Babylon, where he was preparing an Arabian expedition, he caught a fever, and within a few days he died, not yet thirty-three.

Alexander is a historical figure of such size and power that he defies easy interpretation. He is probably the most famous man in Greek history, yet there is no one about whom more sharply differing biographies are written. Part of our difficulty is that our best narrative source for his life, Arrian, lived four centuries later, in the Roman Empire, and Arrian, for all his merits, was not the kind of probing historian who can explain just what Alexander was trying to accomplish. If it was a stable empire embracing his vast conquests, he failed, for the empire exploded on his death. A renowned British scholar, W. W. Tarn, asserted again and again that Alexander had a vision of the brotherhood of mankind and was trying to establish an empire in which different peoples would live in harmony, but this view is widely, and rightly, rejected as sentimental and idealistic. By focusing on certain acts of cruelty and vindictiveness in his career, one could portray him as a paranoiac tyrant, but this view may also be too one-sided. However we interpret him, he has remained the image of a world-conqueror. Some of his successors put his head on their own coins, and later Roman emperors also issued medallions portraying him, as if to borrow his glory for their often threatened reigns.

V. CLASSICAL GREEK CULTURE (Ca. 500–323 B.C.)

Greek Drama

Historians call the period from about 500 to 323 B.C. the Classical Age of Greece. Athens was preeminent in this era, and in many ways the history of Greek culture must focus on Athenian artists. The greatest poetry of the middle and late fifth century is found in dramatic tragedies. Tragedy originated in Athens, at festivals honoring the god Dionysus, and it never lost touch with its religious roots. The playwrights derived most of their plots from the familiar tales of gods and heroes in Greek mythology. Their central themes are the questions fundamental to all religions: What is mankind's relationship to the gods? What is justice?

MAP 3.3. ALEXANDER'S EMPIRE 336–323 B.C.

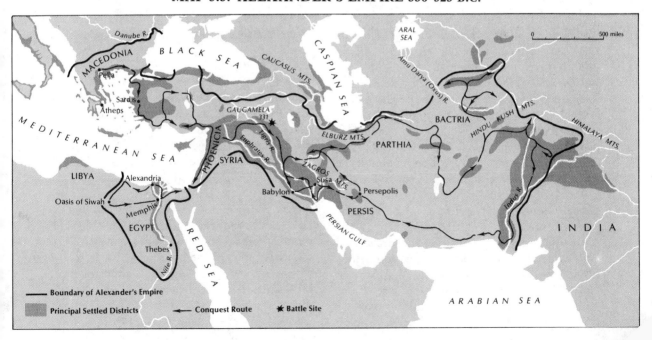

And if the gods are just, why do they make people suffer?

The Greeks invented drama; Egyptians, it is true, had certain ceremonies with musical accompaniment, but this and other Asiatic practices influenced Greek writers little if at all. Aristotle credibly says, in his *Poetics,* that drama originated from the "dithyramb," a choral song in honor of Dionysus. Probably shortly before 500 B.C. a single actor began to sing or talk with the chorus, thus allowing the story to become more complex. In its developed form drama became, like another Greek invention, history, a vehicle for interpreting human experience.

In the fifth century dramas were presented before audiences of several thousand; they were practically an education in ethics for citizens. The surviving plays combine, in amazing fashion, dramatic power with subtle moral problems. The stature of the main characters gives the dramas additional force, for they deal with heroic, strong-willed men and women like Oedipus and Antigone, powerful personalities who are caught in fearful dilemmas. These tragedies are still performed, filmed, and used as the basis for operas and ballets, over two thousand years after their creation.

Playwrights commonly presented dramas in sets of three, but only one such trilogy has survived, the tragedy of Orestes, son of Agamemnon (the *Oresteia*), by Aeschylus (525?–456). The central theme is the nature of justice, which Aeschylus explores in a tale of multiple murders and vengeance. Even before the trilogy opens, the problem has been exposed: the Greek king Agamemnon sails against Troy in accordance with his oath, but on the way his fleet is becalmed. If the fleet is to continue, he must sacrifice his daughter Iphigeneia to the gods (this episode recalls another archetypal myth, in which the god of Israel commands Abraham to sacrifice his son Isaac). Agamemnon must decide which is the more just action, to kill his daughter and thus fulfill his oath, or to spare her and thus break his promise to attack Troy.

He follows the gods' orders but on his return to Greece his wife, Clytemnestra, avenges the girl's death by murdering Agamemnon and assuming the throne with her lover. The chain of vengeance continues as Orestes, Agamemnon's son, kills Clytemnestra and the lover in turn. But now he too must expiate his (partly justified) crime. Orestes is pursued by the Furies, hostile demons who nearly drive him mad. Finally, in Athens, he is tried for homicide by the court of the Areopagus, with the goddess Athena presiding. When the jury's vote is tied, Athena herself acquits Orestes by casting her vote in his favor. Thus he has been forgiven in the sight of the gods. For the Athenian audience, the final scene reveals that their system of justice, divinely inspired by Athena, has supplanted the old tribal custom of personal vengeance.

The characters in Aeschylus are dramatic types rather than sharply characterized individuals, and at times his dramas lapse into narration rather than maintaining action. Sophocles (496?–406) carried the evolution of drama further by adding a third actor, a device that enabled him to concentrate more on the interplay of characters. He also shows a greater interest in personality. His *Oedipus the King* is the most famous tragedy and perhaps the most nearly perfect specimen that survives. Freud drew on it in his theory of the Oedipus complex, which describes a child's desire for the parent of the opposite sex and rejection of the parent of the same sex. The play is about Oedipus, king of Thebes, who had unknowingly committed the terrible crimes of killing his father and marrying his mother. As the play opens, a religious curse has brought a plague on the people. Oedipus orders a search to eliminate the offender who has polluted the city, but the search narrows with terrifying logic to Oedipus himself. His crimes of patricide and incest, though unintentional, have disturbed the order of the uni-

A detail from the Parthenon frieze (completed in 432 B.C.) showing horsemen in the festal procession organized every four years to honor Athena, titulary goddess of the city-state of Athens.
(Photo: Alinari-Scala)

verse, and he must atone for them. When the truth emerges, Oedipus' wife-mother hangs herself. Oedipus, in a frenzy of remorse over this action, plunges her brooches into his eyes and begins a life of wandering as a blind outcast.

The third Athenian tragic poet, Euripides (480?–406?), was virtually a contemporary of Sophocles, but his plays show a still later stage of evolution. The interest in individual characters is now greater than ever. Euripides is interested in how the inner workings of the mind and emotions shape a person's destiny. The passions of the characters rather than the workings of fate determine the course of events in his plays. Euripides' characters are intense and even fanatical, and he carries psychological analysis much further than his predecessors.

Euripides' most familiar play is *Medea.* Jason, the husband of Medea, has deserted her for a princess of Corinth. To avenge herself, Medea kills the Corinthian girl and then her own children. She is a woman of strong, often conflicting, emotions. She weeps over her children but, despite a momentary weakening of her resolve, fulfills her plan to kill them. Medea is driven into viciousness by emotion, and Hellenic rationality is unable to come to her aid. She is nonetheless heroic and terrifying in her determination.

Comedy

Comedy is the other side of the dramatic coin. Almost the only comedies that have come down to us are those of the Athenian Aristophanes (448?–385?), who saw his mission as that of extracting the ridiculous from any situation. Unlike tragedy, comedy treats the real world. Aristophanes satirized the Peloponnesian War, political leaders, intellectuals—including Socrates—and the failings of democracy, using fantasy and burlesque to demolish his targets. He was a complete master of the Greek language;

he could imitate the dignified style of Pindar or Aeschylus and then make a split-second shift into comic patter, invented words, or nonsense.

The first of his eleven surviving plays is the *Acharnians* (425 B.C.), an antiwar comedy from the early years of the Peloponnesian War. He continued his antiwar theme in other plays, notably *Lysistrata,* which he wrote after the disastrous Athenian expedition to Syracuse. In this comedy the women of Athens, despairing of any rational means of ending the long war, go on a sex strike.

Aristophanes reserved some of his sharpest attacks for the democratic leaders who succeeded Pericles. In *The Knights* (424 B.C.) a general tries to persuade an ignorant sausage-seller to unseat Cleon, one of those demagogues:

SAUSAGE-SELLER: Tell me this, how can I a sausage-seller, be a big man like that?
GENERAL: The easiest thing in the world. You've got all the qualifications: low birth, marketplace training, insolence.
SAUSAGE-SELLER: I don't think I deserve it.
GENERAL: Not deserve it? It looks to me as if you've got too good a conscience. Was your father a gentleman?
SAUSAGE-SELLER: By the gods, no! My folks were scoundrels.
GENERAL: Lucky man! What a good start you've got for public life!
SAUSAGE-SELLER: But I can hardly read.
GENERAL: The only trouble is that you know anything. To be a leader of the people isn't for learned men, or honest men, but for the ignorant and vile. Don't miss the golden opportunity.[2]

Historical Writing

Drama is one way of examining the human condition. Another way of doing this is to

---

[2] From L. S. Stavrianos, *Epic of Man to 1500,* 1970.

write history—to analyze the past and compare it with the present. Herodotus (484?–425?) is rightly called the "Father of History," for he was the first to write an analysis of political events, in his case the Greek war with Persia. In his investigation he grasped the essential fact that large historical events are often the result of a meeting between two differing cultures. He therefore sought to learn the history of the Persian Empire and the reasons for its pressure on Europe.

Herodotus traveled throughout the Greek world and the Near East to gather the data for his *History*. He was a curious and open-minded traveler; he judged each society on its own terms rather than according to Greek standards of behavior. Though he often displays a shrewd scepticism, Herodotus did not always try to separate truth from legend. He sometimes reports two versions of one event, leaving it to the reader to make his own assessment. He partly disarms critics by saying "my duty is to report what is told me, but not to believe it all." He attributed the Greek victory in the Persian Wars to the inevitable triumph of a free society over a despotic one. The most impressive dimension of his work is his demonstration that all the cultures of the ancient world were interconnected: Greece and Persia were both parts of the whole. To tell this story, he had to reduce centuries of Near Eastern history into order, with comprehensible dynasties and successions from one monarch to another. He did this without the help of any earlier narrative, and the structure he gave to the history of the Persian Empire has not been shaken.

Thucydides (455?–399?), the successor of Herodotus, participated in the Peloponnesian War and wrote its history; in fact, he did not live to finish his work, which breaks off within 411, seven years before the end of the war. Thucydides perfectly represents the relentlessly analytical thought of the late fifth century. Throughout his work he presents a series of speeches and debates about various issues and

decisions. The speakers are usually contemptuous of any moral principles. Arguments based on justice and mercy, if brought up at all, are ruthlessly swept aside by whichever individual or force has the upper hand. It is by no means clear that Thucydides himself had no use for compassion, but he presents the whole war as a coldly realistic pursuit of power.

In his view, the Athenian state was in good order under Pericles because that statesman could control the masses. His political successors allowed the masses to influence decisions, with tragic consequences for Athens. Thucydides also perceived that "war teaches men to be violent." The lust for power caused Athens, in 416, to commit one of the worst atrocities of the war. We do not know which politician thought of the plan, but Athenian forces sailed to the neutral island of Melos and ordered the Melians to join the Athenian empire. Thucydides describes the negotiations in a brilliant composition called the Melian Dialogue, in which envoys of each side present the respective cases. At one point, the Athenians say,

> Our opinion of the gods and our knowledge of men lead us to conclude that it is a general and necessary law of nature to rule whatever one can. This is not a law that we made ourselves, nor were we the first to act upon it when it was made. We found it already in existence, and we shall leave it to exist for ever among those who come after us. We are merely acting in accordance with it, and we know that you or anybody else with the same power as ours would be acting in precisely the same way.[3]

The Athenians acted on the cynical principles they expounded. Melos finally had to surrender; the Athenians killed all the men of military age (probably two or three thousand) and sold

---

[3] Thucydides, *The Peloponnesian War,* 5.105, tr. Rex Warner, 1954.

the women and children into slavery. Without explicitly stating any moral message, Thucydides clearly shows the Athenian state giving way to the corrupting influence of war.

Thucydides' literary art is superb, particularly when he describes a scene of horror. No reader can avoid feeling a chill over the clinical description of the plague that attacked Athens in 430 or the shattering defeat of the proud armada that sailed against Syracuse. He is the undisputed standard among ancient historians, and for gripping narrative power and philosophical breadth he is an unsurpassed model.

Art and Architecture

As we have stated previously, painted pottery had reached greatness in the sixth century through the Black Figure style. About 530 B.C. some potters began to reverse the color scheme. By painting around the figures in black and leaving the figures themselves in the natural reddish-orange of the clay, they created the Red Figure style. This style allowed more subtlety and finer details than did the black silhouettes.

But the future did not lie with painted pottery, which declined in skill after about 440. Architecture and sculpture became the leading art forms of the fifth century. Fifth-century architects did not try to improve on the dignity and simplicity of the basic design of the temple, nor did they make it more grandiose in scale. Rather, they concentrated on perfecting its proportions and details. One subtle touch in the Athenian Parthenon, for example, is the architect's avoidance of perfectly straight lines; the columns lean slightly inward and swell in the middle, so that the building lacks any appearance of heaviness.

Sculptors in the fifth century, and even more in the fourth, departed widely from the rather rigid form of the earlier kouros. Sculpture became more graceful and freer, as artists learned how to show the body in action. Yet

the realism was touched with ideal qualities: with the typical Greek love of analysis and study of form, artists tried to present the image of men and women in their perfection. This idealized realism appears in a bronze statue of Zeus (or perhaps Poseidon) about to hurl a missile. The body is perfect, the left arm pointing toward the target and the right drawn fully back. Every muscle is tensed with power. The unknown sculptor of about 460 has captured the precise moment of action.

The statuary of the Parthenon is the best-known collection of classical Greek sculpture, largely because of the work of Lord Elgin, who brought to London many of its statues and large sections of its decorative frieze. Around the outside of the building, at the top, were

The most significant stylistic change in Greek sculpture of the fifth century is illustrated in this bronze statue of Zeus. The figure has a special dynamism; strength, resolve, and action are implicit in its form, a striking contrast to the earlier kouros.
(Photo: Himer Fotoarchiv München)

ninety-two decorative panels (metopes) showing battles between Greeks and mythological figures. On the top of the wall surrounding the inner room ran a long frieze portraying not mythology but a true scene from human life, the Panathenaic procession that took place every four years. The aim of the procession was to bring a newly made robe as a birthday present to Athena, and in the crowd we see bearers of vessels, musicians, horsemen, and ordinary citizens on foot. The total effect is one of bustling movement, fluidity, and energy. The work is said to have been supervised by Phidias, and the skill of the sculptors is such that five or six superimposed planes are often shown even though the depth of the relief is only some two inches.

Sheltered by the gables, or pediments, on the east end of the building was the depiction of the birth of Athena from the head of Zeus; on the west end, Athena and Poseidon were shown competing for ownership of Athens. The uncanny perfection of these pedimental statues is nearly beyond description. An interesting detail is that they were wholly finished in the round, even though no one would ever see their backs after they were mounted in the pediments. Like all other Greek statuary, these works were painted.

Greek sculptors, in harmony with the general absence of complex dogma in Greek religion, humanized the gods. One famous relief in the Acropolis Museum shows Nike (Victory) stooping to adjust her sandal—a pose of less then perfect dignity that would have been inconceivable to an Egyptian or Mesopotamian sculptor wishing to portray a god. Another portrait, in the same spirit of humanism, is a relief of Athena, leaning on her spear. She gazes at a tablet, perhaps a list of men who fell in battle. If this is so, it would justify the name often given this relief, the "Mourning Athena."

About 400, or a little later, sculptors began to seek realism even in the portrayal of less attractive persons. Busts of the plump, snub-nosed Socrates abandon all striving after ideal beauty and lead the way to statues of such subjects as old women, or a boxer with cauliflower ears acquired over years in his sport.

Philosophy

Historical writing, drama, and artistic depiction are all ways of looking at human experience and subjecting it to a critique. Another, and one that the Greeks invented, is philosophy—the attempt to use reason, and argument if necessary, to discover why things are as they are. Philosophy comes into existence when people are no longer satisfied with supernatural and mythical explanations. It is hard to say just why Greeks gradually became skeptical about the accounts that they found in their own mythology. Gradually they began to suspect that there was a logical order to the universe and that humanity had the capacity to discover it.

The first Greek philosophers lived in the city of Miletus, on the western shore of Asia Minor in the region of Ionia. The site is significant: Miletus was a prominent trading center, and its citizens had direct contact with the ideas and achievements of the Near East. These intellectual currents must have fertilized Miletus as a center of thought. In any case, soon after 600 B.C., certain Milesians discovered a world of speculation in an apparently simple yet profoundly radical question: "What exists?" They sought their answer in some single primal element. Thales, for example, taught that everything in the whole universe was made of water, a notion that echoes Babylonian myths of a primeval flood.

A pupil and follower of Thales, Anaximander of Miletus (610?–547?), held that the origin of everything was an infinite body of matter, which he called "the boundless" (*to ápeiron*). A whirling motion within the boundless divided its substance into the hot, which rose to form the heavens, and the cold, which sank and as-

sumed form in the earth and the air surrounding it. A further separation into wet and dry created the oceans and the land. This theory points toward a later classification of matter into the four elements (earth, air, fire, water). Anaximander also suggested what modern biology has confirmed: that people and other animals developed from fishlike beings.

Other philosophers had other candidates for the basic matter (fire, vapor). One of the most influential theories was that of Pythagoras of Samos; he emigrated from this island to south Italy in 532. He approached the universe through the study of numbers. He discovered the harmonic intervals within the musical scale and stated the Pythagorean theorem about the sum of the sides of a right triangle, which is familiar to all students of geometry. He and his pupils found special inspiration in the *tetraktús,* a triangular arrangment of dots representing the first four numbers:

$$
\begin{matrix}
& & \bullet & & \\
& \bullet & & \bullet & \\
\bullet & & \bullet & & \bullet \\
\bullet & & \bullet & \bullet &
\end{matrix}
$$

This figure has various meanings. It demonstrates that the sum of 1, 2, 3, and 4 is 10; it also shows that 10 is the smallest sum containing an equal number of prime (1,3) and divisible (2,4) numbers. Pythagoras went on to say that all objects are similar to numbers, by which he must have meant that within them there is a numerically balanced arrangement of parts. Pythagoras thus anticipated the modern discoveries of mathematical relationships within all things, including even the genetic code in our bodies. Such statements show the

Athena leaning on her spear, ca. 450 B.C.
(Photo: Acropolis Museum, Athens)

ability of the Greeks to attain a blinding flash of knowledge, even though they lacked the means of proving it.

Another approach to the universe was that of Heraclitus of Ephesus, in Asia Minor, who wrote about 500. He rejected the idea that there could be one permanent substance in the world of which all things are made. Rather, he proclaimed that everything in the universe was constantly changing and moving toward its own apparent opposite. Birth moves toward death and death toward birth. The elements are tranformed into one another; the world order is not really an order, it is a process. Strife is the father of everything. He said that the world had always been and would always be Fire, which perhaps symbolized for him the constant process of transformation. Heraclitus replaced the harmony and consistency of earlier thinkers with the view that everything changes; "you cannot step in the same river twice."

A contemporary of Heraclitus, Parmenides of Elea in south Italy, gave another answer to the riddle of the universe. First, he rejected the apparent evidence of our senses: reason, not our perceptions, is the way to truth. This view was to be developed by Plato, who maintained that nothing we see around us is truly "real." Next, Parmenides declared that whatever is, is: A thing cannot both be and not be. That which is can be known; that which does not exist cannot be known or named. Moreover, whatever exists cannot change, move, perish, or be transformed. For him, Heraclitus was wrong in accepting transformation; so were those thinkers who saw the world as many things made out of one material. So everything partakes not of water, or vapor, but simply of Being.

Let us also notice the theory first stated by one Leucippus (of Miletus? ca. 450 B.C.) and his contemporary, Democritus of Abdera. They sought reality in a world of space that is partly filled up by solid, invisibly small particles or atoms (Greek *a-toma,* "things that cannot be divided"). Only by constantly changing their location and position do the atoms make up everything in the world; they fall together and cohere at random. Death is only the redistribution of the atoms that make up our body and soul and is thus not to be feared. The atomic theory later inspired the philosophy of Epicurus, who also sought to liberate people from the fear of death; and its scientific truth had to wait until the modern era for its recognition.

The Sophists and Socrates

By about 450, speculations about the nature of the material in the universe had become less productive and interesting, and the emphasis in philosophy turned toward the study of human beings and the dilemmas in their lives. Greek moral philosophy has inspired debate in all subsequent ages, and technical journals in the field of philosophy still treat problems that Greek philosophers discovered. Take, for example, the conception of moral obligation: Is there anything that we should do, as our duty, even though it may bring no reward whatever—or is there some trace of self-interest concealed in every apparently "moral" act?

The first Greeks to undertake this study were the Sophists (Greek *sophistés,* expert or learned man). One of the early Sophists, Protagoras, gave us the famous declaration that "man is the measure" of everything: That is, human beings are the only measure of whether a thing exists at all, and even the existence of the gods, whom mankind cannot really perceive, is only an undemonstrable assumption. The Sophists also drew an important distinction between man-made customs (*nomos*), on the one hand, and the law of nature (*physis*) on the other. Thus they could argue that what was man-made was arbitrary and inferior; what was natural was immutable and proper. This argument called into question all accepted canons

of good behavior. Freed of moral constraints, the Sophists made intellectual activity something of immediate practical advantage. They accepted pupils and claimed to be able to train them for success in any calling, since in every line of work there are problems to be solved through reasoning. They taught the art of rhetoric, persuasive speech-making that could be used to sway an assembly or to defend oneself in court. Their pupils could supposedly gain political power through a cool analysis of the mechanics of politics. The Sophists, men like Gorgias, Protagoras, Prodicus, clearly attacked accepted beliefs.

The main critic of the Sophists was Socrates (469–399). He transformed philosophy into an inquiry about the moral responsibility of people. His basic question was not, What is the world made of? but, What is right action and how can I know it is right? He was concerned with the loss of ethical values during the Peloponnesian War. His mission, as he saw it, was to persuade young men of Athens to examine their lives in the pursuit of moral truth, for "the unexamined life is not worth living." His technique was to question his pupils—even many who were not his pupils—refuting, correcting, and guiding them by his "Socratic" method to the right answers. He held that no man is wise who cannot give a logical account of his actions; this belief led to the statement that "knowledge is virtue," one of several Socratic theses that seem paradoxical, for even ignorant men may have virtues. But such paradoxes were invented to make people think critically in order to discover the truth.

Socrates' doctrines and his insistent questioning annoyed many Athenians. He also had political critics, for he had been the tutor of several Athenians who had opposed democracy during the last years of the Peloponnesian War (Alcibiades had been one of his hearers). In 399 he was brought to trial on charges of "worshiping strange gods and corrupting the youth"—a way of hinting that Socrates had connections with enemies of the democratic state. In a fever of misguided patriotism, an Athenian jury condemned him to death. He accepted his fate and drank the famous cup of poison with simple courage.

Plato and Aristotle

Our knowledge of Socrates' thought comes mainly from the writings of his most famous pupil, Plato (428–347), for Socrates wrote nothing. Plato continued Socrates' investigation of moral conduct. He has left a massive series of philosophical books, mainly in the form of dialogues in which Socrates is the main speaker. But Plato went far beyond the homely paradoxes of Socrates and sought truth through a complex system that is still endlessly discussed and probed by critics.

Plato made his greatest impact on the future of philosophy with his theory of knowledge. Some Sophists, as we have seen, practically denied that it was possible to know anything: in the absence of objective knowledge, the only recourse was to make your way through the world by coolly exploiting any situation at hand. Socrates rebelled against this view, but his answer to the question, How can I know what is right? was simply that one must listen to one's conscience.

Plato believed that we must go beyond the evidence of our senses to find ultimate reality. We see objects as real, but in fact they are only poor reflections of ideal models, or "forms," which are eternal, perfect originals of any given object or notion.[4] To illustrate our lack of true perception, Plato uses a famous metaphor in his *Republic*. Imagine men sitting in a cave, facing a wall, with a fire at their rear. As others carry objects through the cave, in front of the

fire, the men see only vague shadows of the objects and therefore cannot make out the reality. So what we think we see as justice, for example, is only an approximation of the true form of justice. Only through long training in philosophy can we learn how to perceive and understand these forms, which exist somewhere outside our world.

Plato presents this thesis in several dialogues, of which the most read is *The Republic*. Like other Athenian intellectuals, Plato was an opponent of democracy, and his repudiation of this system was strengthened when a jury of 500 was persuaded to condemn Socrates to death, even though the master had served the state as a soldier and had committed no crime. Disillusioned by the excesses of democracy, Plato wanted to deny that the masses should exercise any power. In the first place, they had no grasp of reality, since they were unable to perceive the forms. Government must remain in the hands of statesmen who had received an education in philosophy. This ruling elite would see to it that "everyone will do his proper task." In Plato's system, a second class, warriors, would defend the state; a third, workers, would produce the needed material goods. Plato sums up his conception of good government in the epigram, "the state will be ruled well when kings become philosophers and philosophers become kings."

Like other visions of utopia, Plato's *Republic* had little effect on actual constitutions, but it seems to touch nearly every problem of philosophy, from statesmanship to perception, linguistics, and psychology. Through this rich book run many threads, but one above all: the question, What is justice? As we have seen, this had been worked over in the legendary material of Greek drama and in some of the debates in the history of Thucydides. The pupil of Socrates, who had seen his teacher condemned in a brutal distortion of justice, could hardly be indifferent to this question.

Plato, in turn, had an equally famous pupil,

---

[4] Plato used the Greek word *idéa,* which means something that can be seen. Thus "form" is a better translation of *idéa* than the English "idea," even though the latter is widely used.

Aristotle (384–322), who was for a time the teacher of Alexander the Great of Macedonia. His investigations, in which he was assisted by his pupils in Athens, extended to all fields of learning known to the ancients: logic, metaphysics, astronomy, biology, physics, politics, and poetry among them. His contributions to each of these subjects were not to be surpassed for many centuries; not until the fourteenth century did anyone seriously question Aristotle's theory of motion (see Chapter 12).

Aristotle departed from Plato's theory of ideal forms that cannot be perceived by the senses. He believed that every object has both form and matter, which are inseparable and can be studied only in that object. When we generalize about a group or class of objects, we are not referring to some ideal form but merely making a statement about what the particular objects in that group have in common. Form shapes matter; thus the form of a human being in the embryo makes the child and, eventually, the adult. For Aristotle each object had a purpose as part of a grand design of the universe. "Nature does nothing by accident," he said. The task of the philosopher is to study individual objects to discover their purpose; then, from the conclusions drawn, he may ultimately be able to perceive the grand design.

Aristotle made that task his life's work. He and his pupils devoted themselves to collecting and systematizing knowledge in all fields. For his *Politics* he studied the governments of over 150 contemporary states, comparing the merits of each. In the work he distinguishes three different types of constitution: monarchy, aristocracy, and moderate democracy. But he warns that monarchy can turn into tyranny; aristocracy into oligarchy; and moderate democracy into radical democracy, or anarchy. Of the three pure forms, Aristotle expresses a preference for moderate democracy. The chief end of government, in his view, is the good life, for both the individual and the community as a whole. This is an extension of the view expressed in his *Ethics* that happiness is the greatest good of the individual. To achieve it people must seek moderation, a mean between extremes of excessive pleasure and ascetic denial. This is in accord with the Greek principle of harmony and balance.

Aristotle also achieved a conception of the whole universe that was to remain a strong influence in all later speculations. By his time, philosophers recognized four elements. Of these, Aristotle taught that air and fire naturally move upward and earth and water downward. To these elements he added a fifth, ether, the material of which the stars are made. The stars move in a natural circular motion. Outside the whole universe there exists an eternal "prime mover," which imparts the impulse toward movement throughout all the other parts. This prime mover, or God, as Aristotle finally designates him, does not move or change; God is a kind of divine thought or mind.

Aristotle was the last of the great Greek philosophers. The techniques of logical argument perfected in the polis had been the mother of philosophy, but by Aristotle's death in 322, the self-contained polis had been absorbed into a larger world of empire. Greek philosophy then became narrower in focus, concentrating on practical rules for ethical conduct.

VI. THE HELLENISTIC AGE (323–30 B.C.)

We have dated the Classical Age of Greek civilization from about 500 to 323. The latter date is the year of the death of Alexander the Great. This larger-than-life figure conquered the Persian Empire and opened its vast territory to Greek culture. The mere presence of Greeks inevitably exposed the East to the influence of their ways. Many features of Eastern life were thus changed: the process is called Hellenization, and the period from the death of Alexander in 323 to that of Cleopatra in Egypt in 30 is known as the Hellenistic Age.

Dissolution of Alexander's Empire

After Alexander's death his generals struggled for control of his empire. By about 275, after years of warfare and diplomatic intrigue, the empire had been carved into three large kingdoms ruled by the descendants of three of these generals: Macedonia under the Antigonids; Egypt under the Ptolemies; and western Asia under the Seleucids. A fourth kingdom was formed about 260 around the city of Pergamum in western Asia Minor. The division of the empire did not end the strife. The subsequent history of these kingdoms is one of continual warfare until they were eventually absorbed by the Roman Republic.

The king of Macedonia controlled northern Greece. The poleis in the south continued to retain their autonomy. To protect their independence from the monarchy they formed defensive leagues, the most influental of which were the Aetolian League in western Greece and the Achaean League on the northern coast of the Peloponnese.

The Greek rulers of Egypt and the Seleucid kingdom transformed themselves into absolute monarchs. The inhabitants of these areas had long worshiped their rulers as divine or semi-divine beings, and the Hellenistic rulers exploited this tendency to identify man and god. Such propaganda lent authority and stability to their rule; they presented themselves to their subject as saviors and enjoyed the worship offered to benefactors in the ancient world.

An important trend in the Hellenistic Age was the re-emergence of women as rulers. Perhaps this trend began in Macedonia, where Olympias, the mother of Alexander, was a more important political figure than any woman in classical Greece. Dido, the queen of Carthage in Virgil's Latin epic, the *Aeneid,* is such a queen, and the most famous and skillful of all Hellenistic queens was Cleopatra of Egypt. Through diplomacy and, frankly, through sexual means she manipulated such Roman military leaders as Julius Caesar and Mark Antony.

Hellenistic monarchs ruled through strong armies and large bureaucracies; their systems of taxation were efficient, to say the least. Certain products were royal monopolies and could be traded only at official prices. Greeks usually held the chief public offices in the army and bureaucracy. Rulers did allow some democratic institutions to function in the Near Eastern cities, but the autonomy of these cities was limited to local affairs; they had no independent foreign policy within the monarchic framework.

Economic Life

One of the sharpest contrasts between the classical and Hellenistic worlds is in the scale of their economic operations. In classical Greece farmers worked small plots of land, and industry and commerce were ventures of small entrepreneurs. In the Hellenistic states of Egypt and the Seleucid kingdom vast estates predominated. Industry and trade operated on a larger scale than ever before in the ancient world, requiring the services of bankers and other financial agents.

The Hellenistic world prospered under Greek rule. Ambitious Greeks emigrating from their homeland to make their fortunes brought new vigor to the economies of Egypt and the Near East. They introduced new crops and new techniques in agriculture to make production more efficient. In Egypt, for example, they encouraged the cultivation of grapes for wine and improved and extended the irrigation system. They also devoted more acreage to pasturing animals, which provided leather and cloth for the people and horses for the cavalry.

The growth of industry and trade was even more remarkable. The Hellenistic rulers encouraged these efforts by establishing a sound money system, building roads and canals, and clearing the seas of pirates. Traders ventured eastward to India and, in the west, beyond the Mediterranean to the Atlantic coasts of Africa and Europe.

The resulting prosperity, however, was unevenly distributed. Rulers and members of the upper classes (usually Greek) amassed great fortunes, but little of this wealth filtered down to the peasants and laborers. This great disparity between rich and poor led to increasing social conflict. Moreover, mainland Greece did not share in the new prosperity. And the departure of the more venturesome Greeks for the Near East and Egypt depleted Greek cities of the leadership that might have reversed the economic decline.

Hellenistic Cities

Hellenistic civilization, like classical Greek civilization, was predominantly urban. Though the greater part of the vast lands of the kingdoms was devoted to agricultural pursuits, it was in the numerous Greek cities founded by Alexander and his successors that the culture of the Near East was transformed into the civilization that we call Hellenistic. Most of these new cities were in western Asia, in the Seleucid kingdom. Alexander himself had founded the brilliant city of Alexandria, in Egypt, but the Ptolemies did not follow him with many new foundations, for a docile, rustic civilization was easier to control than citizens of a politically active urban society.

The Hellenistic cities were centers of government, trade, and culture. They were extremely large by ancient standards. Some had ten times as many inhabitants as the average polis in Greece; Alexandria, the largest of them, had at least a half-million inhabitants.

Besides their political institutions the Greeks brought from their homeland many of the amenities of polis life: temples, theaters, gymnasiums, and other public buildings. Natives in the upper classes copied Greek ways and sent their children to Greek schools. Moreover, a version of their language, *koiné* ("common") Greek, based mainly on the Attic dialect, became an international tongue. Now, for the first time, an individual could travel to any city in the known civilized world and make himself understood.

This traveling and intermingling account for the cosmopolitanism seen within the Hellenistic cities. None was more cosmopolitan than Alexandria, the greatest of them all. The city attracted scholars from all over the Greek world, for there the Ptolemies had built a museum and the largest library of ancient times. Though Athens still retained its leadership in philosophy, Alexandria became the cultural center of the Hellenistic Age. Scholars at Alexandria specialized in literary, historical, and scientific research.

The specialization of scholars was characteristic of the growing professionalism of the age. Whereas the citizen of fifth-century Athens could in turn be a farmer, a politician, a soldier, and even an actor (all the performers in the great dramas were amateurs), now these roles were filled by professionals. The army consisted of professional soldiers. Though the private citizen could cast a vote in the city's assembly, the professional bureaucrats ran the government.

Literature, Art, and Science

The Hellenistic Age was not a particularly notable period in literature. Poets were concerned chiefly with style. Many of them achieved a certain technical perfection in their lyrics, but the works had little emotional depth. One of the few to rise above mere technical proficiency was Theocritus, a third-century poet who

The theater at Epidaurus, built probably in the 200s B.C., **is testimony to the importance of drama in Greek life. The theater was designed to seat more than 12,000 people.**
(Photo: Alison Frantz)

wrote charming lyrics about nature. His influence is evident in Virgil's *Bucolics* (or *Eclogues*) and, in a later period, in some of the work of Spenser and Milton.

The most significant literary achievements of the Hellenistic Age came from scholarship, a sign of the growing professionalism of the period. The literary capital of the Greek world was no longer Athens but Alexandria. By about 200 B.C. the library there probably housed a half-million papyrus rolls, predecessors of the book. Scholars in Alexandria worked to preserve the literature of earlier times. Their outstanding achievement was the standardization of the text of Homer. By comparing the many versions that had been handed down in manuscripts over the centuries, they were able to establish the text on which modern versions of Homer are based.

Hellenistic rulers subsidized art and architecture. As a result the architecture of the age tends to emphasize size and grandeur, as compared with the simplicity and human scale of classical architecture. An example is the Altar of Zeus from Pergamum (now in Berlin). A great stairway leading to the altar is flanked by a frieze 400 feet long. The figures on the frieze are typical of Hellenistic sculpture. They are carved in a high relief, with a realism that makes them seem to burst out of the background. The almost extravagant emotionalism of the work is only one of the characteristics that distinguishes Hellenistic sculpture from that of the classical period. Instead of idealized figures, artists now showed genuine individuality in faces and bodies (see Plate 5). They often depicted physical imperfection or even frank ugliness. Their attempts to portray strong emotions in their subjects sometimes led merely to exaggeration.

The most remarkable example of the cross-fertilization of cultures in the Hellenistic Age was in the field of science. The Greeks had long speculated about the nature of the universe, and the Near East had an even longer scientific tradition, particularly in the fields of astronomy and mathematics, as we have seen. After Alexander's conquests joined the two cultures, other conditions favored scientific advance: the increased professionalism of the age, the use of Greek as an international language, and the research facilities established in Alexandria. The result was an age of scientific achievement that was not surpassed until the seventeenth century.

In mathematics, Euclid (about 300) compiled a textbook of geometry that is still the basis for the study of plane geometry. Some of his theorems were already known, and others (for example, his demonstration that nonparallel lines must meet somewhere) may seem obvious. What he did was to construct a set of elegant proofs—incidentally, a typical Greek procedure, for, as we have seen, the insistence on analytical method runs like a thread through Greek civilization. The greatest mathematician of all antiquity—indeed, one of the greatest ever—was Archimedes of Syracuse (287?–212). He calculated the value of *pi* (the ratio between the circumference and diameter of a circle); developed a system for expressing large numbers in words, by using one hundred million as the base; and discovered the ratio between the volumes of a sphere and a cylinder circumscribing it (2:3; he had this proportion engraved on his tombstone). Archimedes was also interested in physics; he demonstrated that a floating body will sink only so far, until it displaces its own weight in a liquid. He perceived the powers of the lever for lifting massive weights and is said to have proclaimed, "Give me a place where I can stand and I will lift the earth."

About 250 Aristarchus, an astronomer and mathematician, advanced a heliocentric theory of the movement of the planets. The view that the earth revolves around the sun was not new, but Aristarchus refined it, stating that the earth revolves on its own axis while it, and the other planets, circle the sun. It remained for Copernicus in the sixteenth century to prove the soundness of Aristarchus' system. Meanwhile, the Greek astronomic tradition continued to follow the geocentric theory of Hipparchus (190?–after 126). This was the basis for the great work of Ptolemy of Alexandria (about A.D. 140), the *Almagest*. This astronomy textbook brought Greek study of the subject to its zenith; the work became canonical and remained so for more than one thousand years.

One of the most important contributions of Hellenistic scientists was the development of more nearly precise measurements. Hipparchus calculated the length of the average lunar month to within one second of the accepted figure. Eratosthenes (275?–194?) computed the circumference of the earth to be about 28,000 miles, only 3000 miles more than the actual figure. Other scientists worked out the division of time into hours, minutes, and seconds and of circles into degrees, minutes, and seconds.

Philosophy and Religion

The change in life style from the security of the polis to the sophistication, variety, and loneliness of a large cosmopolitan world produced corresponding changes in Greek philosophy. Plato and Aristotle had been philosophers of the polis in the sense that they were concerned with the individual's role in the intimate world of the city-state. But now the state was a large kingdom headed by a remote ruler. Individual men and women could hardly influence its policies and yet were caught up in wars and other changes of fortune. In such conditions, philosophies were needed that offered the possibility of survival in this world. The two most important schools of Hellenistic philosophy, Stoicism and Epicureanism, were addressed to an individualistic age in which people sought guidance in their personal lives and were less concerned about the nature of the political framework.

Zeno (335–263), who founded Stoicism, taught that a single divine reason, or plan, governs the universe; and that to find happiness one must act in harmony with this plan. One should be patient in adversity, for it is a necessary part of the divine plan and one can do nothing to change it. By cultivating a sense of duty and self-discipline, people can learn to accept their fate; they will then become immune to earthly anxieties and will achieve inner freedom and tranquility. The Stoics did not advocate withdrawal from the world. They believed that all people, as rational beings, belong to one family. Therefore, they should be tolerant. Moreover, to ensure justice for all, the rational person should consider it a duty to participate in public affairs.

The Stoics were advancing ideas that were to have a profound influence on later Western history: universal membership in the human family, the virtue of tolerance, and compassion for the less fortunate members of the human race. The concept of the brotherhood of all human beings was the product of a cosmopolitan society. Furthermore, most earlier Greeks had accepted the institution of slavery, but the Stoics believed that the practice of exploiting others corrupted the owner (the slave could endure bondage by achieving inner freedom). Stocism became the most influential philosophy among the educated of the Hellenistic Age and achieved great influence among the Romans.

Like the Stoics, Epicurus (341–270) believed that people should strive for tranquility, but he differed from them on the means of attaining it. He adopted the atomic theory of Leucippus and Democritus. Our bodies and souls are made up only of atoms that, for a time, cohere.

When we die, the atoms will be redistributed into the universe again, and there will be nothing left of us that will suffer desire for the life we have lost. Thus death holds no terrors and the gods will not punish us. We should therefore concern ourselves only with leading pleasurable lives, avoiding physical and mental pain. But emotional commitment and passionate love are equally unrewarding, since we are on earth for such a short time. Thus the wise person withdraws from the world to study philosophy and enjoy the companionship of a few friends.

The search for meaning in life existed at all levels of Hellenistic society, but nowhere so much as among the great masses of the poor. The answers of philosophy were addressed to an intellectual elite—wealthy scholars, as it were, meditating in the study. But the poor lacked the education, leisure, and detachment for such a pursuit. They sought spiritual and emotional sustenance for their daily encounters with the harshness of Hellenistic life.

For many the mystery religions of the Near East filled this need. The influence of the old Greek civic religion had declined along with the polis and by now had almost disappeared. Thus Greek religion was never firmly transplanted in the East. Rather, the religious influence gradually moved in the opposite direction until finally Eastern religions dominated the West. Thus the younger societies in the Greek world turned to older ones for guidance.

There were numerous mystery cults that had some features in common as a result of the frequent intermingling of cultures in the cosmopolitan Near East. They centered on the worship of a savior whose death and resurrection would redeem the sins of mankind; their rituals were elaborate, often wildly emotional; and they nourished hope by promising an afterlife that would compensate for the rigors of this one. Among the more important mystery cult was the worship of Isis and Osiris, deities from Egypt.

The Eastern god who was to achieve the greatest acceptance in the West was Yahweh, the god of the Israelites and then of the Jews and Christians. Much in the development of Christianity was Israelite in origin, but some of its practices emerged from other Near Eastern religions. Baptism, the confession of sins, sacrificial meals, and a general growth of mysticism all were part of the spiritual heritage of the Hellenistic Age. We might indeed say that Christianity became the most widespread and successful of all the mystery religions.

The Greeks of the Classical Age established standards of beauty and wisdom that have inspired people ever since. Greek civilization at its height explored and analyzed nearly every aspect of humanity and its potential. Even when the world of the polis was shattering, philosophers reaffirmed that people have reason and can therefore devise a more just society.

The long Peloponnesian War between Athens and Sparta caused the decline of the polis and opened the way for the domination of Greece by Philip II of Macedonia. His son Alexander was responsible for a dramatic expansion of Greek culture; with his conquering armies he brought Greek civilization into Asia Minor, Syria, and India.

A fusion of cultures took place as different societies were drawn into the orbit of Greek language and thought. A new Hellenistic civilization emerged as the polis gave way to the "cosmopolis." The Greeks themselves underwent some changes. They transplanted many institutions of the polis to the Near East, but the ties within the community that had characterized the society of the polis were weakened. The cultural interchange in the Hellenistic world was to have a profound influence on religion in the West. Christianity started as a small cult in the Near East. The man who brought its message to the Greeks, and then to the Romans, was Paul of Tarsus, a Hellenized Jew from Asia Minor.

But the Greeks could not maintain permanent control over the Hellenized world. Another state was to succeed even beyond the achievements of Alexander. Not Greece but Rome became the uniting force that passed the legacy of the classical world to medieval and then to modern Europe.

RECOMMENDED READING

Sources

Aristotle. *The Athenian Constitution.* P. J. Rhodes (tr.). 1984. The great philosopher's brief history and description of the Athenian state, with helpful commentary.

Arrian. *Life of Alexander the Great.* Aubrey de Sélincourt (tr.). 1958.

David Grene and Richmond Lattimore (eds.). *The Complete Greek Tragedies.* 1959. The best collection of translations.

Thucydides. *The Peloponnesian War.* Rex Warner (tr.). 1954.

Studies

Adkins, Arthur W. H. *Merit and Responsibility: A Study in Greek Values.* 1975. An attempt to summarize the ethical beliefs of the Greeks.

Burn, A. R. *Persia and the Greeks.* 1962. Especially good for an accurate narrative of the Persian Wars.

Dover, K. J. *Greek Popular Morality in the Time of Plato and Aristotle.* 1974.

———. *Greek Homosexuality.* 1980. Dispassionate study of this feature of Greek life.

Ehrenberg, Victor. *From Solon to Socrates.* 1968. Mainly a political textbook on the central period of Greek history, with good references to primary sources.

Ellis, John R. *Philip II and Macedonian Imperialism.* 1976. Good modern study of the rise of the kingdom that was to dominate Greece.

Forrest, W. G. *A History of Sparta, 950–192* B.C. 1968. At times adventurous, always stimulating.

Guthrie, W. K. C. *Socrates.* 1971. Excellent study of the man and his thought.

Hamilton, J. R. *Alexander the Great.* 1973. A balanced assessment of this controversial figure.

Hatzopoulos, Miltiades, and Louisa Lykopoulou. *Philip of Macedon.* 1981. Narrative with the latest archaeological evidence about Macedon.

Kitto, H. D. F. *The Greeks.* 1950. Classic appreciation of Greek culture, written with sympathy and wit.

———. *Greek Tragedy: A Literary Study.* 1969. Possibly the best general book on this literary form.

Meiggs, Russell. *The Athenian Empire.* 1972. For advanced students; discussion of many historical problems, especially good at interpreting evidence from inscriptions.

Ross, W. D. *Aristotle.* 1956. Comprehensive study by a great master.

de Ste Croix, G. E. M. *The Origins of the Peloponnesian War.* 1972. Really a detailed history of the fifth century; many appendixes on special topics.

Staveley, E. S. *Greek and Roman Voting and Elections.* 1972. Illuminates many practices in the Athenian constitution.

Walbank, F. W. *The Hellenistic World.* 1982. The best introduction to this period.

EXPERIENCES OF DAILY LIFE

Slavery

Slavery is one of the most troubling features of ancient social life. It is an institution that has perhaps not even now wholly disappeared. But in the ancient world it was accepted; the only criticisms of it were warnings about the need to manage it efficiently. The Greek philosopher Aristotle, whom we have no reason to consider especially cold or heartless, explained that slavery was a product of nature, for nature had divided humanity into natural masters and natural slaves, the latter class including all "barbarians" such as Asians (*Politics,* Book 1). Romans such as Cicero and Livy echoed this theme, and no one recommended the abolition of slavery on the ground that it was morally wrong.

M. I. Finley, a profound scholar of ancient economic history, has suggested three conditions needed for the rise of slavery: private ownership of land and the need to obtain labor outside the owner's family; the production and trading of commodities, since slaves must be bought with surplus income; and the unavailability of extra labor within the society itself. These conditions were present in both Greek and Roman society, but slavery had various contradictory features that make it hard to describe briefly. For example, the helots of Sparta differed from individual slaves in other states: they could not be bought and sold by anyone, since they were owned by the state; and they were not imported from abroad but were recognized as Greeks by other Greeks.

A community obtained slaves mainly

Men working in a clay pit. (Staatliche Museen zu Berlin)

through conquest of other territory, though kidnapping and even the sale of children added to recruitment. We have scattered information about the number of slaves. A Greek farmer with a small plot might own a slave or two; his wife would probably have a domestic girl. The father of the orator Lysias had a shield factory with 120 slaves, and the general Nicias owned 1000 slaves, whom he rented out to work in the Attic silver mines; these mines employed over 10,000 slaves in prosperous times. In Rome the numbers were larger. One senator had a staff of 400 slaves to serve his home, and slaves worked Italian farms in gangs. Roman conquests brought in many more slaves than any Greek state needed.

The only occupations almost always assigned to slaves were mining and domestic service. Law, politics, and administration were reserved for free citizens (so was military service in general, though slaves sometimes took part in times of need, for example as rowers in ships during Rome's wars with Carthage). All other labor was shared; as the Athenian Xenophon said, "A man buys a slave to have a companion at work." In a unique exception to these divisions of labor, the Athenians had a police force of public slaves from Scythia.

We have no accounts of slavery written by slaves, but our evidence seems to show that their treatment depended on the kindness of the master. Since the slave was considered a piece of property, the law never intervened in favor of human rights. The emperor Constantine issued decrees protecting masters who had beaten slaves to death, since this was viewed as maintaining order (but apparently someone had raised the question whether the action was right).

A slave might leave slavery through being freed by the owner (manumission); the slave might bring this about by saving small sums and repaying his or her purchase price. Masters were often willing to free slaves when they were about thirty, since ill health might not justify continuing to maintain them. Prices of slaves could vary widely (Nicias is said to have paid a talent, 6000 drachmas, for a skilled supervisor), but about 150 drachmas, roughly 100 days' pay for a laborer, has been reckoned as an average for Greece about 400 B.C. The master could probably recover his investment out of the slave's work within the first year.

Modern critics of slavery have sometimes sponsored the myth that slavery was not economically efficient. If this was so, it went unnoticed by ancient owners, who used slaves apparently under the impression that they were making a living. This myth also overlooks the fact that no ancient labor or industry was at all efficient in comparison with modern practices. The ancient world was poor in machines to multiply the labor of one worker (water-driven mills are an exception), and the obvious way to increase production was to acquire more human beings. But we lack the means to express in statistics how efficient slavery was, or to judge how well or badly industry would have done without slavery.

Slavery outlasted the world of antiquity, though it does appear to have declined during the later Roman Empire. Why did it pass away? Not through revolts, for slaves appear to have resigned themselves to their fate and rarely rebelled. Some have suggested that Christianity successfully preached against slavery; it would be pleasant if we could believe this, but there is little evidence for it and (in the continued ownership of slaves by the Church) good evidence against it. Finley offers a more probable answer. The reasons for the decline of slavery lay within Roman society itself, especially in the total domination of citizens' lives by the imperial bureaucracy of the fourth and fifth centuries. The trading of commodities shrank decisively as the state requisitioned more and more goods from the people. These payments "in kind" did not return money to the contributors, with which they could buy slaves. It appears, too, that in the depressed conditions more free citizens had to become willing to work for others; thus there was less need for an infusion of slave labor to meet the needs of industry.

Chapter 4
The Roman Republic

The basic theme of Roman history in the republican period is conquest, domination. The Romans themselves may not have seen that this was their constant aim, but a historian can often see a pattern that was not evident to persons alive at an earlier time. And, in fact, the collective behavior of the Romans was so consistently conquest-oriented that one may guess they had a clear idea of this purpose. The best way to achieve conquest is to turn society into a military machine. An army is not a democracy, but a disciplined body governed by a few experienced men—an oligarchy.

The Roman state, indeed all Roman society, was so organized. This was not achieved through internal brutality or terror: Rather, the people never insisted on having the kind of democracy or control by the masses that Athens had in the Greek world. The machine thus formed united first the Italian peninsula, then the area of the Mediterranean. In the process, certain military dynasts became so powerful and ambitious that the republican constitution was destroyed in the Roman revolution. This revolution, a long battle among several warlords, killed whatever elements of political freedom existed in the Republic and established an even more powerful autocracy, the Roman Empire.

I. THE UNIFICATION OF ITALY (TO 264 B.C.)

Geography of Italy

Italy is not, like Greece, divided into many small valleys. The main geographic feature is the Apennine range, which runs diagonally across Italy in the north and then turns southward to bisect the peninsula. The central portion of this peninsula has plenty of water and good soil, benefits that most Greeks would have envied, but the south is poor and sunbaked. North of the Apennines is the fertile valley of the Po River, irrigated by this and other rivers that drain the Apennines and the Alps, which lie farther north. The rich Po valley was for centuries the home of Celtic peoples collectively known as Gauls. The hills of Italy are gentle enough for pasturing, unlike those of Greece, and wood, scarce in Greece, was

plentiful. The landscape, especially in the center and north, is of unsurpassed beauty; some of the best Roman poetry, by Virgil, Horace, and Catullus, hymns the delights of the land and the pleasure of farming.

The Origins of Rome

The legends about the founding of Rome by Aeneas or by Romulus and Remus are myths, so we must depend on evidence gathered by archaeologists to describe early Roman history. Scraps of pottery suggest that the site of Rome was inhabited as early as 1400; certainly between 900 and 600 there was a series of cemeteries on the famous seven hills that bound Rome.

Ancient scholars relied on myths to date the "founding" of Rome in 753 B.C. (slight variations from this date occur in our sources). This date is not to be taken seriously as the moment when Rome came into existence, but there must have been considerable habitation in the area by that time. Early settlers lived on and near the seven hills that ring the city (see Map A-7 in the Cartographic Essay). About 625 they drained the marshes below the hills and built a central marketplace, the Forum. This was forever the center of Roman history.

Two other peoples are especially important in the early history of Rome. The first is the Etruscans, who actually dominated early Rome and provided its kings. The origin of the Etruscans is obscure and forms a famous controversy. Some ancient sources say they were a native European people, while the Greek historian Herodotus asserts that they arrived from Asia Minor. In any case, they appeared in Italy soon after 800, in the region north of the Tiber River known as Etruria (modern Tuscany). Their language was not an Italic dialect; it is still undeciphered even though thousands of short Etruscan inscriptions exist.

During their period of rule the Etruscans left their stamp on the future Roman civilization; indeed, the name "Roma" is an Etruscan word. Theirs was a sophisticated culture—urbane, literate, and technologically advanced—and they traded with Greeks and Phoenicians; Greek vases, especially, have been found in Etruscan tombs. The Etruscans passed on to the Romans the technique of building temples. They also introduced the worship of a triad of gods (Juno, Minerva, Jupiter) and the custom of examining the innards of animals to foretell the future.

The second non-Roman element was the Greeks. Beginning about 750, they established about fifty poleis on the southern and western shores of Italy and on the island of Sicily. The Romans called the area of southern Italy Magna Graecia ("Great Greece") and thus gave us the name "Greeks" for the people who called themselves Hellenes. Greek culture from the colonies influenced the Etruscans and, in turn, the Romans. For example, from the village of Cumae, the oldest Greek colony in Italy, the Etruscans learned the Western version of the Greek alphabet and passed it on to Rome. These Greek colonies survived until the third century, when they were brought under the control of the Roman Republic.

About 500 (the Romans reckoned the date as 509) Etruscan sovereignty over Rome ended. The legends invented to account for this revolution need not be taken seriously, but somehow Rome freed itself of its last king and established a republican form of government. Afterward the Etruscans gradually declined as a power until they were finally absorbed by the Roman Republic in the fourth century.

The Early Constitution

Much of the history of the Roman Republic concerns the development of the constitution; it was never a written document but rather a set of carefully observed procedures and customs. Romans had a deep reverence for law and tradition; indeed, their term for "revolution" was *res novae,* literally "new things."

The Roman system, like those of Athens and Sparta, had three major components, which tended to offset and balance each other. The executives were two officers called consuls, who were the supreme civil and military magistrates.[1] There was also an advisory body of elder statesmen and heads of clans, called the Senate. Finally, there were popular assemblies of all citizens. The Greek historian Polybius (200?–118?) admired the Roman system and found it in an ideal mixture of constitutions: The consuls represented monarchy; the Senate, aristocracy; and the assemblies, democracy.

---

[1] There is ancient evidence (Livy 3.55) that the executive officers were originally called praetors. But from 366 at the latest the term *consul* was used, and Roman writers also employed it for the supreme magistrates of earlier years; we shall follow this convention, as most historians do.

International and Military History	Political History
pre-600 Etruscan rule over Rome	
625	
	509 Traditional date of founding of Republic
	494–287 Struggle of Orders
	494 Tribunes
	450 Laws of Twelve Tables
400	
390 Gauls invade Rome	
	366 First plebeian consul
264–241 First Punic War	
219–202 Second Punic War	
216 Cannae	
200	
149–146 Punic War	
133 Conquest of Spain	133 Tiberius Gracchus tribune
	123 Gaius Gracchus tribune
	107 Marius consul
91–88 Italian ("Social") War	81–80 Sulla dictator
58–50 Gallic War	70 Pompey and Crassus consuls
48 Pharsalus	60 Triumvirate
42 Philippi	49 Civil War
31 Actium	44 Death of Caesar
Death of Cleopatra	

625–27 B.C./TIMELINE

Social and Economic History	Cultural and Intellectual History

— c. 625 Forum drained

445 Lex Canuleia allows patrician–plebeian marriages

— 400

250–184 Plautus' comedies
239–169 Ennius translates Greek plays

— c. 200 Growth of slavery — c. 200–118 Polybius, historian
190–159 Terence

c. 136 Slave revolt, Sicily

106–43 Cicero, orator, essayist
94–55 Lucretius
84–54 Catullus

45 Reform of Julian calendar — c. 50 Caesar's *Commentaries*
— 27

The consuls were elected annually by the Assembly of the Centuries (*comitia centuriata*), which comprised the entire army; in this assembly the wealthier citizens voted first and could often determine the result if they all voted the same way. This arrangement illustrates the conservative nature of the Roman mind; so does the law that, in cases where the two consuls disagreed, one could block the action of the other, and the consul advocating no action should prevail. Consuls (and lower-ranking officers called praetors) possessed imperium, which gave them the power to command troops and to execute any other assignments they might receive from the Senate.

There were two other political bodies besides the Assembly of the Centuries. The Assembly of Tribes *(comitia tributa)* included all citizens, arranged in the final number of thirty-five voting units, or tribes; the criterion for membership in a specific tribe was place of

A sixth-century Etruscan chariot, done in bronze sheathing over a wood frame.
(Photo: Metropolitan Museum of Art, Rogers Fund, 1903)

birth or (if a man had moved) his residence. This tribal assembly elected officers who did not command troops and therefore did not have imperium. These magistrates, known as quaestors and aediles, looked after various financial matters and public works. Finally, there was the Assembly of Curiae, or wards of the city *(comitia curiata);* this body met only to validate decisions taken elsewhere and gradually lost importance. Over the centuries, the Assembly of Tribes became the most powerful and active of the three assemblies. It was this one that passed most of the major laws.

The Senate, in turn, was the nerve center

This sarcophagus is from a late sixth-century Etruscan tomb. The reclining couple on the lid reflects the influence of Greek art on the style of the Etruscans.
(Photo: Alinari-Art Reference Bureau)

of the whole state. It was originally an advisory body to the kings (the word *senatus* means "council of elders"), but in time it took control of both foreign and domestic policy. It did not, in the Republic, pass laws, but it appointed commanders, provided and assigned funds, and generally set the direction of the state. The Roman Senate house, which still stands, though often rebuilt, is thus the cradle of Roman domination. The senators (usually about 300) were recruited from ex-consuls and other officers, and membership was for life. Its solid conservatism acted to restrain hotheaded politicians, and more than once it provided the moral leadership that saw the state through a military crisis. Rome had no political parties in the modern sense, but the Senate did break up into smaller units, rivals in the struggle to hold power.

But the real location of power was the family—indeed, modern historians have learned how to tell the story of the Republic through the study of the family. Alliances, divorces, marriages, and adoptions could all add to the political power of the family. A larger unit was the *gens,* or clan; this was a group of related families, like the clans of Scotland—for example, all Romans whose second name was Cornelius or Aemilius (this was the "gentile" name). The great clans and their subdivisions contrived to maintain such firm control over high office that by about 100 B.C. it was rare for any man to attain the consulship who did not have ancestors who had already been consuls. Such an outsider (for example, the orator Cicero) was referred to as a "new man" *(novus homo)*. Throughout all Italian history, even down to the present, the family unit has remained the focus of social and political life, providing allies and weapons in time of defeat and sharing in the spoils of victory.

The Struggle of the Orders (494–287 B.C.)

Within the citizen body, the Romans established a distinction that had no parallel in any Greek state. The patricians, a small number of families (about 5 to 7 percent of the whole people), were recognized as being socially and legally superior to the vast majority, who were called plebeians. Ancient sources do not explain how the distinction arose; it was probably based on wealth gained by owning land and on the less easily defined criterion of social leadership.

Rome was built on oligarchy. Originally, only patricians could belong to the Senate and hold office. Plebeians could vote in the assemblies, but the upper classes could manipulate these bodies. Also, richer citizens acted as patrons to the poorer, who were known as their clients; this relationship was even formally recognized in Roman law. It was natural for clients to vote as their patrons wished, and for most of the duration of the Republic voters had to declare their votes openly.

The control of affairs by the upper classes was never dissolved: As we have said, the common people never insisted on gaining the real direction of the state. Still, the plebeians did demand and slowly gain more privileges. This long process of adjusting the constitution, which fell short of what we might call a revolution, is known as the struggle of the orders (or classes). When the struggle ended, the people could point to significant gains, but the great families were still secure in their domination. Indeed, the struggle of the orders had the effect of making the state an even more efficient machine for conquest, since the people could now feel that they were better integrated within the system and were willing to fight for their country.

Their first victory in the legal battle came in 494 B.C., when they evidently threatened to secede from the state (this may have meant undertaking a kind of general strike).[2] They now obtained the right to elect two men annually to represent them. These were called tribunes, and eventually there were ten elected, from plebeians only, every year. The powers of the tribunes dramatically show the Roman genius for political compromise in the interests of a united state. The patricians evidently recognized that spokesmen for the people were a necessary evil, and they took an oath that it would be a religious crime to violate or injure the body of a tribune. This sacred vow has no parallel in history, but, with the rarest exceptions, it was respected. The "sacrosanctity" of the tribunes allowed them to interfere in any action, since no one could lay hands on them. Out of this right arose the famous veto power of the tribunes (sometimes called "intercession"); they could forbid any magistrate from acting and could even arrest consuls. (By exception, tribunes could not veto actions of commanders in war or those of dictators, extraordinary officers appointed in emergencies who could hold supreme power for no longer than six months.)

Next the plebeians demanded that the law should be published for all to know. In 450 the law was indeed codified and published on twelve wooden tablets. The resulting code, called the Laws of the Twelve Tables, concerned only civic matters, the definition of various kinds of crime, and relations among citizens and members of families. That is, it was not a constitution defining the form of the state, like that of the United States. None of the original tablets still exist, but from later writers we can assemble quotations of the abrupt declarations that made up the code. For example:

If a man summons another to court, he must go. If he does not go, the other man may call witnesses; only then may he take him by force.

If a man is mad, power over him and his property shall belong to his kinsmen.

A man must mend his road. If he does not keep it laid with stones, people may drive their wagons wherever they like.

If a man kills a thief by night, he shall be considered rightly killed. If a patron has defrauded his client, he may be killed without penalty.

Soon after, in 445, by the passing of the Lex Canuleia, plebeians obtained the right of intermarriage with patricians.[3] This was a measure of great importance, for now richer plebeians could seek out patrician spouses. Over the years this led to the formation of an aristocracy that blended the two classes; thus in a way a new patrician–plebeian aristocracy replaced the one that had consisted of patricians only. In 366 the first plebeian consul held office, and from that time on it was customary for one of the annual consuls to be a plebeian. The patricians retained one consulship, and because of their much smaller number they could still arrange to pass this office around within a favored circle. In 366, too, another magistracy was created, that of praetor—a kind of assistant consul, who also held imperium. Eventually there were eight praetors elected every year.

The final concession to the plebeians came in 287, when a law (the Lex Hortensia) made decisions of the Assembly of Tribes, or *comitia tributa,* binding on the whole state without further action by any other body. Thus the common people now had the absolute legal right to pass laws; but in practice most legislation

---

[2] The sources give contradictory dates for, and accounts of, many events in Roman history down to about 280; the order that we adopt is tenable but cannot always be proved right in every detail.

[3] Every Roman law (Latin *lex*) was named for its sponsor, in this case one Canuleius; since *lex* is a feminine noun, the adjective with it must always end in *-a*.

had the sponsorship of the Senate before it came before the Assembly of Tribes. It was also possible for any faction opposed to certain legislation to gain control over some tribune within the group of ten. Any one tribune could, through his veto, paralyze the action of the others or of the state itself; thus the Senate could disrupt any activity of the assembly that it found uncongenial. As a result, public debate was usually ineffective on all but the senatorial level. The struggle of the orders was real, and it led to greater power for the plebeians, but the upper class managed to control this revolution before it could lead to the actual direction of affairs by the masses. We might ask why the plebeians did not try to press their victory further and overturn conservative control totally. One answer must be that the whole state was soon involved in extending and solidifying the holdings of the Roman people.

Early Expansion of Rome

While the Romans were developing their form of government, they were also expanding their holdings on the Italian Peninsula. They had managed to free themselves from Etruscan domination, but there remained the possibility of an immediate reconquest by the Etruscans. To guard against this, the Romans formed alliances with their neighbors in the surrounding area of the plain of Latium and created the so-called Latin League (about 493 B.C.). Thus from the start Roman imperialism was partly inspired by fear and the need for allies.

Roman historians of the early wars of conquest saw them through a haze of legend, but their narratives convince us that the battles were sometimes long and severe. About 405, for example, they set out to capture the last remaining Etruscan stronghold, the town of Veii, which they captured and destroyed in 396. This outright conquest was one method of expansion, but with some other tribes the Ro-

mans were able to pursue a strategy of more peaceful diplomacy.

The period of conquest was punctuated by one major disaster. About 390 a large force of Gauls left their stronghold in the Po valley and captured part of Rome. They exacted a ransom as the price of their withdrawal. Rome then renewed its policy of expansion, showing the resilience that made it, in the words of the historian Edward Gibbon, "sometimes vanquished in battle, always victorious in war." Shortly after 300 Rome dominated the Italian peninsula as far south as the Greek city-states of Magna Graecia.

A series of quarrels led to a war between Rome and these city-states. At this point Roman history emerges into clear light, with secure dates and no legendary decorations. The Greek city of Tarentum summoned Pyrrhus, a prince from the half-Greek region of Epirus (modern Albania), to direct the campaign against Rome. Pyrrhus fought two successful battles in 280, but at a heavy cost in casualties to his own men (the phrase "a Pyrrhic victory" comes from this).

Pyrrhus sent an envoy to invite the Romans to surrender; but a veteran statesman (Appius Claudius, for whom the famous Appian Way was named) rose in the Senate to declare that "Rome never negotiates with an enemy so long as he is on Roman soil." His statement epitomizes the Roman spirit, and Rome indeed fought on. Pyrrhus might have achieved more than he did if he had stuck to his war, but he became diverted to military adventures in Sicily, and in 275 he abandoned Italy, leaving the Romans to pursue their conquests. By 265 Rome controlled the entire Italian peninsula, but had not yet mastered the Po valley (see Map 4.1).

The Roman Federation

Rome's treatment of conquered communities shows the political skill of its administrators.

MAP 4.1. ITALY 265 B.C.

Rather than holding them down by brutality or direct occupation, Rome devised a system that made them partners, in a way, and so made the state an even more efficient instrument for dominion. Rome organized these communities by establishing several different degrees of privilege and responsibility among them. Residents of a few favored communities were granted the most highly prized status, full Roman citizenship. This meant that they were on the same legal footing as the Romans; they enjoyed the protection of Roman law and could hold office in Rome. Members of some other communities became citizens who could not vote; such citizens had the right of intermarriage with Romans and had to supply troops to the Roman army on demand. At a lower level of privilege were the allied states *(socii)*. They received Rome's protection from other peoples and were also liable for troops. None of these groups, once joined to Rome in whatever status, could follow independent foreign policies, but progress upward within the ranks of citizenship was possible. This system of confederation enabled the Romans to solve an administrative problem that had frustrated the Greek poleis: how to control a large territory without having to demolish or transform the conqueror's own institutions.

II. THE AGE OF IMPERIALISM (264–133 B.C.)

The Punic Wars

After unifying peninsular Italy, Rome possessed extensive resources, especially in manpower. Indeed, it now had the means to become a world power. And Rome—by which we now refer not only to the ancient city but also to the whole group of peoples in Italy allied with the city—achieved this in three wars with Carthage. This city had been founded by Phoenicians about 700; within the next century Carthage established its own Mediterranean empire. By the time Rome had unified the Italian Peninsula, Carthage controlled cities in northern Africa, parts of Spain, the islands of Corsica and Sardinia, and much of Sicily. It was beyond comparison the leading naval power in the western Mediterranean and could live off the tribute paid by possessions. With good reason a modern German historian called Carthage "the London of antiquity."

The confrontation with Rome began in 264 as a minor conflict over the presence of Carthaginian troops in the Sicilian city of Messana (modern Messina), which lay outside the Carthaginian territory there. Messana had invited the troops into the city as protection against other enemies but then decided to replace them with a Roman force. When Carthage refused to tolerate Roman interference, war broke out between Carthage and Rome. The war soon became a contest for control of the island of Sicily itself and it was the first of the three Punic Wars, so named from the Latin word *Poeni,* or Phoenicians, who had founded Carthage. Roman tenacity finally won this war in 241, but with heavy casualties. Carthage abandoned Sicily entirely, and large parts of the island passed to Rome. In 238 the Romans seized the Carthaginian islands of Corsica and Sardinia. These islands, together with Sicily, became the first Roman provinces.

The second Punic War (219–202) was the most critical. The conflict arose in Spain, where Rome protested to Carthage about its treatment of a town friendly to Rome, Saguntum. But, since Saguntum lay well within the agreed Carthaginian sphere of influence in Spain, the Romans had only weak grounds for protest. During negotiations Hannibal, the brilliant Carthaginian general, seized Saguntum, and this action made war inevitable. He welcomed a chance for war against the power that had humiliated his nation, and he decided to carry the war to the enemy. During the autumn of 218 he led his army from Spain across the Alps and down into Italy. Once there he hoped to arouse the Gallic tribes in the Po valley and break up the alliances of the various peoples with Rome; then he planned to go on to conquer Rome itself. Thus this strategy would test the loyalty of the allies to Rome and would show whether the Roman system was well constructed. In the end, Hannibal's twofold strategy failed. He won a stupendous victory over the Romans at Cannae, in central Italy, in 216, which has remained a classic study for strategists ever since, but not even then could he arouse the allies to revolt. At least half of them chose to remain loyal to Rome, and without such revolts Hannibal's manpower was no match for that of the Romans.

While Hannibal was in Italy, the Roman commander Publius Cornelius Scipio carried the war into Spain. In 209 he captured the important city of New Carthage and by 206 he controlled most of Spain. In 204 he landed in Africa, near Carthage itself. His victories here brought about the recall of Hannibal from Italy and set the stage for a final clash between these two great generals and their forces. Scipio won the decisive battle in 202, at Zama in North Africa. In honor of the victory Scipio received the name "Africanus," and proudly added it to his traditional Roman name. Besides paying Rome a huge indemnity, Carthage had to give up all its territory except that immediately around the city in Africa, and it was forbidden to raise an army without Roman permission.

The third and final Punic War was a squalid affair, lasting from 149 to 146. There was in Rome a bitterly anti-Carthaginian group, led by a hard-bitten former consul, Marcus Cato, whose name has become symbolic of narrow conservatism. He succeeded in provoking this war and making it a campaign of punishment against Carthage, which had broken the peace terms by raising an army against a nearby aggressor. Another Scipio, Aemilianus, captured and destroyed Carthage in 146. The city was utterly destroyed and cursed (the tale that Rome poured salt into the soil is, however, a modern fiction), and the territory became the Roman province called simply Africa. In the aftermath of the victories over Carthage, Rome went on to conquer almost all Spain in a series of wars lasting until 133.

Rome's Eastern Wars

War against Macedonia

In the 220's the Romans began to intervene along the shore of Illyria (modern Yugoslavia), when piracy and disturbed political conditions threatened their trade and commerce in this region. Philip V, who became ruler of Macedonia in 221, was alarmed by this extension of Roman interest. During the second Punic War he thought he saw his chance to remove the Roman presence; he formed an alliance with Hannibal after the battle of Cannae. To frustrate this combination, the Romans sent a force toward Greece. Thus by drawing the Romans across the Adriatic into Greek lands, Philip unwittingly opened the gate through which, over several centuries, Roman troops and administrators poured as far east as Armenia. This is one of the milestones in European history.

The war against Philip (214–205) was the first of four wars between Rome and Macedonia. At first the Romans tried to avoid entangling commitments in the Greek world. For example, in 197 they won a decisive victory over Philip in the second Macedonian War, but a year later they withdrew from Greece. In doing this they were not acting in a spirit of innocent devotion to liberty, for they expected the Greeks to remain loyal and obedient subject allies and to respect Roman leadership.

Warfare in Asia Minor

Almost at once the Romans had to plunge back into Greek affairs. Antiochus III, the Macedonian king of the Syrian Empire, invaded Greece in 192 at the request of the Aetolian League, one of the groups of city-states that acted as a counterbalance to Macedonian monarchy (see page 99). The Aetolians were allies of Rome in the Macedonian Wars against Philip, but now betrayed Rome because they had not been allowed to expand their holdings as much as they had wanted after the recent defeats of Macedonia. The Romans had no choice but to drive Antiochus out of Greece. It is true that no single Hellenistic power could challenge Roman hegemony; all the same, a coalition of the Aetolians, Philip, and Antiochus might try to contend with Rome on equal terms.

In 191 the Romans defeated Antiochus at Thermopylae and decided to pursue him into Asia Minor—another important step in the Roman conquest of the Mediterranean world, as Roman legions first left Europe for warfare in Asia. Scipio Africanus, the man who had defeated Hannibal, and his brother Lucius won a crushing victory over Antiochus at the town of Magnesia in 190. Antiochus was not actually disarmed, but he was forced to pay huge reparations and was excluded from western Asia Minor.

Annexation of Greece and Asia Minor

Rome now found it impossible to withdraw from Greek affairs. A further quarrel with Macedonia—the third Macedonian War—ended with a Roman victory at the village of Pydna in 168. The Romans divided Macedonia into four separate districts, but even this severe policy did not produce a calm situation. Further disturbances provoked the Romans into invading again and thus opening the fourth war in 149. By this time the Senate realized that outright annexation was the only way to secure its interests. Therefore, in 147 or 146, Macedonia was officially made a province—Rome's first acquisition of territory in the Greek world. In 146 Rome added most of southern Greece to this province, which was placed under the authority of the governor of Macedonia (in 27 B.C. this newer region became the separate province of Achaea). Thus the Romans brought to an end the independent political life of mainland Greece, and from this time on their dominance in the Mediterranean could not be denied or reversed.

The experienced rulers in the region were shrewd enough to perceive this, and a long process of accommodation to Rome began among them, a process that went on until the death of Cleopatra of Egypt in 30 B.C. For example, in 133, the last king of Pergamum died without leaving a successor and willed his kingdom to Rome. In doing so he was aiding destiny, for Rome's influence in the East practically assured that the kingdom of Pergamum could not long survive without Roman protection. Four years later Rome created the province of Asia, based on the territory of Pergamum (see Map 4.2). This province possessed great wealth, and great were the opportunities for a governor of Asia to enrich himself; the post of governor thus became highly desirable for ambitious politicians and also brought with it a posting to the pleasant climate of the beautifully built Greek cities.

The Nature of Roman Imperialism

What distinctive strength made Rome so successful in its rise to imperial power? Early in Rome's history, events had forced the city to seek defensive alliances. After the expulsion of the Etruscan monarchs, Rome had to unite militarily with its Latin neighbors against a possible Etruscan attack. Constant wars in the fourth and third centuries—for example, the invasion by the Gauls in 390—reinforced the need for common security. The other Italian tribes and cities that joined the Roman system probably valued independence less than military success under Roman leadership. The Romans could therefore pursue a highly effective and (when necessary) utterly ruthless policy of imperialism. Scipio Aemilianus, for example, forced the people of Numantia, in Spain, to surrender in

133 by reducing them to cannibalism, and cut off the hands of 400 young men in a neighboring city who had advocated aiding their Spanish brethren. The Senate at home considered Aemilianus' achievements worthy of a triumphal parade, the highest military honor that Romans could bestow on a successful commander.

The Romans, unlike the Athenians, did not intervene in the internal affairs of their allies. They offered the allies protection from foreign enemies in return for a supply of troops in battle. Both parties were expected to show "friendship," but in the context of Roman imperialism friendship was a more binding obligation than the mild English word suggests.

Provincial Administration

The Latin word *provincia* means any duty assigned to a magistrate, and the Romans extended it to include the governing of the various regions that they had acquired through their conquests. They found governors for the earliest provinces simply by raising the number

MAP 4.2. THE ROMAN REPUBLIC 197–44 B.C.

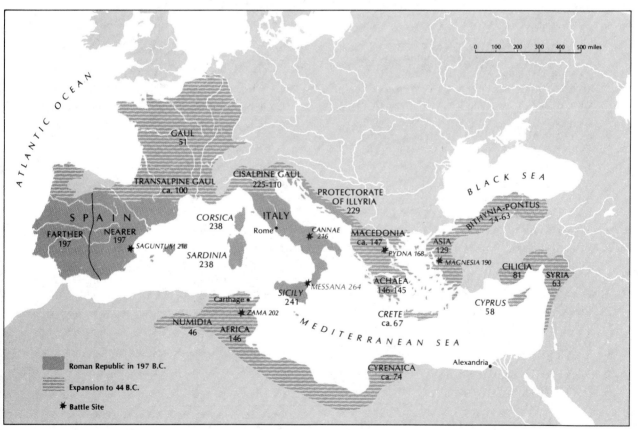

of praetors from two to four; the two new ones governed Sicily and the combined province of Corsica and Sardinia. They used the same expedient in Spain. There were two Spanish provinces, Nearer and Farther Spain, and to provide governors for them the Romans created two more praetors. Because of the distance from Spain to Italy and the importance of the Spanish provinces, these praetors held a higher rank of imperium than the governors of Sicily and Corsica-Sardinia, but the Roman politicians would not raise the number of consuls, the supreme officers, beyond two. Instead, they called these higher-ranking governors *proconsul* ("in place of a consul"), thus giving them the higher grade of authority without the actual office of consul. Similar officials ruled in other provinces.

Governors of provinces were appointed by the Senate. They ruled the provinces with absolute power, though they could not violate Roman law or act illegally against Roman citizens. Some provinces were well ruled, but others were notorious for their corrupt governors. From the Roman view the system was efficient: Rebellions were not common, and troops stationed in the provinces did not resort to massacres to maintain control.

The provinces furnished the financial support for the Roman Republic. Some had to pay tribute in various forms, usually food, while others were assigned a fixed sum of money. In order to obtain these taxes the state devised a convenient, but corruptible, system of tax collection. Companies of tax collectors bid for contracts to collect the taxes of certain provinces, especially Asia. They paid the state a fixed sum in advance and then tried to make their profit by collecting taxes in excess of what they had paid. The natives of the provinces were nearly helpless against the raids of the *publicani*, as tax collectors were called. Their only protection was the governor of the province, who was supposed to see that the *publicani* did not collect more than a reasonable amount.

Unfortunately, however, sometimes the collectors could use their funds as bribes to persuade the governor to overlook their rapacity.[4] These tax collectors came from the nonsenatorial class known as *equestrians* (their name, *equites*, originally meant cavalry; the common translation "knights" is misleading). Besides collecting taxes, equestrians formed companies to build roads and aqueducts, owned land, and managed businesses of all kinds. Senators were forbidden to be in business, and some equestrians could far outstrip senators in wealth through their multiple enterprises; but they held no political office.

The Roman Family

We have mentioned the forceful part played by the family in Roman politics. But what of organization within the family itself? The Romans were content with direction from the top in many areas of their society, and this kind of social structure was also built into the family. The father of the family, the *paterfamilias,* was considered the absolute owner of the whole family, which included children, land, other property, animals, and slaves. So long as he lived, his sons, even if married with their own households, were still in his power. Roman law even recognized his right to execute his children, but we can hardly believe this right was often used (a story that this was done by Marcus Brutus, one of the first consuls, was probably invented to illustrate the legal right). On the death of the father, each of his sons became a paterfamilias in turn over his own family. Such a severe system differs from anything known in Greece but has parallels in Israelite society.

---

[4] Cicero, a firm supporter of the *publicani,* called them "the flower of the Roman equestrians, the ornament of the state, and the foundation of the Republic."

In early Rome, wives were also legally within the power of their husbands (again we may look to Israel), and their chief virtues were silence and obedience. But this system could not last forever. As Rome became wealthier—and the luxury of life style in Rome left Greece far behind—the narrow framework of women's lives was loosened, although our sources do not tell us by what stages. Especially within the capital itself, women of prominent families began to move in society. In apparent alarm at the emancipation of women, the elder Cato sponsored a law forbidding women to possess jewelry and wear colored dresses, which practically tells us that they were doing so in the second century B.C. By the late Republic, the emancipation of some women, at least, had become a matter of moral concern. The poet Catullus wrote lovingly, later bitterly, of his love affair with Clodia, the sister of a prominent politician: she was in fact notorious for her alleged immorality. Again, Julius Caesar's wife, Calpurnia, was said to have taken part in a forbidden religious rite (for which Caesar divorced her).

As in Greece, women could not hold office or vote, but they became important factors behind the scenes. Livia, the last wife of the emperor Augustus, is said by the historian Tacitus to have been an influence toward the adoption by Augustus of her son Tiberius, who became the second emperor, and by the time of the later Empire the mothers of some emperors were practically queens. In many more cases, the chief political importance of women was as a link between prominent families in a marriage alliance. We cannot test the Romans psychologically for the degree of affection within their families; but, as in Greece, sarcophagi and tomb reliefs portray men with their wives and seem to show that the married partners wanted to be remembered together. But even on some inscriptions, the women are praised for modest domestic virtues: "She was chaste, she was thrifty, she remained at home, she spun wool."

Religion

Roman religion consisted largely of forms of worship that upheld Roman tradition. Within the household, the father acted as the priest and led the family in its worship of household gods—for example, Janus, the god protecting the doorway; Vesta, the spirit of the hearth; and household spirits known as Lares and Penates. The main concept underlying religion was that some objects possessed divine power, or *numen,* which probably means "the power to influence things." For example, a boundary or terminal stone marking the edge of a family's property was sacred and had numen, perhaps the power to deter intruders.

Public religion, on the other hand, was closely connected with the interest of the state. Priesthoods were mainly political offices, from which women were excluded. By exception, however, women held one of the most important religious duties: it fell to six virgins to maintain the sacred fire of Vesta that guarded the hearth of the state. These Vestal Virgins were held in high honor and lived in an elegant villa in the Forum. Roman rites seem mainly designed to placate the gods, almost to keep them at arm's length through sacrifices. Eventually the rites hardened into patterns whose original meaning had sometimes been forgotten, but so long as the priests did not deviate from routine, the Romans assumed that the gods were satisfied and would not frustrate their enterprises.

As for mythology, nearly all of it was an adaptation of Greek legend, and Roman gods were often Greek deities with Roman names. The Greek father-god Zeus became Iuppiter, or Jupiter; his wife Hera became Juno; Athena became Minerva, Hermes became Mercury, and so on. These gods were the ones officially worshiped in public, and also in the home along with the household deities. Perhaps because Greek myths often show gods behaving spitefully or immorally, the Romans also created certain uplifting ideas, such as Virtus (manly conduct), Pax (peace), Fides (loyalty), and Pudor (modesty), and transformed them into gods.

Earlier Roman Literature

The historian must be surprised at how long it took the Romans to develop a literature. Homeric epic is older than the Greek city-states themselves, but Rome had been independent of the Etruscans for the better part of three centuries before literature emerged. Evidently the Romans needed contact with Greek civilization, which came about during the age of imperialism, to stimulate their own literary efforts.

The real founder of literature written in the Latin language—the Roman Chaucer, as he has been called—was Quintus Ennius (239–169). His writings now survive only through quotations in other works. He was not a Roman (almost none of the more famous Latin authors were from Rome) but an Italian who lived near Tarentum. His most important original work was his *Annales,* a patriotic historical poem. Ennius was the first poet to translate into Latin the Greek tragedies, which were to influence the still immature Latin literature.

The influence of Greek comedy appears in the plays of Plautus (250?–184?) and Terence (190?–159?). These playwrights imitated Greek New Comedy, as it is called, in which the plays were entirely fiction. The Romans did not approve of Old Comedy, such as the plays of Aristophanes, which savagely lampooned active politicians. Plautus filled his comedies with stock situations, such as mistaken identities, frustrated romances, and the like. One of his plays about mistaken identities, the *Menaechmi,* was used by Shakespeare as the model for his *Comedy of Errors.* Terence wrote comedy in a more refined and delicate style than did Plautus. His influence on later ages was strong, for he

became the model for the comedy of manners of Molière and Sheridan.

The Greek Polybius (200?–118?), though not a Latin writer, deserves a place here as a historian of the Roman Republic. Along with several other prominent Greeks, Polybius was deported to Rome as a hostage in the 160s; there he met many Roman statesmen and became an expert in Roman history. He wrote a general history of the Greco-Roman world from the first Punic War down to his own times, largely to demonstrate the inevitable domination of the Mediterranean by the Romans. He is the only surviving source for some of the wars of Greece and Rome.

Polybius believed that much of Rome's success in government was due to its well-designed constitution, an example of the commendable mixed form of state that would probably preserve the Roman system, despite the difficulty of preserving any constitution in the unstable world of Mediterranean politics. Polybius traveled widely and insisted on the need to visit sites in order to grasp the importance of geography to history. His work is professional and methodical and is an attempt to revive the high standards of historical writing that Herodotus and Thucydides had established. He is both the most important historian of the Hellenistic Age and the most reliable guide to earlier Roman history.

III. THE ROMAN REVOLUTION (133–27 B.C.)

The Changing World of Italy

The breakdown of the Roman Republic has been called Hannibal's legacy, and there is some truth in the epigram. A century of successful warfare saw Carthage destroyed and Rome become the ruler of the Greek-speaking Hellenistic world; but the ravages of years of fighting up and down Italy, and long periods of military service at home and abroad, had impoverished the Italian peasantry, bringing great numbers of them to ruin. After the second Punic War, pacification of the new province of Spain meant more long terms of service abroad and therefore more time away from the farm. Ironically, Rome's great successes in the East made matters worse, for the booty brought back by some of the Roman legionaries and their generals was to have a catastrophic effect on economic and social conditions in the peninsula. Disruption of the socio-economic structure of Italy eventually created turmoil within politics, which ended only when the institutions of the Republic gave way to an imperial autocracy.

The flood of new wealth from the East, the result of war-profiteering, was unevenly distributed. Wealthy citizens into whose hands had come booty and the spoils of war had not only capital, but also a market in which to invest it. The less fortunate, who lacked the cash to maintain or repair their farms, often lost their land or were willing to sell it. There was also a great increase of the slave population on Italian soil from prisoners of war. The new slaves decreased the demand for the labor of independent farmers and depressed wages when private laborers did manage to find work. Often the displaced farmers had little choice but to join the ranks of the permanently unemployed.

New conditions of farming also made it difficult for the small farmer to survive. The market in one important product, wine, was now expanding. This crop demands a heavy outlay for pressing machinery and periodic replacement of stocks. Even the cheapest wines cannot be put on the market at once; thus wine growing requires capital that must be invested for some years. It is not an occupation for a poor man, unless he is backed by a cooperative movement. The wealthy had both the opportunity and a market. Posidonius, who was born

This bust of Julius Caesar shows the realistic style of portraiture that is typical of Roman art. It also expresses the discipline of the Roman commander and the person of Caesar, the supreme general in all Roman history.
(Photo: Art Resource)

about 135, wrote from personal knowledge that Gauls were prepared to trade a slave for a jar of wine and that the slave was likely to become a unit in the production of many more jars. Archaeological evidence is even more convincing. Ancient inhabitants of hill forts in Provence and Languedoc, in France, strewed their area with so many broken wine jars that the fragments impede cultivation even today. And in Rome still stands a great heap of discarded wine jugs, Monte Testaccio, where excavation has shown that Spanish wines, cheaper than

Italian, were capturing more and more of the market in the first century B.C.

Strains on the Constitution

For some years before 133 the small farmers displaced by large landowners had added to the economic problems of the state, and the decline in their fortunes threatened to impede the recruitment of soldiers into the Roman army. Rome had nothing like a modern war treasury, and only men who had enough money to arm themselves could be drafted into the legions. Without sufficient recruits, the gains of imperialism might be lost.

About 136, a revolt among the slaves in the province of Sicily dramatically emphasized the need for a strong army. The revolt directly threatened a part of the Roman food supply since grain was imported from Sicily. Thus in the late 130s two crises faced Rome: a decline in military manpower and the possibility of a serious grain shortage.

Tiberius and Gaius Gracchus

Two ambitious young Roman aristocrats, Tiberius and Gaius Gracchus, moved to solve these problems. Their mother, Cornelia, was a well-known matron from a great family: Her father was the Publius Cornelius Scipio Africanus who had won the war against Hannibal. She had married a prominent plebeian politician, Tiberius Gracchus, and thus her sons were plebeian, though descended from the loftiest aristocracy. Tiberius, the older brother, became tribune for 133 and proposed a land bill to the Assembly of Tribes that would allow the state to assign parcels of public land, reclaimed from the wealthy, to dispossessed farmers, with the double aim of increasing both the supply of potential recruits for the army and his own political support. The bill was opposed by another tribune, who tried to veto it on behalf of vested interests. Tiberius persuaded the people to remove this tribune from office, a dangerous action barely within the constitution. Once this was done, what tribune would be safe in the future from a similar threat? But the people followed Tiberius, and the bill was passed.

The distribution of land was in progress when Tiberius decided to run for reelection. This was a breach of custom, for tribunes held office for only one year. Some of his opponents feared that he might seize permanent leadership of the propertyless as a demagogue. A group of senators, late in 133, took the law into their own hands, raised a gang of thugs, and hunted Tiberius down. He was clubbed to death in a riot. His death gave grim warning of a new intensity in the political struggle. Above all, the taboo against assassination had been violated and this first step, once taken, became easier to repeat. Despite Tiberius' death, the distribution of land continued, and his enemies even took credit for the success of the project.

Gaius Gracchus became tribune ten years later, in 123. He authored several measures with a common theme, mainly limiting the prerogatives of the Senate. One of the most important concerned the extortion court, which investigated cases of alleged extortion by provincial governors and tax collectors. The jurors, all senators, were usually not severe in judging governors, who were fellow members of the Senate. Gaius had a bill passed that assigned the seats on this jury to members of the equestrian class.

All tax collectors were equestrians, and when Gaius Gracchus placed equestrians on the jury of the extortion court, it was now they who had the potential to favor members of their group who might be accused and brought to trial. Provincial governors, who were senators, were now at risk, since they feared unfavorable decisions handed down by equestrian jurors. Gaius' arrangements were later revised, but he was the first to make the extortion court the subject of a bitter political quarrel. Since money and politics were as deeply entwined in Rome as they are in America, Gaius' concessions to these wealthy nonsenatorials may not have been entirely disinterested, especially in a society where favors always created obligations.

To further his brother's program of relocating farmers on the land, Gaius also sponsored the founding of several colonies. The choice of one of them—near the site of the hated Carthage, which only about twenty years earlier had been destroyed in the third Punic War—exposed him to criticism and seriously weakened his standing with the masses. He also proposed that Roman citizenship be offered to large numbers of people in rural districts who were not yet Roman citizens. They had been asking for this status to protect themselves against having their land confiscated for distribution to those whom the Romans were resetting. But the voters of Rome, warned by Gaius' opponents that they would be sharing their privileges with outsiders, refused to extend their citizenship.

Like his brother, Gaius Gracchus came to a violent end. After he left office his enemies asserted that he was planning a revolution. The Senate then instructed one of the consuls for the year 121 to "see to it that the state suffered no harm," thus inviting the consul to use force to suppress the younger Gracchus. When the consul raised an armed force to hunt him down, Gaius, at his own instructions, was killed by one of his slaves.

The Gracchi had tried to adapt Roman procedure to new social and economic realities. When he began to lose support, Gaius turned to new political groups—Italians who lacked Roman citizenship and equestrians who now stood against senators through their control of the extortion court. Above all, the Gracchi had unleashed a force whose working could not easily be controlled when they invited the Assembly of Tribes to take a more activist role.

It is true that the people had long possessed the right to legislate in this Assembly, but they had not always had the will; nor had ambitious tribunes always dared to use this weapon. The Gracchi greatly increased the activity of the assembly. From this moment began the slow but sure Roman revolution.

Marius, the First Warlord

The Gracchi could not protect themselves from the violence of the Senate because they had no army. But as Roman imperialism brought the state into further wars, powerful generals appeared who did have the support of their armies and used their military machine to achieve political supremacy. The Gracchi, no matter what their opponents might have said against them, were not trying to lead a revolution or to overturn the state. Looking generally at the group of warlords we are about to meet, we can probably say the same about them. Each man wanted political power, the supreme control of affairs, within the Republican system. The trouble was that each one had in effect a private army of indebted followers; and, as each one played his own hand with increasingly higher stakes, the Republican constitution—which was never a set of clearly written laws—proved unable to maintain itself and finally collapsed into dictatorship. We may even guess that many Romans welcomed an end to constant civil war, even if it meant the death of the Republic and permanent monarchy.

The first general to play this game was Gaius Marius (157?–86), a "new man" from the country near Rome. He is crucial to the historian because he changed, radically and forever, the membership of the Roman army and the direction of its loyalty. He gained high prestige in a war against a king in North Africa, Jugurtha; the historian Sallust has left us a narrative of this conflict. Marius' reputation grew even more after he drove back an attempted invasion by some Germanic tribes moving toward

This Roman temple (to a still uncertain deity) dates from the first century B.C. and is a combination of Greek forms on a basic Etruscan pattern. Note the high basement, the porch at the front, and the cella closed with half-columns. In its union of Greek and Etruscan forms, the temple is the physical embodiment of the two cultural bases of Roman civilization and thus of the historical development of Rome itself. Similar temples are found in southern France (Nimes, Vienne), in Tunisia, and even in the south of Russia (Georgia).
Photo: Art Resource)

northern Italy. Even though this Germanic invasion was unsuccessful, it points toward later collisions between Germanic and Latin peoples that will be one of the main themes of later European history. Such was Marius' stature in this period that he was consul in five consecutive years and dominated politics from 107 to 100.

In order to raise large numbers of men for these German wars, Marius abolished the old requirement that a soldier must own at least a modest amount of property, and he also accepted volunteers instead of just drafting men for service. As a result, the army came to be composed largely of poor men who served their commander, received booty from him, relied on him as their main patron, and expected him to obtain a grant of land for them, which they could then farm after they were discharged. Thus Marius became involved with the problem of displaced farmers that the Gracchi had addressed. He may not have foreseen the political results of his action, but he converted the army into an instrument for ambitious commanders down through the Republic and indeed throughout the history of the Roman Empire.

The War with the Italians

In the 90s the dispute over citizenship for the allies of Rome in Italy reached a crisis. Neither the Senate nor the people had shown much willingness to grant the allies citizenship, which brought with it the privileges of voting, holding office, and making a will that would be guaranteed by Roman law. These allies became convinced that only outright rebellion would achieve their goal; so in 91 some Italian tribes proclaimed themselves independent and opened a war that continued until 88. In the end the Romans negotiated with the Italians and allowed them to acquire citizenship. But the fact that it required a war to obtain this concession shows that both the upper classes—the senators and equestrians—and the common people as well were still jealous of their privileges.[5]

Senatorial Reaction Under Sulla

The Italian War helped make the reputation of another powerful general, Lucius Cornelius Sulla (138?–78). In the 80s civil war broke out in Rome among various factions of senators. One group rallied behind Sulla and his legions, seeing in them the best vehicle for their own ambitions. In 88 Sulla invaded the city of Rome with his supporters—the first but not the last time that the ancient city was thus seized by Romans themselves. At this time Sulla wanted for himself the command of a war against Mithridates, who ruled the kingdom of Pontus (extending inward from the south coast of the Black Sea) from 120 to 63 B.C. Sulla departed for this campaign in 87. During his absence other politicians, just as unscrupulous as he was, seized Rome in turn.

As soon as Sulla was free of his eastern war he returned to Italy and once more occupied Rome (November 82). He killed hundreds of his opponents and had himself named dictator without limit of time; thus he suspended the customary six-month limit for holding that office.

Sulla used his supreme power to reshape the state on strictly conservative lines. Two forces, he thought, had menaced the rigid control over Rome that the Senate should enjoy: the tribunes of the people, who had made the Assembly of Tribes more conscious of its power, and the strong generals who had used the loyalty of their armies to gain political leverage. To deal with the first of these threats, Sulla passed a law forbidding tribunes to offer legislation without prior approval from the Senate, a clear historical rebuke to Tiberius Gracchus. An-

---

[5] Historians have compared the Italian War to the American Civil War of 1861–1865. Each war finally decided whether the nation was to split apart or remain united.

other law prevented tribunes from ever holding another office, a stratagem that was designed to make the office of tribune unattractive to young men with political ambitions.

Sulla handled the army commanders by restricting their service as governor of a province to a period of one year. This scheme neatly assured that no commander would remain on the scene long enough to become a familiar hero to his troops and possibly the leader of a new march on Rome. It would appear that there were to be no Sullas after Sulla.

Sulla further established minimum ages at which a man might hold the various offices in a political career (a consul, for example, must be 42 or over) and raised the number of the minor offices that admitted a man to the Senate. He also canceled the work of Gaius Gracchus on the jury system; as one might expect from this strict conservative, he gave all the seats on juries to senators. To provide enough jurors, and probably to reward some of his supporters, Sulla raised the membership of the Senate to about 600.

It is sometimes said that Sulla's arrangements were soon abolished, but this is an overstatement. It is true that his rules were soon broken, owing to the weakness of the state in enforcing them, but by and large, his legislation remained in place until the collapse of the Republic. He himself resigned the dictatorship in 79, a rare act in any supreme ruler, but he evidently thought he had put the Senate so firmly in control that he was no longer needed; he died in 78. To his enemies he was pitiless,

and his executions of Roman citizens were brutal, but he was also a clever political strategist. He had done his part for the conservative cause by putting the Senate in charge, but this body proved unable to manage the next generation of warlords.

The Rise of Pompey

The new military threat to the state was Gnaeus Pompeius, usually called Pompey. He first gained a reputation in 77, when he was sent to Spain with instructions to end a revolt there. After completing this task and while his army was still intact, he helped to suppress a rebellion of slaves in Italy led by the famous Thracian slave Spartacus. This campaign was already in the hands of another ambitious Roman, Marcus Licinius Crassus, the richest man of his time. No sooner was the slave revolt crushed in 71 than the joint commanders, Pompey and Crassus, marched their armies to the gates of Rome and demanded both consulships for the year 70. Pompey was legally unqualified for this office, for he was only 36 and had never held any previous magistracy. The Senate, however, had not the will to resist the two men, and they were elected consuls.

During their consulship Pompey and Crassus canceled several other of Sulla's arrangements. They restored to the tribunes their right to propose legislation, and they mixed senators and equestrians in the always controversial juries. At the end of their year in office both consuls retired without demanding any further appointment. This action, at first surprising, was really consistent with Pompey's ambitions. He wanted a position of the first rank in the state, but he disliked committing himself to open revolution. A modern historian has compared him to Shakespeare's Macbeth—he would not play false and yet would wrongly win.

Pompey was given an extraordinary command in 67 to deal with pirates operating in the

A first-century-B.C.** wall painting from the cubiculum of the Villa at Boscoreale, a town in southern Italy. Note the artist's skillful use of perspective, a technique that would disappear for centuries in Europe.**
(Photo: Metropolitan Museum of Art, Rogers Fund, 1903)

Mediterranean who were interfering with the grain supply for Rome, a critical matter since the city had to live on grain shipped to its harbor. Pompey fulfilled his orders and cleared the seas in a swift campaign. Then in 66 he received an even more important command in Asia Minor, where Rome was involved in war with Mithridates, Sulla's old enemy, still on his throne. Cynical political considerations played a part in getting Pompey this large new command. The previous governor, Lucullus, had tried to protect the helpless provincials from the tax collectors and had drastically lowered the amount the equestrian tax collectors could collect. Therefore the equestrian class, representing their own financial interests, demanded the governor's removal and his replacement by Pompey. They were a powerful pressure group in Rome and obtained the support of the politician Cicero, who spoke in favor of Pompey's command.

Pompey successfully fought the difficult war in Asia Minor and established a secure base for Roman interests there. He annexed the province of Syria in 64–63 and enlarged two provinces in Asia Minor (Cilicia and Bithynia). Around these provinces he created a system of client kings, rulers of smaller states whose loyalty to Rome was assured by the familiar device of "friendship." For some time this group of kingdoms, to the east of the province of Asia, offered a solid defense against any threats to Roman territory from enemies to the east.

Cicero and Catiline

During Pompey's absence overseas Marcus Tullius Cicero (106–43) became the chief non-military statesman in Rome. Like Marius, he was a "new man" from the countryside, but unlike him he chose a career in law and administration. His administrative skill won for him each successive political office at the earliest possible legal age. He was genuinely dedicated to compromise and political negotiation and

thought that such procedures would establish a rule of the two upper classes, senatorial and equestrian. This potential system he often called *concordia ordinum*—harmony between the senatorial and equestrian orders. But other, less scrupulous men believed that while orators debated, the sword would decide the issue.

One such renegade was a fiery patrician of undoubted courage, Lucius Sergius Catilina, usually called Catiline. He had gone heavily into debt through extravagance, and in 63 he formed a conspiracy to murder the consuls, seize the state, and pass laws to abolish debts. Cicero, one of the consuls that year, easily frustrated the plot.[6] He hoped that this success would enable him to form a circle of eminent men, including the powerful Pompey, who would be dedicated to traditional, lawful government, but future events would prove his hope vain.

The First Triumvirate

When Pompey returned to Rome in 62 from his Eastern victories, he had two political aims. He wanted the Senate to ratify the arrangements he had made in Asia Minor; and he requested a grant of land for his men. This latter request, as we have seen, was now nothing unusual. It reflected the relationship between a general and his troops, which was that of a patron to his clients—one of the oldest traditions in Rome. But some influential senators resented Pompey's prestige. Some were jealous of his eminence, some had old political scores to settle, and some feared that he might become a second Sulla but might not step aside as Sulla had finally done. His enemies in the Senate therefore combined to frustrate his wishes. This short-term victory practically doomed the Senate and the Republic, for it drove Pompey into

---

[6] Cicero tells his version of the suppression of the conspiracy in his four orations *In Catilinam (Against Catiline);* see also Sallust's *War with Catiline.*

a political alliance with Julius Caesar, who proved to have the revolutionary will that Pompey lacked.

Gaius Julius Caesar (100–44), the brilliant descendant of an old patrician family, was now returning from his post as governor of Spain. He, too, had enemies within the Senate. On his way up in politics he had had to borrow heavily for campaign expenses and was deeply in debt to the wealthy Crassus, who had served as consul with Pompey in 70. To solve his financial problems, Caesar hoped to win the consulship for 59 and then obtain another provincial command, which would provide enough income from the spoils of war to pay off his debts. A small faction in the Senate looked on Caesar as a brash upstart. First they refused him the honor of a triumphal parade through Rome on his return from Spain. Then they tried to block his plans to secure a major provincial command after his consulship of 59. Faced with this obvious affront to his dignity, Caesar made a political bargain with Pompey and with Crassus, who was also at odds with some powerful senators over a financial matter. The three formed a coalition known to modern historians as the First Triumvirate, and their united influence at the polls elected Caesar as one of the consuls for 59.

Caesar's Consulship and the Gallic War

Pompey's aims were met after Caesar himself introduced a bill in the Assembly of Tribes that would provide allotments of land for his army; a tribune then offered another bill ratifying Pompey's arrangements in the East. Both bills were passed by the Assembly of Tribes, which supported the triumvirate against such opposition as the Senate could put forth. Crassus' financial quarrel was also settled to his satisfaction. Lastly, Caesar, looking to his own future command, arranged to have a bill passed that gave him the command over Cisalpine Gaul

From the second century B.C. **onward, a Roman citizen could cast a private ballot. This coin was issued in 137** B.C. **It shows a Roman dropping a small wooden tablet into a basket. On the tablet is written "V," the first letter of V(TI ROGAS), "as you propose": that is, an affirmative vote.**
(Photo: Service Photographique Bibliothèque Nationale)

(the Po valley) and the coast of Illyria (Albania and Yugoslavia) for a guaranteed period of five years beginning on March 1, 59. About this time the governor of Transalpine Gaul (Provence, in the south of France) died, and Caesar also acquired this province within his command.

Caesar actively sought opportunities to extend Roman rule outside the borders of the province. He intervened in the politics of the Gallic tribes and opened a series of campaigns that finally brought the whole area of modern France and Belgium under Roman rule. The Romans implanted in Gaul the Latin language, the mother of modern French, and Roman culture. One notable symbol of Romanization was the network of roads (see Map 4.3), which imitated and extended the system of highways

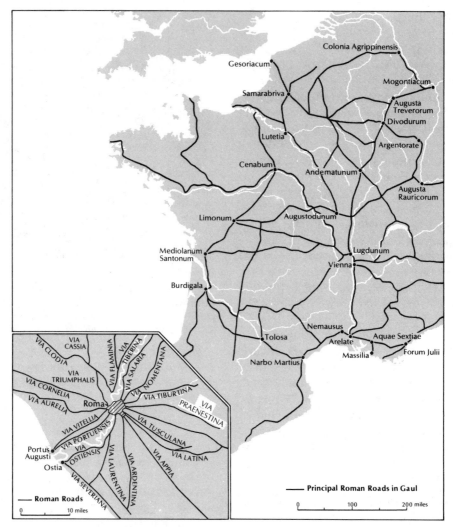

**MAP 4.3. THE NETWORK OF ROMAN ROADS
(A) FROM THE CITY AND (B) IN GAUL**
(From Chevallier, Raymond, "Roman Roads,"
University of California Press, 1976)

within Italy (even today many of these road names are still used—the Via Appia, the Via Salaria, and so on). Caesar narrated his actions and justified his motives in his *Commentaries on the Gallic War.* To this day the book remains a superb textbook in political-military decision making.

The Gallic War lasted from 58 to 50 B.C. Caesar's two partners in the triumvirate, Pompey and Crassus, were always suspicious of each other, but they did maintain fairly good relations and even held a second consulship together in 55. At Caesar's wish, they had his command in Gaul renewed for another five years, so that it would not expire until March 1, 49.[7] Through the Assembly of Tribes Pompey and Crassus also took on commands for themselves. Crassus became proconsul of Syria and fought against the Parthian kingdom on the Syrian frontier, where he was killed in 53. Pompey was given command over the two provinces of Spain, which he governed through assistants (legates), preferring to remain near Rome and thus at the center of power.

The Break Between Caesar and the Senate in 49 B.C.

Caesar's conquest of Gaul greatly enriched the state, but to his enemies it was a cause of terror. They feared that he might use his victories, and his popularity among the people, to become another, and perhaps a permanent, Sulla. As protection against Caesar, his enemies in the Senate began to draw Pompey into their camp. Some of them had quarreled with him in the past, but they were willing to gamble that they could eliminate him when they no longer needed him. "Divide and conquer" was a Roman maxim that did not apply to foreign affairs only.

Caesar planned to return to Rome in 49 after his command in Gaul ended. He would seek the consulship in 48 and then would probably accept another command such as the one Crassus had had in the East. Our evidence does not suggest that Caesar was planning a revolution—he hardly needed it. Yet he would not shrink from revolution if his personal position was at stake.

As 49 opened, the Senate met in a state near hysteria. Caesar's enemies were seeking some way to strip him of his command in Gaul even before it expired. Some cooler heads proposed that both Caesar and Pompey should end the

tension by resigning their commands at the same time. Caesar would have agreed to this, but the small band of implacable senators forced through a motion ordering him to lay down his command, even though he was then taking no action beyond remaining in his province of Cisalpine Gaul. The Senate passed a decree establishing martial law and ordering Pompey to command the armies of Rome against Caesar. The ill-advised Pompey accepted the command, probably in part out of what he saw as loyalty to the state; but in doing so he signed his own death warrant and unknowingly condemned the Republic to extinction in yet another civil war. Finally, the Senate, now dominated by Caesar's enemies, defied the oldest of Roman traditions by threatening the lives of any tribunes who opposed these extreme measures. They thus handed Caesar a superb theme for his own propaganda: He could proclaim that he was defending the rights of the tribunes, the common people of Rome who had elected them, and the men in his army who had loyally served in the Gallic wars.

Caesar's Invasion of Italy

While some hot-blooded senators were driving Rome into civil war, Caesar was stationed in his province just across the Rubicon River, a tiny stream that divided Italy from Cisalpine Gaul. Learning that his enemies were challenging him to war, he decided that he had no course but to fight for his dignity and, as he could now claim, for the people and their sacred tribunes. On about January 11, 49, he invaded his own country at the head of Roman legions.

Caesar's own men supported him loyally, and as he moved southward through Italy more and more people joined his cause. Pompey and his followers had to retreat to Greece; Caesar pursued them and won a decisive battle in 48 at the town of Pharsalus, in Thessaly. Pompey tried to find refuge in Egypt, but as he stepped

---

[7] The exact date on which Caesar's command was to expire is still a controversial question. March 1, 49, seems to accord best with the ancient evidence.

on shore he was murdered by advisers to the pharaoh, since they realized that Caesar had been victorious and that Pompey would be an embarrassment. Caesar also reached Egypt in 48, where he found the pharaoh and his sister, the famous Cleopatra, at odds. In a brief campaign, Caesar settled the quarrel in favor of Cleopatra, whom he placed on the throne of Egypt. This most brilliant and astute of all queens of the Hellenistic Age was a descendant of Ptolemy, the Macedonian general of Alexander the Great, and was thus the last Macedonian ruler of any kingdom. She beguiled Caesar with her beauty, and he is said to have toured with her up the Nile during their love affair; a boy known as Caesarion was rumored to have been their son (but historians have never been able to establish his parentage securely). Caesar then returned to battle and, after victories in Africa and Spain, came back to Rome in 46.

Caesar's Rule to 44 B.C.

Caesar now decided to make his rule impregnable and assumed the positions of both dictator and consul. On the model of Sulla he extended his dictatorship beyond the legal six-month limit; then, in 44, he had himself named dictator for life. He swept aside all restraints on his power that Roman tradition might have imposed. He had complete authority to pass laws, declare war, and appoint men to office.

As dictator, Caesar passed a series of rapid reforms in many areas of Roman life. To reward his followers with public office he raised the number of praetors to 16. Along with this expansion he raised the membership of the Senate to about 900. Many of Caesar's veteran officers became members of this body, assuring Caesar a rubber stamp for anything he wanted. Loyalty and discreet service in the Senate might bring important provincial commands, and we may be sure that few senators dared to challenge the dictator's wishes. From this time on-

ward the Senate rapidly lost its former authority as the bulwark of the state. Caesar also divided all Italy into municipal areas, probably for the sake of greater administrative efficiency; he gave each town control over the surrounding countryside.

Caesar settled many of his soldiers in colonies throughout the Roman provinces, especially Spain, Transalpine Gaul, and northern Africa. He also extended Roman citizenship into some of the provinces. His most lasting reform, however, was one by which we still regulate our lives—the establishment of a calendar based on the old Egyptian reckoning of 365 days, with one day added every fourth year (this was done simply by observing February 24 twice; the modern February 29 was unknown to the Romans). This Julian calendar lasted until 1582; it was then revised by Pope Gregory XIII to our present Gregorian calendar.

The Death of Caesar

The full effect of Caesar's plans was not to be realized, for on March 15, 44, after four years of supremacy, he fell to the daggers of conspirators led by two of his lieutenants, Marcus Brutus and Gaius Cassius. His autocracy had been a grave affront to the upper class; they still wanted the chance to win political leadership rather than be appointed by a high and mighty ruler. Because they were being denied these traditional rights of the Roman governing class, they united against Caesar and carried out the most famous political murder in all history. It is said that Caesar was warned that morning of an imminent conspiracy and that he brushed the warning aside, even as he had earlier dismissed his Spanish bodyguard. Suddenly, outside a large curved theater built by Pompey, the killers plunged on him; as he recognized his protégé Marcus Brutus in the gang, he said in Greek, "You, too, my boy?" and covered his head with his toga as he fell. His body was

The Roman aqueduct at Segovia in Spain (first century A.D.), nearly 899 yards long and 100 feet at its highest point, impressively combines strength, elegance, and utility. It still carries the city's water supply.
(Photo: Editorial Photocolor Archives)

carried to the Forum and burned on a rock that still stands there in a small temple built to him after his death.

The image, as we may call it, of Caesar is baffling and controversial, even as it was to his contemporaries. He was pitiless toward Gauls and Germans, and he enriched himself by selling prisoners of war as slaves; but compassion toward captured foreigners was never common in the ancient world, and this does not show that Caesar was more than normally cool toward other human beings. In Rome he showed too little respect for Republican forms once he became dictator, and for this he paid with his life. On the other hand, he often forgave his enemies: In the civil war he dismissed opposing generals whom he had captured, and they lived to fight him another day. Such actions may have rested on cool calculation of their value as propaganda, but they may also show genuine gallantry. No one can question Caesar's fiery leadership. His troops followed him into Italy with enthusiasm and fought with amazing discipline.

Caesar left no memoirs of his later years, and it is difficult to know what he would have done to the Roman system if he had lived to carry out his plans. He evidently thought that the old institutions of the Senate and the assemblies had lost their political potency. "The Republic," he is said to have remarked, "is only a name without body or face, and Sulla did not know the ABCs of politics in resigning his dictatorship." The political weakness of the late Republic largely confirms this harsh evaluation. But in the end his verdict proved unacceptable to the experienced politicians whom Caesar needed for his administration. His career thus blends triumph and tragedy. He rose to the absolute summit of Roman politics, but in doing so he destroyed both the Roman Republic and himself.

There has been much modern discussion about one possible aim of Caesar—to return Rome to monarchy and make himself a semi-divine ruler. Historians who support this view point to his acquaintance with Hellenistic monarchies and argue that he would have imposed some such system in Rome; Caesar is shown wearing a diadem on some coins, and a monarchy would indeed have been the final logical step beyond his perpetual dictatorship. On balance, the evidence does not seem strong enough to prove that he had such a plan. Later rulers did install a cult of the Emperor and were converted into gods after they died—and Caesar's adopted son did much to further this kind of propaganda by calling Caesar the "divine Julius" almost at once.

Literature in the Age of Revolution

The first century B.C. was productive and turbulent not only in the world of politics. One of the most dynamic poets of the Republic was Lucretius (94–55), whose masterpiece, *De rerum natura (On the Nature of the Universe)*, reveals how much Greek thought influenced Latin literature. His model was the Hellenistic philosopher Epicurus, from whom Lucretius adopted the theory that everything in the world, including ourselves and our souls, is made of atoms that will recirculate through the universe. He wanted to spread Epicurean doctrines of tranquility and withdrawal from the world and, above all, to liberate his readers from the fear of death. Epicureanism did gain some converts, but it was less congenial to the Romans than the more austere beliefs of Stoicism, which preached devotion to duty.

Catullus (84?–54?) wrote poetry of a more personal nature. It suggests the subjectivity and emotional qualities of the work of the Hellenistic poets in Alexandria. Many of Catullus' poems are addressed to his mistress, Clodia (whom he calls Lesbia), a flagrantly promiscuous woman. Their affair burned fiercely, as some poems show, but finally turned to disillusion and hate. Catullus also experimented with miniature epic poems in the Alexandrian fashion, and he was capable of a solemn grief, as he demonstrates in a sorrowful poem that he composed at his brother's grave in Asia Minor. In all his works Catullus displays his feelings with a frankness that was rare in a society where external dignity and self-discipline were considered the main social virtues.

Marcus Tullius Cicero (106–43) was the most versatile Latin writer of his time. His polished prose style became the model for clarity and elegance. At the same time his orations, essays, and letters are among the best sources for the political history of the later Republic.

Cicero's philosophical treatises do not follow the doctrines of any particular philosophic school; he was equally interested in Stoicism, the thought of Plato, and several other methods, and he chose whatever seemed persuasive from Greek models for his own theories. In *On the Republic,* for example, he accepted the Platonic view that wise leaders ought to govern the state, but disregarded the more technical points in Plato's philosophical system.

Cicero's political speeches are a continuous record of his career and his frustrated ambitions. He was the first of his family to attain the consulship and therefore ranked as a "new man." He enjoyed his political success and sought a place for himself among the upper classes, believing that they should guide the state along established constitutional lines. Unfortunately, most members of the governing class in the later Republic were willing to be tempted away from their normal allegiance to the constitution and selfishly followed their own personal advantage. Cicero never became a magnetic leader around whom others gathered. His letters are a frank and often painful record of the compromises that he was forced to make in the treacherous world of Roman politics.

IV. THE END OF THE ROMAN REPUBLIC

The Victory of Octavian

After Caesar's death there remained some in Rome who hoped for a return to the old system of government by competitive elections—that is, for the restoration of the Republic. But this was not to be; nothing could stop the slide toward dictatorship. In the end, Caesar's adopted son founded an enduring autocracy. He became the last and most successful of the

line of generals who used their armies as private instruments of power.

The Second Triumvirate

Brutus, Cassius, and the other liberators imagined that republican government could be restored with Caesar out of the way. Yet partisans of Caesar commanded armies throughout the Roman world. The removal of their leader still left them in charge, and they were not men who would meekly surrender their powers to the Senate. One survivor was Marcus Antonius, or Mark Antony, a follower of Caesar and consul for the year 44. He managed to maintain his position, for the liberators had not had the foresight to remove him as well. Antony tried to seize for himself the provincial command in Cisalpine Gaul, even though the Senate had already assigned it to another governor for the year 43. When Antony tried to take over this province and drive out its duly appointed commander, the Senate turned on him with the now senior statesman Cicero leading the attack. The state sent an army out to bring Antony to justice, and it must have seemed to many that the old institutions of the Republic had indeed come back to life.

Among the commanders whom the Senate put in action against Antony was a young man of 19—Caesar's grandnephew and adopted son. His name, originally Gaius Octavius, became Gaius Julius Caesar Octavianus upon his adoption; modern historians call him Octavian, but he called himself Caesar. He used his name skillfully to win a following among Caesar's former soldiers, but he also played the part of a discreet young supporter of the Senate in its battle against Antony. Cicero, one of the chief supporters of the old constitution, wrote of Octavian after their first meeting, "The young man is completely devoted to me."

Octavian and Antony realized that the Senate was committed to the destruction of the

Caesarian faction from which they derived their political support. Therefore, in 43, they made an alliance between themselves, as Octavian turned his back on the duty the state had laid on him, that of attacking Antony. They brought into their partnership a lesser commander, Lepidus, and formed a political union known as the Second Triumvirate. They simply turned their armies around and, as Sulla had been the first to do, they marched against Rome, invaded the city, and made themselves the military rulers of the ancient capital. The Senate had to acknowledge their leadership, and a tribune proposed a law that turned the state over to their control for a period of five years; their official duties were "to provide order for the state"—a charge broad enough to provide a legal basis for nearly any action they might wish to take. In due course their collective power was renewed for another five years.

Brutus and Cassius, seeing that they did not have popular support, went to the East and managed to gain control of the provinces of Syria and Macedonia. But in 42 the triumvirs eliminated these enemies at the Battle of Philippi in northern Greece. To reward their troops with land, the rulers had already marked out the territory of no fewer than 18 prosperous towns in Italy. The rule of the Second Triumvirate was thus made secure by the seizure and redistribution of property. Further security was provided by a series of "trials" against those who had the bad luck to be on the losing side. Now, as in the time of Sulla, autocrats brushed aside the traditional guarantees of Roman law as they coldly purged their enemies. One of those killed without trial was Cicero.

Tension and suspicion now began to grow between the two major partners, Antony and Octavian (Lepidus had been forced into retirement when he tried to take control of Sicily away from Octavian). Antony did his own cause grave harm by remaining in the East for long periods, fighting the Parthian kingdom,

Gaius Octavius, granted the title "Augustus" by the Senate, is portrayed as ruler in this idealized statue.
(Photo: Vatican Museum)

which had taken certain Roman territories after the death of Crassus in 53. The basic cause of enmity between Antony and Octavian was the lust for supreme power. The publicly announced issue, which Octavian skillfully exploited as propaganda, was Antony's romance with Cleopatra; Octavian falsely asserted that Antony was planning to place an Eastern queen in command of the state. The relationship of Antony and Cleopatra did have distinct political overtones. Cleopatra had the resources to support Antony's Parthian War; in return she wanted to extend the boundaries of her kingdom northward along the coast of Palestine.

The final break between the two men came in 32. By this time Octavian had secured control of all western provinces and felt strong enough to challenge Antony in the field. Octavian and his supporters denounced Antony for having granted to Cleopatra and her children (during their affair Antony had fathered two sons with Cleopatra) certain Eastern territories belonging to Rome. Octavian raised a large force from Italy and the western provinces; his allies included many people who had been encouraged to fear an Eastern domination of Rome. Octavian's forces won the only battle, fought in 31 at Actium, a promontory on the western coast of Greece. Antony withdrew to Egypt and took refuge with Cleopatra, and his army surrendered to Octavian.

The next year Octavian unhurriedly advanced on Alexandria for the reckoning with Antony and Cleopatra. Antony took his own life, and Cleopatra was left to confront Octavian. She had skillfully maintained her rule through alliances and love affairs with Caesar, then Antony, but Octavian evidently desired no such arrangement. Her rule was to end and she would be brought to Rome as a captive in a triumphal parade. She proudly scorned such a disgrace and killed herself—according to one account, immortalized by Shakespeare in his *Antony and Cleopatra*, by pressing a poisonous snake to her breast.

With Cleopatra's death ended the last Macedonian kingdom and, therefore, the Hellenistic Age, which had begun with the death of Alexander in 323. The Roman Republic ended at about the same time, as Octavian built the bridge between it and the Roman Empire. He was Caesar's adopted son and also his true and final successor, the last of the series of warlords. He had eliminated every rival and had mastered the use of the machine built for conquest, as we may call the Republic. His personality seems to lack the panache of Caesar, who was invincible in the field and a talented man of letters, but his greatness before history is that he ended the civil wars and formed the structure from which modern Europe has descended—the Roman Empire.

The development of Rome from a village south of the Tiber River into an imperial state follows a course marked by political discipline. No Greek city-state showed such perseverance once a policy was determined. Why did Rome become the empire builder? One answer is the large reserves of manpower that enabled the Romans to overcome Carthage. Another answer, perhaps more abstract, is the rigorous character of the Roman people. In daily life the word of the father was law. In the state the power of the Senate to direct public affairs was unquestioned for many decades. This authoritarian view of life was reinforced by Roman religion, a group of cults with only one fixed doctrine: conservative obedience to established customs.

As Rome extended its power a wealthy aristocracy, composed of both patricians and plebeians, absorbed the small holdings of peasants. The brothers

Gracchus tried to restore displaced farmers to their lands, but another use was finally made of this manpower when poor men were admitted to the Roman legions.

Generals became warlords and troops became their followers. The prizes of supremacy became more valuable. Julius Caesar played for absolute control and won the contest. It is far from certain that he set out to destroy the Roman constitution, which had served him well, but in the civil war between him and his enemies in the Senate that was the result. Another period of intrigues led to the final civil war and to the supremacy of Octavian, Caesar's adopted son.

Rome originally had institutions like those of the Greek city-states—executive magistrates, a council or Senate, and juries. As Roman territory expanded and the army grew into an ever more dangerous weapon, it is remarkable that the city-state's constitution lasted as long as it did. The further existence of Rome and its possessions now demanded a new political structure to manage the Roman Empire.

RECOMMENDED READING

Sources

Julius Caesar. *War Commentaries.* Rex Warner (tr.). 1960. An unsurpassed textbook in political-military decision making.

Cicero. *Selected Political Speeches.* Michael Grant (tr.). 1977.

———— *Selected Works.* Michael Grant (tr.). 1960.

Livy. All surviving parts of his history of Rome are in four volumes published by Penguin (various translators). 1965–1982.

Polybius. *The Rise of the Roman Empire.* Ian Scott-Kilvert (tr.). 1979.

Sallust. *Jugurthine War and War with Catiline.* S. A. Handford (tr.). 1963.

Studies

Badian, E. *Roman Imperialism in the Late Republic.* 1971.

————. *Publicans and Sinners.* 1983. Together, these two books survey the reasons for Rome's acquisition of an empire and the financial administration that managed the regime.

Earl, Donald. *The Age of Augustus.* 1980. Both a social and a political analysis.

Errington, R. M. *The Dawn of Empire: Rome's Rise to World Power.* 1973.

Gelzer, Matthias. *Caesar: Politician and Statesman.* 1968. For more advanced students; contains precise references to ancient sources.

Gruen, Erich S. *The Hellenistic World and the Coming of Rome.* 1984. Full historical narrative, arguing against the view that Rome tried to make Eastern possessions adopt Roman ways.

Heurgon, Jacques. *The Rise of Rome to 264 B.C.* 1973. Good on the rise of the city and its earliest history.

Mommsen, Theodor. *A History of Rome.* Originally 3 vols., 1854–1856; many modern editions. The classic history of the Republic from a liberal point of view, still a gripping narrative.

Ogilvie, Robert M. *The Romans and Their Gods in the Age of Augustus.* 1970. A brief, approachable discussion.

Pallottino, Massimo. *The Etruscans,* rev. ed. 1975. By the leading Etruscologist of our time.

Richardson, Emeline. *The Etruscans: Their Art and Civilization.* 1964. Better illustrated than Pallottino.

Rose, H. J. *A Handbook of Latin Literature.* 1954. The best brief history, better for reference than for continuous reading.

Scullard, H. H. *From the Gracchi to Nero.* 1971. The best textbook for the central period of Roman history, with good references to sources.

Syme, Ronald. *The Roman Revolution.* 1960. Brilliant analysis of the passing of the Republic and the founding of the Empire by Augustus.

Taylor, Lily Ross. *Party Politics in the Age of Caesar.* 1949.

Housing in Rome

Most pictures of Rome show reconstructions or remains of imposing temples, walls, and official buildings, and indeed a visitor during the Empire must have been overwhelmed by the sheer size of buildings in the great capital. Our ideas of Roman housing are also influenced by films and journalism that recreate elegant pools, atriums, loggias, and frescoed walls, with discreet servants in attendance. Some few Romans did live this way, but what was the housing style of a Roman family of, say, the lower middle class?

For such people Rome was much like a large European city today. Single, separate homes accounted for perhaps 4 percent of the dwellings. The rest were apartment houses known as *insulae* ("islands"). Unlike the expensive private homes, which opened onto inner courts, the apartments faced the street and offered little relief from noise and pollution. Real estate within the city became harder to find as the population approached its estimated height of 1 million or 1.2 million, and builders and landlords tried to maximize their profit by piling

An artist's conception of the Sacred Way rising from the Basilica Nova of Maxentius and Constantine. (New York Public Library Picture Collection)

the apartments as high as possible. The poet Martial testifies that he lived on the third floor, but in one of his satires he refers to an unfortunate man who had to plod up two hundred steps to reach his apartment.

The government was aware of the dangers of these tottering structures. Augustus issued laws limiting buildings to some sixty feet in height, but this still allowed apartments to have five or six stories. Construction was fragile and exposed tenants to the dangers of collapse and fire—the latter persisted even after Augustus also formed the first Roman fire brigade. Juvenal, the satiric poet of the first century A.D., writes of the poor wretch who lived on the top floor, right under the tiles, and would have had little chance of escape when a fire broke out below. And in fact Rome was devastated by the great fire of 64, under Nero; but the response was simply to rebuild high apartment blocks under the same unsafe conditions.

The street level might contain a small shop or tavern; the tradition of snack bars everywhere in Rome is an old one. The proprietor and his family would live immediately above the shop. Less well off families lived above, in groups of rooms on successive floors, perhaps even renting out a room to some other lodgers. No glass covered the windows—rather, they were covered with cloth or leather, perhaps even wooden shutters that closed out light and locked in smoke from cooking or, if open, let in air and noise from outside. There were no internal fireplaces: Cooking was done on an open stove or brazier. Within a room the main piece of furniture was the bed, on which people slept, sat, and dined. Chairs were normally backless stools, and cloths, blankets, and pillows made up the rest. Light came from the court or the street or from small lamps inside.

Rome's superb system of aqueducts supplied constant running water in public latrines and the colossal baths, but only the ground floor of a house could expect running water and interior toilets, while tenants on upper floors had to carry up their water. Personal bathing was probably only a quick splash; a full bath was taken later at the public baths, and shaving was done by a barber (without soap, merely with hot water). Wastes had to be carried away, but it is said that some people would simply dump them out the window, to the annoyance of walkers in the street.

One went to bed, or at least retired indoors, soon after dark; the doors on the ground floor were of heavy wood and presented the same blank appearance that the metal rolling doors of many Roman shops do today. The streets were not lighted, and only those who had a bodyguard could walk in safety after dark; the sources tell us of gangs of toughs that roamed the streets along with the emperor Nero. Wheeled traffic during the day had been banned by Caesar, except carriers of material for public building; so the creaking of wheels and shouts of directions threatened sleep at night. Only a few main streets were wide enough to take more than one cart at a time, and the streets themselves were a twisted network, owing to the crowding in of the *insulae*—a situation still visible in older parts of Rome.

Chapter 5

The Empire and Christianity

The history of the Roman Empire is one of both transformation and remarkable continuity. The system of government devised by Augustus and maintained by his successors gave the Empire two centuries of solid prosperity. The provinces were peaceful and soon began to rival Rome in economic strength. Wars on the frontiers did strain the imperial resources at times, but there was no enemy strong enough to threaten Roman domination of Europe.

At the beginning of the third century the Empire entered a period of crisis. Control of the army became the key to power, and emperors and would-be emperors followed one another in rapid succession. When order finally returned during the fourth century, the old Roman Empire was no more. In the East the Byzantine Empire was formed; in the West the Empire steadily declined, finally ceasing to be governed by Roman emperors altogether in 476.

The passing of the Roman Empire marked the end of the ancient world. The undoing of a marvelous civilization has long held a special fascination for historians, perhaps because it reminds them of the impermanence that threatens all human institutions and every civilization. Many factors weakened the Empire—the inadequacies of the slave system, the plight of the poor, the dearth of effective leaders, the desires of subject peoples for autonomy, the insufficiency of classical values to command allegiance and sustain morale among the Empire's inhabitants. There is no single, simple explanation for Rome's decline, but the study of this process can still be instructive.

Even as antiquity was passing, ancient peoples were laying the basis for a new form of civilization. Here the most important innovation was the gradual formation and slow spread of a new set of religious beliefs. This was Christianity, which was destined to inform the life and culture of the Western heirs of the Roman Empire.

The ancient world declined, but the memory of its achievements never entirely faded. Rather, the magnificence and grace of antiquity's monuments, the range and subtlety of its thought, the elegance and interest of its literature—all this remained to fascinate and inspire future generations. So also the social ideals that the Empire embodied—unity among nations, peace throughout the world, the rule of reason, law, and justice in human affairs—retained their appeal to Rome's heirs and successors. The political regime of the Roman emperors ended in the West in 476. But the intellectual and artistic accomplishments and social ideals of the ancient world have survived to form a living, stimulating, challenging part of Western cultural tradition.

I. THE FOUNDING OF THE ROMAN EMPIRE

The Rule of Augustus to A.D. 14

When Octavian returned to Rome in 29 from his conquest of Egypt, his supremacy was beyond challenge. He was the leader of a huge army commanded by loyal generals, and for several years he had been consul with a dedicated political following. The issue now was whether he would solve the problem that had defeated Caesar: how to rule without seeming to be an autocrat. He achieved this by restoring the appearance—but no more—of Republican government. Candidates ran for office, but only when he designated them; a willing Senate executed only the policies that he favored. Republican structures remained intact, but they were staffed by loyal adherents. He also avoided any offensive displays of authority. At no time did he announce that he was converting the Republic into an empire. Therefore historians can find no official beginning for the Roman Empire; the best date is probably 27 B.C., for in that year Octavian laid the foundations of his system.

In 27 Octavian assumed control of an enormous provincial command, including Farther Spain, Gaul (the regions newly conquered by Caesar, not the old province of Transalpine Gaul), and Syria. Most of the legions were concentrated in these provinces; thus Octavian was the legal commander of an unrivaled military force. He ruled his provinces through assistants, or legates, as Pompey had ruled his Spanish command. Egypt was handled in a special manner; it was treated as a private possession of Octavian's and managed by an equestrian appointee who merely directed the governmental machinery that the Ptolemies had set up.

Along with this command the Senate conferred on Octavian the name Augustus, meaning "blessed" or "fortunate." This title brought with it no powers, but its semidivine overtones were useful to Augustus in establishing his eminence. In 23 he received two additional powers from the Senate. His imperium (the word means power of command) was extended to cover not only his former provinces but the whole Roman world. He also obtained the authority of a tribune (*tribunicia potestas*). As a patrician (by his adoption into Caesar's family), Augustus could not actually be a tribune. Yet his having the power of a tribune suggested that Augustus was the patron and defender of the common people of Rome.

Augustus' control really rested on his "authority" (*auctoritas*)—that indefinable quality of leadership that makes it unnecessary for the ruler to murder his critics. Augustus' rule was absolute, and all candidates who gained office had received his approval. No tribunes inflamed the assembly, though they were still elected; and few proconsuls showed indiscretion. He was usually called the *princeps,* an old Republican title denoting the senior ex-consul in the Senate, who had the right to speak first in the carefully controlled senatorial debates. Modern writers often refer to the system of Augustus as the Principate.

The long reign of Augustus from 27 B.C. to A.D. 14 established many abiding features of the autocracy. He provided a cash payment from the public treasury to soldiers who had served for 20 years, thus securing the loyalty of the legions to the state, not to their generals. He also gave security to the Empire by extending and solidifying the northern frontier (see Map 5.1). The provinces north of Italy now reached as far as the Rhine and Danube rivers.

Augustus also created a force of soldiers known as the Praetorian Guard, which was stationed in Rome. This group of some 9000 men was recruited from Italians (no provincials, even if citizens, could serve in it under Augustus) and received higher pay than the soldiers in legions. The guard served as the city's police force and as Augustus' personal bodyguard, but after a few decades it came to play a decisive,

International and Military History	Political History
27 B.C.	27 B.C.–A.D. 14 Rule of Augustus
	Julio–Claudian emperors
	14–37 Tiberius
A.D. 47 Conquest of Britain	37–41 Caligula
	41–54 Claudius
66–70 Jewish revolt	54–68 Nero
A.D. 80	69 Year of Four Emperors
	97–180 The Five Good Emperors
132–134 Jewish revolt	
160s Wars of Marcus Aurelius in East	
180	
	193–284 Crisis of Empire
280	
	284–305 Diocletian; the Tetrarchy
	337 Death of Constantine
380	
395 Division into Eastern and Western Empires	
	476 "Fall" of Western Empire
480	

Social and Economic History	Cultural and Intellectual History
— 27 B.C.	
	9 B.C. End of Livy's history
A.D. 1 Laws of Augustus on family	7 B.C.–c. A.D. 30 Life of Jesus
	17 Death of Ovid
c. 50 Pottery market dominated by Gaul	
	c. 55–c. 120 Tacitus
	c. 70–c. 130 Suetonius
— 80	
	c. 100 Juvenal
c. 120 Hadrian's attempt to codify laws	
	c. 150 Heresies of Marcion, Montanus
160s Attack of plague	
— 180	
193–284 Economic crisis, inflation, collapse of currency	c. 185–255 Origen
250–313 Age of Persecution of Christians	
	c. 260–340 Eusebius
— 280	
284 Period of severe taxation begins	
	318–323 Heresy of Arius
	325 Council of Nicaea
	c. 340–420 Jerome
	354–430 Augustine
— 380	
	451 Council of Chalcedon
— 480	

This superb onyx cameo (carved about A.D. 1) commemorates a triumph accorded Tiberius for victories over the Germans. Tiberius steps down from his chariot (top left) into the presence of the Emperor Augustus and of a personification of Rome; below, warriors with trophies and prisoners.
(Photo: Alinari-Art Reference Bureau)

and violent, role in the designation of new emperors.

Augustus assumed the office of Pontifex Maximus, or high priest, and made attempts to revive the old Roman religion, probably as a device promoting political stability. He also grasped the possibilities of ruler-cult. First he assigned Julius Caesar a place among the Roman gods and built a Temple to the Deified Julius. He also called himself "Divi Filius," or son of the divine one, though he was only the adopted son of Caesar. This verbal trick invited people to imagine that Augustus, though not divine, might some day become so. Virgil and Horace, who were practically court poets, discreetly referred to Augustus as a future deity. He also sponsored the building of temples to

"Rome and Augustus"—a further suggestion, though not an offensive demand, that the Emperor should be worshiped. It became customary to make an offering to the Genius (protecting spirit) of the Emperor and, in fact, Augustus was deified on his death, a political action that was imitated on the deaths of several later emperors who were considered to have ruled well.

Part of the religious revival was the rebuilding of scores of temples; but temples were by no means the only Augustan buildings; a famous saying tells us that "he found Rome made of brick and left it made of marble." The prosperity of the later years of Augustus' rule reflects the general peace that he brought to the Roman world. Freed of the expense of wars, Rome enjoyed a confidence that expressed itself in cultural creativity.

Augustus also legislated in favor of the Roman family. Perhaps he was inspired by the losses in population during the civil wars. In any case, he issued laws aimed at repopulating Italy, including special privileges for fathers of three or more children. He also issued a strong law against adultery, whose effectiveness we can hardly judge. The general spirit of his laws on marriage shows respect for the family and a wish to nurture and maintain it.

Augustus died in A.D. 14. Through his care-

MAP 5.1. THE ROMAN EMPIRE 44 B.C.–A.D. 14

ful control of the army and magistrates, he had given Rome three decades of healing after the civil wars, and the success of his work is shown by the fact that the state did not relapse into civil war after his death. The Empire he designed and guided in its formative years lasted for two centuries in much the same condition as it had been at his death. For centuries more it survived as the Byzantine Empire in the East, and it was the ancestor of the Holy Roman Empire in the West.

II. THE EMPIRE AT ITS HEIGHT

The Successors of Augustus

The last wife of Augustus, Livia, was from a lofty old patrician family. Augustus had but one child, a daughter named Julia, whose two sons died as boys. It seems likely that Livia influenced Augustus to adopt her son, Tiberius, and thus to designate him as his successor. She thus played a leading role in the shaping of the imperial dynasty.

After the death of Augustus, Tiberius became leader of the state. In recognizing Tiberius, the Senate confirmed the principle of dynastic succession and established the fact that an empire, not a republic, now existed. The dynastic line established by Augustus, called the Julio-Claudian dynasty, reigned until A.D. 68.

Much can be said against the rule of the Julio-Claudians. Tiberius was morbid, suspicious, and vengeful. His successor, Gaius, or Caligula, suffered from insanity. Claudius was gullible and manipulated by his wives and freedmen. Nero, the last of the Julio-Claudians, was one of the worst emperors in Roman history. His tyranny led to a rebellion in Gaul. When the revolt spread to Rome, he saw he was doomed and killed himself.

Yet these emperors did maintain, and even increase, the Augustan heritage. Claudius, for example, decided on the conquest of southern Britain. By A.D. 47 Britain had been annexed as a province of the Empire; this completed the work begun by Caesar's brief invasions of Britain in 55 and 54 B.C. Moreover, within the peaceful Empire, the provincial administration that Augustus had established continued to function effectively.

The process of centralization of power continued. Tiberius stripped the assemblies of the right to elect magistrates and gave this responsibility to the Senate. This reform was little more than a recognition of the true state of affairs, for the assemblies were by now only a formality. From this time onward it was but a short step to allowing the emperor to appoint magistrates directly; the Senate merely made the formal gesture of conferring their imperium. Claudius withdrew more affairs of state from the Senate and turned them over to his trusted assistants. These were usually Greeks who had been freed from slavery (thus called freedmen). Claudius' system was, in a way, the beginning of a professional bureaucracy; the use of such civil servants was to become an important feature of government in the Empire.

Another factor that weakened senatorial power was the frequent interference by the Praetorian Guard. The Guard first intervened in politics when it forced the Senate to recognize Claudius as Emperor. It also played a decisive role in the selection of Nero in 54; his mother bribed the Guard for its support, and the Senate had no choice but to acclaim him as Emperor. This repeated invasion of civil authority by the Praetorian Guard was another step on the road toward militarization; within a little more than a century the emperors were to become totally dependent on being able to buy the good will of the soldiery.

The military played a significant role in the struggle over the succession after Nero's death in 68, as troops in various quarters of the Empire backed their own candidates for emperor. The year 69 is often called "the year of the four emperors" because at one time four men claimed to be emperor. Vespasian finally stabilized the situation and emerged as sole ruler late in 69. He founded the Flavian dynasty (so called from his middle name, Flavius), which lasted through the reigns of his two sons.

Vespasian was an efficient administrator, but in providing a strong central government for Rome he further augmented the powers of the emperor. The old republican institutions, the Senate and the assemblies, no longer retained any power. The emperor appointed the consuls and other officers.

The Five Good Emperors

The Flavian dynasty ended in violence in 96, when a group of senators instigated the murder of the Emperor Domitian, Vespasian's despotic son. Domitian had no son, so the Senate picked a quiet older senator, Nerva, to be the new emperor. Nerva in turn adopted Trajan, and designated him as his successor. This system remained in use for nearly a century and solved the problem of succession. An emperor would choose a qualified successor and adopt him as his son, thus assuring a peaceful transfer of power. The system functioned so well, and the men chosen were so capable, that historians have called Nerva and the next four rulers the "five good emperors."

Nerva was little more than an elderly presiding officer without much real force. After less than two years he was succeeded by his adopted son, Trajan, who had been chosen because of his high military reputation. Trajan (98–117) was later viewed as a model emperor; he ruled with an unusual blend of fairness and freedom, even issuing warnings not to hunt down Christians or listen to anonymous accusations. He was followed by Hadrian (117–138), who asserted that Trajan had adopted him.

On the whole, in the period of the five good emperors the Empire remained stable and even expanded. In 116 it reached its farthest extension to the East as Trajan led his troops down the Tigris-Euphrates Valley to the head of the Persian Gulf; he thus added to the Empire portions of the area that had been the most ancient cradle of civilization (see Map 5.2). Trajan formed two new provinces, called Assyria and Mesopotamia; but revolts in the region made it impossible to retain the two provinces, and he had to retreat and fight his way back toward Syria. In the midst of the retreat he fell ill and died in 117. Hadrian, who succeeded him, decided to cut Rome's losses by withdrawing from the extreme eastern positions that Trajan had taken.

Hadrian continued the development of a frank autocracy. The Roman assemblies no longer met in order to pass laws. Instead, Hadrian himself issued laws, often without bothering to obtain the approval of the Senate; these laws were known as "decisions" (*constitutiones*). Hadrian was advised by an informal council known as the "friends" of the emperor (*amici*). This council included the leading experts of the time in Roman law. One of them, Salvius Julianus, took responsibility for collecting the edicts that Roman praetors had issued over the centuries. This was an attempt to standardize the procedures of civil law; it pointed the way toward the great codification of law in the sixth century under the Emperor Justinian. Hadrian's laws, even though issued without any pretense of democratic process, were often fair and humane. He sometimes tried to improve the condition of soldiers and slaves, and women now obtained the same rights in court as men.

Trajan and Hadrian undertook a vast building program. Trajan erected many structures throughout the Empire and added an impressive column to the Roman Forum, on which are carved a series of scenes recording episodes in the wars against the trans-Danubian tribes. He also saw to the largest single extension of

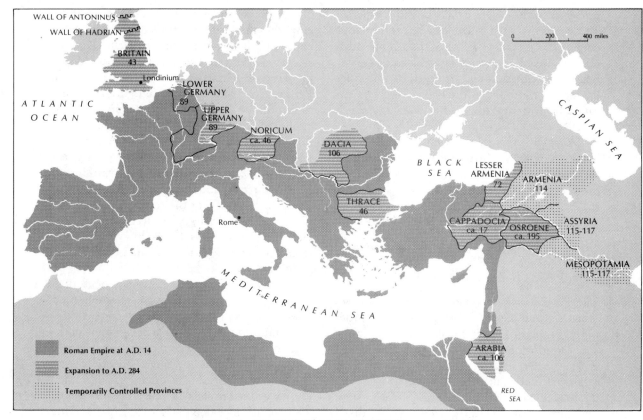

MAP 5.2. THE ROMAN EMPIRE A.D. **14–284**

the Forum by adding a large group of buildings—shops, offices, a library—to the east of his column. Hadrian undertook various building projects in the provinces. Most famous is the wall (much of it still stands) he built across Britain from Newcastle to Carlisle, to protect the frontier between the Roman province of Britain and the areas controlled by Celtic tribes to the north.

Hadrian followed the custom of designating his successor by adoption, and in fact saw to the succession of the next two emperors, Antoninus Pius (138–161) and Marcus Aurelius (161–180), who are the last of the "five good emperors." The rule of Antoninus was peace-

ful, and the Empire enjoyed its last years of prosperity under the reign of Marcus Aurelius. But in his final years the gathering storm broke in all its fury. Marcus had to fight invasions by tribes on the Danube River and in the East. One campaign was especially disastrous, for the army returning from Asia Minor in the 160s brought with it a devastating plague that spread through much of Europe. This plague must have been one cause of the weakening of Rome, but the nearly total lack of records prevents our knowing how many died.

Marcus wanted to advance the position of his worthless son, Commodus (180–192), and this caused him to give up the principle of

This panel from a monumental column erected by the Emperor Trajan in A.D. 113 is a vivid portrait of Roman soldiers attending wounded comrades. Note the standards of a Roman legion carried by soldiers on the right. Such realistic narration characterizes Roman art; Greek artists preferred symbol over reality.
(Photo: Alinari)

adoption in choosing the next ruler. He passed the throne to Commodus, whose extravagance and cruelty were reminiscent of Nero and Domitian. His murder on the last day of 192 opened a period of terrible instability, to which we shall return (p. 169).

Roman Imperial Civilization

Economy

In the late Republic and the first two centuries of the Empire, economic life in Italy and the provinces reached a level of prosperity that Europe would not see again for the next thousand years. The results of Roman censuses, which

---

A detail from the column commemorating Marcus Aurelius' victories shows the beheading of defeated soldiers.
(Photo: Anderson-Giraudon)

have partially survived, indicate that Italy at the death of Augustus (including Cisalpine Gaul but excluding the islands) contained probably 7.5 million inhabitants. (In about 1500, the earliest date at which we can make a comparable estimate, the same area contained about 10 million people.)

A distinctive feature of settlement throughout the Empire was the importance of cities. In the western provinces, these were for the most part small; to judge from the area enclosed by the Roman walls, most towns contained only a few thousand residents. Yet they usually contained temples, markets, arenas, courthouses, and other public buildings, and thus display an authentic urban character. In the East, cities could be much larger. Alexandria in Egypt probably had 400,000 inhabitants; Ephesus in Asia Minor, 200,000; Antioch in Syria, 150,000. The size of the cities in the East is probably one reason why the economy in the Eastern part of the Empire was stronger than that in the Western part. During the era of the decline in the Empire, the Eastern portion managed to survive and was to become the foundation of the Byzantine Empire. Both in the East and West, the cities maintained and extended Roman culture and the Latin language and thus enhanced the unity within the world's largest ancient empire.

Largest of all the imperial cities, and a true wonder of the ancient world, was Rome. Estimates of its size generally reach about 1 million inhabitants. Not until the eighteenth century would other European cities, London and Paris, again contain like concentrations of humanity. The maintenance under crowded conditions of acceptable standards of public hygiene, the supply of enormous quantities of pure water and food, challenged but did not defeat Roman skills in civil engineering and in administration. Rome's central position, both geographically and economically, made the city a metropolis comparable to New York or London today. No other city in the ancient world drew the variety of travelers that came to Rome, and the city's harbor, Ostia, was crowded with goods from the various provinces of the Empire and from such distant lands as China (see Map 5.3). Many writers have portrayed the city as an immense parasite, feeding on the tribute and products of the Empire. This seems unfair. It is true that Rome could not feed itself from the produce of Italy alone, but the city provided economic leadership for the Empire in banking and trade.

In spite of the importance of manufacture and trade, agriculture remained the basic support of the economy; it supplied, according to rough estimates, upward of 75 percent of the total product of the Empire. One important change in Italian agriculture in the last century of the Republic had been the triumph of the great slave-run estates, called latifundia, at the expense of small farms and holdings. At the same time, the managers of these vast plantations favored varied forms of agriculture—the

MAP 5.3. PRODUCTION AND TRADE IN THE ROMAN EMPIRE IN THE 2ND CENTURY A.D.

(From Hayden, *Atlas of the Classical World,* London: Nelson & Sons, Ltd., 1959, p. 151)

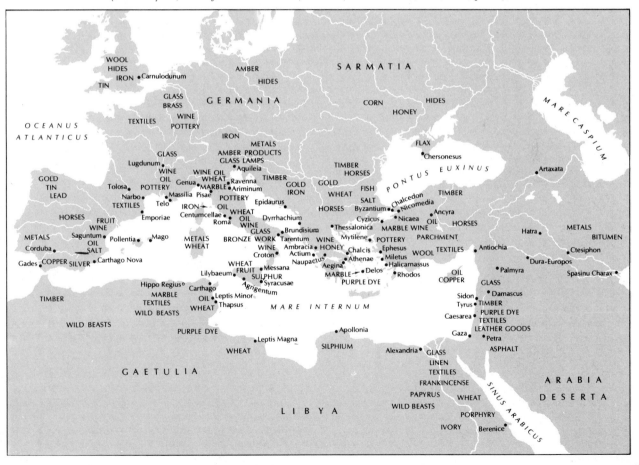

cultivation of vines, olives, and fruit, and the raising of large numbers of cattle, sheep, and goats. Only enough grain was cultivated to feed the *familia,* the resident staff of workers, most of them slaves. On some latifundia, particularly in the south of Italy, cattle were counted in the hundreds and sheep and goats in the tens of thousands. The great estates also supplied the cities with building stone, lumber, and firewood; huge quantities of wood were required, for example, to keep the Roman baths at comfortable temperatures. The widespread abandonment of cereal cultivation left the Italian cities, and Rome especially, critically dependent on imported wheat, which came mainly from Egypt. In the view of some historians, extensive deforestation and overgrazing led inevitably to erosion of the land and the loss of fertile topsoil, and were principal factors in the economic decline of Roman Italy. Even ancient peoples had the power to injure their environments.

Large estates were growing in the provinces as well, but they did not dominate the agricultural economy as in Italy. Moreover, the "Roman peace" favored the development of these once backward areas to the point where they threatened Italy's economic leadership. Provinces such as Spain and Gaul, and those along the Danube River, possessed superior natural resources. The wine market, for example, passed into the hands of Spanish cultivators within the second century, for Spanish wine was better than Italian and was cheaper to produce because of lower labor costs. In some forms of industry, too, the provinces began to outrun Italian production. One of the main Italian industries was pottery, especially the Arretine ware made at Arretium (modern Arezzo). But by about A.D. 50 pottery made in Gaul had replaced Italian pottery even in Italy and had also taken over the market in the provinces and military camps. Thus Rome's success in establishing a commercial network created markets for products of the provinces and eventually contributed to her own economic decline.

Social Conditions

The upper class in Rome lived on a far higher scale, and was more widely separated from the common people, than the rich of Greece. The wealthy had running water tapped into their homes, slaves to tend them hand and foot, and elegant country villas for recreation. These villas approached economic self-sufficiency, for slaves manufactured articles of light industry on the farms.

A modern aspect of Roman cities was the existence of suburbs and resorts. Capri was, as it is now, a resort, and Ostia served as both a harbor and a seaside resort. Pompeii was a commercial town, but its neighbor Herculaneum was a residential suburb. Both towns, buried by the eruption of Vesuvius in 79, provide examples of the airy Roman house, built around an atrium, a central open court, and decorated with graceful wall paintings. The paintings, often showing landscapes, broke the monotony of windowless rooms; the artists even experimented successfully with the creation of perspective, long before this technique reappeared in European painting.

The workers of Rome had no such elegant housing. Their apartments were flimsy and inflammable, though acceptable by ancient standards. They lacked running water, but a complex system of aqueducts gave easy access to water outside the home, and Rome always took pride in its enormous, cheap public baths. There were corporations in Rome for every kind of worker—fishermen, engineers, cobblers, silk workers, and so on. These city laborers had working conditions that were beyond the dreams of a Near Eastern peasant. They worked only about six or seven hours a day, and the Roman year contained about 160

Atrium house, Pompeii. This town was both a commercial center and a summer resort; this elegant home with a courtyard would have belonged to a well-off citizen.
(Photo: Anderson-Giraudon)

holidays. To these the state added from time to time special days of celebration.

The major amusements for the people during days of leisure were public games, especially chariot races, which brought honor and wealth to the skilled charioteers, in one of the arenas such as the great Circus Maximus. Besides races, the Romans gave themselves over to brutal contests, which sometimes went on to death, between gladiators or between men and animals. The main arena for these—to us, deplorable—spectacles was the grandiose Colosseum, begun by the emperor Vespasian in the 70s. It held about 50,000 spectators, and much of it still stands, probably the one monument that most vividly recalls the capital city. Whether Christians were martyred here is still disputed. There were other such arenas in virtually every large city, and some of these also survive; the arena of Verona is the site of operas every summer.

Eating was a species of amusement for the wealthy. Even the most athletic glutton could be more than satisfied at a dinner that began in the late afternoon and lasted until after midnight. Romans always ate in a reclining position without using knives and forks; one enemy of Julius Caesar (the younger Cato) vowed that, until Caesar was captured, he would eat sitting at a table. Servants washed their hands and kept up the flow of wine mixed with water. The Romans' devotion to food is symbolized in their invention, the special place for vomiting, a device that enabled the gourmand to prolong and renew his pleasure.

It is a measure of Rome's prosperity that the city was able to support roughly half its population at public expense, through free allotments of food, especially grain, which was the most common item in the diet. These were the poor, who lived in slums and were able to find little or no work. In the later, less prosperous years the cost of maintaining 50 percent of the city's population was to strain the Empire's economy.

Social mobility became easier within the Empire. Some Greeks who had been freed from slavery enjoyed enviable careers as secretaries to emperors or as businessmen, and they were able to join the wealthier class. The need for troops opened new opportunities for provincials. Italian manpower alone was not enough to patrol Rome's extended frontiers, so the use of non-Italian troops for such service became more common. Men from the provinces entered the Roman legions, especially during the second century and later; they finally made their way into the Praetorian Guard, once recruited from Italians and considered an elite corps. Even the Senate began to include men born in the provinces, often not even Italian in descent. In time the Empire became less "Roman," for Rome was no longer the only center of activity. In both manpower and economic strength the primacy of Italy was of the past. This movement away from Rome as the all-important city led to the transfer of political control from Rome to Byzantium in the fourth and fifth centuries; this in turn points toward the long history of the Byzantine Empire, Rome's successor in the East.

Law

An ever-developing, complex system of law and procedure was one of the chief cultural contributions of Rome. Naturally, Roman law developed under the Republic, but its growth under the Empire suggests that we treat it here. The earliest codified Roman law was the Laws of the Twelve Tables, published about 450 B.C. As the state developed, the Twelve Tables were no longer adequate to the needs of the Romans, and the law began a long process of modification. As we have seen, the assemblies, both that of the Centuries and that of the Tribes, had the power to pass laws. But as time went on, they issued laws mainly regarding large public issues, such as distributions of land or

POPULATION OF THE ROMAN EMPIRE

These estimates of Roman populations were formulated by the German historian K. J. Beloch in 1886. More recent studies would set the totals perhaps as high as 80 million, but Beloch's research still has not been superseded.

Country	Area in km²	Number of Inhabitants	Number of Inhabitants per km²
EUROPE			
Italy	250,000	6,000,000	24
Sicily	26,000	600,000	23
Sardinia	33,000	500,000	15
Spain	590,000	6,000,000	10
Narbonese Gaul	100,000	1,500,000	15
Gaul	535,000	3,400,000	6.3
Danubian Provinces	430,000	2,000,000	4.7
Greece	267,000	3,000,000	11.2
Total	2,231,000	23,000,000	9.7
ASIA			
Asia (province of)	135,000	6,000,000	44
Asia Minor (except Asia)	412,000	7,000,000	17
Syria	109,000	6,000,000	55
Cyprus	9,500	500,000	52
Total	665,000	19,500,000	34
AFRICA			
Egypt	28,000	5,000,000	179
Cyrenaica	15,000	500,000	33
Africa	400,000	6,000,000	15
Total	443,000	11,500,000	26
ROMAN EMPIRE	3,339,500	54,000,000	16

Source: P. Salmon, *Population et Dépopulation* (1974), pp. 22–24.

assignments of commands overseas. The reshaping of laws that affected relations among citizens, private rights, and the like was largely the work of individual magistrates.

Normally, cases came before a judge (*iudex*), who was a private citizen of high standing; judges came from the Senate and later from among equestrians as well. They relied on the advice of other private citizens who were reputed to understand the law. These men were called jurists (*iurisprudentes* or *iurisconsulti*), and their opinions and advice constantly influenced the law. Another impact on the law came from magistrates, especially praetors, who had the right to issue edicts in which they explained how they would interpret the law during their year in office. These edicts acquired the authority of tradition and were a means of revising the law.

The Romans distinguished their own citizens from members of their dominion who did not possess strict Roman citizenship. The citizens were subject to the "civil law" (*ius civile*), or law applying to citizens; the rest were allowed, in various ways, to maintain many of their own customs, and these customs gradually came to form the *ius gentium,* or law of other nations in general. These two kinds of law were assigned, logically enough, to two magistrates for administration, the "urban praetor" (*praetor urbanus*) and the "traveling praetor" (*praetor peregrinus*).

During the earlier Empire the process of modifying the law continued, with a new influence appearing—the intervention of emperors. Their orders and provisions were now also incorporated into the body of law. Jurists continued to play an important part in this process. Sabinus, Gaius, and Papinian were among the most important jurists of the first three centuries. We have seen that the emperor Hadrian recognized the need for a consistent revision of the many edicts laid down by praetors over the decades; he charged Salvius Julianus, one of his jurists, with undertaking such a revision. As the Empire grew and embraced more peoples, the *ius gentium* gradually displaced the *ius civile,* and even the *ius gentium* began to give way to the notion of a kind of universal natural law (*ius naturale*) applicable to all people. Roman legislators never specifically canceled the *ius gentium* in favor of a *ius naturale;* the latter remained only an area of speculation, in which (for example) jurists admitted that a slave could have rights and could be a debtor or creditor; these views played no part in the *ius gentium.*

The Romans' respect for their law is consistent with the remarkable cohesiveness that one sees throughout their society. In war they were often brutal, but then so were many others in all periods of history. Rome's achievement in designing and preserving a system of laws governing the behavior of citizens toward one another has served as a model for the law of Western Europe generally (an exception is the English-speaking nations, which derive their law from the common law of England; this is discussed in Chapter 8). Codes of law, as we have also observed, are a feature of several other ancient societies, but in richness and complexity the codifications of the late Roman Empire easily surpass all the rest.

Engineering and Architecture

The Romans showed remarkable competence in the fields of engineering and construction. The most enduring monument to Roman civilization is the impressive network of roads found everywhere from Britain to Africa. Originally designed as highways for the rapid movement of legions, these roads became trade routes in more peaceful times. The great highways, with their many offshoots, eliminated all barriers to travel; even the mountains and deserts yielded to these everlasting ribbons of flagstone.

From the earliest times the Romans built aqueducts that converged toward the cities, sloping down and carrying fresh water from the mountains; Rome also had an imposing system of sewers, which were constantly flushed by water from the aqueducts.

The Romans placed more emphasis on personal cleanliness than any other civilization down to modern times. Several emperors saw to the building of immense public baths. The grandest set of all was the Baths of Caracalla, built in the third century, and the English city of Bath is named for the facilities that the Romans built there. Like the gymnasiums in Greek poleis, the Roman baths served as social centers.

In architecture the Romans adapted Greek techniques to Roman taste. Their temples, like those of the Greeks, were supported by columns. The Romans especially liked the Corinthian capital, in which the column is crowned with a bell-like acanthus flower. Roman temples had large interiors and were often completely walled at the rear, because Romans performed their ceremonies indoors, while the Greeks performed theirs in front of the temple and reserved the interior as a room for the deity. Roman builders solved the problem of how to create these larger spaces with two devices: the arch and concrete. The Romans were the first to grasp the possibilities of using arches and vaults on a large scale, and this gave their buildings a vastness that the Greeks could not achieve. Arches were prominent in the design of public buildings, sewers, and aqueducts, and the freestanding triumphal arch was an imposing commemoration of various imperial victories. They also invented concrete, which became their principal building material. It has clear advantages over stone and marble: it is inexpensive, its components are readily available, and it can be laid by relatively unskilled labor, which the Romans had in abundance. It can also be shaped into forms impossible in marble, and it is lighter in weight and can easily be supported in vaulted buildings. One of its most successful examples is the spacious Pantheon, built first in the time of Augustus, then

The Forum, originally Rome's central market, became in the period of the late Republic and Empire the political, administrative, and religious center of the city. Its ruins, shown here in a recent photograph, have over the centuries reminded visitors of the Roman achievement.
(Photo: Editorial Photocolor Archives)

rebuilt under Hadrian. Its dome is larger across than that of St. Peter's Church and has a striking opening in the center.

The Forum at Rome was expanded at various times with the addition of libraries, colonnades of shops, and many temples. Its original function was as a town market, but it became a meeting place for various assemblies from the second century B.C. on. Monumental columns and arches, rostra for speakers, and other decorations adorned it. Provincial towns also built forums, bathhouses, temples, and public halls. They often added an arch, an aqueduct, or a theater to express their civic pride and their desire to resemble Rome even in a modest way.

Sculpture and architecture coincided in triumphal arches, which often bore reliefs depicting the historical event that the arch commemorated. Roman sculpture drew on Greek models of the Hellenistic Age, when realism attained at least the same value as the depiction of ideal types; see, for example, the portrait head from Delos (Plate 5). In the later Empire, sculpture moved away from realism toward greater stylization, although realism never wholly vanished.

Our knowledge of Roman painting comes mainly from the wall paintings at Pompeii and Herculaneum. Many of these are the work of Greeks and actually provide our most valuable samples of Greek wall painting, for almost none has survived from Classical Greece. Italian artists learned from their Greek teachers, as they did in other realms of creativity, and began to do more of the decorations. Landscapes were one of the favorite subjects (see Plate 6), for many rooms were built without windows as a refuge from the heat of summer, and landscapes relieved the confining feeling of bare walls. Along with the wall paintings there were many mosaic compositions, also a legacy from Greek art. See, for example, Plates 7–8.

Poets

The leisure provided by Rome's prosperity encouraged the production of literature. During the Empire authors are found all over the Roman world (see Map 5.4 for the origins of many authors of this period). The most famous Latin poet, Virgil (70–19 B.C.), borrowed from Greek models, as Roman poets often did. His early poems, the *Bucolics* and *Georgics,* are polished hymns of praise to the Italian landscape, which reflect the style of Theocritus and Hesiod; but the gentle, human spirit of Virgil himself is always present.

The best qualities of Virgil appear when he treats civilized emotions—mercy, compassion, and sadness; then his work echoes with a grace-

A wall fresco from Pompeii, first century A.D. A young girl (or boy?) pauses in thought during her writing. Roman art cared for realistic portraiture more than did Greek art, and this image shows an accurate realism that would return to European painting only after many centuries.
(Photo: National Museum, Naples/EPA, Inc.)

BIRTHPLACES UNKNOWN
Lucretius ca. 94-55 Poet
Frontius ca. A.D. 30-104 water supply and strategy
Tacitus ca. A.D. 55-ca. 120 historian
Suetonius ca. A.D. 69-ca. 140 biographer
Aelius Donatus 4th cent. A.D. grammarian
Priscianus ca. 400 A.D. medicine
Sedulius 5th cent. A.D. poet

Caesarodunum
Sulpicius Severus ca. A.D. 400 historian
Pictavi
Hilarius A.D. 315-367 bishop, Church Father
GALLIA
Augustodunum

Pliny the Elder A.D. 23-79 scholar
Pliny the Younger A.D. 61-113 letter writer
Catullus ca. 84-54 poet (lyrics)
Livy 50 B.C.-A.D. 17 historian

Lugdunum
Sidonius A.D. 432-489 bishop, poet
Comum
Verona
Patavium
Mediolanum
See of Ambrose
Mantua

Augustonemetum
See of Sidonius
Burdigala
Ausonius A.D. 310-393 poet
Paulinus A.D. 353-431 bishop, poet
Aquitania
Aetheria ca. A.D. 400 abbess

Cornelius Nepos ca. 99-27 biographer
Virgil 70-19 poet
Jerome A.D. 347-419 theologian
to Bethlehem
Stridon

Bracara
Orosius beginning 5th cent. A.D. historian
Sarsina
Pisaurum
Plautus ca. 200 B.C. writer of comedies
Sallust 86-ca. 35 historian
Ovid 43 B.C.-A.D. 18 poet

Calagurris
Quintilian ca. A.D. 38-100 rhetorician
Volaterrae
Asisium
Volsinii
Amiternum
Cicero 106-43 B.C. jurist, orator, philosopher

Caesaraugusta
Prudentius A.D. 348-405 poet
Reate
Sulmo
Varro 116-27 scholar

Bilbilis
Martial ca. A.D. 40-ca. 104 poet
Roma
Pedum
Lucilius 180-102 poet (satires)
Tusculum
Arpinum

HISPANIA
Caesar 100-44 statesman, historian
Symmachus ca. A.D. 340-402 rhetorician
Boethius ca. A.D. 480-524 philosopher
Gregory the Great ca. 550-603 Pope
Aquinum
Suessa
Neapolis
Venusia
Brundisium
Nola
See of Paulinus
Tarentum
Rudiae

Hispalis
Corduba
Seneca the Elder ca. 55 B.C.-A.D. 40 rhetorician
Seneca the Younger ca. 5 B.C.-ca. A.D. 65 philosopher, tragedian
Lucan A.D. 39-65 poet
BALEARES
to Rome
Cato 234-149 orator, historian
Juvenal ca. A.D. 62-ca. 142 poet (satires)
Horace 65-8 B.C. poet (satires, lyrics)
Ennius 230-160 poet

Gades
Columella ca. A.D. 50 agriculture
MARE INTERNUM

Hippo Regius
See of Augustine
Augustine A.D. 354-430 bishop, theologian
SICILIA

Cirta
Carthago
See of Cyprian

to Carthage
Fronto ca. A.D. 100-166 rhetorician
Thagaste
Terence ca. 190-159 writer of comedies
Tertullian ca. A.D. 160-200 apologist

Minucius Felix 2nd cent. A.D. Prose writer
Cyprian ca. A.D. 200-258 bishop, Church Father
Lactantius ca. A.D. 300 apologist
Sicca Veneria
NUMIDIA
Madaura
Apuleius ca. A.D. 125-ca. 180 prose writer

Ammianus Marcellinus A.D. 330-395 historian originating from Antioch →

MAP 5.4. THE MOST IMPORTANT WRITERS WHO USED THE LATIN LANGUAGE
300 B.C.–A.D. 600

---

ful melancholy. These qualities appear in his Roman epic, the *Aeneid,* which borrows and transforms material from Homer. In this work Virgil narrates the wanderings of Aeneas, the Trojan who was the legendary founder of Rome. His aim was to sing the glory of Rome and its salvation by Augustus. No one after Virgil tried to write a patriotic Roman epic. Even in antiquity poets recognized that he used the epic tradition in a way that no other Latin writer could challenge.

A contemporary of Virgil's was Horace, whose *Odes, Epodes,* and *Sermones* (or *Satires*) examine love, amusement, annoyance, contentment—in short, the feelings of everyday life. Now and then Horace makes an attempt at serious patriotic verse, but these poems are self-conscious and moralizing and do not speak with the real Horatian voice of gentle, amusing irony.

The subject of love continued to inspire Roman poets. The most polished poet of love was

Ovid (43 B.C.–A.D. 17?). His most famous work is *Ars Amatoria (The Art of Love),* a witty discourse on how to find and keep mistresses and lovers. The late medieval romances, including many studies of courtly love, draw largely on Ovid. His most complex poem is *Metamorphoses,* a series of fifteen mythological tales about transformations of various kinds. In two famous episodes, for example, Hercules turns into a bull and Julius Caesar into a star. Ovid is a representative of the Roman Empire: elegant, highly civilized, and accomplished. He does not have the elemental power of Homer; rather, he is a poet of wit, rhetoric, and learning.

Juvenal, a more pungent satirist than Horace, wrote shortly after A.D. 100. He took as his motto "indignation inspires my poetry" (*facit indignatio versum*). His poems denounce the excess of pride and elegance in Roman society. His language is colorful, often bitter and obscene. One of his richest and wisest satires concerns the vanity of human wishes. After reviewing the foolishness of man, Juvenal gives his advice in a famous epigram: one should pray for "a sound mind in a sound body" (*mens sana in corpore sano*).

Historians

The histories of Rome written during the Republic were usually the work of men directly involved in politics. Under the Empire this changed, for political contest itself had almost come to an end. It was therefore time for someone to look back on the Republic and write a final history of its politics and imperialism. Livy (59 B.C.–A.D. 17) undertook this task during the reign of Augustus, when the decisive political transformation occurred.

Livy narrated Roman history from its legendary beginnings until 9 B.C. Because he usually drew on the work of earlier historians, he was sometimes unable to escape the influence of the myths that had clouded the history of the early Republic.[1] He was well aware of this problem and complained about the poor sources available to him. Livy is at his best when he uses a good source such as Polybius.

Livy's *Roman History* is a kind of prose epic, filled with patriotism and admiration for the great men who had led Rome when the Republic was conquering the Mediterranean. Just as Virgil became the last Roman epic poet, so Livy was the last writer in Latin to attempt a full history of Rome. His work was accepted as authoritative until soon after 1800. Modern criticism has shown how untrustworthy are the legends that Livy accepted for the earliest period of Rome, but there is no denying the rhetorical skill with which he presented his monument to the Roman Republic.

The best Roman historian, and the one who is most like Thucydides in accuracy and seriousness, is Cornelius Tacitus (55?–120?). One early booklet by Tacitus is his *Germania,* a description of the customs of the Germanic tribes and practically the only portrait of the society that was ultimately to rule over large areas of northern Europe.[2] In it Tacitus carefully describes the tribal organization, the weaponry, and the assemblies of the Germans.

The first major work of Tacitus is the *Histories,* in which he treats Roman history from 69, the year of the four emperors, through the death of Domitian in 96. His chief interest was the analysis of characters during revolution. Deeply influenced by satire, the dominant literary form of his age, Tacitus loved to fashion stinging epigrams aimed at members of the governing class, and he treated nearly all his main characters as selfish or corrupt. His disillusioned attitude was partly the result of his being an outsider, probably from southern

---

[1] Livy's usual sources were "annalists," writers of year-by-year histories, often with a strong pro-Roman bias.

[2] The *Germania* is especially valuable because of the absence of other records concerning the early Germans, but it was probably based on literary sources rather than on Tacitus' personal observation.

Gaul; he saw Roman society through the cool eyes of a provincial who became senator and even consul.

His other major work is the *Annals,* which covers the reign of the Julio-Claudian emperors from Tiberius through Nero (14–68). Tacitus looked back at the early Empire from a vantage point in a higher period, and he saw there little but despotism. By this time his style had reached its perfection. His irony found inviting targets in the Julio-Claudian dynasty, and his epigrams are masterpieces of terse brilliance.

A lesser historian, but one who covers much of the same ground as Tacitus, was Suetonius (70?–130?). He held several posts in the civil service under Trajan and Hadrian, and he must have had access to informative documents. His major preserved work is his *Lives of the Caesars,* biographies of the twelve rulers of Rome from Julius Caesar through Domitian, who died in 96. Suetonius had a fine taste for gossip and sexual scandal, but because of his position in the administration he preserves much information that we cannot obtain from Tacitus and other sources.

III. CHANGES IN ANCIENT SOCIETY

The Period of Crisis

For about two centuries the imperial machine that Augustus had designed worked without having to meet a major challenge. Not even such admittedly tyrannical rulers as Nero and Domitian seriously harmed the Empire, and later ages have looked back, perhaps with envy, on the peace and prosperity of this period. But the centuries of the "Roman peace" ended with the death of the Emperor Commodus in 192. In the following years the political balance shifted to the military. Leaders of the Praetorian Guard and the army began to murder emperors

almost at will and to replace them with new rulers, who in turn were murdered one after another. During the third century dozens of emperors claimed the throne, but many of these men were really no more than political gamblers or warlords who for a short time purchased the loyalty of soldiers within the army.

The Roman Senate, which had once been the inspiration and bulwark of the state, had long ago ceased to act with any political determination. The sheer military dominance of the emperors, and probably the effects of two centuries and more of comparative prosperity, had left this body with neither interest nor power to intervene in affairs of state. The emperors assumed more and more dictatorial powers and governed through court favorites, bypassing the Senate. They also removed the Senate's remaining traditional powers, such as commanding legions and governing provinces, and conferred them on equestrians. This weakening of the Senate, which on the whole had supplied a fairly responsible group of public servants, indicates the radical change that was taking place in the political structure.

The economy of the Empire nearly collapsed during this period. Defense costs had risen as raiders plundered the holdings of the Empire on several frontiers. (The historical effect of these invasions will be discussed in the next chapter.) Moreover, the emperors had been supplying the inhabitants of Rome with free food and public games—a fairly effective means of political domination, but a heavy drain on the economy. Adding to these financial problems was a shortage of silver, on which the imperial currency was based. The emperors resorted to depreciating the currency, but this forced people to hoard what silver they had and actually drove more of the metal out of circulation.[3] The result was a disastrous inflation. In fact, experts conclude that during the third cen-

[3] For example, Caracalla (211–217) tried to stabilize the currency by introducing a large new coin, but this soon became nothing but copper dipped in silver.

tury prices in Egypt soared to between fourteen and twenty times their earlier level.

A further problem faced by the government was the increasing reluctance of people to hold civic office. Servants of the emperor in the imperial bureaucracy drew a salary, but traditional civic offices (consul, praetor, and so on down to local offices in towns) paid nothing; thus only men of independent means could seek political careers. The problem was not new; in the second century the Romans had begun a system of "liturgies"—that is, services performed for the state under official orders. Finally, the government was forced to compel people to take office, a step that pointed to the practice, which was to become common in the fourth century, of binding people to their occupations.

It would be confusing to narrate the careers of the emperors who tried to hold the state together through its period of crisis. Many of them were men of little leadership. On the other hand, some of them must have been among the most able rulers in the history of Rome, for otherwise the Empire would have totally disintegrated. It is also difficult to analyze the exact causes of the crisis. Was it a failure of leadership at the highest level? Did the plague that attacked the Empire under Marcus Aurelius so weaken the army that peoples outside the Empire could at last invade the wealthy domains of Rome? However historians balance the causes, they must also consider what was now happening to ancient society.

Slavery

As in most other ancient states, slaves were widely used in the Roman economy, but no earlier society had organized the institution of slavery to such a degree or used slaves in such large numbers. During the late Republic, the number of available slaves increased dramatically, as Rome overran Greece, Asia Minor,

Spain, and Gaul. Julius Caesar reports in his *Gallic War* that he once sold 53,000 Gauls into slavery in a single day.[4] One owner of a large estate, who died in A.D. 8, mentioned in his will that he owned no fewer than 4116 slaves. Of the 7.5 million inhabitants of Italy at the death of Augustus, an estimated 3 million were slaves. It is easy to appreciate how the prospect of a slave uprising terrified the free classes. Slaves were probably not so numerous in other parts of the Empire, but everywhere they constituted a substantial segment of the laboring population.

Many slaves were employed on the latifundia; they were especially suitable as workers in extensive types of agriculture, which required effort but not much skill or commitment. Indeed, the mounting flood of cheap slaves seems to have been decisive in the expansion of the great plantations during the last century of the Roman Republic. Rural slaves were known in legal terminology as the "talking stock," to distinguish them from the "dumb stock," or farm animals. In most places they lived in modest quarters and were more or less properly fed. On the other hand, in Sicily they were often turned loose without shelter to feed off the land. Usually, they labored in gangs under the supervision of a steward, himself a slave; stewards were, however, usually allowed to marry, in order to assure their loyalty and diligence.

Slaves were better treated in the cities, where they were employed in almost every occupation. They served as artisans, hairdressers, hotel keepers, secretaries, bankers, and, of course, personal servants. Slaves from the East, Greeks in particular, commonly tutored the children of the free classes. Slaves supplied much of the entertainment in ancient society. Girls and boys who could sing, dance, or recite were highly valued; there was also active traffic in beautiful young slaves of both sexes, often

---

[4] These Gauls had violated their pledge to surrender and tried to ambush Roman troops; this partly explains Caesar's ferocious response.

for sexual purposes. Gladiators were slaves, and reputedly fought harder because of it. If they prevailed over an opponent, they might win their freedom; if they lost, they forfeited nothing more than a miserable existence. How slaves were treated depended on the kindness, or lack of it, in their owners. Many urban slaves were highly regarded by their masters, who often expressed their affection and gratitude with the gift of freedom. Moreover, slaves were usually allowed to accumulate some property of their own (occasionally including even other slaves); often, their wealth enabled them to buy freedom. As a freedman, the emancipated slave retained ties of dependence to his former owner, but the master's rights were now narrowly prescribed. Along with slaves, freedmen were everywhere found in ancient cities. A freedman did not necessarily suffer from prejudice in his new life: we have seen that the Emperor Claudius made freedmen his private political staff, and the poet Horace, who moved easily in high circles, including that of Augustus himself, was the son of a freedman.

Judged as an economic system, ancient slavery offered certain substantial advantages. It permitted a rational use of labor in relation to land and capital—an optimum combination of what economists call the "factors of production." The owner of a great estate or an urban shop could maintain his staff of workers at the desired size by purchasing new hands when he needed them or by selling superfluous workers. As long as the market in adult slaves remained favorable, he did not have to pay the costs of supporting unproductive children. Nor was he required to maintain aging slaves. The elder Cato (234–149 B.C.), who enjoyed a durable reputation for wisdom among the Romans, advised estate owners to sell at once worn-out plow animals, diseased sheep, broken tools, aged and feeble slaves, "and other useless things."

But in the long run, the slave system of antiquity also revealed certain serious weaknesses, which we must include in the series of causes for the decline of the Empire in the West.

The Dilemmas of Slavery

Rome declined because its economy could no longer support the huge military expenditures needed to defend the frontiers against the ever-threatening invaders. Why was the economy not equal to the task? One principal reason was this: the slave system, in spite of the short-term efficiencies we have already discussed, revealed in the long term certain fatal flaws. In particular it could not satisfactorily resolve two problems that every economy must face: the creation of incentives, to assure that the primary producers will labor hard and well; and the recruitment of additional workers, to replace the aging and the dead.

Especially in the countryside, the principal incentive that bent slaves to their tasks was coercion, or the dread of punishment. For this reason, they were best employed in work that required little skill, diligence, or effort. (Urban slaves, able to acquire property and enjoy some prospect of eventual freedom, were better off.) The association of slavery with physical labor drained work of its dignity and discouraged even freedmen from engaging in "servile" tasks. The low prestige accorded labor also dampened interest in technological innovation. The great minds of the Classical world, so powerful in the speculative arts, were rarely concerned with practical matters, with easing human efforts, with making life less onerous for chattel. Finally, in the belief of most historians, demoralized slaves were poor producers of children, even when they were allowed to marry. Why pass misery down the generations? The Roman estates counted among their gangs of bondsmen some offspring of slaves, but these *vernae,* as they were called, evidently constituted only a minute part of the corps of workers.

Slaves were recruited primarily from two sources: wars of conquest, which resulted in the enslavement of defeated armies and sometimes entire communities; and piracy. But under Augustus and his successors, the tempo of conquests gradually waned, and they ceased altogether from the time of Hadrian. And the government itself struggled long and successfully to suppress piracy and other violations of the Roman peace.

Slaves were the machines of the ancient economy, the basic capital equipment that supported society and the state. Declining numbers of slaves inevitably meant reduced outputs. What would happen if, in our own society, we faced continuously declining numbers of engines or relentlessly shrinking sources of power? To this critical situation, ancient society could not respond by quickly developing labor-saving devices; here, its splendid culture, its grand intellectual traditions, could offer no aid. Society could respond only by providing to the unfree new incentives for working well, new reasons for wanting and rearing children.

One example of this response was the spreading practice of "housing" the slave in the countryside—that is, of providing him with a house, farm, and wife; with her and with their eventual children, he might work the land and enjoy at least part of its produce. The farm he worked and improved was analogous to the wealth acquired by urban slaves. It belonged to his master, but he gained a moral right to its use and to pass it on to his children after him. The numbers of these "housed slaves" multiplied in late antiquity, even as the gangs of landless slaves diminished. This change was clearly in the long-term interest of society, but there were penalties too. From the housed slave, now truly a peasant, the landlord and the state could expropriate in rent and taxes only a limited portion of his output. The effort to provide incentives to the lowest order of society diminished the surplus that might meet the needs of the elites and the state itself. Paradox-

ically, the move to a fairer social system weakened the fiscal resources of the beleaguered Empire.

The trend to freedom was manifest in cities too, where it had begun probably sooner than in rural areas. Highly skilled slaves expected to receive for their services both property and, eventually, freedom. By the time of the Emperor Diocletian, who sought to impose maximum limits on urban salaries, most of the artisans in the imperial cities must have been free.

The Plight of the Poor

Within the free population, contrasts between rich and poor were extreme, and social tensions and violent social uprisings further disturbed the stability of the Empire. In Italy, the spread of the great estates in the last century of the Republic had driven many small cultivators off the land. Many drifted to the Roman metropolis, where bread and circuses, provided free by the government, purchased their docility. In many provinces, too, rural depopulation and the abandonment of cultivated fields had become a major problem in the centuries after Augustus. It has been estimated that one-third of the lands of North Africa passed from cultivation under Augustus' successors. The reasons for the spread of these empty tracts were several: fiscal oppression in the provinces; the taint associated with servile labor; the lure of cities; and, presumably, low birth rates among the poorest rural classes.

Faced with shrinking numbers of cultivators and taxpayers, the Roman government sought desperately to reclaim and resettle the abandoned fields. Marcus Aurelius initiated a policy of settling outsiders on deserted lands within the Empire, even in regions as far removed from the frontier as the Po valley. Emperors or their officials also sought to attract free Roman cultivators back to the countryside. The free cultivator settled on another's land is technically called a *colonus,* and the institutions affecting his tenure are referred to as the *colonate.*

Roman policy toward the *coloni* and other free cultivators was ambivalent and shifting. Their status was determined both by imperial legislation and by customary (also called "vulgar") law, which historians must reconstruct from inscriptions and other records showing private practices. In the customary, or vulgar, law known from North African sources, the *colonus* held the land under favorable terms. He was charged with a light and fixed rent, which he paid to the landlord or *dominus.* He could sell the land he improved or pass it on to his heirs, and he could depart from it at will. This favorable regimen was doubtless characteristic of other provinces too. The imperial legislation, on the other hand, most of which dates from the fourth century, gives a much different picture: the *colonus* was bound to the soil, as were his children after him, and he was subject to the personal jurisdiction of his lord. As envisioned by the emperors, he was already a serf.

This flagrant inconsistency in our sources seems to reflect a basic dilemma in Roman social policy. The long-term interests of society and government dictated that resettlement within family-owned farms should be encouraged. On the other hand, the hard-pressed government could not overlook any source of revenue. Even while favoring resettlement, it frequently resorted to outrageous fiscal practices. It ruthlessly requisitioned food; it forced settlers to pay the taxes of their absent neighbors; it subjugated them to the authority of the great lords, who could be held responsible for collecting from them services and taxes. By the fourth and fifth centuries, under conditions of devastating fiscal oppression, some peasants preferred to flee the Empire rather than face ruin at home.

The plight of the harassed cultivator at times ignited violent social upheavals. In Gaul and northern Spain, for example, peasants known as the Bagaudae rose in revolt against

tax collectors and judges in the third century and were suppressed, but rebelled again with even greater violence in the fifth century, even as the western provinces were succumbing to the invaders. A Russian classical historian of great insight, M. I. Rostovtzeff, maintained that the turmoil of the third century thinly disguised a class war. The peasant masses, notably those settled in the Illyrian provinces, rejected the traditional leadership of Rome. Because they filled the frontier legions, they were able to raise up their low-born commanders to imperial dignity. Several prominent rulers of the third century—Aurelian, who rebuilt the walls of Rome (270–275), and Diocletian—were Illyrians of rural or at least humble origins. Rostovtzeff has been faulted for seeing in the "revolution" of the third century too close an analogy with the downfall of tsarist Russia in 1917. Was the Roman Empire, like the Russian, engulfed by an uprising of the lower classes? The model is assuredly too simple. But we can hardly deny that social and class tensions and a violent rejection of Roman leadership in the provinces were powerful forces, working to undermine the Empire.

The Problem of the Nations

Rome was surprisingly successful in extending and maintaining its rule over many nations (*gentes:* the word means tribes, foreign peoples, as well as clans within the citizen body) and cultures. Its success rested on two strategies. Incorporation within the Empire and loyalty to it guaranteed to the nations peace, protection, and justice. And the elites of the various nations enjoyed wide autonomy and a growing participation in the affairs of the Empire. Local leaders thus continually entered the imperial system and often brought the people with them. Many regions remained loyal to the imperial idea and faithfully maintained Roman culture, or their version of it, long after the Empire itself had passed away.

But Roman practices, and Greco-Roman culture itself, did not always appeal to the broad masses of the Empire. In the East, outside the great cities where Hellenistic culture prevailed, the largely Semitic peoples retained their own languages, cultures, and surely, too, resentments. In the Christian Book of Revelation, which views the world from a Semitic perspective, Rome, "that great city that bears rule over the rulers of the earth," is viciously depicted as a scarlet whore, committing fornication with kings, corrupting peoples, persecuting the just. There is no mistaking this raging hatred of the Roman name.

In western North Africa, Berber cultural nationalism seems to have inflamed from the fourth century onward the protracted war of the *circumcelliones;* the word means literally "those who prowl around storehouses," perhaps in the sense of rural guerrillas. The revolts of the Bagaudae in Gaul and Spain may have reflected the ethnic dissatisfactions of the Celts as well as the social protest of peasants. Other examples could be given of the restlessness of nations under Roman rule.

The problem of the nations extended even beyond the imperial frontiers; there dwelt the peoples whom the Romans, as the Greeks before them, called "barbarians." We shall view them more closely in the following chapter. From the reign of Hadrian, Rome clearly had not the strength to conquer them, but neither could it ignore them. For some two centuries the frontier defenses (the *limes*) kept out organized barbarian armies. But it did not exclude (nor was it designed to exclude) the continuous, peaceful penetration of barbarians into the Empire. The growing *penuria hominum,* "shortage of people," within the Empire, sucked the barbarians in, to work deserted fields and fill other vacant posts in society. The barbarian migrants had little understanding of, or sympathy for, the grand ideals of Rome. They prepared the way for later, larger, violent intrusions across the imperial frontiers.

Rome could never have built and preserved its vast Empire by material force alone. It had to hold out to the classes and nations of the Empire splendid social and cultural ideals that would hold their allegiance when arms could not. The failure of the Roman system was therefore not exclusively military, economic, or political. It was spiritual too; Rome fell when classes and nations rejected the values with which it had sought to woo them.

Cultural Disintegration

The Greco-Roman tradition, which was the spiritual cement of ancient society and of the Empire, succeeded for two centuries and more in maintaining among the nations morale, loyalty, and peace. Essentially, the promise of Classical civilization under the Empire was universal peace. But this message carried conviction only in times of prosperity and success. Amid peaceful conditions, individuals could pursue personal fulfillment as Classical poets and moralists had defined it. The tradition of Greco-Roman thought identified fulfillment with the cultivation and perfection of every human faculty or power—physical or athletic, literary, intellectual, artistic, or aesthetic. The wise man must of course seek his destiny in this life; the hereafter held out no certain hopes. He must live his life according to nature, which was, in the opinion of most ancient philosophers, the best leader, the *optima dux*. In responding to human needs, nature was both sufficient and benevolent. Even death, for all its mysteries, presented no terrors to the wise. Nature treats us well and fairly throughout our life. Will Nature change character and be mean to us in the end?

In spite of its manifest appeal, the cultural system of Classical antiquity had some crucial weaknesses. It spoke preeminently to the privileged and the gifted, the elites of ancient society. Even as they failed to develop a technology that might have eased the labors of slaves and the poor, so also the intellectual leaders of the age could point out little meaning in the lives of the unfree, the unhealthy, the disadvantaged, those without property, those without talents.

Moreover, during the last centuries of the Empire, pagan thinkers were clearly losing the capacity to examine, elaborate, and develop their own ideals. They could no longer guide or inspire. After the Augustan Age Roman civilization produced fewer original thinkers. A certain morose resignation pervades their writings. The earth was in decline, and history was approaching its term; everything worth accomplishing had been done, every limit had been reached. Already in the final decades of the Republican epoch, the Epicurean philosopher Lucretius, in his great poem *On the Nature of the Universe,* proclaimed that the earth "can scarce grow anything, for all our toil." "All," he continues, "is gradually decaying, nearing the end, worn out by the long span of years."

According to this oft-reiterated theme, there were no new worlds to conquer, no beckoning and challenging frontiers, no new destinies to be pursued. Christian authors fully shared this opinion, that life on earth offered nothing, challenged no one. In a remarkable passage, Tertullian, the first major Christian writer to use the Latin language, describes the state of the world in about 200:

> Everything has been visited, everything known, everything exploited. Now pleasant estates obliterate the famous wilderness areas of the past. Plowed fields have replaced the forests; domesticated animals have dispersed wild life. Beaches are plowed, mountains smoothed and swamps drained. There are as many cities as, in former years, there were houses. Islands do not frighten [settlers], nor cliffs deter. Everywhere there are buildings, everywhere people, everywhere communities, everywhere life.[5]

[5] Tertulliani Opera monastica, *Corpus Christianorum,* Series Latina, II (1954), p. 827, tr. D. Herlihy.

In stating that the earth was excessively burdened with people and their works, Tertullian shows an acute lack of information. Even as he wrote, the emperors were settling foreigners on deserted fields and recruiting them for their depleted armies. But his attitude alone concerns us here. Weighed down by the sense that every earthly limit had been reached, both pagans and Christians were psychologically ill-equipped to propose and to lead major social reforms. The pagans, who could see no destiny for mankind beyond the present life, were particularly muted and ineffectual. There is little wonder that they abandoned the rostra of society to the new group of vocal Christians. For Christians triumphantly affirmed that a further and unfulfilled destiny did indeed await mankind, but that man could only achieve it in life after death.

IV. CHRISTIANITY

The triumph of Christianity within the Roman Empire represents one of the most remarkable cultural revolutions in history. The victory of the new religion is the more extraordinary, since the values it preached were opposed to those of classical thought. The great pagan philosophers had for the most part taught that the good life must be sought in the present world. *Carpe diem:* "seize the day"; there is no surety about tomorrow, no hope at all in an imagined life beyond death. To Christians, on the other hand, this visible world was a place of exile, a vale of tears through which we must pass, as we hurry toward our homeland in heaven. Life was a pilgrimage in a foreign, hostile, hated land.

Cultural systems, if they are to survive, must discover and proclaim meaning and purpose in the varied events of life, the joyous and the sorrowful. Classical values, as we have mentioned, were failing to reach important sectors of ancient society: the slaves, the disadvantaged, the subjugated, the losers. There is little wonder that the inhabitants of the Empire sought reason for their existence in new cultural and religious movements.

The Mystery Religions

Part of this spreading religious ferment was the growing popularity of the so-called mystery religions, "salvationist eschatologies." They were eschatologies because they claimed to explain the "last things" (Greek, *eskhata*), the ultimate purposes of human life. They were salvationist because they offered to their adherents personal salvation, life after death. Their common formula for salvation was the association of the believer, through a mystical rite, with a hero who had conquered death. Thus, the cult of Mithras, which enjoyed particular popularity within the Roman army, required that the believer bathe in the blood of a slaughtered ox. Other heroes, conquerors of death, were Orpheus, Adonis, and Osiris.

Jesus was such a hero; he too claimed the faith of his followers because he had risen from the dead: he too (or only he, as Christians believed) had conquered death. But the cult of Jesus also differed from the other mystery religions. Salvation for the Christian required ritual, mysteries, sacraments; but it required too an upright, moral life. The Christian religion was from its origins a complex mixture of ritual and ethics, sacraments and commandments. Then, too, the redeeming Jesus was a historical person, who had come upon earth "in the fullness of time," as Christian texts affirmed. All other cultic heroes were mythical figures, who may never have walked the earth. Finally, the cult of Jesus drew decisive benefits from its close associations with the long Judaic tradition and its imposing body of sacred writings. In particular, Christians claimed that passages in the Old Testament actually foretold the coming of Jesus.

The Jews in the Roman Empire

The Jewish people had been subjects of the Persian Empire until the Greek and Macedonian invasion of the East swept away Persian rule. In the Hellenistic Age they were governed mainly by the Seleucid kings of Syria. During the Syrian rule one event inspired them to a strong reaffirmation of their faith. This was the ill-advised decision of Antiochus IV, the king of Syria, to impose the worship of Greek gods on the Jews. He installed a statue of Olympian Zeus in the sacred temple in Jerusalem and prohibited several Jewish religious practices.

A rebellion of the Jews, led by Judas Maccabaeus, forced the Seleucids to concede religious freedom in Jerusalem. The temple was cleansed and rededicated in 165 B.C., an event that the Jewish feast of Hanukkah commemorates. Eventually, the Jews, led by the family of Judas, gained independence from Syria and established their own kingdom; but in 64 B.C. the Roman general Pompey dissolved this kingdom and the Jews fell under the control of Rome. As Julius Caesar was making his way to supreme power, he was assisted by a Jewish force in 47; and he rewarded the Jews with a reduction of tribute and exemption from military service. Augustus renewed these privileges. Also, the Romans agreed that Jews could not be called to court on the Sabbath and that they could continue to worship in their synagogues, even in Rome itself. Thus, despite the loss of their political freedom, the Jews enjoyed at least some measure of toleration.

For some time Judea, now a small region in the south of Palestine, was ruled by client-kings, leaders who pledged loyalty to Rome; one of them was the notorious Herod the Great (40–4 B.C.). Herod was a harsh dictator, hated by the Jews, but he did maintain order. After his death Rome was forced to take a more direct role in administering Judea: this was done through a series of civil servants, usually called procurators.

Constant quarrels between the Roman officers and the Jews reached a climax in A.D. 66 when Jerusalem burst into rebellion. This great Jewish War, as the Romans called it, lasted until 70; the Romans then entered Jerusalem and demolished the temple, except for one outer wall, known as the Wailing Wall, at which the Jews were allowed to pray once a year. The Romans did not at first try to suppress the Jewish faith itself; but they finally did attempt this after another Jewish rebellion (132–134). Nonetheless, Judaism retained its coherence and strength, and it assured its people that God would one day send them their redeemer.

The Sects

The plight of the Jews under Roman rule raised religious tensions among them; numerous sects appeared, each advancing its own interpretation of the common Jewish traditions. Among them were the Sadducees, who advocated strict adherence to Jewish law, but rejected belief in an afterlife, in angels, and even (if we can believe their enemies) in a personal, redeeming God. The more liberal Pharisees believed in a life after death and in angels; they accepted gentile converts, and were willing to make some modifications of Jewish law to allow some accommodation with Greco-Roman culture.[6] They were popular preachers in the synagogue. The New Testament, in accusing them of hypocrisy—"whitened sepulchers" it calls them—has permanently and unfairly sullied their name.

The Jewish sect that in recent years has attracted the most concentrated attention is the Essenes. The Essenes formed an ascetic community that sought isolation from the world. In 1947, several rolls of leather and papyrus were found in Qumran, a village near the Dead Sea in Jordan. These Dead Sea Scrolls, which are still being found in the region, have given historians an extraordinary view of the beliefs and practices of this pious Jewish sect in the decades immediately preceding the appearance of Jesus.

The most important scrolls are hymns and guides to moral living. The writings mention a Teacher of Righteousness who had died before the scrolls were written and they also predict that three more leaders will save the Jews: a prophet, a Messiah of Aaron, and a Messiah of Israel. Until the day of salvation, the members of a community must observe the laws included in a document called the Manual of Discipline.

The relations of the Essenes to Jesus and the Christians remain obscure. The New Testament mentions them not at all. Essene beliefs seem to reflect Persian (Zoroastrian) influences. A Wicked Priest, serving the powers of darkness, contends with the Teacher of Righteousness, the champion of the forces of light. This pronounced religious dualism is not a dominant theme, although occasionally present, in early Christian texts. On the other hand, the asceticism of the Qumran community and its withdrawal from worldly entanglements anticipate the style of life of the first Christians. And the very existence of the Essenes shows the intensity of religious expectations within Judaism on the eve of Jesus' career.

Origins of Christianity

The historical investigation of Jesus[7] and his message, the "search for the historical Jesus" in the phrase of a modern theologian, presents formidable difficulties. Jesus wrote nothing at all. We can view him only through the writings of others—the writers of the Gospels in the

---

[6] The Latin word *gentiles* (akin to *gens;* see p. 116 means foreigners, thus those born outside Jewish traditions.

[7] "Jesus" was his name: after his death he was called *ho Christos,* "the anointed one" or the Messiah, by his followers. Thus the familiar names "Christ" and "Jesus Christ," though universally used, are not historically correct; and "Jesus, called the Christ" is cumbersome.

New Testament, who had not known him personally, and early converts such as St. Paul, who formed the first Christian communities. Jesus, who often called himself the Son of Man, invited his followers to reflect upon the meaning of his life: "What do men say of the Son of Man? Who do they think he is?" (Matthew 16.13). We can study what some men thought of Jesus; but we cannot penetrate the abiding mystery of the man.

The first Christians recorded nothing of their memories and impressions of Jesus until probably two decades after his death, perhaps because they expected his imminent return in triumph and glory. The oldest parts of the New Testament are the Pauline Epistles, and Paul himself never knew Jesus personally. The youngest books of the New Testament—the Gospel according to St. John and the Book of Revelation—date probably from the 90s A.D. Even within the books of the New Testament, the authors concentrate on the religious message and the miracles of Jesus, not on his whole life in chronological order. It is thus impossible to write his complete biography; of his life as a youth and a young adult we know almost nothing.

As his followers eventually recalled his career, Jesus was born of a virgin named Mary, betrothed but not yet married to a man named Joseph, "in the days of King Herod," at a date that modern scholarship would set at 7 B.C. At about the age of thirty, he was publicly baptized by an ascetic preacher called John the Baptist, quite possibly an Essene, and he entered upon a public life of teaching. In the Sermon on the Mount, the best summary of his ethical principles, he affirmed that the blessings of God went to the poor, the meek, the pure, those who make peace, those who seek justice. He taught that true prayer and piety were movements of the spirit, not public gestures designed to win society's acclaim. But he also engaged in ritual practices ("sacraments" in later terminology), which implied that his followers

formed an organized community or cult. At his last supper with his apostles, he urged them to continue in his memory the ritual consumption of consecrated bread and wine, which he identified with his own body. He called himself the Son of Man, the Son of God, and a king, but affirmed that his kingdom was not of this world. And he promised eternal life to those who accepted him. According to our texts, he worked miracles to show the truth of his mission. Christian sources further say that he was accused by the Jewish high priests of blasphemy. He was then crucified by order of the Roman governor Pontius Pilate (probably about A.D. 30). His followers were convinced that after three days in the tomb he rose again, and later ascended bodily into heaven. But he would, in their belief, come again, to save his followers and establish his kingdom.

Paul and His Mission

After Jesus departed from his followers, they initially formed only one of many sects within the larger body of Judaism. They called themselves Christians, followers of the new Messiah. They seem to have had no clear notion of the persons—Jews only or gentiles too?—to whom he had directed his message; nor did they know what and where the kingdom was that he had promised them. The man who clarified these crucial issues, reformed Christianity into a distinct and autonomous religion, and infused it with burning missionary fervor was a Jew from Tarsus, Saul, or in the name he chiefly used after his conversion, Paul.

Paul is by far the best known of all the early Christian teachers; the book of the Acts of the Apostles is largely concerned with his career, and we have his own epistles. He enjoyed the privileges of Roman citizenship, knew Greek, and was evidently a learned man. As a pious Jew, he initially considered the followers of Jesus blasphemous, and even aided in their early persecution. He held the cloaks of some irate Jews who stoned to death a man named Stephen, now regarded as the first martyr of the Christian Church. Then, as he journeyed to Damascus to organize still further persecutions, he was visited on the road by an apparition of the risen Jesus, who asked him to explain his hatred (A.D. ca. 38). Paul then accepted Christianity. He began to preach in Damascus, and from there he traversed the Roman world, organizing Christian communities and advising and encouraging their members through letters (see Map 5.5). He began the mission of preaching to the gentiles, which would eventually spread Christianity across the Empire.

In his writings Paul elaborated several points of doctrine that have endured throughout the history of Christianity. He developed, in other words, the first coherent Christian theology. He rejected the conservative policy of some early Christians who would have restricted the preaching of the new faith to Jews alone. All peoples ought to worship the true God and hear the message of his only Son. "Is he the God of the Jews only? Is he not also of the Gentiles? Yes, of the Gentiles also" (Ro-

MAP 5.5. THE SPREAD OF CHRISTIANITY

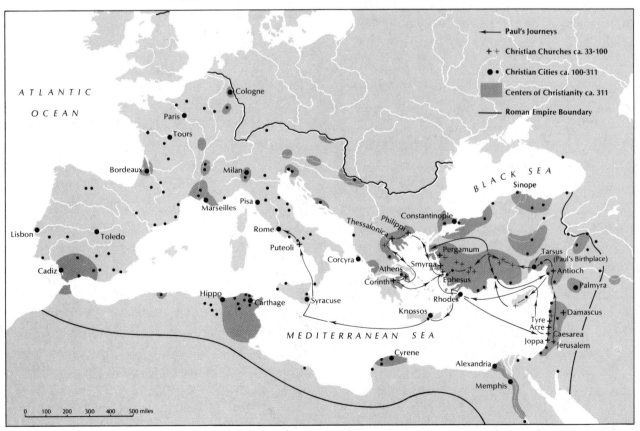

mans 3.29). To facilitate their conversion, Paul did not require Christian gentiles to be circumcised or to follow the Mosaic law.

Paul also began the theological exploration of the notion of grace—the special power by which God redeems sinners. The core of the Christian revelation was initially (as far as we can judge the matter) not so much an idea at all as an emotion, a hope that there was life beyond life. In elaborating a coherent view of the nature of man and the providence of God, Paul and later Christian teachers were deeply indebted to the Jewish tradition, of which they felt themselves the direct heirs and successors. To ancient Israel, they owed their concept of one God and their notions of creation, the fall of Adam and Eve, and the early history of mankind. They also accepted the view that God the creator had not abandoned his creation. Implicit in Old Testament history is the assumption of a return by God to his creation, to achieve, through the Jewish people, a special providence for mankind. God comes back to his creation in order, as it were, to recreate, to undo the damage caused by Adam's disobedience.

To Paul, this idea of a return by God to a humanity enslaved by sin explained at least partially the mystery of Jesus' mission. Through one man (Adam) sin had entered the world, and with sin, death. The offense of one man had condemned all persons of every generation. But also through one man (Jesus), through his willing sacrifice, grace once more abounded, and many would be saved. By nature, Adam was founder and head of the human race. By grace, Jesus was its second founder, its restorer and redeemer.

Paul's writings and thought draw attention to some differences between Jews and early Christians. First and foremost, Paul had to redefine the notion of the Messiah. For Jews, as we have seen, this leader would some day arrive and create another kingdom on earth. But Paul could point to the words of Jesus before Pilate: "My kingdom is not of this world" (John 18.36). To Paul, the kingdom over which Jesus would preside was a spiritual realm, to which one gained admission through faith in Jesus.

In the new Christian perspective shaped by Paul, the universe was organized on two principles: an order of nature, established by original creation but faulted by sin; and an order of grace, founded in God's willingness to save mankind in spite of Adam's fall and brought to fulfillment with the coming of Jesus. The reconciliation of these two powers of nature and of grace, and the determination of their purposes and their limits, have remained over the centuries central problems of Christian theology.

The Church in the Roman Empire

The death of St. John about A.D. 100 brings to an end the so-called apostolic age, the period of origins of the Christian Church. From then until the reign of the Emperor Constantine, the Church remained an illegal, sometimes persecuted sect within the Empire. But it still succeeded in increasing its numbers and in developing remarkably both its theology and its government. Its numbers, to be sure, continued to form a small minority within the Empire, probably never exceeding 10 percent of the population. But, by about 300, the Christian message had penetrated nearly everywhere in the Roman world. At the council of Arles in southern France, held in 314, three bishops from distant Britain made an appearance. But the chief centers of Christian belief remained the regions of the Middle East; among them, Asia Minor (modern Turkey) held a special prominence.

The reasons for the Christian advance were many. The Roman peace facilitated communication and the exchange of ideas. Also, through the movement known as the Diaspora (Greek for "dispersion"), Jews were now scattered far and wide; Christians moved easily from community to community and found a convenient forum for their preaching in Jewish synagogues. By claiming for their own the sacred writings of the Jews (the Old Testament, as Christians call it), they appropriated a rich, impressive collection of religious law and literature. They also pointed to a historical founder, who was to them the central figure in a total explanation of human history. Like the Jews, they made no compromises with paganism—either with pagan polytheism or pagan morality. Above all, they claimed to have an explanation for suffering and misfortune—evils, to be sure, in the pagan view, but benefits, in God's gracious governance, for those who must bear them. The meek, they promised, in a future life and another world, would inherit the earth.

Many converts to the new faith were from lower classes in society. A pagan, writing about 177–180, referred sarcastically to the "superstition" of wool carders, shoemakers, and launderers. But even as he wrote, Christianity was making inroads among the intellectuals, many of whom found the teachings of the pagans stale and unconvincing.

Persecutions

Toward the many religious sects of the Empire, the Roman government adopted, on the whole, a policy of toleration. It asked only that veneration be shown on official occasions to the "genius" (spirit) of Rome, to the traditional gods, and to the persons of deceased and deified emperors. This civic religion asked for little more than a public declaration of loyalty and patriotism, but the Christians, as the Jews before them, refused to make even this small compromise with polytheism. As a result, they earned the hatred and contempt of numerous pagans, who viewed them as enemies of the human race. In 64, the Emperor Nero perpe-

trated the first official persecution of the Christians in Rome. He falsely accused them of setting fire to parts of the city. The opprobrium in which Christians were held made them convenient scapegoats.

Sporadic persecutions, the severity of which is difficult to judge, and long periods of peace marked the history of the Church into the third century. Then only, amid general social crisis, did some emperors attempt a systematic suppression of the Christians. Decius in 250–251, Valerian in 257–260, and above all Diocletian and his successors in 303–313, sought to extirpate the Christian name; their concern with this menace to the state was a tribute to its now established strength. The persecutions probably cost the lives of only a small percentage of the Christians in the Empire, but they did create a list of venerated Christian martyrs. The cult of saints, thereafter an integral part of Christian piety, began originally as a cult of martyrs. And the death of these few but notable members inspired the Christian community with constancy and pride and impressed even pagan observers. Tertullian was right in his judgment that the blood of martyrs was the seed of the Church.

The Conversion of Constantine

The conversion of the Emperor Constantine to Christianity in 312 marked a revolution in the Church and in its relations with the Roman Empire. The circumstances attending this dramatic event are obscure. In the traditional pious story, first appearing in 318–320, Constantine had a dream on the evening before he was to fight a rival emperor for supremacy over Italy, at the Milvian Bridge near Rome. He was instructed in the dream to decorate the shields of his soldiers with the monogram of Christ: "In this sign you shall conquer." Constantine won the battle and recognized the divine power in the name of Christ.

Constantine's conversion was a political as

well as a psychological event. Many of his subjects were now Christians, and the Christian Church had shown itself strong enough to survive persecution. In modern terminology, Constantine was trying to bring the opposition into the government. As emperor of what was still a pagan state, he continued to use pagan titles and symbols on his coinage. He seems to have accepted the cult of Christ as one among many sources of divine help. Only gradually did he recognize its claim to be the true faith. Just before his death in 337 he received baptism from the bishop Eusebius of Nicomedia.

In 313, at a conference held at Milan with a pagan coemperor named Licinius, Constantine extended complete freedom of worship to the Christians and ordered the return of their confiscated goods. This misnamed "Edict of Milan" (the official document was issued some months later and not at Milan) ended the age of persecutions. Other favors followed: churches could own property and enjoyed exemptions from certain taxes; bishops were allowed to judge the legal disputes of the members of their congregations, and their decisions were binding. Christianity did not become the official or established religion of the Empire until Theodosius the Great outlawed heresy (381) and closed the pagan temples (391). But the Church had already acquired a privileged juridical status that it would retain, in many Western lands, until the eighteenth and nineteenth centuries.

This leaf, dated 390–400, is part of the last flowering of paganism. A priestess of Bacchus, at a marriage ceremony, is shown taking a bit of incense to use in the ceremony. During this decade paganism was officially abolished in favor of Christianity in the Empire. This leaf is matched by another in the Cluny Museum, Paris.
(Photo: Victoria and Albert Museum, London. [Crown Copyright Reserved])

This fresco of Adam and Eve is from an underground catacomb in Rome where early Christians met for refuge during the persecutions.
(Photo: The Granger Collection)

Dogma and Government

The Christians within the Roman Empire did not hasten to elaborate a systematic theology, or to develop a systematic government of the Church. Hope in a life after death, not learning or law, was the authentic spirit of the movement. Still, the early Christians inherited from their Jewish origins a strong sense of community. They viewed themselves as the new Israel, members of a holy nation, a chosen people, facing an unbelieving, hostile world. This sense of unity and separateness provided the foundation for a constitution for the Church and for taking fixed dogmatic positions in regard to fundamental beliefs. Usually, the Christian community did not bother to define these matters of dogma or of discipline until the outbreak of disputes threatened its internal unity and peace. The losers in these disputes, if they did not amend their beliefs, were regarded as heretics. The rise and resolution of these controversies forced the orthodox to refine their beliefs. The history of dogmatic and constitutional development in the early Church is related to the history of heresies.

An early dispute was with the Gnostics, beginning even before the year 100 and long persisting. Gnosticism in fact antedates the origins of Christianity, and was more an independent religion than a Christian heresy. The essence of its beliefs was that the mastery of special knowledge (*gnosis*) assured salvation. The Gnostics proceeded to elaborate complicated myths, which constituted the gnosis needed for salvation. They further attempted to incorporate the history of Jesus on earth into their mythological systems. According to modern reconstructions of Gnostic thought, they stated that Jesus was a man into whom miraculous, redeeming powers had descended from above. The divine power in Jesus was, to Gnostics, the anointed one, or the Christ; this power departed from Jesus at his crucifixion. Thus they held that Jesus himself was neither divine nor the son of God. Against this, such orthodox fathers as Ignatius of Antioch in the second century reaffirmed the historical reality of the divine Jesus; his sacrifice was the true redeeming act by which God sacrificed his son for the sake of man.

A heresy that touched on the character of the Christian revelation was that of Marcion, bishop of the town of Sinope in Asia Minor, who taught about the middle of the second century. He was a gifted organizer who attracted followers from Mesopotamia to Africa.

Marcion drew on dualist principles and condemned the God of the Old Testament as the god of darkness, and the Testament itself as a record of abominations. Even among the books of the New Testament, he accepted as binding only the Gospel of Luke and the Epistles of St. Paul.

Another bishop from Asia Minor, Montanus (about 150–200), raised issues of ecclesiastical government. He maintained that certain living believers were prophets who were continuously receiving direct inspiration from the Holy Spirit. Women were prominent among the prophets, and the belief eventually won the allegiance of the great North African writer Tertullian. The movement asked the question: Who should rule the Christian congregations—prophets, who might expect continuing new revelations, or priests, who could only interpret a past and closed deposit of faith?

Christians who accepted standard doctrines of the Church branded these variations in belief as heresy (Greek *hairesis,* "choice"—that is, a wrong choice); the word "schism" (from Greek *schizein,* to split) referred to a sect that would not accept the authority of the regular clergy. Since these heresies have vanished over the centuries, one might well ask: What is their historical importance? The answer is that they stimulated the early Church to redefine its positions. In an age of persecutions, the Church could not tolerate such intellectual luxuries as variations from the accepted faith. Out of the turmoil and disagreement, the Church emerged stronger, even though the price was sometimes the blunt suppression of sincerely held opinions.

Orthodox theologians of the second century, such as Justin, Irenaeus, and Tertullian, replied decisively to Marcion's attempt to eject many writings from the Scriptures. The Church defined its canon of sacred writings to include, in effect, the modern Bible. The Church also declared that the age of divine inspiration had come to an end. This statement was meant to silence the claims of the followers of Montanus, or Montanists, and their orgies of prophecy. All the truths needed for salvation, the Church now said, were complete with the work of St. John, the last inspired author. There was no need for new revelations. In the fourth century the Church refused to accept certain other writings, calling them the Apocrypha (obscure or unclear writings); these include the Gospels of Thomas and of Peter.

More significant still was the development of a formal government within the Church. Evidence from the first century indicates that James, a brother (or half-brother) of Jesus, was the recognized head of the Christians in Jerusalem. During this period, too, we meet the terms "bishop" (*episkopos,* "overseer") and "priest" (*presbuteros,* "elder"), which at first were nearly synonymous. Then, in the second century, the bishop became leader of a group of priests, and priests in turn presided over groups of the faithful. Deacons, a lower rank, also appeared; they were responsible for collecting donations, distributing charities, and managing the material affairs of the community. It is interesting to note that women too enjoyed considerable prominence, which they later lost, in the administration of early churches; they formed recognized orders of widows and virgins, and served as deaconesses.

Slowly but surely the bishops grew in power. They gained the right to appoint priests, basing their claims on the doctrine of apostolic succession. This doctrine holds that Jesus appointed the original Apostles, who were his immediate followers; they in turn appointed bishops, who could thus trace their appointment back to Jesus himself. Bishops assumed the right to define doctrine, maintain discipline among their followers, and oversee morals. This political structure gave Christianity a stable administration that no other ancient mystery religion enjoyed. More important from the point of view of the Romans was that the Church had a government that paralleled, and even rivaled, that of the state. Rome considered this unacceptable until Christianity became a favored religion.

In the West, the number of bishops remained small; thus bishops obtained power over fairly large areas. Those in cities with the largest Christian communities—Rome, Alexandria, Antioch—were the most influential and claimed superior authority. Finally the bishop of Rome, the imperial capital, became the head of the Church in the West. The general name for a bishop was *papa,* or father, but eventually the bishop of Rome was the only one who could call himself pope. The development of papal authority will be discussed in the next chapter.

Thus by about 300 the Church had acquired the characteristics that it was to preserve through the Middle Ages and beyond: faith in a historical redeemer, a canon of sacred books, and a hierarchic government based on the authority of bishops.

Donatists and Arians

The conversion of Constantine and the peace of the Church within the Empire did not bring theological peace. On the contrary, theological controversy mounted in intensity.

In 303, in proclaiming the last persecution of the Christians, Diocletian had ordered priests to surrender their sacred books. Those "traitors" (*traditores*—literally, those who "delivered" the Scriptures) earned the lasting hatred of the more steadfast Christians. At the end of the persecutions in 313, a party of zealous Christians in North Africa, led by a bishop named Donatus, declared that the traitors, even if repentant, had forever lost membership in the Church; all the sacraments they had ever administered—all baptisms, marriages, ordinations, and the like—were worthless. Since the traitors were many, acceptance of the Donatist program would have brought chaos and

revolution to the African church. Moderate Christians won the support of Constantine, who tried to suppress the Donatists by force.

The result was violent schism, which mounted on occasion to civil war. Refusing to accept the rule of traitors, the Donatists established their own bishops and hierarchy. To explain this zeal, modern historians have argued that the movement was in fact an expression of Berber nationalism or an uprising of the oppressed peasantry against the exploitation of the cities. In any case, the schism was still not healed when North Africa was overrun by the barbarian Vandals in 429 and 430.

In response to the Donatists, the orthodox Church determined that the sacraments conferred grace on the recipients *ex opere operato,* "from the work having been worked," automatically, as it were. The spiritual state of the officiating priests did not matter. This remained the accepted position until the issue was raised again in the theological controversies accompanying the Protestant Reformation.

Arius was a priest of Alexandria in Egypt. At some time between 318 and 323 he began to teach that Jesus was not coequal with the Father in the Trinity, but was begotten by him in time: "There was a time when he [Jesus] was not." Arius, in sum, wished to emphasize the monotheistic as opposed to the trinitarian aspects of Christian theology. His teachings raised a furor in Egypt and soon beyond its borders. To restore peace among the theologians, Constantine summoned the first "ecumenical" council (that is, representing the entire inhabited world) of the Christian Church, which met at Nicaea in Asia Minor in May 325. With Constantine in attendance, the council condemned Arius, and in the Nicene Creed—the first authoritative declaration of the principal tenets of the Christian faith—it declared that Jesus was coeternal with the Father, and of one substance with him. The pronouncement hardly placated the Arians, and in the years following Nicaea they spread their teachings widely in the Empire and even among the Goths settled beyond its borders.

The dispute over the nature of the Trinity inspired further speculations—and new heresies—about the nature of Jesus' humanity. Not until the Council of Chalcedon (held in 451 and regarded as the fourth ecumenical council) was the theology of Jesus clearly defined. He was one person with two natures joined in union. He was both true man and true God. As man, he was authentically the son of Mary, and hence a fitting representative of the human race; as God, he was coequal with the Father and had reigned with him and would reign with him eternally. This definition has since remained the belief of orthodox Christians.

The theological turmoil of the fourth and fifth centuries indicates that Christian thinkers were applying the subtleties of Classical philosophy to the deepest mysteries of their faith. Christianity and Classical culture had come into intimate, even explosive, contact and on the highest philosophical levels.

The Church and Classical Culture

Christian writers had consistently pretended to disparage the learning and literature of the Classical world, which were filled, in their estimation, with indecencies, lies, and absurdities. "What has Athens to do with Jerusalem?" demanded Tertullian. But Christians remained indebted to pagan intellectual traditions. They had no choice. The schools of antiquity were all pagan, as were the basic grammars and texts, the authoritative models of argument and style. Moreover, Christianity was a religion based on a book, and the theologians who interpreted the sacred page had to master the arts of exegesis (interpretation), of which the pagans were the accomplished masters. Finally, to defend the faith against pagan detractors, Christian apologists had to master the art of rhetoric; they

had to use the arsenal of pagan learning. As St. Augustine urged, Christians were allowed, like the ancient Israelites, to carry off the treasures of the Egyptians (that is, the learning of the pagans) in order to place them at the service of the one true God. This Christian accommodation with pagan learning had decisive repercussions. Nearly all the texts of the great pagan authors have reached us in copies made by Christians. They preserved them because they believed they would be useful in Christian education and theology. Paradoxically, these outspoken enemies of pagan values were instrumental in the survival of a rich cultural heritage, which they claimed to hate.

The Fathers of the Church

Christianity became the chief religion of Europe partly because it reached the people through the languages and thought of Greco-Roman civilization. Even before the birth of Jesus, Greek-speaking Jews in Alexandria had translated the Old Testament from Hebrew into Greek; this translation is called the Septuagint because it was supposedly made by seventy-two scholars (Greek *septuaginta,* "seventy"). Priests and scholars in the early centuries of Christianity used this version and seldom referred to the original Hebrew text. The New Testament, also written in Greek, was another vehicle that brought Christianity to the educated public in the Western world. Following this body of sacred writing came an ocean of commentary, persuasion, and teaching that goes under the collective name Writings of Fathers of the Church. The study of their thought is patristics (Greek and Latin *pater,* "father").

Several Greek fathers wrote in Alexandria, the successor to Athens as the intellectual center of the Greek world. Clement of Alexandria (150?–215?) was a scholar and teacher thoroughly familiar with Classical Greek literature, which he often cites in his writings. In his *Protrepticus,* an address to the Greeks, he tries to persuade them to give up their religions in favor of Christianity; he criticizes pagan myths as irrational and immoral (as Plato had earlier done in his *Republic,* Book 2). Another work of Clement, his *Stromateis* ("Miscellanies"), is a rambling collection of various studies, also trying to prove the superiority of Christianity to pagan philosophy.

Origen (185?–255?) was a pupil of Clement and held various positions in the Church. He was repeatedly a victim of persecution and, for obscure reasons, was deposed from his position as presbyter in Alexandria. He is considered the most influential of all fathers, except perhaps Augustine, and both the volume and the profound scholarship of his writings were a wonder of late antiquity. He worked especially on the exact text of the Scriptures, by careful comparison between the original Hebrew and the Greek Septuagint. His chief work in defense of Christianity is *Against Celsus,* in which he answers, point by point, the arguments offered by one Celsus in favor of pagan thought. Origen also wrote voluminous commentaries on the various books of the Bible.

Another highly influential Greek father was Eusebius of Caesarea (260?–340?). Like Clement and Origen, he wrote a defense of Christianity, his *Praeparatio Evangelica.* Although Eusebius was sympathetic to the doctrines of Arius, he renounced them at the council of Nicaea in 325. His greatest and most original work was a history of the Church, which became the model for other such histories in later times. Eusebius was considered the most learned man of his time, a reputation that he justified in his *Chronicle,* a kind of universal history arranged chronologically; this is one of our most important sources for ancient history in general.

Among the fathers who wrote in Latin, we may first note Ambrose, bishop of Milan from 374 to his death in 397. His basic doctrine was that the Church must be independent of direction by the emperor and that bishops should have the right to judge rulers. He succeeded in imposing his will on the Emperor Theodosius in 390. Theodosius had massacred the citizens of the Greek city of Thessalonica after they had rebelled. Ambrose, shocked by this crime against humanity, excommunicated the emperor—that is, he could no longer receive the sacrament of the Eucharist and was thus placed outside the body of the Church. Theodosius admitted his guilt and observed a period of penance during which Ambrose forbade him to wear the imperial regalia. Papal statesmen of later centuries owed much of their power to the courageous example of Ambrose.

Jerome (340?–420) succeeded Eusebius as the most learned church father of his time. His translation of both the Old and New Testaments into Latin, usually called the Vulgate version of the Bible, is probably the most influential book ever written in the Latin language. It became the medium through which the Judeo-Christian writings permeated the Latin-speaking nations of Europe and was the biblical text most often used during the Middle Ages.

Augustine

Augustine (354–430), the best known of the fathers, was born in North Africa; his father was a pagan, his mother a Christian. He studied at Carthage, Rome, and Milan and acquired some reputation as a teacher of rhetoric. In early manhood he had been attracted by the teachings of the Manichees—dualists who were impressed by the power of evil, and saw the world in terms of conflict between the principles of darkness and of light. But under the influence of Ambrose, he converted to Christianity (387), the religion of his childhood. He accepted election as bishop of Hippo in northern Africa (395), and spent the last years of his long life writing, preaching, and administering his see. He died even as the Vandals were besieging the city.

Augustine's influence is partially based on his enormous literary output. He had something to say about almost every question of Christian theology. He profoundly influenced, for example, Christian teachings on sexual morality and marriage. His principles were rigorous. Like his pagan contemporaries, he believed that the world was already filled with people. "The coming of Christ," he wrote, "is not served by the begetting of children." "There is not the need of procreation that there once was." He therefore urged all Christians to a life of celibacy, even though this would mean their own declining numbers: "Marriage is not expedient, except for those who do not have self-control."

All sexual activity was, of course, banned for the unmarried. Even within marriage, husband and wife could unite sexually only for procreation. Even so, the pleasure they took in the act, representing a triumph of passion over reason, was at least a small, venial sin. His moral teachings were too rigorous for most pagans, and yet there was one point of agreement between them. Both Augustine and the pagans saw little purpose in further procreation. The human race had already reached the limits of the world.

In theological matters, Augustine was passionately interested in the operations of grace—the special power by which God brought sinful man and faulted creation to their original destinies. He sought to discern the work of grace in his own life, and the result was his *Confessions,* an intensely personal autobiography and a celebration of the providence that had guided him. This masterpiece of introspective analysis represents a type of literature virtually unknown in the classical tradition.

In questions of dogma, Augustine distinguished between God the creator (the author of nature) and God the redeemer (the source of grace), and insisted that these two operations

WOMEN'S MARRIAGE AGES AND MEN'S ENLISTMENT AGES COMPARED

Age of Roman Women at Date of Marriage.

Age	Number of Women	Age	Number of Women	Age	Number of Women
7	1	17	1	28	1
10	3	18	4	30	1
12	7	19	2	31	1
13	6	20	6	32	1
14	6	21	2	56	1
15	8	24	1		
16	5	25	2		59

Age of the Soldiers of the Roman Garrison on Entering the Army.

Age	Number of Soldiers	Age	Number of Soldiers	Age	Number of Soldiers
15	2	24	8	33	1
16	15	25	12	38	1
17	28	26	7	43	1
18	72	27	9	45	1
19	59	28	1	47	2
20	91	29	2	52	1
21	31	30	3		
22	29	31	2		
23	18	32	4		400

Source: MacDonnell, "On the Expectation of Life in Ancient Rome," *Biometrika,* 9, 1913.

not be confused. God as creator, or the nature he has created, gives mankind certain powers, but those powers, injured by the original fall, are insufficient for him to earn his salvation. When an Irish monk named Pelagius declared that people might gain salvation through good works, Augustine sprang into debate against him. If people by their unsupported, natural acts might merit salvation, then the crucifixion of Christ was foolish and unneeded. Only through a special power (grace), which Jesus' sacrifice had earned, could mankind hope to be saved. Moreover, God had known and decided from eternity to whom he would make this gift of grace; hence, even before we are born, we are all predestined either to heaven or hell.

Augustine did not limit his meditations on grace to the living community of believers. He further believed that the whole course of human history was touched by its power. In his greatest work, the *City of God,* he set forth to show that there was order in history, in the sense that behind the manifold events of the human past there was evident the hand of God, directing people through his grace along the ways of his providence. Into this immense panorama, Augustine brought the sacred history of the Jewish Testament, the secular history of his own times, and the Christian expectation of a future resurrection. This total picture of human history and human destiny resembles an epic poem of unrivaled grandeur.

At the same time, Augustine envisioned that the grace and love of God united the chosen in a form of community or city, which was set against the community of those joined by the love of earthly things. The city of God, in which live the chosen, was as yet invisible, and the elect who were its members should recognize that this present earth was not their homeland. The earthly city, identified with the Empire, was not totally evil; it kept the peace, which the elect also enjoyed. Still, it is remarkable how coldly Augustine viewed the wondrous accomplishments of Rome. At all events, to Christians of his own troubled age and to those of later ages, he held out the beckoning vision of a heavenly city, a celestial Jerusalem, where at last they would be at home.

V. THE LATE ROMAN EMPIRE

Restoration and Reform

The severe political crisis of the third century (see p. 169) finally ended in 284 when Diocletian, a high army officer, seized the throne. He was from the peasantry of Illyria (modern Yugoslavia) and was a strong, ruthless, and heroic man. In order to strengthen the administration, he ruled through an elaborate bureaucracy. His system was authoritarian, almost Oriental in its despotism.

Recognizing that the Empire was too large and too unstable to be directed any longer by one man, Diocletian reorganized it into smaller units that could be ruled by a single official. He enlisted three other men to share his rule with him, forming the Tetrarchy (rule of four). Diocletian gave himself and one of the other three the title "Augustus," and the other two took the title "Caesar." The two Caesars, who were younger men, were expected to become Augusti in their turn. There was no precise division of the Empire into four parts; each ruler was placed where it seemed most appropriate.

In order to solve the financial crisis and guarantee income for the Empire, Diocletian devised a new system of taxation under which every plot of land was assessed a certain amount, based on productivity and available labor, to be paid to the emperor's agents. There were also taxes on trades and professions so that the burden would not fall solely on landowners. The cities in the Empire each had a local city council, or *curia;* the officials, called *curiales,* were personally responsible for the required tax and had to pay it themselves if they could not collect it from others. Diocletian also strengthened the secret service unit that was responsible for seeing that taxes were collected. Further, he tried to hold back inflation with a famous Edict on Prices, which fixed a maximum price for nearly all goods. But natural economic forces evidently led to further inflation, and he had to let the edict lapse after a few years.

Diocletian's severe rule was necessary for the stabilization of the Empire, though it is hard to find in it much to praise. Many of his practices continued throughout the fourth century, especially his establishment of an Oriental despotism. Indeed, the historian must notice a general return to the East as the political center of gravity. Diocletian resided almost entirely in eastern cities and visited Rome only once, late in his career; the ancient city on the Tiber was in no way the true center of the Roman Empire.

Diocletian retired in 305 and forced the retirement of Maximian, the other senior partner or Augustus. The two younger partners of the Tetrarchy, who held the title Caesar, moved up to the rank of Augustus, but they could not maintain stable rule. They did appoint two new Caesars in an effort to continue the system of the Tetrarchy, but the arrangement soon broke down. Years of complex intrigue and civil war followed, as several leaders fought for the throne. One of the Augusti was Constantius, the father of Constantine. When Constantius died in 306, Constantine decided to fight for the supreme power. Finally, in 324, Constantine overcame the last opposition and gained recognition as sole emperor of Rome. Thus forty years after the accession of Diocletian the Empire once again had a single ruler.

Constantine and the Bureaucracy

Constantine inherited and expanded the bureaucracy that Diocletian had established. By the end of his reign in 337 Constantine had set the pattern that remained throughout the fourth and later centuries. The whole state was now one rigid structure, almost one massive corporation, that brutally discouraged individual initiative.

For the sake of administrative efficiency, there were now about 120 provinces. In no case did the governor of a province actually command troops, as had been the custom earlier; instead, *duces* (leaders, or dukes) were the military leaders. This reform separated the governors from any force that they might have used in order to revolt. The provinces were grouped into 14 (later 12) units called dioceses, each of them having a *vicarius* ("vicar") in charge.

The old Roman Senate was now simply the town council of Rome, but the title "senator" continued in use, denoting civil servants close to the emperor. There were further bureaucratic posts just below this new order. Far lower in the bureaucratic hierarchy were the local city councils, whose members, the *curiales,* served under compulsion. These councils were the foundation of the whole administrative structure.

Economic progress was in virtual stagnation. Members of all trades and professions

---

The Emperor Constantine tried to increase his glory by commissioning colossal portraits of himself, such as the one shown here. The original full-length statue was some 40 feet tall. (Photo: Himer Fotoarchiv München)

were grouped into *corpora,* or corporations, and to change profession was difficult. To make certain that the various services would be performed, the state made professions hereditary. We have seen that the state bound the tenant farmers, or *coloni,* to the soil. A small class of independent farmers clung to their existence, but the general trend was toward converting agricultural workers into near slaves.

The Empire appears to have been unable to change its policy of economic confiscation. Constantine installed a system by which farmers paid taxes in the form of goods, but it is not clear that this change improved the lot of common citizens. There was a deep gulf between the monarch's court and the common people. Even within the court the emperor stood apart from the rest, surrounded by Oriental ceremony. Fourth-century rulers wore expensive cloaks dyed in purple, and courtiers had to kiss a corner of their robes when approaching the throne. Diadems, the custom of kneeling before the emperor, and other marks of royalty became traditional and have remained so in European monarchies.

Constantine, it is true, was never worshiped as a god. Rather, he chose to exploit his new position as patron of the Christian faith to claim for himself a sacred aura. Even when still unbaptized, he consorted with the bishops at Nicaea as their equal, or rather as their mentor. He appropriated the adjective "sacred" for his person, his family, his officials, his army, and his palaces. He was the first ruler to discern and exploit the divinity that hedges, but does not quite infuse, the Christian king.

The reforms of Diocletian and Constantine won two additional centuries of survival for the Western Empire (to 476). Even more lasting were the benefits conferred on the Eastern Empire. In 330 Constantine renamed the old Greek city of Byzantium as Constantinople and established it as his capital. This city stood as a living monument to his name for more than 1000 years, until taken by the Ottoman Turks in

1453. The reforms of these two emperors, in sum, helped the Eastern Empire to become one of the most long-lived states in human history.

Problems of the Western Empire

The Western portion of the Empire was less fortunate. When Constantine designated Constantinople as the capital it was a further sign that the Western lands were in a period of decline. After Constantine's death in 337, the chief administrative question for more than a century was whether one man could be strong enough to rule as sole monarch. For most of the time this proved impossible, and some kind of shared rule on the pattern established by Diocletian became regular. On the death of Theodosius, in 395, the Empire was divided into an Eastern half and a Western half, with the dividing line just east of Italy.

In the last centuries of the Western Empire, society became more and more rigid; it did not, and perhaps could not, allow people to move freely from one class to another. The *coloni* were bound to the soil chiefly because foreign conquest could no longer provide a regular flow of slaves who might replace them in agriculture. As the central government weakened, estates, usually called villas, became more independent, and the *coloni* became more dependent on the owners for protection; thus the villas developed into the political units to which the *coloni* felt allegiance. Many villas were self-sufficient units resembling the later manors of the Middle Ages, with hunting lands and workshops that supplied the goods that the local population needed; they therefore became the main economic and political units of the Western empire. The strength of the Empire was thus no longer centered in Rome. At the same time, trade was declining because of a shortage of new markets and the constant threat of invasions along the frontiers. Moreover, a shortage of labor caused fertile lands to lie fallow and mines to remain unexploited.

The Decline of the Western Empire

Such was the background, in part, for the dramatic turning point in history that is the end of the Western Empire. History is always in transition, and the milestones that we fix to mark the highway are largely matters of intellectual convenience; we cannot think about long periods of history without dividing them in some way. The formal end of the Western Empire is traditionally dated to 476, when a Germanic warlord deposed the youth whom we call the last Western emperor, Romulus Augustulus, and the Senate resolved not to try to name any further Western emperors. Modern readers inevitably think of this event in the terminology imposed by the historical masterpiece of Edward Gibbon—that is, as the "decline and fall" of the Empire. But, of course, no political structure as large as the Roman Empire really falls like a tree in a forest without further influence or legacy—and the eastern portion did not "fall" until the capture of Constantinople in 1453. The survival of the Christian religion through the medium of Classical languages alone is sufficient proof that the Empire and its heritage did not vanish without a trace. Moreover, some emperors, notably Justinian in the sixth century, saw themselves as the head of the whole traditional Empire and tried to reunite the two geographic parts.

Yet even though historians take care to speak of the transformation of the Empire rather than of its disappearance, there is no doubt that the Empire in the West did pass away while the Byzantine Empire in the East survived for nearly another thousand years. The problem is to explain why the regions of Italy, Spain, and Gaul could not maintain themselves under a continuous government and why

CHRONOLOGY OF THE "FALL" OF ROME

A.D. 476 is known to all readers of history as the year of the fall of Rome, but the true chronology is more complex.

393: Theodosius I, ruling as emperor in Constantinople, installs his son Honorius as emperor in the West.

395: Death of Theodosius; the division of the Empire into East and West is maintained.

423: Death of Honorius in West; other Western emperors continue to be appointed.

474, June 24: Leo I, emperor in East, appoints Julius Nepos as emperor in West.

475: Nepos appoints Orestes, a former lieutenant of Attila the Hun, as Master of the Soldiers. Orestes insists that his young son, Romulus Augustus (or Augustulus), be recognized as Western emperor. Nepos flees to Salona in Dalmatia. Romulus is proclaimed emperor in Ravenna, October 31, but the act is without legal force and Nepos continues to be recognized as official Western emperor.

476: The Germanic warlord Odovacar (sometimes Odoacer) leads a rebellion against Orestes and kills him, August 28. He deposes Romulus in Ravenna (September 4) and exiles him with a pension to Campania. The Roman Senate sends an embassy to Zeno, the Eastern emperor (474–491), proclaiming that there is no further need for a Western emperor; but Zeno continues to recognize Nepos until his death.

480, April or May: Nepos is murdered in his villa at Salona.

about 520: Marcellinus, in his Latin *Chronicle,* written in Constaninople, states that the Western Empire *(Hesperium imperium)* "perished" with the deposition of Romulus Augustulus in 476, thus establishing this date for the "fall" of Rome.

at the same time no dissolution threatened the Eastern regions of the Empire. In other words, the causes for Rome's decline that the historian identifies must operate only in the Western half of the Empire.

A great many historians have been enticed into trying to state the one great cause for the fall of Rome—and this may be an impossible quest. Gibbon, for example, assigned the cause to the destructive work of "barbarism and religion." But to say that Rome declined because of invasions by Germans, Franks, and Goths only pushes the inquiry back one step: Why were these tribes at last able to defeat an Empire that had ruled the civilized world through disciplined armies for centuries? And why did not the Eastern part of the Empire decline along with the Western?

Some historians have said that the mixing of peoples within the Empire, a process that certainly did take place during the centuries, produced an inferior population that lacked the virility to withstand the invasions of the third and fourth centuries. This racial theory is, however, highly unscientific and would appeal to few historians today. After all, the Greeks, Germans, and Slavs who mixed with the Romans were not physically inferior to them and could have fought effectively enough in the armies. A more plausible supplement to this theory is the view that the emperors unintentionally paved the way for the fall of Rome by exterminating possible political rivals in the upper class; thus they weakened this class and prevented it from contributing leadership to the state. It is true that the Senate of the later Empire became feebler and less able to resist the dictatorial rule of emperors, a condition caused largely by the arbitrary execution of senators at the hands of emperors. Recently, an older theory of lead poisoning among the aristocracy has been revived. The wealthier Romans adopted Greek methods of cooking with lead utensils and drank water that was funneled through lead pipes. The theory postulates that the diluted lead poisoned the upper classes, making them progressively sterile; thus they failed to reproduce potential leaders.

Some scholars have advanced an economic argument, saying that the Empire was bound to decline because it never really emerged from a domestic economy to an industrial one. But this theory is hardly convincing, for some societies—admittedly much less complex than the Empire—have existed for many centuries with no more than a domestic economy. If there had been no convulsions and strains in the Empire, the production of goods and food could have continued more or less unchanged. Soil exhaustion and fluctuating cycles of rainfall and drought have also been proposed in order to explain Rome's economic depression, but there is little exact knowledge about the cycles of crops and weather conditions that would indubitably account for the fall of the Empire.

Others have suggested that the weakness of the Western Empire was due to a shortage of manpower. This explanation does seem fairly sound; the Eastern cities appear to have been more populous than the Western ones, and they had more strength and resilience. The numerical inferiority of the West became even more serious when the villas began to operate as self-sufficient units and the population no longer manned an army that was directed by a central authority. It was much easier for outsiders to invade the Empire when they met haphazard resistance from local forces. The relocation of the capital to Constantinople moved the administrative center even farther from the Western provinces; probably this accelerated the dissolution of the regions of Italy and Gaul.

But the shortage of manpower was not the only factor in the weakening of the Western Empire. Its physical geography doomed it to be more vulnerable to invasion than the Eastern Empire. Warlike tribes streamed along the Danube valley and through the terrain of Central Europe into the Western provinces, a less hazardous route than the journey south through the difficult mountains of the Balkans, Greece, and Asia Minor into the Eastern Empire.

Other conditions made the Western Empire less able to resist destructive invasions. In the late second and third centuries the emperors had deliberately increased the prestige of the army and depressed the Senate and the civil service. The creature that they fashioned soon began to rule them, for the armies and their leaders made and unmade emperors at will. The only way to preserve civilian control over the military machine would have been to entrust more responsibility to the Senate and maintain strong civil servants. But the emperors simply continued along the path of absolute coercion. This repression stifled initiative and made the lower classes apathetic and resentful. Nearly the whole economic strength of the state was now devoted to paying and equipping the army, and the system of tax collecting probably left little to the citizens for expanding or repairing their possessions. These conditions gave citizens only slight motivation to defend their oppressive government; domination by invading tribes may have seemed not much worse than being in the grip of the Roman state.

One must also look at the great number of holidays and forms of amusement within the city of Rome: To what degree did laziness and luxury contribute to the fall of the Empire? It seems clear that the masses in the city, scarcely required to work and pampered with free amusements, gradually lost their feelings of responsibility. In 69, as Tacitus reports, the crowd cheered with pleasure as rival troops fought in the streets for the throne. When the masses no longer had to exert more than minimal effort to survive, they abandoned the discipline and civic cooperation that had created

the Empire. Public office was shunned, non-Italians supplied the troops, and appeals to the people to show traditional Roman firmness in danger found little response.

Finally, historians must consider the great upheaval in the sphere of ideas and faith. We cannot express this view in the language of science or statistics, but Christianity must also have weakened the defenses of the Empire. In the Roman scheme the emperors, governors, and administrators stood far above the people, and the objective in life was to attain a higher position. Roman religion offered little spiritual compensation for a low rank in the world. The Judeo-Christian faith, as we have seen, offered something better: the message that all persons are potentially equal in the eyes of God and may hope for a better afterlife through salvation. Were the increasing numbers of Christians really prepared to fight for the preservation of the old system? This spiritual rejection, as we might call it, worked along with the mighty pressures of invasion to cause the "fall" of Rome—an event that the modern world sees as a possible model of its own fate. The fall, a challenge and a warning to all who read history, is the recognized end of the ancient world and the beginning of a long period in which new nations would use the legacy of antiquity in their own development.

The first Roman emperor, Augustus, founded a system that gave the Roman Empire two centuries of peace. The economy attained a material prosperity that surpassed anything in Western Europe for the next thousand years. Populous cities dotted the Empire; Rome itself, with about a million people, was a wonder of the world. Gifted writers—Virgil, Tacitus, and others—made this a resplendent age for Latin letters.

And yet the imperial colossus concealed certain fatal flaws, which became manifest in the rampant chaos of the third century. The slave economy demanded a constant supply of human chattel, which it rapidly consumed. The end of aggressive wars and the suppression of piracy cut off this critical recruitment of slaves. And the values preached by pagan philosophy, urging the pursuit of the good life here and now, had little to offer to the enslaved, the exploited, the subjugated.

Ancient society responded to these pressures with new ways of organizing and rewarding labor and with new cultural attitudes. In agriculture, the small farm, run by housed slaves of free tenants called *coloni,* slowly replaced the large slave-run estate. In towns, the victory of free labor over slavery seems to have been even more rapid and decisive. But in committing a larger and fairer share of the social product to its humblest classes, ancient society deprived itself of the disposable resources it needed to meet the menace of invading peoples beyond the imperial frontiers.

Values, too, were changing. The peoples of the Empire, disillusioned with or unconvinced by the official paganism, sought new visions of the cosmos, new reasons for living. Mystery religions, holding out the promise of eternal life, gained unprecedented popularity. But Christianity eventually won out over all its rivals; with the conversion of Constantine, it became the favored and, not long after, the established religion of the late Empire.

Witness to profound changes in every sector of its life, Rome could not maintain the continuity of its rule in all its provinces, across this tumultuous age. But in economy and culture, the late Empire had already laid the foundations upon which would rise the new states of the Middle Ages.

RECOMMENDED READING

Sources

Ayer, Joseph Cullen. *A Source Book for Ancient Church History.* 1913.

Early Christian Writings: The Apostolic Fathers. M. Staniforth (tr.). 1968.

Suetonius. *Lives of the Caesars.* Robert Graves (tr.). 1972.

Tacitus. *Complete Works.* A. J. Church and W. J. Brodribb (trs.). 1942. Though the translation is old, the book has the merit of completeness.

Studies

Brown, Peter. *Augustine of Hippo: A Biography.* 1967.
———. *The World of Late Antiquity, A.D. 150–750.* 1971. Together, superb historical and cultural discussions.

Chambers, Mortimer (ed.). *The Fall of Rome—Can It Be Explained?* 1970. A collection of modern essays attempting to explain the decline of Rome.

Cross, Frank M. *The Ancient Library of Qumrân and Modern Bibilical Studies.* 1976. A balanced introduction to the study of the Dead Sea Scrolls.

Daniélou, Jean, and Henri Marrou. *The First Six Hundred Years.* Vol. I of *The Christian Centuries,* L. J. Rogier and others (eds.). 1964. The most comprehensive study of the early Catholic Church.

Dodds, E. R. *Pagan and Christian in an Age of Anxiety: Some Aspects of Religious Experience from Marcus Aurelius to Constantine.* 1970. On the inner reasons for the great change of gods in the Roman Empire.

Frend, W. H. C. *The Rise of Christianity.* 1984. Now the most extensive single discussion.

Garzetti, Albino. *From Tiberius to the Antonines: A*

History of the Roman Empire, A.D. 14–192. 1974. The best political narrative of this important period.

Gibbon, Edward. *The History of the Decline and Fall of the Roman Empire*. Originally 6 vols., 1776–1788; many modern editions, the best by J. B. Bury, 7 vols., 1896–1900.

Grant, Michael. *The Army of the Caesars*. 1974. Comprehensive discussion of the development of the Roman army in the Empire.

———. *The Fall of the Roman Empire: A Reappraisal*. 1976.

Jones, A. H. M. *The Later Roman Empire, 284–602*. 1964. Encyclopedic narrative, with detailed citation of primary sources. For advanced students.

———. *The Decline of the Ancient World*. 1975. Essentially a shortened version of the foregoing.

MacMullen, Ramsay. *Enemies of the Roman Order*. 1966. On the internal causes for the weakening of Rome.

———. *Paganism in the Roman Empire*. 1981.

Millar, Fergus (ed.). *The Roman Empire and Its Neighbors*. 1981. With chapters by various experts on the nations bordering on the Empire.

Nock, Arthur Darby. *Conversion*. 1961. The best book on the reasons for the transition from paganism to Christianity, by a towering scholar.

Syme, Ronald. *Tacitus*. 1958. Not only a study of the historian, but also a microscopic analysis of the politics of the Empire.

Watson, G. R. *The Roman Soldier*. 1969.

THE IMAGE
OF HUMANITY

In Ancient and
Medieval Art

"Human beings," however else we choose to define them, are the only creatures on this earth capable of asking, "Who am I?" Not only are we capable of asking this question, but we have been asking it so persistently that we
seem to be "the animal with the built-in identity crisis."

The question can be asked in a thousand ways, and the responses to it have
been equally varied. Modern men and women tend to define themselves in
terms of relationships to other people. Until recently, however, the definition
related to unseen forces, immeasurably more powerful than humans, whose
presence they sensed in the world of nature and to whose will they felt they
must submit. We do not know when in the dawn of history people first attained
the degree of self-awareness that made them inquire into their identity. It
seems likely that this stage of evolution coincided with the emergence of language and the making of images. Language enabled people to name things and
thereby to gain a degree of control over them. For that reason, the name of God
remains a carefully guarded secret in some religions; even if known, it may be
invoked only on solemn occasions, and profaning it is a grave offense. On the
other hand, according to the Bible, Adam named the animals in the Garden of
Eden and in doing so became their master. Images, too, confer a kind of power
over the things they represent. This is their everlasting fascination, attested by
the snapshots in our wallets as much as by the biblical prohibition against
"graven images" of the Lord.

By giving names or making images, then, mankind was defined in relation to
that which was named or represented. Representation implies the idea of substitution; the image is a stand-in for its model. But if the model is known only
through a substitute, as was true for images of spirits or deities, then the
substitute tends to assume the reality of the original; it becomes an idol, the
dwelling place of the god. Early man believed that by providing a dwelling
place for the god he compelled the disembodied spirit to inhabit it; and since
the dwelling place, the image, was under human control, the spirit within it
was too; that is, it was ready to be coaxed, bargained with, or propitiated by
sacrifice and prayer.

If this need to gain control over the uncontrollable was a primary impulse in
the development of art, it is not surprising that for many thousands of years
images of people played only a minor role. There are numerous human images
in the art of the Old and New Stone ages, but they are incidental rather than
dominant in relation to those of animals, which usually strike us as far more
organic and keenly observed. The human form in these images is subject to
radical abbreviation, distortion, or transformation, often merging with animal
features. Clearly, prehistoric men and women did not yet claim a privileged
status for themselves with respect to their fellow creatures; they resolved their

identity crisis by relating their own existence to the rest of nature through an intricate system of magic kinship expressed in the concepts of totem and taboo.

In the course of the fourth millennium B.C. several interdependent developments occurred in Egypt and the Middle East that gave people a radically different view of themselves: the growth of cities and of a more highly organized society divided into distinct classes, the invention of writing, and the emergence of a new concept of divinity. Totem and taboo gradually gave way to the belief in gods that had human shape, although many of them retained animal heads or wings to differentiate them from ordinary mortals; and people learned how to see themselves in relation to these gods rather than to rocks, plants, or animals. It was this claim to a special relationship with the gods that differentiated humans from all other creatures and so, provided a unique, privileged status. The words of the Old Testament, "And the Lord said, Let us make man in our image and likeness," have their counterpart in the mythology of many peoples in the ancient world.

It now became the artist's task to make gods in the image and likeness of humans. Faced with this challenge, the artist evolved a stable concept of human perfection, an ideal image; and the same ideal served when portraying individuals, for only those were so honored who could claim kinship with the divine. In Egypt, where the ruler himself had the status of a god, this included members of his royal family and court, such as Ankh-haf (see Plate 1). The bust is a majestic likeness; over and above all its personal traits, it reflects a well-defined ideal of human perfection in the broad shoulders, the emphasis on smooth, rounded shapes, the proportional relationship of head, neck, and body. Yet this ideal physical image, however impressive, gives no hint of animation or action.

The very opposite may be said of Abikhil, Ankh-haf's Mesopotamian contemporary (see Plate 2). His physical presence is unimpressive, but he radiates a quality of spiritual communication with the deity that is lacking in Egyptian art. Although motionless, the figure acts, through the energetically clasped hands, the smile, the huge eyes. The image of Abikhil's god, had it been preserved, would show the same qualities in still more emphatic form; he would be communicating with his worshipers. These contrasting conceptions of humanity's relationship to the divine—the Egyptian emphasis on physical beauty, the Mesopotamian emphasis on communication—became the basis for the image of men and women in Greece, which in turn bequeathed it to Rome, to the Middle Ages, and to the Renaissance. The Greeks, after borrowing first from the Mesopotamians (see Plate 3), then the Egyptians, arrived at a balanced synthesis that was to remain a model for Western civilization until modern times (see Plate 4). Cicero defined the classical image of mankind for all posterity when he spoke of man as a "mortal god"; that is, a being who, though mortal, shares not only the physical beauty of the gods but their power to act and communicate. Even the portrait heads of Hellenistic Greece and the Roman Empire, however much they may reflect the troubled uncertainties of the individual psyche, still reveal a kinship with the physical nobility of the gods (see Plate 5).

The early images of Christ and the saints followed this classical tradition (see Plate 10); they could be distinguished from their pagan models only by such external attributes as haloes. Christ in his human incarnation was assumed to have looked like any other man. When the Christian emperors, claiming to rule by divine grace, wanted this special relationship to God conveyed in visual terms, the Mesopotamian tradition of man's spiritual likeness to the divine reasserted itself and the classical balance of body and spirit was lost; the figures became rigid and attenuated, their structure concealed behind heavy ceremonial garments, and expression was centered in the head, with its huge staring eyes (see Plates 7 and 11). The image of Christ, too, evolved from that of a man among men to that of the awesome ruler of the universe (see Plate 8). Not until the twelfth and thirteenth centuries did the humanity of Christ return to Western art and, in its train, the humanity of those to whom he had brought redemption, be they participants in the drama of the lamentation (see Plate 14) or simple peasants working their fields (see Plate 15). The image of people that evolved during the later Middle Ages conveys an openness to emotional experience, human vulnerability and humility—qualities never stressed before. Yet it was the soil from which grew the Renaissance, the rebirth of the classical concept of man as a "mortal god."

These two figures in Plates 1 and 2, about the same date and similar in material, show how differently the oldest historic civilizations conceived the image of man. In ancient Egypt, the sculptor's most important task was to carve tomb statues of the Pharaoh—the divine ruler—and of the members of his court who could claim a share of his divinity through their relationship to him. Such statues were not meant for the eyes of ordinary mortals, but were permanent substitutes for the mummified body, so that the soul might always have an abode to come back to. The bust of Ankh-haf is a fully individual portrait —it fits no other soul but his— yet we could not possibly call it a speaking likeness. No hint of action—physical or psychological— disturbs the calm of its powerful shapes. The bust is a work designed for eternity, waiting to be animated by the recurrent visits of the spirit.

The statue of Abikhil, by contrast, is a portrait in name only, through its inscription, which also tells us that the figure was a present for the goddess Ishtar. Its purpose was to serve as a substitute for Abikhil in the act of communicating with the deity, and this act it conveys with extraordinary concentration. The hands are firmly locked in the Sumerian gesture of worship; a smile—denoting aliveness rather than a specific emotional state— makes the corners of the mouth curl upward. But the chief instruments of communication are the huge, luminous eyes, inlaid with shell and lapis lazuli and outlined in black, with their fixed wide-open stare. These clearly were the essential aspects for both sculptor and patron. Individuality is established by the written name, not by the facial features, which here simply repeat the racial type. Nor, unlike the Egyptian sculptor, does the artist show any interest in the subtleties of anatomy; in Ankh-haf the sculptor shows the firm presence of the skull beneath the flesh, but in Abikhil the artist makes no differentiation except in the fleecy waves of the beard. Yet the figure speaks, while Ankh-haf is forever mute.

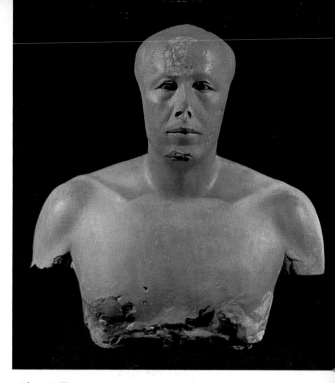

Plate 1. Egypt, BUST OF PRINCE ANKH-HAF
ca. 2600 B.C., *painted limestone, lifesize*
Museum of Fine Arts, Boston

Plate 2. Mesopotamia, ABIKHIL
SUPERINTENDENT OF THE ISHTAR TEMPLE AT MARI
ca. 2750 B.C., *alabaster, height of portion shown about 10"*
Louvre Museum, Paris

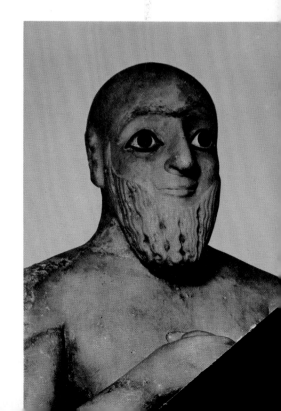

Plate 3.
Greece, THE BLINDING OF POLYPHEMUS
ca. 675–650 B.C., *Proto-Attic amphora,*
height of portion shown about 16"
Museum, Eleusis

Greek artists built on the work of their predecessors in Egypt and Mesopotamia, but they profoundly transformed this heritage in keeping with the dynamic, man-centered world view that is the hallmark of Greek civilization. The gods now became human, not only in shape but in their relations with men; they no longer dominated life on earth or in the hereafter, and eventually were rationalized as the glorified memories of heroes. Such a hero was Odysseus, whose greatest exploit, the blinding of the one-eyed giant Polyphemus, is depicted on the neck of the two-handled storage jar (amphora) in Plate 3. The huge vessel, 56 inches tall, once held the body of a child. Its decoration, however, is not concerned with afterlife; instead, it celebrates mankind's victory over the forces of darkness. It takes three men to thrust the spear into the giant's eye, and their action is portrayed with great directness and expressive force. The heads, with their large noses and oversized eyes, still recall the art of the ancient Near East (compare Plate 2), but the muscular bodies and agitated movements bespeak the Greek painter's emphasis on doing rather than being.

Odysseus and his companions do not yet show the ideal of physical beauty we have come to expect of Greek art. That ideal made its appearance only two hundred years later in what we call the classic period of Greece—classic because its achievements set a standard of perfection which Western civilization has acknowledged ever since. We can see it in the graceful outlines, the harmonious proportions, and the balanced, self-contained pose of the lyre-playing maiden in Plate 4. She is painted on the body of a slender oil jug (lekythos), a funerary offering found in the grave of a girl. The instrument is Apollo's, and Mount Helicon is his abode; perhaps, then, the Muse was meant to commemorate the musical gifts of the deceased. Painted pottery, despite its narrow range of means—outline drawing, flat color, and a severely limited choice of pigments—was highly prized by the Greeks. Its finest masters, such as the Achilles Painter, were great artists of such individuality that we can recognize their personal styles even if we do not know their names. By careful observation of nature, they learned how to draw the human form in such a way that the outlines alone convey its roundness and weight.

Plate 4.
The Achilles Painter, MUSE ON MOUNT HELICON
ca. 445 B.C., white-ground lekythos,
height of portion shown about 6"
Private Collection, Lugano

Individual portraiture became an important concern of Greek artists only after the classic ideal of physical beauty had been established, and even the most striking portraits reflect a residue of this ideal. The ideal serves as a kind of matrix within which the sitter's unique features are embedded and lends him a heroic air although, as in Plate 5, his personality may be quite unheroic. The somewhat flabby features, the plaintive mouth, the unhappy eyes under furrowed brows, reveal a man beset by doubts and anxieties strangely akin to our own. Such men had surely existed earlier in the Greek world as they exist today, but only now, near the end of Greek independence, could the artist grasp such psychological complexity. This intensely private view of the sitter immediately captures our sympathy.

Landscape made its appearance in Greek art even later than portraiture. How indeed could a civilization that viewed man as the measure of all things be expected to celebrate the unbounded immensity of nature? Yet at some point—perhaps only after they had become part of the Roman world—the Greeks added this achievement to their many others. It matters little whether the artist who painted the impressive series of *Odysseus Landscapes* (of which Plate 6 shows one section) on the walls of a house in ancient Rome was a Greek or a Roman. What he shows us, framed by pilasters as if seen through a window, is the sun-drenched shore of the Mediterranean with masses of rock abruptly rising from deep blue waters that stretch to the very limits of our vision. A fine haze marks the meeting of sea and sky at the line of the horizon. In this timeless world, the human drama of the foreground is merely a passing episode; Odysseus, the great hero whose blinding of Polyphemus had been so impressively celebrated on the Proto-Attic amphora, no longer dominates the scene. His adventures have receded from the center of consciousness. Here, they are no more than an excuse for the landscape painter's art.

Plate 5. Greece, PORTRAIT HEAD *(from Delos)*
ca. 80 B.C., *bronze, lifesize*
National Archeological Museum, Athens

Plate 6. Rome, ODYSSEUS LANDSCAPE
late 1st century B.C., *wall painting*
Museo Profano, Vatican

Plate 7. Byzantine
THE EMPEROR JUSTINIAN AND ATTENDANTS *(detail)*
ca. 547, mosaic
San Vitale, Ravenna

The classical ideal of beauty had begun to decay from the third century on when the Roman world entered an ever deepening social and political crisis. A new ideal emerged only after Christianity became the official religion of what remained of the Roman Empire and artists had learned how to give visible form to the truths of the new faith. How remote this image of mankind is from the classical tradition can be seen in the portrait of Justinian and his entourage in Plate 7: the human body—flattened, attenuated, motionless, rigidly frontal—disappears behind a screen of ceremonial garments; it is these garments that signal rank, dignity, and station in life, which now are far more important than the individual's physical appearance. All the faces tend to look alike, sharing a dominant feature: the huge staring eyes, which recall those of the superintendent of the Ishtar Temple (compare Plate 2) and are meant to convey the same intense relationship to the deity.

This style, called Byzantine (after Byzantium, the old Greek name of the capital of Justinian's empire), was created by painters rather than by sculptors. Free-standing statuary soon disappeared

Plate 8. Byzantine
CHRIST IN MAJESTY
ca. 1148, mosaic
Cathedral, Cefalù

altogether, not to be revived until the Italian Renaissance. Among all the techniques of painting, mosaic was the one best adapted to the new ideal of beauty. Greeks and Romans had used colored marble cubes in floor mosaics; the Byzantines used cubes of tinted glass and glass backed with gold leaf to cover the walls and vaults of their churches with images of dazzling brilliance and luminosity. What ancient artists must have regarded as the limitations of the medium—its patternlike flatness and lack of delicate tonal gradation —now became its chief virtues: if mosaic could not create an illusion of reality such as the landscape in Plate 6, it was superbly suited to project an illusion of celestial space. The huge image of Christ in Plate 8 that fills the half-dome behind the altar in the Cathedral of Cefalù in Sicily is a truly awesome figure whose intense gaze endows the concept of the all-present God with overpowering reality.

Plate 9. Irish
ST. MARK AND THE SYMBOLS OF
THE FOUR EVANGELISTS
(from a Gospel Book)
8th century, miniature
Stiftsbibliothek, St. Gall

Plate 10. Carolingian
ST. MATTHEW
(from the Gospel Book of Charlemagne)
ca. 810, miniature
Kunsthistorisches Museum, Vienna

Far removed as it was from that of the Greeks and Romans, Byzantine art remained true to the classical past in that its central concern continued to be the human form. The Celtic and Germanic peoples of northwestern Europe shared an artistic heritage of a radically different sort: theirs was an art of ornament, mingling abstract linear rhythms, geometric patterns, and animal motifs. In accepting Christianity, they also accepted the Mediterranean tradition of the image of mankind, but their first impulse was to assimilate it as much as possible to their own sense of design. The strange result may be seen in the St. Mark in Plate 9: the figure shows no feeling for the organic continuity of the human body. It resembles an intricate knot that seems far more closely related to the ornamental panels surrounding it than to the classical model from which the image is ultimately derived.

The model must have been a picture in another Gospel manuscript, produced in one of the ancient centers of the Mediterranean world from which the missionaries set out to convert the heathen of the North. Christianity was a scriptural religion, hence the book containing the Word of God became a precious object, the copying and embellishment of the sacred text a pious act. The portraits of the evangelists in the earliest Gospel books were patterned on those of Greek and Roman artists. We can infer this from such miniatures as the St. Matthew in Plate 10, which was painted less than a century after the St. Mark but with a wholly new understanding of the classical tradition. Except for the large halo, the visible symbol of his sanctity, this evangelist is easily recognizable as a descendant of the *Muse on Mount Helicon* (compare Plate 4), even though separated from her by no less than 1,250 years. How could this picture have been done in northern Europe around the year 800? We know nothing about the artist, but his work is striking evidence of the Carolingian Renaissance, the classical revival in politics, art, and literature radiating from the court of Charlemagne, the first medieval ruler to assume the mantle of the Roman emperors of old. His empire did not survive long, but he revived the classical tradition that continued to inspire medieval civilization.

If the connection linking the Carolingian St. Matthew and the Greek Muse (Plates 10 and 4) is readily apparent, it takes a sharp eye indeed to perceive any relationship between the head of Sainte-Foy in Plate 11 and the portrait in Plate 5. Yet such a link exists, for the face of the saint was originally the portrait of a late Roman ruler reworked and adapted to its present purpose in the wake of the Carolingian Renaissance. The large eyes and impersonal features betray a closer kinship to the Justinian mosaic (compare Plate 7) than to the Greek head; still, it is a product of pagan antiquity, and we are surprised to see it surviving in a Christian context.

How was this possible? Free-standing sculpture had disappeared with the victory of Christianity, and ancient statues had been destroyed by the thousands as pagan idols. The Middle Ages knew only applied sculpture, that is, sculpture which was an integral part of the architecture of churches and palaces or of their furnishings. The one apparent exception are reliquaries, but even these obey the rule: as sculptured containers of holy relics, they too had a service function which saved them from the evil odor of idolatry.

Let us turn once more to the two evangelists in Plates 9 and 10. What might be the outcome if two styles as different as these could somehow be merged? This is what happened in the years after the Carolingian Renaissance; and the new style, called Romanesque, emerged everywhere in Western Europe toward the end of the eleventh century. The *Annunciation* miniature in Plate 12 is a powerful example, combining the Celtic-Germanic sense of linear pattern with the Mediterranean figurative tradition. Unlike the St. Matthew, this miniature has no depth; all forms remain on the surface. Yet the picture plane is not simply flat, it is a field of force. The urgency of the angel's message, conveyed through his glance and gestures, is matched by the response of the Virgin Mary, awestruck and submissive at once. The contrast of active and passive could hardly be expressed with greater eloquence.

Plate 11. Medieval, RELIQUARY OF SAINTE-FOY
9th–10th century, gold, enamel, and gems,
height of portion shown about 9"
Abbey Church, Conques

Plate 12. Romanesque, THE ANNUNCIATION *(from the* St. Albans Psalter)
ca. 1120, miniature
St. Godehard, Hildesheim

Plate 13. Gothic
CHARLEMAGNE BUILDING A CHURCH
ca. 1220, stained glass
Chartres Cathedral

Plate 14. Giotto
LAMENTATION
1305—1306, wall painting
Scrovegni Chapel, Padua

The great Gothic cathedrals which rose in France between 1150 and 1250 reflect a religious fervor among all strata of the population such as the Middles Ages had not known before. This newly felt devotion profoundly transformed the image of man as seen in the sculpture and painting of the time: the harsh expressiveness of the Romanesque yields to a gentler, more realistic art stressing the human aspect of Christ and the saints. This is true even of stained glass, a pictorial technique that does not lend itself to realism. Plate 13 shows

a small part of one of the windows at Chartres Cathedral, devoted to the deeds of Charlemagne (who wears a halo, having become a saint). The unknown artist does not present him as an awesome figure; the workmen busily erecting the church on the right are the same size as the emperor and attract our attention as much as he does. There is an attempt, by means of curving, hooklike lines, to endow the drapery folds with a measure of three-dimensionality, but such realistic impulses are severely limited by the nature of stained-glass

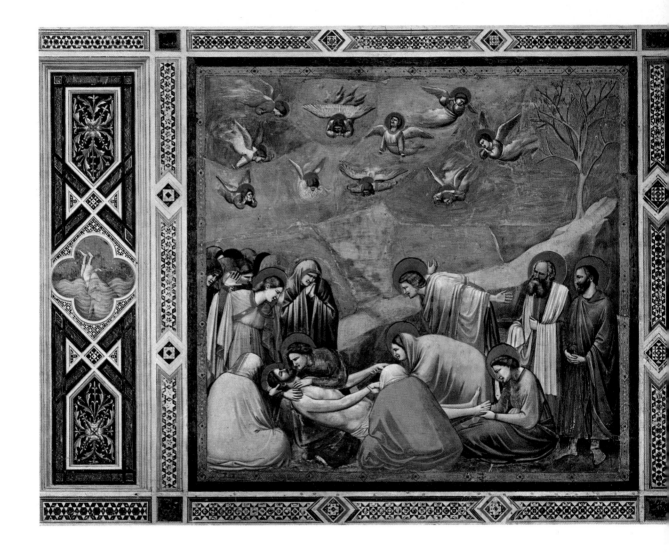

images (black outline drawings on pieces of brilliantly tinted glass).

It was in Italy, less than a century later, that Gothic realism was to bear its most important fruits. Compared to our sample of stained glass, Giotto's *Lamentation* over the dead Christ in Plate 14 looks like a direct revival of ancient painting (compare Plate 10) with its full-bodied, weighty figures seen against a background of landscape and blue sky. Giotto had surely studied the remains of ancient Roman murals, yet the way he approaches his subject—as an emotion-filled human drama rather than as solemn ritual—derives from the Gothic north. To his contemporaries, Giotto's pictures seemed as real as nature itself: not only did the figures have all the solid, tangible qualities of statues, they were animated by feelings that made the beholder see himself as a participant of the scene. Giotto thus became the fountainhead of a great new tradition which was to transform all of European painting within the next hundred years.

Plate 15.
Ambrogio Lorenzetti, GOOD GOVERNMENT *(detail)*
1338–1340, wall painting
Palazzo Pubblico, Siena

If Giotto's *Lamentation* impresses us with its simple and direct humanity, the setting of the figures is severely limited—a stage barely deep enough to hold them and a minimum of props. The exploration of spatial depth was left to younger Italian painters such as Ambrogio Lorenzetti. In his view of country life in Plate 15, the setting is no longer a backdrop, but an environment within which men move as they do in the *Odysseus Landscape* (compare Plate 6). Cottages, fields, and orchards, peasants harvesting, threshing, and driving their heavily burdened donkeys—

every detail of this scene will seem familiar to the traveler who knows the countryside between Florence and Siena.

In the fourteenth century, such travelers included a number of painters from north of the Alps who went south while some of the Italian masters went north to the art centers of Paris or Prague. As a consequence of these exchanges, there developed toward 1400 the International Gothic style, so called because it prevailed all over Europe with only minor local variations. It was the last phase of medieval art, soon to give way

Plate 16.
The Limbourg Brothers, APRIL
(from the Très riches heures
du Duc de Berry)
1413–1416, miniature
Musée Condé, Chantilly

to the revolutionary developments of the following century. And the dawn of a new era announced itself in at least one respect: most medieval art was supported by the patronage of institutions, but the International Gothic was to a large extent sustained by the taste of individual collectors such as the duke who commissioned the *Très riches heures.* This is a book of hours, a personal prayerbook, but one designed as a magnificent showpiece rather than for actual use. Our miniature in Plate 16 belongs to the calendar that forms part of a book of hours. Clearly, the Limbourg Brothers must have

known landscapes such as Lorenzetti's; how else could they have caught the seasonal features of country life—the flowering trees in the walled garden, the fishermen on the river—with such fidelity? But the seasonal activity of the foreground, a tender betrothal scene, relates directly to their patron. It probably shows the betrothal of the duke's granddaughter, and the participants are portraits, even though differentiated mainly by their extravagantly lavish costumes. In a history of fashion, the International Gothic must figure as the earliest Age of Elegance.

Chapter 6

The Making of Western Europe ca. 500–1000

Three new civilizations fell heir to the Classical tradition after the fall of Rome. A distinctive system of religious belief marked each of them— Roman, or Catholic, Christianity in Western Europe; Eastern, or Orthodox, Christianity in Asia Minor, the Balkan Peninsula, and Russia; and Islam in the Middle East and North Africa. These new civilizations differed from their common parent in two fundamental ways. The new societies were predominantly peasant; they were based upon willing, if not exactly free, labor. Although slavery remained important, it no longer provided a principal support to their economic systems. The new cultures were dominated by the Christian and Muslim visions of an afterlife and the hope of personal salvation. Teachers and scholars in both East and West sought to reconcile these religious views with the cultural heritage of Greece and Rome.

These "higher religions," as they are sometimes called, offered to even the humblest members of society a sense of individual dignity and destiny. Unlike the slaves of antiquity who lived and died with little sustaining hope, the peasants believed that their lives and labors, however hard and cruel, were not meaningless. They learned from Christianity and Islam that God had created them and that, if they did God's will on earth, they would ultimately attain eternal life.

Many other changes accompanied the change in religion. A vast movement of peoples took place. Celts, Germans, and Slavs in the north and east, Arabs in the south, and other peoples shifted or enlarged the areas of their former settlements; their migrations permanently affected the composition of the populations in Europe and the Middle East. In spite of these migrations and the violence that accompanied them, the Western and Eastern inhabitants slowly rebuilt their economies.

Technological innovations aided the peasants in carrying on intensive agriculture in areas, principally in northern Europe, that had not been efficiently cultivated before. These medieval societies also developed new economic and social institutions, such as the large estate or manor, based in Europe on semifree or serf labor. Upon these institutions they raised new political structures. Western and Eastern peoples also combined elements from both the barbarian and Classical inheritances to form their distinctive cultures.

This chapter examines the emergence of Western Europe—one of the three successor civilizations to arise in the Early Middle Ages upon the twin supports of peasant labor and a confident expectation of life after death.

I. THE NEW COMMUNITY OF PEOPLES

The civilization that took root in the west and north of Europe after the decline of the Roman Empire was unmistakably the direct ancestor of the modern Western world. Traditionally, historians have called the millennium between the fall of the Empire and approximately 1500 the Middle Ages of European history. Today, almost all historians further divide the European Middle Ages into three distinct periods:

Early Middle Ages	500–1000
Central Middle Ages	1000–1350
Late Middle Ages	1350–1500

The Early Middle Ages witnessed the emergence from the shambles of the Roman Empire of the first recognizably Western civilization.

Early medieval Europe was founded upon a new community of peoples, which embraced both the former subjects of the Empire and "barbarians" beyond its borders. The Romans (and the Greeks before them) called these peoples "barbarians" because of their unintelligible languages and strange customs. Modern historians use the word with caution. It suggests that there was a single barbarian nation. In fact these peoples were many, and differed considerably, one from the others, in language and culture. And the modern use of the word conveys a tone of disparagement. This is unfortunate. The business of the historian is to seek to understand, and not to judge and rank, the societies of the past. With these reservations, we too may call these peoples, as did the Romans, the barbarians. They had been settled for centuries beyond the frontiers of the Roman Empire and had played only minor roles in the cultural life of the ancient world.

The Great Migrations

On the island fringes of northern Europe were Celtic tribes, Gaels in Ireland and Picts in Scotland, who had escaped the Roman domination to which their cousins, the Britons and the Gauls, had fallen subject. More numerous and more formidable than the Celts were the Germans, who were settled in a great territorial arc that stretched from Scandinavia to the Black Sea and rimmed the Roman frontier on the Rhine and Danube rivers. The Germans had benefited from strong Mediterranean influences and were culturally the most advanced of the barbarian peoples. From about 350, through the preaching of a missionary called Ulfilas, Christianity spread among the Germans north of the Danube, but in its Arian form (see p. 185). The adherence of many Germanic tribes—Goths, Vandals, and Lombards—to Arianism later obstructed their assimilation with the largely orthodox Romans. Beyond this Germanic cordon lived the still pagan Slavic tribes, probably the most numerous of the barbarians.

The Germanic tribes had for centuries challenged the Roman frontiers. Their primitive and poorly productive economies forced them to search constantly for new lands to plunder or settle. They were probably more prolific in producing children than the Mediterranean peoples. Several Classical authors affirm (incorrectly) that the name Germany derives from the word *germinate*. Understandably, the Germans were attracted by the wealth and splendor of the Roman world. Even while resisting their armies, the Romans had admitted barbarians into the Empire. Initially, the barbarians came as slaves or prisoners of war, then as free peasants to settle on deserted lands of the Empire, and finally as mercenary soldiers and officers.

This barbarian penetration into the Roman Empire acquired a new urgency and a new violence in the fourth century. Pressed by nomadic hordes from central Asia, the Germanic tribes that lived beyond the frontier moved to find more protected homes; and the Roman Empire, weakened by internal troubles, could no longer mount an effective guard over its borders.

300–1000/TIMELINE

International and Military History	Political History

300

376 Visigoths, pushed by Huns, cross Danube River
378 Visigoths defeat Romans at Adrianople
406 Vandals and Suevi cross Rhine frontier
410 Visigoths under Alaric sack Rome
418 Visigoths at Toulouse establish first autonomous
    kingdom within territory of Roman Empire
429 Vandals cross into North Africa and establish kingdom
451 Gallo-Roman army turns back Huns under
    Attila at Chalons
452 Attila invades Italy; Pope Leo I saves Rome*
453 Death of Attila
455 Vandals under Gaiseric sack Rome
476 Traditional date for end of Roman Empire in the West
487 Ostrogoths besiege Constantinople
489 Ostrogoths under Theodoric pass into Italy
535–554 Byzantines reconquer Italy; destroy
        Ostrogothic Kingdom
550–700 Slavs penetrate Balkans
568 Lombards invade Italy

425–455 Reign of Valentinian III, last effective Western emperor

481–511 Reign of Clovis, first Merovingian king of the Franks

489–526 Reign of Theodoric the Great; heyday of Ostrogothic kingdom in Italy

687 Pepin of Heristal, Mayor of the Palace, unites East and West Frankland
714–741 Charles Martel, Mayor of the Palace
747–768 Pepin the Short ruler of the Franks

711–715 Muslims overthrow Visigothic kingdom in Spain
732 Charles Martel, Frankish mayor of the palace, defeats Muslims at Tours

751 Pepin elected king; last Merovingian deposed
754 Pope Stephen II annoints Pepin; alliance of papacy and Frankish monarchy
756 Donation of Pepin establishes Patrimony of St. Peter
768–814 Reign of Charlemagne

773–774 Charlemagne campaigns in Italy; takes title, king of the Lombards
778 Ambush of rear-guard of Frankish army at Roncesvalles; inspiration for Song of Roland
785 Charlemagne initiates conquest and conversion of Saxons
787–788 Charlemagne deposes duke of Bavaria and takes his territory
787 First Viking raid into England

800

800 Coronation of Charlemagne as emperor by pope at Rome
814–840 Louis the Pious emperor; breakup of empire begins

827 Saracens (Muslims) invade Sicily and southern Italy
842 Saracens raid Rhone valley
846 Saracens sack Rome

843 Treaty of Verdun; empire divided among Lothair, Louis the German, and Charles the Bald
871–899 Reign of Alfred the Great in England

911 Viking Rollo acquires Normandy

919–936 Henry I Fowler king of the Germans, first of the Saxon line
936–973 Otto I the Great, king of the Germans

955 Otto I defeats Magyars at Lechfeld

962 Otto crowned emperor in Italy; restoration of Western empire

1000

1013 Danish king Swein conquers England

1016–1035 Canute the Great rules Denmark, Norway, and England

*e events printed in white type are discussed in other chapters.

300–1000/TIMELINE

Social and Economic History	Cultural and Intellectual History
—300—	
	313 Edict of Milan extends toleration to Christians
	343 Council of Sardica confirms right of appeal to popes
	350 Ulfilas converts Germans north of Danube to Christianity
	412-424 Augustine composes *City of God*
c. 451-568 Refugees from mainland settle Adriatic islands, found city of Venice	440 Pope Leo I affirms primacy of Roman pontiffs in Church
	451 Council of Chalcedon recognizes papal authority in deciding dogmatic questions
	496 Conversion of Clovis, king of the Franks, to orthodox Christianity
c. 500 Diffusion of heavy plow among Germans and Slavs	526 Boethius, author of *The Consolation of Philosophy*, executed by Theodoric
	529 St. Benedict founds monastery at Monte Cassino; writes Benedictine rule
—550—	550-750 Great age of Irish monasticism
	585? Death of Cassiodorus, author of *Divine and Human Readings*
	590-604 Pontificate of Gregory the Great
632-732 Muslim conquests jeopardize Mediterranean trade	597 Augustine, dispatched by Gregory, begins conversion of the English
	663 Council of Whitby determines that English should follow Roman rather than Celtic Christianity
	673?-735 Bede the Venerable, greatest scholar of his age
763 First documentary reference to the three-field system	
768-814 Charlemagne reforms coinage; new system based on silver *denarius*	
	782-794 Alcuin of York leader of the Carolingian Renaissance
— 800 —	c. 800 Development of Carolingian minuscule
c. 820 Survey of the lands of St.-Gérmain des Pres near Paris; first full view of manorial organization	
	842 Earliest surviving text in old French
	871-899 Alfred the Great promotes learning in England
	886 Conversion of Danes in England
	c. 950-1050 Rapid spread of Christianity in Scandinavian countries
992 Byzantine Empire grants trade privileges to Venice	
—1000—	
	1001 Stephen, king of Hungary, accepts Christianity and receives papal crown

The nomads who sowed tumult in the barbarian world were the Huns, a people probably of Mongolian or Tatar origin. For reasons still not fully understood, but perhaps in reaction to weather changes and the desiccation of their pastures, they swept out of their Asiatic homeland and terrorized Western Europe. In 375 the Huns subjugated the Ostrogoths, who were settled in what is now the Ukraine, and routed the Visigoths on the Dniester River. Their great chief Attila (433?–453), the "scourge of God" according to Christian writers, established his horde on the plain of the middle Danube, and from there led them on raids into both Gaul and Italy. With Attila's death in 453, the Hunnic empire disintegrated, but the Huns had already given impetus to the great movement of peoples that better than any other event marks the beginning of the Middle Ages.

The Visigoths were the first of the Germanic tribes to be dislodged. In 376 they petitioned the Emperor Valens, the ruler of the Eastern Roman Empire, to settle within its borders. They were admitted, but the hungry barbarians soon rebelled at the high prices that Roman officials demanded for food. To put down the uprising, Valens led an expedition against them but rashly disdained to await reinforcements from the West. The Visigothic cavalry scattered the ranks of the Roman legions at Adrianople in 378. This battle marked the end of the Romans' military advantage over the barbarians and showed the superiority of the mounted warrior (the prototype of the medieval knight) over the foot soldier. The Visigoths settled for a while in the Balkan Peninsula, then continued on a westward movement. They sacked Rome in 410 and crossed the Alps into Gaul, where they established the first autonomous kingdom on Roman soil in 418. At its height in the mid-fifth century the kingdom of the Visigoths extended from Gibraltar to the Loire River. The Franks conquered the kingdom in Gaul in the sixth century; the Saracens, the surviving kingdom in Spain in the eighth century.

Another tribe pushed by pressure from the Huns was the Vandals. They broke across the Rhine River into Gaul in 406. Within three years, they passed over the Pyrenees into Spain and moved south to the shores of the Mediterranean Sea. Perhaps 80,000 in number, the Vandals crossed to North Africa, where they established a permanent kingdom in 429. Arians, they persecuted the orthodox Christians. Their cruelty earned them a reputation for senseless violence, which the modern word *vandal* still reflects. They were the only barbarians to become a power on the Mediterranean Sea. In 455 they plundered Rome. They also harassed shipping on Western waters until they were destroyed by the Byzantines in the next century.

The Burgundians followed the Vandals into Gaul, probably in 411. These Germans established an independent kingdom in the valleys of the upper Rhone and Saône rivers in 443. The region they settled retained thereafter the name of Burgundy.

The ease with which these Germans invaded the Roman frontiers indicates that the authority of the Empire had almost vanished by the middle of the fifth century. The Emperor Valentinian III was the last Roman to exercise any real power in the West. After his death in 455 a series of feeble emperors followed. They were raised to the throne, deposed, or murdered by German officials in the palace, who were the effective rulers. One of those barbarians, Odoacer, deposed the last emperor in 476. Although no more than a palace mutiny, this coup marks the final passage of power from Roman to German hands.

Odoacer remained in control until overthrown by Theodoric, who was the leader of the Ostrogoths. After the disintegration of the Hunnic empire the Ostrogoths penetrated the Roman frontiers in the East and besieged Constantinople in 487. As a diversionary tactic the Eastern Emperor Zeno persuaded Theodoric to invade Italy, which he did in 489. Odoacer resisted tenaciously, but after years of struggle Theodoric tricked, ambushed, and murdered him, and established his own Ostrogothic kingdom in Italy in 493. A shrewd ruler, he gave Italy more than 30 years of peace and even some prosperity. Romans and Germans learned to live together in the Ostrogothic kingdom. Although it was not destined for long survival, it may justly be regarded as the first medieval state.

In the third and fourth centuries the Germanic tribes living just beyond the Roman frontier in the Rhine valley coalesced into two large federations, the Alemanni in the upper valley and the Franks in the lower valley. The Alemanni pushed beyond the Rhine into the middle of Gaul and founded a kingdom in 420. They give to both modern French and Spanish their names for Germany (*Allemagne, Alemania*). The Franks slowly penetrated into northern Gaul, moving across the valley of the Seine up to the Loire River. By the fifth century they had separated into two peoples: the Salian, or "salty," Franks, who occupied the lands from the shores of the British Channel to the Loire valley (excluding only Brittany); and the Ripuarian, or "river bank," Franks, whose history is wrapped in obscurity, but who seem to have settled between the Rhine and Meuse rivers. The first-mentioned king of the Salians, a figure who stands on the dark margin between legend and history, was called Merovech, and he gave his name to the first dynasty of Frankish kings, the Merovingians. The true founder of the kingdom of the Franks, however, was his putative grandson Clovis (481–511).[1]

At the time of Clovis's accession the various Germanic tribes were contending for supremacy over each other and the native Gallo-Romans. Clovis's great accomplishment was the political unification of nearly the whole of Gaul. Already king of the Salians, he had himself elected king of the Ripuarians and thus ruled a united Frankish people. He then con-

quered the Gallo-Romans at Soissons, the Alemanni, and the Visigoths at Vouillé (see Map 6.1). His sons added both Burgundy and Provence to the kingdom, nearly completing the conquest of Gaul.

No less important for unification was Clovis's conversion, probably about 496, to Roman, rather than Arian, Christianity. This step won him the sympathy and support of the orthodox Gallo-Romans, facilitated his conquests, spared his kingdom the religious divisions between ruler and ruled that debilitated the regimes of the Visigoths and Vandals, and made possible the peaceful assimilation of the diverse peoples he ruled. As the first barbarians to accept Roman Christianity, the Franks became the "eldest daughter" of the Western Church and soon its acknowledged sword and champion.

The Germanic invasions of Britain differed from the conquests on the Continent. The Germans—Angles, Saxons, Jutes, even some Franks and Frisians—did not enter Britain as single tribes or nations. Rather, they came in small bands under the authority of chiefs. These Germans did not settle and assimilate with the native peoples (the Britons), as they did in most other Roman provinces; they either exterminated the Britons or pushed them westward into Cornwall and Wales. While seeking safer homes some Britons crossed the Channel to settle in the Roman province of Armorica, which therefore came to be called Brittany or "little" Britain, as distinct from Great Britain, their former homeland. For a few decades in the early sixth century the Britons rallied against the Germanic incursions under a king whom later sources call Arthur, but they could not permanently resist the inundation of their home. After 550 the Germans rapidly consolidated their conquests and imposed their language on the region. So sharp is the linguistic break that modern English, apart from place names, shows little trace of the speech of the original inhabitants.

The Slavic tribes to the east of the Germanic cordon embarked on their own extensive mi-

---

[1] His name is really a cognate of Louis; thus, by this historical oddity, all the Louis's in the long line of French kings are misnumbered.

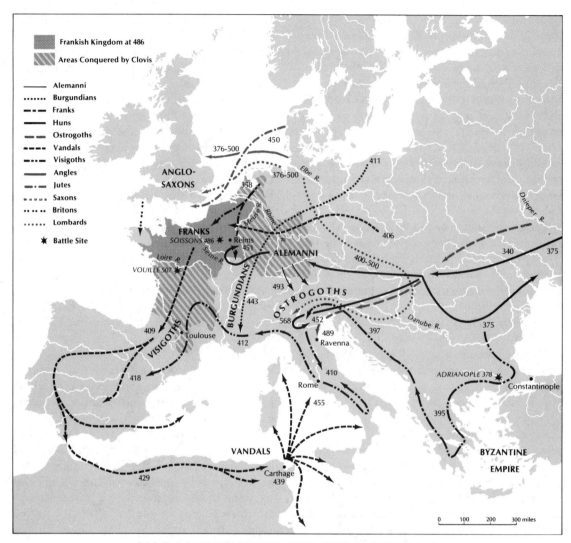

Frankish Kingdom at 486

Areas Conquered by Clovis

Alemanni
Burgundians
Franks
Huns
Ostrogoths
Vandals
Visigoths
Angles
Jutes
Saxons
Britons
Lombards
✳ Battle Site

MAP 6.1. INVASIONS 4TH–6TH CENTURIES

grations. In the fifth and sixth centuries some Slavic tribes pushed their settlements as far west as the Elbe River and as far north as the Baltic Sea; they are the ancestors of the modern West Slavs, the Poles, Czechs, and Slovaks. During the same years other Slavic tribes penetrated into the Balkan Peninsula and Greece; their descendants are the modern South Slavs, the

Serbs, Croats, Bulgarians, and Macedonians. Still other tribes moved east beyond the Dnieper River and north into the forest regions of Russia; they are the ancestors of the modern East Slavs, the Russians, Ukrainians, and Byelo-, or White, Russians.

No other Indo-European peoples came to occupy so extensive a geographic area as the

Slavs, although distance inevitably weakened their ethnic and cultural unity. The West Slavs were influenced primarily by Germanic and Latin culture, and the East Slavs and most of the South Slavs by the civilization of the Eastern or Byzantine Empire.

Germans and Romans

Historians have estimated, although on flimsy evidence, that the Germans who settled within the Roman Empire constituted no more than 5 percent of the total population. The Germanic chiefs and armies were apparently allocated one-third of the tax revenues from the land; this was the share traditionally allotted to an army quartered in a Roman province under an established practice known as "hospitality." With time (and the disintegration of Roman administration) this right to taxes gave them a claim to perhaps a third of the land itself. The kings and chiefs seem to have retained the greater part of the acquired land. Most of the humble freemen apparently settled as cultivators, obligated to pay rents and perform services to the owners of the property; but, unlike the *coloni* in the Late Roman Empire, these freemen retained their liberty of movement.

The Germans did not exterminate the Roman curial and senatorial classes or establish an exclusively Germanic aristocracy; rather, they gradually intermarried and made use of the inhabitants' skills. The Germans, great or humble, rich or poor, thus adopted lives that made them almost indistinguishable from their Roman counterparts. This favored assimilation.

Historians no longer speak confidently, as they once did, of specifically Germanic contributions to medieval and Western civilization. Even before entering the Empire, many Germans, particularly those settled near the frontiers, had achieved a cultural level that resembled that of the Romans. Moreover, the great majority of the Roman subjects probably could not read and did not share the sophisticated culture of the Roman aristocracy. Some historians point to the existence, under the Late Roman Empire, of a vulgar culture—that is, one that reflected the lives of the majority of the people rather than the aristocracy; it did not respect political boundaries, and was already joining invaders and Romans in one cultural community.

The Germans reinforced certain pronounced characteristics of late Roman and early medieval civilizations. The destruction they wrought and their apparent reluctance to settle in cities accelerated the decline of urban life in the West. The centers of economic, social, and cultural life shifted to the countryside. This was a critical change, for cities had dominated the economy and culture of the Classical Mediterranean world.

Germanic Society
The Role of Women

A sensitive indicator of social values, in the study of any society, is the status of women. Under the Roman Empire in the Classical age, girls did not fare well. Given the toleration of infanticide, baby girls were more likely to be abandoned or killed than their brothers. Those who survived were married (at least within the aristocratic classes, about which we are best informed) at a young age—usually about 16— to men who were usually about 10 years older, and under unfavorable terms. The bride, or her family, had to provide a substantial dowry to the groom. Many young Roman men were thus persuaded to delay marriage until they could make the most profitable match.

Germanic (and barbarian) society was much different in its treatment of women. The Roman historian Tacitus praises the Germans for their chastity and fidelity, but he notes that men "of high position" took several wives. A system in which rich men marry several times is

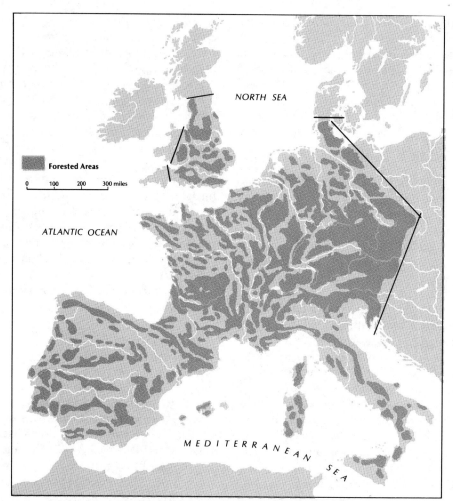

**MAP 6.2. FORESTED AREAS OF WESTERN EUROPE
IN THE EARLY MIDDLE AGES**

**Geographers estimate that three-quarters of
the surface area of Western Europe remained
heavily forested in the Early Middle Ages.
Human settlements in the small clearances
sometimes achieved a high density of inhabitants but remained separated from one another
by vast reaches of wilderness.**

German women, Tacitus also tells us, were
mature at first marriage, and their husbands
were equal in age. To his surprise, the family
of the groom paid a dowry to the bride, which
was hers to keep and to pass on to her heirs.

Why this contrast? Historians are not certain. The most likely explanation is that resource polygyny heightened the competition
for brides. Moreover, women made essential
contributions to the Germanic household at
every social level. The free German male as-

called "resource polygyny." Polygyny of this
kind seems to have been more common among
the Germans than Tacitus implies.

pired to be a warrior; he needed someone who would tend his fields and watch over his flocks and herds during his absences. A wife who worked enabled him to fight. The chief or king similarly looked for someone who could collect his dues, pay his retainers, and manage his lands. Germanic women did these things, and were valued. In Classical Mediterranean society, slaves or freemen fulfilled these services. The social importance of Germanic women was not, however, an unmixed benefit. Still according to Tacitus, they worked harder than the men. In a violent society they were often the prized booty for raiding expeditions, and constant targets of abduction. Their life expectancy seems to have been shorter than that of males, but their smaller number added to their social value.

The Germanic attitude toward children was also distinctive. The dominant cultures of the Mediterranean world, based on literacy and learning, required for their preservation that heavy investments be made in the education of the young. But in spite of its aura of affluence, Classical society was poor. Typically, Classical peoples opted to make that high investment, but in a limited number of offspring. The illiterate Germans, on the other hand, selected another option: they reared many children, but invested little in their upbringing. Tacitus notes that the Germans, unlike the Romans, did not practice infanticide, but they also treated their children with benign neglect. Children of rich and poor were reared with equal indifference. This contrast in cultures helped assure that the Germanic peoples would eventually overwhelm the Roman world, by dint of sheer numbers.

Social Structure and Law

The German chief had an ambiguous position in relation to the tribe and its members. Before their invasions these peoples did not usually have kings; only the invasions, which required a continuing military command, made kings usual within Germanic society. The king was thus primarily a military leader and chief priest. He could not change the old customs. His power rested less on the accepted prerogative and law and more on the naked violence he could threaten or apply.

The uncertain powers of the chief left to the family or kinship group the responsibility for avenging the injuries done to its members. Custom regulated this violent practice by defining in monetary terms how much compensation could be demanded for a person's life (the *Wergeld*), arm, eye, or nose; but the responsibility and initiative in punishing or avenging a crime remained the family's and not the chief's.

Because the family was frequently unable to protect its members, Germanic societies were prolific in forming associations of self-help. Tacitus wrote a description of such an association, which he calls a *comitatus* ("following").[2] Young warriors would join the retinue of an established chief, follow him to battle, and fight under his leadership in return for his protection, a share of his booty, and a reflection of his glory. The social and moral tie between chief and follower much resembles the relationship between lord and vassal in the later feudal system. Another association of self-help was the guild. Unlike the *comitatus* this was an association of equals, and in its early appearances had no relation to economic life. The guild brothers offered gifts to the gods, feasted and drank together, and aided one another against common dangers. Like the *comitatus,* the guild was to have a long and important "afterlife" in medieval social history.

Writing, though not unknown, was little utilized in Germanic societies, and this explains several salient peculiarities of their institutions. To record the creation of contractual obliga-

---

[2]*Agricola and the Germania,* Hugh Mattingly (tr.), 1971, chaps. 13-14. Among the Eastern Slavs the comparable institution was the *druzhina.*

tions, the Germans (and the medieval world after them) relied heavily on symbolic gestures publicly performed. In conveying property, for example, the former owner would hand a twig or a clod of earth to its recipient; witnesses would note the act and later testify to its occurrence. But depending on the testimony of witnesses was a very precarious method for solving juridical disputes. Therefore, the Germans determined truth or falsehood, guilt or innocence, by investigating the characters of the litigants or appealing to magic. In a practice known as compurgation 12 good men who typically knew nothing at all about the facts at issue would swear to the honest reputation and presumed innocence of the accused. Or the accused would undergo an ordeal (the word originally meant "judgment"). He would run barefoot over hot irons or immerse his hand in a cauldron of boiling water; if his feet or hand showed no severe burns, he was declared innocent. Sometimes two contenders in a litigation would simply duel before the court on the assumption that God would not allow the innocent to be vanquished. To set and maintain policies, the Germans relied on old and respected men of the community to recall and state the ancient customs. This explains one of the most distinctive features of tribal government: the use of large councils or assemblies. The chief never made decisions alone; he always acted in an assembly or council of freemen who could help him recall the customs and aid him in making his judgments.

These practices influenced the development of several institutions of medieval law and government. The use of juries in trials, a common practice in Europe in the Middle Ages, was based on the assumption that the entire community, represented by sworn men, and not by the judge alone, should determine when a law was broken. The medieval king, like his early Germanic predecessor, was also expected to make his major decisions with the advice of the great men of the realm, assembled in councils

or parliaments. The connection between the later juries and parliaments and these tribal practices is admittedly distant, but certainly exists.

Germanic Culture

Since the Germans made little use of writing, their literature was preserved by oral transmission. Poetry, more easily memorized than prose, was the favored form of literary expression. The earliest surviving examples of Germanic poetry were not written down until the ninth century, but they still provide an authentic reflection of barbarian culture. Military values saturated barbarian literature, appropriately in a violent age. In the Anglo-Saxon epic *Beowulf* the king of the Danes, Hrothgar, is powerless against the terrible monster Grendel; his plight illustrates the weakness of tribal kingship. Hrothgar must appeal for help to the hero Beowulf. This great warrior offers to the community its one hope of salvation. There is little wonder that the Germans (and medieval society after them) looked upon warriors and their virtues with awe and admiration.

Religion displayed an abiding sense of pessimism. The Germans saw nature as a cruel and hostile force controlled by two sets of gods. Minor deities and spirits, both good and bad, dwelt in groves, streams, fields, and seas and directly affected the human community. Through incantations, spells, or charms people tried to influence the actions of these spirits. These magical practices (foreign to the paganism of the ancient world) strongly influenced popular religion and mixed with it a large element of superstition, which would persist for the entire length of the Middle Ages and for a long time thereafter.

The high gods lived in the sky and took a remote interest in the affairs of men. Chief among them was Woden or Odin, god of magic and victory, whom Tacitus equates with the Roman Mercury. Woden, his wife Friia or

This Anglo-Saxon buckle belonged to an East Anglian king who died in 654. It is made of gold and niello, a black metallic substance that lends itself to incision of a design; the cuts are then filled in to produce the ornamental effect. The interlaced beasts in the ornamentation illustrate the Animal style of barbarian art. The buckle is one of forty-one solid gold items recovered from the ship burial at Sutton Hoo, England, and shows the great value given to gold jewelry by the barbarian kings.
(Photo: British Museum)

Frig, Thor the thunderer, Ti or Tyr the god of war—all give their names to days of the week in all Germanic languages, including English. According to late Scandinavian myth, warriors who died in battle joined the following of Odin in a great banquet hall, Valhalla. War, in other words, was a holy, redemptive exercise. But the entire company of gods and heroes was doomed to destruction by fire during a cosmic twilight when the ravaged earth would sink entirely into the sea. It is not known whether the early Germans shared this elaborate myth. They certainly shared in the exaltation of heroes and in a deep pessimism about mankind's ultimate fate.

The fundamental circumstances of Germanic life also influenced artistic forms. Because they changed their homes so frequently, the Germans developed no monumental art—no temples, palaces, or large statues—before they were settled within the empire. Their loveliest form of artistic expression was jewelry—buckles, brooches, necklaces, and crowns—made from precious metals. Many of these pieces show the Animal style, which embodied the forms of animals in the design of the jewelry. This style seems to have originated in the steppe region of Eastern Europe and Asia and then to have spread westward among both Slavs and Germans. The Animal style exerted a wide influence upon early medieval art; even the lettering and illuminations in the manuscripts of that epoch reflect some of its motifs (see Plate 9).

The period after the invasions witnessed a near triumph of vulgar, nonliterate culture over the literate, urban culture of the Roman aristocracy. The invaders were not alone responsible for the triumph of a popular, non-aristocratic culture in the West. Undoubtedly, the great, unlettered masses of the Roman Empire shared many of the tribal attitudes and practices; but the invasions did lend this vulgar culture a new strength and visibility.

II. THE NEW ECONOMY, 500–900

The great achievement of the Early Middle Ages was the emergence of the single-family farm as the basic unit of agricultural production. Europe became and long remained a peasant society. Several factors contributed to the formation of the medieval peasantry. The declining supply of slaves induced many villa owners to settle their slaves on family farms rather than to work them in gangs. The changes in warfare, specifically the new supremacy of the mounted warrior, made fighting an expensive, hence exclusive, profession and forced many freemen into the ranks of full-time cultivators. And a series of technological innovations in agriculture aided the peasant in supporting himself, his family, and the new society.

Agriculture

The most fertile agricultural region of Europe is the great alluvial plain that stretches from southeast England and France to the Urals. The peoples of the ancient world had not been able to farm it efficiently. The light plow of antiquity only scratched the earth, though it was suitable enough for the thin soil and dry climate in the Mediterranean areas. Cultivation there required that the surface be pulverized to retain moisture, but not cut deeply. On the northern plain, however, the earth had to be cut and turned to form the furrows needed to carry away excess water from the abundant rains. Thus a heavier plow was necessary, one that was more complex and powerful. An obscure passage in Pliny suggests that the Germans had such a plow as early as the first century after Christ; but most historians date its diffusion, simultaneously among the Germans and the Slavs, only from the sixth century.

The light plow, which continued to be used in Mediterranean lands during the Middle Ages, was dragged by two oxen. The heavy plow, used on the plain of northern Europe, required the use of teams of as many as eight oxen. The Romans had harnessed the horse with almost incredible inefficiency. He was bound to his load by pliant straps around his throat and belly that rewarded his best efforts by strangling him. Moreover, he was hitched to his load so high on his withers that he could not throw his full weight against the harness. Northern Europeans did not develop a collar and harness that made efficient use of the horse as a draft animal until the ninth century. At about the same time the tandem harness, which permitted teams of horses to be hitched one behind the other, and the horseshoe, which gave the animal better traction and protected his sensitive hooves, came into common use in Europe. By virtue of all these devices the Early Middle Ages, in the words of one historian, "discovered horsepower."[3]

Northern Europeans also developed a new method of crop rotation: the three-field system, first documented in 763. This routine of cultivation was based on a triennial cycle. The field was planted in winter wheat, then in a spring crop—oats, barley, peas, or beans—then permitted to lie fallow for a year. The older two-field system, which continued to be used in Mediterranean lands, was based on the yearly alternation of winter wheat and fallow. Spring crops were difficult to raise in the south because rain was scarce in the spring and summer months, but they grew well in the north because of the abundant year-round rainfall.

The three-field system kept a larger portion (two-thirds) of the soil under crops. It raised the productive efficiency of the peasant's labor by an even higher degree; the fallow, although it returned no crop, still had to be worked, and

---

[3] Lynn White, Jr., *Medieval Technology and Social Change,* 1966, pp. 57–69.

tatis: qui fingis laborem in precepto.
Captabunt in animam iusti: t san
guinem innocentem condempnabut.

The Luttrell Psalter, produced in England about 1340, is particularly known for its scenes of rural life. This fragment from the psalter illustrates the act of plowing. The heavy plow used on the plain of northern Europe included three indispensable parts: a colter or knife to cut the soil, a share or wedge to widen the breech and break up the clods, and a mold-board to lift the earth and turn the furrow.
(Photo: British Museum)

with a smaller fallow (one-third rather than one-half the land) the peasant had more time for productive labors. The spring crop restored fertility to the soil, provided a more varied diet for the people, and lessened the risk of total failure because two crops were planted in one year. Since the spring crop was often intended for fodder, it also helped support a larger number of animals. The animals in turn provided manure for more abundant crops. For the first time the agricultural resources of the northern plain were used with some measure of efficiency.

These technological innovations did not transform agriculture overnight. Their use spread through Europe at a glacial pace, and not without resistance; but it remains accurate to say that these technological innovations profoundly affected the character of the new Western civilization. They allowed the regions of northern Europe to support a denser population and established a tradition of technical innovation that has remained alive and unbroken to the present.

The Manor

Europeans developed a new form of agricultural organization: the manor, or large estate. Its origins are obscure. Documents from the Continent do not mention the manor with any clarity or frequency until the middle of the eighth century. The first full view we have of manorial organization is a survey of the lands of a Parisian monastery, St.-Germain-des-Prés, done about 820. Manors do not fully appear in English sources until the eleventh century. The manor may have emerged directly out of the Roman villa. However, certain contrasts distinguish the manor from the villa. The Roman

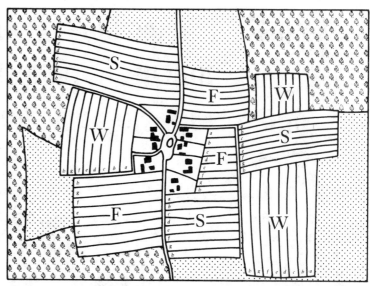

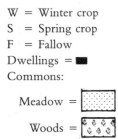

W = Winter crop
S = Spring crop
F = Fallow
Dwellings = ■■
Commons:

Meadow = [ ]

Woods = [ ]

This figure is a simplified reconstruction of a medieval village under the "open field" system of cultivation. Each peasant household owns a strip of land in each of nine large, cultivated fields. The holdings of each family (its hide, or *mansus*) are designated by the letter *a, b, c,* etc. The strips are "open"—that is, no fence or barrier encloses them. The village, and not the individual owners, determines the rotation that each cultivator must follow. Here, the large fields are cultivated according to a three-course rotation—winter crop, spring crop, and fallow. The owners of the separate strips also have the right to graze a set number of animals in the common meadow and woods. If the village formed part of a manor, the lord's demesne would probably also consist of open strips distributed across the large fields.

---

coloni were not obligated, as far as sources inform us, to the labor requirements that were imposed on the medieval serfs. The lord of the villa was primarily dependent upon slaves or hired labor to work his lands, whereas the lord of the manor relied upon his serfs. It seems, then, that the manor was not truly an inheritance from the late Empire but acquired its characteristic organization during the opening centuries of the Middle Ages.

Manorial organizations never extended over the whole of Europe and perhaps never included even a majority of the peasants. The manor was characteristic of southeast England, northern France, western Germany, and certain areas of the south, such as the Rhone and Po valleys. These were regions of fertile soil where cereals in particular could be cultivated intensively. In its idealized form the manor may be defined as a tightly disciplined community of peasants organized under the authority of a lord. The manor should be thought of as a fundamental unit of economic, political, and social organization.

The lands of most manors were divided into two roughly equal parts: the small farms (called

hides in England and *mansi* on the Continent) that belonged to the peasants, and the large demesne that the peasants worked for the lord. All manors possessed extensive meadows, forests, and wastelands where the lord hunted and the peasant grazed his animals or collected firewood. Forests and wastelands were usually part of the lord's demesne; but the peasants too would often have their own commons, a collectively owned meadow in which each resident had the right to graze a fixed number of animals. Many manors also had workshops that produced garments, tools, and other products needed by the community. Self-sufficiency, in other words, remained an ideal in manorial organization, although it could never be completely realized.

The lord was the chief police officer and judge. He or his steward ran the court, which was an important source of revenues. The lord held the rights to operate the bakery, brewery, mill, and winepress on the manor and to sell the peasants salt or iron. He was also the chief military officer, recruiting soldiers from among the free peasants and leading them to war. For many peasants the manorial lord was the only government they ever directly confronted.

Most of the peasants inhabiting the manor were serfs; they, and their children after them, could not leave the land without the lord's permission. Men were usually obligated to work three days a week upon the lord's demesne and to provide additional services at other times of the year, particularly at harvest. Women were required to spend some time in the workshops producing cloth and clothing. The serfs paid, usually in kind, a yearly rental on their land and sometimes a small head tax to the lord. They also honored him with yearly gifts, such as eggs in the spring or a capon in the fall. When a serf died and his farm passed to a son, the family usually paid an inheritance tax, either the best animal or piece of furniture, to the lord. If a serf wished to marry someone outside the manor, he had to seek, and usually purchase, the lord's permission. Besides the serfs most manors had a smaller number of free peasants. They had to pay a yearly rent for land they held but were not subject to the labor obligation or (usually) to the head tax.

Although serfs lived harsh lives, their condition was still superior to that of the Roman slave. Serfs had a moral right to their land, and

the lord who took it away from them committed, in the opinion of the age, a grievous sin; therefore, they and their children could profit from the improvements they made on the land. Moreover, the serfs' obligations were traditional and fixed and could not be raised.

This highly disciplined community was well adapted to the age. The manor offered protection to its members and promoted group cooperation. Few peasants could afford, as individuals, the expensive heavy plow and the large team of animals required to pull it. In working collectively for the lord, the peasants learned to work collectively for one another. From what historians can reconstruct, the great manors supported the best and most progressive technological innovations in agriculture; thus, they served as a kind of formal school for the peasantry.

The Exchange of Wealth

Even as the descendants of Roman slaves and *coloni* and the tribal freemen were learning the ways of peasant agriculture, a new set of economic relations was binding together the kings, chiefs, and great personages in early medieval society. These relations—an "economy of gift and pillage" in the phrase of one historian—were defined in large part by the flow of treasure, of brooches, rings, plates, cups, armor, and coins. The exquisite jewelry, which the Early Middle Ages has bequeathed to us in substantial quantities, not only pleased the eye but served an important social function: it rewarded accomplishment, advertised status, and cemented the social structure.

Kings gained treasure through pillage, gifts, or tribute from their neighbors, and in turn distributed the precious objects among their warriors and retainers. In *Beowulf* (written probably in the tenth century, but reflecting older practice) King Hrothgar is lauded as the "ring-giver." In the moral sense of the age, a gift placed an obligation upon the recipient to reciprocate, either through a return gift or through service. The gift thus established an enduring social bond between donor and recipient. The ethic of the gift even affected religious life. Gifts made to churches that housed the bodies of saints placed these heavenly potentates under the obligation to reciprocate, to bless and favor the donor. Finally, the flow of treasure defined social status and made clear the lines of authority. The king was ring-giver, but also the master of important hoards of wealth. Even in death, the treasure buried with him proclaimed his royalty to another world. On the other hand, the humble participated in this gift economy only in their obligation to provide food to those who defended and ruled them.

The gift economy all but replaced the market economy of the Classical Roman world. The Romans had relied heavily on commerce to meet their essential needs, and maintained an elaborate network of trade routes, roads, ports, and markets. The Mediterranean in particular had served as a great commercial artery. Metals, wood, pottery, and raw materials from the Western provinces were exchanged for the wines, spices, and fine cloths of the Levant, and papyrus and grain from Egypt. By the seventh century, this once vigorous trade had dwindled to an unsteady trickle. Some historians claim that the Islamic incursions (see p. 261) transformed the Mediterranean from a highway to a battleground, and ended this trade. But the more profound reason seems to have been social and cultural changes in the West. The new society, composed of warriors and peasants, did not have the skill, and perhaps not the desire either, to maintain export industries, routes and roads, and large commercial markets.

The West in the Early Middle Ages, with its withered cities and limited commercial exchange, was a poor society. But it was not stagnant. Eventually, the new peasant economy would support advances, both agricultural and industrial, that would surpass the highest material achievements of the ancient world.

III. THE LEADERSHIP OF THE CHURCH

The Church exercised an unrivaled leadership in the Early Middle Ages. In an age of turbulence this institution retained the Roman tradition of effective social organization and social action. It also kept alive the classical tradition of literacy, rhetoric, and logic amid the upsurge of a nonliterate culture. One of history's great paradoxes is that the Church, so hostile to many values of the Classical tradition, was more effective than any other institution in assuring their survival.

Origins of the Papacy

The papacy is the oldest living institution in the Western world; it is the only institution that can trace its history back without interruption to the age of the Caesars. According to the traditional Catholic (and medieval) view Jesus himself endowed the apostle Peter with supreme responsibility for his church.

> And I say unto thee, thou art Peter and
> upon this rock I will build my church, and the
> gates of hell shall not prevail against it.
> [*Matthew 16:18*]

In the Aramaic language that Jesus spoke, as well as in Greek and Latin, "Peter" and "rock" are the same words, implying that the Church was to be founded upon Peter. This play on words has been called the most momentous pun in history. Medieval tradition further held that Peter became the first bishop of Rome and was martyred there about A.D. 60.

Modern historians can neither confirm nor refute this traditional interpretation. Records show that the pronouncements of the Roman bishops were often accepted by the bishops of other churches with extraordinary reverence. The earliest nonscriptural text showing the influence of the Roman bishops is a letter that Clement, fourth in the traditional list of popes, wrote to the Corinthians in 95. Clement clearly considered it his duty to counsel them. In the second century Ignatius, bishop of Lyons, taught that beliefs accepted by the Roman bishops as orthodox should be considered orthodox by the entire Church. But in the third century Cyprian, bishop of Carthage, maintained that all bishops were equal in responsibility and authority; there could be within the Church no "bishop of bishops."

Whatever the validity of these arguments, it is hardly surprising that the church at Rome should have acquired preeminence. Rome was, after all, the city of the Caesars, the capital of the world, and the center of Latin culture; people were accustomed to seeking guidance from Rome. The Christian community there dated from apostolic times, and it had no Western rival in age, size, wealth, and talent. Furthermore, the Roman bishops, although not distinguished speculative theologians, had an uncanny ability to recognize and support dogmatic positions which the Church was ultimately to accept as orthodox. In contrast some bishops in other cities supported positions that later became heresies. These bishops could not rival the Roman bishops' reputation as defenders of orthodox belief.

This small (8⅝ inches) ivory depiction of the Virgin was probably executed at Aachen, one of the capitals of Charlemagne, in the ninth century. Note that the Virgin holds spindles in her left hand; spinning was typically woman's work. But surprisingly, she also wears armor—gauntlets on her wrists and what look to be shoulder pieces. Though a woman doing woman's work, she is a militant, imperious figure, strikingly different from the sentimental madonnas of later medieval art.
(Photo: Metropolitan Museum of Art, gift of J. Pierpont Morgan, 1917)

Growth of Papal Primacy

The idea of a Roman primacy gained support and was expressed with clarity in the fourth and fifth centuries. The emperors, anxious to use the Church as an adjunct to their own imperial administration, favored the concentration of religious authority in Roman hands. The Council of Sardica (modern Sofia) in 343 affirmed the right of the Roman bishop to hear appeals from bishops deposed by provincial councils. Damasus (366–384) was the first pope to base his authority on the text of Matthew and the first to attach the term *apostolic* permanently to the Roman bishopric, or see. The most effective promoter of the conception of

Roman primacy was Pope Leo I (440–461). In numerous letters and sermons Leo identified the person of the living pope with the person of Peter and with his divine commission to rule the Church. At the Council of Chalcedon in 451 the bishops received the declaration of the papal legates with the words "Peter speaks through Leo."

These claims for Roman primacy, however, went largely unsupported by any administrative apparatus; there was no machinery for taking appeals to Rome. Furthermore, the popes rarely intervened in the affairs of local churches outside Italy. The Western churches chose their own bishops, managed their own affairs, and had little occasion to invite intervention. Although the popes were not exercising an autocracy over the Church, their prestige in the Western world was unrivaled.

Gregory the Great

In the absence of effective secular authority, the popes had to assume responsibility for the security of Italy and the defense of the Church. They negotiated with a sequence of invaders— Huns, Vandals, Ostrogoths, and Lombards— and repeatedly sought help from the distant and distracted Eastern emperors. The pope who best exemplifies the problems and accomplishments of the early medieval papacy is Gregory I (590–604).

Gregory was both a writer of great influence and a man of action. His career illustrates the survival of Roman governmental skill in the service of the Church. As a layman he had been a prefect of Rome, its highest official. Then he became a priest and served as papal emissary to Constantinople and as deacon of the Church, managing its estates and supporting its charitable services. When Gregory became pope, the Lombards were plundering the Roman countryside and threatening Rome with destruction and starvation. Under these difficult conditions he maintained the productive capacity of the Church's estates, kept food coming to Rome,

ransomed captives, aided widows and orphans, and organized the defense of the city. Gregory finally negotiated a truce with the Lombards in 598, although they continued to pose a threat to the security of Rome for more than a century.

Gregory was no less solicitous for the welfare of the entire Church. During his pontificate Gregory gave new momentum to missionary efforts and achieved some momentous successes. He sent a monk named Augustine and 30 companions to bring Christianity to England. The missionaries encountered strong opposition from the Anglo-Saxons, but ultimately converted them to Christianity. The new converts developed a strong veneration for St. Peter and a firm loyalty to Rome; some, including many kings, went on pilgrimage to Rome, and others became missionaries who carried the message to other barbarians. The Spanish Visigoths were also converted from Arian to Roman Christianity. By establishing a tradition of active involvement in the affairs of the world, to which most of his medieval successors would faithfully adhere, Gregory widened enormously the influence of the Roman see.

Monasticism

Even more effective than the papacy in shaping medieval civilization was monasticism. The ascetic ideal of fleeing the world in order to devote oneself to worship is common to many religions and is often considered the natural fulfillment of religious aspiration.

Christian monasticism began in the third century in Egypt. There, St. Anthony entered the desert to live a solitary life of rigorous asceticism. But severe practical difficulties limited the spread of this solitary or "eremetic" monasticism. The lone hermit could not easily find food or participate in the common liturgical prayer required of all Christians; moreover, the harsh, solitary life often brought on all sorts of psychological disturbances. To meet these practical needs and spiritual dangers, Pachomius, another "desert father," grouped his followers into a community and drew up for them the first monastic rule. He enjoined upon his monks the practice of chastity, poverty, and obedience to a spiritual abbot (from the Semitic *abba,* "father"). Pachomius's cenobitic (literally, "living in common") monasticism was readily received in other lands.

The Benedictine Rule

By the fifth century cenobitic monasticism had gained a powerful appeal in the West; but it developed into a bewildering variety of forms because all the great fathers of the Church—Augustine, Jerome, and Ambrose—gave advice in their writings to monks and ascetics. The monastic idea evoked a particularly fervent response among the Irish. Entire clans and tribes adopted the monastic life, with the chief assuming the title and functions of abbot. In the sixth and seventh centuries Irish monks gave their land and their people a preeminence in Western piety and letters. Roaming the Continent, the monks founded monasteries, preached to the heathen, reformed the Church, and corrected kings. Their work kept alive learning and intellectual life amid the chaos of the age.

The monk who brought uniformity and order into the movement, the great legislator of Western monasticism, was St. Benedict (480?–543?) from Nursia, in Italy. His rule is the only surviving literary work from his own hand, and much obscurity surrounds its origin and composition.[4]

As a young student at Rome Benedict was

appalled by the vice he encountered there and fled into the wilderness. His growing reputation for sanctity soon attracted numerous disciples. He organized them into cenobitic communities, initially at Subiaco. When a jealous priest drove him from Subiaco, Benedict founded a new community at Monte Cassino in 529. Near the end of his life he drew up his famous rule for this community.

The Benedictine rule was a constitution meant to be generally applicable to many individual communities. It was the product of a conscious reflection upon the purposes and

---

Pope Gregory the Great was one of the key figures in the transition from the ancient world to the Middle Ages. He is regarded, along with Jerome, Ambrose, and Augustine, as one (and the last) of the four fathers of the Latin Church. His efforts to defend Rome against the Lombards and to advance missionary work reaped added prestige to the papal see.
(Photo: Alinari/EPA, Inc.)

---

[4] Historians still discuss the relationship of the Benedictine rule to an apparently older, longer, and cruder monastic code known as the *Regula magistri.* The best opinion now seems to be that Benedict made wide use of this older code but still impressed his own personality and genius upon the rule which bears his name. For a discussion of the controversy see David Knowles, "The *Regula Magistri* and the Rule of St. Benedict," *Great Historical Enterprises: Problems in Monastic History,* 1963, pp. 135–196.

needs of monastic life. Monasteries were thus the one social group of early medieval Europe to possess a written, carefully constructed constitution. The monastic constitution is another example of the survival of Roman governmental genius in the service of the Church. The rule endowed the abbot with full authority (sovereignty, really) over the community; he was to be elected for life and could not be replaced. To assure that the monastery was a disciplined and stable community the rule instructed a monk not to wander from house to house or refuse obedience. The abbot was to consult regularly the elder brothers and, in important matters, to consider even the opinions of the youngest members, on the scriptural ground that God frequently makes known his will to children.

The Benedictine rule also included references to all the principal problems, practical and spiritual, of monastic life; but Benedict made the regulations simple and elastic. In order to test a monk's suitability for the monastic life, for example, he was to take his vows only after a trial period of one year. In setting the daily schedule of the monk he was to say prayers at regular intervals throughout the day (the liturgical hours) rather than as private acts of asceticism. One of the most famous regulations enjoined upon the monks some manual labor, lending to it a dignity which both the Romans and the barbarians had denied. "Idleness," said the regulation, "is the enemy of the soul."

The Role of the Monk

The monks exerted an extraordinary influence on every level of medieval civilization. They were the most successful agriculturists of the age, first as farmers in their own right and then gradually as managers of ever larger estates; thus, they set an example of good farming practices from which laymen could benefit. The weak governments relied heavily on monastic farms to supply food for their administrations and armies and often appropriated part of the monks' income from estates to finance their own needs. Monks were almost the only people who were literate and learned. The Benedictine rule assumed that the monk could read; and the monasteries, although not expressly obliged to do so, maintained both libraries and schools for the training of young monks and, sometimes, lay children. The monks also organized *scriptoria,* or writing offices, in which manuscripts that were needed for liturgy or education were copied. The great bulk of the surviving Latin literary works of both pagan and Christian antiquity were preserved in copies made in monasteries. Sometimes monks decorated, or illuminated, the manuscript pages; manuscript illuminations are among the loveliest art forms that have come from the age. Because they maintained the schools and libraries, the monks were virtually the only intellectuals in society. Rulers recruited their counselors and officials from the monasteries; and nearly all the administrative records that have survived were written by monastic scribes. Finally, the monks, as holy men, were thought to assure God's blessings for the world, and this helped support the morale of the troubled peoples of the Early Middle Ages.

Why were monks so important in medieval society? One reason is that the communal organization enabled the monks to cope more effectively with the problems of a turbulent age. They could divide essential tasks among their members, assigning some monks to work the earth, others to arrange for the defense of the community, and still others to read and study. The community was also, in a real sense, immortal and could maintain continuity of effort over generations.

Spanish manuscript illumination of daily life in the monastery.
(Photo: The Pierpont Morgan Library)

A second reason is that the ascetic temperament equipped monks to be powerful instruments of both economic and cultural change. Early medieval society was desperately poor. Like every poor society its hope for a better future rested on an ability to save and invest some part of the current, meager production. Grain uneaten, cattle not slaughtered, meant more abundant harvests and larger herds the next year; whether the motivation that saved the grain or cattle was religious or economic hardly matters. Monks were the great savers and investors of the age, and this partially explains their own considerable economic success.[5] Asceticism seems also peculiarly suited to an age of transition. The ascetic by his life calls into question the accepted attitudes of his age. The monks rejected both the Classical and barbarian systems of values·and helped uproot or weaken such attitudes as the Classical aversion to physical labor and the barbarian love of violence. They thus prepared the way for the elaboration of the new values and the new culture of the Middle Ages.

IV. THE NEW POLITICAL STRUCTURES

The Frankish Empire

Clovis had established a strong Frankish kingdom in Gaul; but his Merovingian successors, known traditionally as the "do-nothing kings," showed the weaknesses of tribal monarchy. Unable to conceive of the kingdom as anything but a private estate, they divided and redivided

their lands among their heirs. They showed no sense of political responsibility and relied primarily upon violence to define their powers. The history of their reigns is largely a dismal story of intrigue and destructive feuds.

Yet amid the wars and rivalries the character of Frankish society was changing; the decisive shift was in the technique of making war. The introduction of the stirrup, probably in the early eighth century, gave a final advantage to the mounted warrior over the foot soldier (he could now strike a hard blow without falling from his horse) and confirmed the superiority, which had been evident for several centuries, of the cavalry over the infantry. Since horses were expensive, war became a preeminently aristocratic occupation. A new functional and social division appeared in Frankish society. In the past most freemen had been both peasants and warriors. Now those freemen who could not afford horses and arms—they were a majority of the population—became full-time peasants and soon serfs; those freemen who could afford the new implements of battle became full-time fighters. They constituted the new military aristocracy.

Because of the negligence of the Merovingian kings, their chief household official, known as the mayor of the palace, gradually took over the real powers of government. The mayor's functions were to manage the palaces and supervise the royal lands; he was also able to distribute the lands largely as he saw fit. Using this privilege, some of the mayors began to supply the aristocracy with the estates they needed to maintain the expensive animals and arms in return for their service. The mayors thus built a following among the new military aristocracy that supported them in their acquisitions of further territory and power. One mayor, Pepin of Heristal, who already administered the Eastern lands of the kingdom, gained control over the Western lands in 687, unifying nearly all of the kingdom under him.

Pepin's son and successor, Charles Martel,

---

[5] Some historians have discerned a similar link between religious asceticism and economic investment in the growth of capitalism in the sixteenth and seventeenth centuries. Specifically, they have argued that the ascetic attitudes of the Calvinists, especially the Puritans, aided their success in business. For this viewpoint see R. H. Tawney, *Religion and the Rise of Capitalism*, 1926.

cultivated the support of the warrior aristocracy. With their military assistance and the help he gave Christian missionaries, Charles began to extend Christianity and Frankish domination (the two were virtually indistinguishable) over the Germanic tribes settled beyond the Rhine River.

Charles's son, Pepin the Short, courted the allegiance of the other aristocracy of Frankish society, the great churchmen, by making a lasting alliance with the pope. The continuing support of the military aristocracy and the new sympathy of the ecclesiastical aristocracy enabled Pepin to effect a major constitutional change. In 751 an assembly of Frankish notables declared that the last Merovingian king was not truly a king, and they recognized Pepin as their legitimate sovereign. The pope confirmed the wisdom and justice of the act. In return for this expression of support Pepin confirmed papal possession of the Patrimony of St. Peter (Rome and its environs) and defeated the Lombards, who had been harassing the papal lands in Italy. Later popes would repeatedly point to this Donation of Pepin as establishing the Papal States.

Roman tradition affirmed that the king exercised sovereign power; by exposing the character of Frankish kingship to strong Christian and Roman influences, Pepin strengthened and transformed it. He bequeathed to his successors a monarchy founded on the support of great warriors and priests and dignified by association with the Christian and Roman past.

Charlemagne

Pepin's son, Charles the Great, or Charlemagne (768–814), followed the policies of his predecessors; but, pursuing them with unprecedented energy, he achieved unprecedented success. His biographer, the court scholar Einhard, says that he was a large man, "seven times the length of his own foot," and that he delighted in physical exercise, particularly hunting, riding, bathing, and swimming. His taste for food

Pepin the Short reformed the coinage of the Frankish realm, basing it upon a single minted coin, the silver *denarius* or penny. Twelve pennies made a *solidus* or shilling and twenty shillings made a pound, but the latter were exclusively monies of account—not minted coins. This illustration shows a rare surviving specimen of Pepin's new coin.
(Photo: The American Numismatic Society)

and women seems to have been no less exuberant. Perhaps more remarkable in this man whose very life was war were his intellectual curiosity and alertness. He was probably illiterate; at least, Einhard says that he kept tablets by his bed to practice forming letters at night though with "ill success." But Einhard also says that he spoke and understood Latin, comprehended Greek, and enjoyed the company of learned men. The vast empire Charlemagne built was in large measure a personal accomplishment, a tribute to his bounding physical energy and open intelligence.

Charlemagne's success as king depended on

his success as a military leader. On every frontier he waged long wars. His chief concern was to spread Christianity and thus subservience to Frankish authority among still pagan peoples. If permanent conquest and conversion were not possible, the expeditions would still weaken neighboring enemies and prevent them from striking into the Frankish domains. At the pope's request he campaigned four times in Italy against the Lombards and against factions at Rome opposed to the pope. He suppressed the independent Bavarians and overcame the Saxons after 33 years of fighting, bringing these peoples fully and finally into the community of Western peoples. These victorious wars added new territories to his empire (see Map 6.3). Charlemagne also organized punitive expeditions against the Danes, Slavs, and Avars beyond his eastern borders and against the Saracens beyond the Pyrenees.

On Charlemagne's fourth visit to Italy in 800, when he was praying before St. Peter's altar on Christmas night, Pope Leo III crowned him emperor of the Romans. The coronation of 800 added nothing to his possessions, but still retained great symbolic importance. It confirmed the alliance of the papacy and the Frankish monarchy, defined the political axis of subsequent Western history, and gave it its pronounced north-south orientation. It was a public declaration of the independence of the West, a final rejection of even a theoretical submission to the Eastern Empire. The coronation of 800 marks the birth of Europe, for it proclaimed the complete political and cultural autonomy of the Western community of peoples.

Government

The coronation gave Charlemagne no new powers; but it added much to his dignity, and a grandiose imperial ideology developed around his person. The cult of the emperor played a vital role in preserving the unity of the empire because the government did not

have the material force to hold it together. Charlemagne was presented to the people as the new David (the ideal king of the Old Testament), the new Augustus (the greatest of the pagan emperors), and the new Constantine (the champion of the Church). By presenting the emperor as a figure of such sanctity and brilliance, the government hoped to make rebellion against him unthinkable. Ideas might thus accomplish what armies could not do alone.

The emperor was, of course, the head of the government; and he was aided by several officials. The head of the palace clergy, and the chief ecclesiastic of the realm, was the chaplain, who advised the emperor and the entire court in matters of conscience. The chaplain also supervised the chancery, or secretariat, where the official documents were written. The chief lay official was the count of the palace, who supervised the administration, judged cases that the emperor did not personally handle, and acted as regent during the emperor's frequent absences. The chamberlain took care of the royal bedroom and the treasury, the seneschal kept the palace provisioned with food and staffed with servants, the butler supplied the beer and wine, and the constable cared for the horses. These officials and others whom the emperor invited made up the court that advised him.

At the local level the fundamental administrative unit was the county, which in many parts of the empire resembled in its extent the Roman provinces or *civitates.* The count was the administrator, judge, and military leader of the county. The county was further divided into small judicial units under a *vicarius,* who heard minor cases.

Charlemagne's great administrative problem was to maintain an effective supervision and control over the local officials. He used three devices to resolve this problem. Charlemagne himself traveled widely to ascertain how the land was being administered and to hear appeals from the decisions of the counts. He

MAP 6.3. FRANKISH EMPIRE UNDER CHARLEMAGNE

The dates indicate the years when the regions were added to the empire. Marches were the frontier provinces (except Brittany, which was a maritime province) specially organized for the military defense of the empire. Magdeburg was the episcopal see that took the leadership in the conversion of the Danes and Slavs to Christianity. Aix-la-Chapelle also called Aachen was the capital of the empire. The tributary peoples were those beyond the frontiers of the empire over whom the emperor exercised a loose authority. They owed allegiance to him but were never integrated administratively into the empire.

This twelfth-century silver reliquary from Aachen represents Charlemagne as emperor, saint, and protector of the Church. After his death, through all the subsequent medieval centuries, Charlemagne was remembered and viewed as the ideal Christian emperor.
(Photo: E.P.A./Scala)

appointed special traveling inspectors, called *missi dominici,* to inspect a particular county every year. They scrutinized the behavior of both the lay and ecclesiastical officials, heard complaints, published imperial directives, and reported their findings to the emperor. They were in fact surrogate emperors who made the emperor's power felt everywhere in his vast domain. Charlemagne further required that the great men of his realm, both laymen and ecclesiastics, attend a general assembly almost every year. There they reported on conditions in their local areas, advised the emperor on important matters, and heard his directives. Many of the imperial directives have survived. Divided into chapters (*capitula*), these informative records are known as capitularies.

To promote unity, Charlemagne also standardized weights, measures, and money throughout his empire. The monetary system came to be based on a single minted coin, the silver *denarius* or penny. Twelve of these made a solidus or shilling (not a minted coin but a "money of account"), and twenty shillings made a pound. The Englishman who reckons price in pounds, or the Italian in *lire,* still today uses terms of Carolingian origin.

Decline of the Empire

Charlemagne passed on to his single surviving son, Louis the Pious, a united and apparently strong empire at his death. His successors in the ninth century proved unable to maintain that unity. Louis, a weak and indecisive man, soon lost control over his own family; and his sons rebelled against him. After his death the three surviving sons partitioned the empire at the Treaty of Verdun in 843 and established their own kingdoms (see Map 6.4).

As the family of Carolingian rulers divided amid civil wars and partitions, the loyalty of the military aristocracy also waned. The new rulers conquered no new lands; so they had no new offices or properties to buy the loyalties of the aristocracy. The office of count, appoin-

tive under Charlemagne, became hereditary under his successors. The Carolingian rulers no longer summoned the great men of the realm to the yearly assemblies and no longer dis-

---

The division of the Frankish Empire at Verdun was only one of several partitions in the ninth century, but historians have traditionally considered that the date 843 marks the beginnings of the separate national histories of France, Germany, and Italy. The kingdom of Lothar I was soon divided into Lorraine, Burgundy, and Italy.

MAP 6.4. PARTITION OF THE FRANKISH EMPIRE

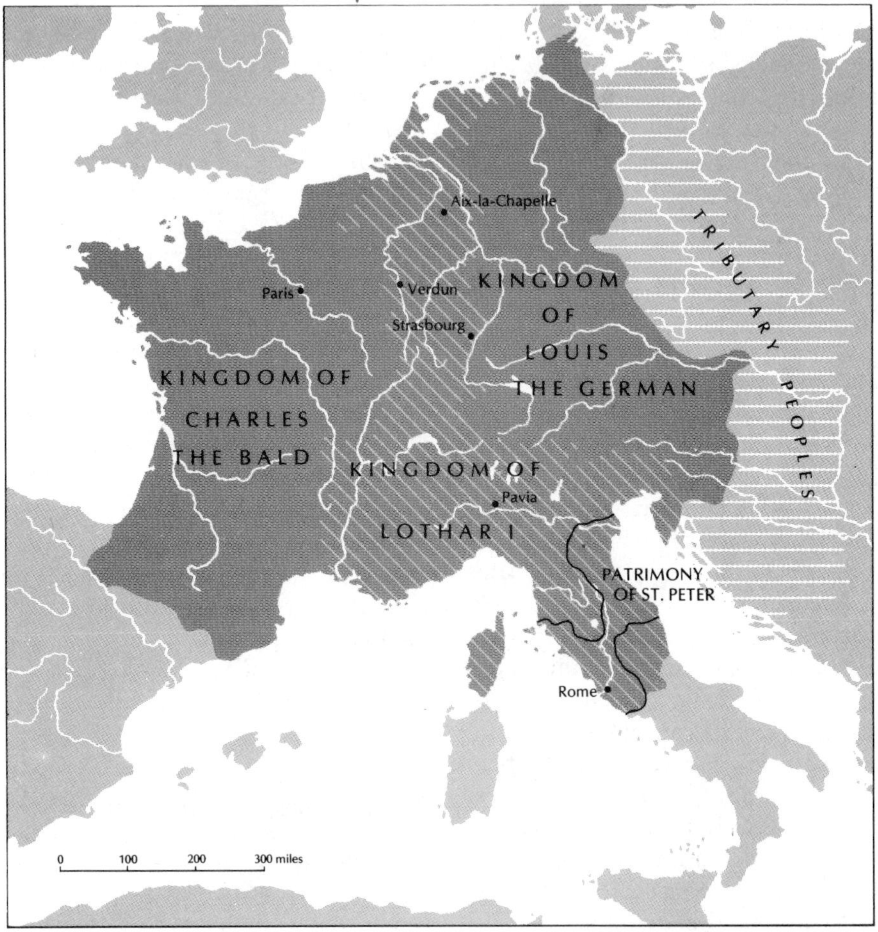

patched the *missi dominici* on their circuits. The institutional and moral bonds tying their central governments to the peripheral territories were thus broken or abandoned.

Renewed Invasions

Charlemagne's military successes had kept the borders of his empire relatively secure against invaders; but under his weak successors the invasions resumed, and they added critically to the centrifugal forces tearing at the empire. From the south, Saracens established in North Africa invaded Sicily and southern Italy in 827, attacked the valley of the Rhone in 842, and raided Rome in 846. They held a pirate fortress at Fraxinetum (Freinet) on the French Riviera, threatening Western ships and even harassing travel over the Alpine passes between Italy and France for over a century. From the East a new nomadic people, the Magyars, established themselves by about 895 in the valley of the Danube; and from this base for the next 50 years they struck repeatedly into France, Germany, and Italy.

The most wide-ranging of the new invasions were those mounted by the Northmen, or Vikings, who were the Germanic tribes settled in Scandinavia. Their movements may be considered the last phase of the Germanic invasions begun in the fourth century. Several facts explain their invasions. The tribes could not support a large population in the harsh northern climate; through commercial contacts and mercenary service they were familiar with the attractive wealth of the neighboring areas. The tribes were constantly at war with one another because there was no stable kingdom; a defeated chief, rather than accept a demeaning vassalage under his conqueror, often preferred to seek out new land overseas. The Vikings were skilled and versatile seamen; their ships enabled them to master both the rivers of the Continent and the open ocean. Explorations took them as far as a western territory they called Vinland, which was undoubtedly part of

the North American continent. Iceland, settled as a result of these explorations, became the great center of medieval Scandinavian culture.

In England and on the Continent the Vikings appeared first as merchants and pirates, then as conquerors and colonists. Vikings, chiefly Danes, began raiding England in 787; then in 866 a Danish army landed in eastern England and established a permanent settlement. The Vikings followed the same pattern on the Continent. They attacked cities along the western coast of Europe, penetrated into the Mediterranean Sea, and invaded the valley of the Rhone. They sailed over the Russian river system to reach the Black Sea and raided Constantinople (see Map 6.5). This initial period of piratical forays led to the establishment of permanent settlements. In 911 the Viking Rollo secured from King Charles the Simple the territory near the mouth of the Seine River, which henceforth was known as Normandy.

This new wave of invasions was not as disruptive as the great movements of peoples in the fourth and fifth centuries, but they were for Western Europe a new dark age. Amid the violence, however, the work of Christianizing the pagan peoples continued and helped to abate the invasions. Missionaries in the tenth century successfully converted the Magyars, Poles, and Vikings. With their acceptance of Christianity and simultaneous establishment of a stable kingdom, the Magyars, alone among the many nomadic tribes of Europe, succeeded in preserving their linguistic and ethnic identity until the present; they are the modern Hungarians. From about the year 1000 these peoples no longer represented a foreign and heathen threat to Christian Europe; rather, they had become full partners in the association of Western peoples.

Anglo-Saxon England

England was divided among more than a score of petty dynasties and kingdoms as a direct result of the Germanic invasions in the fourth

TO GREENLAND AND
NORTH AMERICA

ICELAND

874

FAEROES
800

SHETLANDS
700

V I K I N G S

Novgorod
820

ATLANTIC OCEAN

Dublin
839

DANELAW

866-878

841-884

Hamburg

WESSEX

Rouen
Seine Paris
R.

Aix-la-Chapelle

Rhine R.

Kiev
882

Dnieper R.

Volga R.

895

NORMANDY
896-911

Tours

Loire R.

900

M A G Y A R S

843-882

Bordeaux

917

899

895

866, 907, 941

BLACK SEA

Santiago

Marseilles

Nice

Fraxinetum

Danube R.

Barcelona

859-861

CORSICA

Rome
846

Constantinople

Lisbon
844

BALEARICS

SARDINIA

Monte
Cassino

Valencia

Seville
844

842

SICILY
827

840-896

S A R A C E N S

M E D I T E R R A N E A N   S E A

0 100 200 300 miles

MAP 6.5. INVASIONS OF THE 8TH–10TH CENTURIES

through sixth centuries. These many petty dynasties became fused into a single kingdom, but the climax of this trend toward political unity was not reached until after the Norman Conquest in 1066.

England achieved religious unity before political unity. Augustine and his fellow missionaries dispatched by Pope Gregory arrived in Kent in 597; but other Christian missionaries, the Franks and particularly the Irish, were already evangelizing the island. Irish, or Celtic, Christianity differed from Roman Christianity.[6] Not until 663 or 664 did the Council of Whitby finally determine that the English Church should follow Roman rather than Celtic practices. Later in the century Theodore of Tarsus, a monk from the Middle East who served as archbishop of Canterbury, completed this work of ecclesiastical unification. He reformed monastic education, held numerous councils, made the authority of Canterbury felt throughout the land, and helped give England one of the most vigorous and learned churches of the age.

Political unity came more slowly. The numerous petty dynasties coalesced into seven fairly stable kingdoms, traditionally known as the heptarchy: Northumbria, Mercia, East Anglia, Essex, Sussex, Kent, and Wessex (see Map 6.6). The first kings to exert a stable hegemony over England were the rulers of Northumbria in the seventh and eighth centuries. This was the golden age of Northumbrian culture; the monastery at Wearmouth-Jarrow then counted among its members Bede the Venerable, the greatest scholar of his day. By the late eighth century the hegemony over England passed to the rulers of Mercia. King Offa, a contemporary of Charlemagne, was known even to the pope as King of Britain. Mercian leadership was, however, short-lived; and after Offa's death the honor passed to Egbert of Wessex and his successors.

Alfred the Great

To the kings of Wessex fell the task of defending England against the Danes. The greatest of these kings was Alfred (871–899). After experiencing military defeats by the Danes in the early years of his reign, Alfred reorganized the

Norwegian burial mounds have yielded to archaelogists some specimens of Viking ships, although it is nearly impossible to know how closely these ceremonial barges correspond to the ships in daily use. One of these barges, found at Gokstad, is shown here. It is only 76 feet long, 17.5 feet wide, and 6.5 feet deep. It was propelled by 16 pairs of oars. This seems a small ship to challenge the North Atlantic. (Photo: Universiteteis Oldsaksamling, Oslo)

---

[6] Irish Christians calculated the date of Easter in a different fashion, applied the tonsure (the cut of hair symbolizing clerical status) in their own distinct way, and had a different concept of the role and powers of the bishop.

defense of the kingdom. He reformed the militia to keep a larger and more mobile army in the field and built fortresses to defend the land and ships to defend the coast. His reforms proved successful. In 886 the Danes agreed to accept Christianity and settle in the Danelaw, a region north and east in England. Alfred was the first king effectively to rule over the entire English people. He also renewed intellectual activity. Alfred gathered a group of scholars and began a program of translating into Anglo-Saxon the works of several historians and theologians. During his reign an official record of events in England, the *Anglo-Saxon Chronicle,* was begun. It is an indispensable source for early English history.

The English resurgence initiated under Alfred continued under his successors for almost a century. However, by 991 King Ethelred was unable to overcome the renewed Danish advances and agreed to pay tribute to the Danes. The tax he imposed to meet the tribute was called the Danegeld. Its payment was a mark of weakness, but the Danegeld was

still a national tax and shows the solid and continuing unity achieved by the kingdom. In 1013 the Danish King Swein invaded and conquered England, which became a province in a great northern empire. His son Canute ruled both Denmark and England; but at his death in 1035 the empire disintegrated and Edward, a descendant of Alfred, became the king of England. The work of building a unified community and effective monarchy in England was left to the Norman conquerors to complete after 1066.

V. LETTERS AND LEARNING

The great movement of peoples in the fourth and fifth centuries nearly extinguished in the West the urban, literate, aristocratic culture of the ancient world. Early medieval Europe almost lost entirely the great Classical heritage of literature and learning, in the sense that the nonliterate, nonurban, vernacular culture of the invading peoples and the unlettered masses of the Roman Empire all but triumphed. But the tradition of Classical learning did not entirely succumb. It survived in a peculiar context and for a peculiar purpose: to serve the Christian Church and to promote the interests of the Christian religion.

The Church and Classical Learning

Because Christianity rebelled against Classical values, it is understandable that many prominent Christian writers condemned Classical literature as foolishness and an incitement to sin. Yet almost from the beginning Christianity had to make some accommodation to secular learning. Christianity was a religion founded on a book, the Bible. God had spoken to his people through the written word, and Christian theo-

MAP 6.6. ANGLO-SAXON ENGLAND

logians had to have the skill to read and interpret the sacred texts. The only way they could obtain this skill was to study at secular schools, because the Church had no schools of its own. The leaders of the Christian community, therefore, had to study under the same teachers, read the same authors, and master the same techniques of philosophical argument and rhetorical expression as their pagan neighbors.

Christian scholars preserved a tradition of literacy in the fifth and sixth centuries, but their output accurately reflects the difficult conditions of their times and the biases of their own mental outlook. An important part of their literary effort was devoted to the preparation of textbooks that would preserve a modicum of ancient learning and the ability to read the ancient authors. One of the most influential of these textbooks was the *Introductions to Divine and Human Readings* by the Italian official, finally monk, Cassiodorus (490?–585?). In it he listed the religious and secular books that he felt a monk should copy and read. This book is about as appealing to modern readers as a library catalog, but it was carefully studied and helped to determine the holdings of medieval libraries. A contemporary Italian scholar, also a Christian, was Boethius, who translated into Latin some of Aristotle's treatises on logic. Through this work early medieval writers acquired their limited, but significant, familiarity with Aristotelian logic. Boethius was even more famed for his *Consolation of Philosophy,* a meditation on death that does not mention the Christian religion. It helped to preserve the dignity of learning by showing the role that reason and philosophy play in solving human problems. Less elegant than the *Consolation,* but equally popular, was the *Etymologies* by Isidore, bishop of Seville, which was a vast encyclopedia of ancient learning, covering in 20 books subjects from theology to furniture. It provided a rich source of Classical lore and learning for medieval writers.

Besides providing the medieval world with textbooks, translations, and compendia of Classical learning, scholars also helped through original works to shape the character and interest of the age. Many of them were monks who believed that the highest human calling was the contemplation of the boundless wonders of God. Chief among these wonders was the Bible itself; and a primary concern of the scholars was exegesis, or comment and interpretation, of the sacred text. In this field the most important writer after St. Augustine was Pope Gregory. In his *Moralia in Job,* a commentary on the Book of Job, Gregory made extravagant use of allegory in explaining the biblical text and set the style for biblical exegesis in the medieval world. Another wonder of God was the lives of the saints and the miracles he wrought through them. In this field, too, Pope Gregory educated tastes, notably through his *Dialogues,* a record of the lives and miracles of the holy men of Italy. Since history was viewed as a vast panorama illustrating and proclaiming God's miraculous providence, it too evoked great interest among scholars. One of the most influential accounts was the *History of the Franks* by Gregory, bishop of Tours. Beginning with Creation (to show the entire range of God's providential concern with human affairs), Gregory recounted the history of the human race up to 591.

Modern readers are often surprised by the endless parade of miracles and slightly stunned by the apparent gullibility of the scholars who reported them, but they must view the miracles as did the authors who recorded them. For these writers the miraculous interventions of God leading his people to salvation gave purpose to human life and order to an otherwise chaotic world. In a universe shaped by the operations of grace, the miraculous was the natural and the expected.

Scholarship on the Continent sank to its lowest level in the seventh and early eighth centuries. The most important centers of scholarship were Ireland in the seventh and England in the early eighth century. Scholars there enjoyed the relative shelter of an insular home. They had the zeal of new converts and a strong monastic system that supported the schools. They had never shared deeply in pagan Classical culture and could study it without fear of contaminating their Christianity. Since they did not speak a vernacular language derived from Latin, they could learn a correct Latin in schools without being confused by related vernacular forms.

The finest English scholar was undoubtedly Bede the Venerable (673?–735), whose *Ecclesiastical History of the English People,* an account of the conversion of the English and the growth of their Church, established his fame even until today. His high sense of scholarship is evident in the careful way he collected and used documents and interviewed witnesses. Bede, of course, accepted miracles, and the story of salvation is the principal theme of his history. But his views on the ultimate purpose of history did not lead him to do violence to his sources. He is a man whom any age would recognize as a scholar.

The Carolingian Renaissance

The Frankish rulers—Pepin, Charlemagne, and their successors—sought energetically to promote learning within their domains; and historians call the results of their efforts the Carolingian Renaissance. These rulers were interested in learning for several reasons. In the sixth and seventh centuries, when the Continent was divided among many small kingdoms, different styles of writing, known as national hands (Visigothic, Merovingian, Lombard, Beneventan, and so forth), had developed, and numerous variant readings had slipped into such basic texts as the Bible and the Benedictine rule. The Latin grammar used by scholars had also absorbed many regional peculiarities. Literate persons in one part of Europe thus had great difficulty recognizing or reading a text written in another. The widespread decline in education had left few persons who could read at all. The paucity of readers and the illegibility and diversity of texts undermined the cultural unity of Europe and deprived governments of learned men to employ in their administrations. Furthermore, poorly educated priests could not properly perform the liturgy, upon which God's blessings on the community were thought to depend; and variations in religious rituals were also growing. Both situations weakened the unity of the Church as well as the state.

Pepin and Charlemagne attempted to develop a standardized curriculum, based on the same versions of the same texts and written in the same form of handwriting. They invited to court scholars from all over Europe for this purpose. To increase the supply of locally trained scholars both Pepin and Charlemagne ordered all bishops and monasteries to establish schools to educate boys; however, only the monasteries apparently had the resources to follow this order to any significant degree. Charlemagne himself set the example by founding a palace school for the sons of his own courtiers, but the school seems to have had little permanent impact upon the intellectual life of the age.

One great achievement of this educational revival was a reform in handwriting. About the year 800, monks at the monasteries of Corbie and Tours devised a new type of formal, literary writing, a "book-hand," based on lower-case letters and now called the Carolingian minuscule. Previously, the book-hands used for important texts had been based on various styles of capital letters only. Lower-case letters appeared only in informal, cursive scripts. But a book page written entirely in capitals is difficult to read rapidly; the eye is not aided in distinguishing letters by protrusions above and below the line. The Carolingian minuscule, the first book-hand based on lower-case letters, made rapid reading easier. In addition, more letters could be written on a page with this new script; thus, more books were produced at less expense. Use of this graceful new script eventually spread across Europe.

Another achievement of this educational revival was the development of a common scholarly language. Carolingian scholars perfected and standardized a distinctive language known as Medieval Latin, which largely retained the grammatical rules of Classical Latin but was more flexible and open in its vocabulary, freely coining new words to express the new realities of the age. Medieval Latin was also clearly different from the vulgar, or Romance, Latin spoken by the people. The establishment of Medieval Latin as a distinct language of learning thus freed the Romance vernaculars to develop on their own. One of these vernacular languages is Old French. The earliest surviving text in this language dates from 842.[7]

The Latin created by the Carolingian scholars enabled travelers, administrators, and scholars to make themselves understood from one part of Europe to another; and it continued to serve this function until the modern era. Even when it disappeared as an international language, it helped to promote European unity. All the modern vernacular tongues of Europe developed under the strong influence of this scholars' Latin. One of the reasons it is possible to translate quickly and accurately from one European language to another is that their learned vocabularies are in large measure based upon common Latin models.

A further achievement of the educational revival was the standardization of important texts. Pepin "decorated all the churches of the Gauls with the songs of the Roman church";

The ninth-century manuscript illumination from the first Bible of Charles the Bald displays the Carolingian minuscule, which is the model for the lower-case letters used today in what printers call Roman type. (Photo: Bibliothèque Nationale)

that is, he sought to standardize the liturgy on the basis of Roman practice. Charlemagne continued this policy of standardization. He had the English scholar Alcuin of York, who served as a sort of minister of cultural affairs from about 782 until 794, prepare a new edition of Jerome's Vulgate translation of the Bible. This edition became the common biblical text for the entire Western Church. Charlemagne procured from Monte Cassino a copy of the Benedictine rule and had it copied and distributed, so that monks everywhere would follow a standard code. He also initiated standardization into the school curriculum, based on the seven liberal arts. Alcuin divided the curriculum into the trivium, or verbal arts (grammar, rhetoric, and logic), and the quadrivium, or mathemat-

---

[7] At Strasbourg in 842, Charles the Bald and Louis the German, two of the sons of Louis the Pious, took an oath that was recorded in Latin, Old French, and German. The oath at Strasbourg not only preserves the oldest surviving text in Old French but also marks the first use of German in a formal legal document.

ical arts (arithmetic, astronomy, geometry, and music).

Carolingian scholars wrote lengthy educational tracts and huge quantities of didactic poetry, but little of their work can be considered notable for original thought or rhetorical grace. This is understandable. Most of the scholars were grammarians and educators, engaged in producing teachers' manuals, textbooks, and school exercises; they went back to the Latin classics to find models of correct grammar, usage, and vocabulary but not for aesthetic satisfaction or philosophical insights. Their work was nonetheless of the greatest importance for the intellectual growth of Europe. The revived mastery of correct Latin equipped scholars of later generations to return to the Classical heritage and to recover from it philosophic and aesthetic values. The Carolingian Renaissance made possible all subsequent renaissances in the history of Western thought. The establishment of Latin as a universal language permitted easy communication within Europe and made possible that vigorous and creative dialogue across linguistic frontiers upon which the growth of Western scholarship has since depended.

Europe, in the sense of an association of Western peoples preserving their individual cultural identities and yet sharing certain fundamental attitudes and values, did not exist in the ancient world. This association was formed during the Early Middle Ages. After the politically and culturally disruptive tribal migrations ended Roman rule in the West, medieval people sought to create a new stability out of the chaos. Charlemagne's conquests brought together a new community of peoples over a wide area of Western Europe. Although his empire was not permanent, it left to every region included in it common institutions and a lasting memory of former unity. The missionary success extended the religious and moral unity of the West even beyond the frontiers of his empire.

Early medieval society was desperately poor. Trade declined; commercial contact with the East was broken; cities shrank in size. Yet some remarkable achievements mitigated this misfortune. The labor of the settled peasant family replaced that of the gang slave as the basis of agricultural production. Technological innovations made possible the efficient exploitation of the fertile plain of northern Europe. The three-field system of cultivation and the new manorial organization gradually produced a surplus of food.

By about the year 1000 the population began expanding for the first time since perhaps the second century A.D. A distinctive Western culture was taking shape, based on the customs and practices of the tribal invaders and the unlettered masses of the former Roman Empire, the teachings of Christianity, and the heritage of Classical learning, which the Church largely preserved. The

Early Middle Ages left no brilliant cultural monuments, but it did lay the foundations upon which the achievements of all subsequent periods of Western history have rested.

RECOMMENDED READING

Sources

Einhard. *The Life of Charlemagne.* 1962.

*Herlihy, David (ed.). *Medieval Culture and Society.* 1968.

Hillgarth, J. N. (ed.). *The Conversion of Western Europe: 350–750.* 1969.

Mattingly, H. (ed.). *Tacitus on Britain and Germany. A Translation of the "Agricola" and the "Germania."* 1967.

Studies

Boussard, Jacques. *The Civilization of Charlemagne.* 1968.

Burns, Thomas S. *A History of the Ostrogoths.* 1984. Based on archaeological as well as literary evidence.

Cambridge Economic History of Europe. 1941–. Four volumes to date comprise the standard reference for all economic questions. A revised edition of the first volume on medieval agrarian life was published in 1966.

Cambridge Medieval History. 1911–1936. The eight volumes that make up this work are partially outdated, but still indispensable.

*Duby, Georges. *The Early Growth of the European Economy: Warriors and Peasants from the Seventh to the Twelfth Century.* Howard B. Clark (tr.). 1974. The early medieval economy viewed in terms of "gift and pillage."

*Fichtenau, Heinrich. *The Carolingian Empire.* P. Munz (tr.). 1963. An unsympathetic view and treatment of Charlemagne and his policies.

Goffart, Walter. *Barbarians and Romans, A.D. 418–584: The Techniques of Accommodation.* 1980. A careful inquiry into the obscurities of barbarian settlement within the empire.

Horn, Walter W., and Ernest Born. *The Plan of St. Gall.* 1979. An elaborate reconstruction of the architecture and the life of a major Carolingian monastery.

Laistner, Max. *Thought and Letters in Western Europe: A.D. 500 to 900.* 1955. Basic guide to writers of the period.

Leclercq, Jean. *The Love of Learning and the Desire for God.* Catherine Misrah (tr.). 1961. Monastic culture of the Middle Ages interpreted by a modern Benedictine.

Musset, Lucien. *The Germanic Invasions: The Making of Europe, A.D. 400–600.* Edward and Columba James (trs.). 1975. Excellent recent survey.

Riché, Pierre. *Daily Life in the World of Charlemagne.* Jo Ann McNamara (tr.). 1975. A fine survey of Carolingian life and society.

Sawyer, P. H. *Kings and Vikings: Scandinavia and Europe, A.D. 700–1100.* 1984. Excellent summary of recent research on the Vikings.

Stenton, Frank. *Anglo-Saxon England.* 1971. Basic introductory text.

*Wallace-Hadrill, J. M. *The Barbarian West.* 1962. Brief and readable essays.

Wemple, Suzanne Fonay. *Women in Frankish Society: Marriage and the Cloister, 500 to 800.* 1981. A recent, important study of a neglected topic.

---

* Available in paperback.

EXPERIENCES OF DAILY LIFE

Carolingian Families

The spread of peasant agriculture over Europe and the triumph of Christianity profoundly influenced domestic life. In the Classical world, households varied greatly in size and structure across society. A rich senator might shelter in his palace hundreds of persons—relatives, servants, concubines, and clients. In contrast, the pitiable slaves who worked in gangs and slept in barracks hardly experienced any domestic life at all. Among the barbarians, too, the chiefs often claimed several wives and concubines. But if some men take more than one wife, then others may have no mate at all. Even in tribal society, the households of rich and poor were very different.

The Early Middle Ages witness the settlement or resettlement of large areas of Europe on the basis of peasant agriculture. Peasant agriculture is based on the labor of families, all of them very similar. Moreover, according to the teachings of the Christian Church, men and women, rich and poor, barbarians and Romans, were all obligated to follow one and the same law of sexual morality. Marriage had to be monogamous and permanent. The Church also strictly prohibited close marriages (that is, marriage between blood relatives) and extended the degrees of relationship within which marriage was prohibited to an extraordinary seven (it had been four under Roman law). Young persons had to look outside their kindred to find a mate, and one partner, usually the bride, left home at marriage. The rule of monogamy and the incest prohibition prevented the household of the rich and powerful from gathering in more than its fair share of women, forced a circulation of women through society, and enhanced the chances that even poor males could find a mate.

The new peasant economy and the new rules of marriage worked to reduce the range of variations across households. It made them comparable and commensurable. In the early eighth century, the English monastic historian Bede the Venerable calculated the size of regions of England (and also of estates) in terms of the number of "families" they contained. He meant family farms (hides), but this is perhaps the earliest example of the use of the family or hearth to measure the size of communities. The practice assumes that all families, whether rich

A medieval farm scene.
(Culver Pictures)

or poor, possess a fundamental similarity. The humble household of peasants and serfs, monogamous and stable, was no longer fundamentally different from the household of its lord. It is likely too that the improved chances of finding a mate reduced rapes and abductions and levels of violence generally in early medieval society.

To judge from the peasants living on the estates of St.-Germain-des-Prés near Paris in the early ninth century, the average size of households was 5.79 persons, though many included more than a single family. In the subsequent centuries of Western history, peasant households would continue to contain roughly the same number of members. Among the peasants of St.-Germain, men outnumbered women; those resident on the land included 119 men for every 100 women. It does not seem likely that these Carolingian peasants practiced female infanticide. Women were valued in this society; in Germanic law, the woman typically carried a higher *Wergeld* (fine that had to be paid to her relatives if she was killed or injured) than did the male. There are two likely explanations for this apparent shortage of women. The lords of the manor wanted servants for their manor houses and workers to produce cloth at the workshop or *gynecaeum*. As the latter name suggests, they preferred women for both tasks. Typically, they seem to have taken young, unmarried girls into their direct service, and returned them to the farms when they attained marriageable age.

Another survey of the Carolingian period, listing the peasants of the monastery of St. Victor of Marseilles in southern France, gives us indications of marriage age. The survey includes a population of 1,027 persons, and divides them into children (for whom ages are given up to 15), unmarried adult men and women, and married adults. Clearly, both boys and girls were considered marriageable from age 16, but clearly, too, many of them were slow in taking a spouse. The number of unmarried adults is very large—127 men and 120 women—within the population of 1,027 persons. Both men and women must have delayed marriage until their late twenties, and both groom and bride must have been of approximately the same age when they married. The pattern corresponds closely with Tacitus' description of Germanic marriages; according to the Roman historian, Germanic men and women were mature at first marriage and also nearly equal in age.

It is harder to penetrate the cultural life of these early peasant families. The survey of St.-Germain-des-Prés yields 6,046 male names and 4,036 female. Names with a biblical or Christian connotation are very rare. Jacques (Iacobus) appears only 3 times, and Jean (Iohannes) only 24. The Carolingian rulers maintained a special veneration for St. Martin of Tours, but the number of Martins among the peasants is only 31. St. Geneviève saved Paris from the Huns, but only 2 peasant women recall her name. Even the name of Germain, patron of the monastery, appears only 10 times. The most common names are Ermenarius (223 appearances) for men and Ermengardis (178 times) for women—names with no religious content. If the choice of names is any indication, Christianity, while it influenced governing elites and their laws, had not yet penetrated deeply into peasant culture.

Although we have no direct evidence, there are some hints that family life in the Early Middle Ages could be affectionate. The legend of St. Severus, written down in the ninth century, pretends to tell the story of a poor wool worker from Ravenna in Italy, who lived in the fifth century and who labored at his trade together with his wife and daughter. Severus is miraculously summoned to become bishop of Ravenna, but he does not forget his relatives and their common labors. At his death, he asks to be buried with them. "We who lived a common life in this world," he states, "should also have a common burial." Severus loved the company of his wife and daughter; if his legend is any indication, early medieval people were not strangers to family affection.

Chapter 7

The Early Medieval East ca. 300 –1100

The Early Middle Ages was a period of profound social and spiritual change in the East as well as the West. In both regions a new peasant economy replaced the slave systems that had principally supported ancient civilizations. Unlike Classical beliefs, the triumphant new religions of Christianity and Islam taught their followers that human destiny or salvation lay in a life beyond death, to which even the poorest and the humblest could aspire.

The three most prominent civilizations of the East—Byzantine, Kievan, and Islamic—were nonetheless very different from the less developed societies of the West. The Roman Empire did not fall in the East, and Roman governmental institutions lived on in the Byzantine Empire. The Hellenistic cultural heritage, based on the Greek language, also survived in the East and gave to Byzantine civilization a distinctive character. The new religion of Islam grew up among a people, the Arabs, who (like the Germans in the West) had lived on the fringes of the Classical Mediterranean world. But the expansion of Islam brought it into lands—Egypt, Palestine, Syria, Persia—that had ancient and rich traditions of literate culture. Islamic civilization, in turn, was deeply affected by the Hellenistic, Semitic, and Persian cultures that flourished in the areas it overran.

A further, decisive contrast between the East and West was the survival of cities and an authentic urban life in both the Byzantine and Islamic worlds. Even the Principality of Kiev, founded by a new people—the East Slavs—rapidly developed cities and an urban culture. The presence of cities in the East helped maintain the vigor of commercial exchange, sophisticated governmental institutions, and high levels of learning. All these accomplishments gave the Eastern civilizations a marked superiority over contemporary Western societies in the Early Middle Ages.

After about 1050, however, new invasions as well as internal changes undermined or transformed these Eastern civilizations. But all of them left cultural heritages that have profoundly influenced Eastern societies until the present day; all of them, likewise, played a role in stimulating the Western revival in the eleventh and twelfth centuries.

I. THE BYZANTINE EMPIRE

The name "Byzantine" is, strictly speaking, a historical misnomer. The inhabitants of the Eastern Empire recognized no break in continuity between their own civilization and that of Classical Rome. Throughout their history they called themselves Romans, even after Rome had slipped from their power and they had adopted Greek as their official language. The inhabitants of the Eastern Empire acknowledged what modern Western historians sometimes forget: the Roman Empire did not fall in the East until 1453. Historians differ in the periodizations of Byzantine history, but the following one probably enjoys the widest acceptance:

Early Byzantine Period	324–632
Middle Byzantine Period	632–1071
Late Byzantine Period	1071–1453

Early Byzantine Period

The Emperor Constantine transferred the capital of the Roman Empire from the West to the East in 324. This act marks the beginning of Byzantine history. The emperor's motives were primarily military. Many powerful enemies—Persians beyond the Euphrates River, Germans beyond the Danube River, and Germanic pirates on the Black Sea—were menacing the Eastern provinces, the wealthiest and most populous in the Empire.

Constantine chose as his new capital the site of the ancient Greek colony of Byzantium. The colony had been founded about 660 B.C. on a narrow peninsula that juts into the Sea of Marmara like a hand extended from Europe toward Asia. The official name of the rebuilt city was New Rome; however, it soon came to be called the City of Constantine, or Constantinople, after its founder.

The location of this capital influenced the character of Byzantium and the course of its history. The city stood at the intersection of two of the most traveled routes: the overland highway from the Balkans to Asia Minor and the maritime route between the Black and Mediterranean seas. Inevitably, the city came to serve as the commercial and cultural link among many peoples and cultures.

Constantinople at once acquired the aura of a Christian city, the capital of the Christian empire. No ancient monuments or old families were present to remind men of the past glories of pagan Rome. Because of his close association with the emperor, the bishop of New Rome enjoyed the high status of patriarch. In the entire Church only the bishop of Rome ranked above him.

The successors of Constantine had no intention of abandoning the territories or the powers of the old Roman Empire in either the West or the East. Memories of the old empire dominated their policies; and they struggled continuously, if in vain, to restore the empire to its former size, power, and glory. The emperor whose actions best illustrate the ideals and policies of these early rulers was Justinian (527–565).

Justinian the Great

Historians have much information, or at least many allegations, about Justinian, his family, and his household from the court historian Procopius. While the emperor lived, Procopius praised him in two histories: *On the Wars* recounts Justinian's victorious campaigns, and *On Buildings* describes his architectural achievements. But after Justinian's death, Procopius also wrote one of the most vicious efforts at character assassination in history. The *Secret History* paints Justinian, Empress Theodora, and several high officials of the court as monsters of public and private vice. Historians still have not satisfactorily reconciled the contradictory portraits left to us by the two-tongued Procopius.

Justinian seems to have been a vacillating man; but his will was made strong by his ambitious wife Theodora and made effective by capable men in his service. Born about 500, the daughter of the keeper of the bears in the circus, Theodora became a famous actress and a celebrated courtesan before she was 20. She traveled through the cities of the empire, earning her way, according to Procopius, by skillful prostitution. In her early twenties she returned to Constantinople, mended her morals but lost none of her charm, and married Justinian. She was, in sum, an outsider, with no roots in the social establishment of the capital and no incli-

300–1100/TIMELINE

International and Military History	Political History

300

	324 Constantine I moves capital of empire to Constantinople
535–554 Justinian destroys Vandal kingdom of North Africa	527–565 Reign of Justinian
535–554 Justinian destroys Ostrogothic kingdom of Italy	529 Publication of *Codex Justinianus*
540–562 Justinian fights exhausting and indecisive war against Persians	532 Justinian, encouraged by Theodora, puts down Nika Insurrection
568–573 Lombards overrun most of Italy, except Rome and Ravenna	533 Publication of *Digest*
	565 Publication of *Novellae*
622–630 Heraclius destroys Persian empire of Sassanids	610–641 Reign of Emperor Heraclius; introduction of themes
632–732 Muslim expansion beyond Arabia	
661–750 Omayyad Caliphate; capital moved to Damascus; Islam a world power	

700

International and Military History	Political History
711–715 Muslims under Tariq conquer Spain, destroy Visigothic kingdom	717–741 Reign of Leo III the Isaurian
717–718 Emperor Leo III beats back Muslim attack on Constantinople	
732 Charles Martel defeats Muslims at Tours; highwater mark of Muslim westward expansion	
827–831 Muslims conquer Sicily	
c. 830 Varangian Rus come to Novgorod	
860 First Rus attack on Constantinople	
	873?–913 Oleg unites Novgorod and Kiev to form first Russian state
907 Oleg, prince of Kiev, raids Contantinople	
	1015–1054 Reign of Yaroslav the Wise
1055 Seljuk Turks seize Baghdad	
1061 Cumans invade southern steppe, cut Rus off from sea	
1071 Seljuk victory over Byzantines at Manzikert	

Social and Economic History	Cultural and Intellectual History

300

301 Diocletian's Edict on Prices

313 Edict of Milan extends toleration to Christians
325 Council of Nicaea; first ecumenical council

537 Completion of Hagia Sophia

542 Great Plague; recurrent until c. 600

610 Muhammad begins preaching at Mecca
622 The Hegira, Muhammad's flight from
Mecca to Medina; year 1 of the Muslim calendar
632 Death of Muhammad
651–652 Redaction of the Koran

700

726 Leo III inaugurates iconoclastic policy

843 Restoration of image veneration in Byzantium
c. 850 Great age of Byzantine culture

c. 950 Book of the Prefect names 21 guilds

996 Beginning of governmental effort in Byzantium to
block growth of great estates

988 Conversion of Vladimir, Prince of Kiev, to Christianity

998 Byzantine trade concessions to Venetians

1038 Completion of Church of St. Sophia at Kiev
1054 Schism between Eastern and Western churches

1117 Probable date for composition of Rus
Primary Chronicle

1082 Further concession to Venetian traders within
Byzantine empire

1100

nations to respect its conventions. In this she resembles other active rulers of history—Catherine the Great, the German empress of Russia; Napoleon; Eva Perón in twentieth-century Argentina; and many others.

Theodora's influence on her husband was decisive from the start. In 532, for reasons not entirely known, the popular factions of Constantinople rose in rebellion. Justinian panicked, and decided to flee. But in a moving speech, as recorded by Procopius, Theodora urged her husband to choose death rather than exile. Justinian remained and crushed the uprising. The suppression of this rebellion freed Justinian to pursue the three principal goals of his reign: the restoration of the Western provinces to the empire, the reformation of laws and institutions, and the promotion of physical splendor through an ambitious program of public works.

To restore imperial rule over the lost Western provinces, Justinian directed his armies against the kingdoms of the Vandals, Ostrogoths, and Visigoths and sought at the same time to maintain a precarious peace with the menacing Persians beyond his eastern frontier. By 554 his troops had destroyed the Vandal kingdom in North Africa and established Byzantine rule there, had triumphed, at least for a while, over the Ostrogoth kingdom in Italy, and had forced the Visigoths in Spain to cede the southern tip of the peninsula (see Map 7.1). Justinian sought to reconcile the Eastern and Western branches of the Church, which were bitterly divided over a theological question concerning the nature of Christ.[1] He had the pope abducted from Rome and taken to Constantinople, where he bullied him into accepting an unwelcome compromise. His coercive tactics did not bring union and peace to the Church and were bitterly resented by all the conflicting parties.

One of the chief glories of the Roman Empire, its laws and imperial decrees, had fallen into disarray by the early sixth century. Imperial edicts had been added to edicts over the centuries, but they had been placed in no systematic order. Lawyers could not readily ascertain which laws were relevant to which cases or which law should be followed in instances of conflict. Moreover, the great Classical jurists had produced extensive legal comments, which rivaled in importance the laws themselves. But these opinions were preserved in no organized way, and lawyers could not easily consult this important body of commentary.

In 528 Justinian appointed a commission to prepare a systematic codification of Roman law. The result was the *Corpus Iuris Civilis* ("Body of Civil Law"). It consisted of four compilations: the *Codex Justinianus,* an arrangement of the imperial edicts according to topics in an easily consulted order; the *Digest,* or *Pandects,* a summary of legal opinions; the *Institutes,* a textbook to introduce students to the reformed legal system; and the *Novellae,* a collection of new imperial edicts issued after 534.

It would be hard to exaggerate the importance of the *Corpus Iuris Civilis.* It has remained for all subsequent generations the largest and richest source of information concerning the legal institutions and thought of Roman antiquity. Paradoxically, it ultimately exerted a more profound influence upon the juridical development of the Western peoples than upon the Byzantines or their heirs. It profoundly influenced the canon law of the medieval and modern Church. The modern legal systems of most Western countries are based on the principles of Roman law as preserved in the *Corpus.*[2]

The destruction caused by the rebellion in Constantinople gave Justinian the chance to ini-

---

[1] The Monophysitic theory holds that Christ has one nature, partly divine and partly human; he was not, in other words, true man. Condemned as heretical at the Council of Chalcedon in 451, the belief remained strong in the East. The orthodox position holds that Christ has two natures, one human and one divine; he was both true God and true man.

[2] The British Commonwealth and the United States (except for Louisiana) follow common law, based on cases decided in medieval England. But common law too was strongly influenced by Roman legal concepts.

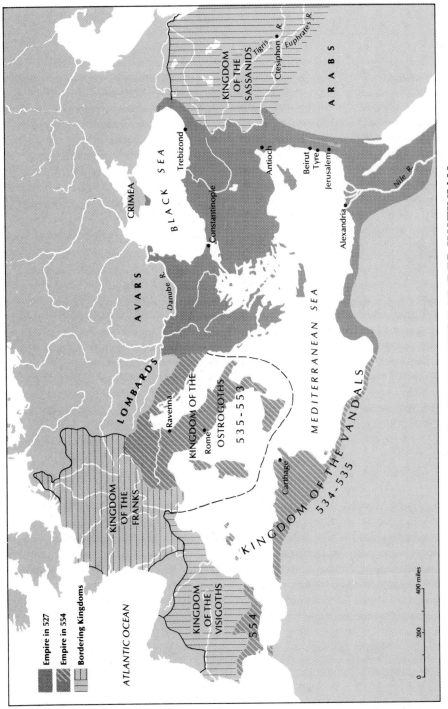

MAP 7.1. BYZANTINE EMPIRE UNDER JUSTINIAN

KINGDOM OF THE SASSANIDS

Tigris R.

Euphrates R.

Ctesiphon

A R A B S

Trebizond

Antioch

Beirut

Tyre

Jerusalem

Nile R.

Alexandria

B L A C K   S E A

CRIMEA

Constantinople

A V A R S

Danube R.

MEDITERRANEAN SEA

LOMBARDS

Ravenna

KINGDOM OF THE OSTROGOTHS
5 3 5 - 5 5 3

Rome

KINGDOM OF THE VANDALS
5 3 4 - 5 3 5

Carthage

KINGDOM OF THE FRANKS

ATLANTIC OCEAN

KINGDOM OF THE VISIGOTHS
5 5 4

Empire in 527
Empire in 554
Bordering Kingdoms

0   200   400 miles

tiate an extensive rebuilding of the capital. His desire was to make Byzantium reflect the physical splendor of Rome. The most spectacular of his many new churches, palaces, and public works was the great church of Hagia Sophia, or Holy Wisdom.

Justinian was remarkably successful in all his ambitious policies until the last years of his reign. Beginning in 542, terrible plagues—not again equaled in virulence until the Black Death (1348)—repeatedly struck the imperial lands. By then he was waging a two-front war against the Persians to the east and the resurgent Ostrogoths on the western frontier. Justinian simply did not have the military power to fight on both fronts. At his death the Byzantine troops were everywhere on the defensive.

Modern historians have tended to view Justinian's policies as unrealistic, excessively ambitious, and ultimately disastrous. Memories of ancient Roman greatness blinded him to the inadequacy of his own resources. Yet Hagia Sophia and the *Corpus Iuris Civilis* assure him a permanent and brilliant reputation in both the East and the West.

In the years following Justinian's death new invaders overwhelmed the frontiers and wrested from his successors most of the emperor's territorial acquisitions. The Lombards' invasion of Italy in 568 undid many of Justinian's conquests there; his successors were able to retain control only over Ravenna, Rome, Naples, and the extreme south of the peninsula. They also held on to Carthage and Sicily. These emperors were not able to recover the Western provinces of the old Roman Empire, and because of this, the Byzantine Empire could no longer aspire to the status of a universal state. It had to find its way as an Eastern, and exclusively Hellenic, empire.

Middle Byzantine Period

The reign of the Emperor Heraclius (610–641) was pivotal in giving Byzantine policy and civilization their new Eastern orientation. His reign began amid repeated military disasters. The aggressive Persians took Antioch, Jerusalem, and Alexandria. With the aid of treasures donated by the churches, Heraclius reorganized and strengthened the army and then boldly took the offensive against the Persians in 622. His success was astonishing. In campaigns waged over six years Heraclius fought his way to the Persian capital of Ctesiphon. The Persians agreed to a humiliating peace. Then a new menace arose. After the death of Muhammad in 632 his Muslim followers embarked upon a tidal wave of conquests, overrunning most of the empire in scarcely more than 10 years.

At the same time that Heraclius was defending the empire against invaders, he was also reforming its administration. One of his predecessors had begun to give land to the soldiers to work for themselves in exchange for military service. The military units and the provinces where they were settled were called themes. Heraclius and his successors extended this system to the navy and the entire empire. The soldier or sailor settled upon his own farm and fighting in his provincial army or navy proved to be far more effective as both a worker and a warrior than the slave, conscript, and mercenary upon whom the empire had earlier and chiefly relied.

A century elapsed before the Byzantines were able to take the offensive against the Muslims. The Emperor Leo III (717–741) beat back a Muslim attack on Constantinople in 717 and 718 and then began a reconquest of Asia Minor.

In 726 Leo forbade the veneration of images within the churches of the empire. Historians still do not agree about his motives. His iconoclastic (image-breaking) policy may have been a legal pretext for seizing the land of the monasteries, which strongly advocated image worship; he needed monastic lands to support his army. Or it may have been an attempt to make Christianity more appealing to the Muslims whom he was seeking to conquer, by emulating the Islamic condemnation of image worship. Whatever the reasons, his iconoclastic policy had a disastrous effect on relations with the West; it antagonized the popes and was a major factor in their decision to seek out a Frankish champion. The veneration of images was restored in the Byzantine Empire between 784 and 813 and permanently after 843. But the iconoclastic policy helped to widen the cleavage between the Western and Eastern churches.

The military revival reached its height under the great warrior emperors of the ninth through eleventh centuries. They pushed the Muslims back into Syria and waged successful wars in southern Italy, the Balkan Peninsula, and the Caucasus. Their principal military accomplishment was in the Balkan Peninsula, where they defeated the Bulgars, a nomadic people who had set themselves over a Slavic population in the lands south of the Danube River. The Bulgars had abandoned their nomadic ways, adopted the language and culture of the Slavs, and established a kingdom during the ninth century. The modern Bulgarians, who are entirely Slavic in language and culture, retain only the name of the original nomadic conquerors.

Byzantine Civilization

Political philosophers of the Hellenistic world, chiefly Epicureans and Stoics, had maintained that all men were one in nature and subject to a single natural law; therefore, all men should be included in a single state. The Byzantines adopted these assumptions and gave them new meanings. As there was one God, one true faith, and one universal Church, so there should be only one empire to rule all Christian peoples, to protect and aid the Church, and to advance the faith among nonbelievers. The empire was thus given the sacred, quasi-messianic function of aiding the salvation of the human race. The Byzantines believed that if the empire served this function, then God would never permit its destruction. This idea (the French would call it an *idée force,* an idea exerting power, comparable to ideas of nationalism or patriotism in the modern world) helped preserve unity among the many nationalities that composed the empire. It gave the Byzantines the spirit they needed to resist for centuries a nearly continuous onslaught of invaders.

The Byzantines also believed that the emperor was a holy figure. He was, after all, the head of a state with a sacred function. Of course, a Christian emperor could not claim divinity; but the emperor lived surrounded by ceremony that imparted an aura of sanctity to his person, and the term *sacred* was liberally applied to his person, palace, and office. The word *sacred* was used as much as we use the word *public,* a usage that illuminates the character of Byzantine civilization.

Modern historians have traditionally used the term *caesaropapism* to describe the emperor's position in the Church. This term suggests that the emperor was both caesar and pope, the true head of both Church and state. Recently, objections have been raised against the use of this term because the emperor's powers over the Church were restricted. He could not repeal the Nicene Creed or personally flout laws of Christian morality. He was not a priest and therefore could not say mass or administer the sacraments.

Yet the emperor exercised an impressive authority over ecclesiastical affairs. He supervised the discipline of the Church, set the qualifications for ordinations, created bishoprics and changed their boundaries, investigated the monasteries and reformed them when necessary, and appointed patriarchs and at times forced their resignation. Even dogma was not beyond his influence. The emperor summoned councils, supervised their proceedings, and enforced their decisions. Some emperors believed they had the right to settle dogmatic disputes through edicts.

Because the emperor was responsible for the peace and welfare of the Church, the clergy was largely limited in its functions to the work of mediation, the performance of the sacred liturgy, and the administration of the sacraments. Even in matters closely touching ecclesiastical interests the clergy characteristically deferred to the wishes of the emperor.

The Eastern Church

The Eastern Church developed and functioned under close secular supervision. In the West, on the other hand, the vacuum of public authority following the collapse of the Roman Empire gave to the clergy a position of leadership in secular affairs. These contrasting experiences in the Early Middle Ages deeply affected the character and spirit of the two major branches of Christianity. The differences between the two Churches are worth reviewing because they help to make understandable other contrasts in the history and cultural development of the Eastern and Western peoples.

Both the Eastern Church and the Western Church considered themselves catholic (that is, universal) and orthodox (that is, holding true beliefs); the terms *Roman Catholic* and *Greek Orthodox* used to identify the Churches today are exclusively modern usages. The two Churches maintained nearly identical beliefs. Perhaps the principal, or at least the most famous, disagreement was, and still is, the *filioque* dispute (meaning "and the son"), which concerns the relationship among members of the Trinity: the Father, Son, and Holy Spirit. The Eastern Church held, and still holds, that the Holy Spirit proceeds only from the Father; whereas the Western Church maintained that the Holy Spirit proceeds from the Father "and the Son." The Eastern Church did not share the Western belief in purgatory, an intermediate state between heaven and hell where some souls are cleansed of minor faults before entering heaven. Both Churches, however, prayed for the dead to ensure that the departed souls would get into heaven.[3] In discipline, too, the

differences in fasting, penitence, and morality were minor. The Eastern Church permitted, as the Western Church did not, divorce for reasons of adultery and the ordination of married men to the priesthood, although bishops had to be celibate.

The differences between the two churches in liturgy were many but not momentous. The most significant difference was that the Eastern Church tolerated the use of vernacular languages—Greek, Coptic, Ethiopian, Syriac, Armenian, Georgian, Slavonic, and others—in the liturgy. Liturgical usage added great dignity to these Eastern languages and stimulated their development. The East Slavs, for example, possessed a rich literature in Slavonic within a century after their conversion to Christianity. Western vernacular literature was much slower in developing. On the other hand, the toleration of many vernacular languages weakened the unity of the Eastern Church. An Eastern cleric who needed to know only his vernacular language for liturgical purposes could not easily communicate with clerics from other regions, whereas a Western cleric who had to learn Latin could make himself understood anywhere in the West. Because of language differences Eastern churches tended to develop in isolation from one another; they could not learn easily from their neighbors. Moreover, the toleration of many vernacular languages made difficult the revival of Classical learning. A Western cleric in learning Latin also acquired, whether he wanted it or not, the ability to read the great Latin classics. An Eastern cleric who did not have to learn Greek never acquired the ability to read the great Greek classics. Eastern cultures were thus deprived of one avenue of enrichment.

The Western Church and the Eastern Church also differed in their organization and relations with secular authority. In the Early Middle Ages the Western Church began to separate itself from secular authority and develop a centralized government under the papacy. By the late twelfth century the pope had become

---

[3] The present disagreements concerning papal infallibility, the Immaculate Conception, and the Assumption of the Virgin Mary (dogmas all recently defined by the Roman Catholic Church) did not disturb relations in the Middle Ages.

the absolute ruler of the Western Church, which he governed with the aid of an elaborate bureaucracy and a sophisticated system of canon law common to the whole Western Church. The Eastern Church, however, remained thoroughly decentralized. It developed into a loose confederation of independent national churches that relied upon secular authority to defend their temporal interests.

The close ties between Church and state in the East conferred advantages on both. The Church devoted itself to its essential functions of liturgical service and the administration of the sacraments; the state made full use of the great wealth and spiritual power of the Church. This was a critical advantage for rulers and peoples struggling to survive on the eastern frontier of Europe, where all resources had to be enlisted in the battle for existence. The East was largely spared, and could have ill afforded, the prolonged disputes between Church and state which marked Western history.

Yet the disputes between Church and state in the West, while often damaging and unseemly, served as a powerful stimulus to intellectual and constitutional changes. The disputes led to fruitful and original analyses of the nature of society and of authority and favored the emergence of balanced constitutions, in which neither the king nor the Church exercised a monopoly of power. Even today, in Communist Poland, the Catholic Church maintains this ancient tradition of independence vis-à-vis the government, while the Orthodox Church in other East European Communist states remains submissive to the state. In the Byzantine Empire, the withdrawal of the Church from temporal concerns established a pattern of Church–state relations that has lived on until the present.

Byzantine Society

The outstanding feature of Byzantine civilization, compared with Western civilization, was the continuing vitality of cities. To be sure, the great plagues of the late sixth century, and the invasions and wars of the seventh, were especially damaging to cities. Many fell in population, and became mere castles or fortresses. Still, some centers survived, and most Byzantine towns enjoyed a period of resurgence in the tenth and eleventh centuries.

At one time the empire included such great urban centers as Alexandria, Antioch, Beirut, Constantinople, Trebizond, and Tyre; the loss of all these except Trebizond and Constantinople after the Muslim conquests of the seventh century still left the empire with two of the greatest cities of the age. At its peak under Justinian, Constantinople probably contained more than 300,000 inhabitants. The city possessed paved and illuminated streets and many splendid churches and palaces. Urban society was marked by a wide division between rich and poor. The rich lived among magnificent surroundings in huge palaces; the poor in sprawling slums. Crimes committed in broad daylight were commonplace. The cities seem to have faced most of the social problems with which our own great cities are painfully familiar.

Rural society consisted largely of peasants, whose status changed greatly over the centuries. An agrarian law, dating probably from the early eighth century, mentions slaves; but clearly the society it describes consisted of free peasants. The most striking feature revealed in the law is the highly developed village government. The peasants owning property assembled together, made decisions concerning the use of uncultivated or common lands, assumed (or were required to assume) collective responsibility for the payment of taxes, and elected judges and other officials to supervise the village government. Serfdom is not mentioned in the law; it probably began in the tenth century.

The Byzantine Empire was wealthy compared with other political entities of the age. One great source of wealth came from the commerce that passed through the ports and gates of Constantinople. Russians and other Slavs

This Byzantine gold cup, dating from the sixth or seventh century, was found at Durazzo in modern Albania. Four female figures in gold repoussé symbolize the cities of Rome, Cyprus, Alexandria, and Constantinople. The detail shows the figure of Constantinople. The representation of cities in allegorical form shows the prominence of urban centers in Byzantine thought and society. (Photo: Metropolitan Museum of Art, gift of J. Pierpont Morgan, 1917)

weight and purity were kept constant from the reign of Constantine to the late eleventh century; no other major system of coinage can match its record of stability.

Another source of wealth was the numerous active guilds. The "Book of the Prefect," written about 950 and describing the duties of a city's chief admininstative officer, mentions 21 professional and craft guilds; most of these were involved with making luxury products, especially silk cloth. Byzantine craftsmen were also famed for goldwork, cups, ivories, jewelry, and reliquaries. These items were shipped to all parts of the known world. The government closely supervised merchants and artisans, regulating prices and the movement of goods. It also maintained state monopolies, particularly over silk products. The best silk, rich purple cloths, could not be exported. The strict regulations enabled the government to profit from this active commerce and were not injurious to it, at least not before the eleventh century.

The empire had a strong central government. The emperor, like his predecessors in the old Roman Empire, enjoyed absolute authority to make or unmake laws at will. He governed with the aid of an elaborate civil service. A master of offices served as a prime minister, a quaestor of the sacred palace presided over the courts and ran the chancery, a count of sacred largesses supervised the treasury, a count of private properties ran the imperial estates, and a provost of the sacred bedroom administered the household affairs. Military affairs were entirely separated from civil administration and entrusted to masters of the soldiers directly responsible to the emperor. All these offices functioned with the aid of a large professional bureaucracy. These great offices were decentralized and simplified when Heraclius reformed the government in the seventh century; then civil and military administrations were combined on the local level under the general who governed the themes. All justice was considered to flow from the emperor, and he or

from the north carried amber, fur, honey, slaves, wax, and wheat; Armenians and Syrians from the east brought clothing, fruit, glass, steel, and spices; merchants from the west contributed arms, iron, slaves, and wood. The vigorous commerce attracted large colonies of foreign merchants who maintained their own churches, mosques, residences, storage houses, and even baths in Constantinople. The commercial importance of Byzantium is revealed in the prestige of its gold coin, the bezant. Its his chief official could hear appeals from any local court in the empire.

There were great contrasts between the Byzantine government and Western governments of the same era. Even after Heraclius reformed the government, it continued to be served by a well-organized local administration and an elaborate, professional bureaucracy. Western kingdoms, on the other hand, functioned with a rudimentary administration and without a professional civil service. The Byzantine government supported such refinements as an effective fiscal system, a state post, and even a secret police, ominously called the *agentes in rebus* ("those doing things"). Western governments had none of these. At a time when Western governments operated almost without a budget, the Byzantine government collected large revenues from the 10 percent tariff it imposed upon trade and from the profit it received from the state monopolies. The government also enjoyed the services of trained diplomats,

As shown in this stone roundel from the late twelfth century, a Byzantine emperor holds the symbols of sovereignty: a scepter and an orb and cross. Note how the sash he wears forms a cross; he is a holy figure.
(Photo: courtesy of the Dumbarton Oaks Collection)

who were celebrated by contemporary observers for their ability to keep enemies divided and their liberal use of bribes, tributes, and subsidies.

The bureaucracy was largely staffed by literate and trained laymen. Eunuchs were preferred for important positions in the government because it was believed that they would not be tempted by sexual intrigue and would have no wife or children to compete with the emperor for their loyalties. Reliance upon eunuchs in palace administration had an interesting social effect. They performed managerial functions that in the West were assumed by queens and women of the court. The services of eunuchs thus restricted the private and public influence of women and led to their progressive seclusion within the inner reaches of the household. This was a gradual tendency, but unmistakable in direction, and set a model for the heirs of the Byzantine Empire.

Byzantine Culture

Byzantine wealth supported a tradition of learning that benefited not only the clergy but also many laymen. There were three types of institutions of higher learning: a palace school trained civil servants in language, law, and rhetoric; a patriarchal school instructed priests in rhetoric and theology; and monastic schools taught young monks the mystical writings of the past. The poor people were dependent on the guilds for what education they received.

Scholars used the Greek language almost exclusively after the sixth century. They composed large numbers of school manuals, histories, saints' lives, biblical commentaries, and encyclopedias of ancient science and lore. Their greatest accomplishment, however, was the preservation of Classical Greek literature. With the exception of some few works preserved on papyri, virtually all the Western world possesses of Classical Greek authors has come down through Byzantine copies, most of which date from the tenth to the twelfth centuries.

The first flowering of artistic achievement occurred in the sixth century, when Justinian literally rebuilt Constantinople. Among his many buildings is Hagia Sophia, designed by Isidore of Miletus and Anthemius of Tralles. Work was begun in 532 and completed in 537. As Procopius described it, its great dome seemed to float in the air, as if suspended by a chain from heaven. Hagia Sophia is one of the acknowledged architectural masterpieces of the world. Hagia Sophia, like other Byzantine churches, was decorated with brilliant mosaics, but most of these were destroyed by the iconoclasts in the eighth and ninth centuries. Because of the iconoclastic movement the richest examples of the early mosaics are not to be found in Constantinople and Asia Minor, but rather in areas that were no longer under Byzantine rule in those centuries. San Vitale and Sant' Apollinare in Ravenna, Italy, are particularly noted for early Byzantine mosaics.

With the final rejection of iconoclasm in the middle of the ninth century there was a resurgence of artistic endeavor. Byzantine artisans designed and decorated many churches throughout the empire. Their work is found in such places as Messina and Palermo in Sicily and Venice in Italy. Artists were summoned to such distant places as Kiev in Russia to aid in the design, construction, and decoration of churches.

The mosaics make vividly concrete the Byzantine concepts of empire, emperor, and church. The emperor is always presented as the august figure that Byzantine ideology made of him (see Plate 7). Christ is never shown as suffering; he is, in other words, always God and never man (see Plate 8). The reason for this seems to have been the close association which the figure of Christ bore to the living emperor. To show Christ as suffering would suggest that the emperor too might be a weak and vulnerable man. The mosaics have no sense of movement, admission of human frailty, or recognition of the reality of change. Operating within this picture of the world, the artists nevertheless

The greatest monument of the Byzantine Empire is the church of Hagia Sophia (Holy Wisdom) in Istanbul, which was begun in 532, during the reign of Emperor Justinian. The four minarets were added when the church became a mosque after the Turkish conquest. (Photo: G. E. Kidder Smith, New York)

portrayed their solemn figures with a rich variety of forms and garments and illumined them with a splendid array of colors. Byzantine mosaics may be static, but they are neither drab nor monotonous.

Decline of the Empire

The military power of the empire in its middle period was largely based upon the system of themes (see p. 244) that created an army and navy of free peasant-warriors. But from the early tenth century these free peasant-warriors, apparently to escape mounting fiscal and military burdens, began to abandon their farms to more powerful neighbors. In the eleventh century many of them became serfs. The disintegration of the theme system reduced the military manpower and contributed to the growth

of a rural aristocracy of landlords, which in turn weakened the strength of the central government.

The weak emperors of the late eleventh century sought to purchase the loyalty of the rural aristocracy by distributing imperial estates to them. During the same time, the aristocracy was gaining control over the ecclesiastical lands. The Church had been granting to them entire monasteries as *charistikaria* (literally, "charitable donations") to administer in the best interest of the monks and the Church. But in fact these concessions represented virtual gifts of monastic properties.

Socially, Byzantium was being transformed from a disciplined society of peasant-warriors under a strong central government to a feudal society with a dependent peasantry, strong local landlords, and a weak central government. The transition was costly in a military sense; the emperors had to seek outside help to compensate for the shrinking contingents they could marshal from among their own subjects. Control of the sea was essential to the security of Constantinople. To assure sufficient naval strength the emperors sought the support of the growing naval power of Venice. In 998 and 1082 they gave generous trading concessions to the Venetians, which were major steps in the growth of Italian (and Western) naval strength in the waters of the eastern Mediterranean. The problem of land defense was even more pressing. The eastern frontiers were being threatened by a new people, the Seljuk Turks, who had recently emerged from the steppes.

The Seljuks

The Byzantines gave the name "Turk" to a number of nomadic tribes who lived in the region east and north of the Caspian Sea (modern Soviet Republic of Turkestan). They had long posed a threat to the settled Islamic and Christian populations. In the eleventh century members of one of the nomadic tribes, the Seljuks, penetrated beyond the eastern borders of the empire into Asia Minor. Emperor Romanus Diogenes tried to expel them but succeeded only in provoking open war. The Seljuks shattered the largely mercenary army of the Byzantines and took Romanus himself captive at Manzikert in 1071.

The disaster at Manzikert broke down the eastern defenses of the Byzantine Empire and opened Asia Minor to the Seljuks. One Turkish chieftain, Suleiman, established himself and his warriors at Nicaea, only a few miles from Constantinople. He founded what eventually became the most powerful Turkish principality in Asia Minor: the Sultanate of Rum. The virtual loss of Asia Minor forced the Byzantine emperor to appeal to the West for help. This was the immediate prologue to the First Crusade and also the end of the Byzantine Empire as a great power in the East.

Schism with the West

The second disaster of the eleventh century was the formal schism between the Eastern and Western branches of the Church. The schism was provoked not by major dogmatic differences but by rivalry, disputes, and snobbery. For years the popes at Rome and the patriarchs at Constantinople had been rivals in converting the East Slavs and had been bitterly disputing the ecclesiastical jurisdiction over southern Italy and Illyria (modern Yugoslavia). Furthermore, the Byzantines resented the papal claim to primacy within the Church. Rome by this time appeared to them as a provincial town without an empire and subject territory, whereas Constantinople was the seat of wealth and power; it was, therefore, the more appropriate capital for the Church.[4]

Perhaps even more fundamentally the rupture of relations reflected the breakdown in communications between the East and West, which had begun when Justinian failed in the sixth century to reconcile the two branches of the Church within the old Roman Empire. After his reign the two halves of the Roman Empire ceased entirely to speak or understand a common language; misunderstandings came easily and were overcome with difficulty. Commercial and diplomatic contacts between the East and West also became sporadic.

---

[4] In the tenth century the Byzantines told Liutprand, bishop of Cremona, that they, and not the residents of Rome, were the true Romans and that Rome was a town inhabited exclusively by "vile slaves, fishermen, confectioners, poulterers, bastards, plebeians, underlings."

Personalities played a major role in the actual schism of 1054. A dedicated but rigid reformer, Cardinal Humbert of Silva Candida, led a papal delegation to Constantinople. Failing to secure satisfactory concessions from Patriarch Michael Cerularius, the papal legates deposited a bull of excommunication on the high altar of Hagia Sophia and left the city in anger. Cerularius, a haughty and ambitious prelate who welcomed a break with the Western Church and had labored to provoke it, publicly declared to the other Eastern patriarchs that the supporters of the pope were steeped in heresy and had taken themselves out of the true Church since the sixth century.

The schism of 1054 destroyed the hope for a united Christian Church, although only later centuries showed the full extent of the damage. Even today, more than nine hundred years after the event, adherents of the Western and Eastern traditions are trying to overcome the rift. Only in 1965 did the pope and the Greek patriarch formally remove the excommunications of 1054.

The Western Debt to Byzantine Civilization

The East Slavs were the true, direct heirs of Byzantine civilization; but the Western peoples also accumulated a large debt to this civilization. Byzantine scholars preserved the Classical Greek literature. This permitted Western scholars to establish direct contact with the most original thinkers of the ancient world. Neither the Western Classical Renaissance nor modern European culture would have been the same without their contribution.

The very existence of the Byzantine Empire, guarding the approaches to Europe, gave the Western peoples a measure of immunity from the destructive incursions of Arabs, Persians, Turks, and others. The sophisticated Byzantine economy and government served as a kind of school of civilized practices from which less advanced peoples could learn new techniques. The greatest contribution Byzantine civilization made to the West was that, through its own achievements, it showed the uncouth Western peoples the possibilities and rewards of civilized life.

II. THE PRINCIPALITY OF KIEV

During the Early Middle Ages a new people, the East Slavs, set about building a civilization that was based primarily on the values of Eastern Christianity. Three modern Slavic peoples—the Russians, Ukrainians, and White (Byelo-) Russians—trace their ancestry directly to these East Slavs, and all regard the foundation of the first East Slavic state as the beginnings of their own national histories. For this reason, it is inappropriate to speak, as is often done, of the first Russian state, as the Russians are not its exclusive heirs. In referring to these East Slavs we shall rather use a contemporary term, the *Rus,* a name of obscure origins, which first referred to a dominant tribe or group and then came to signify the entire people.

The Foundations of Kiev Rus

The East Slavs greatly expanded their area of settlement between the sixth and ninth centuries. Some East Slavic tribes pushed to the east as far as the Volga River. There they encountered on the lower course of the river a Turkish-speaking people called the Khazars. The Khazars (or at least their upper classes) practiced Judaism; their obscure history has its own special fascination. Other Slavic tribes moved to the north nearly to the Baltic Sea. Two of their most important settlements were Kiev on the Dnieper River and Novgorod on

Lake Ilmen, within easy access of the Baltic Sea.

In about 830, Vikings from Scandinavia, embarking upon a vigorous wave of expansion in all directions, penetrated into the lands of the East Slavs in quest of booty and profit. They also established trade routes that ran from the Baltic Sea over the rivers of Eastern Europe to the Black Sea and thence to Constantinople, thus linking Scandinavia with Byzantium. The invasions brought the Vikings and East Slavs into close contact. Out of this encounter emerged the first East Slavic state.

The most detailed and important source for the birth of the Rus state is the *Primary Chronicle*. Many hands contributed to this work; and it was not written down in its present form until 1117 or 1118, some 250 years after the events it describes. According to the *Primary Chronicle* the Varangians, as the East Slavs called the Vikings, ruled Novgorod until the Slavic population rebelled against them and drove them back beyond the sea. Soon, however, the people of Novgorod fell to fighting among themselves. Unable to overcome their discord, they invited the Varangians to rule them once again. In response a prince named Rurik, his two brothers, and "all the Rus" came to govern Novgorod in 862. "On account of these Varangians," the *Primary Chronicle* explains, "the district of Novgorod became known as Russian land."

Historians have long argued vigorously and even bitterly over the dating and terminology used in this account. The date of 862 is certainly wrong, and the meaning of "Rus" is obscure. Byzantine sources mention a Rus attack on Constantinople in 860, and there are earlier references to a mysterious people by that name settled in what is now the Ukraine.

The *Primary Chronicle* goes on to say that Rurik soon left Novgorod and that his follower Oleg assumed authority in Novgorod and then Kiev. Oleg (873?–913) is thus considered the true founder of the Rus state because he united under his rule the two chief cities of Kiev and Novgorod. In 907 he led a fleet, allegedly containing 2000 ships, on a raid against Constantinople. The Byzantine emperor granted both tribute and trading concessions in order to purchase peace with the Rus. Oleg's successors completed the unification of the East Slavic tribes. This brought under their rule an area that stretched from the Baltic to the Black seas and from the Danube to the Volga rivers. They also made war against the nomadic peoples of the steppes and strengthened commercial, diplomatic, and cultural ties with the Byzantine Empire. In 988 the ruler, Vladimir, converted to Christianity (the Eastern Church) and imposed baptism on his subjects. These people, the most numerous of all the Slavs, were thus brought within the Eastern cultural world.

Yaroslav the Wise

The Principality of Kiev reached its height of power under Vladimir's son Yaroslav (1015–1054), who might well be termed the Slavic Justinian. Like Justinian, Yaroslav was a successful warrior, administrator, and builder. He defeated the Pechenegs, a nomadic people who roamed the grasslands south and east of Kiev and hampered contact with the Black Sea, and extended his territory to the north at the expense of the Finns (see Map 7.2). He won self-government for the Rus Church from the patriarch of Constantinople in 1037. The head of the Church was called the metropolitan. Kiev became the ecclesiastical as well as the political capital of the East Slavs. During his reign Yaroslav had prepared the first written codification of East Slavic law, the *Russkaia Pravda*. He built many churches and brought in skilled Byzantine artisans to decorate them. His masterpiece was the cathedral at Kiev. The *Primary Chronicle* says that Yaroslav loved books "and read them continually day and night," and that he wrote many books himself. He tried to pro-

MAP 7.2. PRINCIPALITY OF KIEV

mote learning in his principality and assembled many scribes to translate religious books from Greek into Slavic.

The Principality of Kiev maintained closer ties with Western Europe than any other Rus state for centuries. Russia is mentioned in the eleventh-century French epic the *Song of Roland*. The family of Yaroslav had marriage connections with the ruling dynasties of Byzantium, England, France, Germany, Norway, Poland, and Hungary. Yaroslav's own daughter Anna married King Henry I of France. Charters with her signature survive, carefully inscribed with Cyrillic letters; she seems to have been the only layperson in the French court who could write. Kiev was also a refuge for Western princes; Edwin and Edward, sons of the English king Edmund Ironside, fled there during Canute's reign in England.

Kievan Civilization

The Kievan economy was both vigorous and balanced. Agriculture was productive on the fertile steppes. The *Primary Chronicle* describes peasants plowing with horses at a time when the less efficient oxen were the more common draft animals in the West. Trade was conducted with the Scandinavians, the steppe peoples, the Muslims at Baghdad, and especially the Byzantines. Every year a great fleet of boats assembled at Kiev and floated down the Dnieper River to the Black Sea and across to Constantinople. The princes themselves led these expeditions. Amber, fur, honey, slaves, and wheat were exchanged for silks, spices, and other luxuries of the East. In recent years Russian archaeologists excavating at Novgorod have uncovered numerous commercial documents written on birch bark that illuminate this lively trade. These documents indicate that the Rus merchants were not as sophisticated in their business practices as the Byzantines, but they establish the variety and quality of the products the Rus offered for trade.

Most of the population was free peasants, but there were slaves and some enserfed peasants. Although its foundations were agricultural, Kievan society had an important urban life. Within the many towns a wealthy aristocracy of princes, warriors, and great merchants rubbed shoulders with artisans, workers, and large numbers of destitute persons. The princes had to concern themselves with such social problems as the oppression of the poor, usury, and enslavement for debt.

Kiev in the eleventh century was one of the great cities of the age. The German chronicler Adam of Bremen considered Kiev a rival in size to Constantinople; Metropolitan Hilarion described it as "glittering with grandeur"; another German chronicler, Thietmar of Merseburg, said it had 400 churches, 8 marketplaces, and unnumbered inhabitants. In 1124 a fire allegedly destroyed 600 churches. Kiev must have included 20,000 to 30,000 people, which would be above the size of any contemporary Western city.

The head of the Kievan government was the prince, who selected nobles, called boyars, to aid him in governing. The boyars formed the prince's *druzhina* ("friendship").[5] In all important matters the prince consulted his boyars for advice. The towns had large citizen assemblies, called *veches,* that the prince also consulted for advice. The government was thus based on a balance of monarchical, aristocratic, and popular elements. The prince, unlike the Byzantine emperor, was not the fountain of justice. Most cases were settled in popular courts from which there was no organized system of appeal. Kievan justice was closer to the Germanic system than to the Byzantine system. The limitations upon princely autocracy imposed by the boyars and the *veches* make the Kievan period distinctive in Russian constitutional history.

The central event in Kievan cultural devel-

---

[5] The *druzhina* was the equivalent of the Germanic *comitatus* (see Chapter 6).

opment was the acceptance of Eastern Christianity in 988. The arrival of some Byzantine clergy in Kiev changed the character of its culture. They established a formal educational system primarily to train a clergy; but their schools were open to the sons of ruling families, and a number of women, too, were educated in convents. Monks, as the first scholars in Kiev, used a modification of the Greek alphabet that missionaries had devised years before to convert the Slavs. They employed this alphabet in the translations of parts of the Bible and other ecclesiastical writings. These works constituted the dominant body of contemporary literature, and their religious themes served as models for the native writers.

The literary masterpiece of the age is the *Primary Chronicle*. Its principal theme is the conversion of the Rus to Christianity and their battles against the pagan peoples who surrounded them. This work gave to the East Slavs a sense of national identity within a Christian scheme of history. Although the account is of questionable accuracy in its earliest passages, it remains a classic of medieval literature. Few Western chronicles of comparable age can equal it in the wealth of information and liveliness of narration. The monks, of whom Metropolitan Hilarion was perhaps the most gifted, also produced many sermons, doctrinal and devotional tracts, and lives of the saints. These histories and the *Primary Chronicle* provide the best picture of the society and culture of medieval Rus. The poetry of medieval Rus is represented by the short heroic epic the *Song of Igor's Campaign*.[6] The poem records an unsuccessful campaign that the Rus princes conducted against the pagan Polovtsi in 1185 and depicts with considerable feeling the tragic but

necessary costs of battle against the people of the steppes.

Christianity also had an immense influence on architectural and artistic development. After the conversion the East Slavs built many churches based on Byzantine models. The familiar onion domes of the Russian churches, for example, were a late effort to imitate in wood the domes on ecclesiastical structures at Constantinople. The East Slavs loved magnificence and splendor in their churches and li-

---

Prince Yaroslav built St. Sophia Cathedral at Kiev in 1038, modeling it after Hagia Sophia at Constantinople. It is famous for its outstanding mosaics and frescoes. The present domes were built in the seventeenth century in Ukrainian baroque style. In 1934 it was declared a state museum.
(Photo: Novosti from Sovfoto)

---

[6] The original manuscript was discovered about 1790 by Count Aleksey Musin-Pushkin but was destroyed during the Napoleonic invasion in 1812, when Moscow was burned. Those who accept its authenticity usually date its composition to 1187. The *Song* is available in a fine English translation by the distinguished novelist Vladimir Nabokov.

turgical services. They learned the art of painting from the Byzantines and decorated their churches with icons (from the Greek, *eikón,* meaning "image"). The icon is a representation in painting or enamel of some sacred personage, such as Christ, a saint, or an angel.

Christianity imparted to the East Slavs a sense of world history and of their own place in it. They came to view their country as Holy Rus, the defender of the true faith, facing and fighting a sea of pagan barbarians. Even though many accomplishments of the Kievan era were not maintained in the succeeding periods of East Slavic history, the Russians, Ukrainians, and Byelorussians themselves did not lapse into barbarism.

Decline of the Principality

Both internal and external troubles destroyed the peace of the land after Yaroslav's death. To select his successor Yaroslav introduced an extraordinarily complex procedure known as the rota system. The entire land was considered to be the property of the ruling family, and the towns were ranked in order of their importance and allotted to the princes according to their position within the family. When the senior prince of Kiev died, each of the junior princes transferred his rule to the next greater town; brothers were given preference over sons. This cumbersome system of succession led to a constant movement of princes, to frequent bickerings, and often to civil wars. The political history after the reign of Yaroslav becomes an involved and dismal story of unending princely quarrels.

These struggles left the people unable to resist the renewed menace of the steppe nomads. In 1061 the Cumans began harassing the frontier, and they eventually cut off Kiev from contact with the Black Sea. This sundering of the trade route to Constantinople was a disaster for commerce and culture because it deprived

Kiev of contact with the Byzantine Empire and the Western world.

Pressure from the nomads pushed the area of East Slavic settlement to the north and west, where extensive forests offered protection from their forays. This dispersal prepared the way for the eventual differentiation of the East Slavs into three culturally distinct peoples. The Rus of the north—soon Russians—were forced into a kind of isolation, removed and remote from the major centers of civilization. A new city, Moscow (not mentioned in the sources until 1147), assumed the arduous task of forming a united Russian state. In 1169 the soldiers of a northern prince, Andrew Bogoliubsky of Suzdal, sacked Kiev. With the ruin of Kiev, perpetrated by the steppe nomads and by the Rus themselves, the first major chapter of East Slavic history closes.

III. ISLAM

Sometime about 610 in the Arabian town of Mecca, a merchant's son named Muhammad began to preach to the people, summoning them to repentance and reform. Gradually, he brought his teachings together to form a new system of religious belief that he called Islam. The explosive impact of his preaching must be reckoned as one of the most extraordinary events of world history. Within a century after Muhammad's death his followers had conquered and partially converted territories larger than the old Roman Empire. Even today Islam remains the faith of more than 513 million people, about an eighth of the world's population.

The Arabs

The Arabian Peninsula, the homeland of the Arabs, profoundly influenced their culture and history. Its vast interior and northern regions are dominated by steppes, wastelands, and some of the hottest and driest deserts of the world. The Arabs, however, had adapted to this harsh environment. They supported themselves by raising sheep and camels. These animals provided nearly all their necessities: meat, milk, wool and skins for clothes and tents, and fuel from dried camel dung. The Arabs were extremely proud of their family, race, language, skill, and way of life. The harsh environment and fierce pride made them spirited, tenacious, and formidable warriors.

The Arabian Peninsula was in a state of intense political and social ferment on the eve of Muhammad's appearance. The stronger political powers—the Persians, Byzantines, and Abyssinians across the Red Sea—tried repeatedly to subdue the Arabs, but they could not dominate them in their desert home. Religious ferment was no less pronounced. Several prophets, preaching new religious beliefs, had appeared in Arabia before Muhammad; and this indicates a growing dissatisfaction among the Arabs with their traditional paganism that gave no promise of an afterlife and offered no image of human destiny and the role of the Arabs in it. Both Christianity and Judaism had won numerous converts, but neither one was able to gain the adherence of the larger part of the people. The Arabs awaited a man who by the force of his vision could fuse these contending ideas—pagan, Christian, and Jewish—into a single, commanding, and authentic Arabian religion.

Muhammad

Historians have little information that is certain about the founder of Islam. Muhammad was born at Mecca about 570 or 571. His father died before his birth, and his mother when he was six. After being raised by his uncle, Muhammad worked as a camel driver in mercantile caravans. He may have been illiterate and may have had no direct knowledge of the Jewish and Christian scriptures; but he did acquire a wide, if sometimes inaccurate, knowledge of the history and teaching of those two religions. About the age of 25 Muhammad married the widow of a rich merchant; thus freed from economic concerns, he gave himself to religious meditations in the desert outside Mecca.

In 610 the voice of the angel Gabriel spoke to Muhammad, and he continued to receive revelations in increasing frequency and length for the remainder of his life. After that event Muhammad began to preach publicly about personal moral reform, but only his wife and a small group of relatives initially accepted his teachings. The people of Mecca feared him because his strictures against paganism seemed to threaten the position of Mecca as a center of pilgrimages. Mecca possessed a renowned shrine containing the Kaaba, a sacred black stone that was the object of pagan worship. Rejected in his native city, Muhammad accepted an invitation to come to Yathrib, a trading town 270 miles to the north, which he later renamed Medina.

Muhammad's flight from Mecca to Yathrib is called the Hegira and occurred in 622; it later became the year 1 of the Islamic calendar. The Hegira was a turning point in Muhammad's career for two reasons: he became the political leader and governor of an important town, which gave him a base for the military expansion of the Islamic community; and his responsibilities as head of an independent town affected the character of his religious message. More and more it was concerned with public law, administration, and the practical problems of government.

Muhammad was more successful at Yathrib than he had been at Mecca in making converts. He told them that God ordered them to convert or conquer their neighbors; through enthusiastic proselytizing and war the community of believers grew rapidly. With this support Muhammad marched against the Meccans, defeating them at Badr in 624 and taking Mecca in 630. By his death in 632, Muhammad had given his religion a firm foundation on Arabian soil.

The Religion of Islam

Instructed by the angel Gabriel, Muhammad passed on to his followers the words or prophecies of Allah (from *al ilāh,* "the God"). The collection of prophecies is known as the Koran; and Allah, in Islamic theology, is its true author. The Koran was written down in its present, official version from 651 to 652. The Koran often impresses the non-Muslim reader as chaotic and repetitious, but to the sympathetic reader it imparts a powerful mood, one of uncompromising monotheism, of repeated and impassioned emphasis upon the unity, power, and presence of Allah. The mood is sustained by constant reiterations of set formulas praising Allah, his power, knowledge, mercy, justice, and concern for his people.

The chief obligation which Muhammad imposed upon his followers was submission (the literal meaning of "Islam") to the will of Allah. Those who submit are Muslims. ("Muhammadan," which suggests that Muhammad claimed divinity, is an inappropriate usage.) Muhammad was little concerned with the subtleties of theology; he was interested in defining for Muslims the ethical and legal requirements for an upright life. Unlike Christianity, Islam retained this practical emphasis; jurisprudence, even more than speculative theology, remained the great intellectual interest of scholarship. Also in contrast to Christianity, Islam did not recognize a separate clergy and church, for there was no need for specialized intermediaries between Allah and his people. Allah was the direct ruler of the faithful on earth; he legislated for them in the Koran and administered through Muhammad, the Prophet, and his successors, the caliphs. Church and state were not separate entities, at least in theory. There was only the single, sacred community of Allah.

Expansion of Islam

The message of Islam exerted a powerful appeal to the Arabs. Compared with Christianity and Judaism, Islam was a starkly simple belief, easily explained and easily grasped. It was an effective fusion of religious ideas from Christianity, Judaism, paganism, and perhaps Zoroastrianism. Judaism influenced the legal code regulating diet and behavior. Judaism and Christianity provided the notion of prophecy (Muhammad considered himself the last of a line of prophets that began with Abraham and included Christ). Christianity gave the concepts of Last Judgment, personal salvation, heaven and hell, charity to the poor and weak, and a universal religion. Christianity or perhaps Zoroastrianism suggested the figures of Satan and evil demons. Paganism contributed the veneration of the Kaaba at Mecca and the requirement of pilgrimage to the sacred city. Islam was the fulfillment of religious ideas already familiar to the Arabs. Perhaps most important, Islam appealed strongly to the intense racial and cultural pride of the Arabs. The Koran was written in their native language, Arabic, and only in Arabic could Allah be addressed. Islam was the final revelation, bringing to completion the message that God had partially conveyed through the Hebrew prophets and Christ. The Arabs, a semibarbarous people who had hitherto played a negligible role in history, were given an important mission in life: to carry to the world the ultimate saving message. Even as Muhammad supplanted Christ as the supreme prophet, so the Arabs replaced the Jews as God's chosen people, with a sacred right to his holy places, including Jerusalem.

It is remarkable that these ideas retain power even in the contemporary world. The present conflict in the Middle East between Israelis and Arabs, among Jews, Muslims, and Christians, is not primarily a reflection of modern political and economic rivalries. Rather, it is grounded in ancient theologies and ingrained cultural pride; it is history's anguished legacy.

Allah instructed his followers to convert or

conquer nonbelievers. Several factors aided the extraordinary expansion of Islam in the first century of its existence. Islam fused the once contending Arab clans and tribes into a unified and dedicated force. The Arabs, long familiar with camels, were masters of desert warfare. Their enemies, relying on horses, could not challenge them on desert terrain. Using the desert much as English imperialists later used the sea, the Arabs moved armies and supplies with facility across vast arid stretches, struck the enemy at places and times of their own choosing, and retreated to the safety of the desert when the odds turned against them. Moreover, the Arabs' immediate neighbors, the Byzantines and Persians, were mutually exhausted by their recurrent wars. Both empires included large Semitic populations that were linguistically and culturally related to the Arabs and, therefore, could comprehend the message of Islam. The Arabs were able to make and hold their conquests through a unique combination of fanaticism and toleration. They were inspired to battle by the Prophet's promise of vast rewards to those who died in the Holy War against the nonbelievers and by the very real prospect of considerable booty if victory accompanied their efforts. The Prophet, however, also enjoined a policy of partial toleration toward the Christians and Jews, the "people of the Book." They were permitted to live under their own laws, but they paid a special tax for the privilege. Finally, because the Arabs did not have the numbers and the skills to govern all the territories they conquered, they opened the ranks of government to men from the newly conquered and converted peoples. This added stability to Islamic rule.

The period of most rapid expansion of Islam followed Muhammad's death in 632 and coincided with the rule of the first four caliphs. Arabian forces seized the Byzantine provinces of Palestine and Syria, overran Persia, and conquered Egypt. By 661 Islam was firmly established as a world power. Islamic conquests continued under the Omayyad caliphs, the first line of hereditary rulers. The Omayyads moved the capital from Mecca to Damascus. Under their rule the Muslims conquered North Africa and overran the kingdom of the Visigoths. After crossing the Pyrenees into the kingdom of the Franks, Muslim raiders were finally defeated by Charles Martel at Tours in 732. This battle, 100 years after Muhammad's death, marked the extent of the western advance and stabilized the frontier of Islam for the next several centuries (see Map 7.3).

As the territory under Islamic control grew to enormous size, powerful movements threatened and finally shattered Islamic unity. Jealousies and frictions disturbed the relations among the various peoples who had accepted Islam, and religious divisions also appeared. Islam had been an open and fluid religion at the death of Muhammad, but scholars and teachers gradually elaborated a theology that a majority of the believers accepted as orthodox. The scholars based the new orthodoxy not only upon the Koran but also upon the Sunnas, or traditions, which were writings that purported to describe how the first companions of Muhammad or Muhammad himself dealt with various problems. Some Muslims, however, rejected the new orthodoxy of the Sunnites, as they came to be called. Those who opposed the Sunnites were called the Shiites, or schismatics.

This earliest schism was more a political than a religious protest. The Shiites maintained that only the descendants of Muhammad's son-in-law, Ali, who was the fourth caliph, could lawfully rule the Islamic community; therefore, they rejected the Omayyads (and later the Abbasids) as usurpers. Shiism soon became a cloak for all sorts of antagonisms, protests, and revolts. It struck deep roots among the mixed populations, reflecting the dissatisfactions of non-Arabs with Arab preponderance and channeling the antagonism between the poorer classes and their masters.

The growing social and religious dissensions finally broke the Omayyad caliphate. A descendant of Muhammad's uncle Abbas re-

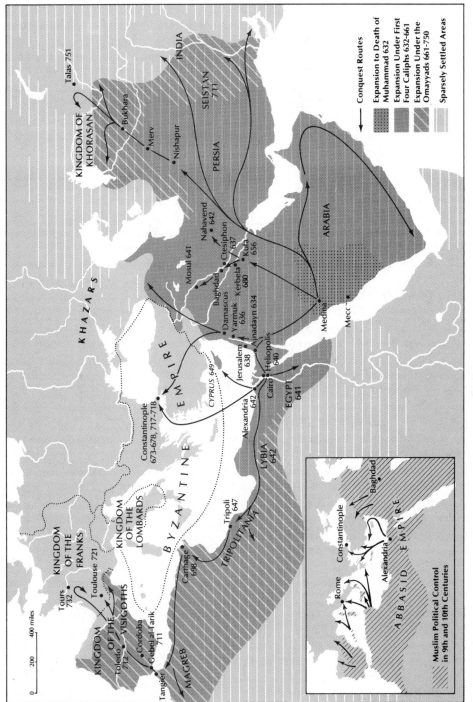

MAP 7.3. EXPANSION OF ISLAM

volted against the Omayyads, captured Damascus, and ruthlessly massacred the caliph's family in 750. Only one member escaped, Abdurrahman. He fled to Spain, where he set up an independent caliphate at Córdoba in 755. Other split-offs soon followed: Morocco in 788, Tunisia in 800, eastern Persia in 820, and Egypt in 868. All became virtually independent under their local dynasties. The new Abbasid caliph moved the capital from Damascus to a new city, Baghdad. The community of Islam was never again to be united.

Islamic Civilization

Medieval Islamic civilization reached its peak of prosperity, refinement, and learning in the ninth and tenth centuries. The name of Caliph Harun al-Rashid is known throughout the world by virtue of the tales of the *Arabian Nights*. These exotic stories, put into their present form in the fourteenth century, convey a glamorous and idealized, but not a false, picture of the luxurious life at Baghdad during its most splendid age. Harun's son Al-Mamun reigned even more splendidly than his father. He was also a patron of learning. Al-Mamun founded an observatory for the study of the heavens and established a "House of Wisdom" (sometimes referred to as the first Islamic institution of higher education), where translations could be made and a library collected for the use of scholars.

Spain was also a center of medieval Islamic civilization. The brilliance of Islamic-Spanish civilization is best reflected in three great architectural monuments: the mosque (now a cathedral) at Córdoba, the Alhambra Palace in Granada, and the Alcazar at Seville. Jewish communities in Spain contributed to the high quality of intellectual life. It was in Spain that Western Christians came into intimate contact with Islamic learning and drew from it the greatest benefits.

The expansion of Islam brought within the Muslim world a great variety of economic systems. The Bedouins in the Arabian Peninsula, the Berbers in North Africa, and the Turkish peoples on the Eurasian steppes continued to follow an essentially pastoral economy. The

---

The Book of the 1001 Nights, **first composed in Arabic at Baghdad in the ninth century, made use of much Persian and Indian material and remains a world classic of imaginative storytelling. This bizarre representation of a monster, taken from a late-medieval Urdu (Hindustani) edition of the work, illustrates both its romantic content and lasting appeal.**
(Photo: The Granger Collection)

majority of the population in Egypt, Persia, Sicily, and Spain lived from settled agriculture. The inhabitants of cities, particularly those found along the caravan routes which tied the Middle East to India and central Asia, depended on commerce.

Islamic religion contributed to the economic life of these many peoples and regions by facilitating communication and commercial exchange. The imposition of a universal language, Arabic, enabled travelers and merchants to make themselves understood from Spain to India. The obligation of pilgrimage to Mecca assured that travel would be frequent. Moreover, Muhammad had been a merchant, and the earliest centers of his religion, Medina and Mecca, were important caravan cities; therefore, Islamic law was favorable to commercial transactions, and Islamic society held the merchant in high esteem. Merchants not only continued the caravan trade, but also developed an important maritime commerce in the Mediterranean Sea, the Red Sea, and the Indian Ocean. Their ships provided until the sixteenth century the chief commercial link between India and the West. Egypt served as a vital link between these two great zones of maritime commerce (the Mediterranean Sea and the Red Sea–Indian Ocean). There have survived letters of Jewish merchants, resident in Cairo, that date chiefly from the eleventh and twelfth centuries. They marvelously illuminate trade and many other aspects of social life in the medieval East.[7]

Commercial exchange stimulated agriculture. Cultivators in Sicily and Spain learned of, and adopted, new plants from Asia, such as rice, and new techniques of cultivation, such as the irrigation of fields. Muslims from Persia to

Spain practiced an agriculture remarkably advanced for the age. Commercial exchange also stimulated urban artisans to improve the quality of their products. The steel of Damascus, the leather of Córdoba, and the fine cotton, linen, and silk of many Eastern towns were desired and imitated in the West. These same products were shipped to India and Indonesia, where they were traded for spices and other products.

The practice of a common religion assured that there would be similarities in Islamic societies everywhere in the world. Religious law allowed the male Muslim to have as many as four legal wives and an unlimited number of concubines. In fact, only the very rich could afford to have several wives. More important than polygamy in determining the position of women were the relative ease of divorce and the life of seclusion imposed upon all women after puberty. Religious laws permitted the husband to dismiss his wife almost at will and prohibited a woman from revealing her face except to her husband. These laws were not enforced everywhere with equal rigor; they primarily weighed upon women of the upper classes. Moreover, within the cities, at least in certain periods, women enjoyed relative freedom. Variety, in other words, rather than uniformity, was the more prominent characteristic of medieval Islamic society.

That society was also distinguished by a vigorous urban life, concentrated in the cities of Baghdad, Cairo, Córdoba, and Damascus. According to travelers' reports, Damascus had 113,000 homes and 70 libraries. Baghdad surpassed all cities with the number of palaces, libraries, and public baths. In all the major cities products from almost all parts of the known world could be purchased at the markets, or bazaars. The streets teemed with slaves, servants, artisans, merchants, administrators, and beggars. The aura of the Islamic cities was preeminently cosmopolitan.

Muhammad died before making provision

---

[7] They are called the "Geniza" documents. The geniza was a storeroom attached to synagogues; records mentioning God's name (including merchants' letters) could not be destroyed and were placed in the storeroom. The geniza of the Cairo synagogue was sealed up and forgotten in the late Middle Ages, and not rediscovered until the nineteenth century. For examples of these extraordinary records, see S. D. Goitein, *Letters of Medieval Jewish Traders,* 1973.

for the government of Islam, and his immediate followers elected Abu Bakr as his successor, or caliph. Because Islam recognized no distinction between church and state, the caliph was the supreme religious and civil head of the Muslim world. But he was not free to change the laws at will since Allah had already provided all the laws his people needed; therefore, he was primarily a military chief and a judge. The government tended to retain the administrative institutions of the preceding rulers in territories that were overrun. Among the Muslims the chief administrator on the local level was the kadi. He was primarily a judge, and his importance reflects the concern of the faithful to live according to the dictates of the Koranic law.

The Islamic conquests brought the Arabs into intimate contact with older and more accomplished civilizations than their own, particularly the intellectual achievements of Hellenism, which they were eager to preserve. During the eighth and ninth centuries scholars translated into Arabic many Greek authors: Aristotle, Euclid, Archimedes, Hippocrates, and Galen. These works, most of which were translated from the Syriac rather than directly from the Greek, provided the foundations for Islamic learning.

Scholars were especially interested in astronomy, astrology, mathematics, medicine, and optics; and in these areas their writings exerted a great influence on the Western world. Al-Razi (known as Rhazes in the West) of Baghdad wrote some 140 medical treatises, including an admirable description of smallpox. Mathematicians took the numbers from the Hindus, but made the critical addition of the zero, which is itself an Arabic word. Italian merchants became familiar with the Arabic numbers shortly before the year 1200 and carried them back to the West. Mathematicians also developed algebra. Astronomers and astrologers invented an improved astrolabe (which measures the angular declination of

heavenly bodies above the horizon) and were able to improve the astronomical tables of antiquity.

Scholars also wrote philosophical and theological treatises. The most important Islamic philosopher was the Spaniard ibn-Rushd, or Averroës (1126?–1198), who wrote commentaries on Aristotle and exerted a profound influence on Christian as well as Islamic philosophy in the subsequent Middle Ages. Islamic philosophical speculations aided intellectual life in the West in two ways: Western philosophers gained a much broader familiarity with the scientific and philosophical heritage of Classical Greece through translations made from the Arabic, chiefly in Spain, and Islamic philosophers explored issues central to religious philosophy much earlier than Christian thinkers. What is the relation between faith and reason, between an all-powerful, all-encompassing God and the freedom, dignity, and individuality of the human person? In posing these problems and in suggesting answers, the Muslims stimulated and enriched thought in the West.

Decline of Medieval Islamic Civilization

The earliest indication of decline was the growing military debility of the various Islamic states in the face of new invasions in the middle of the eleventh century. In the West, Christian armies embarked on the reconquest of the Iberian Peninsula, and Christian fleets broke the Islamic domination of the western Mediterranean islands. The Christian offensive blends imperceptibly with the First Crusade, which wrested Jerusalem from Islamic control in 1099. In the East, Turkish nomads infiltrated the Abbasid caliphate in considerable numbers, and the Seljuks seized Baghdad in 1055. Turkish rulers gained supremacy in all the Eastern Islamic states over the next few centuries.

The economic basis was also changing.

Commerce had been vigorous and was the chief economic resource. By the thirteenth century, however, maritime and commercial supremacy on the Mediterranean Sea passed to the Italians and other Westerners. Arabian coins largely disappeared from circulation in the West, documenting a headlong retreat from commerce. Simultaneously, the Islamic states were no longer supporting their warriors by salaries but by grants of land, which weakened central authority. The growing importance of an aristocracy of rural warriors seems to have brought a new rigidity into society.

Caution, to be sure, must be used in speaking of the decline of medieval Islam. Islamic civilization continued to support some great cultural centers and to inspire some great individuals; but after the eleventh century Islamic civilization lost those qualities of openness, flexibility, and intellectual daring that had so distinguished it in the ninth and tenth centuries.

The Western Debt to Islamic Civilization

Almost every aspect of medieval Western life was influenced by Islamic civilization. Western farmers imitated the techniques of irrigation developed by the Muslims and learned to grow many new plants, such as rice, citrus fruits, and peaches. Western merchants adopted the system of numbers and probably some forms of business partnerships. Western physicians, philosophers, and theologians were influenced by Islamic scholars.

However, what Western civilization took from Islamic civilization did not decisively change the course of Western cultural devel-

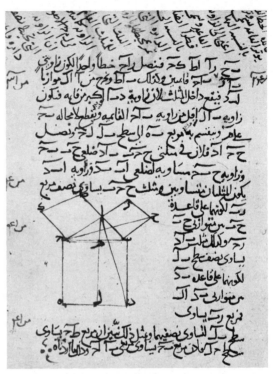

This thirteenth-century Arab commentary on the *Geometry* of Euclid illustrates the proof of the Pythagorean theorem. Mathematics was one science in which the Arabs not only persevered, but even surpassed the Classical achievements.
(Photo: British Museum)

opment. The more remarkable aspect is really how little these two medieval civilizations affected one another in their fundamental cultural attitudes, apart from specific techniques and institutions. The Islamic historian Sir Hamilton Gibb remarked that a civilization will resist foreign borrowings which threaten the character of its aesthetics, philosophy, or religious thought and will "absorb elements from other cultures only within a limited range and in

The Alhambra Palace in Granada.
(Photo: G. E. Kidder Smith, New York)

forms adapted to its own temperament and psychological structure."[8] The medieval West

was not much influenced by, and in fact poorly understood, the fundamental theology or the spirit of Islam. But it still enlisted many Islamic accomplishments in the service of its own civilization.

[8] "The Influence of Islamic Culture on Medieval Europe," in Sylvia L. Thrupp (ed.), *Change in Medieval Society,* 1964, p. 167.

The East preserved the urban culture of antiquity better than the West, and this largely explains the evident superiority of the East in the Early Middle Ages. Even in Classical times the Eastern provinces of the Roman Empire had been more populous and more urbanized than the Western ones, and the Islamic conquests did not disturb the continuity and vitality of urban life. The Principality of Kiev, although the creation of a people only recently emerged from tribal society, still benefited from its close proximity to the ancient Mediterranean centers of civilization.

These Eastern communities performed inestimable services for Western civilization. The Byzantine Empire and the Principality of Kiev helped shield the West from destructive invasions coming out of Asia. Byzantium and Islam offered the West enlarged access to the Classical Greek heritage. They further passed on numerous techniques and skills and were for the backward West models of high accomplishment. From about the year 1000 the West embarked on a great age of growth. Its chance to work in relative security, to take full advantage of the heritage of antiquity, and to learn from gifted neighbors was in no small measure due to the presence and the splendor of these Eastern civilizations.

RECOMMENDED READING

Sources

Cross, Samuel Hazard (ed.). *Russian Primary Chronicle: Laurentian Text.* O. P. Sherbowitz-Wetzor (tr.). 1968.

★Ibn, Khaldun. *The Muqaddimah: An Introduction to World History.* Franz Rosenthal (tr.). 1969.

★*The Meaning of the Glorious Koran.* M. Marmaduke Pickthall (tr.). 1948.

Procopius. *Secret History.* Richard Atwater (tr.). 1961. Full of scandal, sure to hold reader's attention.

★Vernadsky, George (ed.). *Medieval Russian Laws.* 1969.

Studies

★Baynes, Norman H., and Henry Moss (eds.). *Byzantium: An Introduction to East Roman Civilization.* 1948. Elegant essays written by leading scholars.

Fine, John V. A. *The Early Medieval Balkans. A Critical Survey from the Sixth to the Late Twelfth Century.* 1983. The first of two volumes; the only work of its kind in English.

★Geanakoplos, Deno J. *Byzantine East and Latin West: Two Worlds of Christendom in the Middle Ages and Renaissance.* 1966.

★Gibb, Hamilton A. *Mohammedanism: An Historical Survey.* 1962. Reflections of a distinguished scholar.

Goitein, S. D. *A Mediterranean Society: The Jewish Communities of the Arab World as Portrayed in the Documents of the Cairo Geniza.* 1967–. Reconstruction of Jewish social life on the basis of the remarkable Geniza documents.

Grekov, B. D. *Kiev Rus.* Dennis Ogden (ed.). 1959. From the viewpoint of a modern Soviet historian.

Hodgson, Marshall G. *The Venture of Islam: Conscience and History in a World Civilization.* 1974. A lengthy examination of the traditional beliefs and values of Islam.

*Lewis, Bernard. *The Arabs in History.* 1966. Short, graceful, and thoughtful.

Mango, Cyril. *Byzantium: The Empire of New Rome.* 1980. An introduction to the civilization of the Eastern Empire, with effective use of archaeological data.

Ostrogorski, George. *History of the Byzantine State.* Joan Hussey (tr.). 1969. The basic reference for all matters of political history.

*Runciman, Steven. *Byzantine Civilization.* 1933. An essay, many times reprinted, by a prominent English scholar.

*Vasiliev, A. A. *History of the Byzantine Empire: 324–1453.* 1953–1959. Stronger on cultural matters than Ostrogorski, by a great Russian scholar.

*Vernadsky, George. *A History of Russia.* 1946–1963. In five parts and six volumes, the most comprehensive history of early Russia by a single historian in any language.

*Von Grunebaum, Gustave E. (ed.). *Medieval Islam: A Study in Cultural Orientation.* 1966. By one of the great figures in Islamic studies.

* Available in paperback.

Chapter 8

Two Centuries of Creativity ca. 1000–1200

The present historical view of the Middle Ages recognizes the year 1000 as a watershed between two contrasting periods. Before 1000, Western civilization changed slowly, nearly imperceptibly. Europe's population was small, and the economy remained overwhelmingly agricultural. Trade was sporadic, and the few towns that survived the repeated invasions played only a minor role in economic life. Governments tended to be weak and unstable. In art and literature, there were few works produced which we would today regard as masterpieces.

After 1000, change came rapidly on virtually every level. Population, stagnant or declining since the last years of the Roman Empire, increased. People cleared and settled new lands and extended Europe's land frontiers in every direction. Commerce grew; and the resulting expansion of wealth restored vitality to the cities. Rulers reorganized their governments in an effort to adapt the institutions of feudalism to a more stable political environment. Western philosophers embarked on a penetrating and even audacious examination of Christian theology, and the Church itself was subject to a major reform. Artists were once again productive, primarily in service to the Church.

Only recently have historians come to appreciate the dimensions of these changes, and this appreciation has led many of them to make a radical reassessment of the contribution of the Middle Ages to Western development. From the time of the Italian Renaissance, humanists and other scholars had dismissed the period as barbarous, and the prejudice against the Middle Ages remained strong in scholarly circles until the twentieth century. Today, however, many historians actually speak of a medieval renaissance. They have, in fact, gone so far as to propose a new periodization of Western history that dispenses with the old division between the medieval and modern periods. For these historians the eleventh and twelfth centuries, more than the Italian Renaissance or the Reformation, created the civilization they label "traditional Europe." This civilization lasted until the revolutionary upheavals of the eighteenth and nineteenth centuries, the beginning of the authentically modern world. Not all historians would want to discount, as this view does, the impact of the Renaissance and the Reformation; but nearly all agree that the eleventh and twelfth centuries gave new impetus and new directions to the course of Western history.

I. THE ECONOMIC AND SOCIAL CHANGES

From the year 1000, European society showed many signs of growth, in its human numbers and in its geographic area of settlement. Moreover, these greater numbers of people were earning their living in novel ways; in particular, there occurred a revival of trade and a rebirth of urban life. Simultaneously, Europeans were creating new forms of social and political organization and of cultural expression.

The Beginnings of Expansion

Europe's population in the Early Middle Ages, to about the year 1000, was small in absolute numbers and was not distributed evenly across the countryside. Rather, the people tended to cluster into crowded communities—"population islands" they are sometimes called—separated from one another by vast stretches of wilderness. Within these islands there is much evidence of acute population pressures, even though there was little or no absolute growth. Peasant farms (the *mansi*), each intended for the support of a single family, often contained several by the ninth century. Average family size tended to be small—fewer than five persons per family, for example, on the estates of the monastery of St.-Germain-des-Prés near Paris in the early ninth century.

Why did the population not spread out from these impacted settlements and clear new farms in the extensive surrounding wilderness? Many factors obstructed such an exodus; among them were the trammels of serfdom, the safety provided by close settlement in a period of invasions, the bonds of kinship, and a traditional fear of the wilderness.

This pattern of settlement changes from about the year 1000. Peasants pour out of their older centers of settlement to newly opened frontiers, both within Europe and beyond its former borders. What had happened? Perhaps improving conditions of climate encouraged the colonization of new lands. By the middle and late tenth century, the incursions of Vikings, Hungarians, and Saracens were waning, and the new security made the wilderness less intimidating. Beginning in the late tenth century many lords and princes began to encourage the settlement of the wilderness areas they controlled; others assumed leadership in the expansion of the external frontier. They offered land to new settlers under favorable terms and assured them protection in the work of colonization. Their interest in increased rents perhaps indicates that the warrior aristocracy of Europe could no longer live, as it had in the past, predominantly from royal gifts and pillage taken in the frequent wars. The Church too, Europe's largest landlord, by the late tenth century actively sought to increase its own revenues from the land in the interest of supporting a celibate and reformed clergy (see p. 298). These changes further imply that Europeans, or at least their lay and ecclesiastical leaders, were developing a new self-consciousness. They were able to analyze their situation, evaluate their needs, and act rationally in order to obtain them.

The opening of new lands encouraged reproduction. Children became an asset to families engaged in the hard work of clearing land. Women survived better than before. More land in cultivation meant more food. For the first time since the fall of the Western Roman Empire, Europe's population gives evidence of sustained and substantial growth.

Frontiers

In England, France, and Germany, the peasants leveled forests and drained marshes; in England and the Low Countries they won land from the sea by building dikes and polders. Other pioneers, chiefly German peasants and knights looking for new lands to settle, pushed eastward beyond the former borders of the Frank-

International and Military History	Political History
1000	
1015–1016 Pisan and Genoese fleets free Sardinia from Islamic rule	
c. 1015 Norman knights come to south Italy as mercenaries	
1054 Schism of Eastern and Western churches	
1066 Harold Godwin repulses Viking army at Stamford Bridge	
1066 Battle of Hastings; Norman conquest of England	**1066–1087** William of Normandy king of England; formation of Norman fuedal state
1076 Emperor Henry IV does penance at Canossa	
1085 Alfonso VI of Castile takes Toledo	**1086** Salisbury Oath; William recognized as liege lord of all free Englishmen
1095 Pope Urban II preaches First Crusade at Clermont	**1086** Domesday survey
1099 Crusaders take Antioch and Jerusalem	
1100	
	1108–1137 Louis VI king of France; consolidation of royal authority over Île-de-France
1113–1115 Christian fleet under Pisan leadership takes Balearic Islands	
1124 Foundation of Norman Kingdom of Naples and Sicily	
1144 Muslim retaking of Edessa occasion of Second Crusade	
1146 Bernard of Clairvaux preaches Second Crusade	
1149 Acre taken but Crusade fails	**1152–1190** Frederick I, Barbarossa, emperor
	1152 Marriage of Eleanor of Aquitaine and Henry of Anjou
	1154–1189 Henry II king of England
1176 Lombard League defeats Frederick Barbarossa at Legnano	**1170** Assassination of Thomas à Becket
1183 Peace of Constance between emperor and Lombard communes	**1180–1226** Philip II Augustus king of France
1187 Saladin retakes Jerusalem	
1189 Richard Lionhearted of England, Philip II of France and Frederick Barbarossa of the Empire embark on Third Crusade	
1200	
1212 Battle of Las Navas de Tolosa; greatest Christian victory of Reconquista	

1000–1200/TIMELINE

Social and Economic History	Cultural and Intellectual History
c. 1000 Beginnings of substantial population growth	c. 1000 Beginnings of extensive construction of churches in the Romanesque style
	c. 1033–1109 Anselm of Canterbury; beginnings of intellectual revival
	1049–1054 Pontificate of Leo IX, first reform pope
	1054 Schism of Eastern and Western churches
	c. 1065–1100 Probable dates for composition of *Song of Roland*
	1073–1085 Gregory VII pope; climax of Investiture Controversy
1081 First free communes in northern Italy and Flanders	1075 Papal condemnation of lay investiture
1086 English population 1.1 million, based on Domesday Book	1079–1142 Peter Abelard, who helped establish reputation of Bishop's School at Paris
c. 1095 Italian cities establish commercial colonies in East, in wake of crusades	
c. 1100–1300 Great age of Champagne fairs	c. 1100 Beginnings of tradition of troubadour poetry
c. 1100 Appearance of merchants' guilds	
	1122 Concordat of Worms ends Investiture Controversy
	1122 Peter Abelard publishes *Sic et Non*
c. 1130 Earliest charters establishing free villages	1142 Gratians *Decretum;* first official code of canon law
1143 Foundation of Lübeck	c. 1150 Heyday of Bishop's School at Chartres
	1160–1200 Building of Notre Dame cathedral, Paris; development of Gothic style of architecture
	c. 1182 Romances of Chrétien de Troyes
	c. 1182–1226 St. Francis of Assisi
c. 1200 Multiplication of artisans' guilds	1200–1216 Innocent III pope
	1200 Earliest charter given University of Paris

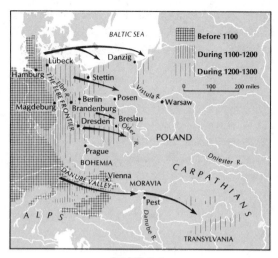

**MAP 8.1.
GERMAN MIGRATION EASTWARD**

ish Empire (see Map 8.1) into territories that were thinly inhabited by Slavs, Prussians, Letts, and Lithuanians. Some Germans settled just beyond the Elbe River and established the Principality of Brandenburg. Other Germans advanced along the shores of the Baltic Sea at the same time that Swedes began to move across Finland. The Russian prince of Novgorod, Alexander Nevsky, defeated the Swedes on the Neva River close to the Baltic Sea in 1240, and repulsed the Germans at Lake Peipus in 1242. Although these defeats halted further advances in northeastern Europe, the Germans and Swedes controlled the shores of the Baltic Sea. The Germans had by then pushed through the middle Danube valley and founded another principality: Austria. By the mid-thirteenth century the *Drang nach Osten* ("drive to the east") had clearly spent its strength, but it had tripled the area of German settlement over what it had been in Carolingian times (see Map 8.1).

Settlers also moved into the Iberian Peninsula. In the mid-eleventh century the Christian kings, whose kingdoms were confined to the extreme north of the peninsula, began an of-fensive against the Muslims, who ruled most of Iberia. These kings actively recruited Christian settlers for the territories they reconquered and gave them land under favorable terms. The Christian domination of the peninsula was confirmed in 1212 at Las Navas de Tolosa, when an allied Christian army defeated an invading Muslim army from North Africa. Only the Principality of Granada in the south remained under Muslim rule; the Iberian frontier remained almost unchanged for the next 280 years. The reconquest and resettlement of the Iberian Peninsula, known as the *Reconquista,* are the dominant themes of medieval Iberian history.

In Italy, too, pioneers pushed the Christian frontier to the south. In the early eleventh century knights from Normandy began fighting in southern Italy against Muslims, Byzantines, and local lords who had long been disputing dominion there. In 1124 they finally drove the Muslims and Byzantines from southern Italy and Sicily and united the two regions into the Kingdom of Naples and Sicily.

European power swept over the sea as well as the land. The leaders were the maritime cities of Pisa and Genoa. In 1015 and 1016 fleets from Pisa and Genoa freed Sardinia from Islamic rule; and between 1113 and 1115 an allied Christian army, carried by a Pisan fleet, drove the Muslims from the Balearic Islands.

Social Changes

In many regions of Europe the expansion in settlement shifted the balance between the free and unfree classes. To attract settlers onto previously uncultivated lands, lords had to offer generous terms, frequently guaranteed in a written charter. Many landlords established on their properties free or new villages. The peasant who settled in a free village usually paid only a small, fixed rent for the lands he cleared and was not required to labor for the landlord.

He could leave the village at will, selling his lands and the house he had built at their market value. A runaway serf who resided in a free village for one year and one day without being claimed by his owner was thenceforth free. The settlers in the free villages were usually given the right to run their own courts and, for all but the gravest offenses, to judge their peers according to their own customs.

The social conditions of the serfs also improved; a number of factors contributed to this. Emancipation was considered a religiously meritorious act, and the period was one of marked religious enthusiasm. The increase in population eliminated the need for landlords to keep the entire labor force tied to the soil. Moreover, since the new frontiers attracted the serfs, only better terms, not brute force, could hold the laborers on the lord's land. Revived trade enabled some serfs to sell their produce at market; they could thus earn money with which to buy their freedom. Finally, serfdom bound landlords as well as serfs. Enterprising lords who wished to raise their rents or even change routines of cultivation were blocked by the custom making servile obligations fixed and immutable. To reorganize their estates, to free their lands, to free themselves, the landlords had also to free their serfs.

By the early thirteenth century serfdom had almost disappeared in France, Spain, Italy, and western Germany, although some vestiges of it were to remain until the eighteenth century. In England serfdom also declined until the thirteenth century; but the growing cities of the Continent created a large, profitable market for cereals, and English landlords were eager to produce for it. Rather than leasing out their estates, they continued to cultivate them directly. To find the necessary laborers, English lords maintained, or reimposed, conditions of serfdom over their peasants. But this Indian summer of English serfdom did not last much beyond the fourteenth century.

The changes in agriculture altered the char-

acter of noble life. Most landlords now rented their lands to peasants to cultivate; they were no longer direct cultivators but rent collectors. Since this new function did not require the constant supervision of their lands, the lords were free to live away from home for extended periods, perhaps traveling as pilgrims or crusaders to distant lands or mingling with their peers at the courts of great nobles. The new agricultural system, and the physical freedom it allowed the lords, permitted the growth of a courtly society, which in turn brought with it a rich lay culture.

Life continued to be very hard, of course, for the peasants of Western Europe, but there were some improvements. To judge from skeletons found in medieval churchyards and from other slight evidence, the incidence of violent death declined, and the life expectancy was growing; by the thirteenth century, the average newborn might expect to live as long as 40 years. But rural conditions continued to be taxing for women. In the typical peasant village, men continued to outnumber, and presumably to outlive, women.

Although most peasants no longer lived in packed settlements, they still saw a good deal of their fellows. Markets and market days became a characteristic feature of rural life in Europe. Peasants slowly grew accustomed to selling or exchanging their surplus produce, purchasing their needs, borrowing money, or simply sharing information with their neighbors at the markets. The influence of markets further stimulated the growth of cottage industries, especially in the vicinity of towns. Within their homes, after their agricultural tasks were accomplished, the peasants and their families spun yarn, wove cloth, cured leather, made wood products, and produced other commodities which they could exchange at the urban markets.

The rural Church acquired new importance, and it is to this period that the rural parishes of Europe (and the Christianization of the countryside) must be dated. Churches were built at an extraordinary pace. A contemporary remarked that churches came to cover the landscape like a white blanket. The parish priest was usually of peasant origins and was often assisted by a young cleric or clerics in training for the priesthood (there were no seminaries). Because the priest was frequently the only member of the community who could read, he aided the peasants in their contacts with merchants, tax collectors, and other representatives of the literate culture of the city. Sundays and feast days brought the people together for divine services and for boisterous celebrations too. Church councils repeatedly condemned dancing and singing in the churchyard, especially since the songs on such occasions tended to be indecent, but the denunciations had scant effect. Many of these boisterous customs continued to mark rural life in the West until the twentieth century.

Commerce

The European economy remained predominantly agricultural, although new forms of economic endeavor were emerging. Trade, which had dwindled to small importance in the Carolingian Age, became more vigorous. Most of the trade was local, between rural areas or between city and countryside, but there was a dramatic rebirth of trade with regions beyond the European frontiers. Three trading zones developed; they were based upon the Mediterranean Sea in the south, the Baltic Sea in the north, and the overland routes that linked the two seas (see Map 8.2).

The leaders of this commercial revolution were Venice, Pisa, and Genoa. In 998 and again in 1082 the Venetians received from the Byzantine emperors charters that gave them complete freedom of Byzantine waters. In the twelfth century, Pisans and Genoese negotiated formal treaties with Islamic rulers that allowed them to establish commercial colonies in the Middle East and North Africa. Marseilles and Barcelona soon began to participate in the profitable Eastern trade.

In this Mediterranean exchange, the East shipped condiments, medicines, perfumes, dyes, paper, ivories, porcelain, pearls and precious stones, rare metals such as mercury—all of which were known in the West under the generic name of "spices." It also sent a variety of fine linens and cottons (damask, muslin, organdy) as well as brocades and other silks. Western North Africa supplied animal skins, leather, cheese, ivory, and gold. Europe shipped wood, iron, and products made from them (including entire ships), grain, wine, and other agricultural commodities. By 1200 manufactured goods, especially woolen cloth woven in Flanders and finished in Italy, began to play an increasingly important role in the Mediterranean exchange. This cloth gave European merchants a product valued in the Eastern markets; with it they were able not only to pay for Eastern imports but also to generate a flow of precious metals into Europe.

Trade in northern Europe among the lands bordering the Baltic Sea linked the great ports of London, Bruges, Bergen, Cologne, Lübeck, and Novgorod with the many smaller maritime towns. The eastern Baltic regions sold grain, lumber and forest products, amber, and furs. Scandinavia supplied wood and fish. England provided raw wool and cereals. Flanders was the great industrial area of the north, taking food and raw material for its excellent cloth.

The northern and Mediterranean trading zones were joined by numerous overland routes. After 1100 the most active exchange between north and south was concentrated at six great fairs, held at various times of the year in the province of Champagne in France. Merchants could find at least one fair open no matter what time of year they came. They were guaranteed personal security at the fairs, low tariffs, and quick and fair justice. For two centuries the fairs remained the greatest markets in Europe.

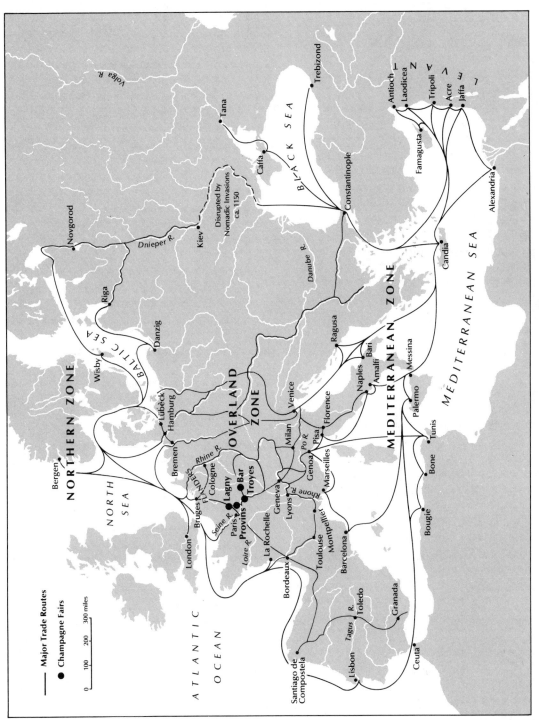

MAP 8.2. MEDIEVAL TRADE ROUTES

The Rebirth of Urban Life

Although the towns in Western Europe were increasing in size and social complexity, their growth was very slow even in this age of economic expansion. Before 1200 probably no town in Western Europe included more than 30,000 inhabitants. These small towns, however, were assuming new functions.

In the Early Middle Ages the towns had been chiefly administrative centers, serving as the residence of bishops—or, much more rarely, of counts—and as fortified enclosures to which the surrounding rural population fled when under attack. (The original sense of the English word *borough* and of the German *Burg* is fortress.) As the revival of trade made many of them centers of local or international exchange, permanent colonies of merchants grew up around the older fortresses. These merchant quarters were sometimes called a *foris burgus,* or faubourg ("outside the fortress"), or a *vicus* ("street" or "neighborhood"; preserved in such names as Brunswick and Greenwich). Many European towns, especially in the north, still show these two phases of their early history in their central fortress and surrounding settlements (see Map 8.3).[1] Some towns in the twelfth century added to their administrative and commercial services a third function: they became centers of large-scale industrial production, especially of woolen cloth. However, the great industrial town of the Middle Ages is more characteristic of the thirteenth century.

While growing in size, town populations, or at least their richest merchants, began demanding a greater measure of liberty from the bishop or lords who ruled them. They resented the lord's cumbersome, expensive, and undis-

cerning justice (he probably knew little about commercial needs); they feared his powers to tax and to demand military service. The instrument by which the medieval townsmen sought to govern themselves was the commune, a permanent association created by the oath of its members and under the authority of several elected officials. Communes first appear late in the eleventh century in northern Italy and Flanders, the two most heavily urbanized areas of Europe. Through force, persuasion, or purchase, many communes acquired from their lords charters that recognized their right to judge and tax themselves. Others gained similar rights by simple usurpation.

Urban society also began to show considerable complexity. At the top of the social scale was a small aristocracy; historians now usually call its members the patricians. In Italy this aristocracy included many nobles and great landlords from the countryside, who lived for part or all of the year in the towns. In Flanders nobles and great landlords tended to keep to their rural estates, whence they viewed with disdain and fear the growing wealth of the towns. The powerful urban families in the north came chiefly from common origins, and most of them founded their fortunes upon commerce or the management of urban property. Social and cultural contrasts between town and countryside, then, were much sharper in the north than in Italy.

Below the patricians were the small merchants and shopkeepers, who were at first unspecialized in their economic interests. Most towns in the twelfth century still had only a single guild, or association of merchants. Soon after 1200, however, the guilds multiplied, showing an ever greater diversification in the commercial enterprises of the mercantile classes. At the same time the small merchants and shopkeepers were disputing, often with violence and soon with some success, the political domination of the patricians. Before the coming of industries the cities did not support a large class of artisans and workers. But here,

---

[1] In Italy, for example, it is rare to find a physical contrast between a central fortress and surrounding faubourgs, but population growth is amply documented by the successive circles of walls built to protect the urban settlement. By comparing the oldest, or Roman, circle of walls with those constructed in the thirteenth century, historians have concluded that some Italian towns must have expanded from 5000 or 6000 inhabitants in about 1100 to some 30,000 or more by about 1300.

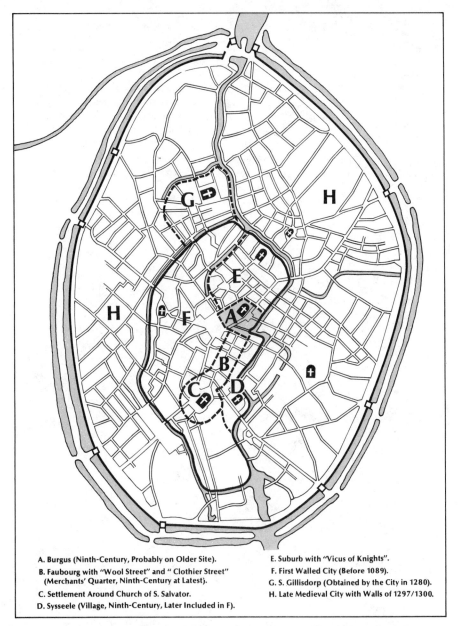

A. Burgus (Ninth-Century, Probably on Older Site).

B. Faubourg with "Wool Street" and " Clothier Street"
(Merchants' Quarter, Ninth-Century at Latest).

C. Settlement Around Church of S. Salvator.

D. Sysseele (Village, Ninth-Century, Later Included in F).

E. Suburb with "Vicus of Knights".

F. First Walled City (Before 1089).

G. S. Gillisdorp (Obtained by the City in 1280).

H. Late Medieval City with Walls of 1297/1300.

MAP 8.3. THE GROWTH OF MEDIEVAL BRUGES

Bruges (in modern Belgium) presents a fine example of the topographical dualism of many commercial towns of northern Europe. The town grew from two centers: the central fortress (A) and the merchants' settlement (B), gradually absorbing surrounding parishes and villages. The size of the late medieval walls conveys an accurate impression of the dimensions of medieval urban growth.

(*Grosser historischer Weltatlas, II: Mittelalter, Munich,* 1970, p. 129)

p:mces telles choses p:ouffitables selon le langaige du puis pour
instituer toue les assistens. Donc cestes choses ainsi tractees du
regime de maison en passant soub: silance auanes choses puis
aillieurs dignes de narration. Nous faison fin de ce second liure
ou quel nous auons buille air du regime domestique selon me
saence par laide de celui dont toute saence et boute vient.

¶ Icy fine le second liure du regime des princes ou quel est tracte
du gouuernement de maison. Et comance le tiers liure le quel tracte
du regime de cite et communisme. Dont le premier chapitre declaire
que la comunite de cite est auuimemet p:mapale et est constituee
pour cause de bien.

too, the city presents a dynamic picture, and the commercial growth in the twelfth century was laying the basis for industrial expansion in the thirteenth. Perhaps the most distinctive feature of urban society, even in the twelfth century, was the fluid division of the classes. Vertical social mobility was easier in the city than in any other part of the medieval world, the only possible exception being the Church. The patrician class was always admitting new members, chiefly recent immigrants from the countryside whom the buoyant economy of the city had carried to wealth and power. The towns of the Middle Ages were much more efficient than rural society in recognizing, utilizing, and rewarding talent.

The dynamic towns of the Middle Ages, like the cities of the ancient world, shaped culture more than size alone might indicate. Urban commercial life required skill in calculations and a high level of literacy. The towns provided adept administrators who soon figured prominently in the governments of both Church and state. The urban milieu fostered new cultural attitudes, an approach to life based on exact observations and reasoned decisions. Medieval townsmen were by no means indifferent to religion or the afterlife, but they wanted the Church to respond more directly to the moral and religious problems characteristic of the city, in terms comprehensible to them. From the eleventh and twelfth centuries the medieval towns exerted a profound influence on the developing culture of the Middle Ages; moreover, that influence was growing.

This illustration from a French manuscript of the early sixteenth century shows the narrow streets, tall houses, and numerous ground-level shops that were characteristic of European cities in the Middle Ages.
(Photo: Photographie Bulloz)

II. FEUDALISM AND THE SEARCH FOR POLITICAL ORDER

Growth in population, expansion in trade, and changes in society in the eleventh and twelfth centuries were in part made possible by, and in part helped produce, a higher degree of security and political order than Europe had possessed in the chaotic tenth century. The European communities sought to achieve this renewed stability through a set of institutions that constituted what is traditionally called the feudal system. Although in different ways, the governments of England, France, the Holy Roman Empire, and other European states may all be called feudal.

Feudal Institutions

Feudalism, feudal systems, la féodalité must be reckoned among the most abused and confusing terms in the historical vocabulary.[2] These terms were unknown in the Middle Ages. Lawyers in the seventeenth century first devised them to denote the combination of laws and customs governing the kind of land tenure known as the fief. Among enlightened liberals and reformers in the eighteenth century *la féodalité* meant the unjustified privileges enjoyed by the nobles and the Church. Nineteenth-century socialists, especially Marx, used the term "feudalism" to mean an economic system based upon serfdom; they considered it a stage in economic development that followed slavery and preceded capitalism. To Marxists today the essential feature of feudalism is that it exploits peasants by binding them to the soil and forcing them to pay rent to the landlords. Many books, even some recent ones, treat feudalism as if it meant no more than decentralized and weak

---

[2] Perhaps more than any other medieval institution, the feudal system invites comparisons with similar arrangements in other cultures. See especially, in this regard, Peter Duus, *Feudalism in Japan*, 1966.

government, or simple chaos. In popular usage *feudal* is often indistinguishable from *backward*.

Most non-Marxist scholars now use *feudalism* in reference to systems of political and social, *not* economic, institutions. Large estates and serfdom were not central to the feudal system and are better referred to as the manorial system. Still, *feudalism* remains an elastic term and is used in both a narrow and a broad sense. In its restricted meaning *feudalism* refers to a set of distinct social and political institutions, defined by free contract, that established the relationship between two freemen of differing social station, a lord and his vassal of lower rank. In practice both lord and vassal came from the upper echelons of society. Feudal institutions did not include the serfs, who could not enter into a contract, and they touched only remotely and rarely the poorer freemen. In its broad sense *feudalism* refers to the society and government in which social and political institutions created by contract played a major role in defining relationships within the upper classes. Perhaps the most distinctive feature of feudal government is that the powerful men in society defined their political rights and obligations through individual contracts. In the ancient Roman Empire (as in our own society) one's rights and obligations were defined by the public law of the state, which, with only minor exceptions, applied equally to all citizens.

Following the guidance of a great French historian, Marc Bloch,[3] many historians now divide Western feudalism into two periods. The first feudal age, which lasted from the disappearance of Roman government in the West until about 1050 or 1100, witnessed among the free classes of Europe the spontaneous development of feudal practices out of the early medieval and post-Carolingian chaos. In the second feudal age, which spans the period from about 1050 to 1300, princes began self-consciously to use and manipulate these institutions in order to buttress their own authority.

The Feudal Milieu

To understand the growth of feudalism we must first recall the chaotic conditions prevailing in the Early Middle Ages, especially in the ninth and tenth centuries. In a milieu in which governmental authority counted for little, the individual freeman had to seek his security through his own efforts. He might appeal to his family, which has always been the first and most natural bastion of defense for the harassed individual. In Celtic areas of Europe (Ireland, Scotland, Wales, Brittany) traditionally powerful clans could extend such protection; therefore, a true feudalism never developed in those lands. Similarly among the South Slavs, the persistence of a social organization based on the clan (*zadruga* in Serbian) made superfluous the creation of authentically feudal relationships. Northern Italy was also an exceptional area in the history of feudalism. Perhaps because of the early importance of towns, the quest for security primarily favored the development of communal associations, linking social equals, rather than lords and vassals, in what might be considered artificial families or clans. The power of the urban communes in northern Italy stunted, although it did not entirely suppress, the extension of feudal ties even in the countryside.

The true homeland of Western feudalism was the region between the Loire and the Rhine rivers. The institutions that developed there were subsequently exported to England in the Norman Conquest, to southern Italy, and even to Palestine, and they greatly influenced government and society in southern France, Spain, and Germany beyond the Rhine. In this region the family seems to have been too scattered or too weak to guarantee security for its members.

---

[3] As proposed in his *Feudal Society*, L. A. Manyon (tr.), 1963, one of the most important works in medieval history to be published in this century.

The freeman in search of protection had little recourse but to appeal to a neighbor stronger than himself. If the neighbor accepted, the two men entered by implied contract into a close, quasi-familial relationship. Like the bonds between father and son, the feudal relationship between the strong "lord" and the weak freeman was initially far more ethical and emotional than juridical. It remained so until the thirteenth century, when lawyers systematically began to clarify and define its juridical implications and, by so doing, diluted its earlier ethical and emotional force.

Vassalage

The honorable personal bond between the lord and his man is called vassalage, a term that derives from a Celtic word meaning "boy" or "servant." Vassalage was created by an act of homage (from the French *homme,* "man," a common synonym for "vassal"), the prospective vassal placing his hands within those of his lord (sometimes too a kiss was exchanged) and perhaps swearing an oath of fidelity. The *immixio manuum* ("joining of hands") was the central act in the ceremony of homage.

Vassalage imposed obligations on both the vassal and his lord. The vassal owed his lord primarily loyalty or, in its feudal term, fealty, which meant that he had to render aid and counsel, or material and moral help, to his lord. He had to perform military service in the lord's army and usually had to bring additional men in numbers proportionate to his wealth. As the duty of service became more precisely defined in terms of nature and duration, military service became more a matter of law than of the heart. The vassal might be expected to serve, for example, forty days a year in a local war and still less time if the lord intended to fight in foreign lands. The vassal could not refuse this service, but if asked by the lord for more time than custom allowed, he could demand compensation or simply return home, on the argument

that the lord's need was not real. The lord could also demand financial aid, and there were four occasions or, in traditional terminology, "incidents," which required that the vassals provide money without question: the ransoming of the lord, the knighting of the lord's eldest son, the marriage of the lord's eldest daughter, and the lord's own departure on crusade. At other times the vassal still had to consider requests for financial aid but could grumble and, if the lord was weak enough, refuse.

The obligation of counsel required the vassal to give good advice, to keep the lord's secrets, and to help him reach true judgments in legal cases which came before his court. If he lived at a distance, the vassal might be required to attend the lord's court at regular intervals—for example, on Easter, Michaelmas (a feast day celebrated in September), and Christmas. The ordinary work of the court was the adjudication of disputes among the vassals and the hearing of complaints brought by the lord against his men. Feudal custom held that a vassal could be judged only by his own peers, that is, his fellow vassals. By the thirteenth century many great feudal courts were claiming the right to hear appeals from the courts of the individual vassals. The acceptance of such appeals was one of the principal ways by which royal governments were able to strengthen their authority in the second feudal age.

The vassal's duties toward his lord were further complicated in the second feudal age by the development of multiple vassalage—acts of homage by the same man to several lords. In case of conflict among his different lords, whom should he serve? To escape this dilemma feudal custom required that the vassal select one of his lords as his liege, that is, the one whom he would serve against all others. The growth of multiple vassalage and liege homage was itself a sign of the waning emotional content of the feudal relationship.

The lord in turn owed his vassal protection and maintenance, or military and material support. He had to come to his vassal's aid when requested, repel invaders from his possessions, and even help him if he was sued in another's court. Failure to extend such help allowed the vassal to "defy" his lord, that is, to remove his faith from him and cease to serve him. In the formative period of feudalism the lord's obligation of material support was often carried out at his own table, but as vassals became more numerous and more distantly located and as great princes came to be included among them, sheer logistics prevented the lord from feeding all his men. Since a lord often had no cash revenues for making monetary compensations, he would distribute land as a form of payment for the vassal's allegiance. This concession of land was the fief. The granting of a fief superimposed upon the personal relationship of vassalage a second relationship, involving property, between the lord and his man. The close union of personal and property ties was, in fact, the most characteristic feature of the Western feudal relationship.

The Fief

The lord granted the fief in a special ceremony called investiture (it usually immediately followed the act of homage), in which he extended to his vassal a clod of earth or sprig of leaves, symbol of the land he was receiving. In a strict juridical sense the fief was a conditional, temporary, and nonhereditary grant of land or other income-producing property, such as an office, toll, or rent. At the vassal's death, disability, or refusal to serve, the fief at once returned, or escheated, to the lord who granted it. The juridical origins of the fief seem to go back to forms of ecclesiastical land tenure which grew up in the Early Middle Ages, the *precarium* (or *beneficium*). Churches were canonically forbidden to sell or give away their property, but they could grant its "use" while retaining ownership over it. In Carolingian times the emperors took to ordering churches

and monasteries to make such concessions to favored laymen; this grant was called the "*precarium* by order of the king." The true fief, however, involving only laymen and linked with vassalage, does not appear until after the Carolingian Age.

Although technically not inheritable, the fief became gradually assimilated to the allodium (property held in absolute ownership), which was unconditional, permanent, and hereditary. From the start lords had found it convenient to grant a fief to the adult son of a deceased vassal, since he could at once serve in his father's stead. The son had only to make a special payment (the "relief") to the lord in order to acquire the fief. Feudal custom also soon recognized the right of a minor son to inherit, but the lord retained the privilege—the right of wardship—of serving as his guardian or of appointing someone to fulfill that function. Feudal practice was less inclined to admit daughters to the inheritance of a fief since they could not perform military service. Nevertheless, in some areas of Europe (Spain, southern France) women did acquire a right of inheritance. Their lord, however, could select their husbands for them, inasmuch as their spouses had to assume the obligations of service. Initially, vassals were forbidden to sell the fief, grant it to a church, or otherwise transfer it in whole or in part. By the thirteenth century, however, fiefs were commonly sold or granted—but only with the lord's permission, and that almost always had to be purchased.

The fief was the dominant form of land tenure in northern France and western Germany from the late ninth and tenth centuries. The Norman Conquest carried it to England in the eleventh. In the same period it became common in southern France, but it never entirely supplanted the allodium. It was still later in arriving in Spain, and in Italy its importance always remained restricted. The diffusion of the fief, even if slow and incomplete, had important social effects nonetheless. Because vassals could not dispose of their lands without the lord's consent, property relationships (and society, indirectly) remained fixed and stable for long periods. Moreover, the economic pressure superimposed upon the moral force of vassalage gave the princes of the age an effective means of retaining the loyalty of their dependents: the disloyal vassal not only violated the ethics of his times, but also risked losing the lands that supported him.

Private Justice

In granting a fief, the lord gave his vassal all possible sources of revenue the land could produce, including, usually, the right to hold court and to profit from its fines and confiscations. This contributed to another characteristic of feudal society, private justice (the wide exercise of governmental powers by persons other than the king—that is, the exercise of public powers by private individuals as a right associated with their tenure of land). Lords and vassals, in other words, at every level of the feudal pyramid, could tax, judge, and punish their dependents.

By the second feudal age lawyers were arguing that the king, as the font of all justice, had the right of hearing appeals from the courts of his chief vassals (as well as those "rear vassals" who stood lower on the feudal ladder) and could also accept cases in the first instance, which his vassals had traditionally heard. The exertion of these royal prerogatives brought about the gradual but unmistakable decline of private justice.

Stages of Feudal Development

Although there were significant local variations in the character and chronology of medieval feudal institutions, it remains possible to speak of certain broad stages of feudal development. In the ninth and tenth centuries Carolingian administration on the local level disintegrated. The power of the count waned, and the *vicarii*

disappeared. Authority in the countryside largely passed into the hands of petty lords, most especially the castellans, or holders of castles. The eleventh and twelfth centuries saw a remarkable upsurge in the construction of castles in Europe. To cite one example, in the Diocese of Florence in Italy only 2 castles are mentioned in the sources before 900, 11 before 1000, 52 before 1050, 130 before 1100, and 205 before 1200. The proliferation of these fortresses reflects both the violence of European life and the growing effort to find protection from it.

The castellans initially had no official status in the shadowy structure of the post-Carolingian state, but they dominated the communities which lived in or near their fortresses. The castellan was the judge, tax collector, and military leader, and he usually controlled the local church as well. Within the confines of these small societies the institutions of feudalism developed spontaneously. The castles with their lands constituted fairly stable units.

From about the year 1050, counts, dukes, and some few kings were attempting to integrate these castles into fairly centralized principalities, insisting that the petty nobles assume toward them the obligations of vassals and fief holders. The use of these feudal concepts and institutions to serve the interests of princely authority initiates the second feudal age—the age of the feudal principality.

Norman and Angevin England

We could use the history of any one of several principalities—the Duchy of Normandy, the County of Flanders, the Kingdom of Naples and Sicily, among others—to illustrate the political reorganization characteristic of the second feudal age. But England offers the best example of feudal concepts in the service of princes. The growth of feudalism in England was in turn intimately connected with the Norman Conquest of 1066, the central event of English medieval history.

The Norman Conquest

Duke William of Normandy (1027–1087), the architect of the Conquest, is the epitome of the ambitious, energetic, and resourceful prince of the Central Middle Ages. A bastard who had to fight twelve years to make good his claim over his own Norman duchy, William early set his ambitions on the English crown. His claims were respectable, but not compelling. He was the first cousin of the last Saxon king, the childless Edward the Confessor, who allegedly had promised to make William heir to the throne. However, before his death Edward in fact selected the Saxon Harold Godwin to succeed him, and his choice was supported by the Witan, the English royal council.

Edward died in 1066. William immediately recruited an army of vassals and adventurers to support his claim to the throne and gained a papal blessing for his enterprise, but unfavorable winds kept his fleet bottled up in the Norman ports for six weeks. Meantime Harold Hardrada, king of Norway, who also disputed Harold Godwin's claim, invaded England with a Viking army but was shattered by the Saxons at Stamford Bridge near York on September 28, 1066. The same day the channel winds shifted and William landed in England. Harold Godwin foolishly rushed south to confront him. Although his army was not, as was once thought, technically inferior to the Norman army, it was tired and badly in need of rest and reinforcements after the victory over the Vikings. At the Battle of Hastings on October 14, fatigue seems eventually to have tipped the scales of an otherwise even struggle. The Normans carried the day, leaving Harold Godwin dead upon the field. Duke William of Normandy had won his claim to be king of England.

After years of study the exact importance of the Norman Conquest in English history is still disputed. Today, however, most historians believe that while the Norman Conquest did not radically alter the course of English development, it did add a new speed and decisiveness to changes already in evidence. For example, the Conquest oriented England away from Scandinavia and toward the Continent and established a French-speaking aristocracy. Norman and Continental influences, however, were growing well before 1066; Edward had been raised in Normandy, and Normans were familiar figures in the English court and Church. Nor did William radically change the political and social institutions of Anglo-Saxon England; rather, he built upon them.

The basic unit of local administration remained the shire under the supervision of the sheriff, who had primary responsibility for looking after the king's interests. The sheriff administered the royal estates, collected the taxes (notably the Danegeld), summoned and led contingents to the national militia (the fyrd), and presided over the shire court. William left all these institutions of local government intact.

The real impact of the Conquest was felt at the upper levels of Anglo-Saxon society. The Saxon earls, as the great nobles were called, and most of the lesser nobles, or thanes, lost their estates, which William redistributed among his followers from the Continent—his barons (a title of uncertain origin, now used to connote the immediate vassals of the king). Al-

---

The *Bayeux Tapestry,* **reputedly woven by the wife of William the Conqueror, is a strip of linen 231 feet long and 20 inches wide depicting the Norman Conquest of England in 1066. In the portion shown here, William arrives at Pevensey (top); King Harold fights in the Battle of Hastings (bottom). The tapestry was completed toward the end of the eleventh century.**
(Photo: La Ville de Bayeux, Giraudon)

HIC EXEV...

hAROLD·REX·INTERFEC
TVS·EST

though the fiefs that William allotted were large, they were not compact blocks of land; rather, they were strewn hither and yon across the countryside—fit to support service but not rebellion.

William did, however, redefine the relations between the king and the great men of the realm on the basis of essentially feudal concepts. The Anglo-Saxons had a form of lordship under which protection was extended to a man of lesser station in return for loyalty and service. Lords might further support their retainers with grants of land, but they gave the properties in full title. They did not make tenure conditional upon service—the essential feature of the Continental fief. William now insisted that all English land be considered a fief held directly or indirectly from the king. The barons had to serve the king, and the knights the barons, or risk losing their estates.

In 1086 William conducted a comprehensive survey of the lands of England, the report of which was the *Domesday Book,* probably so called because its judgments in their finality resembled those to be made on the Last Day. This survey, unique for its age among the European kingdoms, served two main purposes: it gave the king a clear record of his own holdings and those of his barons, and it enabled him to know how much service the land could support. In the Salisbury oath of 1086 every vassal had to swear loyalty to the king as the liege lord of all. Feudal concepts thus brought a greater precision to the obligations of English freemen toward their king and placed a new ethical and material force behind royal prerogatives.

In order to maintain close contact with his barons and vassals William also took from the Continent the institution of the great council, or Curia Regis. Essentially, it was an assembly of bishops, abbots, barons—in fact, anyone whom the king summoned. The great council fulfilled the feudal functions of giving the king advice and serving as his principal court in reaching judgments. It was a much larger assembly than the Saxon Witan. However, as the great council could not be kept permanently in session, a small council, consisting of those persons in permanent attendance at the court whom the king wished to invite, carried on the functions of the great council between its sessions. The development of the great and small councils had major importance for English constitutional history. The great council was the direct ancestor of Parliament, while the small council was the source of the administrative bureaus of the royal government.

Angevin Kingship

William was succeeded by his second son, William Rufus, one of England's worst kings. He terrorized his subjects and antagonized the Church. At his death in 1100, probably from assassination, his younger brother, Henry I, became king. Henry began a series of administrative reforms, but a dispute over the succession at his death and a protracted civil war undermined his accomplishment. By 1154, however, a unified and pacified England passed under the rule of Henry II of Anjou, grandson of Henry I and the first of the "Angevin" kings of England.

Through combined inheritances and his marriage to Eleanor of Aquitaine in 1152, Henry II ruled over a sprawling assemblage of territories, including, besides England, nearly the entire west of France from the English Channel to the Pyrenees Mountains (see Map 8.4). A man of great energy who carried to completion many of the reforms of Henry I, he ranks among the most gifted statesmen of the twelfth century and among the greatest kings of England.

It was in the sphere of English government and law that Henry left a permanent mark. He made royal justice the common justice of the kingdom through the use of itinerant officials, or "justices in eyre" (*in itinere,* i.e., "on jour-

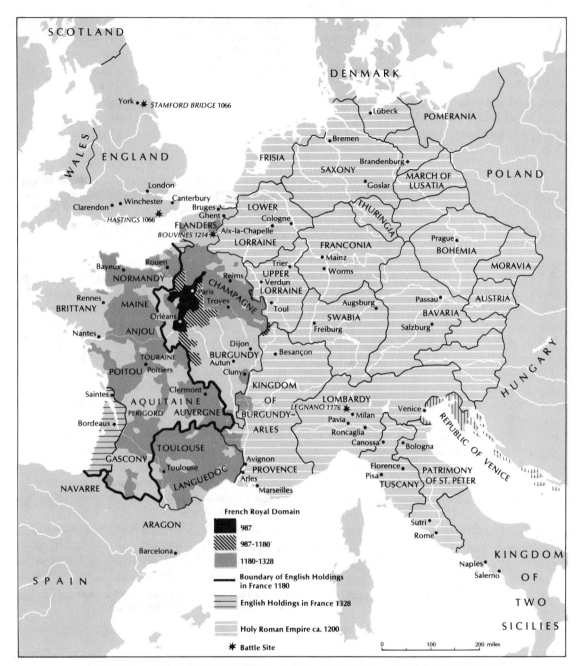

MAP 8.4. MEDIEVAL ENGLAND, FRANCE, AND GERMANY

ney"), who were endowed with all the authority of the king himself. The itinerant justice traveled regularly to the courts of the shires, investigating and punishing crimes. Upon his arrival the justice would impound 12 "good men" and inquire of them under oath what crimes they had heard about since his last visit and whom they suspected of guilt. (This sworn inquest is the direct ancestor of the modern jury of presentment, or grand jury.) Those indicted by the 12 "good men" were still tried by the ancient ordeals of fire and water, which were retained until the Church condemned these procedures at the Fourth Lateran Council in 1215. Thereafter, the small, or petty, jury was used, as it is today, to judge guilt or innocence.

The itinerant justice did not forcibly interfere in civil disputes, but he did offer for sale the services of the royal court in settling them. Barons receiving fiefs from the king had also been given the right to hold a court and judge the disputes of their own knights and dependents. Normally, therefore, litigants in a civil dispute appeared before a baronial court. But as a result of Henry's reforms a litigant could purchase one of many royal writs, which ordered the sheriff to bring the case under the scrutiny of the royal court presided over by the justice in eyre. The great superiority of royal justice in civil matters was that it relied, not on ordeals or duels, but on sworn inquests or juries. These juries in civil cases were composed of "good men" from the neighborhood who were likely to know the facts at issue and were able to judge the truth or falsity of claims. Henry made no effort to suppress baronial courts, but the better justice offered by the royal court left them with a progressively shrinking role in the juridical life of England.

In time the justices built up a considerable body of decisions, which then served as precedents in similar cases. The result was the gradual legal unification of the realm, the development, in other words, of a "common law" of England—common in that it applied to the entire kingdom and was thus distinct from the local customs by which cases were formerly decided. It differed from Roman law in that it represented not the will of the king or legislator but the principles, formed by custom, that were followed in deciding cases. This marks the beginnings of the tradition of common law, under which most of the English-speaking world continues to live.

The justices performed one other service in the interests of royal authority. They investigated the behavior of the sheriffs and saw to it that the king's business was handled capably and honestly at the level of the shire.

Central administration and bureaucracy also grew stronger under Henry's rule. The great officers who aided him were the justiciar, who governed the realm in his absence, the chancellor (secretary), and the chamberlain (treasurer). The Exchequer, or treasury, enjoyed a remarkable development in Henry's reign and assured the king substantial revenues in money. It received its name (which means "checkerboard") for the reason that calculations were performed by moving counters across a table into squares, much as one calculates with an abacus.

The Exchequer combined the functions of an accounting office and a court. The accounting office, the lower Exchequer, received twice a year from the sheriffs an accounting of the moneys they had received—whether from the royal estates in their shires; fees or fines; the Danegeld; or scutage, which was the payment knights had to make when they did not serve personally in the royal army. The upper Exchequer was a court which heard disputes about the king's fiscal prerogatives.

Thomas à Becket

The judicial reforms of Henry II led him into a bitter conflict with the English Church, which maintained its own canonical courts. In Henry's

The Romanesque mural from the Church of Sts. Giovanni e Paolo in Spoleto portrays the murder of Thomas à Becket. The archbishop of Canterbury was murdered in 1170 after six years of opposition to Henry II's judicial policies.
(Photo: André Held)

opinion the penalties these courts meted out to the guilty were too mild to deter them from future crime, and in 1164 he claimed the right to retry before his royal courts clerics accused of crime. The archbishop of Canterbury, Thomas à Becket, rejected this claim. He argued that both the Bible and canon law forbade what we now call "double jeopardy"—that is, a second trial and punishment for the same crime.

Thomas had been a warm personal friend of Henry's and had served him ably and faithfully as his chancellor, the chief official of his realm. Royal friendship and favor had brought him his election as archbishop of Canterbury in 1162. In the course of the six-year struggle between these former friends, Thomas first submitted, then broke with Henry and fled to France, and then was reconciled once more in 1170. A few months later he suspended those bishops who had supported the king. Henry, then in France, demanded in fateful rhetoric whether no man would free him of this pestilential priest. Four of the king's knights took the words to heart, journeyed to England, found Thomas in his cathedral, and cut him down before the high altar on December 29, 1170. His death accomplished what his life could not. Henry revoked the objectionable reforms and performed an arduous personal penance for his unwise words.

Although Henry II was unable to dominate the Church, the English monarchy at his death in 1189 was the strongest in Europe. It remained for the thirteenth century to discover how the great power of the king might be managed and controlled.

Capetian France

In France the pattern of feudal development was much different from that of England. Central government all but disappeared in the turmoil following the age of Charlemagne. What governmental functions could still be performed amid the chaos were carried out by counts, castellans, and other lords of small territorial units. These factors alone would have made the rebuilding of an effective national monarchy in France considerably more difficult than in England, but, in addition, France was a much larger country, and its regions preserved considerable cultural diversity.

Nonetheless, the second feudal age did witness considerable changes in France. There are two notable developments. We can discern the emergence of several compact and effectively governed principalities, especially in the north—the Duchy of Normandy, the counties of Flanders and Champagne, the royal lands of the Île de France, and others. Second, the French kings sought with some success to establish a lord-vassal relation with the great dukes and counts who governed these principalities. The kings did not envision, and could not have achieved, the unification of the entire realm under their own direct authority. The goal of monarchical policy was a kind of federation of principalities bound together by a common fealty to the king on the part of distant dukes and counts.

The Capetians

In 987 the great nobles of France elected as their king Hugh Capet, whose descendants held the throne until 1792. Hugh was elected primarily because his small possessions in the Île de France, which included Paris and the surrounding region, made him no threat to the independence of the nobles. He and his successors for the next century made no dramatic efforts to enlarge their royal authority, but they carefully nursed what advantages they had: the central location of their lands; the title of king, which commanded a vague prestige; and a close association with the Church, which gave them an avenue of influence extending beyond their own territory. They also pursued a remarkably prudent policy of consolidating control over their own lands, and they had the good luck to produce sons. For 200 years the kings crowned their sons during their own lifetimes and thus built the tradition that the crown was theirs, not by election, but by hereditary right.

The Capetian policy first bore fruit under Louis VI, the Fat (1108–1137). His aim was to be master of his own possessions, and he successfully reduced to obedience the petty nobles and castellans who had been disturbing his lands and harassing travelers seeking to cross them. By the end of his reign he had established effective control over the lands between the cities of Paris and Orléans. This gave him a compact block of territory in the geographic heart of France. Louis VI promoted the colonization of forests and wastelands by establishing free villages, and he courted the support of the town communes. The economic growth encouraged by the king added to his own fiscal resources. He staffed his administration with new men from the middle ranges of society at the expense of the older, entrenched, and unreliable nobility. One such man of humble origins was Abbot Suger of the monastery of Saint-Denis near Paris; Suger was in fact the chief architect of these successful policies.

Louis VI bequeathed to his successors a

strong base of power in the Île de France, but his weaker son, Louis VII, could do little with it. At Suger's insistence Louis VII married Eleanor of Aquitaine, heiress to the extensive lands of the Duchy of Aquitaine. This marriage promised to more than double the lands under direct royal control. But manifest incompatibility of character and Eleanor's failure to produce a male heir set the spouses feuding, and the marriage was annulled in 1152. Eleanor, or at least her possessions, proved irresistible to Henry II of England, who married her two months later, although he was her junior by some 10 years. The loss of her vast inheritance to the English monarchy was a major blow to the Capetian fortunes.

Louis VII's son by a later marriage, Philip II Augustus, set out to reclaim from the English the provinces of Aquitaine and Normandy, and to break the near encirclement by Angevin lands of his royal demesne. To achieve this goal he skillfully exploited the quarrels of Henry II with Queen Eleanor and with his sons, Richard the Lion-Hearted and John. John, who succeeded Richard as king of England in 1199, paved the way to his own humiliation by marrying the fiancée of a noble of southern France, a flagrant violation of feudal custom. The offended noble appealed for justice to their common lord, Philip, who eagerly summoned John before the French court to answer for his crime. When John failed to appear, Philip declared his fiefs forfeit.

John then showed himself as maladroit in war as he was in love. While he dallied in England, French troops invaded Normandy and after an eight-month siege took the fortress of Château Gaillard, which Richard the Lion-Hearted had erected to defend the province. Normandy thus became part of the French royal domain (see Map 8.4). Finally, John bestirred himself to action. He organized a coalition of Philip's enemies, including Emperor Otto IV of Germany and the count of Flanders who, though Philip's vassal, viewed with considerable apprehension the growth of royal authority. Philip beat back the invading army at Bouvines in 1214, a victory that confirmed England's loss of Normandy and brought new prestige to the Capetian throne. It was convincing proof of the power the king now could wield.

Under Philip royal influence began to penetrate to the south of France. In 1208 Pope Innocent III declared a crusade against the Albigensian heretics of the south (see Chapter 9), who enjoyed the protection of many powerful nobles. Philip's vassals flocked to the call, overwhelmed the counts of Toulouse and other prominent nobles, and seized much of their lands. The defeat of the southern nobility left a vacuum of power, which the king's authority soon filled.

Administration

In addition to increasing his lands, Philip strengthened the administration of his royal demesne (he still made no effort to interfere directly in the governments of the fiefs of the kingdom). On the local level the representative of the king—the French counterpart of the English sheriff—was the *prévôt*. About 1190, apparently in imitation of the English itinerant justices, Philip began to appoint a new official, the *bailli*, to supervise the work of the *prévôt*. (When the king acquired territory in southern France, the same officer was called the *sénéchal*.) The *bailli* supervised the collection of rents and taxes, the administration of justice, and all the king's interests within a certain prescribed circuit or area, but he never assumed the full range of functions and powers that the English justice in eyre had acquired. The central administration was also developing specialized bureaus, although less advanced than the English, and the *Chambre de Comptes,* a special financial office, equivalent to the English Exchequer, gradually assumed responsibility for the royal finances.

Louis VI and Philip Augustus made the French monarchy the unquestioned master in the Île de France, greatly enlarged the royal demesne, and insisted with considerable success that the great dukes and counts of the realm serve the king loyally. In France, as in England and widely in Europe, feudal practices did not necessarily mean weak government; on the contrary, the able and energetic princes of the age utilized these concepts and institutions to redefine the relationship between ruler and ruled in the interest of achieving a stronger central authority. The feudal system, as it was constructed in these principalities, was thus a major step toward a more ordered political life and toward the sovereign state of the early modern period.

The German Empire

In the tenth and eleventh centuries the German lands east of the Rhine show a pattern of political development very different from that of France or England. Whereas in France after the collapse of the Carolingian Empire, power became fragmented among many petty lords and castellans, in Germany it came to be concentrated in certain relatively large territorial blocks. Saxony, Franconia, Swabia, and Bavaria, known as "Stem" duchies (from the German *Stämme,* meaning a distinct people, tribe, or ethnic group), were originally districts of the Carolingian Empire that became independent political entities under powerful dukes. Because these duchies were close to the hostile eastern frontier, their inhabitants learned to appreciate the advantages of a unified leadership.

Moreover, in Germany the old idea of a Christian empire, which we have seen both in Byzantium and in the West under Charlemagne, retained considerable appeal. Perhaps because they were so close to the frontiers of Christendom, the German dukes considered themselves to be in a special way the champions of the Christian faith, and they mounted a missionary effort among the unconverted peoples. Their leader should appropriately be an emperor who, like Charlemagne, would aid the Church against its foreign enemies while promoting its interests at home.

Otto I, the Great

The last direct descendant of Charlemagne in Germany, a feeble ruler known as Louis the Child, died in 911. Recognizing the need for a common leader, the German dukes in 919 elected as king one of their number, Henry of Saxony. His descendants held the German monarchy until 1024. The most powerful of this line of Saxon kings, and the true restorer of the German Empire, was Otto I, the Great (936–973). Otto was primarily a warrior, and conquest was a principal foundation of his power. He routed the pagan Magyars at Lechfeld near Augsburg in 955 and ended their menace to Christian Europe; he organized military provinces, or marches, along the eastern frontier and actively promoted the work of German missionaries and settlers beyond the Elbe River; and in 951 he marched into Italy.

Historians are not certain what exactly drew Otto to the south. Perhaps he feared the formation of a large kingdom, including Provence, Burgundy, and Lombardy, which would eventually threaten Germany. Perhaps like Charlemagne he hoped to rescue the papacy from the clutches of the tumultuous Roman nobility, to which it had once again fallen victim. It does appear at any rate that Otto conceived of himself not just as a German king but as the leader of all Western Christians. He could not allow Italy, especially Rome, to remain in chaos or permit another prince to achieve a strong position there. And, indeed, during a second campaign in Italy in 962 Pope John XII crowned Otto Roman emperor. The title gave him no new powers, but it did provide him high prestige, inasmuch as he could claim to be the special protector of the Church and the most exalted ruler in Christendom.

The coronation of 962 not only marked the restoration of a "Roman" empire in the West (in fact it was German) but also confirmed the close relations between Germany and Italy that lasted through the Middle Ages. Although the German emperors claimed to be the successors of the Caesars and of Charlemagne, and thus the titular leaders of all Western Christendom, their effective power never extended beyond Germany and Italy and the small provinces contiguous to them—Provence, Burgundy, and Bohemia. Government of his far-flung territories presented Otto with problems even more formidable than those which confronted the English and French kings. He distributed the Stem duchies among his relatives, in the poorly founded hope that they would be loyal to him, and placed great reliance upon the Church both in Germany and Italy, using its lands and officials as adjuncts to his own fisc (crown lands) and administration. He therefore insisted upon the right to nominate or approve the nominations of the great prelates of his empire—bishops, abbots, and popes. Control of Church offices and Church lands gave the emperor enclaves of power in the Stem duchies and in Italy which no potential rival could match.

When Otto died in 973, his state was the strongest in Europe, but it was troubled by several difficulties. Foremost among them was the growing discontent of the Church with the imperial domination of ecclesiastical life. (This will be examined in the following section.) Reformers sought to liberate the Church from the emperor's tutelage, and they succeeded in undermining a principal foundation of imperial authority. But the reform did not end the efforts of the German kings to build a strong empire that would unite Germany and Italy and allow them to exercise a moral leadership over the whole of Western Europe.

Frederick I, Barbarossa

The emperor who came closest to building a lasting foundation for the German Empire was Frederick I (1152–1190) of the House of Hohenstaufen. He was called Barbarossa, meaning "red beard." Large, handsome, gallant, courageous, Frederick, like Charlemagne before him, gained a permanent place in the memories and myths of his people. He much resembles in his policies, if not quite in his achievements, the other great statesmen of the twelfth century—Henry II of England and Philip II of France. Frederick showed a broad eclecticism in his political philosophy. He claimed to be the special protector of the Church and therefore a holy figure. During his reign the German Empire was first called the "Holy Roman Empire," the title by which it was to be known until its demise in 1806. But Frederick also used the new institutions and concepts of political feudalism and effectively exploited ideas concerning the emperor's powers that the revived study of Roman law was providing.

Frederick pursued three principal goals. He hoped to consolidate a strong imperial domain consisting of Swabia, which he inherited; Burgundy, which he acquired by marriage; and Lombardy, which he hoped to subdue. These three contiguous territories would serve him much as the Île de France served the French king, giving him a central base of power from which he could dominate those more distant areas that he could not rule directly. In Germany he sought to force the great princes in the north and east to become his vassals. In Italy he claimed, as successor of the Caesars, to enjoy the sovereignty that Roman law attributed to the emperors.

Frederick's Italian ambitions disturbed the popes and the town communes, which from about 1100 had become the chief powers in the northern half of the peninsula. Both feared that a strong central government could be established only at the cost of their own independence. With active papal support the northern Italian towns, led by Milan, formed a coalition known as the Lombard League and defeated the imperial forces at Legnano in 1176. The Battle of Legnano not only marked the failure of Frederick's efforts to establish full sovereignty over the Lombard cities; it was also the first time in European history that an army of townsmen had bested the forces of the established army under noble leadership. At the Peace of Constance in 1183 Frederick conceded to the towns almost full authority within their walls; the towns in turn recognized that their powers came from him, and they conceded to him sovereignty in the countryside. Frederick did not gain all that he had wished in Italy, but his position remained a strong one.

In Germany he was able to achieve a more resounding victory, this time over the powerful duke of Saxony, Henry the Lion, who had refused to aid him in his Italian war. Making effective use of feudal custom, Frederick summoned him in 1180 to face trial as a disloyal vassal. The court condemned Henry and confiscated his Saxon fief. With Henry humiliated and deprived of his lands, Frederick seemed to be the unchallenged master in Germany (see Map 8.4).

Frederick now wanted to advance the empire's prestige in Europe and sought out a position of leadership in the Third Crusade, as it is traditionally numbered. But the aged emperor drowned while trying to ford a small stream in Asia Minor, bringing to a pathetic end a crowded and brilliant career.

His successors proved unable to build upon, or even maintain, his accomplishments. The chief powers in Italy, the pope and the towns, maintained their opposition to the establishment of a strong imperial government under German auspices. Their deep involvement in Italian affairs prevented Frederick's successors from building their base of authority in Germany. The very extent of the lands they sought to dominate, and their great cultural diversity, worked against them. The heritage of the medieval empire was to be a divided Germany and Italy—divisions that would not be overcome until the nineteenth century.

III. THE REFORM OF THE WESTERN CHURCH

Along with lay governments, the Church, too, experienced fundamental transformations in the eleventh and twelfth centuries; it then acquired characteristics it was to retain in large measure to the present day. The reform of the Church was the direct result of revolt against the traditional system of lay domination over ecclesiastical offices and lands.

Moral Crisis

After the disintegration of the Frankish Empire a kind of moral chaos invaded the lives of the clergy. Since the fourth century the Church had demanded that its clergy remain celibate, but this injunction was almost completely ignored in the post-Carolingian period. Also rampant in the Church was the sin of simony—the buying or selling of offices or sacraments. Many bishops and even some popes purchased their high positions, and parish priests frequently sold their sacramental services (baptisms, masses, absolutions of sins, marital blessings) to the people.

The constitution of the Western Church seems to have contributed to this moral breakdown. On the highest level the tradition of lay domination made the king or emperor effective head of the Church in all its temporal affairs. At the local level, ecclesiastical offices and lands were largely under lay control. Landlords were considered to own churches built upon their property. They therefore could name the priests who served in them and profit from donations made to them, freely sell the offices they controlled, or distribute Church lands to their relatives and friends. The results were disastrous. The Church was flooded with unworthy men who were little concerned with their spiritual duties, and the pillaging of Church lands and revenues left many clerics without adequate livings. For these, simony was often an essential means of support.

Early Attempts at Reform

According to canon law, the bishops bore the chief responsibility for the moral deportment of the clergy. A few reforming bishops in the tenth and eleventh centuries tried to suppress clerical marriage and the simony of their priests, but they could make little headway. The powers of a single bishop were perforce limited to his own diocese, and to his own lifetime, since he could not name his successor.

Monastic discipline was the focus of a more effective attempt at reform, the center of which was the monastery of Cluny in Burgundy, founded in 910. Cluniac monasticism was marked by two constitutional novelties. The monastery was placed directly under the pope (neither lay lords nor bishops could interfere in its affairs). While formerly monasteries had been autonomous communities, electing their own abbots and supervising their own affairs, the administration was now centralized under the abbot of Cluny. He retained authority over the many daughter houses his monks had founded or reformed and could visit them at will, freely correcting any abuses. The congregation of Cluny grew with extraordinary rapidity in the eleventh and twelfth centuries until it included no fewer than 1184 houses, which were spread from the British Isles to Palestine.

The restoration of the German Empire in 962 opened another avenue of ecclesiastical reform. Otto I and his successors repeatedly condemned clerical marriage, simony, and the un-

authorized usurpation of Church lands, but in the interests of their own authority they could not abandon their traditional control over ecclesiastical offices and lands. Their efforts did not satisfy a growing group of radical reformers who believed that complete freedom of the Church from lay domination was the only means to effective reform. To win and defend this liberty they looked for leadership to the long-degraded office of pope.

Papal Reform

The first of the reforming popes—selected, ironically, by the Holy Roman Emperor—was Leo IX (1049–1054). He traveled widely and presided at numerous councils, where he promulgated decrees ordering reforms, summoned suspect bishops, and deposed many of them. He was the first pope to make wide and regular use of papal legates, who, like Charlemagne's *missi dominici,* traveled through Europe, inspecting, reprimanding, and reforming. For the first time lands distant from Rome were subject to the close supervision of the papacy.

Under Pope Nicholas II the movement toward ecclesiastical liberty took several forward strides. By allying himself with the Normans of southern Italy, Nicholas freed the papacy from military dependence on the German Empire. He was the first pope who expressly, if vainly, condemned the practice of "lay investiture"—that is, receiving churches and Church offices from laymen. In 1059 a Roman council reformed papal elections and defined the principles by which popes to this day have been elected.

Tradition required that the pope, like all bishops, be elected by the clergy and people of his diocese. In practice, however, the emperor named him, or in his absence the powerful noble families and factions of Rome did. However, the election procedures set up by the council of 1059 conferred this prerogative upon the cardinals, the chief clergymen associated with the Church at Rome, thereby assuring that the College of Cardinals, and the reformers who controlled it, could maintain continuity of papal policy. (Even today all cardinals, no matter where they live in the world, hold a titular appointment to a church within the archdiocese of Rome.) Both the emperor and the Roman nobility were simultaneously deprived of one of their strongest powers.

Gregory VII

The climax of papal reform came with the pontificate of Pope Gregory VII (1073–1085), who brought to his office a high regard for its powers and responsibilities and a burning desire for reform. With regard to Church matters Gregory asserted that the pope wielded absolute authority—that he could at will overrule any local bishop in the exercise of his ordinary or usual jurisdiction. His ideas on the relations of Church and state, however, are less than clear. According to some historians, he believed that all power on earth, including the imperial power, came from the papacy. According to others, Gregory held merely that the normal function of kings—the suppression of crime—was far lower than the sacred authority of popes. This much at least is beyond dispute: Gregory believed that all Christian princes must answer to the pope in spiritually significant matters and that the pope himself had a weighty responsibility to guide them.

Gregory VII believed that the pope had a weighty obligation to defend the liberty of the Church against all lay encroachments. In this nearly contemporary drawing, he receives an abbot under papal protection.
(Photo: The Granger Collection)

The Investiture Controversy

The major collision between the papacy and the Holy Roman Empire that occurred during the pontificate of Gregory VII is traditionally called the Investiture Controversy. The name suggests that the principal issue was the practice of great laymen, most notably the emperor, of "investing" bishops with ring and staff, the symbols of their spiritual office. More fundamentally, the struggle revolved around the claims of laymen to dispose of ecclesiastical offices and revenues by their own authority and in their own interests.

At a Roman council in 1075 Gregory, convinced that Emperor Henry IV had no sincere interest in reform, condemned lay investiture and excommunicated some of Henry's advisers. Henry reacted with unexpected fury; he summoned a meeting of imperial bishops and declared Gregory not the true pope but a false monk. Not one to pause in what he thought to be the work of God, Gregory in turn excommunicated Henry, deposed him, and freed his subjects from allegiance to him. These acts struck at the fundamental theory of the Christian empire, according to which the emperor was supreme head of the Christian people, responsible only to God.

Gregory's forceful appeal to spiritual power gained remarkable success in Germany. Henry's enemies leagued against him and demanded that the emperor be judged before an assembly of lords and prelates to be held at Augsburg in February 1077. They invited Gregory to preside, and he readily accepted. Henry resolved to fight spiritual weapons with spiritual weapons. He slipped across the Alps and intercepted Gregory, then on his way to Germany, at the Apennine castle of Canossa near Modena. He came in the sackcloth of a penitent, radiating contrition, pleading for absolution. Gregory, who doubted the sincerity of the emperor's repentance, refused for three days to receive him, while Henry waited in the snow. Finally, in the face of such persistence Gregory the suspicious pope had to give way to Gregory the priest, who, like all priests, was obligated to absolve a sinner professing sorrow.

The incident at Canossa is one of the most dramatic events of medieval history. Through the centuries since, the picture of the supreme lay magistrate of Christendom begging forgiveness from the pope has symbolized a victory of spiritual over material power, or a triumph of Church over state. The reality was more complex. Henry was the immediate victor. He had divided his opponents and stripped his German enemies of their excuse for rebelling. They named a rival emperor anyway, Rudolf of Swabia, but he was killed in battle in what seemed a divine judgment in Henry's favor. Gregory appears to have become unsure of himself after Canossa. He finally excommunicated Henry a second time in 1080 but was forced to flee Rome at the approach of an imperial army. Gregory died at Salerno in 1085 in apparent bitterness, avowing that his love of justice had brought him only death in exile.

After years of confused struggle Pope Calixtus II and Emperor Henry V settled the In-

vestiture Controversy through the Concordat of Worms in 1122. The terms of agreement were that the emperor would no longer invest prelates with the symbols of their spiritual office, and the pope would allow the elections of imperial bishops and abbots to be held in the presence of the emperor or his representative. This clearly permitted the emperor to influence the outcome of elections. In addition, the emperor retained the right of investing prelates with their temporalities—that is, their imperial fiefs. The essence of the agreement was that the great bishops and abbots of the realm would have to be acceptable to both parties—worthy and religious men to please the Church and loyal and capable servants to please the emperor. The agreement fell short of both papal and imperial demands, but it shows the emergence of a new and important principle in Western political life: a recognition that major appointments in the Church ought to be made through consultation and compromise.

The Consolidation of Reform

In the twelfth century the popes continued to pursue Gregorian ideals—reform, liberty, and centralization—and to consolidate past advances. In their struggle to be free of lay authority the reformers had insisted that certain persons, such as clerics, widows, orphans, crusaders, and other wards of the Church, should be judged only in ecclesiastical courts, and that matters such as cases touching on sacrilege, heresy, marriage, testaments, contracts, and the like should also, because of their religious nature, be under ecclesiastical jurisdiction, no matter who the parties might be. In the twelfth century a complex system of ecclesiastical courts developed according to this premise, paralleling and at times rivaling the courts of the kings. Judicial decisions from these courts could be appealed to Rome.

Legal scholars simultaneously sought to compile and clarify the canons of the Church—

the authoritative statements from the Bible, Church councils, Church fathers, and popes that constituted the law of the Church. The compilation ultimately recognized as official and binding was the Concordance of Discordant Canons, or the *Decretum,* put together by the Italian jurist Gratian about 1142. With systematic compilations came trained canon lawyers to comment upon, interpret, and apply the law. These men helped make the law of the medieval Church one of the West's great juridical monuments.

Centralization gained in other ways. The popes came to exert a progressively tighter control over the canonization of saints, hitherto a local matter, and they gained a stronger voice in the election of bishops, until finally papal approval was accepted as essential to a valid choice. In papal tithes imposed upon the clergy and in the administration of the census (yearly payments made by many churches to Rome), the outlines of a centralized financial administration appear, though it remained rudimentary in the twelfth century.

The Reform and Medieval Society

The reform of the Church in the eleventh and twelfth centuries left an indelible mark on both religious and secular life in the West. The suc-

This bronze tomb cover from Merseberg cathedral in Germany depicts Rudolf of Swabia, whom the supporters of Pope Gregory VII elected emperor in 1077, in place of Henry IV. This is the oldest existing tomb figure in the medieval West, but already shows remarkable skill in bronze casting. Note the cross and orb, symbols of a holy and universal kingship, which Rudolf carries. He was killed in 1080, in what seemed a judgment of God in favor of Henry.
(Photo: Bildarchiv Foto Marburg)

cessful establishment of sacerdotal celibacy set the clergy apart from the laity to a degree unknown in the ancient or Eastern Church. (The ideals of the reform have continued to influence the life of Catholic priests until the present.)

The movement for ecclesiastical reform touched nearly all aspects of contemporary life. The reform clergy gave powerful support to the efforts of princes to suppress private warfare and to establish an internal peace of which the Church was a chief beneficiary. They also helped revive intellectual life in the West. The Church actively set about building an educational system for its clergy. The bishop's school, and then the university, were the principal fruit of the reform. The dispute between Church and state also greatly stimulated fruitful speculations on the nature of Christian society and an intensive investigation of the ancient sources that defined its character.

Finally, the Gregorian reform was based on the assumption that the good man facing an evil world need not timidly flee it; rather, he can and should seek to correct its abuses and bring it closer to what God intended it to be. The reform thus helps mark the emergence of a new faith in human power and in the possible improvement of this present world—both cultural attitudes that Western people have not since abandoned.

IV. THE CULTURAL REVIVAL

The reorganization of European life in the eleventh and twelfth centuries affected institutions of learning and even the direction and methodology of Western thought. Its impact was profound in the fields of vernacular literature and art also. The Western peoples entered upon a period of high creativity, which marked all forms of cultural expression, and many of the cultural attitudes developed in this period have affected Western culture until the present.

The Rise of Universities

During the Central Middle Ages, a new institution came to assume a role in the intellectual life of Europe, which it has not since relinquished. This was the university; it ranks as one of the most influential creations of the medieval world.

Up to about 1050, monastic schools had dominated intellectual development in the West (see Map 8.5). But the monastic devotion to prayer, asceticism, and mystical meditation was not especially favorable to original thought, while the isolation of monasteries restricted the experiences of the monastic scholar and made difficult the exchange of ideas that intellectual progress requires.

From about 1050 to 1200, the cathedral, or bishop's, school assumed the intellectual leadership in Europe. Traditionally, bishops had been obliged to provide for the education of their clergy, but the disorders of the Early Middle Ages and the decline of urban life had prevented their schools from assuming a prominent role in cultural life. From the late eleventh century the growth of cities, the Gregorian emphasis upon a trained clergy, the shock of the Investiture Controversy, and the stimulus of a more intimate contact with non-Christian areas all served to revitalize the long-moribund cathedral schools.

The cathedral schools were at first very fluid in their structure. The bishop's secretary, the chancellor, or a special officer of the cathedral clergy known as a *scholasticus* was usually in charge of the school and had the responsibility of inviting learned men, or "masters," to lecture to the eager students. Both masters and students roamed from town to town, seeking the best teachers, the brightest (or best-paying) students, or the most liberal atmosphere for their work. The twelfth century was the age of the wandering scholars, or *clerici vagantes,* who have left us charming traces of their spirit or at least that of their more frivolous members, in the form of Goliardic verses, largely concerned

MAP 8.5. GREAT MONASTIC CENTERS OF LEARNING

with such unclerical subjects as wine, women, song, and their attendant joys.[4] We also know of student life through model letters composed by master rhetoricians for students without the time or eloquence to write their own letters. Such models always include letters directed to parents and almost always mention that if the affectionate and dutiful son is to continue his studies, he will need more money. Another side of student life is made manifest by disputes with the permanent residents of the towns where the schools were found. Townsmen frequently registered protests with the bishops or with the king against the students, whom they resented because of their boisterous ways and because their clerical status gave them immunity from the local police and courts. Riots involving town and gown were commonplace events, another medieval tradition which has continued to the present. To impose some order on this flux, and to protect young students from incompetent or unorthodox teachers, the twelfth-century cathedral schools gradually insisted that masters possess a certification of their learning, a "license to teach." The chancellor or *scholasticus* awarded this *licentia docendi*, the ancestor of all modern academic degrees.

The throngs of masters and students, many of them strangers to the city where they lectured and studied, eventually grouped themselves into guilds to protect their common interests. It was out of these spontaneously formed guilds of masters and students that the medieval university grew (*universitas* was a widely used Latin word for guild). The guild formed by the masters in Paris, for example, received a royal charter about 1200 and a papal bull, *Parens Scientiarum,* in 1231. These documents confirmed the guild's autonomy and powers to license teachers. The University of Paris may thus claim to be the oldest of the

north European universities. From about 1200 we may also date the beginnings of the age of the university in European intellectual life.

The university in Italy sprang from slightly different origins. Even in the Early Middle Ages professional schools for the training of notaries, lawyers, and doctors survived in some Italian cities. The Italian schools, too, seem to have enjoyed rapid growth from the late eleventh century, and growth in turn led to the formation of guilds. Here, however, the students rather than the professors constituted the dominant "university." At the oldest of these schools, the University of Bologna, the students regulated discipline, established the fees to be paid to the professors, and determined the hours and even the content of the lectures.

Like all guilds, the university sought to protect and advance its "art" of thought and teaching and to preserve that art over generations through the appropriate training of the young. The ancient world, although it possessed several famous schools, had never developed a university system, in the sense of numerous institutions of higher learning, specifically organized for the pursuit and preservation of learning. The rise of the universities also marks the appearance in Western society of a social class professionally committed to the life of thought. These institutions, and the people associated with them, have ever since played a role of unsurpassed importance in the intellectual growth of the West.

Scholasticism

In its broadest sense Scholasticism refers to the teaching characteristic of the medieval schools, that is, all the subjects taught in the four great faculties: the arts (traditionally numbered as seven), canonical and Roman law, medicine, and theology. But in a narrower and perhaps more usual sense the term refers to theology, the medieval "queen of the sciences," in which

---

[4] The exact etymology of the word *Goliardic* remains unknown. It possibly derives from Goliath the Philistine, who was honored as a kind of antisaint by the boisterous students.

the character and originality of Scholastic reasoning appear most clearly.

Theology had similarly dominated the monastic thought of the Early Middle Ages, but the monks had largely limited their interests to biblical interpretation, or exegesis. They sought in the sacred Scriptures four traditional levels of meaning (literal, moral, allegorical, and mystical) and wrote voluminous commentaries without constructing a rigorously logical system of theology.

The novelty of Scholasticism was, specifically, its application of dialectic to Christian theology. Dialectic is the art of analyzing the logical relationships among propositions in a dialogue or discourse. The monastic theologian, through exegesis, wished to discover what was true; the Scholastic, on the other hand, sought to learn how propositions of faith joined one another within a larger, consistent, and logically forceful theological system.

The first thinker to explore, although still not in rigorous fashion, the theological applications of dialectic was St. Anselm of Canterbury (1033–1109). Anselm defined his own intellectual interests as *fides quaerens intellectum* ("faith seeking to understand"—in actuality faith seeking to find logical consistency among its beliefs). In a work known as the *Proslogium*

The university as a community of scholars, teachers, and learners was a medieval innovation. Its structure was such that students exercised a degree of control that they rarely possess today. Since there were no salaries, professors relied upon tuition fees for their daily bread, and students could starve out unpopular teachers merely by refusing to attend their classes. However, in other aspects student life then was much the same as it is today. These scenes from a fifteenth-century manuscript show students gambling, opposing each other in disputations (class debates), and engaging in other activities of dormitory life.
(Photo: University Library of Freiburg-im-Breisgau)

he tried to show that there is a necessary, logical connection between the traditional Judeo-Christian dogma that God is a perfect being and the dogma that he really exists. A perfect being must possess the perfection of existence. Otherwise, our concept of him would be absurd and unthinkable.

This ontological argument for God's existence has challenged philosophers for centuries. Its great historical interest is this: it marks the revival of logical inquiry, the eagerness to know the "whys" of things, to find order and consistency among statements accepted as true. The Scholastic interest in dialectical relationships much resembles Classical Greek thought with the important exception, of course, that the Scholastics initially sought order among propositions presented by faith. (Later, they would take further propositions from the ancient pagan philosophers and even, to a limited degree, from their own observations.) From the time of Anselm Scholastic thought assumed that the human intellect was powerful enough to probe the logical and metaphysical patterns within which even God had to operate.

Peter Abelard (1079–1142), a second father of Scholasticism, brought a new rigor and popularity to dialectical theology. Abelard came to Paris in the early years of its intellectual growth, and his brilliant teaching helped give that city its reputation as Europe's leading center of philosophical and theological studies.

Abelard's major contribution to the growth of Scholasticism was his book *Sic et Non* ("Yes and No"), the first version of which probably appeared in 1122. Using what became the classical method of Scholastic argumentation, the posing of formal questions and the citation of authorities on both sides, Abelard assembled 150 theological questions. For each question he marshaled authorities from the Bible, Church councils, and Church fathers. In every case there was conflict. He made no effort to reconcile the discrepancies but left the authorities standing in embarrassing juxtaposition. His

method was an ingenious retort to those who maintained that dialectic could make no contribution to Christian theology and that it was enough to hold fast to the ancient writings. *Sic et Non* implied that one must either enlist dialectic to reconcile the conflicts or concede that the faith was a tissue of contradictions.

In the early phases of the medieval intellectual revival dialectic had to contend for supremacy with humanistic studies, which emphasized familiarity with the Classical authors and the ability to appreciate and write good Latin. Chartres, a small cathedral town near Paris, was the center of this twelfth-century humanism. But by the end of the century dialectic, as cultivated at Paris, predominated partly because it seemed to offer to the inquisitive men of the twelfth century a certain avenue to truth and a sound means for organizing the truths they had inherited. Another factor was that after the middle of the twelfth century, translators working chiefly in Spain and Sicily introduced European scholars to hitherto unknown works of Aristotle, as well as to the great commentary that the Muslim Averroës had written on them. Christian thinkers now had at their disposal the full Aristotelian corpus, and it confronted them with a thoroughly naturalistic and rationalistic philosophical system. Aristotle's philosophy was built on reason alone, and his assumptions drove Western scholars to examine his works and their own faith through dialectic. The difficult task of reconciling Aristotelian reason and nature with Christian revelation and divine grace remained the central philosophical problem of the thirteenth century.

Vernacular Literature

Scholasticism reflected the cultural interests of only a small group of intellectuals in medieval society. What the broader masses of the people valued must be sought in vernacular literature. Here, too, the themes treated and characters described largely reflect the life of the nobility, not that of the common people. But there is much reason to believe that this literature, or some oral version of it, was appreciated well beyond aristocratic circles. Townsmen and even peasants seem to have delighted in hearing of the doings of the great.

Of the vernacular literatures of Europe only Anglo-Saxon possesses a substantial number of surviving writings that antedate the year 1000. For most of the major languages of Europe an abundant tradition of literary work dates only from the eleventh and twelfth centuries. In forming the literary tastes of Europe, the Romance tongues (the vernacular languages descended from Latin) achieved a particular importance, especially the two great dialects of France, the langue d'oïl spoken north of the Loire River and the langue d'oc, or Provençal, used in the south. Castilian was slightly later in producing an important literature, and Italian, perhaps because of its similarity to Latin, did not emerge as a major literary language until the late thirteenth century.

There were three principal genres of vernacular literature: the heroic epic, troubadour lyric poetry, and the courtly romance. Heroic epics, or chansons de geste, have survived in great abundance. The oldest and probably the best of them is the *Song of Roland,* which was composed in the langue d'oïl probably in the last quarter of the eleventh century. The basis of the poem is the ambush of the rear guard of Charlemagne's army under the command of Roland by the Basques at Roncesvalles in 778, but poetic imagination (or, perhaps, older legend) transformed this minor Frankish setback into a major event in the war against Islam.

With fine psychological discernment the poem examines the character of Roland. The qualities that make him a hero, his dauntless courage and uncompromising pride, are at war with the qualities required of a good vassal—obedience, loyalty, cooperation, and common sense. Roland is in serious danger but refuses for reasons of personal dignity to sound his horn in time for Charlemagne to return and save him and his men. By the time his pride relents and he does blow the horn, their deaths are assured. The sensitive examination of the conflict between Roland's thoughtless if heroic individualism and the demands of the new feudal order gives this poem its stature as the first masterpiece of French letters.

Very different from the heroic epic is troubadour lyric poetry, initially written in the langue d'oc of the south. The novelty of this complex poetry is its discovery and celebration of women and of love. The heroic epic was written for the thoroughly masculine society of the battle camp. The troubadours sang at courts, in which women exerted a powerful influence. In a mobile age, when knights and nobles would be away for long periods on crusades and wars, their mothers, wives, and daughters administered their households and estates and achieved considerable social prominence. The women became the arbiters of what constituted "courtly manners"—proper behavior—in their households, and they surely influenced the literature that was heard within their walls.

The troubadour usually addressed a lady of superior social station, almost always someone else's wife, whom he had little chance of winning. Although she was not a likely means of sensual gratification, love for her did offer a hope for inward consolation; it could, if requited, elevate the poet's spirits to unspeakable joy and transform his world to eternal spring. Courtly love (at least as the troubadours present it) was not a dalliance but quite literally a way of salvation, a means of rescuing the lover from despondency and introducing him into an earthly paradise. This discovery and intensive exploration of the emotion of love represents one of the most influential creations of the medieval mind.

The courtly romance, which entered its great age after 1150, combines traits of both heroic epic and troubadour lyric poetry. It is

This panel, from an ivory box made in Paris in the fourteenth century, illustrates the bizarre link between love and war characteristic of the cult of courtly love. Knights are shown besieging the castle of love; ladies defend it, by hurling down from the ramparts not boiling oil, but bouquets of flowers. Young knights, often forced to delay marriage until approximately age 30, doubtless lived and fought under high erotic tensions. This scene may reflect their sexual musings.
(Photo: Metropolitan Museum of Art, gift of J. Pierpont Morgan)

narrative in form like the epic; but, like Provençal poetry, it allots a major role to women and love. Chrétien de Troyes, whose works probably date from shortly before 1182, is the author of the oldest surviving romances about King Arthur of Britain and his coterie of knights. Many of these tales are concerned with an analysis of the tensions that love, the rebellious emotion, creates in society. Western letters have since endlessly explored these themes.

Romanesque Art

The conventional term used to describe the architectural and artistic style of this period is *Romanesque*. It means "of Roman origins" but is, like many terms applied to the Middle Ages, misleading. Artists in the Central Middle Ages did imitate Classical models, but not exclusively; they also drew on nearly every other artistic tradition to which they had access—barbarian, Byzantine, and Arab.

The proliferation of castles across the face of Europe stimulated the techniques of construction. These fortresses were built on a progressively larger scale, in contrast with the castles of the Carolingian Age, and by the thirteenth century, builders were able to work entirely in stone. Crusaders returning from the East brought with them new concepts of fortress design and perhaps also a desire to render castle life more gracious. The crafting of tapestries, furniture, and glass benefited from the new importance of cities, the strength of markets, and the growing number of artisans. Although life about 1200 was still remarkably crude, even for the rich, it was clearly becoming less so.

Art, however, remained in most of its forms the servant of the Church. The religious reform in the eleventh century brought with it a liturgical revival. The monks of the Cluniac monasteries were especially devoted to (and occasionally criticized for) sumptuous religious services. Liturgical needs stimulated the art of metalwork (which produced chalices and other sacred vessels), glass making, and the weaving of fine fabrics for the priests' vestments. Music too advanced. The Gregorian chant (named for Pope Gregory the Great, but in fact representing the traditional plainsong of the Church of Rome) had become established as the common music of the Western Church in the Carolingian epoch. The eleventh and twelfth centuries witnessed, not certainly the origins, but a great development in polyphonic music (part-singing). The coordination of the vocal parts in choral music also required effective systems of musical notation. A monk named Guido d'Arezzo is credited with giving names to the notes, some of which are still used (re, mi, fa, sol, la). The secular songs and melodies of the troubadours were another major source of enrichment for the Western musical tradition.

The most impressive artistic monuments left to us from the Romanesque period are the churches themselves. In engineering the great achievement of the Central Middle Ages was the roofing of churches in stone. From about the year 1000, small, stone-roofed churches began to appear, especially in southern Europe. At first the builders utilized the simple barrel, or tunnel, vault, but this design did not allow for windows because the roof would collapse if holes were put into the supporting sides of the tunnel. Engineers then developed and mastered the use of the groin vault, which is formed by the intersection of two barrel vaults. The area of intersection is called the bay, and the roof over the bay is supported at four points, not by the entire length of the lateral walls. Bays could be grouped next to bays, an entire church could be roofed with stone, win-

dows could be easily cut, and the monotony of tunnel vaulting would be avoided.

Romanesque churches were decorated on the exterior with stone sculpture. Monumental sculpture had been a dead technique in the West since the end of the Roman Empire. Romanesque statues, which exist by the thousands, show a marked quality of antirealism, a refusal to allow visual accuracy to dominate portrayals. In part this was dictated by the odd-shaped crevices, corners, columns, and capitals (upper part of a column) that the sculptor frequently had to decorate, but the artist was also striving to present a world as seen by faith. Christ, for

---

The tympanum (i.e., the recessed façade above the principal doors) of the cathedral at Autun, in France, displays the mixture of mysticism and vitality that characterizes Romanesque works of stone sculpture, particularly those designed for the churches.
(Photo: Jean Roubier)

The Romanesque cathedral at Poitiers in western France is one of hundreds of stone churches built in Western Europe in the eleventh and twelfth centuries, and is a masterpiece of the new artistic and architectural style. (Photo: Dr. Martin Hürlimann—Zurich)

example, had to be shown larger than others, in keeping with his dignity. Demons and monsters, many drawn from the popular imagination, abound in Romanesque sculpture. While similar to Byzantine portrayals in its antirealism, Romanesque style, unlike the Byzantine, overflows with movement, tension, excitement, and the spirit of mystical exhilaration. Romanesque statuary marvelously documents the exuberant spirit of this age of reform and crusades, when people seemed convinced that God was actively at work among them, setting right the world.

Romanesque art makes use of many prior and foreign traditions, but it still manifests its own proper spirit. It is therefore much more than a juxtaposition of borrowed forms. Rather, it is the first style and school that can be called an authentic product of the European West.

The eleventh and twelfth centuries were vigorously creative at every level of European life. By 1200 Europe was very different from the old, or "first," Europe of Charlemagne. Its economy was more diversified and productive, its society more complex, its government more effective, its religion more sensitive, and its thought and art more original and daring. But the very innovations of the age posed severe problems for European society. How could the new forms of economic endeavor be reconciled with the older hostility and suspicion toward a life of buying and selling? How could the rising power of monarchs be reconciled with the self-consciousness and self-interest of the nobility, reformed Church, and privileged towns? How could the new confidence in human reason and in nature, reinforced by familiarity with Aristotle, be synthesized with the older notions that nature was corrupt, men weak, and the afterlife the only hope? From about 1200 the West was trying to consolidate its recent advances and bring them into harmony with its older heritage. This effort at consolidation, reconciliation, and synthesis is the theme of Western history in the thirteenth century.

RECOMMENDED READING

Sources

Anselm of Canterbury. *Basic Writings: Proslogium, Monologium, Gaunilon's On Behalf of the Fool, Cur Deus Homo.* S. W. Deane (tr.). 1962.

Chrétien de Troyes. *Arthurian Romances.* W. W. Comfort (tr.). 1958.

Douglas, David C. (ed.). *English Historical Documents.* 1955. The richest available collection of translated sources bearing on English history.

Fitzneale, Richard. *The Course of the Exchequer.* Charles Johnson (tr.). 1950.

★Herlihy, David (ed.). *The History of Feudalism.* 1971.

John of Salisbury. *The Statesman's Book.* John Dickinson (tr.). 1963.

★*The Song of Roland.* Dorothy L. Sayers (tr.). 1957.

Studies

Barraclough, Geoffrey. *The Origins of Modern Germany.* 1963. Classic interpretation of medieval German history.

Chenu, M.-D. *Nature, Man and Society in the Twelfth Century.* Jerome Taylor and Lester K. Little (trs.). 1968. Seminal essays on cultural and intellectual change, by a French Dominican.

Chrimes, Stanley B. *An Introduction to the Administrative History of Medieval England.* 1966. Clear and authoritative.

*Douglas, David C. *William the Conqueror: The Norman Impact upon England.* 1966. Outstanding among many biographies.

Duby, Georges. *The Chivalrous Society.* Cynthia Postan (tr.). 1977. Essays on feudal society by a prominent French medievalist.

———. *The Knight, the Lady and the Priest: The Making of Modern Marriage in Medieval France.* 1983. An essay in social history.

Ennen, Edith. *The Medieval Town.* Natalie Fryde (tr.). 1979. By a German historian; now the best introductory survey available in English.

*Fawtier, Robert. *The Capetian Kings of France: Monarchy and Nation, 987–1328.* Lionel Butler and R. J. Adams (trs.). 1962.

*Ganshof, François L. *Feudalism.* P. Grierson (tr.). 1964. Standard introduction to feudal institutions.

Hallam, Elizabeth M. *Domesday Book through Nine Centuries.* 1986. Now the best introduction to the great survey.

*Haskins, Charles H. *The Renaissance of the Twelfth Century.* 1927. A classic study.

*———. *The Rise of Universities.* 1957.

*Heer, Friedrich. *The Medieval World: Europe, 1100–1350.* 1964. Thoughtful appraisal by an Austrian scholar.

Le Goff, Jacques. *Time, Work and Culture in the Middle Ages.* Arthur Goldhammer (tr.). 1980. Medieval culture studied through anthropological methods.

*Pirenne, Henri. *Medieval Cities.* Frank D. Halsey (tr.). 1939. Old but worth reading.

*Southern, Richard W. *The Making of the Middle Ages.* 1955. Classic essay on the twelfth century.

Strayer, Joseph R. *On the Medieval Origins of the Modern State.* 1970.

*Tellenbach, Gerd. *Church, State and Christian Society at the Time of the Investiture Contest.* 1970.

*Available in paperback.

EXPERIENCES OF DAILY LIFE

Nobles

All societies in the early Middle Ages possessed an elite of warriors, but they seem not to have had a true nobility. (In a strict sense, nobles not only possess legal privileges but also hold them through birth or blood. Warriors in the early period were certainly privileged, but their sons had no hereditary claim to their fathers' prerogatives.)

A hereditary nobility does not seem to appear in medieval society until after Carolingian times. In fact, within the historic European nobility, very few families can trace their genealogies as far back as the ninth century; most family names, even of the high nobility, do not appear in the documents until the eleventh and twelfth and even later centuries.

The appearance of nobles' lines seems to reflect a fundamental change in the structure of the elite family. In early medieval society, the kindred or set of relatives, even of important persons, was bilateral or cognatic, that is, blood relationship was traced through both males and females. Kindreds were formed, in other words, around a horizontal axis, and did not extend far back in time. The kindred structure of the new nobility was much different. It placed exclusive emphasis on descent from, and relation through, males. And it pushed the line of descent through males far into the past, to the ancestor or founder of the line. It had, in other words, a vertical orientation. This set of male relatives descending through males from

A noble paying homage to his king.
(New York Library Picture Collection)

a common ancestor is called an agnate lineage or patrilineage.

Several factors contributed to the appearance of the noble patrilineage. The division of ancestral lands among many claimants threatened to destroy the economic base upon which their status depended, and to shore up their social position, the elite families sought to limit the number of heirs. The great families accordingly provided their daughters with a dowry, but otherwise excluded them from a full share in the inheritance. They excluded younger sons too. Often, these were denied the chance to marry, unless they could win prizes in war or the hand of an affluent heiress. The family wealth was principally reserved for the support of the eldest son, and with him went the chief hope for the preservation of the lineage.

The old elite also tried to defeat the efforts of new families, including those of bourgeois origin, to enter their ranks. By the twelfth century, they had successfully reserved the status of noble to those whose ancestors had held similar dignity. To proclaim their identity and breeding (and distinctiveness from the rest of society), the nobles adopted family names, which usually recalled the name of the revered founder, or of the ancestral castle. They adopted other symbols of solidarity, such as coats of arms, mottoes, and sometimes fanciful genealogies.

The emergence of noble patrilineages also corresponds with a change in the patterns of aristocratic marriages. The nobles restricted the marriages of their younger sons but wished to find husbands for all their daughters (for them, the only other honorable option was the convent). This created an imbalance on the marriage market, as nubile girls outnumbered eligible bachelors. To attract a husband, fathers had to offer ever larger dowries. The surplus of unmarried girls seems to have exerted downward pressure on the ages of first marriage for women. Fathers were anxious to settle the future of their daughters as early as possible, even as they were requiring sons to marry late, if they were allowed to marry at all.

Noble society, in which the patrilineage was the central institution, thus acquired certain peculiar features. Unattached young males abounded. They drifted from court to court as knights errant and were eager participants in tournaments, mock wars in which they hoped to win a prize that would make their fortunes. Or they wandered off on crusade to Europe's distant frontiers. The young women their own age would likely be married or deposited in convents. The severe restrictions on marriage could not help but raise erotic tensions in this society. But the only lady the single knight could court would most likely be already married, perhaps to the lord of the castle in which he was staying. This situation seems accurately reflected in the literature of courtly love, in which the lover almost always courts a married woman, almost always higher than himself in social status. But it would be wrong to claim, as is sometimes done, that the woman in the courtly love pattern is totally passive. She is very much the mistress of the game, in literary convention and in life.

The new patrilineages did not replace, but were rather superimposed upon, the older, bilateral kindreds. The Church, for example, continued to insist that matrilineal ties (that is, relations through the mother) must be examined in determining eligibility for marriage. The superimposition of one definition of kindred upon another generated domestic tensions. The good of the first-born male was not often the same as the good of all descendants, and the claims of the latter played upon parental consciences. Conflicts involving parents and siblings were commonplace in noble families.

The patrilineage did not win a total victory, but it offered a model of kindred organization that other classes in society would eventually follow. You probably bear, as most people in most Western countries do, your father's name, the same that his father bore, and his father too, and so on up through the generations. Why does your own surname recall your own patrilineage? The custom reflects a tradition of family organization that has its origins in the Central Middle Ages.

Chapter 9

The Summer
of the Middle Ages
ca. 1200 –1350

The thirteenth century (or, more precisely, the period between about 1200 and the Black Death of 1348 and 1349) has been traditionally considered the summer of the Middle Ages. It can claim many impressive achievements: a largely prosperous economy, which supported more people than Europe possessed at any other time during the Middle Ages; reasonably effective systems of government in the feudal monarchies; parliamentary institutions; Gothic cathedrals; the great works of Scholastic philosophy and theology; and the *Divine Comedy* of Dante Alighieri, one of the great masterpieces of Western literature. Moreover, these products of the medieval genius seem to share a certain spirit: a sense of logic and order and a serene confidence, not only in divine grace and faith but also in human reason and effort. Thirteenth-century men and women believed that God had created a harmonious world and that they could describe its ordered structure in their philosophy, imitate it in their art, and use this knowledge to guide their earthly lives.

Today, as research probes ever deeper, we know that these favorable impressions are not entirely accurate. Thirteenth-century society was less placid than the smiles of Gothic angels persuade their admirers to believe. The population may have grown too large to be supported by available resources, and this may have been an important factor in provoking plagues and famines from the middle fourteenth century. The prosperity of the rich often rested on the rampant misery of the poor; the aspirations toward a united and peaceful Europe did not dispel the specter of war; and Scholastic theology did not quench the flames of intellectual and religious revolt. In sum, the effort to achieve order and synthesis was itself a manifestation of acute tensions and conflicts. One must beware of what a historian has recently called the "golden legend" of the Middle Ages.

Medieval society in the thirteenth century could not achieve permanent solutions to the many problems it confronted. But this ultimate failure should not prevent us from recognizing its accomplishments. It strove to build both an ordered society and ordered systems of thought, in which all conflicts, social or intellectual, would be reconciled. The effort was admirable and the achievements magnificent; we may still regard the thirteenth century as the summer of the Middle Ages.

I. ECONOMIC EXPANSION

The Countryside

Population growth, land reclamations, and the expansion of external frontiers continued in the thirteenth century, though at a slackening pace after about 1250. Regional specialization in agricultural production also grew more pronounced. Southwest France (Gascony), for example, exported wine in quantities that rival even modern exports from this same region; the wine flowed principally to England and northern Europe. England itself, and soon Spain, supplied raw wool to the busy textile towns of Flanders and Italy. Peripheral areas—the Baltic lands beyond the Elbe River, Catalonia, Sicily, even parts of the Eastern Empire—delivered wheat to the more crowded central zones. And the agricultural lands surrounding the towns were devoted to market farming and industrial crops, such as vegetable dyes. By raising what the natural endowment of their regions most favored, cultivators worked more productively.

A dense population sustained a strong demand (and high prices) for food, especially for cereals. As peasants competed for land and workers for jobs, rents increased and wages fell, and the profits of landowners and employers rose. In increasing measure, the prosperity of the propertied and entrepreneurial classes was coming to rest upon the deprivation and misery of the humble.

The Cities

Dramatic economic changes were also occurring in the cities.[1] Large-scale production, extensive trade, complex commercial and banking institutions, and the amassing of great fortunes became the commonplace features of urban economic and social life. These urban centers pioneered many of the methods, and show much of the spirit, of modern business enterprises.

Medieval towns developed a new system of producing goods. Usually called the "putting-out system," it remained characteristic of the Western economy until the Industrial Revolution. Most work was performed in the home, little use was made of power, and there were no factories. Increased efficiency was achieved through finely dividing the process of production and through developing highly specialized skills. A merchant or manufacturer, who fulfilled the function of providing capital, acquired the raw material, put it out in sequence to specialized artisans, and then sold the finished products.

The making of woolen cloth, the largest industry of the medieval town, well illustrates the complex character of thirteenth-century manufacturing. The raw wool, often coming from England, Spain, or North Africa, was first prepared by sorters, beaters, and washers. Then the cleaned and graded wool was carded, or combed. The next task, the spinning, was usually done by women who worked in their own homes with a distaff, a small stick to hold the wool, and a spindle, a weight to spin and twist the strands into thread. (The distaff has since remained a symbol of the female sex.) The spinning wheel, apparently first invented in Italy in the late thirteenth century, added a new speed and quality to thread-making.

Weavers, almost always men, wove the thread into huge broadcloths that were 30 yards in length and might contain 2000 to 3000 warp (lengthwise) threads. The cloth was then fulled—that is, washed and worked with special earths that caused the wool to mat. This was arduous work and was often done at a water-driven fulling mill. The giant cloth was then

---

[1] We must of course recognize that the size of towns everywhere in Europe remained small in comparison with the rural population. The largest medieval towns probably never had more than 120,000 inhabitants. In England in the fourteenth century only about 10 percent of the population lived in cities. In Flanders and certain regions of Italy, that figure may have reached 25 percent, but this was exceptional.

International and Military History	Political History
1200	
1204 Fourth Crusade establishes Latin Empire at Constantinople	
	1208–1229 Albigensian Crusade
1204 John of England loses Normandy to Philip II	1212–1250 Emperor Frederick II Hohenstaufen, "wonder of the world"
1214 Battle of Bouvines; Philip II defeats coalition led by John of England	1215 English barons force King John to grant Magna Carta
	1216–1272 Reign of Henry III in England
	1226 Louis VIII completes conquest of the south
	1226–1270 Louis IX king of France
1242 Alexander Nevsky, prince of Novgorod, defeats Teutonic Knights on Lake Peipus	
1242 Louis IX repulses English at Saintes	
1248 Louis IX leads crusade against Egypt	
1250	**1250–1273 Interregnum in Holy Roman Empire**
1258 Treaty of Corbeil between France and Aragon	1258 Barons extract Provisions of Oxford from King Henry III
1259 Treaty of Paris between France and England	
	1264 Simon de Montfort's Parliament
	1265 Simon defeated and killed at Battle of Evesham
1270 Death of Louis IX while on crusade against Tunis	1272–1307 Edward I king of England
1282 The Sicilian Vespers; Angevins expelled from Sicily	
1284 Edward I seizes Wales	
	1291 Perpetual Compact among Swiss Cantons
1296–1303 Conflict of Philip IV with Pope Boniface VIII	1295 Model Parliament
1300	
1302 Flemish towns defeat Philip IV at Courtrai	1302 First meeting of French Estates General
	1306 Philip IV expels Jews from France
	1307 Philip IV suppresses Knights Templars
	1328 Death of Charles IV; end of direct line of Capetian kings
	1328 Philip of Valois elected king of France (Philip VI)
1350	

1200–1350/TIMELINE

Social and Economic History	Cultural and Intellectual History

—1200—

1204   Fourth Crusade gives Venetians colonial empire in East

1208   Pope Innocent III approves first Franciscan rule

1215   Fourth Lateran Council
1215   Bishop of Toulouse approves new order founded by Dominic

1231   Pope Gregory IX institutes the Inquisition
1234   Pope Gregory IX publishes collection of decretals (papal letters)

— c. 1250   European population growth slackens —
1252   Minting of gold florin, earliest successful gold coin

c. 1266–1274   Aquinas writes *Summa Theologica*

1275–1292   Marco Polo travels in China

1296   Bull *Clericis laicos* forbids royal taxation of clerics

— c. 1300   Probable peak of medieval population —

1302   Bull *Unam Sanctam;* broadest statement of papal powers
1303   Boniface VIII humiliated at Anagni
1309   Pope Clement V establishes papal court at Avignon, beginning of Avignon exile
1313–1321   Dante composes *Commedia*

1315–1317   Great famine in northern Europe

1342   Failure of Bardi and Peruzzi banks in Florence

1348   Black Death strikes mainland of Europe
—1350—

tentered, or stretched on a frame, so that it would dry properly and shrink evenly. Next, the dry cloth was rubbed with teasels to raise the nap, and the nap was then carefully cut. Several times repeated, this last operation gave the cloth a smooth, almost silky finish, but it was extremely delicate work; one slip of the scissors could ruin the cloth and the large investment it represented.

At various stages in this process the wool could be dyed—whether as unspun wool, thread, or woven cloth. Medieval people loved bright colors, and dyers used a great variety of animal, vegetable, and mineral dyes and special earths, such as alum, to fix the colors.

The medieval woolen industry thus came to employ a large and remarkably diversified labor force, which worked materials brought from all corners of the known world. Capital and labor were sharply divided; a few great entrepreneurs controlled huge masses of capital. In Florence in about 1300, the number of wool shops ranged between 200 and 300; the number of big broadcloths produced were between 80,000 and 100,000, with a value surpassing 1.2 million gold florins; the number of persons who earned their living from the industry was upward of 30,000.

The Guilds

To defend and promote their interests in a world still ruled by warriors and priests, the merchants and artisans took to forming associations of self-help known as guilds. The first guilds were organized by merchants, and appear about 1000.[2] By the twelfth century both artisans and merchants in special trades—for example, dealers in wool, spices, or silk—had organized their own independent guilds. A large industrial town such as Florence had more than 50 professional guilds.

The guild members exercised wide powers over their own affairs. They usually met once a year in their church or hall to approve changes in the statutes and to elect permanent officials. These consuls, as the officials were often called, enforced the statutes, adjudicated disputes among the members, administered the properties of the guild and supervised its expenditures, maintained the quality of the product by regulating both the materials and processes, protected the members from unfair competition, and restricted the number of working hours, the number of employees, and the type of advertising. The personal security and welfare of members were also principal concerns. The guilds aided those who lost goods through fire or flood; they supported the widows and educated the orphaned children of their deceased members. Banquets, public processions, and religious ceremonies enriched the social life of the membership. Many guilds assumed a further responsibility for the beauty and welfare of their town. They were among the principal donors to hospitals and charities, and they usually built and maintained their own church, or at least a chapel in the city cathedral.

One of the chief contributions of the guilds was the apprenticeship system; the guilds were in fact the most important institutions of lay education functioning in the Middle Ages. They stipulated what the apprentice had to be taught and what proof of skill he had to present to be admitted into the brotherhood, how long he had to work and learn in the shop of the master, and what the master had to give him by way of lodging, food, and salary. (The apprentice really earned his education by helping the master produce his goods, and the salary he received was always small.) The young man might be required to produce a "masterpiece"

---

[2] Merchant guilds appear at the small town of Montreuil-sur-Mer probably before 980, at Tiel from about 950 to 1024, at Valenciennes between 1051 and 1070, at Cologne in 1070, and at Saint-Omer between 1072 and 1083. Leather workers had a guild at Rouen between 1100 and 1135, and fishermen at Worms between 1106 and 1107.

to show his skill, or at least treat the brothers to a lavish banquet. If, after finishing his training, he was too inexperienced or poor to open his own shop, he could work as a paid laborer, or journeyman, in the shop of an established master. By carefully saving his wages, the apprentice might eventually become a master in his own right and a full-fledged member of the guild, but most medieval artisans continued to work as salaried laborers for their entire lives. The medieval guild has thus been called, with some justice, not a union of workers but a union of bosses.

Only rarely did girls serve as apprentices, but most wives and daughters helped their husbands and fathers in their labors. Many widows continued in their own name the trade of their deceased husbands. Women's contribution to the town economy was less visible than men's, but no less essential.

In protecting commercial skills under difficult conditions, offering a measure of insurance and social security to their members, and promoting education, the guilds played a crucial role in forming an environment favorable to commerce and manufacture. They were the incubators of modern economic enterprise.

Business Institutions

The growth of trade and manufacturing stimulated the development of sophisticated commercial and banking institutions. Christian ethics traditionally condemned the taking of usury (which then meant any profit on a loan, however tiny); therefore, the medieval business community developed alternative instruments of credit.

Most important for properly commercial purposes was the bill of exchange, in essence a loan, but requiring repayment at a specified time in another place and currency. Thus a Florentine might borrow 100 pounds at Florence and agree to repay three months later in local money at a Champagne fair. He then bought goods at Florence, sold them in Champagne, and repaid the money. The rate of exchange between the currencies almost always concealed a substantial profit for the investor, but technically he earned it for changing money, not for making the loan.

Partnerships and business associations were another important means of recruiting capital. At Venice, Genoa, and Pisa overseas ventures were most often financed through special temporary partnerships, usually called a *commenda*. In its simplest form an investor, who remained at home, gave a sum of money to a merchant traveling abroad in return for a share of the eventual profits (usually three-quarters); the investor bore the entire loss if the ship sank or the venture failed. A merchant would usually accept many of these investments simultaneously or might himself invest in one voyage while sailing on another. The partnership lasted only for the length of the specified voyage.

The Companies

In the inland Italian towns a more permanent kind of partnership developed known as the *compagnia* (literally, "bread together," a sharing of bread). These earliest companies seem to have been partnerships among brothers. The sons of a deceased merchant, for example, might decide to leave their inheritance undivided and to trade together as a single company. By the thirteenth century two changes were transforming the character of these fraternal companies. They now quite commonly included as partners persons who were not blood relatives but could contribute capital and services, and they also accepted deposits from nonpartners in return for fixed yearly payments of interest that were called "gifts," lest they be considered usurious. The capital supplied by the partners was called the *corpo*, or "body" of the company. Money accepted in deposit from nonpartners was considered *sopra corpo* ("above the body") and could reach substantial amounts.

These companies performed a wide variety of functions and became colossal in size. They traded in any product that promised a profit, wrote bills of exchange, and fulfilled other banking services. From the late twelfth century they served the Roman Curia as papal bankers and were largely responsible for building and maintaining the financial system of the medieval papacy. They were also drawn into the risky business of extending loans to prelates and princes.

Before its failure in 1342 the Bardi Company of Florence had loaned King Edward III of England almost 900,000 florins and the Peruzzi Company had provided 600,000. These were gigantic amounts: in 1348, Pope Clement VI purchased Avignon for only 80,000 florins.[3] Clearly, the capital of these Florentine banks was the price of kingdoms.

Medieval Views of Economic Life

The thinkers of the thirteenth century were coming to new and more favorable, if not exactly enthusiastic, views concerning wealth. The Church fathers had taught that difference in wealth in human society was a necessary evil arising out of sin. Sin had aroused the concupiscence of men and threatened to make social life a "war of all against all." Private property, defended by the power of the state, restrained concupiscence and promoted peace. In contrast, Thomas Aquinas, the great thirteenth-century theologian, drew his principal argument for private property from natural law. Private property, he argued, provided incentive, assured good care of belongings, and promoted

---

[3] These figures are taken from Yves Renouard, *Les hommes d'affaires italiens du moyen âge,* 1949, p. 124.

peace and order. He thus gave property and wealth more dignity than the thought of an earlier age had accorded them.

Even commercial wealth was losing some of its ancient taint. As late as about 1150, Gratian in the *Decretum* had quoted with approval the aphorism that "rarely or never can a merchant be saved." By the thirteenth century, however, preachers in commercial cities were eloquently comparing merchants to Christ. After all, they, like Christ, lived by peaceful enterprise and not by violence. Moreover, Christ, like a good and worthy merchant, had repurchased or "redeemed" the human race from the devil's ownership.

Nevertheless, the social thought of the thirteenth century was far from espousing laissez-faire liberalism in the marketplace. The rich man could not use his wealth as his personal inclinations might dictate. Property could be private in possession, but it had to be used to promote the common good. The individual, in other words, was morally obligated to use his wealth to benefit the entire community, not just himself.

II. THE STATES OF EUROPE

Through its practices and institutions the thirteenth-century European economy acquired a more stable structure. Governments, too, were moving toward a new level of constitutional stability. The thirteenth century was an age of great laws, which helped define and fix governmental and legal procedures. They thus served to implant in the West a strong tradition of constitutionalism, a lasting belief that people should be governed by fixed procedures. The thirteenth century made one other lasting contribution to Western political development: the representative assembly. European princes extended to the great estates, or classes, of society—namely, the clergy, nobility, eventually

Nel vano tutta sua coda guizzava,
torcendo in su la venenosa forcha.
cha guisa di scorpion la punta armava.
Lo duca disse or conuien che si torcha.
la nostra via un poco in fina quella.
bestia maluagia che colla si torcha.
P ero scendemmo a la destra mamella.
co diece passi femmo in su lostremo.
per ben cessar la rena e la fiamella.

A detail from a fourteenth-century manuscript copy of Dante's *Divine Comedy* illustrates the section of hell reserved for usurers. The Church regarded usury as one of man's many earthly sins that condemn him in the eyes of God.
(Photo: British Museum)

even the townsmen—the opportunity to hear and approve the major decisions of government. To make this participation possible, parliaments or assemblies of estates came to assume a recognized if still humble place among the institutions of government.

England

At the death of Henry II in 1189, the English monarchy wielded exceptional authority, but neither in practice nor in theory was it clearly established within what limits, if any, royal powers should operate, or how, if at all, the great men of the realm might participate in government.

Henry's son and successor was Richard I, the Lion-Hearted. Although Richard had all the virtues of a model knight—boldness, military skill, stately bearing, even a flair for composing troubadour lyrics—he had none of the attributes of a good king. He loved battles and shunned conferences. In 1191 and 1192 he was off fighting in the Holy Land on the Third Crusade, where he won some significant victories and gained some concessions for the Christians from the Muslim chief Saladin. Chivalry, which gave him his reputation, also took his life. He died in 1199 from a neglected wound received while besieging a castle in a minor war in southern France. Richard's presence in England was restricted to two visits, lasting less than ten months, but the English government continued to function efficiently even in the absence of its chief; this is testimony to its fundamental strength.

Richard was succeeded by his younger brother John, who rightly or wrongly is considered a wicked king (significantly, no other English monarch has borne the name). While the towns and the common people supported him, he gratuitously antagonized his powerful subjects by his insolence and capricious cruelty. His reign is largely a record of humiliations suffered at the hands of the pope, Philip II of France, and his own barons.

In 1206 John brazenly tried to make a worthless favorite archbishop of Canterbury. The clergy of Canterbury appealed to Pope Innocent III, who selected for the office the learned, pious, and popular Stephen Langton. To force John to acquiesce, Innocent laid England under interdict in 1208. The interdict was a command to the English Church to go on strike. Priests were not to baptize babies, marry couples, or bury the dead in public ceremony. (In case of need, private conferral of the sacraments was still allowed.) Parish bells were silenced, and the rhythm of life must have changed across England. But the Church's strike did not sway John at all. Only when he wanted papal support in his war against the French over the loss of Normandy did he finally submit in 1213. After his defeat at Bouvines John had to reap the bitter harvest that his long years of misrule at home and failures abroad had sown.

Magna Carta

To meet the extraordinary expenses of war, the English kings had traditionally requested, and almost always received, special aids or contributions from their barons. But after Bouvines, when John's policies proved to be disastrous, the enraged barons refused further help. Encouraged by the Church, they took to arms. At Runnymede in June 1215 they forced John to grant the "Great Charter" of liberties, which had probably been inspired, if not largely composed, by Archbishop Langton. The Magna Carta resembled oaths that English kings since Henry I had taken upon their coronation; it obligated the king to respect certain rights of his subjects. But no previous royal charter of liberties equaled it in length, explicitness, and influence.

The Magna Carta disappoints most modern readers. Unlike the American Declaration of Independence it offers no grand generalizations about human dignity and rights. Its sixty-three clauses, arranged without apparent order, are largely concerned with technical problems of feudal law—rights of inheritance, feudal relief, wardship, and the like. But it did establish, more clearly than any previous document, that the king ought not to disturb the estates of the realm—Church, barons, and all free subjects—in the peaceful exercise of their customary liberties. It thus guaranteed to the clergy the freedom to elect bishops and to make appeals to Rome, protected the barons against arbitrary exactions of traditional feudal dues, and confirmed for the men of London and other towns "all their liberties and free customs." It called for one standard of weights and measures in the kingdom, which facilitated trade and, therefore, undoubtedly pleased the townsmen. To all freemen it promised access to justice and judgment by known procedures. "No free man shall be taken or imprisoned or dispossessed," the charter reads, "except by the legal judgment of his peers or by the law of the land." Finally, the king could impose new taxes only with the common consent of the realm. On the other hand, it offered almost nothing to the unfree classes, the serfs or villeins who constituted perhaps 80 percent of the population.

The Magna Carta marked a major step toward constitutionalism, that is, toward government by recognized procedures that could be changed only with the consent of the realm. Of course, the barons and the bishops never anticipated that subjects other than themselves might be called upon to give consent, but this limitation in no way compromises the importance of the principle established. Finally, future generations of Englishmen were to interpret the provisions of the Magna Carta in a much broader sense than its authors had intended, making it truly part of the "Bible of the English constitution." The document is of importance not only for what it said but for what it allowed future generations to believe about the traditional relationship in England between authority and liberty.

Provisions of Oxford

Under John's son Henry III (1216–1272) two issues—appointments to royal offices and the imposition of taxes—again raised the storms of baronial revolt. In selecting the high officials of state and Church, Henry favored over his own English subjects Frenchmen from Poitou and Provence (the homeland of his queen) and Italians put forward by the popes. The popes also involved him in ill-considered foreign adventures: to establish his younger son, Edmund, as king of Sicily and to secure the election of his brother Richard as German emperor. The barons once more protested against the heavy charges placed upon them to support these costly failures.

At a meeting at Oxford in 1258 the barons forced Henry to accept the Provisions of Oxford, which required him to govern England under the tight control of several baronial committees. Almost at once the king and barons fell to arguing over the implementation of the provisions, and both sides agreed to accept the arbitration of the saintly king of France, Louis IX. In 1264 Louis decided in Henry's favor and

exonerated him from his promise to respect the provisions; the pope concurred. But the disgruntled barons under the capable leadership of Simon de Montfort took up arms. With the support of the king's own son Edward, Simon defeated and captured Henry at Lewes and for a little more than a year was the effective ruler of England. However, the barons were too unruly to maintain a united opposition against the king. Edward changed sides, defeating the baronial army at Evesham in 1265, and Simon himself was killed in the fray. The issue was thus decided: the king, not the barons, would be the chief power in England.

Legal Reforms

The powers and procedures of the royal government received a still clearer definition under Edward I (1272–1307). Pious without being weak, committed to crusading but also concerned with the welfare of his realm, Edward ranks as one of the greatest and most influential of medieval English kings. In 1284 he seized Wales and later gave it as an appanage (a province intended to provide "bread," or support) to his eldest son. (Since 1301 the heir presumptive to the English throne has borne the title Prince of Wales). Edward left his strongest mark on English law and institutions, and is often referred to, somewhat extravagantly, as the English Justinian.

Edward produced no systematic codification of English law, which remained based principally on custom and court decisions of the past, but he did seek to correct and enlarge the common law in certain critical areas and to give the system a new pliancy. He issued the first Statutes of the Realm, initiating a series in which all the public laws of England have since been entered. Edward's statutes required the barons to show by what warrant (quo warranto), or royal license, they exercised jurisdiction in their courts, and this marked an important step in the decline of baronial justice. His laws also limited the growth of mortmain, that is, land held by the Church. The statutes were especially important in determining the land law of England, regulating inheritance and defining the rights of lords, vassals, and the king when land changed hands through inheritance or purchase. Edward laid the foundations upon which the English (and eventually American) law of real estate rested for centuries. In enacting these statutes and in governing the kingdom Edward also placed a new emphasis on securing the consent of his subjects through Parliament.

Parliamentary Origins

Since the time of William the Conqueror the plenary meetings of the great council, or Curia Regis, had included the great barons, bishops, abbots, royal household officials—anyone whom the king wished to invite. During the reign of Henry III these plenary sessions of the royal court grew more frequent and clearly more important, and came to be called parliaments. (The word means only "conversation" and, derivatively, an assembly where discussion occurs.) It also became customary, but by no means mandatory, to invite knights from the shires to these sessions. In 1264 Simon de Montfort summoned a parliament that included two knights elected from every shire and two townsmen or burgesses from every town. Edward followed him in this precedent.

Historians cannot assign an exact date for the division of Parliament into separate houses of Lords and Commons. The knights and burgesses seem to have met informally together since the time of Edward I, and these meetings gained official recognition at least from the reign of Edward III. Two unique features of the English Parliament helped enhance the influence of Commons. First, the lower aristocracy (that is, those knights who were not the tenants in chief or immediate vassals of the king) sat with the burgesses and learned to act

together in their mutual interests. (On the Continent the lower aristocracy and the townsmen sat as separate groups and rarely developed or supported common causes.) Second, representatives of the upper clergy gradually gave up active participation in the English Parliament, preferring to meet at their own convocations, and this weakened the influence of the House of Lords, which lost the function of representing the Church, and benefited the House of Commons.

Parliamentary Functions

We now think of Parliament as a limitation on royal power, but it was not this at all in its earliest development. Parliament, as the assembly of the king's vassals, had the obligation merely of giving the king advice. In addition, the king found Parliament a valuable adjunct to his own administration, for it promulgated and enlisted support for his decisions, strengthened royal justice, and facilitated the collection of taxes. It was therefore in the king's interest to make the assembly broadly representative of the free classes. In summoning the Parliament of 1295 Edward cited a dictum taken from the Justinian Code: "What touches all, by all should be approved."

Parliament's role in the collection of taxes led to the development of a true system of representation. The Magna Carta, feudal custom, and prudence had required that the king seek the consent of his subjects for new taxes. He could not ask all freeholders of the realm individually. He might seek the consent of the separate shires and the towns, but this was slow and awkward. Edward ingeniously simplified the procedure of consent. Through special writs, he ordered the shires and the towns to elect representatives and to grant them *plena potestas* ("full power") to grant him money. These representatives, gathered in Parliament, thus had authority to consent to taxes and to bind their electors back home. Paradoxically,

To secure his dominion over Wales, Edward I constructed in the years after 1277 eight great castles. These huge structures give testimony to the resources and organizational skills that the English monarchy commanded. Edward's Welsh castles represent the culmination of castle building in the Middle Ages. Shown in the photograph is Harlech castle, begun in 1283.
(Photo: Black Star)

the unique powers of the English king laid the basis for the eventual, unique powers of Parliament.

As the supreme feudal council, Parliament was also England's highest court (an honor the House of Lords retains today). The members attending its sessions would carry petitions or appeals from decisions made in lower courts; whereas a sheriff or shire court might have been subject to intimidation, Parliament would not be. By welcoming petitions, the king thus made his justice better known and respected throughout the realm. Some historians see in the role of Parliament as high court the ultimate source of its sovereignty.[4] As with our own Supreme Court the decisions of Parliament determined the future policies of all English courts. The decisions were thus nearly the equivalent of legislation, and from them there was no appeal.

---

[4] The idea was first strongly argued in C. H. McIlwain, *The High Court of Parliament: A Historical Essay on the Boundaries Between Legislation and Adjudication in England,* 1962.

At Edward's death in 1307 the English constitution had acquired certain distinctive features. The constitution was not contained in a single written document but was defined by both custom and statute law. The king was the chief of the state, but it was recognized that the important men of the kingdom should have some participation in the decision-making processes, especially regarding taxes. Parliament gave this policy its practical implementation. In spite of later changes these principles still underlie the English constitution. This extraordinary continuity over centuries is testimony to the sound construction that the medieval English kings, lords, and commoners gave to their government and their realm.

France

In France as in England the thirteenth century was primarily an age of constitutional consolidation. The successor of Philip Augustus, Louis VIII, ruled for only three years (1223–1226), but his reign was notable for several reasons. He was the first Capetian king not to be crowned in his father's lifetime; the Capetians had finally established that their claim to the monarchy was based on inheritance and not upon election. He campaigned personally against the Albigensian heretics in southern France, and his victories prepared the way for the eventual inclusion of Toulouse and Languedoc in the royal domain (these were the last major additions to the royal lands until the late fifteenth century). He adopted the policy of supporting younger sons and younger brothers by granting them territories, the so-called appanages. This policy, continued by his successors, ultimately created powerful and troublesome princely lines in France.

St. Louis

At Louis's death in 1226 the throne passed to Louis IX, St. Louis, one of the great figures of the thirteenth century. Louis was recognized as a saint even during his lifetime. He attended at least two masses a day, was sternly abstemious in food and drink, often washed the feet of the poor and the wounds of lepers, and was scrupulously faithful to his wife, Margaret of Provence, who, like her husband, bore an aura of sanctity.[5] However, his personal asceticism did not preclude a grand conception of royal authority. He added new pomp to court ceremonies and freely acted against the pope's wishes whenever the interests of the monarchy or his people seemed to require it. Three great ideals informed his policies as king: more effective justice within his kingdom, peace with its neighbors, and war against the Muslims, who still held Jerusalem.

Legal Reforms

Louis made no attempt to extend the royal domain at the expense of the nobles of the realm or to deprive them of their traditional powers and jurisdictions, but he did expect them to be good vassals. He forbade wars among them, arbitrated their disputes, and insisted that his ordinances be respected; he was the first king to legislate for the whole of France. Although Louis did not suppress the courts of the great nobles, he and his judges listened to appeals from their decisions, so that royal justice would be available to all his subjects. The king liked to sit in the open under a great oak at Vincennes near Paris to receive personally the petitions of the humble. The prestige which the piety and fairness of his decisions lent to royal justice was his great contribution to its growth.

During Louis's reign jurists began to clarify and codify the laws and customs of France. The most important of these compilations was the

---

[5] One of Margaret's burdens was the intense jealousy of her mother-in-law, Blanche of Castile. In the early years of his marriage, Louis supposedly had to meet with his wife secretly on the palace staircase to escape his mother's watchful eye. This did not, however, prevent the royal couple from having 11 children.

In this fourteenth-century manuscript illumination, St. Louis hears the pleas of his humble and defenseless subjects, chiefly women and a monk. Note the hanged felons in the left panel. The picture illustrates the abiding reputation for justice that St. Louis earned for the French monarchy.
(Photo: New York Public Library/Picture Collection)

Establishments of St. Louis, drawn up before 1273 and once wrongly attributed to the king himself. It contained, besides royal ordinances, the civil and feudal customs of several northern provinces and seems to have been intended for the guidance of judges and lawyers. It was not an authoritative code, but it and other compilations helped bring a new clarity and system to French law.

Louis strengthened the royal administration in other ways. He established the *enquêteurs,* or special wandering inspectors, who investigated the performance of the local officials of the royal domain, namely, the *baillis* and the *sénéchaux*. In his reign the Parlement of Paris became fully independent of the royal court. (The Parlement of Paris was never, like the English Parliament, a representative assembly, but was always a tribunal or court of law.) Louis confirmed its status as the highest court in France, a position it retained until 1789.

Peace and War

Louis sought peace with his Christian neighbors. French monarchs had traditionally claimed some land south of the Pyrenees Mountains, which had formed the Spanish March under Charlemagne (see Map 6.3), and the Spanish kings of Aragon in turn claimed large areas of Languedoc in southern France (see Map 8.4). Rather than settling this dispute through war, Louis negotiated the Treaty of Corbeil (1258) with the Aragonese king, with each side renouncing its claims. This settlement defined the French-Spanish border for the next 200 years (see Map 9.1).

Peace with England was harder to attain. The English still held Aquitaine and Gascony and were not reconciled to the loss under King John of their extensive fiefs north of the Loire River. Louis repulsed an English invasion at Saintes in 1242 but then actively sought peace with his English foe. At the Treaty of Paris in

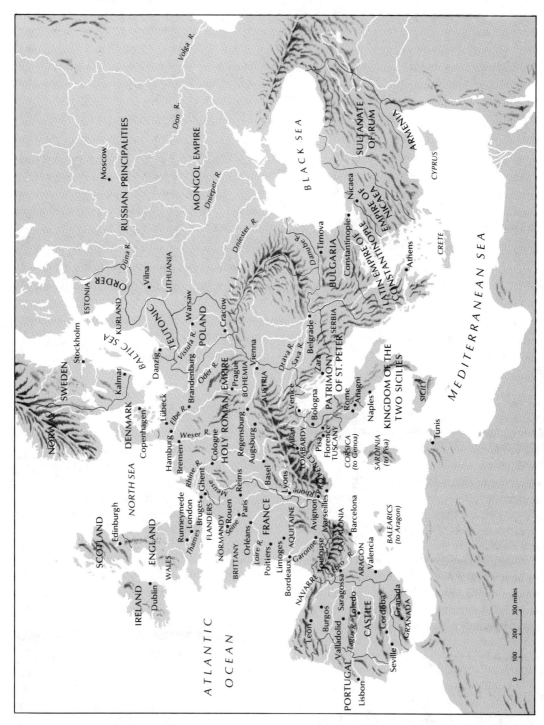

MAP 9.1. EUROPE CA. 1250

1259 Louis relinquished several territories that his troops had occupied along the borders of Gascony, and in return King Henry III of England abandoned his claims to the lands that John had lost and agreed to perform liege homage to Louis for his fief of Gascony. The Treaty of Paris was unpopular in France; many believed that in ceding the Gascon borderlands Louis had given away more than the military situation warranted. Louis replied that these liberal terms might enable Henry's sons and his own to live thereafter in peace, as was proper for vassals and lords.

Louis, who believed that a principal duty of a Christian king was to lead a crusade, led two, one in 1248 against Egypt and the other in 1270 against Tunis. Both expeditions proved to be fiascos, but they were significant in at least one way: these were the last major Western crusades.

Philip IV

Louis's successors were able to preserve the strength, but not the serenity, of his reign. His grandson Philip IV, the Fair (1285–1314), is perhaps the most enigmatic of the medieval French kings; neither contemporaries nor later historians have agreed on his abilities. To some, Philip has seemed capable and cunning; to others, phlegmatic and uninterested, content to leave the business of government almost entirely to his ministers. If Philip lacked the personal ability to rule, he at least had the capacity to select strong ministers as his principal advisers. They were usually laymen trained in Roman law and possessing a high opinion of royal authority. They considered the king to be not merely a feudal monarch who ruled in agreement with the magnates of his realm but rather an "emperor in his own land" whose authority was free from all restrictions (the root sense of *legibus solutus,* "absolute") and subject to no higher power on earth. According to some historians, Philip's reign registers the triumph of

a new "lay spirit," which overthrew the ecclesiastical and clerical domination of the earlier Middle Ages.[6]

The greatest obstacle to the advance of Philip's power was Edward I of England, master of the extensive fief of Gascony. Philip's resolve to drive England from the Continent resulted in intermittent wars from 1294 to 1302. To punish the English economically Philip tried to block the importation of English wool into Flanders. The Flemish towns revolted. Philip marched against them but was overwhelmed at Courtrai in 1302 by the towns' militias. This defeat deprived Philip of all hope of expelling the English from the Continent.

These costly wars had placed a heavy burden on the royal finances. To replenish the treasury Philip confiscated all the property of the Jews and drove them from his realm; he also imprisoned foreign merchants to extort money from them and arrested the members of the Knights Templars within France and brought them to trial, hoping to obtain their extensive possessions.

The Templars were originally a military-religious order, founded to aid pilgrims and to support crusades in the Holy Land. Through donations the order had grown enormously wealthy over the years, so that by the fourteenth century it had enough riches and influence to function as an international bank. To Philip, suppression of the order and confiscation of its properties offered a means to fill a depleted royal treasury. He brought the Templars to trial on false charges witnessed to by his hand-picked cronies and pressured a reluctant pope to suppress the order. But instead of transferring the order's French possessions to the royal treasury, the pope gave the properties to another religious order, the Knights Hospitalers. The royal treasury received only compensation for the costs of the trial.

---

[6] The most extensive statement of this important thesis is Georges de Lagarde, *La naissance de l'esprit laïque au déclin du moyen âge,* 3rd ed., 1956–1963.

Finally, Philip insisted on his right to demand from the Church "free gifts" that were actually taxes. The issue led to a protracted dispute with Pope Boniface VIII (see pp. 344–345). In seeking to dominate these international powers—the Templars and the Church itself—Philip showed his determination to become truly sovereign in his own lands.

Philip's Heritage

In trying to achieve an absolute monarchy, Philip upset the delicate feudal equilibrium of the France of St. Louis. He left at his death a deeply disturbed France. The Flemish towns remained defiant, and the strained relation of the monarchy with its principal vassal, the king of England, threatened to produce a major war. Under Philip's successors, with the outbreak of the Hundred Years' War, France entered one of the darkest periods of its history.

The Iberian Kingdoms

The Christian *Reconquista* had achieved all but final victory by 1236 with only Granada still in Muslim hands. The principal challenge now was the consolidation of the earlier conquests under Christian rule and the achievement of a stable constitutional order.

The three major Christian kingdoms that emerged from the Christian offensive were Portugal, Castile (including León), and Aragón (including Catalonia and Valencia), but they were not really united within their own territories. The Christian kings had purchased the support of both old and new subjects through generous concessions during the course of the *Reconquista*. Large communities of Jews and Muslims gained the right to live under their own laws and elect their own officials, and favored towns were granted special royal charters, known as *fueros,* that permitted them to maintain their own forum, or court. Barcelona

and Valencia in the kingdom of Aragon and Burgos, Toledo, Valladolid, and Seville in the kingdom of Castile were virtually self-governing republics in the thirteenth century. Among other groups, the military aristocracy was highly privileged. The magnates,. or *ricos hombres,* particularly in Castile, the largest of the Iberian kingdoms, held much of their lands not as fiefs but as allods (properties in full title), and this reinforced their independent spirit. The clergy of course formed still another powerful and privileged group. Moreover, the Iberian kings had to reckon with three wealthy religious orders of knights, the Calatrava, Santiago, and Alcántara, which had been founded about 1200 to aid in the struggle against the infidel and that were now able to wield independent financial and military power.

To hold all these elements together under a common government was a formidable task, but the kings retained real advantages. The tradition of war against the infidel gave to kings a special prestige. And their rivals were too diverse and too eager to fight one another to be able to present a united challenge.

Sooner than other Western monarchs, the Iberian kings recognized the practical value of securing the consent of their powerful subjects to major governmental decisions, particularly regarding taxes. By the end of the twelfth century they made frequent use of representative assemblies, called Cortes. Although they never achieved the constitutional position of the English Parliament because there were too many of them, the Cortes were the most powerful representative assemblies in Europe during the thirteenth century.

In order to impose a stronger, essentially feudal sovereignty over their subjects, the Iberian kings set about systematizing the laws and customs of their realms, thus clarifying both their own prerogatives and their subjects' obligations. For example, King Diniz of Portugal reorganized royal finances and administration, suppressed the Templars, and won from the papacy concessions that gave him wide powers over the Portuguese Church. Alfonso X of Castile issued an encyclopedia of legal institutions, meant to instruct lawyers and guide judges. This code, known as the *Siete Partidas* ("Seven Divisions"), was thoroughly imbued with the spirit of Roman law and presented the king as the source of all justice. Alfonso was in no position to achieve a true absolutism in his government, but the code did serve to educate the people to the high dignity of kingship. Even more than in England and France, feudal government in the Iberian kingdoms rested on a delicate compromise between royal authority and private privilege, and this apparently fragile system worked tolerably well.

With the achievement of fairly stable governments the Iberian kingdoms were free to play a larger role in the affairs of Europe. Aragon in particular, with an opening on the Mediterranean Sea, made its power felt. In 1229 James I captured the Balearic Islands. His son Peter III made himself king of Sicily, after a revolt known as the Sicilian Vespers (1282) drove from the island a French dynasty of rulers. Sardinia was taken from the Pisans in 1326. A seemingly invincible company of Catalan mercenaries besieged Constantinople (1302–1307), then captured Athens and subjugated it to Catalan domination until 1388. The expansion of the Iberian kingdoms was to be a major theme in European history for the next several hundred years.

The Holy Roman Empire

While the English, French, and Iberian kingdoms were moving toward greater unity under more centralized governments, the German and Italian territories of the Holy Roman Empire were disintegrating into a large number of small and virtually autonomous principalities. Frederick Barbarossa had negotiated an uneasy peace with the pope and the Italian towns in the last years of his reign, but the struggle was renewed soon after his death in 1190. Barbarossa's son Henry VI had married Constance, heiress to the Norman Kingdom of the Two Sicilies. Their son Frederick II thus had a legal claim to southern Italy as Constance's heir, and a moral claim to the German throne. The prospect of Italian unification under German auspices disturbed both the papacy and the free cities of Lombardy. The towns feared the direct domination of the emperor, while the papacy believed that its liberty would not survive were it to be encircled by German lands. In his brief reign of seven years Henry VI had little chance to effect the "union of the Kingdom with the Empire," as contemporaries called this fateful policy. It was a dream that was to elude his son too.

Frederick II Hohenstaufen

Frederick II (1194–1250) is one of the most fascinating personalities of the Middle Ages. A contemporary called him *stupor mundi* ("wonder of the world"). Later historians have hailed him as the first modern ruler, the prototype of the Renaissance despot, the cold and calculating statesman, a Machiavellian before Machiavelli. Frederick spoke six languages, loved learning, patronized poets and translators, founded a university at Naples, and, after a fashion, conducted scientific experiments. It had been said, for example, that a baby who hears no voices will grow up speaking Hebrew, which supposedly was man's first and most natural language. He therefore had an infant raised in total silence, to see if this were true. He wrote a scholarly tract on hunting with falcons. He also corrected Aristotle by writing on the margins of his works in several places, "It isn't so."

Several princes had contended for the German throne upon Henry VI's death. Pope Innocent III, disappointed in them all, supported Frederick's candidacy. Innocent's successor,

Emperor Frederick II, in the ship showing the imperial eagles, watches his soldiers assaulting prelates on their way to a council summoned by Pope Gregory IX in 1241. This contemporary illustration of the emperor's sacrilegious behavior, taken from a manuscript, is a good example of the war of propaganda by which both pope and emperor sought to win public sympathy.
(Photo: The Granger Collection)

Honorius III, crowned Frederick emperor in 1219 on the double promise that he would renounce his mother's inheritance of southern Italy and lead a crusade to Palestine. Frederick procrastinated on both agreements, creating lasting difficulties with the Church.

Emperor Frederick influenced German development in several fundamental ways. He established on the empire's eastern frontier a military-religious order, the Teutonic Knights, who eventually created the Prussian state; recognized Bohemia as a hereditary kingdom and

Lübeck as a free imperial city; and issued the earliest charter of liberties to the Swiss cantons. His most important policy, however, was to confer upon the German ecclesiastical princes and the lay nobles virtual sovereignty within their own territories. The emperor retained only the right to set the foreign policy of the empire, make war and peace, and adjudicate disputes between princes or subjects of different principalities. All other powers of government passed to the princes; no later emperor could regain what Frederick gave away.

In Italy Frederick pursued a much different policy. For the government of the Kingdom of the Two Sicilies he relied upon a trained lay bureaucracy. He rigorously centralized his administration, suppressed local privileges, imposed a universal tax in money upon his subjects, recruited his army from all classes and from Muslims as well as Christians, and issued a constitution which, in the spirit of Roman

Art historians speculate that Emperor Frederick II himself commissioned this fierce bronze falcon, perhaps to surmount his staff. It is, in any case, of Italian manufacture and dates from ca. 1200. Frederick was devoted to falconry and even wrote the standard medieval text on the sport.
(Photo: Metropolitan Museum of Art, The Cloisters Collection)

law, interpreted all jurisdiction as stemming from the emperor.

While seeking to build a strong and centralized government in Italy, Frederick had to face the increasingly bitter opposition of the popes and the free cities of the north. Pope Gregory IX excommunicated him in 1227 because of his failure to lead an Eastern crusade. Frederick then departed on the crusade but preferred to negotiate rather than fight and made a treaty with the Muslims that guaranteed unarmed Christian pilgrims access to Jerusalem. The more militant among the Western Christians believed that this treaty was dishonorable. He returned to Italy in 1229 and came to terms with Pope Gregory a year later.

The Lombard towns remained fearful of his designs and finally leagued against him. He defeated them at Cortenuova in 1237, but his success once more awakened in Gregory fears of encirclement, and Frederick was again excommunicated. Both sides struggled to win the public sympathy of Europe, but the tide of history began to turn against Frederick. To break the power of the Lombard towns he unsuccessfully besieged Parma in 1248. In 1250 death cut short his efforts to unify Italy under imperial auspices.

There are some historical figures whose careers seem to summarize a given epoch and to predict the one to come. Frederick is such a figure. In Germany he reinforced a political fragmentation that had become ever more pronounced since the eleventh century. In southern Italy he completed the constitutional reorganization that the Norman kings, his forebears, had begun. He does resemble the later Renaissance tyrant and the modern statesman, but he was also perhaps the last emperor to take seriously the grand vision of the Christian empire. The chronicler who called him the wonder of the world wrote with perspicacity.

III. THE CHURCH

Since the time of the Gregorian reform of the eleventh century, the papacy had sought to build in Europe a unified Christian commonwealth, one based on faith and on obedience to Peter, in which European princes and peoples might work out their salvation in fraternal peace. In the thirteenth century, the Church came close to achieving this grand design, but it still had to face powerful challenges to both Christian unity and its own leadership.

The Growth of Heresy

From the fifth until nearly the eleventh century no major heresies had troubled the Western Church, a sure indication of intellectual and spiritual torpor. From about the year 1000, however, chroniclers begin to note with growing frequency the appearance of heretics and sporadic attempts to suppress them.

The spread of heresy in the eleventh and twelfth centuries was partially a reaction to abuses within the established Church. Angered by the wealth and moral laxity of the clergy, heretics rejected the claimed privileges of the official priesthood. Heresy had social roots also. The continuing increase of population brought many social dislocations in its wake. The young were too numerous for the positions and jobs left to them by the aged. Young men, frustrated in their hopes for a career, and unmarriageable young women filled society. The movement into new territories, the growth of towns, the appearance of new trades and industries all created strong psychological tensions, which often found an outlet in heretical movements. Within the towns, for example, heresy offered a form of social protest to the urban poor. It held potential for rich townsmen, too, inasmuch as traditional Christianity had been highly suspicious of wealth, particularly when earned in the marketplace, and gave the rich merchant little assurance of reaching heaven. Nobles envied the property and power of the Church; to them, heresy offered a justification for seizing the wealth of a corrupt Church for themselves. Heresy had a particular appeal to women. Many could not marry because of the large dowry demanded, and could not enter a religious order, as this also required a monetary contribution. Without a firm and stable social niche, many women had cause for intense dissatisfaction with both Church and society. Many heretics made a special effort to recruit women, conducting schools for them and teaching them how to read the Scriptures at a time when the established Church largely ignored their needs.

This was also an age of spiritual tension. Many laymen wanted a more mystical and emotional reward from religion, but were denied such satisfaction because they were given no opportunity to study the Bible, to hear it read in the vernacular, or to be moved by sermons. These were the exclusive activities of monks. A principal effort of both the new heresies and the new movements within the Church was to break this monastic monopoly of the religious experience.

The Waldensians and Albigensians

The first heretics appeared about the year 1000 and seem to have been reformers who denounced the Church for its failings but offered no solutions for its problems. Then about 1170 a rich merchant of Lyons, Peter Waldo, adopted a life of absolute poverty and gave himself to preaching. He soon attracted followers, who came to be known as "the poor men of Lyons" or Waldensians. The Waldensians attacked the moral laxness of the clergy and extended their denunciations to the sacraments they administered. This group was declared heretical by the Lateran Council of 1215, but the Church never succeeded in suppressing the movement. The Waldensian Church still exists, although its theology was later much transformed by Protestant influences.

Far more powerful in their own day, though not destined to survive the Middle Ages, were the Cathari, or Albigensians, named for the town of Albi in Languedoc. The Albigensians' religious attitudes were greatly influenced by Manicheanism, a belief that antedated Christianity. It continued to survive among various small sects in Asia Minor and the Balkans. The Albigensians, like the Manicheans, believed that two principles, or deities, a god of light and a god of darkness, were fighting for supremacy in the universe. The good person must help the god of light vanquish the evil god of darkness, who had created and ruled the material world. The true Albigensians led a life of rigorous asceticism. They abstained from sexual intercourse, as procreation replenished the earth, the domain of the god of darkness. Marriage they regarded as hypocrisy, and intercourse within it worse than any other sexual sin. They abstained from meat, since it was sexually reproduced. Fish was, however, allowed, as the Albigensians were not familiar with the mating habits of aquatic animals. Because a sect that preached against marriage and procreation risked bringing about its own extinction, the Albigensians reached a practical compromise: those who abided by these stringent regulations were the *Perfecti* (they formed the priesthood); those who did not live by this stern code were the believers. A believer at the point of death could hope to be initiated into the ranks of the perfect through a kind of sacrament known as the *consolamentum,* which could be received only once.

The Albigensians, like the Waldensians, denied all value to the sacraments and priesthood of the established Church. They, of course, denied that Christ had ever taken on human flesh and saw no coming resurrection of the body. The Albigensians more truly constituted a non-Christian religion than a Christian heresy. Their appeal came principally from their use of a vernacular Testament and their willingness to preach in the vernacular to laypersons and from their moral fervor. Eventually they developed a strong organization with councils and a hierarchy of *Perfecti* under a chief resembling a pope.

The Suppression of Heresy

The Church initially responded to the heretics by attempting to reconvert them. One of the first and greatest leaders supporting the policy of reconversion was a priest from Castile named Dominic. About 1205 he began to preach among the Albigensians of Languedoc. Dominic insisted that his followers—whose mission was to preach—live in poverty and support themselves by begging; they thus constituted a mendicant, or begging, order. This new Order of Preachers grew with amazing rapidity, and was approved by the bishop of Toulouse (1215) and shortly afterward by the pope. To prepare its members for their work the Dominican Order stressed education, and thus eventually became the intellectual arm of the medieval Church. It counted among its members Albertus Magnus, Thomas Aquinas, and many other important religious thinkers of the thirteenth century.

Reconversion through preaching, persuasion, and example remained, however, a slow and uncertain process. Moreover, canon law failed to provide an effective remedy against the powerful, organized heresies of the twelfth century. The law did give the bishop the right to try a suspected heretic before his own court, but a heretic protected by important men in the community was virtually immune to prosecution, inasmuch as the bishop often feared offending the lay powers of his diocese. The lack of any effective legal way of dealing with heretics led to frequent riots against them—the medieval equivalent of the lynch law.

By the early thirteenth century the Church began to suppress heresy systematically by force. Pope Innocent III, of whom more will be said later, favored peaceful solutions to heresy until his legate Peter of Castelnau, who had excommunicated the count of Toulouse for tolerating heresy, was murdered by one of the count's retainers. Innocent concluded that as long as the nobility of Languedoc abetted heresy, nothing short of force would be effective against it. He therefore proclaimed a crusade against the Albigensians and the nobles who supported them. Knights from the north of France responded with zeal, but more out of greed for plunder than concern for orthodoxy. They defeated the nobles of Languedoc, but the problem of suppressing heresy remained.

In 1231 Pope Gregory IX instituted a special papal court to investigate and punish heresy. This was the famous papal Inquisition, which was to play a large and unhappy role in European history for the next several centuries. Through the Inquisition the popes sought to impose ordered and effective procedures upon the hunt for heretics. Like the English justices in eyre, the inquisitors were itinerant justices who visited the towns within their circuit at regular intervals. Strangers to the locale, they were not subject to pressures from the important men of the region. While the Inquisition was doubtless an improvement over riots, the procedures it adopted, which were a conscious break with traditions of canonical and medieval justice, were unfortunate. It accepted secret denunciations and, to protect the accusers, would not reveal their names to those denounced; at times it used evidence that was not even revealed to the accused; it denied the right of counsel and tortured obdurate heretics. The suspected heretics were, in fact, considered guilty before even being summoned to court. They could confess and repent, with the likely consequence of a heavy penance and usually the confiscation of their property. But they had little chance to prove their innocence.[7] As an ecclesiastical court the Inquisition was forbidden to shed blood, but here too its procedures were novel: it delivered relapsed or unrepentant heretics to the secular authority with full knowledge that they would be put to death.

The weaknesses of this system soon became apparent. Secret procedures protected incompetent and even demented judges. Inquisitors such as Bernard Gui in northern France or Conrad of Marsburg would today probably be considered psychotics; they shocked and disgusted even their contemporaries with their savage zeal. In addition, the Inquisition could function only where it had the close cooperation of the secular authority. It was never established in areas (for example, England) where strong kings considered themselves fully competent to control heresy. (Kings characteristically equated religious and civil rebellion and considered heresy to be identical with treason; even Frederick II, in spite of his bitter dispute with the papacy, imposed the death penalty upon heretics.) Dependence on the secular arm meant that the Inquisition ultimately became an instrument of royal as much as ecclesiastical policy. Philip IV of France, for example, used the Inquisition for the suppression of the Templars.

The number of heretics who were executed is not known exactly, but they were probably not more than several hundred. Fines, confiscations of property, and imprisonment were the usual punishments for all but the most obstinate heretics. There is no denying the unfortunate effect of the Inquisition upon the medieval papacy and Church, chiefly the association of the papacy with persecution and bloodshed to the inevitable erosion of its own prestige. And moral prestige has been, in all ages, the true basis of papal authority.

The Franciscans

Crusades and the Inquisition could not alone preserve the unity of the medieval Church. A spiritual regeneration was needed; the Church

---

[7] The one defense the accused had was to show malice and prejudice by identifying in court the otherwise anonymous accusers. This meant, however, that defense depended too often upon a good guess.

This fresco from the basilica of St. Francis at Assisi, traditionally attributed to the Florentine painter Giotto, shows the saint preaching to the birds. He congratulates them on their bright plumage and bids them sing in praise of God. The implication is that if people too recognize God's providence over them, they will respond with gratitude and joy.
(Photo: Alinari/Scala)

had to reach laypeople, especially those living in towns, and provide them with a spiritual message they could comprehend. The Dominicans were the first religious order to undertake this task as their primary mission. A major role was also played by a contemporary of St. Dominic's, St. Francis of Assisi.

Francis (1182?–1226) is probably the greatest saint of the Middle Ages and possibly the most sensitive poet of religious emotion. He succeeded in developing a style of piety that was both faithful to orthodoxy and abounding in new mystical insights. Since most of Francis's life is screened by legend, it is nearly impossible to reconstruct the exact course of his spiritual development. He seems to have devoted his young manhood to a self-conscious search for happiness, or, in the troubadour terminology he favored, for perfect joy. He first tried the rowdy amusements of the city. But dissatisfaction lingered; a biographer, Thomas of Celano, relates that after a severe illness Francis wandered on a May morning out to the blossoming fields but did not feel his accustomed joy. He then became a knight, but contentment still eluded him. Finally he turned to the religious life, instructed to do so, according to legend, by Christ himself, and adopted a life of poverty. Still, he believed that the test of true living, and indeed of true religion, ought to be joy: if all creatures, including men, recognized God's good providence over them, they would respond with joy. Joy would in turn assure universal harmony in the world and bring a kind of golden age.

Disciples began to gather almost at once around the "little poor man" of Assisi. In 1208 Francis obtained papal approval for the formation of a new religious order. This Order of Friars Minor (Lesser Brothers) grew with extraordinary rapidity; within ten years it reached some 5000 members and spread from Germany to Palestine; before the end of the century it was the largest order in the Church. Although the problems of administering a huge order did not command Francis's deepest interests, he did write a brief rule for the Friars and shortly before his death gave them some further recommendations in a document known as his Testament, in which he stressed the importance of poverty and simplicity.

He visited Palestine twice to preach to the infidels. In 1224 he is said to have received the stigmata, the marks of Christ's five wounds, thus becoming the first Christian saint to exhibit these signs of profound sanctity.

The success of the Friars Minor was an authentic triumph for the Church. Like the Dominicans, they carried their message primarily to laypeople in the growing towns, to the social classes where the heretics had hitherto won their greatest successes. Giving themselves to poverty and preaching, the Friars Minor came to include not only a second order of nuns but a third order of laypeople. Francis and his followers thus opened orthodox religion to delight in the natural world, to mystical and emotional experience, and to joy, which all people, they believed, including the ascetic and the pious, should be seeking.

Papal Government

In this period of profound social change and religious crisis the papacy faced serious obstacles in achieving its ideal of a unified, peaceful, and obedient European community. The pope of the thirteenth century whose reign best illustrates the aspirations and the problems of the medieval Church is Innocent III (1198–1216).

Innocent was somewhat ambiguous in defining his own powers.[8] He once stated that God had given him "not only the universal Church, but the whole world to govern," yet he also declared to Philip II of France that he

---

[8] For a good presentation of the ambiguities of Innocent's statements, see James M. Powell, *Innocent III—Vicar of Christ or Lord of the World?*, 1963.

had no wish to "lessen or disturb the jurisdiction and power of the king." Although he seems to have been willing enough to leave the princes undisturbed in the routine exercise of government, he did insist that they obey him in matters concerning the rights of the Church, the peace and common interests of Christendom, and their own personal morality. He sought with vigor and with remarkable, if always partial, success to achieve three major goals: the unity of Christendom, the hegemony of the papacy over Europe, and the clarification of Christian discipline and belief.

Within Europe heresy was the greatest threat to Christian unity, and though he ordered the crusade against the Albigensians, Innocent primarily looked to the new mendicant orders to counter the appeal of the heretics. Beyond Europe he sought reunion with the Eastern Church. At first condemning the Fourth Crusade, which was directed against fellow Christians, Innocent came to consider the fall of Constantinople to the crusaders a providential act, meant to achieve unification of the Western and Eastern churches. From 1204 to 1261 an imposed union did hold the members of the Eastern Church, or at least some of them, in obedience to Rome, but the violence of the Western Europeans during the crusade sowed among the conquered a lasting hatred that frustrated later efforts at permanent union.

The pope also sought to exert his leadership over the princes of Europe in all spiritually significant affairs. Some of his efforts to bend kings to his will have already been mentioned: his struggle with King John to install Stephen Langton as archbishop of Canterbury and his support of Frederick II as candidate for emperor. He also excommunicated Philip II of France for refusing to live with his queen. Innocent had occasion to reprimand the kings of Aragon, Portugal, Poland, and Norway. Indeed, no prior pope had scrutinized princely behavior with so keen an eye. Nevertheless, his interventions had uneven results, especially with regard to his dearest goal, the establishment of permanent peace among the European princes.

The Fourth Lateran Council

Trained in canon law, Innocent wanted to bring a new order to Christian belief and government. In 1215 he summoned some 1500 prelates to attend the Fourth Lateran Council. The Lateran Council identified the sacraments as exactly seven and reaffirmed that they are essential to salvation, imposed an obligation of yearly confession and communion on the faithful, and defined the dogma of transubstantiation, according to which the priest in uttering the words of consecration at mass annihilates the substance of bread and wine and substitutes for them the substance of Christ. Transubstantiation unambiguously affirmed the mass as miracle, and thus conferred a unique dignity and power on the Catholic priesthood. The council also pronounced on a wide variety of disciplinary matters—the qualifications for the priesthood, the nature of priestly education, the character of monastic life, the veneration of relics, and other devotional exercises. Only the councils of Nicaea, Trent, and Vatican II have had a greater influence on Catholic life.

The Papacy in the Thirteenth Century

Innocent's successors pursued his goals of ecclesiastical unity, though with only moderate success. Further attempts were made to heal the schism with the Eastern Church. At the Council of Lyons in 1274 representatives of the Eastern patriarch formally submitted to papal authority, but the union soon proved illusory. Innocent's successors also continued the work of codifying Church law. In 1234 Gregory IX

This ivory panel shows a bishop extending a blessing to a kneeling man and woman. Note the expressions worn by all. Harmony would prevail in a society guided by the Church. This was the principle governing the policies of Innocent III.
(Photo: Victoria & Albert Museum, London)

the finished constitution of the medieval Church.

Papal administration, and especially papal finances, continued to expand during the thirteenth century. Often desperate for funds to carry on their ambitious policies, the popes extracted substantial payments for appointments to office, imposed tithes (a tenth of income) upon the clergy, and sold exemptions and dispensations from the regulations of canon law. By the late thirteenth century the popes were clearly exploiting their spiritual powers for financial profit, and this was to prove a disastrous precedent.

Boniface VIII

By the late thirteenth century the papacy was facing a rising challenge from the princes of Europe, who sought to dominate the churches within their own territories. Both Philip IV of France and Edward I of England had been taxing the clergy through the fiction of asking, and always receiving, gifts, or subventions. In 1296 Pope Boniface VIII forbade all clergy to make grants without papal permission. Such a restriction would have given the pope a powerful if not controlling voice in royal finances, which no king could tolerate. The English simply ignored the order, but Philip retaliated by forbidding all exports of coin from his realm to Rome. Boniface, surprised by the forceful reaction, dropped his demands a year later.

In 1301 Philip arrested for treason a French bishop who also happened to be a papal legate, thus striking directly at the sovereignty of the pope and the immunities of his representatives. Boniface reprimanded Philip for his behavior, but the king responded by circulating defamatory accusations against the pope. Naturally Boniface felt that both his personal character and the papal authority were being threatened. He therefore issued a bull (all solemn papal letters were called bulls because they were closed with a seal, or *bulla*), known from its

published an authoritative collection of decretals (papal letters) to which additions were made in 1298 and 1314. Together with the *Decretum* of Gratian, these collections formed the Body of Canon Law, which in turn made up first two words as *Unam Sanctam,* declaring that Philip must submit to his authority or risk the loss of his immortal soul. In no mood to accept a rebuff, Philip sent one of his principal advisers to Italy, who with the aid of a Roman faction opposed to Boniface broke into the papal palace at Anagni and arrested the pope. The citizens of Anagni rescued Boniface shortly afterward, but he died in Rome only a few months later. The vulnerability of the papacy had been clearly demonstrated.

The succeeding popes capitulated to the French king and even revoked *Unam Sanctam.* Philip's victory was complete when a Frenchman was elected pope in 1305. Clement V never reached Rome, settling in the French-speaking, though imperial, city of Avignon in 1309. For the next 68 years the popes lived within the shadow of the French monarchy.

The medieval papacy hoped to serve as the vocal conscience of Europe. It was aided in this ambition by magnificent theological and legal systems and by a huge administrative apparatus. But the growth of papal power weakened the bishop's ability to maintain the moral discipline of his clergy and people, the result being an increasing measure of local chaos that permitted abuses to grow unchecked. Even the new intellectual rigor of Christian belief carried with it a certain risk for the spiritual life; cold intellectualism or a suffocating legalism might well threaten and dilute authentic piety. The Church has lived for hundreds of years with the achievements and unresolved problems bequeathed to it by the thirteenth century.

IV. THE SUMMER OF MEDIEVAL CULTURE

Whereas the twelfth century was the period of discovery and creation in the cultural growth of the medieval world, the thirteenth century was an age of intellectual synthesis. As the statesmen of Europe tried to unite law and custom in ordered constitutional systems, the cul-tural leaders tried to bring earlier intellectual traditions into harmony.

The Medieval Synthesis

An appreciation of thirteenth-century culture requires an understanding of the ideas and values the period was seeking to combine. The Scholastics were trying to reconcile the fundamental assumptions of Aristotelian philosophy with the fundamental attitudes of Christianity, the former asserting that human reason could probe the metaphysical structure of the universe unaided, the latter insisting on the necessity of divine revelation and grace.

In their attempt to reconcile these views medieval intellectuals aimed at nothing less than uniting two historical and cultural experiences, for medieval civilization was itself the product of two quite different epochs. The violence and desperation of the late Roman and early medieval periods had implanted in the medieval mind a deep conviction that the natural powers of human beings were inadequate to control their destiny, that they needed help through grace. The experiences of society after 1000 had, on the other hand, bred a new confidence in human capabilities. Aristotelian philosophy lent intellectual force to what experience seemed to be teaching: that human beings could attain, through their own efforts, some measure of truth and fulfillment in this present world.

In seeking to reconcile faith and reason, medieval people were trying to extract the common denominator of truth from the vastly different experiences through which they had passed. They wanted to construct an open intellectual system that would give a place to all truth and all values, wherever found, however they had been learned. The general nature of this effort at synthesis can be seen in three of the major achievements of the period: the Scholasticism of Thomas Aquinas, the Gothic cathedral, and the *Comedy* of Dante Alighieri.

MAP 9.2. MEDIEVAL UNIVERSITIES

Thomas Aquinas

The most gifted representative of Scholastic philosophy, and the greatest Christian theolo-

gian since Augustine, was St. Thomas Aquinas (1225?–1274), whose career well illustrates the character of thirteenth-century intellectual life. At 17 Thomas entered the new Dominican Order, perhaps attracted by its commitment to scholarship; he studied at Monte Cassino and Naples, and later, as a Dominican, at Cologne and Paris (see Map 9.2). His most influential teacher was another Dominican, Albertus Magnus, a German who wrote extensively on theological matters and questions of natural science, especially biology. Thomas was no intellectual recluse; he lectured at Paris and traveled widely across Europe, particularly in the business of his order and the Church.

In his short and active life Thomas produced a prodigious amount of writing: commentaries on biblical books and Aristotelian works, short essays on philosophical problems, a lengthy compendium of Christian apologetics, the *Summa contra Gentiles,* which was probably intended for Dominican missionaries working to convert heretics and infidels. However, his most important work was one he did not live to finish. Divided into three divisions on God, Man, and Christ, the *Summa Theologica* was meant to provide a comprehensive introduction to Christian theology and to present a systematic view of the universe that would do justice to all truth, natural and revealed, pagan and Christian.

Thomas brought to his task an extraordinary, subtle, and perceptive intellect, and his system (not unlike the feudal constitution) rests upon several fundamental, delicate compromises. In regard to faith and reason he taught that both are roads to a single truth. Reason is based ultimately on sense experience. It is a powerful instrument, but insufficient to teach people all that God wishes them to know. Nature is good, and humans can achieve some partial, temporary happiness in this life. But nature alone cannot carry them to ultimate fulfillment. Grace is still needed to bring nature to perfection and human beings to eternal salvation.

With respect to the fundamental structure of the universe, Thomas sought the common ground between two interpretations of reality,

inherited from the ancient philosophers and called in the medieval schools realism and nominalism. The realists maintained that universal terms—the common nouns that can be predicated on many individual objects, such as man or stone—refer to "real" entities that exist independently of the mind. Somewhere, in other words, there exists a "manness" or "stoneness" in which individual men or stones somehow participate. These general natures form a hierarchy or chain of being leading up to God. Their critics, the nominalists, said that the universal term, or common noun, is merely a *nomen* ("name"), a "breath of air," with no existence outside the mind. In the nominalist view, the universe has no knowable structure. It must be viewed as an aggregate of unique and autonomous beings. Philosophers can discern similarities among objects and place those objects into species and genera, but they cannot be certain that their classifications have a basis in reality.

Thomas, who was technically a moderate realist, argued that both views are correct. Each object in the universe is autonomous and unique but it is also representative of general species or classes. To possess this double dimension of meaning, each object must also be metaphysically a composite of two principles, one of which explains its unity with other objects and the other its individuality.[9] In broadest terms, the principle of unity is "act," meaning the act of being, as it is ultimately in their being that objects resemble one another. The principle of individuation is "potency," which limits act and renders an object unique. Motion or change in the universe is essentially a transition from potency to act. Only God is unlimited, unindividuated Being—"pure act" in Thomas's

---

[9] This two-dimensional view of reality is also reflected in Gothic art, in which the statues are at once individuals and yet manifestations of a higher order, and in Dante's *Comedy,* where the figures he encounters on his journey through the other world are both individual personalities and representatives of common human types.

definition. Only God cannot change, but He ultimately supports all change. In his proofs of God's existence, Thomas argued that instability, imperfection, and change, which we see all around us, point to the existence of an "unmoved mover," a principle of absolute perfection, stability, and power.

The *Summa* shows certain characteristic weaknesses of Scholasticism. Thomas affirmed that natural truth is ultimately grounded in observation, but in fact he observed very little. His critical distinction between act and potency, which he borrowed from Aristotle, was not founded on observation or experimentation. (He admitted these principles were in fact supersensory.) Many later thinkers found his system too speculative, too elaborate. Nonetheless, the *Summa* remains an unquestioned masterpiece of Western theology. It offers comment on an enormous range of theological, philosophical, and ethical problems, and it consistently attracts with its openness, perception, and wisdom.

John Duns Scotus

Thomas's system fell under critical scrutiny already in the generation following his death. Among his early critics the most influential was a Scottish Franciscan, John Duns Scotus (1265?–1308). Drawing inspiration from St. Augustine, Duns Scotus affirmed that faith was logically prior to reason; that is, unless faith had first suggested to reason that spiritual beings—God and angels—could exist, reason would never have arrived at a concept of them. Once the mind accepted the idea of God from faith, it could then prove the necessity for God's existence. To Duns Scotus the proof of God's existence was not based, as with Aquinas, on the perception of change in the universe, for he did not trust the accuracy of sense observation; rather, it derived from an exclusively intellectual analysis of the concept of God as a necessary being. In effect, he was restating

in revised form the "ontological proof" for God's existence, first formulated by Anselm of Canterbury (see p. 306). Later, in the seventeenth century, René Descartes, regarded as the founder of modern philosophy, would present still another version of the same argument. It has continued to tease philosophers until the present.

Because of the complexity of his thought, Scotus is traditionally called the "subtle doctor." His followers, who continued the tradition of sometimes unintelligible speculations, were "dunces" to their derisive critics. Scotus marks the transition between the synthetic, or constructive, period of medieval philosophy and a new period of analysis and criticism, which begins in the fourteenth century.

The Gothic Cathedral

Artists as well as theologians were attempting to present a systematic view of the universe reflective of all truth. The artistic counterpart to the Scholastic *Summas* was the Gothic cathedral.

The word *Gothic* was coined in the sixteenth century as an expression of contempt for these supposedly barbarous medieval buildings. In fact, the Goths had disappeared some 500 years before any Gothic churches were built. As used today, "Gothic" refers to the style of architecture and art that initially developed in the royal lands in France, including Paris and its surroundings, from about 1150. The abbey church of Saint-Denis near Paris, built by the Abbot Suger in 1144, is usually taken as the first authentic example of the Gothic style. The early Gothic churches were almost all urban cathedrals and were characteristically dedicated to the Virgin Mary. In the thirteenth century the Gothic style spread widely through Europe and found special application in the large churches built by the Franciscan and Dominican orders. The growth of cities also led to its expression in secular architecture: town halls, guildhalls, towers, gates, and private houses.

Technically, three engineering devices helped stamp the Gothic style: the broken rather than rounded arch; ribbed vaulting, which concentrated support around the lines of thrust and gave the buildings a visibly delineated skeleton; and the flying buttress, an external support that allowed the walls to be made higher and lighter. The flying buttress also freed sections of the walls from the function of supporting the roof and therefore permitted the use of large areas for windows. Romanesque architects had pioneered all three devices, but the Gothic engineers combined them and used them with unprecedented vigor and boldness.

Innovations were also made in the statues that adorned the buildings. Romanesque sculpture often conveyed great emotion and power but did not reflect the visible world. Sculptors now wanted their works to emulate reality, or at least its handsomest parts (decorative foliage, for example, was carved with such accuracy that the botannical models can be identified). Their statues were real and usually cheerful people, subtly exerting their own personalities without destroying the harmony of the whole.

The Gothic Spirit

These magnificent churches with their hundreds of statues took decades to construct and decorate, and many were never completed. The builders intended that the churches provide a comprehensive view of the universe and instruction in its sacred history. One principal element of the Gothic aesthetic is a strong sense of order. The naked ribs and buttresses and the intricate vaulting constitute a spectacular geometry that instills in the viewer a vivid impression of intelligence and logical relationships. The churches, reflecting the structure of the universe, taught that God, the master builder, created and still governs the natural world with similar logic.

This interior view of the nave of Reims Cathedral shows the ribbed vaulting that was characteristic of Gothic churches.
(Photo: ND–Giraudon)

The most distinctive aspect of the Gothic style is its use of light in a manner unique in the history of architecture. Once within the church, the visitor has entered a realm defined and infused by a warm, colored glow. In Christian worship light is one of the most ancient, common, and versatile symbols. It suggests to the worshiper mystical illumination, spiritual beauty, grace, and divinity itself.

The impressions rendered by the architecture and the stained glass were further developed by the performance of the sacred liturgy. Here music was also enlisted to convey the sense of an intricate and sublime harmony in God's care of the world. Paris in the thirteenth century witnessed a marked development of polyphonic music; the choirmasters seem to have sought a musical style that would parallel the complexity and the harmony of the surrounding cathedral. Through architecture, sculpture, and music, the believer was encouraged to feel the presence of God, to discern a universe permeated with his wisdom, sanctity, and loving concern.

Dante

Literary output in most vernacular languages grew continuously more abundant during the thirteenth century, except in English, which was retarded in its development by the continued dominance of a French-speaking aristocracy. Of several masterpieces the one that best summarizes the culture of the age is the *Comedy* of Dante Alighieri.

Dante was born in Florence in 1265. Little is known of his education, but he seems to have acquired a broad learning. The *Comedy* is one of the most erudite, and hence most difficult, poems of world literature.

Two experiences in Dante's life profoundly influenced his attitudes and are reflected in his works. In 1274, when he was (as he himself affirms) only nine years old, he fell deeply in love with a young girl named Beatrice. Much mystery surrounds her, but she seems to have been Beatrice Portinari, who later married into a prominent family and died in 1290. Dante could have seen her only rarely; we do not know if she ever returned his love. Still, in his youthful adoration of Beatrice he seems to have attained that sense of harmony and joy that the troubadours considered to be the great reward of lovers. In 1302 an experience of a much different sort shattered his life. For political rea-

In contrast to Romanesque sculpture which overflows with great displays of emotion, Gothic sculpture evokes a sense of calm and orderly reality, as can be seen in the jamb figures on the central portal of Chartres Cathedral.
(Photo: Marburg–Art Reference Bureau)

sons he was exiled from Florence. He spent the remaining years of his life wandering from city to city, a disillusioned, even bitter man. He died in 1321 and was buried at Ravenna.

The Comedy

Dante composed his masterpiece from 1313 to 1321. He called it a *commedia* in conformity with

The cathedral of Notre Dame in Paris, built ca. 1160–1200, is one of the early representations of the new Gothic style. That style sought to impart a sense of airiness and grace. Note here how the structure avoids any impression of massive support of its upper levels. Heaven, and not earth, was supporting these buildings.
(Photo: Rapho/Photo Researchers)

the Classical notion that a happy ending made any story, no matter how serious, a comedy; the adjective *divine* was added to its title only after his death. The poem is divided into three parts, which describe the poet's journey through hell, purgatory, and heaven.

The poem opens with Dante "in the middle of the way of this our life." An aging man, he has grown confused and disillusioned; he is lost in a "dark forest" of doubt, harassed by wild animals, symbols of his own untamed passions. The theme of the poem is essentially Dante's rediscovery of a former sense of harmony and joy. Leading him back to his lost peace are two guides. The first, Virgil, who represents human reason, conducts Dante through hell and then up the seven-storied mountain of purgatory to the earthly paradise, the vanished Eden, at its summit. In hell Dante encounters people who have chosen as their supreme goal in life something other than the love of God—riches, pleasures, fame, or power. Virgil shows Dante that the good life cannot be built upon such selfish choices. Reason, in other words, can enable humans to avoid the pitfalls of egoistic, material existence. Reason can accomplish even more than that; for, as embodied by Virgil, it guides Dante through purgatory and shows him how to acquire the natural virtues that are the foundations of the earthly paradise—a full and peaceful earthly existence. In the dignity and power given to Virgil, Dante shares the high regard for human reason characteristic of the thirteenth century. However, reason can take humans only so far. To enter heaven Dante

needs a new guide—Beatrice herself, representative of supernatural revelation and grace. She takes the poet through the heavenly spheres into the presence of God, "in Whom is our peace." The peace and joy of the heavenly court set the dominant mood at the poem's conclusion, in contrast to the confusion and violence of the dark forest with which it had opened.

Like many literary masterpieces the *Comedy* has several dimensions of meaning. On a personal level it summarizes the experiences of Dante's own life; it affirms that the youthful idealism and joy he had once so easily found were not proved false by age and bitter exile. The poem further reflects the great cultural issues that challenged his contemporaries—the relations between reason and faith, nature and grace, human power and the divine will. Dante, like Aquinas, was trying to combine two opposed views of human nature and its abilities to shape its own destiny. One, rooted in the very optimism of the twelfth and thirteenth centuries and in the more distant Classical heritage, affirmed that human beings were masters of themselves and the world. The other, grounded in the Judeo-Christian tradition, saw them, fundamentally, as lost children in a vale of tears. Both views had helped support human life and were therefore worth preserving. Dante's majestic panorama summarizes not only the medieval vision of the universe but also his estimation of what it meant to live a truly wise, truly happy, and truly human life.

In the thirteenth century, medieval civilization attained a new stability, and medieval institutions functioned with considerable success. Large-scale manufacture, long-range commercial exchanges, and sophisticated business practices gave the economy a distinctly capitalistic aura. In political life feudal governments consolidated and clarified their constitutional procedures, and parliaments and representative assemblies came to play a recognized role in the processes of government. Confronted with heresies that threatened its unity and dominance, the Church responded in part with crusades and the Inquisition, ultimately to its own detriment. At the same time orthodox religion enjoyed an authentic spiritual renewal, of which Francis of Assisi was the chief inspiration. The papacy energetically sought to lead the Western princes as their guide and conscience, but secular entanglements and fiscal problems threatened and gradually diluted its moral authority.

In cultural life this was a period not so much of new creations as of reordering and synthesis. The masterpieces of the age aimed at bringing together all parts of the medieval heritage into an ordered whole which would offer people a comprehensive understanding of the universe and a wise formula for living.

Medieval society in the thirteenth century seemed close to resolving its principal problems, whether economic, political, or cultural. In fact, however, the relative prosperity and peace, the institutional stability and intellectual synthesis were not to survive much beyond the year 1300. In the fourteenth century a new era of turmoil dawned for the medieval world. The close of the Middle Ages was a period of spectacular disasters, but also of profound changes. These changes greatly altered the character of the civilizations in both Eastern and Western Europe.

RECOMMENDED READING

Sources

Alighieri, Dante. *The Divine Comedy.* Louis Biancolli (tr.). 1966.

Aquinas, Thomas. *Basic Writings.* Anton C. Pegis (ed.). 1945.

★Brown, Raphael (ed. and tr.). *The Little Flowers of St. Francis.* 1971. Legends collected in the early fourteenth century exemplifying the style of Franciscan piety.

DeJoinville, Jean. *The Life of St. Louis.* René Hague (tr.). 1955.

Studies

Bisson, Thomas. *Medieval Representative Institutions.* 1973. Introductory essays.

Boase, T. S. R. *Boniface VIII.* 1933. Standard biography of the controversial pope.

★Copleston, Frederick. *Aquinas.* 1955.

Duby, Georges. *William Marshal: The Flower of Chivalry.* 1986. Sensitive biography of an Anglo-Norman knight.

Hillgarth, J. M. *The Spanish Kingdoms, 1250–1516.* 2 vols. 1978. Recent survey of Spanish history across the Late Middle Ages.

Holt, J. C. *Magna Carta.* 1965. Gives useful guidance to extensive literature.

Kantorowicz, Ernest H. *Frederick II.* E. O. Lorimer (tr.). 1957. Stimulating interpretation of the career of the great Hohenstaufen emperor.

Keen, Maurice. *Chivalry.* 1984. Sympathetic survey of the culture of medieval knights.

★ Le Roy Ladurie, Emmanuel. *Montaillou: The Promised Land of Error.* Barbara Bray (tr.). 1978. Social life in a small village in the Pyrenees, a center of heresy.

Little, Lester. *Religious Poverty and the Profit Economy in Medieval Europe.* 1978. Examines changes in economic attitudes in the thirteenth century.

Lyon, Bryce. *A Constitutional and Legal History of Medieval England.* 2nd ed. 1980.

Mundy, John H. *Europe in the High Middle Ages.* 1973. A general survey.

*Panofsky, Erwin. *Gothic Architecture and Scholasticism.* 1966. Examines the relationships between two great cultural monuments of the thirteenth century.

Powicke, F. M. *The Thirteenth Century, 1216–1307.* 1953. Basic survey of English political history.

Vacandard, E. *The Inquisition.* 1924.

Von Simson, Otto. *The Gothic Cathedral: Origins of Gothic Architecture and the Medieval Concept of Order.* 1962. Interprets Gothic style primarily in terms of its use of light.

---

* Available in paperback.

Chapter 10

The Crusades and Eastern Europe ca. 1100–1550

The peoples of Western Europe had remained fairly isolated from the East during the Early Middle Ages, a factor that added considerably to their economic and cultural backwardness. This isolation began to break down after the year 1000. Western pilgrims and crusaders in large numbers visited the Christian holy places in the East and for some two centuries maintained in the Latin Kingdom of Jerusalem a colony in Palestine. Western merchants established contact with the principal ports of the eastern Mediterranean and Black seas. A vigorous trade developed across the waters of the Mediterranean, and Westerners once more came to enjoy the spices and other products of the East. In the thirteenth century, some missionaries and merchants penetrated into Central Asia, and a few traveled as far as China. This greatly enlarged the geographic horizons of Europeans and made them aware that rich and brilliant civilizations existed beyond their borders. Westerners entered into intense military competition, close trade relations, and fruitful cultural exchanges with their Eastern neighbors. An appreciation of Western history therefore requires a knowledge of these Eastern peoples and the results of the increasing contact with them.

The East after the year 1000 was itself in a state of flux. The three states that dominated the region in the Early Middle Ages—the Byzantine Empire, the Arab Caliphate, and Kievan Rus—were all in manifest decline. Turkish peoples—first the Seljuks and then the Ottomans—built states that, in large part, claimed the territorial heritage of both Byzantium and the caliphate. By the fifteenth century the Ottoman Empire had come to dominate the land bridge between Europe and Asia and presented the West with a formidable military challenge. This powerful and aggressive empire gave Europeans strong incentive for searching out new trade routes around Ottoman territories to the more distant East.

The spiritual and cultural heritage of both Byzantium and Kievan Rus largely passed to a new Russian state that had its capital at Moscow and was the direct ancestor of the modern Russian Empire and the Soviet Union. Like Byzantium before it, Muscovite Russia assumed the function of guarding the eastern frontiers of Christian Europe.

The contacts, the rivalries, the economic and cultural exchanges begun or restored in the second half of the Middle Ages have continued to play a major role in the history of the peoples in both these areas of the world.

I. THE CRUSADES

In the eleventh century the Western peoples launched a series of armed expeditions to the East in an effort to free the Holy Land from Islamic rule. These expeditions are traditionally known as the crusades. Not long ago it was fashionable to consider the crusades a central event in medieval history that stimulated trade, encouraged the growth of towns, and contributed to the establishment of a stable political order in the West. More recently, many historians have alleged that the campaigns in the East were costly failures, that they worsened relations not only with the Muslims but with Eastern Christians, and that the crusading enthusiasm in Europe all too frequently found an outlet in riots and pogroms directed against those most accessible infidels, the Jews.[1]

Whatever their net effect, the crusades manifest more dramatically than any other event the spirit of Western society in the eleventh and twelfth centuries—its energy, brash self-confidence, compelling faith, and frequent bigotry. At the same time that they helped acquaint the Western peoples with ideas and techniques of civilizations more sophisticated than their own, the crusades were an initial phase in the expansion of the West—the massive exportation of European people and skills beyond the confines of their narrow continent, a movement that has since influenced civilizations in every part of the world.

Origins

The origins of the crusades must be sought in a double set of circumstances: the social and

---

[1] One of the leading modern historians of the crusading movement, Sir Steven Runciman, concludes his three-volume study with the following strong condemnation: "The Holy War itself was nothing more than a long act of intolerance in the name of God, which is the sin against the Holy Ghost." *A History of the Crusades,* vol. 3, 1954, p. 480.

religious movements in the West and the political situations in the East. In the Christian West a favorite form of religious exercise was the pilgrimage, a personal visit to a place made holy through the lives of Christ or his saints or sanctified by the presence of a sacred relic. Common in the West since the fourth century, pilgrimages gained in popularity during the eleventh century as Europe experienced religious revival and reform. Bands of pilgrims, sometimes numbering in the thousands, set forth to visit the places sacred to their religion, and of these Palestine was the most holy.

Inevitably, this pilgrim traffic was jeopardized by the Seljuk Turks, Muslim nomads who in the eleventh century had overrun most of the Middle East. It does not appear that the Seljuks consciously sought to prevent the pilgrims from reaching Palestine, but they did impose numerous taxes and tolls upon them, and many Christians became incensed at the domination of the holy places of Palestine by a strong, aggressive Islamic power.

Perhaps still more disturbing was the prospect that the Christian empire of Byzantium would also be overrun. The Seljuks had crushed a Byzantine army at the Battle of Manzikert in 1071, and the road to Constantinople seemed wide open. The fall of Byzantium would remove the traditional barrier to Islamic advance to the West and would be a major disaster to the Christian world. In 1095 a delegation from the emperor of Byzantium requested the help of Pope Urban II, who resolved to appeal to the Western knights and princes to go to the aid of their fellow Christians in the East. Social and religious conditions in Europe helped assure that Urban's summons would evoke a powerful response.

The Motives of the Crusaders

The crusades were viewed by those who participated in them primarily as acts of religious

International and Military History	Political History
1071 Byzantine defeat at Manzikert by Seljuks	
1095 Urban II preaches First Crusade	
1099 Great crusader victory at Antioch; Jerusalem taken	
1100	
1147–49 Second Crusade ends in failure	
1189–1192 Third Crusade; climax of crusading effort	
1200	
1204 Fourth Crusade; establishment of Latin Empire at Constantinople	
1223 First Mongol raid into Russia	
1237–1242 Mongols invade Russia and Hungary; establishment of Khanate of the Golden Horde	
1291 Fall of Acre, last crusader outpost on Asiatic mainland	1261 Restoration of Greek empire
1299–1326 Othman begins expansion of Ottoman lands	1290–1326 Osman organizes Ottoman state in Asia Minor
1300	
1328–1341 Ivan I, prince of Moscow, begins "gathering of the Russian land"	1326 Moscow becomes principal see of Russian church
	1328–1341 Ivan I, Kalita, prince of Moscow
	1328 Ivan obtains *yarlik* from Mongol kham
1380 Prince Dmitri Donskoi defeats Mongols at Kulikovo on the Don	
1400	
	c. 1430 Organization of Janissaries, elite corps of Ottoman army
	1451–1481 Mohammed II, the Conqueror, Ottoman sultan
	1453 Fall of Constantinople; end of Byzantine Empire
1453 Fall of Constantinople to Ottomans	1462–1505 Ivan III, the Great, ruler of Russia; first national sovereign
1471–1478 Ivan III, the Great, takes Novgorod	1472 Ivan III marries Sophia, niece of last emperor of Constantinople
	1497 Ivan promulgates *Sudebnik*, first code since *Russkaia Pravda*
1500	
1521 Suleiman II, the Magnficent, takes Belgrade	
1526 Suleiman annihilates kingdom of Hungary	
1529 Suleiman besieges Vienna; highwater mark of Ottoman expansion into Europe	

1100–1550/TIMELINE

Social and Economic History	Cultural and Intellectual History

— 1071 ——————————————

— 1100 ——————————————

— 1200 ——————————————
1204–1261   Period of Latin rule in Constantinople;
empire never fully recovers

c. 1200   *Song of Igor's Campaign;* if authentic,
oldest Russian epic

1274   Council of Lyon achieves temporary reunion
of the churches

— 1300 ——————————————

1347   The Black Death in the East

1370?–1430?   Painter Andrei Rublev active in Russia

— 1400 ——————————————

c. 1400   Flight of scholars and manuscripts out of
Constantinople to West intensifies

1439   Council of Florence proclaims renunion of churches

c. 1450   Ottomans introduce the *devshirme,* or levy of boys

1462–1505   Ivan III of Russia introduces new form of
land grant, the *pomest'e*

1485–1495   Ivan the Great brings in Italian architects to
aid in rebuilding of Kremlin

— 1500 ——————————————

This drawing, from the twelfth-century West-
minster psalter, captures in graceful lines some
characteristics of the crusading knight. Crosses
are everywhere about him, reminding the
viewer of the religious purpose of his venture.
The man, dressed for war, affects a gesture of
prayer. He is young, even his horse appears to
be young. The crusades had great appeal to
the superfluous young warriors of a growing
Europe. They eagerly sought to win their fortunes in the East; if they failed to do so, they
could at least hope that they had done God's
will.

(Photo: © The British Library)

devotion. Even before Urban made his appeal,
the idea had gained currency in the West that
God would reward those who fought in a good
cause; that is, that wars could be holy. The
crusaders also shared the conviction manifest in
the movement for Church reform that the good
man ought not simply to endure the evils of
the world but should attempt to correct them.
This active, confident spirit is in obvious contrast to the resignation to evil and the withdrawal from the world recommended by most
Christian writers of the Early Middle Ages.

Social and economic motivations also contributed to these holy enterprises. The age of
mass pilgrimages and crusades, from about
1050 to 1250, corresponds to the period in medieval history in which the European population was growing most rapidly. The crusades
may be considered one further example of the
expanding Western frontier, similar in motivation and character to the Spanish *Reconquista*
or the German push to the East. Of course, the
crusades differed in at least one significant way
from these other ventures. They were almost
exclusively military expeditions of Europe's
warrior classes; peasants did not settle in Palestine in significant numbers, as they did in the
lands of Eastern Europe or in the Iberian Peninsula.

The knights of Europe were particularly
sensitive to the pressures created by an expanding population, especially with regard to
younger sons, many of whom could not hope
to receive from their parents lands sufficient for
their support. "This land which you inhabit,"
Pope Urban is reported to have told the knights
of France in 1095, "is too narrow for your large
population; nor does it abound in wealth; and
it provides hardly enough food for those who
farm it. This is the reason that you murder and
consume one another." Moreover, the knights
were educated for war, and in war they placed
their chief hope for wealth, honor, and social
advance. The growth of the feudal principalities, the efforts of the Church to restrict fighting, and the slow pacification of European so-

ciety that these policies were bringing threatened to leave the knights poor, unhonored, and unemployed. "You should shudder, brethren," Urban is also reported to have told the knights, "you should shudder at perpetrating violence against Christians; it is less wicked to turn your sword against Muslims. . . . The possessions of the enemy will also fall to you, since you will claim their treasures as plunder." War against the infidel thus offered constructive employment for Europe's surplus and troublesome population of knights. In the following century St. Bernard of Clairvaux, whose preaching inspired thousands to join the Second Crusade, frankly affirmed that all but a few crusaders were "criminals and sinners, ravishers and the sacrilegious, murderers, perjurers, and adulterers." To have them crusading in the East therefore conferred a double benefit. As Bernard remarked, "Their departure makes their own people happy, and their arrival cheers those whom they are hastening to help. They aid both groups, not only by protecting the one but also by not oppressing the other." The crusades, in sum, were in considerable degree a violent means of draining the violence from medieval life.

The First Crusade

In 1095, before a council assembled at Clermont in southern France, Pope Urban II urged the knights to go to the East to aid their endangered Christian brothers and to free the Holy Land from its allegedly blasphemous masters.[2] His sermon was intended for the up-

per classes, but its plea had sensational results at all levels of Western society. In northern France and the Rhineland influential preachers were soon rousing the people and organizing movements that historians now call the Popular Crusade. Bands of peasants and the poor set out for the East, miserably equipped and lacking competent leaders. They marched down the Rhine valley, through Hungary and Bulgaria, to Constantinople. Emperor Alexius of Byzantium, who could only have been shocked at the sight of this hapless army, gave them transport across the Bosporus. The Turks at once cut them to pieces.

Far better organized was the official First Crusade, which was led by nobles: Robert of Normandy, son of William the Conqueror, headed a northern French army; Godfrey of Bouillon, his brother Baldwin, and Robert of Flanders commanded an army of Lotharingians and Flemings; Raymond of Toulouse led the men of Languedoc; and Bohemond of Taranto and his brother Tancred marshaled the Normans of southern Italy. These four armies moved by various overland and sea routes to Constantinople (see Map 10.1), arriving there in 1096 and 1097.

Although the leaders of the First Crusade had intended to conquer lands in the East in their own name, Emperor Alexius demanded from them an oath of fealty in exchange for his provisioning the armies as they marched to Palestine. Grudgingly, they agreed, promising to regard the emperor as the overlord of the lands they might reconquer from the Turks. Subsequently, both the emperor and the Western leaders accused each other of violating the terms of the oath. The failure of the crusaders and the Byzantines to find a firm basis for cooperating ultimately weakened, although it did not defeat, the enterprise.

In 1097 the crusaders entered the Seljuk Sultanate of Rum, achieving their first major joint victory at Dorylaeum. Baldwin, the brother of Godfrey of Bouillon, then separated his troops from the main body and conquered Edessa,

[2] The exact circumstances of Urban's famous sermon remain obscure. He probably was replying to a plea for help from Emperor Alexius of Byzantium; a Greek embassy, bearing such a plea, reached him at Piacenza earlier in 1095. The chroniclers give us four versions of the sermon, but it is almost impossible to determine which, if any, have preserved Urban's own words. At any rate, certainly Alexius wanted from the West mercenary soldiers, not princes bent on establishing their own principalities in the East. The sources dealing with the summoning of the First Crusade have been conveniently gathered and translated by Peter Charanis, "Byzantium and the West," in Kenneth M. Setton and Henry R. Winkler (eds.), *Great Problems in European Civilization*, 1966, pp. 93–110.

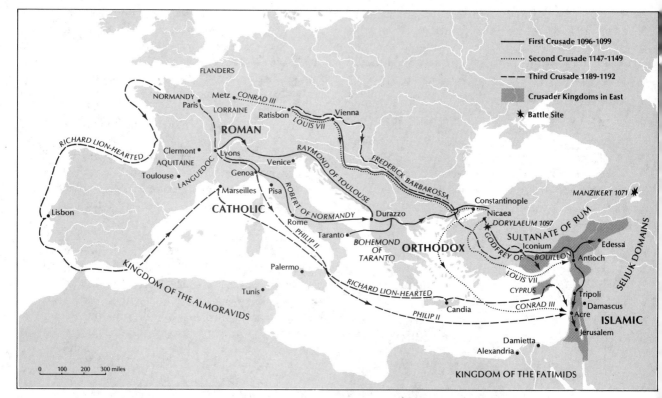

MAP 10.1. THE CRUSADES

where he established the first crusader state in the East.

The decisive victory of the First Crusade came in the battle for the port city of Antioch. After that, the road to Jerusalem was open before the crusaders. On July 15, 1099, they stormed the Holy City and pitilessly slaughtered the entire infidel population.

Besides a high level of organizational skill and their own considerable daring, the Westerners had a critical advantage in the tumultuous political situation in the East. The Seljuk Turks, newly risen to power, had had little opportunity to consolidate their rule and were contending with the Fatimids, the ruling dynasty of Egypt, over the possession of Palestine. In addition, the ancient schisms among

the Islamic religious sects continued to divide and weaken the community. The inability of Muslims to present a united front against the crusaders was probably the decisive factor in the final success of the First Crusade.

The Kingdom of Jerusalem

The crusaders now had the problem of organizing a government for their conquered territories. They chose as ruler Godfrey of Bouillon, but death cut short his reign in 1100, and his younger brother Baldwin, the conqueror of Edessa, succeeded him.

Baldwin set out to strengthen his realm through the application of feudal concepts and institutions. He retained a direct dominion over Jerusalem and its surroundings, including a stretch of coast extending from Gaza to Beirut. To the north three fiefs, the County of Tripoli, the Principality of Antioch, and the County of Edessa, were made subject to his suzerainty (see Map 10.2). Although King Baldwin and his successors were able to exert a respectable measure of authority over all these lands, profound weaknesses undermined the security of their hold. For one thing, the kings were never

MAP 10.2. CRUSADER KINGDOMS 12TH CENTURY

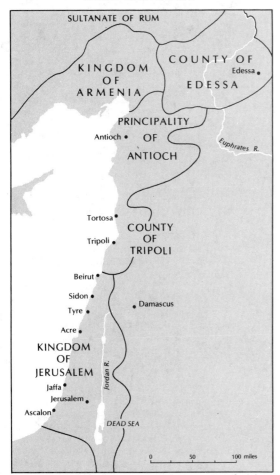

able to push their frontiers to an easily defensible, strategic border, such as the Lebanese Mountains. Furthermore, the administration remained critically dependent upon a constant influx of men and money from the European homeland. Many knights and pilgrims came, but relatively few stayed as permanent settlers. The Westerners constituted a foreign aristocracy, small in number and set over a people of largely different faith, culture, and sympathies. The wonder is not that the crusader states ultimately succumbed, but that some of their outposts could have survived on the mainland of Asia Minor for nearly two centuries.

The Later Crusades

Although historians have traditionally assigned numbers to the later crusades, these expeditions were merely momentary swells in the steady current of Western people and treasures to and from the Middle East. The recapture of the city of Edessa by the Muslims in 1144 gave rise to the Second Crusade (1147–1149). Two armies, led by King Louis VII of France and Emperor Conrad III of Germany, set out to capture Damascus to give the Kingdom of Jerusalem a more defensible frontier. However, they were soon forced to retreat ignominiously before superior Muslim forces.

The capture of Jerusalem by the Muslim chief Saladin evoked the Third Crusade (1189–1192), which was the climax of the crusading movement and its greatest disappointment. Emperor Frederick Barbarossa and kings Philip II of France and Richard I, the Lion-Hearted, of England all marched to the East. (Frederick drowned while crossing through Asia Minor and most of his forces turned back.) Although the crusaders captured Acre, the Third Crusade ended in a stalemate. The Kingdom of Jerusalem remained limited to a narrow strip of the coast from Acre to Jaffa, but unarmed Christian pilgrims were given the right to visit Jerusalem. These were paltry fruits from so grand an effort.

In the thirteenth century the crusades clearly lost their appeal to Western knights. The population expansion in Europe, which had helped lend strength to the earlier crusades, was already leveling off. Moreover, many Europeans were shocked when the popes tried to direct crusades against the Albigensian heretics in southern France and against political enemies such as Frederick II of Hohenstaufen. With dwindling support from the West, the Christians in 1291 lost Acre, their last outpost on the Asiatic mainland. Repeatedly during the Late Middle Ages the popes attempted to organize crusades; many knights and princes vowed to participate; some traveled to the East, but none gained a major victory.

Results of the Crusades

In terms of their principal professed goal the crusaders gained a partial success but not a permanent one: they held Jerusalem for nearly a century and maintained outposts on the Palestinian coast for nearly two centuries. Meanwhile, Christian pilgrims in large numbers were able to visit the holy places in Palestine in moderate safety. Even after the loss of Acre the Westerners continued to hold Eastern possessions acquired during the early crusades. When the Ottoman Turks, successors to the Seljuks, finally seized these last remnants of the crusaders' conquests, the Western peoples had already found new routes to the Far East and were in the midst of the "Atlantic Revolution," which gave them a new position in the world that the

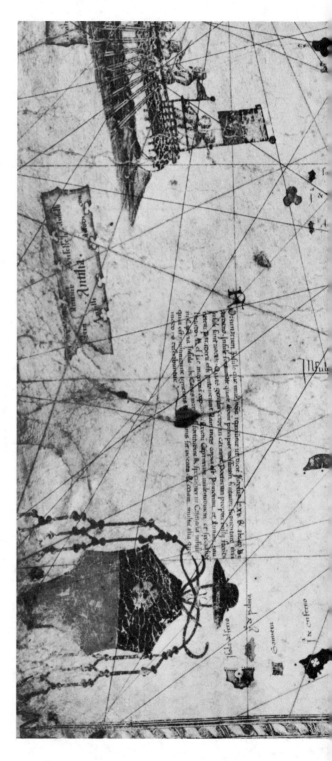

Cartography in the Renaissance benefited from both an increased knowledge of the world and improved skills in illustration and printing. This beautiful map by the Italian cartographer Giovanni Benincasa shows with admirable accuracy and elegance the newly discovered coast of northwest Africa.
(Photo: Scala/EPA Inc.)

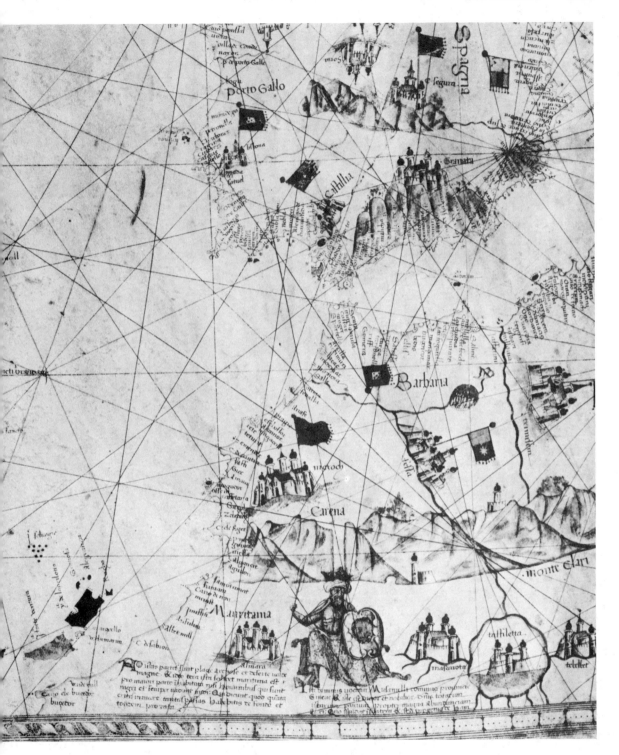

This manuscript rendering of two perfect knights jousting is thought to be a portrayal of Richard the Lion-Hearted and Saladin. (Photo: British Museum)

Turks did not challenge. The crusades enhanced the security of the West by slowing the Turkish advance across the Mediterranean Sea and into Europe.

Militarily, the crusades exerted a powerful influence upon the arts of war. After their initial invasions the crusaders waged a largely defensive war, and they became particularly skilled in the art of constructing castles. The numerous remains of crusader castles still found in nearly all the Eastern lands reflect this fact in such features as the overhanging tower parapets from which oil or missiles could be rained down on attackers and the angular castle entranceways that prevented the enemy from shooting directly at the gates. Islamic castles also show a similar evolution toward a more advanced military design.

The foes continually copied each other, and the Ottoman Turks in particular adopted many Western technical skills. By the fifteenth century the Ottomans, originally landlocked nomads, had begun to build a fleet and challenge Western maritime supremacy in the eastern Mediterranean Sea. They also learned from Western technicians the new arts of firearms, specifically cannons, without which they probably could not have conquered their vast empire.

The crusades naturally presented enormous,

unprecedented problems of financing and logistical support, and therefore exerted a major stimulus upon the growth of financial and governmental institutions in the West. In the early crusades each knight or soldier had largely looked to his own support. He brought money with him (often acquired by selling or mortgaging his estates) and purchased supplies from the natives of the lands through which he marched. He replenished his funds through booty or gifts from his lord and eventually through estates granted him in Palestine. But as the crusader wars became largely defensive in character, the opportunity for booty declined and the armies could no longer live off the land; support had to come primarily from Europe, thus requiring permanent institutional arrangements by which a constant flow of money (and men) could be directed from Europe into Palestine.

Traditional sources of revenue were inadequate, so both the popes and the princes began to impose direct taxes upon their lands and subjects. In 1188, for example, the pope authorized, and the princes collected, the so-called Saladin tithe, a direct tax of 10 percent imposed on all clerical and lay revenues and destined to finance the Third Crusade. (Previously, European governments had made little use of direct taxes because they were difficult to assess and collect.) The imposition of the Saladin tithe and subsequent direct taxes required that institutional methods be devised for assessment, col-

The Krak-des-Chevaliers in Syria is a castle formerly used by crusaders as a bastion of defense. This aerial view reveals the extended parapets and angular entranceways, both innovative features of fortification developed during the crusades.
(Photo: Aerofilms Limited)

lecting the moneys, and transferring the funds to where they were most needed. The crusades, in other words, helped the governments of the West come of age in a fiscal sense.

One other financial course adopted by the papacy had great importance for the future. The popes allowed those Europeans who were too old or too weak to participate in the crusades to gain the spiritual benefits of crusading through monetary contributions, in return for which they were promised an indulgence—that is, a remission of punishment due for their sins. This practice was subsequently to draw the criticism of reformers, and it was the immediate cause of Martin Luther's split with the Roman Church in 1517.

Military-Religious Orders

Soon after the First Crusade a new kind of institution appeared that was founded to offer armed escorts and safe lodgings to pilgrims to Palestine but eventually assumed a major role in the task of supplying the newly acquired Eastern lands. This was the military-religious order, which combined the dedication, discipline, and organizational experience of monasticism with the military purposes of the crusade. The first of three great orders to emerge from the crusades was the Knights of the Temple, or Templars, founded sometime before 1120 by a group of French knights. The knights took the three monastic vows of poverty, chastity, and obedience and, like monks, lived together in their own convents, or communities. The Templars assumed a principal role in the maintenance of safe routes between Europe and the crusader states and in the defense of the Kingdom of Jerusalem. The order also transported and guarded moneys in support of the Eastern war, and thus became the most important banking institution of the age until its suppression by the pope in 1312.

The Knights of the Hospital of St. John of Jerusalem, or the Hospitalers, founded about 1130, enjoyed an even longer history. Never as numerous or as wealthy as the Templars, they still made a major contribution to the defense of the Kingdom of Jerusalem. With the fall of Acre the knights moved their headquarters to Cyprus, then to Rhodes, and finally to Malta. As the Knights of Malta, they ruled the island until 1798. This "sovereign order" of the Knights of Malta survives today as an exclusively philanthropic confraternity and is a principal arm of papal charities throughout the world.

About 1190, German pilgrims organized the Teutonic Knights for the defense of the roads to Palestine. These knights later transferred their headquarters first to Venice, then to Transylvania (in modern Rumania), and finally, in 1229, to Prussia, where they became the armed vanguard of the German eastward expansion and conquered for themselves an extensive domain along the shores of the Baltic Sea. In 1525 the last grand master, Albert of Hohenzollern, adopted Lutheranism and secularized the order and its territories. The German state of Brandenburg-Prussia eventually absorbed the lands, and perhaps something of the militant spirit, of these crusading knights. At all events, the long history of these orders illustrates how organizational and military skills first acquired in the crusading movement continued to affect European life over the subsequent centuries.

Economy

Historians still cannot draw up an exact balance sheet that registers accurately the economic gains and losses of these holy expeditions. Certainly the crusades were costly in blood and treasure. To support its armies Europe exported large quantities of precious metals; the spoils of war and commercial profits undoubtedly brought some moneys back, but probably not enough to recoup the losses. Nevertheless, the crusades seem to have had a powerful and beneficial impact on the European economy, principally by forcing into circulation moneys and treasures that had hitherto been hoarded in the West. Although there are no exact figures, both the volume of money and the speed of its circulation in Europe seem to have increased dramatically during this period. The new abundance of money stimulated commercial exchange and business investments and helped revive the Western economy, though in this respect the crusades were less significant than such factors as population growth and the settlement of new lands within Europe.

The crusades also enlivened trade with the East. After the First Crusade most of the large Western armies went to Palestine by water, creating a lucrative business for the maritime cities of the Mediterranean Sea, especially in Italy. The Italians poured much of their profits from transporting and provisioning crusaders into commercial enterprises and established merchant colonies in many Eastern ports. Moreover, the crusades greatly strengthened the market for Eastern condiments in Europe. Knights and other pilgrims who had become familiar with sugar, spices, and similar products in the East continued to want them upon returning home, and they introduced them to their neighbors.

The Western demand for spices promoted commerce not only on the Mediterranean Sea but between the Middle East and East Asia. Furthermore, it had an impact that went beyond the narrowly commercial. In the Late Middle Ages political disruptions in Central Asia and the high taxes imposed by the Turks and Egyptians hampered trade with the East, but the call for Eastern products continued to be strong within Europe. This situation assured rich rewards to the navigators and nations who discovered surer, cheaper ways to import spices and other Eastern commodities, and thus provided a direct incentive for the geographic explorations and discoveries that introduce the modern epoch.

In familiarizing Europeans with many new products, the crusades helped raise the standard of living in the West, and this in turn intensified the pace of economic activity. From the eleventh century on, Europeans seem to have worked harder, partly perhaps to gain for themselves some of the products and the amenities of life they had observed in the East. Discoveries overseas in the sixteenth and seventeenth centuries seem to have influenced Europe in a similar fashion. New commodities altered the popular appreciation of what was essential for a good life and prompted Europeans to work more energetically to satisfy their newly raised expectations.

Religion and Learning

As acts of piety the crusades inevitably affected the organization and practice of religion, although it is all but impossible to distinguish their impact from that of many other forces at work in the West. Their initial success added to the prestige of the popes who sponsored them, just as their subsequent failures undermined faith in papal leadership. Ecclesiastical finances and even canon law were influenced, as the Church sought to extend economic support and legal protection to both the crusaders and the families they left behind.

It is difficult to assess exactly the importance of the crusades to the intellectual life of Europe. In one area of knowledge, geography, they did make important contributions. Starting from the crusader principalities in the East, first missionaries, then merchants penetrated deep into Central Asia, and by the early thirteenth century reached China. Their reports, especially the memoirs of the Venetian Marco Polo at the close of the thirteenth century, gave Europe abundant information about East Asia, and helped inspire Western navigators to seek new ways to penetrate beyond Islamic lands.

In other fields of knowledge the crusades seem to have brought little enlightenment. Most crusaders were rough warriors who had little interest in the subtleties of Islamic learning. However, the failure of these warriors to absorb new ideas from foreign cultures does not fully measure the cultural debt that the medieval West owes to Islam. Particularly through contacts in Spain and Sicily, Westerners learned new skills (the making of paper, perhaps the use of the compass) and new ideas that influenced the development of courtly love and scientific, philosophical, and religious thought in Europe. But it may also be true that the crusades in fomenting hatred against the infidel made Europeans less receptive to foreign ideas.

In the intellectual field as in all others, then, the crusades did not radically alter the course of medieval history, either in Christian or Islamic societies, but they did powerfully reinforce existing tendencies and accelerate the pace of change on almost every level of life. Through the crusades Europeans learned about the geography of distant lands, became highly motivated to establish permanent, profitable contact with them, and acquired some experience in the conquest and administration of overseas territories. Appropriately, the crusades may be regarded as an initial chapter in the expansion of Europe, which was to be renewed and carried forward even more vigorously in the early modern period.

II. BYZANTIUM AND THE ASCENDANCY OF THE OTTOMAN EMPIRE

After the disaster at Manzikert in 1071, the Byzantine Empire was able to survive until the middle fifteenth century, but it constituted a shrinking enclave around Constantinople and could no longer exercise a strong regional leadership. Nor could it halt the expansion of the Ottoman Turks, who by the early sixteenth century became the unquestioned masters of southeast Europe and the Middle East.

The Passing of East Rome

The beginning of the thirteenth century saw the launching of the Fourth Crusade and, unexpectedly, the subsequent fragmenting of the Byzantine Empire. The expedition was first planned as a campaign against Egypt, but the Venetian Doge Enrico Dandolo bargained the short-funded crusaders into capturing, in return for passage east, the Christian city of Zara in Dalmatia, which was opposing Venice in the Adriatic Sea. Then Alexius IV, a pretender to the Byzantine throne, hired the crusaders to seize Constantinople in return for money, military help in the Egyptian campaign, and the reunion of the Eastern and Western churches. The crusaders restored Alexius, but he could not honor his promises. By way of compensation, the crusaders stormed and looted Constantinople in 1204. They then divided the Byzantine Empire among themselves.

A Flemish nobleman assumed the office of emperor, although he ruled directly only a small parcel of territory surrounding Constantinople. The Venetians gained three-eighths of all Byzantine possessions; this acquisition marks the foundation of the Venetian colonial empire, portions of which were retained until the seventeenth century. Byzantine refugees from Constantinople set up an empire in exile, with its capital at Nicaea in Asia Minor. In 1261 the emperor of Nicaea, Michael III Paleologus, recaptured Constantinople, but neither he nor his successors could restore the shattered unity of the old Byzantine Empire.

The decline of the Byzantine Empire allowed the hitherto subject Balkan peoples to build their own independent kingdoms and to aspire to a position of dominance in the area. First the Bulgarians in the thirteenth century, and then the Serbs in the fourteenth, created large Balkan empires. At the height of their powers these empires seemed destined to absorb the remnants of the Byzantine Empire, but by the fourteenth century it was the Ottoman Turks who presented the greatest menace to Byzantium.

The Fall of Constantinople

Turkish communities and peoples had been assuming a large military and political role in the Middle East since the late tenth century. The Seljuk Turks, who had nearly overwhelmed the Byzantine Empire with their victory at Manzikert in 1071, established the Sultanate of Rum, which dominated western Asia Minor for the next century and a half. This sultanate survived the attacks of the Western crusaders but was defeated by the far more formidable invasion of an Asiatic people, the Mongols, in the thirteenth century. The Ottoman Turks followed the Mongol invasions and settled in the area of the Sultanate of Rum. They established themselves at Gallipoli on the European side of the Straits in 1354, and within a few years their possessions entirely surrounded Byzantine territory.

The Byzantine emperors tried desperately but unsuccessfully to gain military help from the West. In 1439 Emperor John VII accepted reunion with Rome, largely on Roman terms, in return for aid, but he had no power to impose his policy of reuniting the churches upon his people; in fact many Eastern Christians preferred Turkish rule to submission to the hated Westerners.

The Ottomans were unable to mount a major campaign against Constantinople until 1453, in the reign of the Sultan Mohammed II, the Conqueror, when they attacked the city by land and water. Constantinople fell after a heroic resistance; Emperor Constantine XIII, whose imperial lineage stretched back more than 1400 years to Augustus Caesar, died in this final agony of the Byzantine Empire.

The fall of Constantinople changed very little in military or economic terms. The Byzantine Empire had not been an effective barrier

Mohammed II, the Conqueror, here represented in a contemporary painting attributed to the Venetian artist Gentile Bellini, took Constantinople in 1453 and was one of the principal founders of the Ottoman Empire.
(Photo: The Granger Collection)

to Ottoman expansion for years, and Constantinople had dwindled commercially as well as politically. The shift to Turkish dominion did not, as was once believed, substantially affect the flow of trade between the East and West. Nor did the Turkish conquest of the city provoke an exodus of Byzantine scholars and manuscripts to Italy. Scholars from the East, recognizing the decline and seemingly inevitable fall of the Byzantine Empire, had been emigrating to Italy since the late fourteenth century; the revival of Greek letters was well under way in the West by 1453.

The impact of the fall was largely psychological; although hardly unexpected, it shocked the Christian world. The pope sought to launch a new crusade and received from the Western princes the usual promises but no armies. Venice waged a protracted and inconclusive war against the Turks (1463–1479). Perhaps most important, the collapse of the Byzantine Empire gave further incentive to the search for new ways to East Asia, for new contacts with the lands beyond the Islamic territories of the eastern Mediterranean.

Finally, the fall did have great symbolic importance for contemporaries and perhaps even more for later historians. In selecting Byzantium as his capital in 324 Constantine had simultaneously founded a Christian Roman empire that could be considered the first authentically medieval state. For more than 1000 years this Christian Roman empire played a major political and cultural role in the history of both Eastern and Western peoples. To many historians the years of its existence mark the span of the Middle Ages, and its passing symbolizes the end of an era.

Expansion of the Ottoman Empire

The Ottomans took their name from Osman, or Othman (1299–1326), who founded a dynasty of sultans that survived for six centuries.[3] Under Mohammed II, who from the start of his reign committed his governments to a policy of conquest, the Ottomans entered upon a century of expansion. After the fall of Constantinople, which became his capital under the name of Istanbul, Mohammed subjugated the Morea, Serbia, Bosnia, and parts of Herzegovina. He drove the Genoese from their Black Sea colonies, forced the khan of the Crimea to

become his vassal, and fought a lengthy naval war with the Venetians. At his death the Ottomans were a power on land and sea, and the Black Sea had become a Turkish lake.

Early in the following century Turkish domination was extended over the heart of the Arab lands through the conquest of Syria, Egypt, and the western coast of the Arabian Peninsula. (The Arabs did not again enjoy autonomy until the twentieth century.) With the conquest of the sacred cities of Mecca and Medina the sultan assumed the title of caliph, "successor of the Prophet," claiming to be Islam's supreme religious head as well as its mightiest sword.

The Ottoman Empire was brought to its height of power by Suleiman II, the Magnificent (1520–1566), who extended the empire in both the West and the East. In 1521 he took the citadel of Belgrade, which had hitherto blocked Turkish advance up the Balkan Peninsula toward Hungary, and the next year forced the Knights of St. John, after a six-month siege, to surrender the island of Rhodes, a loss that was a crippling blow to Western naval strength in the eastern Mediterranean.

Suleiman achieved his greatest victory by annihilating the Kingdom of Hungary in 1526. Then he launched his most ambitious campaign, directed against Austria, the Christian state that now assumed chief responsibility for defending the Western frontiers. However, this effort, the high-water mark of Ottoman expansion into Europe, failed, and the frustrated Suleiman returned home in 1529, turning his attention toward the East. His armies overran Mesopotamia and completed the conquest of southern Arabia. The Ottoman Empire, which now included southeastern Europe, the Middle East, Egypt, and Arabia (see Map 10.3), then entered a period of stability.

Suleiman brought his empire fully into the diplomatic as well as the military struggles of Europe, taking shrewd advantage of the rivalries that existed there. He hated Charles V, who

---

[3] For a more detailed treatment of the remarkable state and civilization of the Ottomans see Norman Itzkowitz, *Ottoman Empire and Islamic Tradition,* 1972.

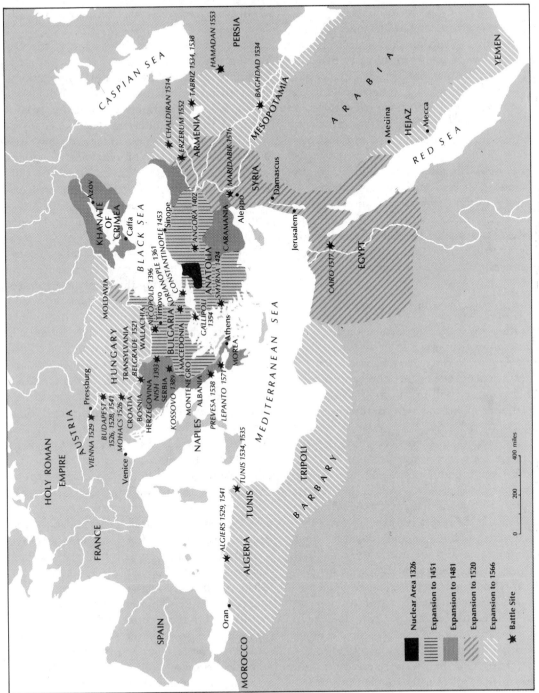

MAP 10.3. THE OTTOMAN EMPIRE 1300–1566

Nuclear Area 1326
Expansion to 1451
Expansion to 1481
Expansion to 1520
Expansion to 1566
★ Battle Site

as Holy Roman Emperor similarly pretended to rule the world, and in 1525 he joined Francis I of France in an alliance directed against Charles, later negotiating a commercial treaty that further cemented cooperation between France and the Ottoman Empire. Through his alliance with France, Suleiman confronted Charles V with the possibility of a war on two fronts and prevented the formation of a common Christian crusade against himself, which the popes were ceaselessly advocating. Indirectly, by weakening Charles, Suleiman contributed to the success of the Reformation, since the Holy Roman Emperor, threatened from both East and West, was unable to take effective action against Martin Luther and the German Protestant princes.

Ottoman Institutions

The Ottomans had expanded a small, landlocked community in western Asia Minor into a great empire. Several advantages account for this achievement, one of them being their geographic position. Set on the frontier between the Islamic and Christian worlds, the Ottomans could claim to be the chief warriors for the faith, and the prestige thereby accruing to them won recruits and moral support from the more interior Islamic communities. Moreover, the Ottomans soon became a power in the political struggles of both Europe and the Middle East and were able to take advantage of favorable opportunities in both regions, even enlisting allies in one area to wage war in the other.

The intense rivalries sundering the Christian faiths also facilitated Ottoman expansion. Some Balkan Christians accepted papal supremacy, others adhered to the Eastern Orthodox traditions, and still others were regarded as heretics by both the Roman Catholics and the Orthodox. Often a Christian sect preferred the rule of the tolerant Ottomans to that of a rival Christian sect. In preserving peace among these dissident Christians, the Ottomans could serve as impartial referees, as Christians obviously could not.

Perhaps the greatest advantage of the Ottomans in their remarkable ascendancy was the character of their own cultural institutions. From their nomadic origins and their long experience as frontier fighters they had preserved a strong military tradition. Their devout adherence to Islam, which advocated holy wars against unbelievers, reinforced their aggressive tendencies; but the Ottomans also showed a remarkable ability to organize conquered territories and gain the support, and in some measure even the loyalty, of the people held under subjugation.

The Ottomans allowed the subject communities to live by their own laws under their own officials, requiring them only to pay taxes and supply men for the Ottoman army and administration. The Ottoman conquests did not greatly disturb the society, economy, or culture of these communities, which were also able to play a role of considerable importance in the social and economic life of the Ottoman Empire. Trade, for example, which remained vigorous in the Black Sea and the eastern Mediterranean Sea, was still largely in the hands of Greeks, Armenians, and Jews. The Ottomans themselves remained aloof from commercial undertakings and confined their careers to government service and the army.

In the course of their enormous expansion the Ottoman sultans faced the formidable problem of developing military and administrative institutions strong enough to hold together their vast empire. Like all medieval rulers the sultan originally governed with the aid of a council of chosen advisers, which was called the divan. From the time of Mohammed the Conqueror, however, the sultan came to be considered too august to participate personally in its deliberations. The function of presiding over the meetings of the divan fell to the grand vizier, who became the chief administrative official of the Ottoman state. The administration

In this woodcut by Peter Coeck van Aelst (1553), the sultan Suleiman is shown riding through the ruins of the hippodrome (stadium) of the Byzantine capital, Constantinople. (Photo: The Granger Collection)

was divided into three major categories: civil, ecclesiastical, and military. The divan retained supreme responsibility over both the civil and military branches; it supervised the collection of taxes and tribute, conscription of soldiers, and conduct of foreign affairs, and made recommendations to the sultan concerning peace, war, or other major decisions of state; it also functioned as a court in disputes which were not religious in character.

Religious affairs were administered by a class of judges specially trained in Islamic law, who constituted a special corps called the *ulema.* At their head the sheikh-ul-Islam served as the supreme judge after the sultan himself in all matters of sacred law.

The army had two principal divisions: unpaid holders of fiefs granted by the sultan in exchange for military service; and paid soldiers, technically considered slaves, who remained permanently in the sultan's service. The holder of a fief was required to provide the military with armed men, the number being set in strict proportion to the revenue deriving from his estates. Among the paid soldiers the most important were those belonging to the highly trained, thoroughly professional, but legally unfree corps of the "Janissaries," meaning new troops. Slave armies had been common in Islamic states, but the Ottomans did not adopt the practice until the fifteenth century. According to the accounts of the earliest chronicles, Sultan Murad learned from a theologian in about 1430 that the Koran assigned him one-fifth of the booty captured by his army, including prisoners. Murad decided to convert his prisoners to Islam, teach them Turkish, and enlist them in a special, highly trained military contingent, the Janissaries. Most medieval monarchs relied upon mercenaries or poorly trained and poorly equipped feudal levies, comprised of vassals with little enthusiasm for fighting, and feudal levies continued to make up the larger part of the Turkish army. But the Janissaries soon became an elite corps of professional fighters, dedicated to the sultan and to Islam, and were in large part responsible for the Ottoman victories.

On the local level the government of the empire was content to leave many administrative responsibilities to the self-governing communities of Christians and Jews and to the holders of fiefs, who collected taxes and mustered soldiers from those settled on their lands. Apart from the fiefs the unit of local administration was the canton, or *kaza,* which was administered by a judge, or *qaid.* The cantons were grouped into departments and provinces, usually under the authority of a pasha, who was both a civil and a military official, since he bore the responsibility of leading the feudal levies of his provinces in time of war.

Sometime in the fifteenth century a new system of recruitment for the civil administration and the military was introduced—the *devshirme,* or levy of boys. In the *devshirme's* developed form, special commissioners every five years selected young boys from among the Christian population to be given special instruction in Turkish and converted to Islam. After their training they were examined and

either assigned to the corps of Janissaries or chosen for the palace administration. In the latter case they were given still more intensive training, and the most talented of them could aspire to the highest administrative offices of the empire. Even the grand vizier was usually a slave. Remarkably, in each generation the most powerful administrators were new men having no family ties with the Turkish aristocracy and no reason to ally with them against the sultan's interests. This practice of requisitioning slaves in the sultan's service is sometimes called the fundamental institution of the empire, for the sultan's power was critically dependent upon its proper functioning.

The Sultan

The sultan united in his own person supreme civil, military, and religious authority. The concept of his office was influenced by Byzantine views of imperial authority, which seem to have contributed primarily to the pomp of court ceremony and the aura of sanctity surrounding the person of the sultan, and still more by Islamic traditions concerning governmental power, particularly the notion that he was the successor of Muhammad, the legitimate ruler of all true believers. In a strict sense the sultan could not be an absolute ruler, for he was, like every member of the Islamic community, subject to the sacred law. But he was also the supreme judge of that law, and there was no way apart from revolution that his decisions could be challenged.

The early sultans devised a striking solution to a problem common to most medieval states: the peaceful transference of power from a ruler to his successor. From the fifteenth to the seventeenth century the Ottomans followed what has come to be called the law of fratricide. The sultans cohabited with numerous slave girls of the harem, who were selected much as were the male household slaves, and characteristically fathered numerous progeny. The reigning sultan selected one of the boys to be his successor. At the sultan's death, the designated heir had the right and obligation to put his brothers and half-brothers to death. (They were strangled with a silken bowstring in order to avoid the shedding of their imperial blood.) The religious judges allowed such massacres, because an orderly and peaceful succession was essential to the welfare of the empire.

The Limits of Ottoman Power

In the sixteenth century Suleiman the Magnificent had brought the Ottoman Empire to unprecedented heights of power, but already certain factors were imposing limits upon its expansion. One was geography. The Ottomans had operated effectively in areas close to their homeland in Asia Minor, but the efficiency of their army and administration inevitably diminished with distance. The unsuccessful campaign against Austria proved that the region was already beyond their reach, and the Ottomans encountered similar walls to further advance in the Iranian Plateau and the waters of the central Mediterranean. With the opening of trade routes around Africa and across the Atlantic, the Ottomans were no longer at the center of the civilized world and no longer the masters of movements east and west. Although they left the commerce of their empire largely in the hands of the subject communities, they were well aware of its importance, and Suleiman therefore sent a force to destroy the Portuguese ships and trading stations in the Indian Ocean. Its failure was an ominous sign for the empire. Economically, the geographic discoveries of the period caused dislocations in the empire—the shift in trade routes, the increase in the stock of precious metal in Europe, and consequent inflation—and brought few benefits.

Within the empire there was also a deterioration in the quality of leadership. For reasons hard to explain, the sultans after Suleiman show little of the energy and ability which had marked out the earlier rulers of the House of Osman. Technical advance was continuing in the West, and it was critical for the empire to keep abreast of these changes. The great sultans had welcomed Western technicians and made use of their skills, especially in armament, but their successors after Suleiman seem distinctly less interested in learning from the West. Declining efficiency appears broadly evident in Ottoman government. The chanceries and secretariats kept precise and informative records in the fifteenth century, but they no longer did so in the late sixteenth century and seem to have been beset by mounting disorder.[4] At the death of Suleiman in 1566, it is still much too early to speak of Ottoman decadence, but the fortunes of the Ottoman Empire were already past their apogee.

III. THE BIRTH OF MODERN RUSSIA

A great Russian historian, V. O. Kliuchevsky, once defined the principal theme in the history of the Russian people to be colonization, the long, arduous, and ultimately successful struggle to settle and subdue the huge Eurasian plain that was their home.[5] The history of that strug-

---

[4] During the period of expansion the basis of organizing conquered provinces was a document called the *defter,* a survey of the population and its possessions. The oldest surviving *defter* dates from 1431 to 1432 and deals with Albania, but the practice is undoubtedly somewhat older. These are remarkable documents, combining the qualities of a census and a property survey, and are comparable to the best records we possess from the same age in Western Europe. They illustrate the high administrative efficiency of the Ottoman government—an efficiency that noticeably deteriorates after the late sixteenth century.

[5] *A History of Russia,* 1911, vol. 1, p. 2, "Thus we see that the principal fundamental factor in Russian history has been migration or colonisation, and that all other factors have been more or less inseparably connected therewith." This theory bears interesting similarities to Frederick Jackson Turner's "frontier thesis" in regard to American history.

gle records defeats as well as victories. From the ninth to the twelfth centuries, the center of Rus civilization had been Kiev, on the fringes of the southern steppe. Although the Rus of Kiev maintained close contact across the steppes to the Black Sea and the Mediterranean world beyond, they could not permanently defeat the invading steppe nomads. From the twelfth century, Pechenegs and Cumans, followed by the still more terrible Mongols, mounted ever more destructive raids against the Rus settlements and cut off their contact with the Black Sea. Eventually the insecurity of the steppe forced the Rus to seek out safer homes in the forested regions to the north and west. In these areas, the Rus formed new institutions and built a new civilization, the direct ancestor of the modern Russian state.

The Mongols

The resurgence of the steppe nomads was a principal factor in the decline of Kievan Rus, especially with the appearance of the Mongols on Europe's borders in the early thirteenth century. The Mongol chief Genghis Khan was then amassing the largest empire the world has ever known. In 1223 a Mongol army penetrated into Eastern Europe in what seems to have been a reconnoitering expedition. The Mongols defeated the allied princes of Rus in a battle on the Kalka River (a tributary of the Don) but almost at once returned home, only to reappear a few years later in still greater force. From 1237 to 1241 a Mongol army under a nephew of Genghis's named Batu conducted raids throughout Eastern Europe and established at Sarai on the lower Volga River the capital of a division of the Mongol Empire that came to be called the Golden Horde. The khans, or rulers, of the Golden Horde maintained suzerainty over the lands of what is now the Ukraine and Byelorussia until the middle fourteenth century and over eastern Russia until the middle fifteenth. The princes subject to the Golden

Genghis Khan (1162–1227), here depicted as the illuminator of a sixteenth-century Persian manuscript imagined him to be, built an empire extending from China to central Europe. He is the most successful conqueror in history. (Photo: The Granger Collection)

Horde had to pay tribute to the khans and secure from them a charter, called *yarlik,* that confirmed them in their office, but otherwise they were not interfered with in their rule. In spite of the duration of the Mongols' power over the East Slavs, the influence they exerted upon their languages and cultures remained relatively slight.

The nomad incursions and the formation of the Golden Horde were particularly destructive in the exposed southern steppes. A chronicler laments that Kiev, once proudly known as the "mother of Rus cities," had only 200 houses left standing in the thirteenth century. Under nomad pressure the Rus population sought out more protected lands. In the twelfth and thirteenth centuries three new areas of East Slavic settlement came into prominence. Colonists moved west into the provinces of Galicia and Volynia along the upper Dniester River and became the forebears of the modern Ukrainians and the Byelorussians, or White Russians. After a short period of submission to the Mongols, these colonies fell under the political domination first of the grand dukes of Lithuania and then of the Polish kings, developed their own literary languages and cultural traditions, and were not politically reunited with their fellow East Slavs until the seventeenth and eighteenth centuries. (The province of Galicia, with a large Ukrainian population, remained under Polish or Austrian rule until 1944.) Other colonists moved north into the vast and empty lands ruled by the city of Novrogod, the region of Russia where Mongol rule had the shortest duration. But the poor soil of the area could not support a dense population. More important was the third new center of settlement: the Russian "Mesopotamia," the lands between the upper Volga and Oka rivers, with dense forests that offered both relative security from the nomads and a productive soil. Those who moved north to Novgorod and the Russian Mesopotamia were the ancestors of the modern Great Russians, still the largest of all the East Slavic peoples, and they formed the nucleus of a new Russian state; hence, their institutions and culture have a special interest.

Historians conventionally call the period between the twelfth and fifteenth centuries the age of feudal, or appanage, Russia—the time when Russia was divided into many princely patrimonies; for nearly all the small towns within the Russian Mesopotamia had their own princes, their own citadels, or kremlins, and their own territories. All the princes were subject to the khan of the Golden Horde, but Mongol government remained limited to the extracting of tribute and the granting of *yarliks*. Russia lacked a central government.

In this feudal period Russian economy, society, and culture acquired distinctive characteristics. With the exception of Novgorod the towns of the north could not, like Kiev, develop an active commerce with distant areas, nor did they have close contact with Constantinople or other centers of learning. The Russian towns in the main were not commercial or industrial centers but fortresses to which the surrounding population could repair in times of danger. The economy was overwhelmingly agricultural, and the energy of the people was primarily directed to clearing the great forests. In social terms, most peasants remained freemen, and their freedom was protected by the proximity of an expanding frontier.

Art continued to serve primarily the Church. Working within the conventions of icon painting established by Byzantine masters, Russian artists were able to achieve a remarkable delicacy and serenity, which stand in sharp contrast to the harsh conditions of Russian life. Russia's supreme religious painter was Andrei Rublev (1370?–1430?), who deserves to be recognized as one of the world's great artistic geniuses, even though little of his work survives.

The Rise of Moscow

In spite of political divisions, the Russians' religion and their common submission to the Mongols preserved a sense of identity and unity among them, but for long it remained uncertain which of the many petty princes would take the leadership in building a politically united nation. The town that perhaps seemed least likely to achieve this hegemony was the new settlement of Moscow, which is mentioned in a chronicle for the first time in 1147. Its early

obscurity proved an advantage because the small town was passed up by raiding nomads in search of richer plunder. This city on the Moskva River had other advantages too. It was in the center of the Russian Mesopotamia, close to the hub of the tributary rivers feeding the Volga River to the north and the Oka River to the south. The princes of Moscow could pursue a "river policy" in their expansion, following the courses of streams in all directions and depending upon this network of water routes to bind their state together. The region between the Volga and the Oka rivers also formed the geographic heart of European Russia and allowed the prince who ruled it to exploit opportunities in almost any part of Russia.

Moscow gained preeminence primarily through the talents of its early princes. Like other rulers in the north they abandoned the disastrous rota system of inheritance characteristic of the Kievan period and after some initial hesitation adopted a policy of primogeniture. A prince's acquisitions were thus kept intact rather than being divided among many heirs, and each prince built upon the accomplishments of his predecessor. The princes set about "gathering the Russian land," as historians traditionally describe the process of reunification, through the simultaneous pursuit of two distinct goals: they acquired new territories at every opportunity, through wars, marriages, and purchases; and they sought to make of Moscow, together with the Church, the symbol and the embodiment of Russian national unity, the representative of all Russians in the

---

Page from the Slavic Gospels. This manuscript illumination from the fourteenth century depicts Alexander, Tsar of the Bulgars "and the Greeks," and his family. The illustration shows how Byzantine conceptions of sacred kingship influenced the South Slavs, and through them (also independently of them) the East Slavs and the Russians.
(British Museum)

face of the Mongols and Western Christians. The prestige that thus accrued to Moscow helped persuade the princes of other cities to submit to its hegemony.

Ivan I (1328–1341) was the first Muscovite prince to raise this obscure little town to a place of prominence. Chiefly through purchases from other princes but occasionally through conquest, he extended his possessions along the entire course of the Moskva River and gained enclaves of territory to the north beyond the Volga River (see Map 10.4). Ivan assiduously courted the favor of the still powerful Mongol khan of the Golden Horde; he repeatedly visited the khan in his capital on the lower Volga River. In 1328 in recognition of his loyalty and gifts the khan gave him a special *yarlik* that made him the chief representative of Mongol authority in Russia with the right to collect the Mongol tribute from all the Russian lands. Thereafter Ivan and his successors permanently bore the title *velikii kniaz* ("great prince," or as traditionally if inaccurately rendered into English, "grand duke"). In collecting tribute for the Mongols, Ivan also increased his own treasury, thereby earning the nickname by which he is best known to history—*Kalita* ("moneybags").

Ivan no less assiduously sought to win the favor of the Russian Church and developed a strong friendship with the holder of its primal see, Peter, successor to the metropolitan of Kiev. Like his predecessor, who had abandoned that decaying city, Peter at first had no fixed see but peregrinated among the new centers of Russian settlement. He visited Moscow frequently and by chance died there in 1326. His tomb became a national shrine, and his successors chose Moscow as their permanent see, thus making it the capital of the Russian Church before it was the capital of the Russian people.

By the late fourteenth century the power of the Mongols was declining, largely because of dissensions within the Golden Horde; the princes of Moscow shifted from their tradi-

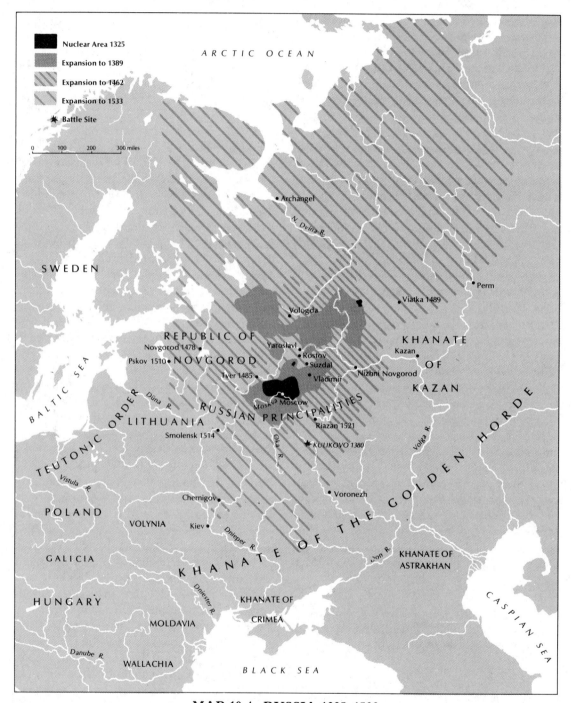

MAP 10.4. RUSSIA 1325–1533

tional role as chief servant of the khan to that of leader in the growing national opposition to Mongol rule. Though far from breaking the power of the Mongols, Prince Dmitri scored the first Russian defeat of a Mongol army in 1380, at Kulikovo on the Don River. In addition to this victory, which earned him the proud title *Donskoi* ("of the Don"), Dmitri also repulsed a Lithuanian invasion. He thus made Moscow the special defender of Orthodoxy against both the infidel Tatars and Western Christians, whom the Russians regarded as heretics, and gave it a prestige no other Russian city possessed.

The sovereign who completed the gathering of the Russian land and laid the constitutional foundations for modern Russia was Ivan III, the Great (1462–1505). His most important acquisition was Novgorod, a commercial city that had strong ties with the West and had gained control of a huge if still thinly populated area to the north. Through its vigorous trade with the Hanseatic League, a mercantile league of German cities, Novgorod had enjoyed considerable prosperity in the fourteenth and fifteenth centuries, but the consolidation of strong states along its borders—Lithuania and Poland as well as Muscovite Russia—threatened its independence. The merchant oligarchy that ruled the town wished to accept the suzerainty of the Catholic Lithuanians, while the populace, which was staunchly Orthodox in religion, looked rather to the prince of Moscow. Ivan could not allow a territory so large and so close to his own to fall under the control of a powerful foreign prince. In 1471 he demanded and received the submission of the city; when the city rebelled again in 1478, Ivan not only subdued it but incorporated Novgorod and its territories into the Muscovite state. Ivan also gathered in the principalities of Yaroslavl, Perm, Rostov, and Tver. He dispelled the shadow of Mongol sovereignty over Russia by confronting an invading army at the Oka River in 1480, although no battle was fought because the river

separated the two foes and neither dared cross its waters. The enemy withdrew, quietly ending more than two centuries of Mongol rule in Russia.

Under Ivan's successor Basil III, the principalities of Pskov, Riazan, and Smolensk were added; Moscow, which in 1462 had ruled some 15,000 square miles of territory, by the middle of the sixteenth century ruled 40,000 square miles, and the borders of the principality of Moscow included nearly all the areas settled by the Great Russians. The princes of Moscow now confronted beyond their frontiers, not another Russian prince, but foreign sovereigns. The reign of Ivan III thus begins a new epoch in the history of diplomatic and cultural relations with non-Russian peoples.

Institutional and Social Change

Ivan III refashioned Russian institutions to suit the newly achieved national unity. The ruler of all the Russians could no longer be considered a mere appanage prince, so Ivan adopted the title *tsar*, the Slavic equivalent of the Latin term *Caesar* and the Greek *kaîsar*, the traditional title of the Roman and the Byzantine emperors. Ivan also sought to depict himself as the successor of the Byzantine emperors. He adopted the Greek title *autokrator* ("autocrat") and introduced at his court the elaborate pomp and etiquette that had been characteristic of Byzantine practice. The Byzantine double-headed eagle became the seal and symbol of the new Russian Empire. Ivan added material as well as ideological splendor to his capital. Under the influence of his wife, Sophia Paleologus, who was the niece of the last Byzantine emperor and had been educated in Italy, he invited Italian artists to Moscow who helped to rebuild the Kremlin, the ancient citadel of the city. The Italians exerted considerable influence on Russian artistic style, especially Aristotele Fioravanti, who designed some of the Kremlin's most graceful churches and palaces.

The throne of Ivan the Terrible (the grandson of Ivan III) resembles a straight high-backed chair. The ivory plates that face the wooden framework are covered with relief carvings featuring mythological, historical, heraldic, and everyday scenes. The detail shown here is of the double-headed eagle, a Byzantine emblem that was adopted by the tsar as the seal and symbol of the Russian Empire.
(Photo: APN)

Ivan was the first prince since the Kievan period to legislate for the whole of Russia. In 1497 he promulgated a new code of laws known as the *Sudebnik,* which was the first national legal code since the *Russkaia Pravda,* compiled by the Kievan Prince Iaroslav the Wise in the eleventh century. The new strength and splendor of the tsar inspired several mon-

astic scholars to elaborate the theory of Moscow as the third Rome. The first Rome had allegedly fallen into heresy, and the second, Constantinople, was taken by the infidel. Moscow alone, the capital of the one Orthodox ruler, preserved the light of true religion.

In administering their state the princes of Moscow had traditionally relied upon the boyars, the hereditary nobles who were obligated to serve the prince in both the army and the civil administration. Many of the boyars held vast estates in full title, and their economic independence sometimes made them unreliable as servants. Without directly attacking the boyars, Tsar Ivan created a new class of serving gentry who were entirely dependent on the tsar's favor for their social position. He inaugurated a land grant called a *pomest'e,* which like the Western fief was made on condition of faithful service. The *pomeshchik,* as the holder of the grant was called, retained the property only so long as he fulfilled his obligations and, initially at least, the concession was not heritable. This new class acted as a counterpoise to the power of the boyars and as a principal support of the tsar's authority.

Although Ivan's reforms were not truly completed until the reign of his grandson, the notorious Ivan IV, the Terrible, who brutally extirpated the old nobility of boyars and imposed on all landowners the status of the tsar's servants, Ivan III may be considered the founder of the modern Russian state. He created the class of serving gentry; he finished the task of gathering the Russian land and unifying its people; he brought a united Russia to face the outside world; and he declared himself to be tsar, autocrat of Russia. Ivan III bequeathed to his successors one of the most characteristic institutions of modern Russia: its centralized, autocratic government.

In the Central and Late Middle Ages the isolation of the West from the East was partially overcome through the crusades and commercial expansion. The period further witnessed the formation in the East of two new states destined to replace both the Byzantine Empire and the Islamic Caliphate as the region's principal powers. Through a combination of military skill, religious fervor, remarkably effective institutions, and the weakness of their foes, the Ottoman Turks reassembled the territories of both Byzantium and the caliphate and established in the Middle East a vast empire, which stretched from Persia to the Danube River, and from North Africa to the Russian steppes. To the north the Russians had overcome by 1500 the political fragmentation of their own "feudal" age and had regained political unity. Although the tsars in the sixteenth century were not nearly so powerful as the Ottoman sultans, they were laying the foundations for the future strength of their empire.

In Western Europe over these same centuries, changes of comparable magnitude were occurring. The West was spared the nomadic invasions that always threatened and frequently struck the Eastern peoples, but it too sustained in the fourteenth and fifteenth centuries a series of disastrous blows—famines, plagues, economic depression, and wars. These catastrophes were the cause of profound dislocations in the society of the medieval West. The following two chapters examine the nature of this crisis, which transformed the medieval world and helped create the civilization of modern Western Europe.

RECOMMENDED READING

Sources

The Chronicle of Novgorod. Robert Mitchell and Nevill Forbes (trs.). 1914. Portrays social and political life of the principal commercial town of medieval Russia.

*DeVillehardouin, Geoffrey, and Jean De Joinville. *Chronicles of the Crusades.* Margaret R. Shaw (tr.). 1963.

Howes, Robert Craig (ed. and tr.). *The Testaments of the Grand Princes of Moscow.* 1967.

Tyre, William of. *A History of Deeds Done Beyond the Sea.* Emily A. Babcock and A. C. Krey (trs.). 1943. One of the most important chronicles of crusader activities.

Studies

Atiya, Azia S. *Crusade, Commerce and Culture.* 1962. An evaluation of the results of the crusades in European history.

Billington, James H. *The Icon and the Axe: An Interpretive History of Russian Culture.* 1966.

Erdmann, Carl. *The Origin of the Idea of the Crusade.* Marshall W. Baldwin and Walter Goffart (trs.). 1977. Perceptive study of the idea that war could be holy, by a German scholar.

Eversley, George, and Valentine Chirol. *The Turkish Empire: Its Growth and Decay.* 1969.

Fennell, J. L. *Ivan the Great of Moscow.* 1963. A political biography.

Halperin, Charles J. *Russia and the Golden Horde: The Mongol Impact on Medieval Russian History.* 1985.

Argues that the Mongol influence on Russia was greater than is usually maintained.

Kliuchevsky, V. O. *A History of Russia.* C. J. Hogarth (tr.). 1911. Classic study, still worth reading.

Lewis, Bernard. *Istanbul and the Civilization of the Ottoman Empire.* 1963. By a prominent student of Islamic cultures.

Mayer, Hans Eberhard. *The Crusades.* John Gillingham (tr.). 1972. Short and excellent.

Merriman, Roger B. *Suleiman the Magnificent: 1520–1566.* 1966.

Meyendorff, John. *Byzantium and the Rise of Russia: A Study of Byzantine–Russian Relations in the Fourteenth Century.* 1981. Byzantine contributions to Moscow's prominence.

Mylonas, George E. *The Balkan States: An Introduction to Their History.* 1947. Clearly written introductory survey.

Queller, Donald E. *The Conquest of Constantinople, 1201–1204.* 1977. Recent reconstruction of the course of the Fourth Crusade.

Runciman, Steven. *A History of the Crusades.* 3 vols. 1951–1954. By a prominent English historian.

Setton, Kenneth M. *The Papacy and the Levant (1204–1571).* 2 vols. 1976–1978. Now the basic survey of papal relations with the Eastern Churches.

———. (ed.). *A History of the Crusades.* 1955–. When completed, this five-volume work will constitute the most comprehensive history of the crusades.

Vernadsky, George. *The Mongols and Russia.* 1953.

———. *Russia at the Dawn of the Modern Age.* 1959. Volumes in the author's monumental *History of Russia.*

Wittek, Paul. *The Rise of the Ottoman Empire.* 1971.

---

* Available in paperback.

EXPERIENCES OF DAILY LIFE

Wood and Russian Culture

The new center of Russian civilization between the Oka and the Volga rivers, in the so-called Russian Mesopotamia, was a heavily forested region. To settle it, the Russian peasants had to carve out cleared areas, in which they built their homes and worked their fields. Understandably, they lived within a material culture dominated by wood. As James H. Billington explains in *The Icon and the Axe,* the Russian peasant hung on the wall of his home the ax, which supplied many of his material needs, and the icon, which gave him spiritual sustenance. And the icon was painted on a wooden panel.

Wood was the fuel that warmed the household during the long Russian winter, and it was the principal material used in building. The princes, great boyars, and foreign merchants (*gosti*), when they could, built their houses in stone or brick, and many towns also constructed their central fortress (kremlin) and cir-

Onion domes on the Church of the Transfiguration on Kizhi Island in northern Russia's Lake Onega. (Erich Lessing/Magnum)

cle of interior walls of the same materials. But stone was scarce on the Russian plain and brick expensive; wood, on the other hand, was abundant and cheap. It was used in a variety of ways. Birch bark was a common writing material. Excavations at Novgorod have recovered the letters of medieval merchants written on bark. Shoes were made of wood, and spoons and tools. Timbers were used to pave the streets of towns, which otherwise became impassable in the spring thaw or under heavy rains.

The Russians became extraordinarily adept in cutting and carving wood, and in the rapid raising of buildings. A Swedish traveler named Olearius, who made several trips to Muscovy in the middle seventeenth century, noted that an entire quarter of the town of Moscow was called Skorodom ("Quick House"). It was very large, as much as five leagues (23 miles) in perimeter. It contained the wood and house market. There the purchaser could buy the parts of a house, which could be put together in another part of the city in just two days. The logs of pine or spruce were already cut and trimmed, and the buyer need only lay out the beams and caulk the chinks with moss. Russian builders were capable of prefabricating entire towns. In 1551, Ivan IV wished to build a fortress on a hill near the confluence of the Sviyaga and the Volga rivers, which would bear the name Sviyazhsk. But he did not want to expose the builders to possible Tatar attack. He therefore had the walls, towers, storehouses, arsenals, bathhouses, bakeries, and some 100 other buildings erected in the interior of Russia. Then the edifices were dismantled and floated on rafts or carried on ships some 620 miles to the designated site. The town was quickly reassembled.

No less remarkable were the "one-day churches." In times of troubles, when the people were threatened by foreign invaders or even by plague, the peasants gathered at sunset to build a temple to God. Women held candles through the night and chanted, while the men labored at raising the church. They would finish it before sunset the following day, in time to celebrate the Eucharist.

The ax applied to the forests not only pro-vided shelter and warmth, but also defended the community. The peasants cut out of the forest long clearings, designed to stop the passage of invaders (sharpened stumps were left standing), of fire, or of plague. To fight fire, the Russians did not use water; rather, they rapidly demolished contiguous houses, in an effort to contain it. The ax was also a principal weapon. The *streltsy,* or "shooters," the first permanent infantry in early Muscovy, initially drilled with axes rather than with guns. The rebellious peasants of the seventeenth century fought with axes, and their leaders were executed by ax when the uprising failed. In a common Russian idiom, the cry "to your axes" had as its equivalent meaning "to arms."

Russian towns were, in the main, wooden cities, and this affected their design and character. The builders could not ring settlements with large circuits of stone walls, and wooden stockades or earthen ramparts were easily dismantled or destroyed. In the West, stone walls gave a clear definition to urban space and sharply separated it from the rural surroundings. Russian towns were not so well defined, and the towns tended to blend imperceptibly into the countryside. This may have hindered the growth of a separate urban law and perhaps an urban consciousness. So also, streets were broader in Russian towns than in the West, as wide streets served as a protection against the spread of fire. It also appears that buildings serving a public function, such as churches, were not expected to survive for long. They were quickly built or rebuilt, and were very small but very numerous. Olearius assures the reader that there were more than 2000 churches, monasteries, and chapels in Moscow; one in every five buildings in the city served religious purposes. Because of the frequent fires, the patriarch sought to have them all rebuilt in stone.

The many conflagrations have not served history well, as countless records were destroyed by them. They also deprived the Russians of many monumental reminders of the past, in the form of ancient buildings, and perhaps weakened their appreciation of the continuity of history.

Chapter 11

The West in Transition: Economy and Institutions 1300–1500

Shadows covered wide areas of European life in the fourteenth and fifteenth centuries. The vigorous expansion into bordering areas that had marked European history since the eleventh century came to an end. The Christian West fought to halt the expansion of the Muslim Turks but did not completely succeed. Plague, famine, and recurrent wars decimated populations and snuffed out their former prosperity. The papacy and feudal government struggled against mounting institutional chaos. Powerful mystical and heretical movements and new critical currents in Scholasticism rocked the established religious and philosophical equilibrium of the thirteenth century.

But for all these signs of crisis the fourteenth and fifteenth centuries were not merely an age of breakdown. The partial failure both of the medieval economy and government and of the established systems of thought and value facilitated change and impelled the Western peoples to repair their institutions and renew their culture. As Chapter 12 will show, there were vigorous developments in philosophy, religious thought, vernacular and Latin literature, and the fine arts. By the late fifteenth century the outlines of a new equilibrium were emerging. In 1500 Europeans doubtless remained fewer in number than they had been in 1300. But they also had developed a more productive economy and a more powerful technology than they had possessed 200 years before. These achievements also equipped Europeans for their great expansion throughout the world in the early modern epoch.

A traditional interpretation of the fourteenth and fifteenth centuries has made them years of renewal, rebirth: the Renaissance. In another interpretation, now equally traditional and reputable, the fourteenth and fifteenth centuries were the "autumn of the Middle Ages," and the somber theme of their history is the decline and death of a formerly great civilization. Today, with our own vastly enlarged fund of information, it is permissible and indeed necessary to consider the age both an autumn and a renaissance. The study of any past epoch requires an effort to balance the work of death and renewal. In few periods of history do death and renewal confront each other so dramatically as in the years between 1300 and 1500.

I. ECONOMIC DEPRESSION AND RECOVERY

The plagues and famines that struck European society in the fourteenth and fifteenth centuries profoundly affected economic life. Initially, they disrupted the established patterns of producing and exchanging goods and led directly to what some scholars now call "the economic depression of the Renaissance." But the effects of this disruption were not entirely negative; in reorganizing the economy under greatly changed demographic conditions, Europeans were able to make certain significant advances in the efficiency of economic production. To understand this paradox we must first examine how these disasters affected the population of Europe.

Demographic Catastrophe

Scholars have uncovered some censuses and other statistical records that for the first time give an insight into the size and structure of the European population. Nearly all of these records were drawn up for purposes of taxation and they therefore usually survey only limited geographical areas—a city or a province—and are rarely complete. But although they give us no reliable figures for total population, they still enable us to discern with considerable confidence how it was changing.

Almost every region of Europe from which we possess such records shows an appalling decline of population between approximately 1300 and 1450. For example, the population of Provence in southern France seems to have been between 350,000 and 400,000 in about 1310; a century later it had shrunk to something between one-third and one-half its earlier size, and only after 1470 did it again begin to increase. The population of the city and countryside of Pistoia, near Florence, fell from about 43,000 in the middle of the thirteenth century to 14,000 by the early fifteenth. The neighboring city and countryside of San Gimignano had approximately 13,000 residents in 1332 and only 3100 in 1428; the region still has not regained its maximum medieval size.

For the larger kingdoms of Europe the figures are less reliable, but they cannot be too far from the mark. England had a population of about 3.7 million in 1347 and 2.2 million by 1377.[1] By 1550 it was no larger a nation than it had been in the thirteenth century. France by 1328 may have reached 15 million; it too was

not again to attain its peak medieval size for several hundred years. In Germany, of some 170,000 inhabited localities named in sources antedating 1300, about 40,000 disappeared during the fourteenth and fifteenth centuries. Since many of the surviving towns were simultaneously shrinking in size, the population loss could only have been greater.

Certain favored regions of Europe, however—the fertile lands surrounding Paris or the Po valley—continually attracted settlers and maintained fairly stable populations, but they owed their good fortune more to immigration than to high birth rates or immunity from disease. It can safely be estimated that all of Europe in 1450 had no more than one-half, and probably only one-third, of the population it had had in the thirteenth century.

Pestilence

The great plague of the fourteenth century provides the most evident, although perhaps not the most satisfactory, explanation for these huge human losses. In 1347 a merchant ship sailing from Caffa in the Crimea to Messina in Sicily seems to have carried infected rats. A plague broke out at Messina and from there it spread throughout Europe (see Map 11.1).

This Black Death was not so much an epidemic as a pandemic, striking an entire continent. It was not the first pandemic in European history. One had raged across Europe in 542, during the reign of Justinian (see p. 244). But

---

[1] The estimate is based on the pioneering researches of J. C. Russell, *British Medieval Population,* 1948, but there is no national census for England in the period immediately preceding the Black Death and the figure of 3.7 million had to be extrapolated on the basis of presumed mortality rates. Recently, M. M. Postan, in the *Cambridge Economic History,* I, 562, stated that the preplague population may have been nearer 7 million and that "to most historians abreast of most recent researches the higher estimates may well appear to be more consistent with the economic and social conditions of rural England at the end of the thirteenth century."

International and Military History	Political History

1300

1328 Philip VI defeats Flemings at Cassel	1328 Philip of Valois elected King of France
1337 Philip VI declares French fiefs of Edward confiscated	
1338 Outbreak of the Hundred Years' War	
1340 English naval victory at Sluys	
1346 Great English victory at Crécy	
1347 English take Calais	
1356 The Black Prince routs French at Poitier	
1360 Peace of Brétigny ends first phase of Hundred Years' War	
1369 Fighting resumes; Bertrand du Guesclin leads French resurgence	
	1378–1402 Gian Galeazzo duke of Milan, Renaissance despot
	1399 Henry of Lancaster (Henry IV) seizes English throne

1400

1415 Henry V of England wins Battle of Agincourt	
1420 Treaty of Troyes; Henry V named heir to French throne	
1428 English begin siege of Orléans	
1429 Joan of Arc raises siege; has Dauphin crowned at Reims	
1430 Joan captured at Compiegne, sold by Burgundians to English	1434 Cosimo de' Medici establishes rule in Florence
1431 Joan burned at stake at Rouen	1438 Pragmatic Sanction of Bourges limits papal authority over French Church
	1445–1446 Companies of Ordinance established in France
1449–1461 English lose Continental posessions, except Calais	
	1455–1485 Wars of the Roses in England
	1461–1483 Louis XI, the "Spider King," rules France
1477 Charles the Bold, Duke of Burgundy, defeated and killed by Swiss at Nancy	1478–1492 Lorenzo the Magnificent ruler of Florence
	1485 Battle of Bosworth Field; Henry Tudor becomes English king
1494 Charles VIII of France invades Italy	

The great social disaster of the Black Death left few traces in the visual arts; perhaps people did not wish to be reminded of its horrors. One exception was the *Triumph of Death,* a mural painted shortly after 1348 in the Camposanto (cemetery) of Pisa in Italy. The author, once thought to be Francesco Traini, is now regarded as unknown. In this detail of the mural, an elegant party of hunters happens upon corpses prepared for burial. Note the rider who holds a handkerchief—scented, undoubtedly—to his nose, to ward off the foul odors.
(Photo: EPA, Inc.)

it was the first in perhaps 800 years, and it struck repeatedly during the century. A city was lucky if more than 10 years went by with-

out an onslaught; in some part of Europe, in almost every year, the plague was raging. Barcelona and its province of Catalonia, for example, lived through this record of misery in the fourteenth century: famine, 1333; plague, 1347 and 1351; famine, 1358 and 1359; plague, 1362, 1363, 1371, and 1397.

Some of the horror of the plague can be glimpsed in this account by an anonymous cleric who visited the French city of Avignon in 1348:

> To put the matter shortly, one-half, or more than a half, of the people at Avignon are already dead. Within the walls of the city there are now more than 7,000 houses shut up; in these no one is living, and all

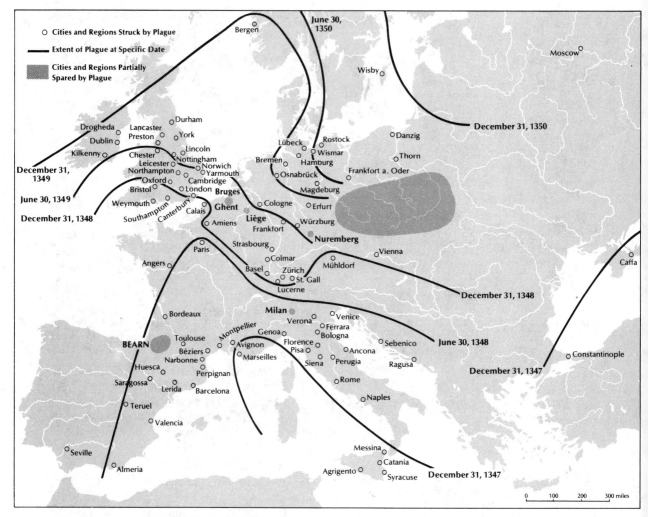

Legend:
- ○ Cities and Regions Struck by Plague
- — Extent of Plague at Specific Date
- ▨ Cities and Regions Partially Spared by Plague

Dates on map: June 30, 1350 · December 31, 1350 · December 31, 1349 · June 30, 1349 · December 31, 1348 · December 31, 1348 · June 30, 1348 · December 31, 1347 · December 31, 1347

0   100   200   300 miles

MAP 11.1. THE BLACK DEATH

[Adapted from Carpentier, E., "Autour de la peste noire; famines et épidémies dans l'histoire du XIVe siècle," in *Annales: Economies, Sociétés, Civilisations*, XVII (1962). Used by permission.]

who have inhabited them are departed; the suburbs hardly contain any people at all. . . .

The like account I can give of all the cities and towns of Provence. Already the sickness has crossed the Rhone, and ravaged many cities and villages as far as Toulouse, and it ever increases in violence as it proceeds. On account of this great mortality there is such a fear of death that people do not dare even to speak with anyone whose relative has died, because it is frequently remarked that in a family where one dies nearly all the relations follow him, and this is commonly believed among the people.[2]

[2] *Breve Chronicon clerici anonymi*, quoted in Francis Aidan Gasquet, *The Black Death of 1348 and 1349*, 1908, p. 46.

Most historians identify the Black Death as the bubonic plague, but they find it difficult to explain how this disease could have spread so rapidly and killed so many, since bubonic plague is more truly a disease of rats and small mammals than of human beings. If bubonic plague is to spread to a human, a flea must bite an infected rat, pick up the infection, and carry it to a human host through a bite. The infection causes the lymphatic glands to swell, but recovery is not uncommon. Only if the infection travels through the bloodstream to the lungs, causing pneumonia, can the disease be spread directly from person to person. The real killer in the fourteenth century seems to have been a pneumonic plague, which infects the lungs directly; it probably was spread through coughing and was almost always fatal.

In spite of the virulence of pneumonic plague it is hard to believe that medical factors alone can explain the awesome mortalities. After all, Europeans had maintained close contact with the East, where the plague had been endemic, since the eleventh century, but not until 1347 and 1348 did it make serious inroads in Europe. In addition, pneumonic plague itself is a disease of the winter months, but the plagues of the fourteenth century characteristically raged during the summer and dissipated with the cooler weather of autumn. Some scholars consider that the weather of the age—it seems to have been unusually cool and humid—somehow favored the disease. Others argue that acute, widespread malnutrition had severely debilitated the population and lowered resistance to all kinds of infections.

Hunger

A second cause of the dramatic fall in population was hunger. Famines frequently scourged the land; and even if they were less lethal than the plague in their initial onslaught, they were likely to persist for several years. In 1315, 1316, and 1317 a severe famine raged in the north of Europe; in 1339 and 1340 another struck the south. The starving people ate not only their reserves of grain but most of the seed set aside for planting. Only a remarkably good harvest could compensate for the loss of grain by providing both immediate sustenance and seed for future planting in satisfactory quantities.

Why was hunger so rampant in the early fourteenth century? Some historians now locate the root of trouble in the sheer number of people the lands had to support by 1300. The medieval population, they say, had been growing rapidly since about 1000, and by 1300 Europe was becoming the victim of its own success. Parts of the Continent were crowded, even glutted, with people. The county of Beaumont-le-Roger in Normandy, for example, had a population in the early fourteenth century not much below the number it was supporting in the early twentieth century. Thousands, millions even, had to be fed without the aid of chemical fertilizers, power tools, and fast transport. Masses of people had come to depend for their livelihood upon unrewarding soils. Even in good years they were surviving on the slim and uncertain margins of existence; a slightly reduced harvest during any one year took on the dimensions of a major famine. Through hunger, malnutrition, and plague the hand of death was correcting the ledgers of life, balancing the numbers of people and the resources that supported them.

Economic Effects of the Decline in Population

What effects did the fall in population have on the economy of Europe? Initially, the losses disrupted production. According to the chroniclers, survivors of the plague frequently gave up toiling in the fields or working in shops; presumably, they saw no point in working for the future when the future was so uncertain. But, in the long run, the results were not altogether negative. In agriculture, for example, the contraction of the population enabled the survivors to concentrate their efforts on the better soils. Moreover, in both agriculture and industry the shortage of laborers was a challenge to landlords and entrepreneurs to save costs either by adopting productive routines less demanding of manpower or by increased investment in laborsaving devices. Thus the decline in population eventually taught Europeans to work more efficiently through more rational productive routines and greater capital investment.

Agriculture

Perhaps the best indication of the forces working upon the European economy comes from the history of prices. The evidence is scattered and rarely precise, but is good enough to reveal roughly similar patterns in price movements all over Europe. Most agricultural products—cereals, wine, beer, oil, and meat—shot up immediately after the Black Death and stayed high until approximately 1375 in the north and 1395 in Italy. High food prices in a period of contracting population seem certain evidence that production was falling even more rapidly than the number of consumers.

The beginnings of an agricultural recovery become evident in the early fifteenth century. With a diminished number of Europeans to be fed, the demand for cereals, the cultivation of which dominated agriculture in the earlier centuries, lessened perceptibly and their prices declined; with fewer available workers, the cost of labor pushed steadily upward. Landlords had to compete with one another to attract scarce tenants to their lands and did so by offering lower rents and favorable terms of tenancy. The upward movement of wages and the downward price of cereals led to a concentration on those commodities that would command a better price in the market or were less expensive to produce. Better wages in both town and

countryside enabled the population to consume a more varied and more expensive diet. While the price of wheat fell, wine, beer, oil, butter, cheese, meat, fruit, and other relatively expensive foods remained high, reflecting a strong market demand.

One branch of agriculture that enjoyed a remarkable period of growth in the fifteenth century was sheep raising. Labor costs were low, since a few shepherds could guard thousands of sheep, and the price for wool, skins, mutton, and cheese remained high. In England many landlords fenced large fields, converting them from plowland into sheep pastures and expelling the peasants or small herders who had formerly lived on them; this process, called enclosure, continued into the sixteenth century and played an important role in the economic and social history of Tudor England.

By the middle of the fifteenth century, agricultural prices tended to stabilize, and this suggests a more dependable production. Farms enjoyed the advantages of greater size, better location on more profitable soil, and greater capital investments in tools and animals. Agriculture was now considerably diversified, benefiting the soil, lowering the risk of famine through the failure of a single staple crop, and providing more nourishment for the people. Europeans were consuming a healthier diet by the middle of the fifteenth century than had their ancestors 200 years before.

Industry and Trade

The movement of prices created serious problems for the entrepreneurs within the cities. As the labor force contracted, wages in most towns surged upward and commonly reached levels two, three, and even four times higher than they had been before 1348. Although the prices of manufactured commodities also increased, they did not rise as much as wages, and this worked to reduce profit margins. To offset these unfavorable tendencies, the entrepreneurs sought government intervention. In various enactments from 1349 to 1351, England, France, Aragon, Castile, and other governments tried to fix prices and wages at levels favorable to employers. The English Parliament in the Statute of Laborers, following a policy typical of the age, forbade employers to pay more than the customary wages and required laborers to accept jobs at those wages. These early experiments in a controlled economy failed. The price and wage ceilings set by law seem to have had little perceptible influence on actual prices.

A related problem troubled the business climate. Competition grew as population fell and markets contracted. Entrepreneurs tried to protect themselves by creating restricted markets and establishing monopolies. Guilds limited their membership, and some admitted only the sons of established masters. Cities too imposed heavy restrictions on the importation of foreign manufactures.

Probably the best example of the monopoly spirit is the association of north German trading cities, the Hanseatic League. The league was a defensive association formed in the fourteenth century to promote German interests and exclude foreigners from the Baltic trade. The cities initially sought this mutual protection because the emperor was too weak to defend their interests. At its height the Hanseatic League included about 70 or 80 cities under the leadership of Bremen, Cologne, Hamburg, and especially Lübeck. Maintaining its own treasury and fleet, the league supervised commercial exchange, policed the waters of the Baltic Sea, and negotiated with foreign princes. By the late fifteenth century, however, the league had begun to decline. It failed to meet the growing threat of the Dutch, who were then vigorously competing for leadership in northern commerce. The Hanseatic League was never formally abolished; it continued to meet at lengthening intervals until 1669.

The Forces of Recovery

Attempts to raise the efficiency of workers proved to be far more effective than wage and trade regulation in laying the basis for recovery. Employers were able to counteract high wages by adopting more rational production procedures and substituting capital for labor, that is, providing the worker with better tools. Although largely inspired by hard times and labor shortages, most of the technical advances of the fourteenth and fifteenth centuries enabled the worker to practice his trade more efficiently and eventually helped make Europe a richer community.

Metallurgy

Mining and metallurgy benefited from a series of inventions after 1460 that lowered the cost of metals and extended their use in European life. Better techniques of digging, shoring, ventilating, and draining allowed mine shafts to be sunk several hundred feet into the earth, permitting the large-scale exploitation of the deep, rich mineral deposits of Central Europe. Some historians estimate (on slim evidence, to be sure) that the output from the mines of Central Europe—Hungary, the Tyrol, Bohemia, and Saxony—grew as much as five times between 1460 and 1530. During this period miners in Saxony discovered a method of extracting pure silver from the lead alloy in which it was often found (the invention was of major importance for the later, massive development of silver mines in America). Larger furnaces came into use, and huge bellows and trip-hammers, driven by water power, aided the smelting and working of metals. Simultaneously, the masters of the trade were acquiring a new precision in the difficult art of casting.

By the late fifteenth century, European mines were providing an abundance of silver bullion for coinage. Money became more plentiful, and this stimulated the economy. Beginnings were also laid for the exploitation of the rich coal deposits of the European north. Expanding iron production meant more and stronger pumps, gears and machine parts, tools, and ironwares; such products found wide application in construction work and shipbuilding. Moreover, skill in metalworking contributed to two other inventions: firearms and movable metal type.

Firearms

Europeans were constantly trying to improve the arts of war in the bellicose Middle Ages; and one weapon, or family of weapons, they sought was a device which would hurl projectiles with great force and accuracy. We do not know how Europeans first learned that certain mixtures of carbon, sulfur, and saltpeter burn with explosive force and could be used to hurl boulders at an enemy, but we do know that cannons were used in the fourteenth century during the Hundred Years' War. Their effect seems to have been chiefly psychological: the thunderous roar, merely by frightening the enemy's horses, probably did more damage than the inevitably misdirected shots. Still, a breakthrough had been made, and cannons gained in military importance. Their development depended primarily on stronger, more precise casting and on proper granulation of the powder to ensure that the charge would burn at the right speed so that its full force pushed the projectile. With firearms fewer soldiers could fight more effectively; capital, in the form of an efficient though expensive tool, was again being substituted for labor.

Printing

The extension of literacy among laypeople and the greater reliance of governments and businesses upon records created a demand for a cheap method of reproducing the written word. One important advance was the replace-

A page from Johannes Gutenberg's Bible marks one of the most significant technical and cultural advances of the fifteenth century: printing with movable type, a process that made possible a wider dissemination of literature and thought.
(Photo: E. Harold Hugo)

ment of expensive parchment by paper, which had originated in the East. But even so, the scribe and copier worked slowly and, like all artisans, were commanding an increased salary. As a solution, printing was first tried by stamping paper or parchment with woodcuts, which were inked blocks with letters or designs carved on them. But the "block books" produced in this fashion represented only a small advance over handwriting, for a separate woodcut had to be carved for each page. And the woodcuts were not sufficiently durable; they tended to split in the press, after short use.

By the middle of the fifteenth century several masters were on the verge of perfecting the technique of printing with movable metal type. The first man to prove the practicability of the new art was Johannes Gutenberg of Mainz, a former jeweler and stonecutter. Gutenberg devised an alloy of lead, tin, and antimony that would melt at a low temperature, cast well in the die, and be durable in the press; this alloy is still the basis of the printer's art. His Bible, printed in 1455, is the first major work reproduced through printing.

In spite of Gutenberg's efforts to keep the technique a secret it spread rapidly. Before 1500 some 250 European cities had acquired presses. German masters held an early leadership, but Italians soon challenged their preeminence. The Venetian printer Aldus Manutius published works, notably editions of the Greek and Latin classics, that are minor masterpieces of scholarship and grace. Manutius and his fellow Italian masters rejected the elaborate Gothic typeface used in the north and developed their own, modeled on the clear script they found in their oldest manuscripts. They wrongly believed that it was the style of writing used in ancient Rome; they were in fact imitating the Carolingian minuscule. Our own term *Roman type* still reflects this old mistake.

The immediate effect of the printing press was to multiply the output and cut the costs of books. It thus made information available to a much larger segment of the population. Libraries could store much bigger quantities of information at much lower cost. Printing also facilitated the dissemination and preservation of knowledge in standardized form; this was of inestimable importance in the advance of technology, science, and scholarship. Printing produced a revolution in what we would call today "information technology." Indeed, this revolution in many ways resembles the profound changes that computers are making in our own lives. Finally, printing could spread new ideas with unprecedented speed and impact, a fact that was appreciated only slowly. The Protestant reformers of the sixteenth century were really the first to take advantage of the potential of printing for propaganda, and Catholics soon followed.

Navigation

People as well as ideas began to travel more easily in the fourteenth and fifteenth centuries. Before about 1325 there was still no regular sea traffic between northern and southern Europe by way of the Atlantic, but it grew rapidly thereafter. In navigation the substitution of capital for labor primarily meant the introduction of larger ships, which could carry more cargo with relatively smaller crews. The large ships were safer at sea; they could sail in periods of uncertain weather, when smaller vessels had to stay in port. They could also remain at sea longer and did not have to sail close to the coastline in order to replenish their supplies. Their voyages between ports could be more direct and therefore speedier.

The larger vessels required more sophisticated means of steering and navigation. Before 1300, ships were turned by trailing an oar over the side. The control provided by this method was poor, especially for sailing ships, which needed an efficient means of steering to take advantage of shifting winds. Sometime during the fourteenth century the stern rudder was developed, enabling the captain to tack effectively against the wind and control his ship more closely entering or leaving ports. Voyages thus were rendered quicker and safer, and the costs of maritime transport declined.

Ocean navigation also required a reliable means for estimating course and position, and here notable progress had been made, especially in the late thirteenth century. Scholars at the court of King Alfonso X of Castile compiled the Alfonsine Tables, which showed with unprecedented accuracy the position and movements of the heavenly bodies. Using such tables along with an astrolabe, captains could shoot the sun or stars and calculate their latitude, or position on a north-south coordinate.[3]

The compass, the origin of which is unclear, was commonly used on Mediterranean ships by at least the thirteenth century. By 1300, and undoubtedly for some decades before, Mediterranean navigators sailed with the aid of maps remarkable for their accuracy. Navigators were further aided by portolani, or port descriptions, which gave an account of harbors and coastlines and pinpointed hazards. All these technical developments gave European mariners a mastery of the Atlantic coastal waters and helped prepare the way for the voyages of discovery in the fifteenth century.

Business Institutions

The bad times of the fourteenth century also stimulated the development of more efficient business procedures. The mercantile houses in the late fourteenth and fifteenth centuries were considerably smaller than those of the thirteenth century, but were more flexible in their structure. The Medici bank of Florence, which

---

[3] Ships could not tell their longitude, or position on an east-west coordinate, until they could carry accurate clocks, which could in turn tell the time of a basic reference meridian (such as that of Greenwich, England) and be compared with the ship's time. Galileo's discovery of the laws of the pendulum made possible the first really accurate mechanical clocks, but they could not function aboard a swaying ship. Not until the eighteenth century were the first accurate "chronometers," or shipboard clocks, developed. Until then navigators such as Columbus who sailed across the Atlantic had no precise idea how far they were traveling.

functioned from 1397 until 1498, offers a particularly clear example of fifteenth-century business organization. It was not a single monolithic structure; rather, it was founded upon separate partnerships, by which its various branches were established at Florence, Venice, Rome, Avignon, Bruges, and London. Central control and unified management were ensured, since the senior partners—members of the Medici family—were the same in all the contracts; but the branches had autonomy and, most important, the collapse of one did not threaten them all. One scholar has compared this system of interlocked partnerships to a modern holding company.

Banking operations also grew more sophisticated. By the late fourteenth century, "book transfers" had become commonplace; that is, one depositor could pay a debt to another without actually using coin by ordering the bank to transfer credit from his own account to his creditor's. At first the depositor had to give this order orally, but by 1400 such an order was commonly written, making it one of the immediate ancestors of the modern check.

Accounting methods also improved. The most notable development was the adoption of double-entry bookkeeping, which makes arithmetical errors immediately evident and gives a clear picture of the financial position of a commercial enterprise. Although known in the ancient world, double-entry bookkeeping was not widely practiced in the West until the fourteenth century. In this as in other business practices the lands of southern Europe, especially Italy, were precocious, but their accounting techniques eventually spread to the rest of Europe.

Another financial innovation was the development of a system of maritime insurance, without which investors would have been highly reluctant to risk their money on expensive vessels. There are references to the practice of insuring ships in the major Italian ports as early as 1318. In these first insurance contracts the broker bought the ship and cargo at the

This illustration from a printed Italian handbook, which gives instructions to merchants and is dated ca. 1496, shows the interior of a bank or counting house.
(Photo: New York Public Library/Picture Collection)

---

port of embarkation and agreed to sell them back at a higher price once the ship reached its destination. If the ship sank en route, it was legally the broker's and he assumed the loss. In the course of the fourteenth century the leading companies of Florence, actively interested in providing insurance to shippers, abandoned the clumsy device of conditional sales and wrote explicit and open insurance contracts. By 1400 maritime insurance had become a regular item of the shipping business. It was to play a major role in the opening of the Atlantic.

Insurance for land transport developed a half-century later and never was intensively practiced. The first examples of life insurance contracts come from fifteenth-century Italy and were limited to particular periods (the duration of a voyage) or particular persons (a wife during pregnancy). But without actuarial tables life insurance of this sort was far more a gamble than a business.

The Economy in the Late Fifteenth Century

In the last half of the fifteenth century Europe had fairly well recovered from the economic blows of a hundred years before, and the revived economy differed greatly from what it had formerly been. Increased diversification, capitalization, and rationalization aided production and enterprise in both countryside and city. Europe in 1500 was certainly a much smaller community than it had been in 1300. Possibly, too, the gross product of its economy may not have equaled the output of the best years of the thirteenth century. But the population ultimately had fallen more drastically than production. After a century of difficult readjustment Europe emerged more productive and richer than it had been at any earlier time in its history.

II. POPULAR UNREST

The demographic collapse and economic troubles of the fourteenth century deeply disturbed the social peace of Europe. European society had been remarkably stable and mostly peaceful from the Early Middle Ages until approximately 1300, and the chronicles have preserved few notices of social uprisings or class warfare. The fourteenth and fifteenth centuries, however, witness numerous revolts of peasants and artisans against what they believed to be oppression by the propertied classes.

Rural Revolts

One of the most spectacular of the fourteenth-century rural uprisings was the English Peasants' War of 1381. Both the policies of the royal government and the practices of the great landlords angered the peasants. As mentioned earlier, the royal government through the Statute of Laborers (1351) sought to freeze wages and keep the workers bound to their jobs. Although this policy had little practical success, the mere effort to implement it aggravated social tensions, especially in the countryside, where it would have imposed a kind of neoserfdom upon the peasants. In addition the government made several efforts to collect from the rural villages a poll tax (a flat charge on each member of the population). Moreover, the great landlords, faced with falling rents, sought to revive many half-forgotten feudal dues, which had been allowed to lapse when rents were high in the thirteenth century.

Under leaders of uncertain background—Wat Tyler, Jack Straw, and a priest named John Ball—peasant bands, enraged by the latest poll tax, marched on London in 1381. They called for the final abolition of serfdom, labor services, tithes, and other feudal dues and demanded an end to the poll taxes. The workers of London, St. Albans, York, and other cities, who had similar grievances against the royal government, rose in support of the peasants. After the mobs burned the houses of prominent lawyers and royal officials, King Richard II, then 15, with considerable bravery personally met with the peasants and was able to placate them by promising to accept their demands. But as the peasants dispersed, the great landlords reorganized their forces and violently suppressed the last vestiges of unrest in the countryside; the young king also reneged on his promises.

The peasant uprising in England was only one of many rural disturbances that occurred between 1350 and 1450, including revolts in the Île de France, Languedoc, Catalonia, Sweden, and another in England (1450). Numerous rural disturbances occurred in Germany in the fifteenth century, and a major peasant revolt there in 1524 played an important role in the history of the early Reformation.

Urban Revolts

The causes of social unrest within the cities were very similar to those in the countryside.

Governments controlled by the propertied classes tried to prevent wages from rising and workers from moving and also sought to impose a heavier share of the tax burden upon the poorer segments of society. In the fourteenth and early fifteenth centuries Strasbourg, Metz, Ghent, Liège, and Paris all were the scenes of riots. One of the most interesting, if not perhaps the most typical, of the specifically urban revolts was the Ciompi uprising at Florence in 1378.

Florence was one of the wool-manufacturing centers of Europe; the industry employed probably one-third of the working population of the city, which shortly before the Black Death included probably 120,000 people. The wool industry, like most industries, entered into bad times immediately after the plague. To protect themselves, employers cut production, thereby spreading unemployment. Since many of the employers were also members of the ruling oligarchy, they had laws passed limiting wages and manipulating taxation and other monetary policies to the benefit of the rich. The poorest workers were denied their own guild and had no collective voice that might have influenced the government. In all disputes they were subject to the bosses' judges and the bosses' law.

The poorest workers—principally the wool carders, known as the Ciompi—rose in revolt. They demanded, and for a short time got, several reforms. The employers would produce at least enough cloths to ensure work; they would refrain from certain monetary manipulations considered deleterious to the interests of the workers; they would allow the workers their own guild; and they would give them representation in communal government. This was hardly a dictatorship of the proletariat, but it was nevertheless intolerable to the ruling oligarchy. Because the Ciompi did not have the leaders to maintain a steady influence on governmental policy, the great families regained full authority in the city by 1382 and quickly abrogated the democratic concessions. Although the Ciompi revolt was short-lived and ultimately unsuccessful, the incident marks one of the first manifestations of urban class tensions that would frequently disturb capitalistic society in future centuries.

The Seeds of Discontent

Each of the social disturbances of the fourteenth and fifteenth centuries was shaped by circumstances that were local and unique. Nevertheless, there were similarities in these social movements: for example, the fact that misery does not seem to have been the principal cause of the unrest. Indeed, the evidence suggests that the conditions of the working classes in both countryside and city were improving after the Black Death. The prosperity of the thirteenth century, which was chiefly a prosperity of landlords and employers, had been founded in part upon the poor negotiating position, and even the exploitation, of the workers. The depopulation of the fourteenth century radically altered this situation. The workers, now much reduced in number, were better able to bargain for lower rents, higher wages, and a fairer distribution of social benefits.

With the possible exception of the Ciompi, the people who revolted were rarely the desperately poor. In England, for example, the centers of the peasant uprising of 1381 were in the lower Thames valley—a region that seems to have been more fertile, more prosperous, and less oppressed than other parts of the kingdom. (Serfdom, for example, was relatively less widespread and onerous here than in other English areas.) Also, the immediate provocation for the revolt was the imposition of a poll tax, and obviously poll taxes, or any taxes or charges, do not alarm the truly destitute, whereas they do alarm people recently arrived at some favorable position and anxious to hold on to their gains.

The principal goad to revolt in both town and country seems to have been the effort of the propertied classes to retain their old advantages and deny the workers their new ones. In the first decades after the Black Death governments failed in their efforts to increase taxes and to peg rents, wages, and prices at levels favorable to landlords and employers; meanwhile they spread hostility among the workers, who felt their improving social and economic status threatened.

The impulse to revolt also drew strength from the psychological tensions characteristic of this age of devastating plagues, famines, and wars. The nervous temper of the times predisposed men to take compulsive action against real or imagined enemies. When needed, ready justification for revolt could be found in Christian belief, for the common teaching of the Christian fathers was that neither the concept of private property nor social inequality had been intended by God. In a high-strung world many of these uprisings involved an emotional effort to attain the millennium, to reach that age of justice and equality that Christian belief saw in the past, expected in the future, and put off for the present.

The revolts of the fourteenth and fifteenth centuries brought no radical changes in governments or policies, but underlying social movements were coming to elevate the status of the workers. If the rich wanted tillers for their lands and workers for their shops, they had to offer favorable terms.

By about 1450, after a century of instability, a new equilibrium was emerging in European society, even if slowly and never completely. The humblest classes improved their lot and were fairly secure in their gains. Serfdom all but disappeared in the West; wages remained high and bread cheap. Life of course was still very hard for most workers, but it was better than it had been two centuries before. Perhaps reflective of better social conditions for the masses, the population once more began to grow, equipping Europe for its great expansion within its borders and beyond the oceans in the sixteenth century.

III. THE GOVERNMENTS OF EUROPE

War was a frequent occurrence throughout the Middle Ages but was never so widespread and so protracted as in the conflicts of the fourteenth and fifteenth centuries. The Hundred Years' War between England and France is the most famous of these struggles, but there was fighting in every corner of Europe. The inbred violence of the age manifests a partial breakdown in the governmental systems, their failure to maintain stability at home and peace with foreign powers.

Crisis and the Feudal Equilibrium

The governmental systems of Europe were founded upon multiple partnerships in the exercise of power under the feudal constitutions. The king enjoyed supreme dignity and even a recognized sacred character, but he was far from being an absolute ruler. In return for loyalty and service he conceded a large share of the responsibility for government to a wide range of privileged persons and institutions: the great secular and ecclesiastical princes, the nobles, religious congregations, powerful military orders such as the Templars, free cities or communes, and even favored guilds such as the universities.

The growth of the feudal constitution in the eleventh and twelfth centuries had been a major step toward a more ordered political life, but it rested upon a delicate equilibrium. To keep an internal peace, which because of the confused borders of most feudal states often meant in-

CHRONOLOGY OF THE HUNDRED YEARS' WAR

1328: Charles IV, last Capetian king in direct line, dies; Philip of Valois elected king of France as Philip VI. Philip defeats Flemings at Cassel; unrest continues in Flemish towns.

1329: Edward III of England does simple homage to Philip for Continental possessions, but refuses liege homage.

1336: Edward embargoes wool exports to Flanders.

1338: Philip's troops harass English Guienne; Edward, urged on by the Flemings, claims French crown; war begins.

1346: Great English victory at Crécy.

1347–1351: Black Death ravages Europe.

1356: Black Prince defeats French at Poitiers.

1358: The Jacquerie, peasants' uprising near Paris.

1360: Peace of Brétigny. English gain major territorial concessions but abandon claim to French crown.

1369: Fighting renewed in France.

1370: Bertrand du Guesclin, constable of France, leads French resurgence.

1381: Peasants' Revolt in England.

1392: Charles VI of France suffers first attack of insanity; Burgundians and Armagnacs contend for power over king. Fighting wanes as both sides exhausted.

1399: Henry IV of Lancaster takes English throne.

1415: Henry V wins great victory at Agincourt.

1420: Treaty of Troyes. Charles VI recognizes Henry V as legitimate heir to French crown; highwater mark of English fortunes.

1429: Joan of Arc relieves Orléans from English siege; Dauphin crowned king at Reims as Charles VII.

1431: Joan burned at the stake of Rouen.

1435: Peace of Arras; Burgundy abandons English side.

1436: Charles retakes Paris.

1453: Bordeaux falls to French; English retain only Calais on Continent; effective end of war, though no treaty is made.

ternational peace, all members of the feudal partnership had to remain punctiliously faithful to their obligations. This governmental system worked well until the beginning of the fourteenth century, but it could not sustain the multiple blows suffered during the period of social crisis. Governments had to be slowly rebuilt, still along feudal lines, still based on shared authority. Many of the new governments that came to dominate the European political scene in the late fifteenth century, although still not absolutistic, conceded far more power to the senior partner in the feudal relationship, the king or prince.

Dynastic Instability

The forces that upset the equilibrium of feudal governments were many. One of the most evident, itself rooted in the demographic instability of the age, was the failure of dynasties to perpetuate themselves. The Hundred Years' War, or at least the excuse for it, arose from the inability of the Capetian kings of France, for the first time since the tenth century, to produce a male heir in direct line. The English War of the Roses resulted from the uncertain succession to the crown of England and the claims that the two rival houses of Lancaster and York exerted for it. In Portugal, Castile, France, England, Naples, Hungary, Poland, and the Scandinavian countries the reigning monarchs of 1450 were not the direct, male, legitimate descendants of those reigning in 1300. Most of the founders of new lines had to fight for their position.

Fiscal Pressures

The same powerful economic forces that were creating new patterns of agriculture and trade were also reshaping the fiscal policies and financial machinery of feudal governments. War was growing more expensive, as well as more frequent. Better-trained armies were needed to fight for longer periods of time and with more complex weaponry. Above all, the increasing use of firearms was adding to the costs of war. To replace the traditional, undisciplined, unpaid, and poorly equipped feudal armies, governments came more and more to rely on mercenaries, who were better trained and better armed than the vassals who fought in fulfillment of their feudal obligations. Many mercenaries were organized into associations known as companies of adventure, whose leaders were both good commanders and businessmen. They took their enterprise where the market was most favorable, sold their services to the highest bidder, and turned substantial profits. To hire mercenaries, and win battles, was increasingly a question of money, which then became, as it has since remained, the *nervi belli* ("the sinews of war").

While war went up in price, the traditional revenues upon which governments depended sank. Until the fourteenth century the king or prince was expected to meet the expenses of government from ordinary revenues, chiefly rents from his properties; but his rents, like everyone's, were falling in the Late Middle Ages. Governments of all types—monarchies, the papacy, cities—desperately sought to develop new sources of revenue. For example, the papacy, because it could not rely on the meager receipts from its lands, built a huge financial apparatus that sold ecclesiastical appointments, favors, and dispensations from normal canonical requirements; imposed tithes on ecclesiastical revenues; and sold indulgences. In France the monarchy established a monopoly over the sale of salt (the *gabelle*). In England the king at various times imposed direct taxes on hearths, individuals (the poll tax), and plow teams, plus a host of smaller levies. The Italian cities taxed a whole range of items from windows to prostitutes. Under acute fiscal pressures governments rigorously scrutinized the necessities, pleasures, and sins of society to find sources of revenue.

Surviving fiscal records indicate that in spite of the disturbed times many governments did succeed in greatly increasing their incomes through these taxes. For example, the English monarchy never collected or spent more than £30,000 per year before 1336; thereafter, the budget rarely sank below £100,000 and at times reached £250,000 in the late fourteenth century.

This new reliance on extraordinary taxes had important political consequences. The most lucrative of them were not limited to the ruler's own demesne but extended over all his realm. They were, in other words, national, or at least territorial, taxes. Moreover, the ruler had no established right to their collection but had to seek the consent of his subjects. He therefore frequently summoned territorial or national assemblies of estates, such as Parliament in England or the Estates General in France, to grant the new taxes. But the assemblies in turn often balked at these requests or offered to grant them only in return for political concessions. Even within the Church many reformers maintained that a general council should have ultimate control over papal finances. The extraordinary expansion of governmental revenues thus raised profound constitutional questions in both ecclesiastical and secular governments.

Factional Conflicts

The aristocracy that had developed nearly everywhere in Europe also entered a period of instability in the Late Middle Ages. Birth afforded the principal access to this class, and membership in it conveyed certain legal and social privileges—exemption from most taxes, immunity from certain juridical procedures, such as torture, and so forth. The nobles looked upon themselves as the chief counselors of the king and his principal partners in the conduct of government.

By the fourteenth century, however, the nobles had long since lost whatever economic homogeneity they may once have possessed. Their wealth was chiefly in land, and they, like all landlords, faced the problem of declining rents. Frequently they lacked the funds needed for the new systems of agriculture. They were further plagued by the continuing problem of finding income and careers for their younger sons. In short, the nobles possessed no immunity from the acute economic dislocations of the times, and their class included men who lived on the brink of poverty as well as holders of enormous estates.

To maintain their position some of the nobles joined the companies of adventure to fight as mercenaries. Others hoped to buttress their sinking fortunes through marriage or by winning offices, lands, pensions, or other favors that governments could provide. Amid these social uncertainties the nobles tended to coalesce into factions, which disputed with one another over the control of government and the distribution of its favors. From England to Italy factional warfare, far more than class warfare, constantly disturbed the peace. A divided and grasping nobility added to the tensions of the age and to its taste for violence.

Characteristically, a faction was led by a great noble house and included numerous persons of varying social station—great nobles in alliance with the leading house, poor knights, retainers, servants, sometimes even artisans and peasants. At times the factions encompassed scores of families and hundreds of men and could almost be considered little states within a state, with their own small armies, loyalties, and symbols of allegiance in the colors or distinctive costumes (livery) worn by their members.

England, France, and the Hundred Years' War

All the factors that upset the equilibrium of feudal governments—dynastic instability, fiscal pressures, and factional rivalries—helped to provoke the greatest struggle of the epoch, the Hundred Years' War.

The proclaimed issue of the Hundred Years' War was a dispute over the French royal succession. After more than 300 years of extraordinary good luck, the last three Capetian kings (the brothers Louis X, Philip V, and Charles IV) failed to produce male heirs. With Charles's death in 1328, the nearest surviving male relative was his nephew King Edward III of England, son of his sister Isabella. But the Parlement of Paris—the supreme court of France—declared that women could not transmit a claim to the crown. In place of Edward the French Estates chose Philip of Valois, a first cousin of the preceding kings. Edward did not initially dispute this decision, and as holder of the French fiefs of Aquitaine and Ponthieu he did homage to Philip.

More important than the dynastic issue was the clash of French and English interests in the county of Flanders, whose cloth-making industry relied on England for wool. In 1302 the Flemings had rebelled against their count, a vassal of the French king, and had remained virtually independent until 1328, when Philip defeated their forces at Cassel and restored the count. At Philip's insistence the count ordered the arrest of all English merchants in Flanders; Edward then retaliated by cutting off the export of wool, which spread unemployment in the Flemish towns. The Flemings revolted once more and drove out the count. To give legal sanction to their revolt they persuaded Edward to assert his claim to the French crown, which would have given him suzerainty over Flanders as well.

The most serious of all points of friction, however, was the exact status of Aquitaine and Ponthieu. Edward had willingly performed ordinary homage for them, but Philip then insisted on liege homage, which would have obligated Edward to support Philip against all enemies. Edward did not believe that, as a king, he could undertake the obligations of liege homage to any man, and refused. Philip began harassing the frontiers of Aquitaine and declared Edward's fiefs forfeit in 1337. The attack upon Aquitaine undoubtedly pushed Edward into supporting the Flemish revolt and was the

A castle under siege during the Hundred Years' War.
(Photo: British Museum)

principal provocation for the Hundred Years' War.

Philip, in his eagerness for glory, had clearly embarked upon a dangerous adventure in his harassment of Aquitaine, and Edward, in supporting the Flemings, reacted perhaps too strongly to the provocation. Both men evidently took their feudal obligation of mutual respect and love very lightly. The coming of this war between the French king and his principal vassal was thus rooted in a breakdown of the feudal constitution of medieval France in both its institutions and its spirit.

The Tides of Battle

The French seemed to have a decisive superiority over the English at the outset of the war. The population of France was perhaps 15 million; England had between 4 and 7 million. But for most of its course the war was not really a national confrontation. French subjects (Flemings, Gascons, later Burgundians) fought alongside the English against other French subjects. The confused struggle may be fairly divided into three periods: an initial phase of English victories from 1338 to 1360; a phase of French resurgence, then stalemate, from 1367 to 1415; and a wild denouement with tides rapidly shifting from 1415 to 1453.

The series of English victories that opened the war were never fully exploited by the English, nor ever quite undone by the French. An English naval victory at Sluys in 1340 assured English communications across the Channel and determined that France would be the scene of the fighting. Six years later Edward landed in France on what was more a marauding expedition than a campaign of conquest. Philip pursued the English and finally overtook them at Crécy. The French knights attacked before their own forces could be entirely marshaled and organized; the disciplined English, making effective use of the longbow, cut the confused French army to pieces. The scenario was repeated in 1356 at Poitiers. John II, who had succeeded Philip, attacked an English army under Edward's son, the gallant Black Prince, and incurred a defeat even more crushing. English victories, the Black Death, and mutual exhaustion prepared the way for the Peace of Brétigny in 1360. The English were given Calais and an enlarged Aquitaine, and Edward in turn renounced his claims to the French crown.

But the French were not willing to allow so large a part of their kingdom to remain in English hands. Nine years later, under John's successor, Charles V, they opened the second phase of the war. The French armies succeeded largely by avoiding full-scale battles and wearing down the English forces. By 1380 they had pushed the English nearly into the sea, confining them to Calais and a narrow strip of the Atlantic coast from Bordeaux to Bayonne. Fighting was sporadic from 1380 until 1415, both sides content with a stalemate.

The last period of the war, from 1415 to 1453, was one of high drama and rapidly shifting fortunes. Henry V of England invaded France and wrought disaster on the French army at Agincourt in 1415. His success was confirmed by the Treaty of Troyes in 1420, an almost total French capitulation. King Charles VI of France declared his son the Dauphin (the future Charles VII) illegitimate, named Henry his successor, appointed him regent of France, and gave him direct rule over all French lands as far south as the Loire River (see Map 11.2). Charles also gave Henry his daughter Catherine in marriage.

The Dauphin of course could not accept this forced abdication, and from his capital at Bourges he led an expedition across the Loire River. Henry drove his forces back and then embarked on a systematic reduction of towns and fortresses north of the river that were loyal to the Dauphin. Then in 1428 the English laid siege to Orléans; its fall would have given them a commanding position in the Loire valley and would have rendered the plight of the Dauphin nearly desperate.

Joan of Arc

The intervention of a young peasant girl, Joan of Arc, saved the Capetian dynasty. Convinced that heavenly voices were ordering her to rescue France, Joan persuaded several royal officials, and finally the Dauphin himself, of the authenticity of her mission and was given an army. In 1429 she marched to Orléans and

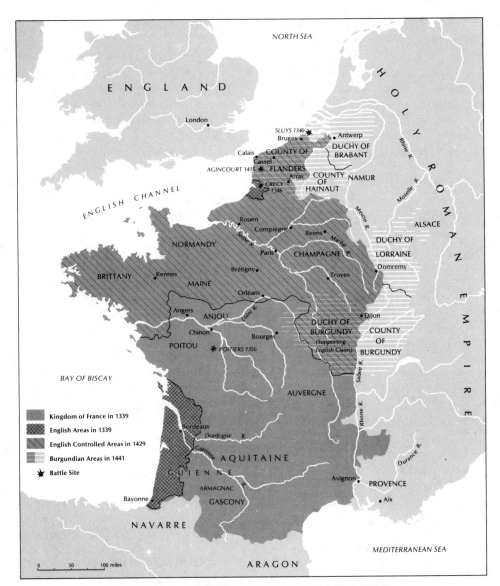

NORTH SEA

ENGLAND

London

SLUYS 1340 ✱
Bruges •
Calais • COUNTY OF
Cassel • FLANDERS
AGINCOURT 1415 ✱ Arras •
CRECY
1346

• Antwerp
DUCHY OF
BRABANT
COUNTY
OF
HAINAUT NAMUR

ENGLISH CHANNEL

Rouen •
Compiègne •
NORMANDY
Paris •

Reims •
CHAMPAGNE
Troyes •

Rhine R.
Moselle R.
Meuse R.
Marne R.

ALSACE
DUCHY OF
LORRAINE
Domremy •

BRITTANY
Rennes •
MAINE
Brétigny •
Orléans •
Angers •
ANJOU
Chinon •
POITOU ✱ POITIERS 1356
Bourges •

DUCHY OF
BURGUNDY
(Supporting
English Claims)

• Dijon

COUNTY
OF
BURGUNDY

BAY OF BISCAY

AUVERGNE

Saône R.
Rhône R.

Bordeaux •
Dordogne R.
Garonne R.

AQUITAINE

GUIENNE

Bayonne •

ARMAGNAC

GASCONY

Avignon •

PROVENCE

• Aix

Durance R.

NAVARRE

MEDITERRANEAN SEA

ARAGON

■ Kingdom of France in 1339
▨ English Areas in 1339
▨ English Controlled Areas in 1429
▨ Burgundian Areas in 1441
✱ Battle Site

0   50   100 miles

MAP 11.2. THE HUNDRED YEARS' WAR

forced the English to raise the siege. She then escorted the Dauphin to Reims, the historic coronation city of France. His own coronation there confirmed his legitimacy and enlisted the support of French royalist sentiment in his cause. The tide had turned.

Joan passed from history as quickly and as dramatically as she had arrived. The Burgundians, allies of the English, captured her in 1430 and sold her to the English, who put her on trial for witchcraft and heresy. She was burned at the stake at Rouen in 1431.

Joan was a manifestation of an increasingly powerful sentiment among the people. They had grown impatient with continuing destruction and had come to identify their own security with the expulsion of the English and with a strong Capetian monarchy. This growing loyalty to the king finally saved France from its protracted agony. A series of French successes followed the execution of Joan, and by 1453 only Calais was left in English hands. No formal treaty ended the war, but both sides accepted the outcome: England was no longer a Continental power.

The Effects of the Hundred Years' War

Like all the disasters of that era, the Hundred Years' War accelerated change. With regard to warfare, it stimulated the development of firearms and the technologies needed for them and helped establish that the infantry, armed with longbow, pike, or gun, was superior in battle to mounted knights.

The war also had a significant effect on governmental institutions in England and France. The expense of fighting forced the kings on each side to look for new sources of revenue through taxation. In England the king willingly conceded to Parliament a larger role in return for grants of new taxes. The tradition became firmly established that Parliament had the right to grant or refuse new taxes, to agree to legislation, to channel appeals to the king, and to offer advice on important decisions such as those regarding peace and war. The House of Commons gained the right to introduce all tax legislation, since the Commons could speak, as the Lords could not, as representatives of the shires and boroughs. Parliament also named a committee to audit the tax records, to be sure that its will was respected. Equally important, Commons could also impeach high royal officials, an important early step in establishing the principle that the king's ministers were responsible to Parliament as well as to their royal master. By the end of the Hundred Years' War, Parliament had been considerably strengthened at the expense of royal power.

The need for new taxes produced a somewhat different outcome in France, actually enhancing the power of the French monarchs while weakening the Estates General, the national representative assembly. In 1343 Philip IV established a monopoly over the sale of salt, determining in many French provinces how much each family had to consume and how much they had to pay for it. The tax on salt, called the *gabelle,* was destined to form a major support of French finance for the entire duration of the monarchy, until 1789. In gaining support for this and other proposed taxes Philip and his successors sought the agreement of both the regional, or provincial, assemblies of estates and the national Estates General. The kings' reliance on the provincial estates hindered the emergence of a centralized assembly that could speak for the entire kingdom. By the reign of Charles VII, during the last stages of the war, the monarchy obtained the right to impose national taxes (notably the *taille,* a direct tax from which nobles and clerics were exempt) without the consent of the Estates General. By then, too, the royal government was served by a standing, professional army (the "companies of ordinance")—the first in any European country since the fall of the Roman Empire.

Both England and France experienced internal dissension during the course of the war. After the death of Edward III in 1377, England faced over a century of turmoil, with the nobles striving to maintain their endangered economic fortunes through factional conflicts—that is, by preying on one another. In time these conflicts led to a struggle between two factions, the Lancastrians and the Yorkists, over the throne itself, with the English nobles quickly aligning themselves on one side or the other. The civil war that followed is known to historians as the War of the Roses (the Lancastrian emblem was a red rose, that of the Yorkists a white one). It lasted some 35 years, ending in 1485, when at Bosworth Field Henry Tudor defeated the Yorkists and acceded to the throne as Henry VII. By this time prosperity had relieved the pressures on the English nobles, and the people in general, weary of war, welcomed the strong and orderly regime that Henry proposed to establish.

In France too the power of the monarchy was threatened by strife between rival factions of nobles, the Armagnacs and the Burgundians. The Armagnacs favored a vigorous prosecution of the war with England, whereas the Burgundians favored accommodation. The territorial ambitions of the Burgundians also posed a threat to the French monarchy. King John the Good of France had granted the huge Duchy of Burgundy to his younger son, Philip the Bold, in 1363. Philip and his successors greatly enlarged their possessions in eastern France, the Rhone and Rhine valleys, and the Low Countries (see Map 11.2). The dukes seem to have taken as their goal the establishment of a Burgundian "middle kingdom" between France and the Holy Roman Empire; such a state would have permanently affected the political geography of Europe and undermined the position of the French monarch. However, this threat ended in 1477 with the death of the last duke. His daughter and heir, Mary of Burgundy, was unable to hold her scattered inheritance together, and a large part of it came under French control.

With the loss of nearly all its Continental possessions in the course of the war, England emerged from the war geographically more consolidated. It was also homogeneous in its language (English had replaced French as the language of the law courts and administration) and conscious of its cultural distinctiveness and national identity. Freed from its Continental entanglements, England was ready for its expansion beyond the seas and for a great growth in national pride and self-consciousness.

France never achieved quite the territorial consolidation of England, but with the expulsion of the English from the Continent and the sudden disintegration of the Duchy of Burgundy the French king was without a major rival among his feudal princes. The monarchy emerged from the war with a permanent army, a remunerative tax system, and no clear constitutional restrictions on its exercise of power. Most significantly, the war gave the French king greater prestige and confirmed him as the chief protector and patron of the people.

In both France and England, government at the end of the Middle Ages must still be considered decentralized and "feudal," if we mean by that term that certain privileged persons and institutions (nobles, the Church, towns, and the like) continued to hold and to exercise some forms of private jurisdiction. They retained, for example, their own courts. But the king had unmistakably emerged as the dominant partner in the feudal relationship. Moreover, he was prepared to press his advantages still further in the sixteenth century.

The Holy Roman Empire

With the death of Emperor Frederick II of Hohenstaufen (1250), the Holy Roman Empire ceased to function as a major power in European affairs. The empire continued to link Germany and Italy, but real authority fell to the princes in Germany and the city republics in Italy. In 1273, after a tumultuous period known as the Interregnum, during which several rivals contended for the title, the princes chose as emperor Rudolf of Hapsburg, the first of that famous family to hold the office. Instead of rebuilding the imperial authority, Rudolf rather sought to advance the interests of his own dynasty and its ancestral possessions. His successors also characteristically sought to use the office of emperor for their own narrow dynastic advantage.

A significant event of the fourteenth century was the issuance in 1356 of the Golden Bull, which defined the constitution of the empire as it would largely remain until 1806. Although issued by the pope, the bull reflected the interests of the great German princes. The right of naming the emperor was given to seven electors—the archbishops of Mainz, Trier, and Cologne, the count palatine of the Rhine, the duke of Saxony, the margrave of Brandenburg, and the king of Bohemia. It assigned no role to the popes in naming or crowning the emperor and thus was a victory for imperial autonomy.

A development of major interest in the empire was the emergence of the Swiss Confederation of cantons (districts), which won virtual autonomy in the Late Middle Ages. In the early thirteenth century Emperor Frederick II of Hohenstaufen had recognized the autonomy of two cantons, Uri and Schwyz, and had given them the responsibility of guarding the Saint Gotthard Pass through the Alps, the shortest route from Germany to Italy. The lands of the cantons were technically part of the ancient Duchy of Swabia, and in the late thirteenth century the Hapsburg princes, seeking to consolidate their possessions in the duchy, attempted to subjugate the Swiss lands as well. To resist the Hapsburg menace the cantons of Uri, Schwyz, and Unterwalden joined in a Perpetual Compact in 1291. They formed the nucleus of what was eventually to become the 22 cantons of present-day Switzerland.

The Swiss had to fight for their autonomy, and they acquired the reputation of being among the best fighters in Europe. Both history and legend, such as the colorful stories of William Tell, celebrate their successes. The confederated governments of the Swiss cantons represent a notable exception to the tendency, evident elsewhere in Europe, for central governments to grow stronger in the fourteenth and fifteenth centuries.

The States of Italy

The free city, or commune, was the dominant power in Italian political life at the beginning of the fourteenth century, at least in the center and north of the peninsula. The Holy Roman Empire exerted a loose sovereignty over much of the peninsula north of Rome and the papacy governed the area around Rome, but almost all the principal cities, and many small ones too, had gained the status of self-governing city-states.

However, the new economic and social conditions of the fourteenth century were unfavorable to the survival of the smaller communes. The economic contractions of the times made it increasingly difficult for industries and merchant houses in the smaller cities to compete with their rivals in the larger ones. Moreover, with the rising costs of war the small communes found it equally hard to defend their independence. Finally, in both large and small towns Italian society was deeply disturbed by factional strife that often made political order impossible.

In response to such pressures two principal tendencies become evident in Italian political development. Much stronger governments, amounting at times to true despotisms, tended to replace the weak governments of the free commune. And regional states, dominated politically and economically by a single metropolis, replaced the numerous, free, and highly competitive communes.

Perhaps the most effective Italian despot was the ruler of Milan, Gian Galeazzo Visconti (1378–1402), who energetically set about enlarging the Visconti inheritance of 21 cities in the Po valley. Through shrewd negotiations and opportune attacks he secured the submission of Verona, Vicenza, and Padua, which gave him an outlet to the Adriatic Sea. He then seized Bologna, purchased Pisa, and through a variety of methods was accepted as suzerain in

Siena, Perugia, Spoleto, Nocera, and Assisi. In the course of this advance deep into central Italy Gian Galeazzo worked with some success to keep his chief enemies, the Florentines and the Venetians, divided, and he seemed destined to forge an Italian kingdom and restore Italian unity.

To establish a legal basis for his power Gian Galeazzo secured from the emperor an appointment as imperial vicar in 1380, and then as hereditary duke in 1395. This made him, in fact, the only duke in all Italy and seemed a step toward the assumption of a royal title. He revised the statutes of Milan, but his chief administrative achievement, and the true foundation of most of his successes, was his ability to wring enormous tax revenues from his subjects. Gian Galeazzo was also a generous patron of Humanism and the new learning, and with his conquests, wealth, and brilliance he seemed to be awaiting only the submission of the truculent Florentines before adopting the title of king. But he died unexpectedly in 1402, leaving two minor sons, who were incapable of defending their inheritance.

Even those states that escaped the despotism of a Gian Galeazzo moved toward stronger governments and the formation of territorial or regional states. In Venice the government was placed under the domination of a small and closed oligarchy. A kind of corporative despot, known as the Council of Ten, looked over and after the Venetian state. Its mandate was the preservation of oligarchic rule in Venice and the suppression of opposition to the government.

Whereas Venice had previously devoted its principal energies to maritime commerce and overseas possessions, it could not now ignore the growth on the mainland of territorial states, which might deprive it of its agricultural imports or jeopardize its inland trade routes. From the early fifteenth century onward Venice too initiated a policy of territorial expansion on the mainland. By 1405 Padua, Verona, and Vicenza had become Venetian dependencies.

Florence, while retaining the trappings of republican government, also came under stronger rule. In 1434 a successful banker named Cosimo de' Medici established a form of boss rule over the city. In his tax policies he favored the lower and middle classes of the city, and also cultivated the support of the middle classes by appointments to office and other forms of political patronage. Further, he took peace in Italy as his supreme goal. In guiding the relations between Florence and other cities and states he earned from his fellow citizens the title *pater patriae* ("father of his country"), and most historians would concur in this judgment.

Cosimo's achievements were a preparation for the rule of his more famous grandson, Lorenzo the Magnificent (1478–1492). Under Lorenzo's direction Florence set the style for Italy, and eventually for Europe, in the splendor of its festivals, the elegance of its social life, the beauty of its buildings, and the lavish support it extended to scholars and artists. With good reason, Lorenzo's lifetime is viewed by many as the golden age of Renaissance Florence.

The Papal States and the Kingdom of Naples

The popes, who were now located in Avignon in southern France, sought to consolidate their rule over their possessions in central Italy, but they faced formidable obstacles. The rugged territory with its many castles and fortified towns enabled communes, petty lords, and plain brigands to defy the papal authority easily. Continuing disorders largely discouraged the popes from returning to Rome, and the attempts to pacify the tumultuous region were causing a major drain on papal finances.

Even after its return to Rome in 1378 the papacy had difficulty maintaining authority. Not until the pontificate of Martin V (1417–

1431) was a stable administration established, and Martin's successors still faced frequent revolts for the entire course of the fifteenth century.

The political situation was equally confused in the Kingdom of Naples and Sicily. With papal support Charles of Anjou, younger brother of St. Louis of France, had established a dynasty of Angevin rulers over the area. But in 1282 the people of Sicily revolted against the Angevins and appealed for help to the king of Aragon. For the next 150 years the Aragonese and the Angevins battled for dominion over Sicily and Naples. Then in 1435 the king of Aragon, Alfonso V, the Magnanimous, reunited Sicily and southern Italy and made the kingdom the center of an Aragonese empire in the Mediterranean. Alfonso sought to suppress the factions of lawless nobles and to reform taxes and strengthen administration. His efforts were not completely successful, for southern Italy and Sicily were rugged, poor lands and difficult to subdue; but he was at least able to overcome the chaos that had prevailed earlier. Alfonso was an enthusiastic patron of literature and the arts, and his court at Naples was one of the most brilliant of the early Renaissance.

Foreign Relations

Italy, by about 1450, was no longer a land of numerous, tiny free communes. Rather, it was divided among five territorial states: the Duchy of Milan, the republics of Venice and Florence, the Papal States, and the Kingdom of Naples (see Map 11.3). To govern the relations among these states the Italians conceived new methods of diplomacy. Led by Venice, the states began to maintain permanent embassies at important foreign courts. Moreover, largely through the political sense of Cosimo de' Medici, the Italian states were able to pioneer a new way of preserving stability. The Peace of Lodi in 1454 ended a war between Milan, Florence, and Venice, and Cosimo sought to make the peace a lasting one through balancing alliance systems. Milan, Naples, and Florence held one side of the balance, and Venice and the Papal States the other. Each state felt sufficiently secure in its alliances to have no need to appeal to non-Italian powers for support. During the next 40 years the balance was occasionally rocked, but never overturned, and it gave Italy an unaccustomed period of peace and freedom from foreign intervention. This system represents one of the earliest appearances in European history of the concept of the balance of power as a workable means of maintaining both security and peace.

IV. THE PAPACY

The papacy also experienced profound transformations in the fourteenth and fifteenth centuries. It continued to envision as its chief objective a peaceful Christendom united in faith and in filial obedience to Rome. But in fact the international Christian community was beset by powerful forces that worked to undermine its cohesiveness and to weaken papal authority and influence. Although the culmination of these disruptive forces came in the Reformation in the sixteenth century, their roots lie deep within the history of the previous two centuries.

The Avignon Exile

The humiliation of Pope Boniface VIII by the agents of Philip IV of France at Anagni in 1303 opened the doors to French influence at the Curia. In 1305 the College of Cardinals elected a French pope, Clement V, who because of the political disorders in the Papal States settled at Avignon. Though technically a part of the Holy Roman Empire, Avignon was in language and culture a French city. The popes who followed

1 MARCH OF MONTFERRAT
2 MARCH OF MANTUA
3 DUCHY OF MODENA
4 REPUBLIC OF LUCCA
5 COUNTY OF ASTI

DUCHY OF SAVOY

Aosta

Turin

Saluzzo

Genoa

GENOA

Milan

Pavia

Lodi

Cremona

Piacenza

Parma

Reggio

Bergamo

Brescia

Trent

Vincenza

Verona

Padua

Po R.

Adda R.

Adige R.

Treviso

Venice

Chioggia

ISTRIA

Ferrara

Modena

EMILIA

Bologna

DUCHY OF
FERRARA

Ravenna

Rimini

San Marino

Urbino

Ancona

ROMAGNA

Lucca

Pisa

Livorno

Pistoia

Florence

Arno R.

TUSCANY

Siena

Arezzo

Perugia

Assisi

Spoleto

MARCHES

SIENA

ELBA
(to Florence)

CORSICA
(to Genoa)

Orvieto

Viterbo

Rome

Tiber R.

Pontecorvo

Naples

Nocera

Benevento

Salerno

Barletta

Trani

Bari

Brindisi

Taranto

Otranto

PUGLIA

SARDINIA
(to Aragon)

TYRRHENIAN SEA

ADRIATIC SEA

DALMATIA

Cosenza

CALABRIA

Palermo

Messina

Reggio

SICILY

Syracuse

THE FIVE GREAT POWERS

Republic of Florence

Duchy of Milan

Kingdom of Naples

Papal States

Venetian Republic

0   50   100 miles

MAP 11.3. ITALY 1454

The palace of Avignon, shown above, was the seat of the papacy from 1308 to 1377. The argument could be made, and was made, that Avignon, more central to the continent than Rome, was a more appropriate capital for the papacy. But the city lacked Rome's prestige, and many people regarded the papacy's long presence at Avignon as a scandal.
(Photo: Black Star)

Clement expressed an intention to return to Rome but remained at Avignon, claiming that the continuing turmoil of central Italy would not permit the papal government to function effectively. These popes were, in fact, skilled administrators, and the period witnessed an enormous expansion of the papal bureaucracy, especially its fiscal machinery.

Fiscal Crisis

Like many secular governments the papacy at Avignon faced an acute fiscal crisis. But unlike the major powers of Europe it had no adequate territorial base to supply it with funds, because the tumultuous Papal States usually drained off more money than they supplied. The powers of appointment, dispensation, tithing, and indulgences were the only resources the papacy possessed, and it was thus drawn into the unfortunate but perhaps unavoidable practice of exploiting them for financial purposes. For instance, the popes insisted that candidates appointed to high ecclesiastical offices pay a special tax, which usually amounted to a third or a half of the first year's revenues. The popes also claimed the income from vacant offices and even sold future appointments to office when the incumbents were still alive. Dispensation released a petitioner from the normal requirements of canon law. A monastery or religious house, for example, might purchase from the pope an exemption from the visitation and inspection of the local bishop. Tithes were a payment to the papacy of one-tenth of the revenues of ecclesiastical benefices or offices throughout Christendom. Indulgences, remissions of the temporal punishment attendant to a sin, were also distributed in return for monetary contributions to the papacy.[4]

These fiscal practices brought the popes greatly enlarged revenues, but they also had many deplorable results. Prelates who paid huge sums to Avignon tended to pass on the costs to the lower clergy. Parish priests, hardly able to live within the incomes left to them, were the more readily tempted to disordered moral lives. The flow of money to Avignon angered rulers; well before the close of the Middle Ages there were demands for a halt to such payments and even for the confiscation of Church property. Dispensations gravely injured the authority of the bishops, since the exempt persons or houses all but escaped their supervision. The bishops were frequently too weak, and the pope too distant, to deal effectively with abuses on the local level. The fiscal system of the papacy thus helped sow chaos in many parts of the Western Church.

[4] Both the tithe and the indulgence originated as means of supporting the crusades, but income from them was frequently, and even usually, applied by the pope to his domestic needs.

The Great Schism

The end of the 70-year Avignon exile led to a controversy that almost split the Western Church. Pope Gregory XI returned reluctantly to Rome in 1378 and died there a short time later. The Roman people, fearing that Gregory's successor would once more remove the court to Avignon and thereby deprive Rome of desperately needed revenues, agitated for the election of an Italian pope. Responding to this pressure, the College of Cardinals found a compromise candidate who satisfied both French and Italian interests—a Neapolitan of French-Angevin extraction. The new pope, Urban VI, soon antagonized the French cardinals by seeking to limit their privileges and by threatening to pack the College with his own appointments. Seven months after choosing Urban, a majority of the cardinals declared that his election had taken place under duress and was therefore invalid; they then named a new pope, who returned to Avignon. Thus began the Great Schism of the West, the period when two, and later three, popes contended over the rule of the Church. The schism was to last for almost 40 years.

Christendom was now confronted with the deplorable spectacle of two pretenders to the throne of Peter, one in Rome and one in Avignon. Princes and peoples quickly took sides (see Map 11.4). The troubles of the papacy were at once doubled. Each pope had his own court and needed still more funds, both to meet ordinary expenses and to pay for policies that he hoped would defeat his rival. And since each pope excommunicated the other and those who supported him, everyone in Christendom was at least technically excommunicated.

The Conciliar Movement

Theologians and jurists had speculated earlier on who should rule the Church if the pope were to become heretical or incompetent; some con-cluded that it should be the College of Cardinals or a general council of Church officials. Since the College of Cardinals had split into two factions, each backing one of the rival popes, many prominent thinkers supported the theory that a general council should rule the Church. These conciliarists, as they were called, went even further. They urged that the Church be given a new constitution to confirm the supremacy of a general council. Such a step would have reduced the pope's role to that of a limited monarch. The critical need for correcting numerous abuses, particularly regarding the fiscal support and morality of the clergy, lent further strength to the idea that a general council should rule and reform the Church.

The first test of the conciliarists' position was at the Council of Pisa (1409), which was convened by cardinals of both Rome and Avignon. The council did assert its own supremacy within the Church by deposing the two popes and electing another. But this act merely compounded the confusion, for it left Christendom with three rivals claiming to be the lawful pope.

A few years later another council finally resolved the situation. Some 400 ecclesiastics assembled at the Council of Constance (1414–1418), the greatest international gathering of the Middle Ages. The council was organized in a fashion novel for the times. The delegates elected to sit and vote by nations to offset the power of the Italians, who constituted nearly half the attendance. The council also gave recognition to the new importance of national and territorial churches, as each national church voted as unit.

The assembled delegates immediately deposed both the new pope and the pope at Avignon after the latter refused to resign; the Roman pope submitted to the demand of the council and resigned. In his stead the council elected a Roman cardinal, who took the name Martin V. Thus the Great Schism was ended, and the Western Church was once again united under a single pope.

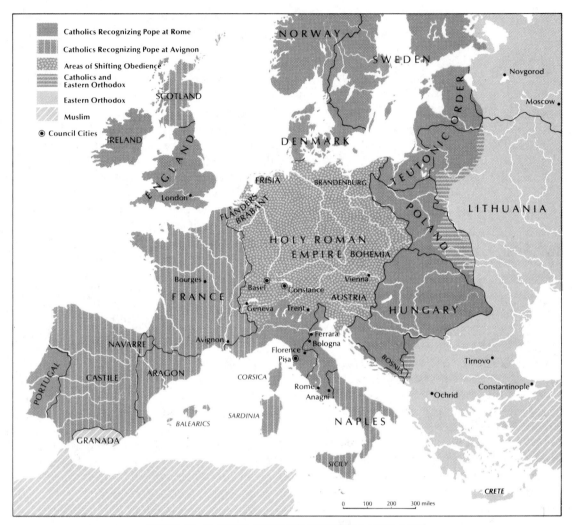

MAP 11.4. THE GREAT SCHISM 1378–1417

As the meetings continued, the views of the conciliarists prevailed. The delegates formally declared that a general council was supreme within the Church. To ensure a degree of continuity in Church government the delegates further directed that new councils be summoned periodically.

In spite of this assertion of supremacy, the council made little headway in reforming the Church "in head and members," to use the language of contemporaries. Those attending the council, chiefly great prelates, were in large part the beneficiaries of the fiscal system. They were reluctant to touch their own privileges and advantages. The real victims of the fiscal abuses, the lower clergy, were poorly represented. The council could not agree on a general program of reform. This failure illustrates a fatal flaw in the vision of conciliar rule over the Church. The council was too large, too cumbersome, and too divided to maintain an effective ecclesiastical government. The restored papacy quickly reclaimed its position as supreme head of the Western Church.

The practical weaknesses of the conciliar movement were amply revealed at the Council of Basel (1431–1443). Because disputes broke out almost at once with the pope, the council deposed him and elected another to replace him, Felix V. The conciliar movement, designed to heal the schism, now seemed responsible for renewing it. Recognizing the futility of its actions, the council at the death of Felix tried to rescue a semblance of its dignity by "electing" the Roman pope Nicholas V in 1449 and disbanding. This ended the effort to reform the Church through giving supreme authority over it to councils.

The popes retained a suspicion of councils, but in fact they had much more serious rivals to their authority in the powerful lay princes, who were exerting an ever tighter control over their territorial churches. Both England and France issued decrees that limited the exercise of papal powers within their kingdoms. The policy was soon imitated in Spain and in the stronger principalities of the Holy Roman Empire. Although these decrees did not establish national or territorial churches, they do document the deteriorating papal control over the international Christian community.

The Popes as Patrons of the Arts

After 1417, when Martin V returned to Rome, the popes faced a monumental task of rebuilding their office and their prestige, in both a political and cultural sense. While seeking to make Rome a cultural capital, the popes wished to remain autonomous, not beholden to the culture of the medieval world, which meant preeminently the culture of France, the home of both Scholastic philosophy and Gothic art. Restored to Rome, the papacy did have an alternate cultural tradition to which it could appeal, even though that tradition had been largely moribund in the Central Middle Ages. In Italy, learned men, chiefly Florentine or Tuscan by birth—Petrarch, Boccaccio, and their followers—had been energetically promoting the Classical heritage. They searched out neglected manuscripts, strengthened their philological skills, and eventually recovered command of the Greek language. They also disparaged the culture of the transalpine regions, including Scholasticism and the Gothic style, as fundamentally barbarous. The popes saw advantage in cultivating this revival of ancient culture, even in its pagan form. It honored their capital and it honored them, and it proclaimed their independence of French tutelage.

Nicholas V (1447–1455), often considered the first humanist pope, vigorously pursued this program of cultural renewal. According to a contemporary, he sought "by the construction of grand and lasting buildings to increase the honor of the Roman Church and the glory of the Apostolic see, and widen and strengthen the devotion of all Christian people." He was an assiduous collector of ancient manuscripts, and his collection became the nucleus of the Vatican Library.

Sixtus IV (1471–1484) also stands out for his brilliant patronage of the arts. "If there is a city in the world," he proclaimed, "which ought to shine by its cleanliness and beauty, it is above all that which bears the title of capital of the universe, and that the honor of possessing the chair of St. Peter incontestably places in the first rank." He gave his name to the Sistine Chapel in the Vatican. To paint the 12 frescoes of its lower walls, he commissioned the best artists of the day—Botticelli, Perugino, Pinturicchio, and others. During the pontificate of Sixtus's nephew Julius II (1503–1513), Michelangelo painted the glorious ceiling of the chapel (see Plate 24). Julius also commissioned the new St. Peter's Church, with the Florentine Bramante (later succeeded by Michelangelo) as architect.

Earlier popes had not been noticeably active as patrons of the arts, and had willingly accepted French cultural leadership. The popes newly reestablished at Rome did so no longer, and they sought to express their new autonomy by favoring the Classical revival. To be sure, there was a danger here. In enthusiastically cultivating Roman memories, the papacy may well have become more Roman, and less uni-versal, than it ought to have been. In particular, the crisis of the Reformation, which struck during the pontificate of Julius's successor, was proof that for all its splendor, the papacy was failing to retain the spiritual allegiance of wide areas of Europe, especially in the north. Perhaps a less Roman papacy might have somehow avoided the great cultural schism between north and south that was the Reformation. But it cannot be disputed that these popes succeeded in what they set out to do: they made Rome once again a cultural capital of the Western world.

In the fourteenth and fifteenth centuries a series of spectacular catastrophes disrupted European life on almost every level. In the wake of plague, famine, and war, all rooted perhaps in overpopulation, the numbers of Europe's peoples fell drastically, and a severe economic depression gripped the Continent. The European nations were forced to reorganize their economies in accordance with the new scarcity of labor and the new structure of the market. By about 1450 they achieved considerable economic recovery, based upon a greater diversification in production and a marked substitution of capital for labor. In the late fifteenth century Europe was a smaller but richer community than it had been 200 years before.

Society and government experienced a comparable crisis, as social unrest, factional strife, and war nearly everywhere disturbed the peace of Europe. But here too a new stability was achieved by about 1450, based on better conditions of life for the humbler classes and on the stronger authority claimed by many princes. The papacy also changed; it developed a huge bureaucratic and fiscal apparatus and successfully withstood the challenge of the conciliar movement. However, it failed to lead the Church to the reform many Europeans were demanding.

In European culture as well as institutions a profound crisis occurred in the fourteenth and fifteenth centuries. Yet even in this aspect of the "autumn" of the Middle Ages there was a renaissance, in the sense that out of a crisis of traditional values there emerged new creative efforts to enrich the culture of the West.

RECOMMENDED READING

Sources

Council of Constance. Louise R. Loomis (tr.). 1961.

★Froissart, Jean. *The Chronicles of England, France, Spain and Other Places Adjoining.* 1961. Covers the first half of the Hundred Years' War.

★Pernoud, Regine (ed.). *Joan of Arc: By Herself and Her Witnesses.* 1969.

Pius II, Pope. *Commentaries of Pius Second.* Florence A. Gragg (tr.). 1970. Personal, often acerbic reminiscences; unique document in papal history.

★Vespasiano da Bisticci. *Renaissance Princes, Popes and Prelates.* 1963. Biographies of prominent Italians of the fifteenth century, written by a contemporary.

Studies

★Ady, Cecil M. *Lorenzo dei Medici and Renaissance Florence.* 1952. Brief introduction to the rule and culture of the Medici.

★Bridbury, A. R. *Economic Growth in England in the Later Middle Ages.* 1962. Rejects thesis of a "Renaissance depression."

Brucker, Gene A. *Florentine Politics and Society, 1373–1378.* 1962.

———. *The Civic World of Early Renaissance Florence.* 1977. Important studies of Florentine politics and society from about 1300 to 1430.

De Roover, Raymond. *The Rise and Decline of the Medici Bank.* 1963. Informative study in business history.

Eisenstein, Elizabeth L. *The Printing Press as an Agent of Change in Early-Modern Europe.* 2 vols. 1979.

Provocative interpretation of the place of printing in early-modern cultural history.

Gillingham, John. *The Wars of the Roses: Peace and Conflict in Fifteenth-Century England.* 1981. Readable political and military history.

Gottfried, Robert S. *The Black Death: Natural and Human Disaster in Medieval Europe.* 1983. A survey with particular emphasis on the medical consequences.

Hilton, Rodney. *Bondsmen Made Free.* 1973. A study of peasant violence in the Late Middle Ages.

Martines, Lauro. *Power and Imagination: City-States in Renaissance Italy.* 1979. Explores the ties between politics and culture.

★Mattingly, Garrett. *Renaissance Diplomacy.* 1964.

Miskimin, Harry A. *The Economy of Early Renaissance Europe, 1300–1460.* 1969.

Oakley, Francis. *The Western Church in the Later Middle Ages.* 1979.

★Perroy, Édouard. *The Hundred Years' War.* 1965. Excellent survey by a French scholar.

Schevill, Ferdinand. *Medieval and Renaissance Florence.* 1963. Old, but still a minor classic.

Seward, Desmond. *The Hundred Years War.* 1978. Short and readable.

Unger, Richard W. *The Ship in the Medieval Economy.* 1980. Recent and authoritative.

Vaughan, Richard. *John the Fearless: The Growth of Burgundian Power.* 1979.

———. *Philip the Bold: The Formation of the Burgundian State.* 1979. Two recent studies of the great duchy of the West.

★Available in paperback.

EXPERIENCES OF DAILY LIFE

Women and Sanctity

In the late Middle Ages, women gained a special prominence in religious life, both in numbers and in influence. We have a rough idea of numbers through the work of a group of Jesuit priests known as the Bollandists, who have been studying saints since the seventeenth century. They have compiled a long list of saints about whom some information, usually a life or biography, has survived; the lists includes 3287 names.

It was much easier to win recognition as a saint in the earlier than in the later Middle Ages. In the early period, holy persons while alive gained a reputation for sanctity, and after their deaths miracles allegedly occurred at their tombs. A cult spontaneously took shape about

their persons. But the proliferation of local cults seemed dangerous to Church leaders. From the late twelfth century, the papacy successfully reserved for itself the right of naming or "canonizing" saints. (Canonization meant that the holy person's name was entered into the canonical or liturgical books of the Church.) The procedures of canonization soon became very elaborate; they closely resembled a trial. Witnesses were summoned to testify to the sanctity of the servant of God, and even a "devil's advocate" was appointed to refute the testimony. Partly because of the complexity and cost of the new canonization procedures, the number of recognized saints declined precipitously over the late Middle Ages.

But the relative number of women saints grew in the same period. Over the entire Middle Ages, 522 out of the 3287 saints listed by the Bollandists were women; for every single female saint, there were five males. Women saints were fewest right in the middle of the Middle Ages, from 1000 to 1150, when they were outnumbered by males by 12 to one. But the ratio drops thereafter, and for the years 1348 to 1500 stood at 2.74 to one. Not even the martyrs who died during the early persecutions showed so high a proportion of women.

Late medieval women saints also represented a particular type of sanctity. The typical female saint of the early Middle Ages was a queen or princess who eventually founded a monastery and became its abbess. Some establishments included an attached house of male monks and were called double monasteries. But the female division was always the larger and the abbess retained the direction of the entire community.

REX ROGAT ABBATEM MATHILDIM SUPPLICAT ATQ;

Henry IV (kneeling) before Abbot Hugh of Cluny and Countess Matilda.
(Vatican Library)

422

This type of female saint became rare in the central Middle Ages, for two reasons. The Gregorian reform, in prohibiting clerical marriage, also distanced women from Church offices and from the male clergy. And the appearance of the patrilineage limited the claims of daughters to the resources of their families. They received dowries if they wished to marry, or smaller payments (also regarded as dowries) if they entered the religious life. But only under special circumstances (such as the total absence of male heirs) did they command the wealth and resources needed to found or endow religious establishments.

The typical women saints of the later Middle Ages were no longer queens, princesses, and abbesses. They were mystics and visionaries, charismatic people who gained the attention of the Church and the world by the power of their message and the force of their own personalities. The supreme representative of this type of saint was Catherine of Siena (1347–1380). She was the youngest of 25 children (her twin sister died at birth) born to a dyer, Giacomo di Benincasa. From young adulthood she pursued a religious life but never joined a cloistered order. She lived in the world as a "sister of penitence of St. Dominic." Her reputation for holiness attracted a company of followers, both men and women, from as far off as England. She traveled much, in an effort to bring the papacy back from Avignon to Rome and to reform the Church. She wrote (or dictated, as she probably couldn't write) more than 400 letters to great and humble contemporaries. Her devotional tracts are monuments in Italian literature and in the literature of mystical experience.

Once, Catherine expressed to God the fear that her sex was an obstacle in her efforts at religious leadership. God reassured her: "Isn't it I who have created the human race, and divided it into male and female? I dispose where I want the grace of my spirit. In my eyes there is neither male or female, rich or poor. All are equal, for I can work my will through all equally."

Among the late medieval women distinguished by their mystical or charismatic qualities were the English matron Margery Kempe, the anchoress Julian of Norwich, Catherine of Genoa, and Bridget of Sweden. Joan of Arc, who achieved what she did through conviction and personality, should also be numbered among these figures.

Women who out of poverty or preference lived a religious life outside cloistered convents were very numerous in late medieval society, especially in towns. Some lived with their families, and others eked out a living on the margins of society. Christina of Stommeln (d. 1312) ran away from her rural home at age 12 and went to the big city of Cologne; for years she lived by begging. Margaret of Cortona in Italy was thrown out of her father's home by her stepmother, and at first earned her living as a prostitute. Still other women lived in spontaneously organized religious houses, communes really. They were called Beguines in northern Europe. The Church looked with suspicion upon these women professing a religious life outside cloisters and without an approved rule. But the movement was too large and powerful for the Church to suppress or control. In the north, the movement raised what historians have traditionally called the *Frauenfrage*, the medieval "women question."

Social changes across the central Middle Ages limited women's access to ecclesiastical office and to material resources, which had earlier lent them importance in the Church. But women were resilient, and they compensated for these losses through the cultivation of a highly personal, mystical, or charismatic style of religion. No contemporary male saint matched Catherine of Siena in the power of her mystical vision, and many women were cultivating a similar style of piety. In the phrase of French historian André Vauchez, the piety of the late medieval world was becoming "feminized."

Chapter 12

The West
in Transition:
Society and Culture
1300–1500

The Swiss historian Jacob Burckhardt published a book in 1860 that has influenced, as few books have, the understanding that most educated men and women in Europe and America have of their own past. In *The Civilization of the Renaissance in Italy* he argued that the fourteenth and fifteenth centuries witnessed a true revolution in values in that country. People allegedly shook off the religious illusions and institutional restrictions of medieval society and rediscovered both the visible world and their own true selves. The essential novelty of Renaissance culture was the accent it placed on the individual and the delight it took in the beauties and satisfactions of life. The humanistic heritage of Greece and Rome, which stressed similar values, appealed to the people of this age, and the revived interest in that heritage constituted the Classical Renaissance. Moreover, according to Burckhardt, the Italy of this period deserves to be considered the birthplace of the modern world.

Modern historians can easily criticize Burckhardt's sweeping assertions. It is difficult to believe that anyone could attain the full release from his society and its traditions that Burckhardt claimed for the people of the fourteenth and fifteenth centuries. He certainly slighted the achievements of the earlier Middle Ages and exaggerated the originality of the period he called the Renaissance. Also, he confined his vision to Italy, and historians have had difficulty applying his formulas to other regions of Europe. Nevertheless, his fundamental insight still commands the respect and agreement of many scholars.

Historians today still discuss the problems raised by Burckhardt, but they are also learning to view those problems from new perspectives. They are penetrating ever more deeply into archives and attempting to apply stronger analytical methods to the data they are gathering. They are exploring aspects of society and social experience inaccessible to Burckhardt and other earlier historians. How long did men and women live and how did they grow, marry, raise children, and meet with death? In the light of these experiences, how did they view the world, and what did they value in life? How and to what extent did their attitudes in fact change? These are the questions for which many scholars today are seeking answers, and that we too shall examine in this chapter.

I. SOCIETY AND CULTURE IN ITALY

In the fourteenth and fifteenth centuries Italy produced an extraordinary number of gifted thinkers and artists, whose collective work constituted the core of the cultural Renaissance and profoundly influenced all areas of European thought and artistic expression. To understand the character of the Renaissance requires, therefore, a consideration of the society that, in Burckhardt's estimation, shaped the culture of the modern world.

Cities

One basic social characteristic clearly distinguished Italy from most European areas: the number and size of its cities, particularly in the northern regions of Tuscany and the Lombard plain. In 1377, for example, only 10 percent of the people in England lived in urban centers with a population greater than 3200—a percentage fairly typical for most of northern Europe—whereas in Tuscany about 26 percent lived in urban centers. The cities were large. Venice, for instance, counted probably 120,000 inhabitants in 1338; 84,000 in about 1422; 102,000 in 1509; and 169,000 in 1563—a figure it was not to reach again until the twentieth century.

This remarkable urban concentration affected Italian culture. The large nonagrarian population depended for its support on a vigorous commerce and active urban industries. All levels of society participated in commerce, including the great landlords, nobles, and knights—classes that in northern Europe remained on their rural estates. Moreover, success in urban occupations required a level of training higher than that needed in agriculture; therefore, many Italian cities supported public schools to assure themselves of an educated citizenry. Frequently even girls were given an elementary education, since literacy was a nearly essential skill for the wives of shopkeepers and merchants. Finally, many towns were politically independent and offered their affluent citizens the opportunity to participate in governmental decisions. To many great families such participation was essential to the protection of their interests, and required a mastery of the arts of communicating with their fellow citizens. In sum, Italian urban society in the fourteenth and fifteenth centuries was remarkably well educated and committed to active partici-

pation in the affairs of business and of government.

Families

The cities were populous, but the households within them tended to be small and unstable. Average household size roughly followed the general population trends of decline and growth in the fourteenth and fifteenth centuries, but remained small over most of this period.[1] At Florence in 1427, the average household contained only 3.8 persons; at Bologna in 1395, 3.5 persons; at Verona in 1425, 3.7 persons. Restricted household size reflected the numerous deaths in a time of plagues, but marital customs also contributed. In particular, urban males tended to be much older than their brides when they married. At Florence in 1427, most men postponed marriage until they were 30, and some did not marry at all. Economic factors—lengthy apprenticeships required of males in the urban trades, extended absences from home on commercial ventures, the need to accumulate capital before starting a family—delayed and sometimes precluded marriage for urban men. Florentine women, on the other hand, were on the average less than 18 years old when they married for the first time; the modal (most common) age of first marriage for these urban girls in 1427 was 15 years.

Several important social and cultural results followed from this distinctive marriage pattern. Because of high mortalities, the pool of prospective grooms (men approximately 30 years old) was distinctly smaller than the pool of eligible young women (in their middle and late teens). Girls (or rather, their fathers and families) faced acute competition in the search for scarce husbands; young women, in consequence, usually entered marriage under unfa-

---

[1] The data on Florentine families are taken largely from a study by D. Herlihy and C. Klapisch-Zuber, *Tuscans and Their Families* (1985).

1300–1500/TIMELINE

Social and Economic History	Cultural and Intellectual History
	1260?–1327 Meister Eckhart, German mystic
	1276–1337 Giotto, Florentine painter
1300	**1300?–1349** William of Ockham, nominalist philosopher
	1309–1378 Papacy at Avignon
1315–1317 Great famine in northern Europe	
	1324 Marsilius of Padua writes *Defender of Peace*
1328 First mention of firearms	
	1341 Petrarch crowned poet laureate at Rome
1347–1351 The Black Death revishes Europe; one-third population dies	
1351 Statute of Laborers in England	1351? Boccaccio writes *Decameron*
	c. 1360 William Langland writes *Piers Plowman*
	1365–1384 John Wycliffe, English heretic, active
	1369–1415 John Huss, Czech heretic
	1374–1400 Froissart composes the *Chronicles* of the Hundred Years' War
1378 Revolt of poor wool workers (Ciompi) at Florence	1378 Pope Gregory XI returns to Rome
1381 Peasants' Revolt in England	1378–1417 Great Schism; popes at Rome and Avignon
	1384 Death of Gerhard Groote; Brethren of the Common Life popularize *devotio moderna*
1397 Founding of Medici bank	1385?–1440 Jan van Eyck, Flemish painter
	1386–1400 Chaucer writes *Canterbury Tales*
1400	1401–1429? Florentine painter Masaccio
	1402–1472 Leon Battista Alberti, Florentine architect and author
	1409 Council of Pisa fails to heal schism; three popes claim supremacy
	1414–1418 Council of Constance; schism ended
	1417 Martin V returns to Rome
	1425 Thomas à Kempis writes *Imitation of Christ*
	1421–36 Hussite wars in Bohemia
	1447–1455 Pontificate of Nicholas V, first humanist pope
	1452–1519 Leonardo da Vinci
	1458–1464 Pontificate of Pius II, only pope to leave personal memoirs
1455 Gutenberg Bible; first printed book	1469 *Theologia Platonica* of Marsilio Ficino
	1471–1484 Pontificate of Sixtus IV, designer of Sistine Chapel
	1475–1564 Michelangelo Buonarroti
	1482 Pico della Mirandola proposes disputation at Rome
	1483–1520 Raphael Santi
1492 Columbus discover America	
1498 Vasco da Gama reaches India	
1500	

vorable terms. In particular they or their families normally had to pay substantial dowries. Families with many daughters to marry faced financial ruin. This was one reason why girls were married so young; their fathers or families were eager to settle their uncertain futures as soon as possible. Those girls who could not be married before the age of 20 had no honorable alternative but to enter convents. In the words of a contemporary saint, Bernardine of Siena, these unwilling nuns were "the scum and vomit of the world."

Given the wide age difference separating the spouses, the urban marriage was likely to be of short duration, ending usually with the death of the husband. Often, too, the young widow did not remarry. Florentine husbands typically tried to discourage their spouses from remarrying after their own deaths; their widows, once remarried, might neglect the offspring of their earlier unions. Accordingly, the wills of Florentine husbands characteristically gave to their widows special concessions that would be lost in the event of remarriage: use of the family dwelling, the right to serve as guardians over their children, sometimes a pension or annuity. Moreover, at her husband's death the substantial dowry, paid by her family at her marriage, was returned to the widow to be used as she saw fit. For the first time in her life, she was freed from male tutelage, whether of father, brothers, or husband. Many widowed women obviously relished this newfound freedom. At Florence in 1427, more than one-half of the female population, age 40 or over, were widowed. The city teemed with mature women, many of them widows, many attracted to the city from the countryside, some of them wealthy and able to influence urban culture.

Even while her husband lived, the Florentine woman soon attained a special position within the household. Her husband was likely to be fully occupied by affairs of business or politics. The wife assumed primary responsibility for running the household and for bringing up the children. She was also usually destined for longer contact with her children. The average baby in Florence in 1427 was born to a mother of 26; the father was 40. To many Florentines of the fourteenth and fifteenth centuries, the father was a distant figure, routinely praised but rarely intimately known; the mother dominated the formative years of the children. A friar named Giovanni Dominici, writing in the first decade of the fifteenth century, complained that Florentine mothers were spoiling their children, both girls and boys. They dressed them in elegant clothes and taught them music and dancing, presumably elevating their aesthetic tastes. They did not countenance violent or brutal games or sports. The result, Dominici implied, was an effeminization of Florentine culture. Women served primarily as intermediaries between the urban generations, shaping to their own preferences the values and attitudes transmitted to the young. Elegance and refinement are essential attributes of Renaissance culture; elegant and refined tastes seem to have been assiduously nurtured within the bosom of the urban family.

The short duration of the urban marriage, the reluctance of many widows to remarry, and the commitment of many girls to the convent limited the exposure of urban women to the risk of pregnancy, to use the language of modern demography. In the countryside, men characteristically married in their middle twenties and took as brides girls nearer in age to themselves. The duration of rural marriages was longer, and couples had more children. The urban family was less prolific and usually smaller than its rural counterpart. The city thus ran a demographic deficit in relation to the countryside. This too had an important social repercussion. The city was forced to replenish its numbers by encouraging large-scale immigration from the countryside and small towns. This promoted both physical and social mobility, as the city characteristically attracted and rewarded skilled and energetic immigrants. Many of the leaders of the cultural Renaissance—Boccaccio, Leonardo Bruni, Coluccio Salutati, Poggio Bracciolini, Leonardo da Vinci, and others—were of rural or small-town origins and came to the city to meet its constant need for immigrants. The Renaissance city seems to have been eminently successful in identifying the talented and in using well its human capital.

The unstable character of the urban household and of human relations within it prompted much reflection on the family. Earlier, social thinkers had viewed the family abstractly, in relation to man's ultimate destiny; they affirmed that it was a natural society, but did not examine how it functioned in the real world. In contrast, concern for the welfare, even the survival, of families animates writers of the fifteenth century in Italy. Foremost among them was the Florentine scholar, artist, and architect Leon Battista Alberti, who in the 1430s wrote a tract entitled *Four Books on the Family*. In it he explained how children should be reared, wives chosen, domestic affairs managed, and friends cultivated—all to assure the survival of threatened lineages. Closely related to this examination of domestic policies are numerous tracts devoted to the training of children, many of which advocated a reform of education in the humanistic spirit (see p. 431). These tracts show a new awareness of the special psychology of children. Simultaneously, the artists of the period were presenting young people, even the infant Christ, not as miniature adults, but authentically as children, looking and acting as children do. The playful baby angels known as putti appear in even the most solemn religious paintings. The very fragility of the Italian urban family seems to have inspired a deeper appreciation of the values of family life, and the contribution that every member, even the youngest, makes to domestic contentment.

Finally, the weakness of the urban family forced its members to cultivate ties with outsiders in order to seek supplementary material and moral support. Living in constant contact with the outside world, the inhabitants of the Italian cities grew more sensitive to the canons of good behavior and the art of making friends. The age produced an abundance of essays on good manners, the most famous of which was the *Book of the Courtier,* written in 1516 by Baldassare Castiglione. Castiglione intended to describe proper deportment at court, but his work affected the image of the gentleman and the lady for a much broader range of society and was destined to influence standards of behavior all over Europe.

Leadership of the Young

A principal reason for the instability of the urban family was the high levels of mortality that prevailed everywhere in Europe in the fourteenth and fifteenth centuries. On the basis of family memoirs left to us by Florentine merchants, which record births and deaths in the household, life expectancy from birth for these relatively affluent persons was 40 years in about 1300, dropping to only 18 years in the generation struck by the Black Death, and rising to 30 years in the fifteenth century as the plagues declined in virulence. (Today in the United States a newborn may be expected to survive for some 70 years.) To be sure, the high death rates attributable to plague were strongly "age specific"—that is, they varied considerably across the various levels of age. The principal victims were the very young. In many periods, probably between one-half and one-third of the babies born never reached 15. Society swarmed with little children, but the death of children was a common occurrence in almost every family.

According to the most recent studies, the plague (as distinct from other causes of death) took greater tolls among young adults than among the aged. In effect, a person who survived one or more major epidemics had a good chance of living through the next onslaught. This phenomenon allowed some few favored persons to reach extreme old age, in the face of the horrendous mortalities. But it also meant that young adults continued to face high risks of dying. Friars, for example, who entered the Dominican convent of Sta. Maria Novella at Florence in the last half of the fourteenth century survived an average of only 20 years after profession, when most would have been in their late teens. Although there are exceptions, the normal adult career was of short duration.

For this reason, on every level and in every activity of life, the leaders of the fourteenth and fifteenth centuries were often very young, and subject to rapid replacement. The young were not frustrated by the lengthy survival of numerous elders, who clung to the available jobs and blocked their own careers. There was no basis for the kind of generational tensions and conflicts that have disturbed modern societies. The leaders of the age show psychological qualities that may in part at least be attributed to their youth: impatience and imagination; a tendency to have quick recourse to violence; a love of extravagant gesture and display; and a rather small endowment of prudence, restraint, and self-control. High mortality and a rapid turnover of leaders further contributed to making this an age of opportunity, especially within the cities. Early death assured room at the top for the energetic and the gifted, especially in the business and artistic fields, where birth mattered little and skill counted for much.

The power given to the young, the rapid replacement of leaders, the opportunities extended to the gifted, and the thin ranks of an older generation that might counsel restraint worked also to intensify the pace of cultural change. To be sure, notoriously poor communications hampered the spread of ideas. The quickest a person or a letter could travel on land was between 20 and 30 miles per day; to get to Bruges by sea from Genoa took 30 days, from Venice 40 days. The expense and scarcity of manuscripts before the age of printing further narrowed and muffled the intellectual dialogue. On the other hand, new generations pressed upon the old at a much more rapid rate than in our own society and characteristically they brought with them new policies, preferences, and ideas, or at least a willingness to experiment—in sum, ferment. The gifted individual was given his or her main chance early in life and passed early from the scene. In Italy as in all Europe the stage of the fourteenth and fifteenth centuries with its constantly changing characters often appears crowded, but the drama enacted upon it moves at a rapid, exciting pace.

Learning and Literature

Although university and scholastic learning retained considerable vitality in the fourteenth and fifteenth centuries, Scholasticism did not adequately serve the literate lay population. The curriculum remained largely designed for the training of teachers and theologians, whereas men committed to an active life in business and politics wanted practical training in the arts of persuasive communications: good speaking and good writing. Moreover, many laypeople believed that Scholastics failed to meet their religious needs. Coldly analytic in its treatment of religious questions, Scholasticism seemed indifferent to the personal, emotional, and mystical aspects of religion. As Petrarch was to note, education should train people in the art of leading a wise, pious, and happy life. The central concern of the cultural Renaissance was to develop a system of education that would do exactly that.

Humanism

One minor branch of the medieval educational curriculum, rhetoric, or the art of good speaking and writing, was concerned specifically with the skill of communicating well. Initially, the art consisted of little more than memorizing Latin formulas by rote for use in letters or legal documents. With time its practitioners began to search through the Latin classics for further models of good writing. This return to the Classical authors was facilitated by the close relationship between the Italian language and Latin, by the availability of manuscripts, and by the visual evidence preserved in countless monuments of the Classical achievement. By the late thirteenth century in a number of Italian cities, notably Padua, Bologna, and Florence, writers were calling for new directions in education, urging that the classics be studied intensively and that learning be made morally relevant in the sense of helping people to better lives.

These writers were the founders of the intellectual movement known as Humanism. Basically, Humanism means Classical scholarship—the ability to read, understand, and appreciate the writings of the ancient world. In Classical antiquity, and again in the Renaissance, educators called the curriculum most suitable for the training of free and responsible persons the *studia humanitatis* ("the studies of mankind" or "the humanities").[2] The curriculum was designed to develop in the student primarily those qualities of intellect and will that truly distinguished human beings from animals. The ideal product of a humanist education was the individual, trained in the classics, who possessed both *sapientia* and *eloquentia*—the wisdom needed to know the right path to follow in any situation and the eloquence needed to persuade others to take it.

Renaissance Humanism was marked by three principal characteristics. First, it rejected

---

[2] *Humanism* was not actually coined until the nineteenth century. In fifteenth- and sixteenth-century Italy, *humanista* signified a professor of humane studies (the *studia humanitatis*) or a Classical scholar.

the emphasis that the medieval schools placed on professional training, whether in theology, law, or medicine, and advocated a liberal education, based on a knowledge of moral philosophy and a command of eloquence. The truly educated person was not identified by technical mastery of a body of learning, but by the capacity to make the right moral judgments in difficult human situations. Second, Humanism stressed the supreme importance of the Latin language (later, Greek also) and the Classical authors. These were the models of eloquence and the storehouses of wisdom that offered people the best possible guides to life, apart from religion itself. Third, Humanism affirmed the possibility of human improvement through education and study. Ideally, individuals should develop to the fullest all their specifically human faculties—physical, moral, spiritual, aesthetic. There was nothing in this hope for human perfection antagonistic to traditional Christianity and ecclesiastical authority. The modern use of the word *Humanism* to denote a secular philosophy that denies an afterlife has no basis in the history of the Renaissance. Most Renaissance humanists read the Church fathers as avidly as they read the pagan authors and believed that the highest virtues included piety. Humanism was far more an effort to enrich traditional religious attitudes than a revolt against them.

Petrarch

The man who clarified these humanistic ideals and disseminated them with unprecedented success in Italy and to some extent in Europe was the Tuscan Francesco Petrarch (1304–1374), a writer by profession and one of the most attractive personalities of his age. Petrarch possessed an immense enthusiasm—and generated it in others—for the ancient authors, for educational reform, and for scholarship. He personally sought to save from neglect the ancient authors preserved in monastic libraries and launched an eager search for their manuscripts, a pursuit that was to become an integral part of the humanist movement. Petrarch had a dismal opinion of his own times and held up in contrast the ideal world of ancient Rome, when there supposedly flourished both authentic learning and virtue. For this reason he thought that the Latin classics should be the heart of the educational curriculum.

Petrarch wrote prolifically and with consistent grace and flair in both Latin and Italian. His best Latin works are his 500 letters, all clearly composed with an eye to a readership beyond the persons addressed. He was the first to discern personality in the great writers of the past, and he directed some of the letters to them—Cicero, Seneca, Virgil, and especially St. Augustine, his favorite literary companion. He also composed an autobiographical "letter to posterity" to future generations—to us. Even today, his warmth and wit win him friends.

Petrarch pretended to disparage his Italian works, but today they are the foundation of his literary reputation. Especially admirable are his 366 sonnets, most of which express his love for a young married woman named Laura, who died in the plague of 1348. In the sonnets written both before and after her death, love represents for Petrarch not so much passion as a way to inner peace; Laura offers him not so much satisfaction as solace.

In his writings, particularly in his imaginative exchanges with St. Augustine, Petrarch examines at length an ethical dilemma characteristic of his age: how should religious people act who aspire to a life of quiet contemplation but feel themselves responsible for the welfare of family, friends, community, Church, and the world in tumultuous times? He does not resolve this dilemma, but probably no one before him explored its dimensions with equal sensitivity.

Petrarch richly deserves his esteemed place in the history of European thought. More than any writer before him, he set a new standard of excellence for Western letters by imitating the simplicity and elegance of Classical literary style. He also defined a new aim in education—the art of living happily and well, as distinct from the narrow professional goals of the older Scholasticism. Finally, he helped develop a new vision of human fulfillment. To Petrarch, the ideal human type was the one who spent a life in the study of letters, enjoyed them, cherished them, and found God in them.

Boccaccio

A near-contemporary of Petrarch, and second only to him in his influence on fourteenth-century Italian learning, was Giovanni Boccaccio (1313–1375). As a young author, Boccaccio celebrated in poetry the charms of his lady Fiammetta, who, unlike Beatrice and even Laura, did not conduct the poet to idealized rapture and ultimate peace, but instead delighted him with both her beauty and her wit. She was the woman not of mystic love but of daily experience.

Boccaccio's great work, the collection of short stories known as *The Decameron,* was written probably between 1348 and 1351. It recounts how a group of young Florentines—seven women and three men—fled during the Black Death of 1348 to a secluded villa, where for 10 days each told a story. The first prose masterpiece in Italian, and a model thereafter for clear and lively narration, *The Decameron* is often considered a work of literary realism, principally for its frank and frequent treatment of sex. In fact, however, it hardly ever offers a realistic portrait of fourteenth-century life and society, for the narrators are consciously seeking to flee and forget the grim, real world; their servants are even forbidden to repeat unpleasant news within their charming villa. *The Decameron* was composed as an antidote to melancholy—one of the first major works in Western letters intended to divert and amuse rather than edify.

Nastagio's tale, from *The Decameron,* tells of a rejected suitor who encounters a phantom knight in the woods outside of Ravenna. **Every Friday, the knight hunts down and kills the ghost of the lady who, in refusing his love, had caused his death. The suitor invites his own lady and her family to a Friday banquet in the woods, where they too witness the horrifying hunt. The living lady recognizes the cruelty of her ways and accepts the suitor. The depiction of this popular story given here is a detail from panels by the great fifteenth-century Florentine painter Sandro Botticelli.** (Photo: Museo del Prado)

With age this one-time spinner of ribald stories was drawn to the religious life; he took orders in the Church and turned his efforts to the cure of souls. Like Petrarch, he disparaged his vernacular writings and even reprimanded a friend for allowing his wife to read the indecent *Decameron.* He died regretting the work that has earned him immortality.

The Civic Humanists

In the generation after Petrarch and Boccaccio, Florentine scholars were preeminent in promoting humanism, and under the leadership of Coluccio Salutati gave to the revived study of antiquity the character of a true movement. Through the recovery of ancient manuscripts and the formation of libraries Coluccio and his group—Leonardo Bruni, Poggio Bracciolini, and others—made accessible to scholars virtually the entire surviving corpus of Classical Latin authors.

These Florentines further sought to reestablish in Italy a command of the Greek language, which, according to Bruni, "no Italian had understood in 700 years." In 1396 they invited the Byzantine scholar Manuel Chrysoloras to lecture at the University of Florence. In the following decades—troubled years for the Byzantine Empire—other Eastern scholars joined the exodus to the West, and they and Western visitors returning from the East brought with them hundreds of Greek manuscripts. By the middle of the fifteenth century Western scholars had both the philological skill and the manuscripts to establish direct contact with the most original minds of the Classical world and were making numerous Latin and Italian translations of Greek works. Histories, tragedies, lyric poetry, the dialogues of Plato, many mathematical treatises, the most important works of the Greek fathers of the Church—in sum, a large part of the Greek cultural inheritance—fully entered Western culture for the first time.

Coluccio and his contemporary Florentine scholars are now often called civic humanists, since they stressed that participation in public affairs is essential for full human development. They linked their praise of the active life with a defense of the republican liberty of Florence, then threatened by the despot Gian Galeazzo of Milan. The humanists argued that human advance depends on a kind of a community dialogue, which allows individuals to learn from one another. To participate in such a dialogue the educated citizen needs wisdom founded upon sound moral philosophy and also eloquence, without which knowledge will remain socially barren. The best education imparts both qualities, which are themselves best exemplified by the ancient classics. Moreover, if human progress depends on dialogue, the best political institutions are those which invite the participation of the citizens in the councils of government. The republican form of government was therefore deemed superior to the despotism represented by Gian Galeazzo. In one integrated argument the civic humanists thus defended the capital importance of training in the classics, the superiority of the active life, and the value of Florentine republican institutions.

Humanism in the Fifteenth Century

As the humanist movement gained in prestige, it spread from Florence to the other principal cities of Italy. At Rome and Naples one of the most able humanist scholars was Lorenzo Valla (1407–1457). Valla conclusively proved that the document known as the Donation of Constantine—one of the documents upon which the papacy based its claim to supremacy in the West—was a forgery concocted in the eighth century.

Two fifteenth-century scholars from the north of Italy, Guarino da Verona and Vittorino da Feltre, were chiefly responsible for incorporating the diffuse educational ideas of the humanists into a practical curriculum. Guarino launched a reform of the traditional methods of education and Vittorino brought the new methods to their fullest development in the various schools he founded, especially his Casa Giocosa ("Happy House") at Mantua. The pupils included boys and girls, both rich and poor (the latter on scholarships). All the students learned Latin and Greek, mathematics, music, and philosophy; in addition, because Vittorino believed that education should aid physical, moral, and social development, they were also taught social graces such as dancing and courteous manners and received instruction in physical exercises like riding and fencing. Vittorino's Happy House attracted pupils from all over Italy, and his methods were widely imitated even beyond the Italian borders.

By the late fifteenth century, and still more in the sixteenth, Humanism, in the sense of Classical literary scholarship, showed a declining vitality in Italy. Like most reform movements Italian Humanism declined principally because its cause had been won. By about 1450, with only a few exceptions, the monastic libraries had yielded their treasures of ancient manuscripts, and in the latter half of the century printing made the texts readily available among the educated public. Humanists were no longer needed to find the ancient authors, copy them, or propagandize for their wider dissemination. Education too had come to recognize, at least partially, the value of training in the classics. By the late fifteenth century the leaders of Italian intellectual life were no longer the humanists but philosophers, who were now able to use a command of the Classical heritage to enrich and develop their own philosophical systems.

The Florentine Neoplatonists

One major theme of the cultural Renaissance, perhaps generated by the misery and melancholy of life, was an effort to depict ideal worlds in thought, literature, and art. A good example of what some scholars call the Renaissance religion of beauty is provided by a group of philosophers active at Florence in the last decades of the fifteenth century. The most gifted among them was probably Marsilio Ficino, whose career is a tribute to the cultural patronage of the Medici. Cosimo de' Medici befriended him as a child and gave him the use of a villa and library near Florence. In this lovely setting a group of scholars and statesmen met frequently to discuss philosophical questions. Drawn to the idealism of Plato (and usually called the Platonic Academy), Ficino and his fellows were particularly concerned with the place of the human soul within the Platonic cosmos and with the soul's dignity and immortality, which they passionately affirmed. To spread these ideas among a larger audience Ficino translated into Latin all of Plato's dialogues and the writings of the chief figures of the Neoplatonic tradition. He also made an ambitious effort to reconcile and assimilate Platonic philosophy and the Christian religion.

Another brilliant member of the Platonic Academy was the young Prince Giovanni Pico della Mirandola, who thought he could reconcile all philosophies. In 1486 Pico proposed to dispute publicly at Rome on some 900 theses that would show the essential unity of the philosophic experience. But Pope Innocent VIII, believing that the theses contained several heretical propositions, forbade the disputation. By the time of his death at 31 Pico had not made much progress toward the "philosophical

peace," or reconciliation of philosophical systems, which he sought.

Both Ficino and Pico founded their philosophies upon two essential assumptions: all being is arranged in a hierarchy of excellence with God at the summit. Moreover, each being in the universe, with the exception only of God, is impelled through a "natural appetite" to seek the perfection of its kind; it is impelled, in other words, to achieve—or at least to contemplate—the beautiful. As Pico expressed it, however, man is unique in that he is placed in the middle of the universe linked with both the spiritual world above and the material one below. His free will enables him to seek perfection in either direction; he is free to become all things. A clear ethic emerges from this scheme: the good life should be an effort to achieve personal perfection, and the highest human value is the contemplation of the beautiful.

These philosophers believed that Plato had been divinely illumined and therefore that Platonic philosophy and Christian belief were two wholly reconcilable faces of a single truth. Neoplatonic philosophy has a particular importance for the influence it exerted on many of the great artists of the Florentine Renaissance, including Botticelli and Michelangelo.

The Heritage of Humanism

Fifteenth-century Italian Humanism left a deep imprint on European scholarship and education. The humanists greatly strengthened the command of Latin. They also restored a mastery of the Greek language in the West and elevated a large part of the Greek cultural inheritance to a position of influence in Western civilization. Moreover, they began the systematic investigation of other languages associated with great cultural traditions, most notably Hebrew, and in so doing laid the basis of modern textual and (more remotely) historical criticism. They developed new ways of investigating the character of the ancient world—through archaeology, numismatics (the study of coins), and epigraphy (the study of inscriptions on buildings, statues, and the like), as well as through the study of literary texts. Humanistic influence on the study of history was particularly profound. The medieval chroniclers had looked into the past for evidence of God's saving providence, whereas the humanists were primarily concerned with using the past to illustrate human behavior and provide moral examples. Though their approach was not without its faults—such as an aversion to mundane detail and statistical data, and a sometimes bombastic and obscure rhetorical style—they certainly deepened the historical consciousness of the West and greatly strengthened the historian's technical skill. Humanistic influences on vernacular languages helped bring standardization of spelling and grammar; and the Classical ideas of simplicity, restraint, and elegance of style exerted a continuing influence on Western letters.

No less important was the role of the humanists as educational reformers. The curriculum devised by them spread throughout Europe in the sixteenth century; in fact, until the early twentieth century it everywhere defined the standards by which the lay leaders of Western society were trained. Protestants, Catholics, men and women of all nationalities were steeped in the same classics and consequently thought and communicated in similar fashion. In spite of bitter religious divisions and heated national antagonisms, the common humanistic education helped preserve the fundamental cultural unity of the West.

Whatever the achievements of the movement in the fourteenth and fifteenth centuries, it cannot be concluded that Humanism represented a revolt against the intellectual and religious heritage of the Middle Ages. It would be more accurate to say that the humanists, rather than destroying the heritage of the past, opened it to a new and larger audience. In the thirteenth century learning had remained largely a monopoly of monks and Scholastics, and its character reflected their professional and vocational needs. In the fourteenth and fifteenth centuries the humanists introduced a narrow but still important segment of lay society to the accumulated intellectual treasury of the European past, both Classical and Scholastic, ancient and medieval. Simultaneously, they reinterpreted that heritage and enlarged the function of education and scholarship to serve human beings in their present life by teaching them, as Petrarch recommended, the art of living wisely and well.

II. THE CULTURE OF THE NORTH

Most areas of Europe beyond the Alps did not have the many large cities and the high percentage of urban dwellers that supported the humanistic movement in Italy. Moreover, unlike those of Italy, the physical monuments and languages of northern Europe did not offer ready reminders of the Classical heritage. Humanism and the true Classical Renaissance, with a literate, trained laity, did not come to the north until the last decade of the fifteenth century. The court, rather than the city, and the knight, rather than the merchant, dominated northern culture for most of the later fourteenth and fifteenth centuries.

Chivalry

In 1919 a Dutch historian, Johan Huizinga, wrote *The Waning of the Middle Ages,* a stimulating study of the character of north European culture in the fourteenth and fifteenth centuries. That culture, Huizinga argued, should be viewed, not as a renaissance, but as the decline of medieval civilization. Paying chief attention to the court of the dukes of Burgundy, who were among the wealthiest and most powerful princes of the north, Huizinga examined courtly life and manners, and described the courtiers' views on love, war, and religion. He found tension and frequent violence in this society, with little of the balance and serenity that had marked medieval society in the thirteenth century. Instead, its members seemed to show a defective sense of reality, an acute inconsistency in their values and actions, and great emotional instability. Many critics now consider that Huizinga probably exaggerated the negative qualities in northern culture, but that his analysis still contains much that is accurate.

The defective sense of reality that Huizinga noted is manifest in the extravagant cultivation of the notion of chivalry. Militarily, the knight was in fact becoming less important than the foot soldier armed with longbow, pike, or firearms. But the noble classes of the north continued to pretend that knightly virtues governed all questions of state and society; they discounted such lowly considerations as money, arms, number of forces, supplies, and the total resources of countries in deciding the outcome of wars. For example, before the Battle of Agincourt, one French knight told King Charles that he should not use contingents from the Parisian townsfolk because that would give his army an unfair numerical advantage; the battle should be decided strictly on the basis of chivalrous valor.

This was the age of the perfect knight and the *beau geste* and grand feats of arms. King John of Bohemia insisted that his soldiers lead him to the front rank of battle, so that he could better strike the enemy; but he needed his soldiers to guide him, for John was blind. The feats of renowned knights won the rapt admiration of chroniclers but affected the outcome of battle hardly at all. The age was marked too by the foundation of new orders of chivalry—notably the Knights of the Garter and the Burgundian Knights of the Golden Fleece.[3] The basic supposition was that these orders would reform the world by the intensive cultivation of knightly virtues.

Princes rivaled one another in the sheer glitter of their arms and the splendor of their tournaments. They waged wars of dazzlement, seeking to confound rivals and confirm friends with spectacular displays of gold, silks, and tapestries. Court ceremony achieved unprecedented excesses.

Extravagance touched the chivalric arts of love as well. A special order was founded for the defense of women, and knights frequently took lunatic oaths to honor their ladies, such as keeping one eye closed for extended periods. Obviously people rarely made love or war in this artificial way. But men still drew satisfaction in speculating—in dreaming—how love and war would be if this sad world were only a perfect place.

The Cult of Decay

Huizinga called the extravagant life style of the northern courts the "cult of the sublime," or the impossibly beautiful. But he also noted that both knights and commoners showed a morbid fascination with death and its ravages. Reminders of the ultimate victory of death and explicit treatment of decay are frequently encountered in both literature and art. One popular artistic motif was the danse macabre, or dance of death, depicting people from all walks of life—rich and poor, clergy and laity, good and bad—dancing with a skeleton, with their own future selves. Another melancholy theme favored by all European artists was the Pietà—the Virgin weeping over her dead son.

This morbid interest in death and decay in an age of pestilence was not the fruit of lofty religious sentiment. The unbalanced concern with the fleetingness of material beauty shows, if anything, an excessive attachment to it, a kind of inverse materialism. Even more than that, it reveals a growing religious dissatisfaction. In the thirteenth century Francis of Assisi addressed death as a sister; in the fourteenth

---

[3] Jason, leader of the Argonauts, was the first patron of the order, but the question was soon raised whether a pagan hero could appropriately be taken as a model by Christian knights. It was further pointed out that Jason had treated his wife Medea in a most unchivalrous fashion (he left her for another woman). Jason was therefore replaced as patron by the Old Testament hero Gideon.

and fifteenth centuries men clearly regarded it as a ravaging, indomitable fiend. Clearly the Church was failing to provide consolation to many of its members, and a religion that fails to console is a religion in crisis.

Still another manifestation of the unsettled religious spirit of the age was a fascination with the devil, demonology, and witchcraft. The most enlightened scholars of the day argued at length about whether witches could ride through the air on sticks, and about their relations with the devil. (One of the more notable witch trials of Western history occurred at Arras in 1460. Scores of people were accused of participating in a witches' sabbath, giving homage to the devil, and even having sexual intercourse with him.) Fear of the devil and perhaps also a widespread cultivation of the occult arts in the lower levels of society are salient departures from the serene, confident religion of the thirteenth century.

Finally, people showed an inordinate desire to reduce religious images to their most concrete form. The passion to have immediate, physical contact with the objects of religious devotion gave added popularity to pilgrimages and still more to the obsession with relics of the saints, which, more often fabricated than authentic, became a major commodity in international trade, and princes accumulated collections numbering in the tens of thousands.

Huizinga saw these manifestations of northern culture as the disintegration of the cultural synthesis of the Middle Ages. Without a disciplined and unified view of the world, attitudes toward war, love, and religion lost balance, and disordered behavior followed. This culture was not young and vigorous but old and dying. However, Huizinga's root concept of decadence must be used with a certain caution. Certainly this was a psychologically disturbed world that had lost the self-confidence of the thirteenth century; but these allegedly decadent people were not the victims of a torpid spirit. They were dissatisfied perhaps,

but they were also passionately anxious to find solutions to the psychological tensions that unsettled them. It is well to recall that passion when trying to understand the appeal and the power behind other cultural movements—lay piety, northern Humanism, and efforts for religious reform.

Contemporary Views of Northern Society

Huizinga wrote about chivalric society from the perspective of the twentieth century. One of the best contemporary historians of that society was Jean Froissart (1333?–1400?) of Flanders, who traveled widely across England and the Continent, noting carefully the exploits of valiant men. His chronicles give the richest account of the first half of the Hundred Years' War, and he has no equal among medieval chroniclers for colorful, dramatic narration. Nonetheless, Froissart has been criticized for his preoccupation with chivalric society; his narrative treats peasants and townspeople with contempt, or simply ignores them. Yet concerns limited to chivalry suited the purposes for which he wrote. He wished to record the wars of his day, lest, as he put it, "the deeds of present champions should fade into oblivion."

The works of contemporary English writers help to round out the picture of northern society in the fourteenth century. One of them, a poet of uncertain identity, probably William Langland, presents the viewpoint of the humbler classes. His *Vision of Piers Plowman,* which was probably written about 1360, is one of the most remarkable works of the age. The poem gives a loosely connected account of 11 visions, each of which is crowded with allegorical figures, and it is filled with spirited comment about the various classes of people, the impact of plague and war upon society, and the failings of the Church.

Geoffrey Chaucer (ca. 1340–1400) came from a middle-class background; his father was a London vintner, and he himself a diplomat and officeholder. His *Canterbury Tales,* perhaps the greatest work of imaginative literature produced anywhere in Europe in the late fourteenth century, recounts the pilgrimage of some 30 persons to the tomb of St. Thomas à Becket at Canterbury. For entertainment on the road each pilgrim agrees to tell two stories. Chaucer's lively portraits provide an unexcelled view of English society, especially in its middle ranges. The stories also sum up the moral and social ills of the day. His robust monk, for example, ignores the Benedictine rule; his friar is more interested in donations than in the cure of souls; and his pardoner knowingly hawks fraudulent relics. The wife of Bath complains of prejudice against women. But Chaucer's picture remains balanced and good-humored; he praises the student of Oxford, who would gladly learn and gladly teach, and the rural parson, who cares for his flock while others search out benefices, to the neglect of the faithful. Apart from the grace of his poetry Chaucer was gifted with an ability to delineate character and spin a lively narrative. *The Canterbury Tales* is a masterly portrayal of human personalities and human behavior that can delight readers in any age.

III. RELIGIOUS THOUGHT AND PIETY

The Scholasticism of the thirteenth century, as represented by Thomas Aquinas, was based on the bold postulate that it was within the power of human reason to construct a universal philosophy that would do justice to all truths and would reconcile all apparent conflicts among them. The simultaneous growth in ecclesiastical law had also tended to define Christian obligations and the Christian life in terms of precise rules of behavior rather than interior spirit. This style of thinking changed during the next two centuries. Many Scholastics were drawn toward analysis (breaking apart) rather than synthesis (putting together) as they attempted a rigorous investigation of philosophical and theological statements. Many of them no longer shared Aquinas's confidence in human reason. Fundamentally, they hoped to repair the Thomistic synthesis or to replace it with new systems that, though less comprehensive, would at least rest on sound foundations. Piety changed too, as more and more Christian leaders sought ways of deepening interior, mystical experience.

The "Modern Way"

The followers of St. Thomas or of Duns Scotus remained active in the late medieval schools, but the most original of the philosophers were nominalists—that is, those who denied the existence, or at least the knowability, of universal natures—manness, dogness, and the like. The greatest of these late medieval nominalists was the English Franciscan William of Ockham (1300?–1349?). The fundamental principle of his logical analysis later came to be called Ockham's razor. It may be stated in several ways, but essentially it affirms that between alternative explanations for the same phenomenon, the simpler is always to be preferred.

On the basis of this "principle of parsimony" Ockham attacked the traditional problem of ideal forms, such as manness or dogness. He rejected Aquinas's argument that all beings, apart from God, were metaphysically composite of a principle of unity (act) and a principle of individuation (potency). The simplest way to explain the existence of an individual object is to affirm that it exists. The mind can detect resemblances among objects and form general concepts concerning them; these concepts can be further manipulated in logically valid ways. But they offer no certain assurance that ideal forms—principles of unity in which individual objects participate—exist in the real world.

The area of reality in which the mind can effectively function is thus severely limited. The universe, as far as human reason can detect, is an aggregate of autonomous individual beings, not a hierarchy of ideal forms, natures, or ideas. The proper approach in dealing with this universe is through direct experience, not through speculations about ideal or abstract natures, the very existence of which is doubtful. Any theology based upon observation and reason would obviously be greatly restricted. It would still be possible, thought Ockham, to prove the existence of necessary principles in the universe, but man could not know whether the necessary principle, or God, is one or many.

Ockham and many of his contemporaries were profoundly impressed by the power and freedom of God and by man's absolute dependence on him. God's freedom allowed him, if he chose, to reward vice or punish virtue. But if God was free to act in erratic ways, how could there be a stable system of dogma, a fixed theology or ethics? To escape this dilemma the nominalists made a crucial distinction between the absolute and the ordained power of God (*potentia absoluta* and *potentia ordinata*). By virtue of his absolute power, God could act in any way he chose. But through a covenant, or agreement, God assures people that he will act in consistent and predictable ways. On these assumptions, theology becomes the study not of metaphysical reality but of God's will and covenant regarding the human race.

Nominalists lacked Aquinas's high assessment of human powers and his confident belief in the ordered, autonomous, and knowable structure of the natural world. Living within a disturbed, pessimistic age, the nominalists reflect a crisis in confidence, in natural reason and in themselves, that is a major theme of late medieval cultural history.

Nominalism enjoyed great popularity in the universities, and Ockhamite philosophy in particular came to be known as the *via moderna* ("modern way"). Although nominalists and humanists were frequently at odds, they shared certain common attitudes: both were dissatisfied with some aspects of the medieval intellectual tradition; both were impatient with the speculative abstractions of medieval thought; and both advocated approaches to reality that would concentrate upon the concrete and the present and consider them with a stricter awareness of method.

Social Thought

The belief of the nominalists that reality was to be found not in abstract forms but in concrete objects had important implications for social thought. Among the social thinkers clearly influenced by nominalism the most remarkable is Marsilius of Padua. In 1324 he wrote *Defender of Peace,* a pamphlet attacking papal authority and supporting lay sovereignty within the Church. In conformity with nominalist principles Marsilius affirmed that the reality of the Christian community, like the reality of the universe, consists in the aggregate of all its parts. The sovereignty of the Church thus rests in its membership—or, as Marsilius phrased it rather vaguely, in its "stronger and healthier part." This part in turn constituted the "human legislator," which represents the collective, sovereign will of the community. The human legislator delegates the functions of government to six great bureaus: the princely office, the treasury, the military establishment, artisans, cultivators, and finally the clergy.

Marsilius is often considered an architect of the modern concept of sovereignty, and even of totalitarianism. He maintained that only those regulations supported by force are true law. Therefore, the enactments of the Church do not constitute binding legislation, because they are not supported by any coercive power. Only the human legislator can promulgate authentic law, and there is no limit on what it may do. The Church has no right to power or property and is entirely subject to the sovereign will of the state. Sovereignty is in turn indivisible, absolute, and unlimited.

Defender of Peace is noteworthy not only for its radical ideas but also for the evidence it gives of deep dissatisfactions within medieval society. Marsilius and others manifested a hostile impatience with the papal and clerical domination of Western political life. They demanded that the guidance of the Church and the Christian community rest exclusively with laypeople. *Defender of Peace,* in this respect at least, was a prophecy of things to come.

Styles of Piety

Religion remained a central concern of fourteenth- and fifteenth-century men and women, but new forms of piety, or religious practice, began to appear that were designed to meet the needs of laypeople. Mysticism, an interior sense of the presence and love of God, had found its usual expression within the confines of the monastic orders, but by the thirteenth century this monopoly was beginning to break down. The principal mission of the Franciscans and the Dominicans became preaching to the laity, to whom these two mendicant orders hoped to introduce some of the satisfactions of mystical religion. And laypeople wishing to remain in the outside world could join special branches of the Franciscans or Dominicans known as third orders. Confraternities, which were religious guilds largely for laypeople, grew up in the cities and, through common religious services and the support of charitable activities, tried to deepen the spiritual life of their members. Humanism preserved strong overtones of a movement for lay piety. An abundance of devotional and mystical literature was written for laypeople to teach them how to feel repentance, not just how to define it. Translations of the Scriptures into many vernacular languages appeared,

although the high cost of manuscripts before the age of printing severely limited their circulation.

This growth of lay piety was in essence an effort to open the monastic experience to the lay world, to put at the disposal of all what had hitherto been restricted to a spiritual elite. Frightened by the disasters of the age, people hungered for emotional reassurance, for evidence of God's love and redeeming grace within them. Moreover, the spread of education among the laity, at least in the cities, made people discontented with empty forms of religious ritual.

The Rhenish Mystics

The most active center of the new lay piety was the Rhine valley. The first of several leading figures in the region was the Dominican Meister Eckhart. A great preacher and a devoted student of Aquinas, Eckhart sought to bring his largely lay listeners into a mystical confrontation with God. Believers, he maintained, should cultivate within their souls the "divine spark." To achieve this they must banish all thoughts from their minds and seek to attain a state of pure passivity. If they succeed, God will come and dwell within them. Eckhart stressed the futility of dogma and, implicitly, traditional acts of piety. God is too great to be contained in dogmatic categories and too sovereign to be moved by conventional piety.

The Rhenish mystics all stressed the theme that formal knowledge of God and his attributes means little if it is cultivated without love and emotional receptivity. Perhaps the most influential of all of them was Gerhard Groote of Holland. Groote wrote sparingly, exerting his extraordinary influence upon his followers largely through his personality. After his death in 1384 his disciples formed a religious congregation known as the Brethren of the Common Life. Taking education as their principal ministry, they founded schools in Germany and the

Low Countries that imparted a style of lay piety known as the *devotio moderna* ("modern devotion"). Erasmus of Rotterdam and Martin Luther were among their pupils.

The richest statement of the *devotio moderna* appeared about 1425 in *The Imitation of Christ,* a small devotional manual attributed to Thomas à Kempis, a member of the Brethren of the Common Life. *The Imitation of Christ* says almost nothing about fasting, pilgrimages, and other acts of private penitence characteristic of traditional piety. Instead, it emphasizes interior experience as an essential part of the religious life; it is also untraditional in its ethical and social consciousness. The fruit of interior conversion is not extreme acts of personal expiation, but high ethical behavior: "First, keep yourself in peace, and then you shall be able to bring peace to others."

The new lay piety was by no means a revolutionary break with the medieval Church, but it implicitly discounted the importance of many traditional institutions and practices. In this personal approach to God there was no special value in the monastic vocation. As Erasmus would later sharply argue, what was good in monasticism should be practiced by every Christian. Stressing simplicity and humility, the new lay piety was reacting against the pomp and splendor that had come to surround popes and prelates and to mark religious ceremonies. Likewise, the punctilious rules concerning fasts, abstinences, and devotional exercises; the cult of the saints and their relics; and the traffic in indulgences and pardons all seemed peripheral to true religious needs. Without the proper state of soul these traditional acts of piety were meaningless; with the proper state every act was worship.

A generation ago many Protestant scholars considered that the new lay piety was a preparation for the Reformation, while Catholic historians vigorously affirmed that it was authentically Catholic. Today, in our ecumenical age, the desire to enlist Thomas à Kempis among one's spiritual forebears seems pointless. The new lay piety was a preparation for both sixteenth-century reformations, Protestant and Catholic. It aimed at producing a more penetrating religious sentiment. The formal religion of the Middle Ages, for all its grandeur and logical intricacies, no longer fully satisfied the religious spirit and was leaving hollows in the human heart.

Although the *devotio moderna* was a religious movement, it was in many ways similar to Humanism. Both Thomas à Kempis and Petrarch expressed their distaste for the subtle abstractions and intellectual arrogance of the Scholastics. Both stressed that the person who is wise and good will cultivate humility and maintain toward the profound questions of religion a "learned ignorance." Both affirmed that it is more important to educate the will to love than the intellect to the mastery of abstruse theology. Finally, both addressed their message primarily to laypeople, in order to aid them to a higher moral life. The humanists of course drew their chief inspiration from the works of pagan and Christian antiquity, whereas the advocates of the new lay piety looked almost exclusively to Scripture. But the resemblances were so close that in the late fifteenth and sixteenth centuries, men like Erasmus and Thomas More could combine elements from both in the movement known as Christian Humanism.

Heresies

Efforts to repair the traditions of medieval Christianity also led to outright heretical attacks upon the religious establishment, which of course were strengthened by antagonism toward the papacy, reaction against corruption in the Church, and the social and psychological tensions characteristic of this disturbed epoch. Fundamentally, however, the growing appeal of heresies reflected the difficulties the Church was experiencing in adapting its organization and teachings to the demands of a changing world.

The most prominent of the heretics of the time was the Englishman John Wycliffe, who was clearly influenced by the national spirit generated by the Hundred Years' War and the apparent subservience of the Avignon papacy to France. In 1365 he denounced the payment of Peter's pence, the annual tax given by the English people to the papacy. Later he publicly excoriated the papal Curia, monks, and friars for their vices.

Wycliffe argued that the Scriptures alone declared the will of God and that neither the pope, the cardinals, nor Scholastic theologians could tell Christians what they should believe. (In 1382 he began to translate the Bible into English, but he died two years later before finishing.) He also attacked the dogma of transubstantiation, which asserts that priests at mass work a miracle when they change the substance of bread and wine into the substance of Christ. Besides attacking the special powers, position, and privileges of the priesthood in such dogmas as transubstantiation, Wycliffe assaulted with equal vehemence the authority of the pope and the hierarchy to exercise jurisdiction and to hold property. He claimed that the true Church was that of the predestined—that is, those in the state of sanctifying grace. Only the elect could rule the elect; therefore, popes and bishops who had no grace could be justly divested of their properties and had no right to rule. The chief responsibility for ecclesiastical reform rested with the prince, and the pope could exercise only so much authority as the prince allowed.

Wycliffe's adherents, mostly from among the lower classes, were called Lollards, a name apparently derived from "lollar" (idler). Although this group may have survived in England until the age of the Tudor Reformation, Wycliffe's religious system seems to have had no direct influence on subsequent ecclesiastical history. Still, his ideas show many similarities with later Protestantism. His insistence on a purified Church, a priesthood not sacramentally distinct from the laity, a vernacular Bible, a religion more culturally responsive to the people, and lay direction of religious affairs marks out the major issues that, within a little more than a century, would divide the Western Christian community.

In distant Bohemia a Czech priest named John Huss (1369–1415) mounted an equally dangerous attack upon the dominance of the established Church. Historians dispute how much Huss was influenced by Wycliffe's ideas. Certainly he knew the works of the English heretic, but he was more conservative in his own theology—what can be understood of it. Huss's ideas are less than clear, and it is hard even to define how he departed from orthodoxy. He seems to have held that the Church included only the predestined and he questioned, without explicitly denying, transubstantiation.

Huss was burned at the stake at Constance in 1415, more for rejecting the authority of the general council which condemned him than for his doctrinal errors. After his death Huss's followers in Bohemia defied the efforts of the emperor and Church to persuade them to submit; however, the Hussites soon divided into several rival sects—in a manner that anticipates the experience of later Protestantism—and civil war raged in Bohemia from 1421 to 1436 with no clear-cut outcome. The Hussite movement represents one of the earliest successful revolts against the medieval religious establishment. It was also the first withdrawal of an entire territory from unity with Rome.

IV. THE FINE ARTS

The social and cultural changes profoundly affected the arts, making the fourteenth and fifteenth centuries one of the most brilliant periods in Western history. Works of art have survived from this age in unprecedented abundance, a sign that the arts were assuming broader functions in Western society. Princes and townspeople became art patrons, and the artists themselves acquired a new prestige.

Patrons and Values

In the Early Middle Ages architecture, sculpture, painting, and music were primarily liturgical in character, in the sense that their chief function was to enrich Christian worship. There had, of course, always been some lay patronage of the arts—the troubadours, for example, had composed and sung songs for lay patrons—but secular music remained technically behind the music of the Church, and it is difficult today even to reconstruct its sounds.

The Church continued to promote and inspire artistic production in the fourteenth and fifteenth centuries, and many of the greatest creations of the period retained a liturgical character. But the more novel development of the age was the greatly enlarged role that laypeople came to play as patrons—notably the princes of Europe and the rich townspeople in Italy and Flanders. In older histories of the Renaissance the growth of lay patronage was often equated with a secularization of art, but such a view is only partially correct. To a large degree lay patrons favored religious themes in the art they commissioned, even though much of it was no longer liturgical in function. Yet the rise of lay patronage did strongly affect the character of art. In works prepared for liturgical purposes the artist could not draw too much attention to his own work, for the Church objected to art or music that overly intruded upon the consciousness of the worshiping Christian. Moreover, the painter and the sculptor had to accommodate the architecture of the church they were decorating. The lay patronage of religious art— and the use of that art for the decoration of homes as well as churches—in part freed the artists to form their work as they saw fit, knowing that they had the principal attention of the viewer and that the work did not have to be subservient to architecture.

Moreover, the changing religious values that have been mentioned affected artistic styles. Both the humanists and the promoters of the new lay piety insisted that religious values be made more concrete and more immediate to the believing Christian; in terms of art this meant that the viewer should become involved visually and emotionally with the sacred scenes he or she contemplated. The growth of naturalism in art reflected not a waning interest in religious images, but an effort to view them more intimately.

The interest of fourteenth- and fifteenth-century society in elegant living naturally extended to nonliturgical art, providing artists an abundance of opportunities. Both townspeople and nobles wished to live in attractive surroundings. Architects therefore turned their attention to the construction of beautiful homes, villas, palaces, and châteaus; adding to the beauty of these residences were tapestries, paintings, statuary, finely made furniture, and windows of tinted glass. This pursuit of elegance also gave music a new importance. In the books on good manners characteristic of the age the perfect courtier or gentleman was instructed to develop an ear for music and an ability to sing gracefully and play an instrument. No gathering within the higher levels of society could take place without the participation of singers and musicians.

Art and music also fulfilled other functions. The growing awareness of and concern with the family led patrons to commission portraits of their loved ones. In an often melancholy age art and music offered the same sweetness, delight, and spiritual refreshment that Boccaccio meant to convey in his *Decameron*. In Italy the philosophers of the Platonic Academy maintained that the contemplation of ideal beauty was the highest human activity, and it was primarily in art that the ideal beauty could be found. In the north as well, art and music were essential parts of what Huizinga called the cult of the sublime, the effort to conjure up through the mind and senses images of ideal worlds.

Finally, the social position of the artist himself was changing. In the Early Middle Ages many artists appear to have been either amateurs (in the sense of drawing their support from another career such as the monastic or clerical) or poorly paid artisans. The growing market for works of art, however, widened the ranks of professional artists and gave them greater economic rewards and prestige. The growing professionalism of the artist is perhaps most apparent in music. For example, the great churches of Europe relied more and more on professional organists and singers to staff their choirs, governments employed professional trumpeters to add splendor to their proceedings, and professional musicians entertained at the elegant fêtes of the wealthy. The high technical competence required of singers and musicians in much of the music of the Late Middle Ages probably would not have been within the reach of amateurs. The artist too was often accorded special social status; painters such as Leonardo and Michelangelo were actively cultivated by princes.

Techniques and Models

The artist was also acquiring a larger array of technical skills. In music the age witnessed accelerated progress in musical notation. More diversified instrumentation became possible as new instruments were invented and existing ones improved. Thus in strings there were the lute, viol, and harp; in wind instruments, the flute, recorder, oboe, and trumpet; and in keyboard instruments, the organ, virginal, and clavichord.

Technical advances in painting helped artists to achieve greater depth and realism. The fourteenth-century Florentine Giotto used light and shadow, initiating a technique known as chiaro-

Detail from the Campin Altarpiece. This Flemish painting, from the early fifteenth century, shows the intense realism and the attention to detail that were the primary characteristics of Flemish art of this period. It also shows the bustle of urban life.
(Photo: The Metropolitan Museum of Art, The Cloisters Collection, Purchase)

scuro to create an illusion of depth. Less than a century after Giotto, another Florentine, Masaccio, achieved a complete mastery of the scientific laws of perspective, as evidenced in his *Holy Trinity with the Virgin and St. John,* which seems almost three-dimensional (see Plate 19). In 1436, in his essay "On Painting," the Florentine humanist and architect Leon Battista Alberti (1402–1472) presented the first systematic exposition of the laws of perspective. Artists lent their paintings still greater realism through the scientific study of human anatomy. All these techniques made Italian paintings true windows into visionary realms.

The major technical achievement in the north was the development of oil painting in the fifteenth century. Oils provided artists with richer colors and permitted them to paint more slowly and carefully and to make changes on the painted canvas. To create an illusion of reality, the Flemish masters concentrated on precise detail rather than on perspective and chiaroscuro. Because of their painstaking exactitude the Flemish artists were the leading portrait painters of the age.

The artist was also using new models, and here the most important innovation was the heightened appreciation, especially in Italy, of the artistic heritage of the Classical world. Earlier medieval artists had frequently borrowed the motifs of Classical art, but they had made no effort to reflect its values—idealized beauty, admiration of the human form, simplicity, restraint, elegance, and balance. An appreciation of Classical style and the values it conveyed is the achievement of Italian art, particularly in sculpture, in the fifteenth century. One of the greatest sculptors of the age, the Florentine Donatello, demonstrates those values in his *Annunciation;* though the theme is religious, the treatment is Classical (see Plate 17).

Architecture too benefited from the closer reading of Classical writers (notably Vitruvius) and from the conscious effort to introduce harmonious proportions into building design. To embellish their churches the Italian masters borrowed a variety of forms from the Classical style—domes, columns, colonnades, pilasters, and cornices. In the early and middle 1400s the churches and palaces merely combined Classical motifs with conventional medieval designs. Thus, Filippo Brunelleschi (1379–1446), inspired by ancient architecture, raised a huge

dome over the church of Sta. Maria del Fiore in Florence, but the church itself retained the form of a traditional basilica. A pure Classical style did not really triumph until the sixteenth century. Architects then developed central churches, arranged symmetrically around the dome; of these, St. Peter's in Rome is the chief monument. Among the most gifted masters of Classical style was Andrea Palladio (1518–1580) of Vicenza; in numerous villas, palaces, and churches in the lower Po valley, he fully captured all the stateliness and grace of the ancient temples.

The Great Masters

The two major centers of Western art in the fifteenth century were Italy and the Low Countries, then under the rule of the dukes of Burgundy. In Italy the last decades of the fifteenth century and the opening decades of the sixteenth are traditionally called the High Renaissance. But most historians of art believe that the term *Renaissance,* in the sense of conscious imitation of Classical models, is inappropriate in the north of Europe in the fifteenth century, where the chief sources of inspiration remained medieval. All scholars, however, recognize the high level of creativity achieved in the north, especially by the artists and musicians of the Low Countries.

The North

The great period of painting in Flanders began with Jan van Eyck (1385?–1440), whose meticulous concern with detail achieved an intense realism that was to characterize Flemish art. In *The Virgin and Child in the Church,* van Eyck's precision in depicting the jewels of the Virgin's crown and the fabric of her robe heightens the realism; the Virgin's vivid presence seems almost to envelop the viewer (see Plate 18). In an unstable age, when religious confusion was prevalent in the north, van Eyck and the other

Flemish masters seemed anxious to reassure the viewer of the reality and truth of the scenes they were presenting.

The Low Countries enjoyed an equal prominence in music in the late fifteenth century. The choirmasters in the cathedral towns such as Cambrai, Bruges, and Antwerp, with the aid of professional singers, carried four-part choral polyphony to a new level of development. With the perfection of the *a cappella* (unaccompanied) vocal harmony, instrumental music was freed from its traditional subservience to voice. The masters gave their attention almost equally to secular and sacred music. Among many gifted musicians may be cited Guillaume Dufay of Cambrai, author of several impressive masses as well as secular songs; and Josquin Des Prés, perhaps the most versatile of the northern composers, author of masses, motets, and chansons in almost every current style. These masters, musicians, and composers traveled widely in Europe and many of them spent some time in Italy; they therefore learned from, and deeply influenced, the local and regional musical traditions.

Italy

The art of the High Renaissance in Italy is best represented in the work of three men, each of whom stands among the major artistic geniuses of the Western past: Leonardo da Vinci (1452–1519), Raphael Santi (1483–1520), and Michelangelo Buonarroti (1475–1564).

Leonardo is celebrated for his mechanical designs as well as for his art, but his exact contribution to technology and science remains difficult to assess. He failed to complete most of the projects he contemplated, and he purposely worked in a secretive fashion (he wrote his notes in mirror writing). Although he stands somewhat apart from the mainstream of technical and scientific advance, his inventive imagination produced ingenious speculative designs for an airplane, a tank, and a submarine.

In art Leonardo's accomplishment is unmis-

takable. Only 15 paintings survive, but they include some of the greatest masterpieces of Western art. He had two remarkable gifts, an ability to handle groups of people and an extraordinary skill in portraying human psychology, both exemplified by his *Last Supper,* which depicts the psychological reactions of the apostles as they hear Christ say that someone at the table will betray him. The *Mona Lisa,* a portrait of a Florentine matron in her twenties, is a fascinating psychological examination of the woman's personality.

If Leonardo was a master of design, Raphael would have to be called a master of grace. Better than any other artist he reveals the Renaissance admiration for harmony, serenity, pure beauty, and pure form. He was an extremely versatile painter from the point of view of style, readily absorbing the techniques of his masters both in Umbria (his native province) and Florence (where he served his apprenticeship)—the bright colors favored by the Umbrians, the subtle shading of color and the strength of design of Leonardo, and the vitality and power of Michelangelo. Raphael may not be as original a genius as Leonardo or Michelangelo, but he is unsurpassed in the quality of his craftsmanship and the charm of its results.

Michelangelo is probably the best example of the universal genius of the Renaissance, a man of towering accomplishments in architecture, sculpture, and painting. As an artist Michelangelo preferred sculpture to painting, but his work in both mediums is rich with subtle, dramatic vitality. He liked to portray his subjects at the moment of psychological transition. For example, his statue of David catches the young man at the instant he resolves to hurl the stone at Goliath. The statue of Moses shows the old prophet awakening to anger at the idolatry of the Israelites. Adam, painted on the Sistine ceiling, is represented just as his inert body responds to God's life-giving touch (see Plate 24).

Imbued with the Neoplatonic longing to view things not as they are but as they ought to be, Michelangelo did not depict a natural world. His works seem almost a protest against the limitations of matter, from which many of his subjects struggle to be free. There is little that is placid or serene in his art, and this predilection for contorted, struggling, even misshapen figures exercised a profound influence on his successors. His work is traditionally, and justly, considered to mark the bridge between the harmonious art of the Renaissance and the distorted, dynamic style of the Mannerist school.

V. SCIENCE AND THE RENAISSANCE

In the fourteenth and fifteenth centuries numerous changes—social and economic as well as intellectual—prepared the way for the scientific revolution of the early modern epoch. Although the natural philosophers of the period made no dramatic advances in scientific theory, they succeeded in assimilating a large part of ancient science and began the slow process of questioning and revising, which ultimately led to the achievements of Copernicus, Galileo, and Newton.

The Reception of Ancient Science

A critical first step toward the scientific revolution was the mastery of the natural science of the ancient world. Ancient science offered philosophers a full and coherent system or model of the natural world (sometimes called a paradigm) with which they could compare their own observations and speculations. In the twelfth and thirteenth centuries the complete corpus of the scientific works of Aristotle, together with the commentary by the Muslim philosopher Averroës, became known in the West and immediately inspired close study and extensive discussion. Albertus Magnus, for ex-

ample, the teacher of Thomas Aquinas, wrote at length on biological questions; he both reflected and promoted a new interest in the life sciences in Western schools.

In the fourteenth century, nominalists at Paris and Oxford took the first, hesitant steps toward a criticism of Aristotle's world system. At the University of Paris, for example, Jean Buridan proposed an important revision in the Aristotelian theory of motion, or physical dynamics. If, as Aristotle had said, all objects are at rest in their natural state, what keeps an arrow flying after it leaves the bow? Aristotle had reasoned rather lamely that the arrow disturbs the air through which it passes and that it is this disturbance that keeps pushing the arrow forward.

But this explanation did not satisfy the nominalists. Buridan suggested that the movement of the bow lends the arrow a special quality of motion, an "impetus," which stays with it permanently unless removed by the resistance of the air. Although it was inaccurate, Buridan's explanation anticipated Galileo's theory of inertia, according to which an object at rest tends to remain at rest, and an object in motion continues to move along a straight line until it is acted upon by an external force. Buridan and other fourteenth-century nominalists also theorized about the acceleration of falling objects and made some attempt to describe this phenomenon in mathematical terms. Their ideas became the point of departure for other of Galileo's investigations of mechanics. Moreover, their use of mathematics foreshadowed the importance to be given to measurement in scientific work.

The humanists also helped to prepare the way for scientific advance. The growth of textual and literary criticism—a major humanist achievement—taught people to look with greater care and precision at works inherited from the past. Inevitably too, they acquired a sharper critical sense concerning the content as well as the language of the ancient texts. The revival of the classics placed at the disposal of

Europeans a larger fund of ancient ideas, and this increased the awareness that ancient authors did not always speak in unison. Could the ancients therefore always be correct? Furthermore, the idealism of Plato and the number mysticism of Pythagoras maintained that behind the disparate data of experience there existed ideal forms or harmonies, which the philosopher should seek to perceive and describe. Once this assumption gained credence, it was natural to assume that the cosmic harmonies might be described in mathematical terms.

The Middle Ages also nourished traditions of astrology and alchemy; men sought not only to understand natural processes but also to turn that knowledge into power. Natural science and the scientists themselves would for a long time maintain close connections with these intellectual forms of magical practice.

Finally, technological and economic changes contributed to the birth of exact science. The improvement of ships stimulated, for navigational purposes, more accurate observation of the heavenly bodies. Changes in warfare raised interest in the ballistics of cannonballs,

in the design of war machines and fortifications, and in military engineering generally. Artists were able to depict with high levels of accuracy the human anatomy, maps, or astronomical charts. Printing assured that ideas could be disseminated cheaply, accurately, and quickly across wide geographical areas. Craftsmen working in metal and glass were growing more skilled in the course of the Late Middle Ages. Eyeglasses became ever more popular in Europe in the thirteenth century, and glass workers ground lenses more accurately and experimented with their uses. Although the telescope was a seventeenth-century invention, the technical basis for it was laid in the Late Middle Ages.

The scientific revolution was, in sum, supported by a whole range of developments in European cultural life, many of which occurred in the fourteenth and fifteenth centuries. It remained for the founders of modern science to draw upon these various traditions in the sixteenth and seventeenth centuries, and to form out of them and their own observations new systems or models of the natural world.

The culture of the West was changing profoundly in the fourteenth and fifteenth centuries, as it responded to new social needs. In Italy a literate lay aristocracy had come to dominate society. Traditional cultural interests and values seemed too abstract, too removed from the lives of these people, who daily faced concrete problems and wanted moral guidance. To meet this need Italian humanists developed a system of education that emphasized rhetoric and moral philosophy and looked to the works of Classical antiquity for the best models of wisdom and persuasive language.

In the north of Europe the ideals of chivalry continued to dominate the culture of the lay aristocracy until late in the fifteenth century; but those ideals had become exaggerated, and they began to distort reality. The overripe chivalry of the north has helped give the Late Middle Ages its reputation for decadence.

Nominalist philosophers in the universities were effecting a critical reappraisal of the principles of thirteenth-century Scholasticism in the interest of defining precisely the borders between reason and faith. Also evident is a new style of piety that stressed the need to cultivate an interior sense of the presence and love of God.

The humanists, nominalist philosophers, and advocates of the new piety were not revolting against the accumulated cultural heritage of the Middle Ages. Rather, they wished to enrich it and make it accessible to a broader spectrum of the population. Learning, literature, art, and religion, they believed, should help people lead lives that would at once be more cultured, more contented, more pious, and more human.

The fine arts flourished during these years of change. In both Italy and the north artists adopted new techniques and gave brilliant expression to a much fuller range of values. The scientific achievements of the age were more modest, but they foreshadowed the revolutionary changes in science that were to take place in the sixteenth and seventeenth centuries.

RECOMMENDED READING

Sources

★Boccaccio, Giovanni. *The Decameron.* G. H. McWilliam (tr.). 1972.

★Cassirer, Ernst, P. O. Kristeller, and J. H. Randell, Jr. (eds.). *The Renaissance Philosophy of Man.* 1953. Selections from Petrarch, Valla, Ficino, Pico, and others.

★*The Earthly Republic: Italian Humanists on Government and Society.* Benjamin G. Kohl and Ronald G. Witt (eds.). 1978.

Eckhart. *Meister Eckhart, a Modern Translation.* Raymond Bernard Blakney (tr.). 1956.

Kempis, Thomas à. *The Imitation of Christ.* William Benham (tr.). 1909. Great classic of late medieval piety.

Langland, William. *The Vision of Piers Plowman.* Henry W. Wells (tr.). 1959.

★Marsilius of Padua. *Defender of Peace.* Alan Gerwith (tr.). 1956.

Studies

★Baron, Hans. *The Crisis of the Early Italian Renaissance: Civic Humanism and Republican Liberty in the Age of Classicism and Tyranny.* 1966. Fundamental analysis of Florentine "civic humanism."

Beck, James. *Italian Painting of the Renaissance.* 1981. Recent survey.

★Berenson, Bernard. *The Italian Painters of the Renaissance.* 1968. Classic essays in the history of art.

Bergin, Thomas G. *Boccaccio.* 1981. Learned and readable review of Boccaccio's works.

★Burckhardt, Jacob: *The Civilization of the Renaissance in Italy.* 1958. One of the great works of European history.

Clark, J. M. *The Great German Mystics: Eckhart, Tauler and Suso.* 1949.

Crombie, Alistair C. *Medieval and Early Modern Science.* 1961.

Goldthwaite, Richard A. *The Building of Renaissance Florence: An Economic and Social History.* 1980. Imaginative examination of relations between society and architecture.

★Herlihy, David. *The Family in Renaissance Italy.* 1974.

Herlihy, David, and Klapisch-Zuber, Christiane. *Tuscans and Their Families.* 1985.

★Huizinga, Johan. *The Waning of the Middle Ages.* 1953.

★Kristeller, Paul Otto. *Renaissance Thought: The Classic, Scholastic and Humanistic Strains.* 1961. One of many works by a leading student of Renaissance thought.

Leff, Gordon. *William of Ockham.* 1975. Authoritative examination of a difficult philosopher.

Martines, Lauro. *The Social World of the Florentine Humanists.* 1963. The humanists examined in the light of their social background.

★ Available in paperback.

The Worker in the Venice Arsenal

The city of Venice reached its greatest power and influence in the 1400s and 1500s. It controlled a far-flung empire in northern Italy and the eastern Mediterranean, and had to maintain a large army and especially a strong navy. For the city, with a population of about 150,000, was built on a collection of islands in a lagoon, and though it was never seriously threatened by invaders in this period, its command of the seas was essential to its independence. As a result, it developed the most remarkable shipbuilding and arms manufacturing facility in all of Europe: the Arsenal.

Founded in the 1100s, the Arsenal was constantly expanded: in the 150 years before 1460 it doubled in size three times. By 1500 it employed over 10,000 people, nearly 10 percent of the city's adult population. It was not only the largest industrial enterprise in Europe, but also a godsend for the poor: nowhere else was

The Arsenal in 1500. In the foreground freight-carrying round ships or cogs are seen at anchor.
(National Gallery of Art, Rosenwald Collection)

ENTRANCE TO ARSENAL

ROPE BUILDING

there such an opportunity for employment. The workers were not especially well paid. The women who sewed the ships' sails were known to receive the lowest wages in Venice. But there was a welfare system for all employees, which took care of them in sickness and old age and helped the families of workers. It was by no means generous, but it provided far more security than was otherwise available to the poor.

The Arsenal was thought of as one of the marvels of Europe. Venice was already a favorite tourist spot for travelers and pilgrims to the Holy Land. And no visit to the city was considered complete without a tour of the Arsenal. The discipline and efficiency of its workers were legendary. They were capable of producing a fully equipped warship, starting from scratch, in just one day. A wide variety of skills, from carpentry to metalworking to design, were practiced at a very high level. The finest minds of the time were brought in as consultants. Galileo, for example, who was a professor of mathematics at the Venetian university of Padua, was asked for advice about military technology. When he visited the Arsenal, he watched the workers using the methods they had developed over the years for moving huge weights, such as cannon and cannonballs. Impressed by their use of levers and pulleys, he investigated the principles of dynamics that lay behind their actions, and the results helped shape his famous researches into the laws of physics.

Because so many different crafts were needed to produce ships and armaments, there were many different teams of workers at the Arsenal, each in its own area or building. Perhaps a third of the employees were women, and it is likely that entire families came to work there together. Some tasks were purely female. One traveler, for example, described a "hall where about 50 women were making sails for ships; they had already finished more than 10,000, which were lying there waiting to be used." In another area, he said, "we were in-

formed by the head that 100 men and 150 women worked daily in that building and were paid a good weekly wage." Perhaps the most famous site was the rope-making hall, a building over 200 yards long where hemp was stretched and twisted into rope. The same traveler spoke of seeing 100 women there, "spinning and making ropes and doing other work related to ropes."

To maintain the Arsenal at the peak of efficiency, the government gave it first choice in hiring the craftsmen it needed. If, say, someone skilled in grinding gunpowder worked for another employer in the city, administrators of the Arsenal could insist that he come to work for them. But it was also a matter of pride to be involved in maintaining the power of Venice. The employees seemed willing to remain there for life; although they occasionally demanded better wages or made other kinds of protest, on the whole the security of the employment was a major attraction. Even in hard times, the Venetians kept up the Arsenal because it was the mainstay of the city's military strength.

Most of the workers lived in the area around the Arsenal, which was known as one of the poorer districts of Venice. But within their ranks there were quite distinct levels. The master shipwrights were the best paid and thus the aristocracy of the workers. Women were the worst paid, though their earnings might have been quite significant as a second income for a family. Wages were distributed on Saturday afternoons. Although they grumbled at the long time they had to wait in line for their pay— this issue in fact caused one of their few protest demonstrations—the workers regarded Saturday evening as an occasion for relaxation and conviviality. Their expectation that they would have regular times for recreation was another indication of how unique the Arsenal employees were among the ordinary laborers of Europe.

Chapter 13

Overseas Expansion and a New Politics 1415–1560

Between the last quarter of the fifteenth century and the middle of the sixteenth century, a renewed sense of confidence spread through Europe, accompanying a revival of prosperity and political authority. The vigor that returned to economic life was particularly remarkable; this was a period of rising prices, population growth, and a rapid expansion of trade. Overseas the results of this surge of enterprise were even more spectacular: the discovery of new lands and riches, and the founding of colonies which grew into massive empires that endured into the nineteenth and twentieth centuries.

The question of why it was Western civilization that eventually spread around the globe has long fascinated historians. In the fifteenth century Europeans were less advanced in technology than Asians, and their leading rulers had none of the wealth of Indian moguls or Chinese emperors. Some scholars have suggested that Oriental societies, being much larger, were more self-sufficient and that therefore neither explorers nor international traders achieved the status they gained in the West.

Another reason the Europeans seem to have been able to launch the expansion was the strengthening of central authority in political life. A new assurance permeated the government of the rulers of three leading kingdoms: England, France, and Spain. Often called "new monarchs" by historians, they merited the title because of their potent reassertion of royal preeminence in their domains. Their aims were still largely personal and dynastic—they were concerned more with the fortunes of their own families than with the destinies of the people they ruled—but to this end they raised their power at home, particularly against the nobility, to new levels. By the 1550s the new monarchs had emerged from the uncertainties of the Late Middle Ages as the main political force in their realms.

The Germans, Italians, and Eastern Europeans, by contrast, began to fall behind their Western neighbors in this crucial respect. They lacked strong, unifying central governments, and thus local nobles or small political units fragmented political authority. The result was the eventual decline of these countries. From the mid-sixteenth century until the mid-nineteenth century, they slipped to lesser roles in international affairs, victims of the chief political lesson of this period: only a capable central authority could marshal the resources of a territory and win prominence on the international scene.

I. EXPLORATION AND ITS IMPACT

Few great changes in the history of the world have owed so much to the exploits of a handful of daring adventurers as the overseas expansion of Europe. The origins of the movement can be traced back to the crusades, the Europeans' first outward steps after centuries of defensiveness and shrinkage. Travelers such as Marco Polo and traders in the Levant had also contributed to the interest in far-off places. But the enlargement of the Ottoman Empire during the fifteenth century threatened to cut overland contacts with Asia. It was therefore necessary to find an alternative: a sea route such as the one being opened up by the explorers who were inching their way around Africa toward the Indian Ocean.

The Overseas Expansion

The Portuguese

The pioneers in the transformation of Europe's relations with the rest of the world were the Portuguese, occupants of an inhospitable land, whose seafarers had always held an important place in the country's economic life. The need for better agricultural opportunities had long turned their eyes toward the Atlantic islands and the territories held by the Muslims (Moors) to the south. But this ambition had to be organized into a sustained effort if it was to achieve results, and in the early fifteenth century, Prince Henry the Navigator, a younger son of the king, undertook that task.

A talented leader, Henry participated in the capture of the North African port of Ceuta from the Arabs in 1415, a crusading expedition that only whetted his appetite for more victories over the infidels. At Ceuta he probably received information about legendary Christians (the fabled kingdom of Prester John) and mines of gold somewhere in the interior. A mixture of motives—profit, religion, and curiosity—spurred him on, and in 1419 he began patronizing sailors, mapmakers, astronomers (because their contributions to celestial navigation were vital), shipbuilders, and instrument makers who were interested in discovery. They were mainly Italians, and they were united in their hope of finding a way around Africa in order to reach India. The early adventurers did not succeed, but during their gradual advance down the West African coast, they opened a rich new trade in ivory, gold, and slaves.

Then, in 1487, one Portuguese captain, Bartholomeu Dias, returned to Lisbon after an incredible voyage. He had been blown out to sea by a northerly gale and spent 13 days without sight of land. As soon as possible he had headed east, but when he made his landfall it proved to be on the east coast of Africa, beyond the Cape of Good Hope, which thus far no one had been able to pass.

The way to India now seemed open, but before the Portuguese could send out their first expedition the news arrived that a sailor employed by the Spaniards, one Christopher Columbus, had apparently reached India by sailing west. To avoid conflicting claims, Portugal and Spain signed the Treaty of Tordesillas in 1494, which gave Portugal possession of all the lands to the east of an imaginary line about 300 miles west of the Azores, and Spain a monopoly of everything to the west. Portugal thus kept the only practical route to India (as well as the rights to Brazil, which one of her sailors may already have had discovered). Three years later Vasco da Gama took the first Portuguese fleet across the Indian Ocean.

At first, he found it very hard to trade, because the Arabs, who had controlled these waters for centuries, tried to keep out all rivals. Within 14 years, however, the Portuguese merchants had established themselves. The key to their success was naval power, for their ship designers had learned to combine their old square sails, which provided speed, with the

1460–1560/TIMELINE

International and Military History	Political History
1460	1460 Henry the Navigator dies
	1461–1559 New monarchs in France
	1474–1556 New monarchs in Spain
	1485–1547 New monarchs in England
	1492 Fall of Granada, last Muslim stronghold in Spain
1494–1559 Italian wars and Hapsburg-Valois wars	
1494 French invasion of Italy	
Treaty of Tordesillas, dividing the world between Portugal and Spain	
1509–1515 Albuquerque's conquests in Asia	
1519 Cortés expedition to Mexico	1519 Charles V Holy Roman Emperor
	1520 Revolt of comuneros in Spain
	1524–1525 Peasant revolts in Germany
1529 Turks besiege Vienna	1529–1536 Meeting of Reformation Parliament in England
1536 Treaty between French and Turks	
	1547 Henry VIII of England dies
1559 Treaty of Cateau-Cambrésis, ending Italian wars	1559 Henry II of France dies, leaving danger of revolts
1560	

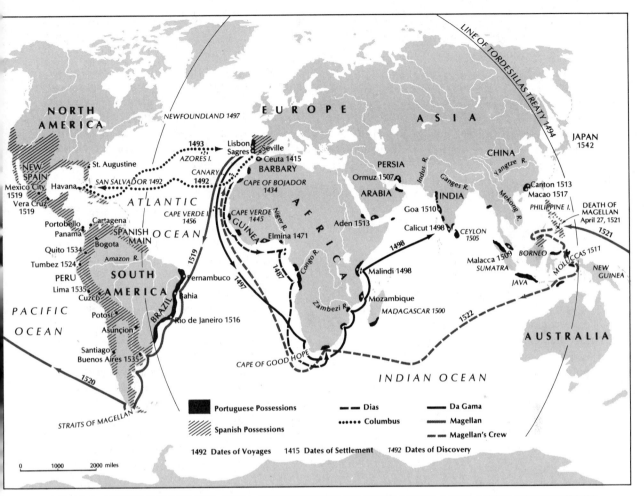

MAP 13.1. EXPLORATION AND CONQUEST IN THE 15TH AND 16TH CENTURIES

Arabs' lateen sails, which increased maneuverability. The Portuguese were also the first to give their fleets effective fire power, realizing that cannon, not soldiers, won battles at sea. In addition, they deployed their ships in squadrons rather than individually, a tactic that further increased their superiority. The result was rapid and overwhelming success. A series of victories at sea reduced Arab naval strength, and bombardments quieted stubborn cities. Guided by the military skill and superb stra-

tegic sense of a brilliant commander, Affonso de Albuquerque, the Portuguese established trading posts in the East that by 1513 extended to the rich Spice Islands, the Moluccas (see Map 13.1).

The empire Portugal created remained entirely dependent on sea power; it rarely tried to colonize overseas areas. Instead the Portuguese set up a chain of trading bases, consisting of warehouses combined with forts that could be supplied and defended by sea, from West Africa to China. Generally the Portuguese restricted contacts with Africans and Asians to maintain friendly relations and missionary and trading rights; they made no attempt to conquer. By the mid-fifteenth century, they were beginning to profit from their explorations—between 1442 and 1446 almost 1000 slaves were brought home from Africa—and in the sixteenth century their wealth multiplied as they became major importers of luxuries from the East such as spices, which were in great demand as medicines, preservatives, and tasty delicacies. By dominating commerce with the rich Oriental civilizations, Portugal's merchants controlled Europe's most valuable trade.

The Portuguese achievement displayed all the ingredients of the West's rise to worldwide power: driving ambition, technical superiority in guns and ships, tactical skills, commercial expertise supported by military force, and careful planning and organization in the home country. Their expansion was sustained by the political and economic revival that was spreading through Western Europe at this time and by the added spur of competition. For Spain soon determined to emulate her neighbor, and when later the Dutch, English, and French took the lead in empire building, they sought to outdo their predecessors and one another. This competition gave the Europeans the crucial stimulus that other peoples had lacked, and it projected them into a dominance over the rest of the globe that would last for more than 450 years.[1]

The Spaniards

Inspired by the same centuries-old crusading ambitions as the Portuguese, the Spaniards rode

the second wave of expansion to wealth and glory overseas. Because Spain was a much larger nation and happened to direct its attention toward a more sparsely populated continent than did Portugal, Spain founded its empire on conquest and colonization, not trade. But it got its start from a stroke of luck.

Christopher Columbus, an experienced Genoese sailor who had some contact with the leading Italian geographers of his day, seems to have believed (it is difficult to know for certain, for he was always a secretive man) that Asia lay only 3500 miles beyond the Canary Islands. He arrived at this figure as the result of two mistakes: he relied on the ancient Ptolemaic estimate that the circumference of the world was 18,000 miles—6000 miles too short—and on Marco Polo's estimate that Asia extended 1500 miles farther east than in fact it does.

Convinced that sailing across the Atlantic to the East was perfectly feasible, Columbus took his proposal in 1484 to the Portuguese government, which refused to underwrite the venture: With a mystic belief in his own destiny, he persisted, gained the financial backing and blessing of Ferdinand V and Isabella I of Spain, and set sail in 1492. He was an excellent navigator (one of his discoveries on the voyage was the difference between true and magnetic north), and he kept his men going despite their horror of being so long at sea without sight of land. After 33 days he reached the Bahamas, and though disappointed that he found no Chinese or Japanese as he investigated Cuba and the west coast of Hispaniola (today's Haiti), he was certain that he had reached Asia, notwithstanding the lack of resemblance between the few natives he encountered and those whom travelers such as Marco Polo had described.

Columbus crossed the Atlantic Ocean three more times, but he made no further discoveries of significance. By the end of his life, in 1506, it was becoming apparent that he had found islands close by a new continent, not Asia. The

---

[1] Current discussions of the differences that led Europe, rather than another civilization, to expand throughout the world are excellently surveyed in Joseph R. Levenson (ed.), *European Expansion and the Counter-Example of Asia, 1300–1600* (1967). See also Robert O. Collins, *Europeans in Africa* (1971), Ch. 1.

This facsimile of a wood engraving depicts the discovery of Santo Domingo by Christopher Columbus. It is based on a sketch attributed to the explorer himself.
(Photo: New York Public Library/Picture Collection)

Asia. But the last remaining hopes were finally dashed in 1522, when the one surviving ship from a fleet of five that had set out under Ferdinand Magellan three years before returned to Spain after the ordeal of having sailed around the world (Map 13.1).

Magellan's 98-day crossing of the Pacific stands as a supreme accomplishment of seamanship in the age of discovery. But the perilous voyage soon persuaded the Spaniards that Portugal had the best route to the East, and in 1529 they finally renounced all claims to trade with the Spice Islands for a payment of 350,000 ducats. The world had been divided, and Spain could concentrate on the Americas, those unexpected continents that were to become possessions of unbelievable richness.

Volunteers were amply available. When the last Muslim kingdom in southern Spain was conquered by the Castilians in 1492, soldiers with long experience of military service found themselves at loose ends. Many were the younger sons of noble families, who were often kept from inheriting land because Spanish law usually allowed only the eldest son to inherit. Naturally the prospect of unlimited land and military adventure across the Atlantic appealed to them, as it did to ambitious youngsters from Castile's lower classes, and thus the conquistador, or conqueror, was born. There were not many of them—less than 1000 at most—but they overran much of America in search of wealth and glory.

The first and most dramatic of these leaders was Hernando Cortés, who in 1519 landed on the Mexican coast and set out to overcome the splendid Aztec civilization in the high plateau of central Mexico. His army consisted of only 600 troops, but in two years, with a few reinforcements, he had won a complete victory. Guns alone made no important difference because Cortés had only 13 muskets and some unwieldy cannon. More effective were his horses, his clever manipulation of Aztec superstitions, and the unshakable determination of

Treaty of Tordesillas reserved the exploration of these lands for the Spaniards, who soon began to perceive them as an asset, not an obstacle.

Other Spanish voyages of discovery followed those of Columbus. In 1513 Vasco de Balboa saw the Pacific Ocean from Central America, and this rekindled the notion that an easy westward passage might be found to East his followers. The conquest of the Mexican Mayas also began under Cortés, while the Incas of Peru fell to Francisco Pizarro. Other conquistadors repeated these successes throughout Central and South America (Map 13.1). By 1550 the conquest was over, and the military leaders, never very good at governing the territories they had won, gave way to administrators who began to pull the huge empire into organized shape.

The Spanish government established in the New World the same pattern of political administration that it was setting up in its European territories (see section II of this chapter). Representatives of the throne, viceroys, were sent to administer the empire and to impose centralized control. Each was advised by a local *audiencia,* a kind of miniature council that also acted as a court of law, but the ultimate authority remained in Spain. And the colonies began to grow only when hardy women pioneers came out to create settlements; families had to be all Spanish, for there was almost no intermarriage. Indeed, the natives were treated with cruelty and disdain. Not only were they to be exploited, but their own traditions were to be ignored. A few humane voices were raised, but in general Europe's empires were characterized, from the start, by almost total indifference to the well-being of the populations they subdued.

To the rest of the world, the overwhelming attraction of Spanish America was its mineral wealth, especially its silver. In 1545 a major vein of silver was discovered at Potosí, in Bolivia, and from those mines—worked by Indian forced labor—came the treasure that made fortunes for the colonists, sustained wars that Spain was fighting against her neighbors, and ultimately enriched all of Western Europe (see accompanying table). For the balance of the sixteenth century, however, despite the efforts of other countries, Portugal and Spain remained the only conspicuous promoters and the major beneficiaries of Europe's expansion.

IMPORTS OF TREASURE TO SPAIN FROM THE NEW WORLD, 1511–1600

Decade	Total Value★
1511–1520	2,626,000
1521–1530	1,407,000
1531–1540	6,706,000
1541–1550	12,555,000
1551–1560	21,437,000
1561–1570	30,418,000
1571–1580	34,990,000
1581–1590	63,849,000
1591–1600	83,536,000
★ In ducats	

Adapted from J. H. Elliott, *Imperial Spain, 1469–1716* (New York, 1964), p. 175.

Economic Growth

Most of the silver from the New World went beyond Spain to Italian and German merchants who financed the wars of the Spanish kings and also controlled the American trade. Although other sources of supply, mainly silver mines in Austria, were appearing at this time, the New World was primarily responsible for the end of the crippling shortage of precious metals, and hence of coins, that had plagued Europe for centuries. By the middle of the seventeenth century, the Continent's holdings in gold were to increase by one-fifth, and, more important, its stock of silver was to triple.

In 1556 a Spanish professor named Azpilcueta suggested that this flow explained a phenomenon that was beginning to cause wide concern—a tremendous rise in prices. The inflation was sharpest in Spain, where money lost three-quarters of its 1500 value by 1600; the depreciation elsewhere was serious but less marked—in England for example it was about two-thirds. Recent historians, however, have shown that the upward movement of prices began before substantial amounts of silver were shipped and that the rate slowed at the very time that imports from South America rose sharply. Although it is still acknowledged that the supply of precious metals directly influenced price levels and contributed to Europe's economic revival, an exclusive correlation can no longer be accepted.[2] Other factors must be taken into consideration to explain the startling changes of the late fifteenth century.

At the simplest level what happened was a gradual revival of confidence. After a century and a half of hard times, economic conditions were improving. Much of the credit for this must be given to the restoration of political stability (see section II of this chapter). Merchants were more inclined to risk long-distance trading under strong governments. Rulers could make treaties with foreign powers for commercial advantage and guarantee that such agreements would be upheld. The growth of population in the sixteenth century was the most dramatic result of the new sense of confidence, and the surge in the number of people was a prime contributor to the inflation because it increased the demand for goods. In general the business community, encouraged by the discovery of new sources of silver, enlarged markets, and the improved profits generated by rising prices, was now able to widen the scope of investments.

Records are far too poor to permit a measurement of the increase in population, but it is likely that by the early seventeenth century, Europe had perhaps 50 percent more people than in the late fifteenth. And cities grew much faster than the population as a whole: London for example had approximately 50,000 inhabitants in the early sixteenth century but over 200,000 a hundred years later (see Map 13.2). Significantly, wide areas of marginal farmland were reoccupied, having been abandoned in the fourteenth and fifteenth centuries because a shrinking population had provided no market for their produce. Now there were more mouths to feed, and the extra acres again became profitable.

The population rise was followed by a staggering jump in food prices. By the early 1600s wheat cost approximately five times more than in the late 1400s, an increase that far outpaced the movement of prices in general. It is not surprising, therefore, that this period witnessed the first wave of enclosures in England: major landowners put up fences around common tilling or grazing ground, traditionally open to all the animals of the locality, in order to reserve it for their own crops or their sheep, whose wool was also in increasing demand. By 1600 about an eighth of England's arable land had been enclosed.

As markets began to grow in response to population pressures, the volume of trade also shot upward; commercial profits thus kept pace with those of agriculture. Customs receipts rose steadily, as did the yield of tolls from ships entering the Baltic Sea, one of Europe's leading trade centers. In many areas, too, shipbuilding boomed. This was the heyday of the English cloth trade and the great Spanish sheep farms, of the central German linen industry and the northern Italian silk industry. Printing became a widespread occupation, and gunmaking and glassmaking also expanded rapidly. The latter had a major effect on European society, because the increasing use of windows allowed builders to divide houses into small rooms, thus giving many people a little privacy for the first time.

Leading financiers who invested in the growing volume of trade of course accumulated large fortunes. For centuries the Italians had been in the vanguard of economic advance but in the sixteenth century firms of other nations were achieving international prominence. The most successful of the new enterprises was run by a family descended from a fourteenth-century weaver, Johannes Fugger of Augsburg. The sixteenth-century Fuggers financed the Spanish King Charles I's campaign for the

---

[2] There is a good introduction to the problem of explaining the rise in prices in J. H. Elliott, *Imperial Spain, 1469–1716* (1964), pp. 172–191.

MAP 13.2. THE GROWTH OF CITIES IN THE 16TH CENTURY

throne of the Holy Roman Empire and his later wars when he became the Emperor Charles V. Great bankers were thus often closely allied with monarchs, and like all merchants, they gained from the mounting power of central governments. Rulers encouraged commerce in the hope of larger revenues from customs duties and taxes, and they gave leading entrepre-

neurs valuable privileges. Such alliances were eventually the undoing of some houses, which were ruined by royal bankruptcies, but until the late sixteenth century, Italian and German bankers controlled Europe's finances (see Map A-19 in the Cartographic Essay).

The continued importance of Italy, and of the Mediterranean in general, indicates that the overseas expansion did not change Europe overnight. In fact, Italy's overland spice trade across Asia continued as it had for centuries, even though the Portuguese found it much cheaper to bring the goods west by sea. But rather than try to squeeze Italy out of the trade, Portugal simply charged the same prices and thus made a larger profit. Not until Dutch and English fleets began to enter the Mediterranean around 1600, and at the same time gained control of Eastern spice shipments, did the balance shift away from the Italians. In the meantime, the boom benefited all areas of Europe.

Indeed, every level of trading activity offered opportunities for advancement. The guild system expanded in the sixteenth century to incorporate many new trades, while the whole structure of mercantile enterprise developed in new ways. The idea took hold that a business firm was an impersonal entity, larger than the person who owned it and vested with an identity, legal status, permanence, and even profits that were not the same as those of its members. Here was yet another indication of the creativity and energy at work in economic affairs.

Social Change

Not everyone shared in the new prosperity. Naturally landowners and food producers benefited most from the inflation and could amass considerable wealth. The tenant could also do well, because rents did not keep pace with food prices. But wages lagged miserably. By the early seventeenth century, a laborer's annual income had about half the purchasing power it had had at the end of the fifteenth, a decline that had its most drastic impact in Eastern Europe, where serfdom reappeared. In the West, large numbers of peasants had to leave the land, which could no longer support all of them; others were forced off by enclosures and similar "improvements." These displaced people turned to begging and wandering across coun-

try, often ending up in towns, where crime became a serious problem. Peasant uprisings directed at tax collectors, nobles, or food suppliers were almost annual affairs in one region of France or another after the mid-sixteenth century, and in England the unending stream of vagrants gave rise to a belief that the country was overpopulated. The extreme poverty was universally deplored, particularly as it promoted disorders; local nobles, not as strong as they had once been, could no longer restrain potential troublemakers, and the two centuries from the mid-sixteenth to the mid-eighteenth were the great days of the highwayman. Nobody could understand, much less control, the forces that were transforming society.

The newly strong governments of the period tried to relieve the distress, but their efforts were not always consistent. They regarded the beggars sometimes as shirkers who should be punished and at other times as unfortunates who needed to be helped. Not until the end of the sixteenth century did the more compassionate view begin to prevail.

Vagrancy was only one of the signs that Europeans were witnessing the beginnings of modern urbanization, with all of its dislocations. Major differences also developed between life in the country and life in the town. Rural workers may have led a strenuous existence, but they escaped the worst hazards of the urban dweller. Whole sections of most large cities were controlled by the sixteenth-century equivalent of the underworld, which offered sanctuary to criminals and danger to most citizens. Plagues were much more serious in towns—the upper classes soon learned to flee to the country at the first sign of disease—and famines more devastating because of the far poorer sanitation in urban areas and their remoteness from food supplies.

On the other hand, the opening of economic opportunities offered many people a chance to improve their status dramatically. At courts, in royal administrations, in law, in the burgeoning cities, and overseas in growing empires, the ambitious won fortunes and titles and founded new aristocratic dynasties. The means of advancement varied: the English monarchy sold to the newly rich the lands it confiscated from monasteries after the religious struggle that split the kingdom from the Church of Rome (see section II of this chapter); France put government offices on the market to raise revenue and build the bureaucracy; the New World gave minor Spanish nobles the chance to acquire vast estates; and everywhere the long boom in commerce encouraged social mobility. By the 1620s, when the upward movement began to subside, a new aristocracy had been born that was destined to dominate Europe for centuries.

It seems a paradox that the disruptive economic and social changes of the sixteenth century should have happened at a time when the "new monarchs" of England, France, and Spain were asserting their control and imposing order in their realms. The two processes were not unrelated—strong central governments gave vital support to economic growth, overseas expansion, and attempts to relieve social distress, while prosperity provided rulers with the tax revenues that were essential to their power—but they clearly had somewhat contrary effects. In the long run, however, it was the restoration of strong political authority that permitted the solution of the problems that arose during the sixteenth century. The creation of well-organized states, structured around powerful central governments, was even more decisive than the economic boom in shaping the future of Western Europe.

II. THE "NEW MONARCHIES"

During the last quarter of the fifteenth century, England, France, and Spain were governed by remarkable rulers, whose accomplishments have led historians to call them "new mon-

archs": Henry VII, Louis XI, and Ferdinand and Isabella.[3] Their reigns are generally regarded as marking the end of more than a century of fragmentation and the beginning of a revival of royal power that would ultimately weaken all the rivals to the crown and create the bureaucracies characteristic of the modern state.

Tudor England

The English monarchs had relied for centuries on local cooperation to run their kingdom. Unlike other European countries, England contained only 50 or 60 families who were legally nobles out of a population of perhaps 2.5 million. But many other families, though not technically members of the nobility, had large estates and were dominant figures at the parish, county, and even national level. They were known as gentry, and it was from their ranks that the crown appointed the local officers who administered the realm—notably the justices of the peace (usually referred to as J.P.s). These voluntary, unpaid officials served as the principal public servants in the more than 40 counties of the land.

For reasons of status as well as out of a feeling of responsibility, the gentry had always sought such appointments. From the crown's point of view, the great advantage of the system was its efficiency: enforcement was in the hands of those who could enforce. As a "great man" in his neighborhood, the justice of the peace rarely had trouble exerting his authority. Thus, the king had had at his disposal an administrative structure without rival in Europe. This

---

[3] An excellent introduction to the scholarship on the "new monarchs" is Arthur J. Slavin (ed.), *The "New Monarchies" and Representative Assemblies: Medieval Constitutionalism or Modern Absolutism?* (1964), which also covers some subjects not treated in this chapter—for example the rise of representative assemblies in the Low Countries and the establishment of a strong central government in Sweden during the sixteenth century.

cooperative approach to the task of governing had created a strong sense of duty among the members of the ruling class, and the king had come to consult them more frequently over the years.

In the sixteenth century an institution that had developed from this relationship, Parliament, began to take on a general importance as the chief representative of the country's wishes; it was increasingly considered to be the only body that could give a ruler's actions a wider sanction than he could draw from his prerogatives alone. Although for a long time to come Parliament would remain firmly subordinated to the crown, England's kings already realized that they could not take such measures as raising extraordinary taxes without its consent.

Another of the monarch's assets was England's common law, the uniform country-wide system of justice based on precedent and tradition. Like Parliament, the common law would eventually be regarded by opponents of royal power as an independent source of authority with which the crown could not interfere. But under the conditions facing the "new monarch" in the 1480s, it proved an effective tool in his work of restoring the authority of the throne after two centuries of weakness.

Henry VII

Henry VII (1485–1509), who founded the Tudor dynasty, came to the throne as a usurper in the aftermath of more than 30 years of civil conflict, the Wars of the Roses. England's nobles had been fighting one another for decades, and the situation hardly looked promising for a reassertion of royal power. Yet Henry both extended the authority of the crown and restored order with extraordinary speed.

His first concern as he set about establishing a stable rule was finance. The crown's income was about £52,000 a year, but Henry's imme-diate expenses were considerably higher.[4] He knew that unless he could balance his budget, his position would remain insecure. Yet extra taxes were the surest way to alienate subjects who expected a king to "live of his own," that is, from the income his lands provided, customs payments, and the traditional contributions made to him at special times such as the marriage of his daughter. It is a testimony to the care with which he nurtured his revenues that by the end of his reign he had paid off all his debts and accumulated between 1 and 2 million pounds as a reserve.

Part of his success was due to his beginning his reign with more property than any of his predecessors, a consequence of forfeitures and inheritances during the civil wars. But Henry also sharply increased the profits of justice—fees and fines—which had the added advantage of cowing unruly subjects. Moreover he radically improved his financial administration by taking the tasks of collection and supervision out of the cumbersome office of the Exchequer and placing them in his own more efficient household. By careful management of this kind, he was able to "live of his own."

Where domestic order was concerned, the revival of royal authority was largely due to the energy of the king and his chief servants. Henry increased the powers of the justices of the peace, thus striking severely at the independence attained by leading nobles during the previous two centuries. Under his leadership, too, his council became a far more active and influential body. The ministers not only exercised executive powers but also resumed hearing legal appeals, because the government was determined to exert all its force to quell disorder. Plaintiffs could be sure that at such a hearing, where there was no jury and where deliberations would not be influenced by the power of a local lord, decisions would be quick and fair,

---

[4] To give a sense of scale, a man who made £100 a year was considered very rich.

and the popularity and business of the councillors' court grew rapidly.[5]

The dual objective of government stability and fiscal responsibility guided Henry's foreign policy. He never became involved in costly adventures, and he allowed no challenge to the Tudor dynasty's claim to the crown. In 1492, for example, after Henry half-heartedly invaded France as a protest against the French annexation of Brittany, Charles VIII signed a treaty promising to pay him £160,000 and guaranteeing not to support any claimants to the English throne. A succession of agreements with other rulers from Denmark to Florence bolstered the position of England's merchants, whose international trade was essential to the crown's customs revenues. Henry encouraged the manufacture and export of the country's great staple product, cloth, and protected English shipping. Turning to more distant possibilities, he granted an Italian sailor, John Cabot, a patent to search for a westward route to China. The result of this undertaking was the discovery of enormous fishing banks off Newfoundland, whose exploitation was to be the basis of the growing prosperity of many English ports in the sixteenth century.

Henry VIII and His Successors

The first Tudor was a conservative, building up his authority and finances through traditional methods and institutions that had long been at the disposal of England's kings but that the founder of the new dynasty applied with exceptional determination and vigor. The young man who followed him on the throne, Henry VIII (1509–1547), was an arrogant, dazzling figure, a strong contrast to his careful father (see Plate 30). Early in his reign he removed a longstanding threat from England's north by inflicting a shattering defeat on an

invading Scots army at Flodden in 1513, and the following year he brought a sporadic war with France to a favorable conclusion. With his prestige thus enhanced, he spent the next 15 years taking only a minor part in European affairs while he consolidated royal power at home with the capable assistance of his chief minister, Cardinal Thomas Wolsey.

Wolsey was not an innovator but a tireless and effective administrator who continued the consolidation of royal power begun under Henry VII. To meet the rising demand for royal justice, he expanded the jurisdiction and activities of royal courts such as the Star Chamber.

Wolsey fell from power in 1529, ruined by the king's wish to obtain a divorce from his wife, who had failed to produce a surviving male heir. Henry had married his brother's widow, Catherine of Aragon, under a special papal dispensation from the biblical law that normally prohibited a union between such close relatives. Obsessed with continuing his dynasty, for which a male heir seemed essential—and infatuated with a young lady at court, Anne Boleyn—Henry had urged Wolsey to ask the pope to declare the previous dispensation invalid. Under ordinary circumstances there would have been no trouble, but at this moment the pope was in the power of Charles V, king of Spain and emperor of the Holy Roman Empire, who not only had a high sense of rectitude but also was Catherine's nephew. When all Wolsey's efforts ended in failure, Henry dismissed him.

For three years thereafter the king tried in vain to get his divorce. He called Parliament and gave it free rein to express bitter anticlerical sentiments; he sought opinions in European universities in favor of the divorce; he attacked his own clergy for having bowed to Wolsey's authority; he even extracted a vague recognition from the clergy of his position as "supreme lord" of the Church. Finally he placed his confidence in Thomas Cromwell, a former servant

---

[5] The room where the royal council met had stars painted on its ceiling; the council sitting as a court eventually came to be known by the name of the room, the Star Chamber.

of Wolsey's, who suggested a radical but simple solution: that Henry break with the pope, declare himself supreme head of the Church, and divorce Catherine on his own authority. The king agreed, thus unleashing a revolution that dramatically increased the powers of the royal government. At the same time, he drew England into the Reformation, a movement that, as we will see in Chapter 14, was sweeping Continental Europe. By identifying his kingdom with the Protestants, in opposition to the Catholics, Henry gave his subjects an emotional cause to support that eventually stimulated a sense of national pride.

The instrument chosen to accomplish the break with Rome was Parliament, the only body capable of giving the move legal sanction and an aura of national approval. Henry called the assembly in 1529 and did not dissolve it until 1536. During its sessions it acted on more matters of greater importance than a Parliament had ever considered before. It forbade litigants from making ecclesiastical appeals to Rome, thus allowing Henry to obtain his divorce and remarry, and finally declared him supreme head of the Church in England in 1534. Royal power gained enormously from these acts, but so too did the stature of Parliament, thanks to its unprecedented responsibilities and the length of its sessions.

Previously, election to Parliament had been considered a chore by the townsmen and landed gentry in the House of Commons, who found the expense of unpaid attendance and the time it took more irksome than did the nobles in the House of Lords (so named during Henry VIII's reign). But this attitude began to change in the 1530s as members of the Commons, returning to successive sessions, came to know one another and to develop a remarkable esprit de corps as guardians of Parliament's traditions and privileges.

Following his successful suggestion for solving Henry's conflict with Rome, Thomas Cromwell rose rapidly in his monarch's service. He was a tireless bureaucrat; he reorganized the administration of the country into six carefully distinguished departments with specific functions and gave himself the chief executive position, the secretaryship. A Privy Council, consisting of the king's principal advisers, was also established to coordinate and direct the administration.

Unquestionably the principal beneficiary of the events of the 1530s was the crown. Royal income rose markedly when Henry became head of the English Church and took over the ecclesiastical fees that previously had gone to the pope. He gained an even larger windfall when he dissolved all English monasteries and confiscated their immensely valuable lands, which were sold over the next few decades. Fortunes were made by speculators, and new families rose to prominence as major landowners.

For all the stimulus he gave to parliamentary power, Henry now had a much larger, wealthier, and more sophisticated administration at his disposal, and he left no doubt where ultimate authority lay. He did not establish a standing army, as some of the Continental kings did, but he had no need for one. He was fully capable of intimidating ambitious nobles or crushing such uprisings as a 1536 revolt against the Reformation.

Where doctrine and the structure of the Church were concerned, Henry was a conservative; he allowed few changes in dogma or liturgy. He even tried to restrain the spread of Reformation ideas and persecuted heresy, but he could not avoid compromises. Perhaps realizing the shape of things to come, he had his son, Edward, tutored by a committed reformer. Moreover in the 1540s a leading Continental reformer, Martin Bucer, spent a few years in Cambridge, deeply influencing a number of future leaders of the English Church.

During the reign of Edward VI (1547–1553), who died while still a minor, the nobility attempted to resume some of their old powers

The anti-Catholic feelings that began to grow in England during the reign of Edward VI are expressed in this painting. The young king sits on his throne. His father, Henry VIII, who started the Reformation in England, points to him as the victor over Catholicism. The crushing of the old faith is symbolized by Christ's conquering of the pope and monks (below) and the destruction of Roman churches and images (through the window). (Photo: National Portrait Gallery, London)

in government, and the Reformation advanced rapidly in England. But Edward's half-sister, Mary I, tried to reestablish Roman Catholicism when she became queen in 1553, forcing many Englishmen into exile and others into two major revolts during her five-year reign. Royal power, however, was strong enough to survive these strains. The revival of the nobles was short-lived, and Mary's death, in 1558, brought an end to the reversal of religions. She was succeeded by Henry VIII's last surviving child, Elizabeth, a woman of determination who demonstrated that the growth of the monarchy's authority had been but briefly interrupted under Edward and Mary.

Valois France

The rulers of France in the fifteenth century, unlike their English counterparts, lacked a well-formed organization for local government. Aristocrats dominated many sections, particularly those farthest from Paris, and great nobles had become virtually independent rulers. They had their own administrations and often their own courts and taxation, leaving the crown little say in their affairs. The size of the kingdom also placed restraints on royal power; it took more than a week to travel from Paris to the remoter parts of the realm—almost double the time for the equivalent English journey. Delays of this nature inevitably hampered central authority.

The monarchy had tried to resolve the problem of ruling distant provinces by granting to close relatives large blocs of territory that came into royal hands. Theoretically the kinsman would devote full attention to these lands and execute the monarch's wishes more effectively than he himself could from Paris. In practice, however, an ambitious family member often became just as difficult to handle as any powerful noble. After 1469 the crown kept control over such acquisitions—an indication that it was becoming capable of exercising authority even in areas far from the capital.

The administrative center of the government in Paris was the royal council and its chief departments: the Chancery, which had charge of all formal documents, and the Treasury. The greatest court of law in the land was the Parlement of Paris, whose members were appointed by the crown and which had remained a judicial body, unlike the English Parliament. As the central administration grew in the fifteenth and early sixteenth centuries, various provinces received their own parlements from the crown, a recognition of the continuing strength of local autonomies. The countervailing force was the dominant system of Roman law, which enabled the monarch to govern by issuing ordinances and edicts. They had to be registered by the parlements in order to take effect, but usually this was a formality.

Representative assemblies, the estates, also reduced the power of the throne. A number of provinces had local estates, and matters such as the raising of taxes had to be arranged through them. But the national representative body, the Estates General, to which clergy, nobles, and townsmen sent delegates, never attained the prestige of the English Parliament and was never able to bind the country together or function as an essential organ of government.

Moreover French kings had a degree of independence that English monarchs never achieved in a critically important area: finances. For centuries they had supplemented their ordinary sources of income, from lands and customs duties, with extraordinary levies in the form of a sales tax (*aide*), a hearth tax (*taille*), and a salt tax (*gabelle*). Consequently the average Frenchman who was subject to taxation (all nobles and many towns were exempt) usually bore a heavier burden than his English counterpart. In earlier days the consent of the localities had been required before such demands could be made, but after 1451 the taxes could be raised on the king's authority alone, although he still had to negotiate the exact rate with provincial estates and be careful not to go beyond what would seem reasonable to his subjects.

But the most decisive contrast with England lay in France's standing army. The upkeep of the troops accounted for more than half the royal expenditures in Louis XI's reign, mainly because their numbers grew with increases in revenues. In the 1480s a force probably larger than 15,000 men, chiefly professional mercenaries and military-minded nobles, was held in permanent readiness every campaigning season from spring to fall. With the invention of the arquebus, a primitive handgun, and the need for large concentrations of pikemen to protect the gunners, the size of armies had to be increased; moreover, the development of cannon demanded the expensive skills and logistics of heavy artillery. These innovations added to the advantages of the central government because it alone could afford the cost of the new technology. At the same time, much larger resources were needed to support the army in the field. Troops were billeted in various provinces, and often the local estates had to contribute to their maintenance. As a result the entire French population eventually had the indirect burden of heavier taxation, and many regions of France had direct contact with royal soldiers. Although frequently short of pay, the troops were firmly under royal control and hence a vital device—rarely used but always a threat—in the strengthening of royal authority.

Louis XI and Charles VIII

When Louis XI (1461–1483) began his reign, he faced a situation as unpromising as that of Henry VII at his succession, for the country had just emerged from the Hundred Years' War, and royal powers were much reduced. English troops, present in France for most of the war years, had finally departed in the 1450s; but a new and equally dangerous menace had arisen in the east: the conglomeration of territories assembled by the dukes of Burgundy.

By the 1460s the dukes, though vassals of the French crown in their southern holdings, were among the most powerful lords in Western Europe. They ruled a loosely organized dominion that stretched from the 17 separate provinces of the Low Countries to the Swiss Confederation, and their Burgundian capital, Dijon, had become a major cultural and political center. In 1474 Louis XI put together a coalition against Duke Charles the Bold, who had been at war with him for some seven years, and in 1477 Charles was killed in battle with the French king's Swiss allies. Louis then reannexed the duchy of Burgundy itself; but Mary, the duke's daughter, retained the Low Countries, which would later form part of the imperial inheritance of her grandson, the Holy Roman Emperor Charles V.

The Burgundian lands added considerably to Louis's sphere of authority. His masterful maneuvering in the tortuous diplomacy of his day soon won him other territories; he was appropriately nicknamed "the Spider," because the prizes he caught in his web were more often the result of waiting or shrewd negotiation than of victories on the battlefield. Such was the case at the beginning of his reign when, by a typical combination of force and fraud, he pried two provinces on his southern border away from Spain. Simple luck enlarged his realm as well: in 1481 he inherited the enormous Angevin lands—the provinces of Anjou, Maine, and Provence. The result was that by the end of his reign, though government procedures had not noticeably changed, royal power had penetrated into massive areas where previously it had been unknown; only one major region, Brittany, remained completely beyond the crown's influence (see Map 13.3).

Louis XI's son and successor, Charles VIII (1483–1498), was equally dedicated to increasing the territories under the Valois dynasty's command. For a start he married the heiress of the duke of Brittany, thereby securing the last independent region of France, though it was not officially incorporated into the royal domain for another half-century.

In 1494, seeking further gains, Charles invaded Italy at the request of the duke of Milan, who was afraid of being attacked by Florence and Naples. After some initial successes the French settled into a prolonged struggle with the Hapsburgs for control of the rich Italian peninsula. The conflicts lasted for 65 years, ending in defeat for the French. Although the Italian wars failed to satisfy the territorial ambitions of Charles and his successors, they provided an outlet for the restless French nobility and gave the monarchy an opportunity to consolidate royal power at home.

The Growth of Government Power

After Charles VIII's reign France's financial and administrative machinery grew in both size and effectiveness, largely because of the demands of the Italian wars. There was rarely enough money to support the adventure; the kings therefore relied heavily on loans from Italian

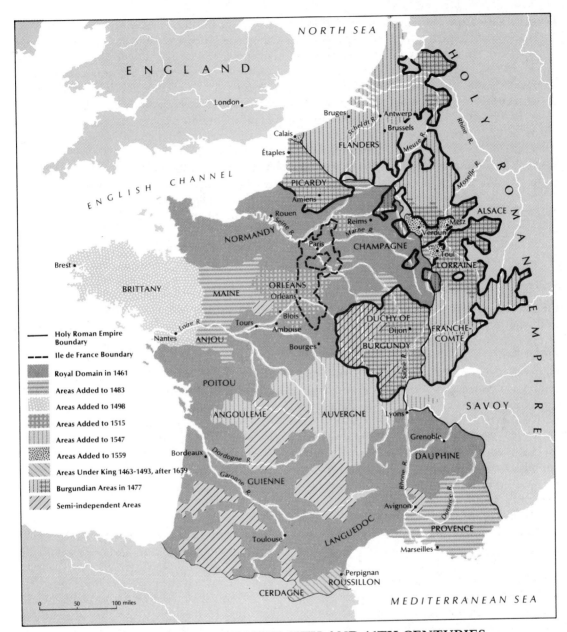

MAP 13.3. FRANCE IN THE 15TH AND 16TH CENTURIES

This map shows in detail the successive stages whereby the monarchy extended its control throughout France.

bankers, who sometimes helped shape France's financial policies. At the same time the crown made a determined and notably successful effort to increase traditional royal revenues.

But expenses were also rising. France was a rich country of 15 million people with the most fertile land in Europe; yet the financial needs of the monarch always outstripped his subjects' ability to pay. Nobles, many towns, royal officeholders, and the clergy were exempt from the *taille* and the *gabelle*. Thus the bulk of the taxes had to be raised from the very classes that had the least to give. Other means of raising revenue were therefore needed to supplement the royal income.

One solution was found in the sale of offices. The kings sold positions in the administration, the parlements, and every branch of the bureaucracy to purchasers eager to obtain both the tax exemption and the considerable status (sometimes a title of nobility) that the offices brought them. From modest and uncertain beginnings under Louis XII (1498–1515), the system widened steadily; by the end of the sixteenth century, it would provide the crown with one-twelfth of its revenues.

Many other rulers were adopting this device, and everywhere it had similar effects: it stimulated social mobility, creating dynasties of noble officeholders and a new administrative class; it caused a dramatic expansion of bureaucracies; and it encouraged corruption. The system spread most rapidly and the effects were most noticeable in France, where the reign of Francis I (1515–1547) witnessed a major increase in the government's power as its servants multiplied. Francis tried hard to continue the widening of royal control by expeditions into Italy, but in fact he contributed more to the development of the crown's authority by his actions at home.

One of the most remarkable of Francis's accomplishments was the power he gained over his formidable rival, the Church. Early in his reign he was highly successful in his Italian campaigns, and he used his position to persuade the pope in 1516 to give France's king the right to appoint all its bishops and abbots. According to this agreement, the first year's income after a new bishop took office still went to the Vatican, but in effect Francis now controlled the French Church. Its enormous patronage was at his disposal, and he could use it at will to reward servants or raise money. Since his wishes had not been blocked by the pope, he did not need to break with Rome in order to obtain the authority over the clergy that Henry VIII was soon to achieve in England.

In the 1520s he also began a major reorganization of the government. Francis formally legalized the sale of offices, and gradually the purchasers replaced local nobles as the administrators of the various sections of France. He also formed an inner council, more manageable than the unwieldy royal council, to act as the chief executive body of the realm. As part of this streamlining, in 1523 all tax-gathering and accounting responsibilities were centralized in one agency. Against the parlements, meanwhile, the king invoked the *lit de justice,* a prerogative that allowed him to appear before an assembly that was delaying the registration of any of his edicts or ordinances and declare them registered and therefore law. The Estates General was no problem because none met between 1484 and 1560.

With the monarchy's authority extended throughout his country, Francis's interests began to move outside of Europe. Jacques Cartier's voyages to North America in the 1530s and a French challenge to the Portuguese monopoly of West African trade were the first stirrings of a maritime effort that was cut short only by civil wars in the late sixteenth century.

By the end of Francis's reign, royal power was thus stronger than ever before; but signs of disunity had begun to appear that would intensify in the years to come. The Reformation was under way in the Holy Roman Empire, and it soon produced religious divisions and social unrest in France (see Chapter 14). As the reign of Francis's son Henry II (1547–1559) came to a close, the Italian wars ended in a French defeat, badly damaging the prestige of the monarchy. The civil wars that followed came perilously close to destroying all that the monarchy had accomplished during the previous 100 years.

United Spain

The Iberian peninsula in the mid-fifteenth century was divided into three very different kingdoms. Portugal, with some 1.5 million inhabitants, was in the midst of an expansion around the coast of Africa that was soon to bring her great wealth from the East. Castile, in the center, with a population of more than 8 million, was the largest and richest of the kingdoms. Sheep farming was the basis of its prosperity, and its countryside was dominated by powerful nobles. Castile was the last kingdom still fighting the Moors, and in the ceaseless crusade against the infidels the nobles played a leading part. They had built up both a great chivalric tradition and considerable political strength as a result of their exploits, and their status was enhanced by the religious fervor that the long struggle had inspired. The third kingdom, Aragon, approximately the same size as Portugal, consisted of three areas: Catalonia, the heart of the kingdom and a great commercial region centered on the city of Barcelona; Aragon itself, which was little more than a barren hinterland to Catalonia; and Valencia, a farming and fishing region south of Catalonia along the Mediterranean coast.

In October 1469, Isabella, future queen of Castile, married Ferdinand, future king of Sicily and heir to the throne of Aragon. Realizing that the marriage would strengthen the crown, the Castilian nobles opposed the union, precipitating a 10-year civil war. But the united monarchy emerged victorious, more powerful, and in control of a new political entity: the Kingdom of Spain.

Ferdinand and Isabella

When Ferdinand and Isabella jointly assumed the thrones of Castile in 1474 and Aragon five years later, they made no attempt to create a monolithic state. Aragon remained a federation of territories, administered by viceroys, who were appointed by the king but who allowed local customs to remain virtually intact. The traditions of governing by consent and preserving the subjects' rights were particularly strong in this kingdom, where each province had its own representative assembly, known as the Cortes. Ferdinand left the system untouched, but he did make the viceroys a permanent feature of the government and created a special council for Aragonese affairs, through which he controlled the kingdom. In Castile, however, the two monarchs were determined to assert their superiority over all possible rivals to their authority. Their immediate aims were to restore the order in the countryside that had been destroyed by civil war, much as it had been in England and France, and to reduce the power of the nobility.

The first objective was accomplished with the help of the Cortes of Castile, an assembly dominated by urban representatives who shared the wish for order because peace benefited trade. The Cortes established special tribunals to pursue and try criminals, and by the 1490s it had succeeded in ending the widespread lawlessness in the kingdom.

To reinforce their authority, Ferdinand and Isabella sharply reduced the number of great nobles in the royal council and overhauled the entire administration, particularly the financial agencies, applying the principle that ability rather than social status should determine appointments. As the bureaucracy spread, the hidalgo, a lesser aristocrat, who was heavily dependent on royal favor, became increasingly important in government. Unlike the great nobles, whose enormous wealth was little affected by the reforms that reduced their role, the hidalgos were hurt because they lost their tax exemptions. The new livelihood they found was in the service of the crown, and they became essential figures in the centralization of power in Castile as well as the overseas territories.

The monarchs achieved even greater control over the nobles in the 1480s and 1490s, when they took over the rich and powerful military orders into which the aristocracy was organized. This required assertiveness and determination, especially by Isabella, Castile's inherited ruler. At one point she rode on horseback for three straight days in order to get to one of the order's elections and control the outcome. The great nobles could not be subdued completely; nor did the king and queen wish to destroy their power, because they were essential servants of the crown, especially in the army and in the higher levels of government. But like the kings of England and France, Ferdinand and Isabella wanted to reduce their autonomy to a level that did not seem to threaten central authority—a process that was accomplished by 1500.

The rulers also succeeded in weakening the Spanish bishops and abbots, who were as strong and wealthy as leading nobles. After Ferdinand and Isabella destroyed the power of the Moors in Castile, the pope granted the monarchy the right to make all major ecclesiastical appointments in the newly won territory, and this right was extended to the New World shortly thereafter. In the following reign the monarchy would gain complete control over Church appointments, making Spain more independent of Rome than any other Catholic state.

Mastery over the towns and the Cortes of Castile did not pose much of a problem. Where local rule was concerned, an old official, the *corregidor,* was given new powers and a position of responsibility within the administrative hierarchy. Usually a hidalgo, he became the chief executive and judicial officer in his region, rather like the justice of the peace in England, and he also supervised town affairs. The Cortes did not seriously restrict the crown because Spanish taxes, like French, could be raised without consent. The Castilian assembly met frequently and even provided additional funds for foreign wars, but it never challenged royal supremacy during this reign.

The king and queen supervised the system of justice directly, hearing cases personally once a week. All law was considered to come from the throne, and they had full power to overrule the decisions of local courts, often run by nobles. Centralized judicial machinery began to appear, and in a few decades Castilian law was organized into a uniform code—always a landmark in the stabilization of a state.

Considering the anarchy at the start of their reign and the absence of central institutions, Ferdinand and Isabella performed greater wonders in establishing royal power than did any of the other new monarchs. A good index of the effectiveness of their growing bureaucracy is the increase in their revenues. As soon as the main administrative reforms were completed, in the 1490s, the yield of the sales tax (the *alcabala*), which was the mainstay of royal income, began to rise dramatically. Total annual revenue is estimated to have soared from 80,000 ducats in 1474 to 2.3 million by 1504, the year Isabella died.[6] Religious affairs, too, helped in the consolidation of the crown's authority. After the civil wars in Castile had come to an end, Ferdinand used his military command to drive the Moors from the peninsula. The reasons for his aggressive policy were clear: first, it complemented the crown's drive for power at home; second, war was a traditional interest for an ambitious ruler, and it helped keep restless

---

[6] There were approximately four Spanish ducats to the English pound, which means that Ferdinand and Isabella had an income nearly five times that of Henry VII or half that of Louis XII.

nobles occupied; and finally, the crusade stimulated the country's religious fervor, which in turn promoted enthusiasm for its rulers.

The tide of religious zeal swept on after the last Arab stronghold, Granada, capitulated in 1492. Less than three months later, all Jews were expelled from Spain. Some 150,000 of the most enterprising people in Aragon and Castile, including many leading doctors, government officials, and others who had made a vital contribution to economic and cultural life, departed overnight. It was only natural that the rulers' determination to remove anything that stood in their way should have focused on a group that did not share the popular religious passion sustaining their authority. The campaign against the Jews thus went hand in hand with growing royal power.

The same drive to consolidate their strength had prompted Ferdinand and Isabella to obtain permission from the pope in 1478 to establish their own Inquisition. Since 1483 this indigenous body had been run by a royal council and given a mandate to root out Marranos and Moriscos—Jews and Moors who, usually under coercion, had pretended to accept Christianity but in fact retained their original beliefs. After the fall of Granada, the Spanish Church attempted to convert the Moors, and in 1502 all Arabs who were not officially Christian were expelled from the country. Nonetheless suspected Moriscos and Marranos kept the Inquisition busy. The persecution welded the country into a religious unity that paralleled and supported the political centralization achieved by the monarchy. Religious policy was thus as much an instrument of political power as it was of ideological conformity.

Foreign Affairs

The fall of Granada extended Spain's dominion southward, but there were also lands to be captured to the north and east. It was in this undertaking that Ferdinand took the lead, because men controlled diplomacy and warfare, and he emphasized these activities during the 12 years he ruled on his own after Isabella's death. His first success had come in 1493, when Charles VIII rewarded Spain's support of the French expedition into Italy by returning to Spain the two provinces on the French border that Louis XI had taken 30 years before. Two years later, however, fearful that France's Italian invasion was threatening his Kingdom of Sicily, Ferdinand decided to enter the war in Italy.

His achievements in the next two decades were due to a combination of military and diplomatic skills unusual even among the highly capable rulers of the age. A reorganization of Spain's standing army made it the most effective force in Europe, and it rapidly achieved a commanding presence in Italy: by 1504 it had conquered Naples, and Spain had become a major power in the peninsula. Ferdinand also built the strongest diplomatic service of his time, setting up five permanent embassies—at Rome, Venice, London, Brussels, and the Hapsburg court. The ambassadors' reports and activities made him the best-informed and most effective maneuverer in the international politics of the day.

Thus by the time of his death, in 1516, the united Spain that he and Isabella created had gained enormously in territory and status both at home and abroad. The successor to the throne inherited a monarchy fully as dynamic and as triumphant over its rivals as those of England and France.

Charles V, Holy Roman Emperor

To bolster their dynasty the joint rulers had married their five children to members of the leading families of Europe. Their daughter Joanna became the wife of the Hapsburg Archduke Philip of Austria, and her son Charles became heir to both the royal throne of Spain and the Hapsburg dukedom.

Early in his reign as king of Spain, however, Charles (1516–1556) had to withstand a major onslaught on the crown's position. Educated in

Flanders, he spoke no Castilian, and when he arrived in Spain late in 1517, he soon aroused the resentment of the local nobility, particularly when members of the large Flemish entourage he brought with him were given positions in the government. The young king stayed for two and a half years, during which time he was elected emperor of the Holy Roman Empire (1519). This enhanced his prestige, but it also intensified his subjects' fears that he would become an absentee ruler with little interest in their affairs. The Cortes, in particular, showed open hostility when Charles requested additional tax funds so that he could leave the country with Spanish troops for imperial purposes. As soon as he left, in 1520, revolts began to break out in Spain's towns, and the risings of these communes racked the country for two years. The troubles Charles now endured were one of the first of many major clashes during the next 150 years between the traditional dynastic aims of the leading European monarchs and the jealous sense of distinctiveness felt by their subjects.[7]

Fortunately for the crown, the communes lacked positive aims; their resentments and hopes were deep but vague. They wanted to reverse the growth of royal power and to restore their traditional autonomy—a grievance that central governments were bound to encounter as they extended their authority. To this end communes asked for the removal of Flemish royal officials and a reduction in taxation, and at first they had the strong sympathy of the Spanish nobles, who particularly disliked the foreign ruler. But the movement soon revealed more complex motives and took on social overtones: the communes launched attacks on the privileged orders of society, especially the nobility, and this lost the revolt its only

chance for success. For now the nobles turned against the communes and defeated them in battle even before Charles returned to Spain.

The king took warning from the uprisings and made sure that his administration was now kept entirely in Spanish hands. Henceforth the energies of his subjects were channeled into imperial missions overseas, where the conquest of Mexico was under way, and against the Ottoman Turks in the Mediterranean. Once again foreign excursions brought a monarch peace at home.

The one notable extension of royal power during Charles's reign was the large empire Spaniards were establishing in Central and South America. Closer to home, however, there was little that gave him or his Spanish subjects cause for pleasure. As Holy Roman Emperor and king of Spain, Charles ruled almost all of Continental Europe west of Poland and the Balkans, with the major exception of France, and he was almost ceaselessly at war defending his territories (see Map 13.4). To the Spaniards most of the wars helped imperial ambitions and were thus irrelevant. As far as they were concerned, aside from the widening acquisitions in the New World, Charles did little to further the expansion started by Ferdinand and Isabella.

The recurrent crises and wars outside of Spain kept Charles away from his kingdom for more than two-thirds of his 40-year reign. But in his absence a highly talented administrator, Francisco de los Cobos, shaped and clarified the government's position. He established the complete supremacy of the crown by greatly enlarging the bureaucracy and elaborating the system of councils that Ferdinand and Isabella had begun. In the 1520s this structure, which was to survive for centuries, received its final form.

There were two types of council. One was responsible for each of the departments of the government—finance, war, the Inquisition, and so on. The other supervised each of the territories ruled by the crown: Aragon, Castile, It-

---

[7] Although this feeling cannot be called nationalism, it was certainly an ancestor of that powerful modern force. Incidentally, the word *communes* as used here refers to the towns and cities of Spain that had distinct legal privileges and some degree of self-government; they were the center of the revolt. Their inhabitants were called, in Spanish, *comuneros.*

MAP 13.4. THE EMPIRE OF CHARLES V

aly, the Indies, and later in the century the Low Countries. At the head of this system was the Council of State, the principal advisory group, consisting of leading officials from the subsidiary councils. All the subsidiary councils reported to the king or to his deputy when he was away, but since each controlled its own bureaucracy, they were perfectly capable of running the empire in the monarch's absence.

What emerged was a vast federation, with Castile at its heart but with the parts, though directed from the center, allowed considerable autonomy. A viceroy in every major area (there

This map indicates both the vastness of Charles's empire and the extent of the fighting in which he became involved. Almost every battle his troops fought—against Spanish communes, German Protestants, the Turks, and the French—is included so as to show the full measure of the emperor's never-ending ordeal.

were nine altogether from Naples to Peru) ran the administration under the supervision of the *audiencia*—the territorial council—and while on the whole these officials were left to do as they wished, they had to report to Castile in minute detail at regular intervals and refer major decisions to the central government.

Although corruption was widespread and delays in communications (it took at least eight months to send a message from Castile to Peru) made the system unwieldy, the centralization gave the monarch the power he wanted. The enormous bureaucracy was carefully staffed, primarily by hidalgos and townsmen, while great nobles were given only viceroyalties or high army posts. Flexibility was allowed at the local level, but through the hierarchy of loyal servants the crown could exercise full control. As a result, Spain's administrative machine was one of the most remarkably detailed structures ever devised for ruling so vast an empire.

The Financial Toll of War

The only serious strain on Charles's monarchy was financial, the result of the constant wars the Hapsburgs had to support. A large portion of the money for the fighting came from Italy and the Low Countries, but Spain had to pay a growing share of the costs. As the sixteenth century progressed, the Spaniards increasingly resented the siphoning away of their funds into foreign wars. It was the tragedy of their century of glory that so much of the fantastic wealth they discovered in Latin America was exported for hostilities from which they drew almost no benefit.

The burden was by no means equally distributed. The stronger Cortes of Aragon was able to prevent substantial increases in taxation, which meant that Castile had to assume the brunt of the payments. To some extent this was balanced by a monopoly of trade with the New World that was granted to the inhabitants of Castile, but eventually the basic inequality among different Spanish regions led to civil war in the next century.

Charles's finances were saved from disaster only by the influx of treasure—mainly silver—from Latin America. Approximately 40 percent of the bullion went into the royal coffers, while the rest was taken by merchants in the Castilian port of Seville, mainly Genoese, who were given the sole right to ship goods to and from America. Starting with an annual inflow of some 20,000 ducats at the beginning of the century, Charles was receiving approximately 800,000 ducats' worth of treasure each year by the end of his reign. Unfortunately it was always mortgaged in advance to the Italian and German bankers whose loans sustained his armies.

The country and the monarchy faced increasing difficulties as the wars continued for more than a century and a half. Seville's monopoly prevented the rest of the nation from gaining a share of the new wealth, and foreigners—notably representatives of Italian and German financiers—came to dominate its economy and its commerce. Spain was squeezed dry by the king's financial demands; yet he only just kept his head above water. In 1557, the first year of the reign of Charles's successor, Philip II, the monarchy had to declare itself bankrupt, a self-defeating evasion of its mammoth debts that it had to repeat seven times in the next 125 years. There has never been a better example of the way that ceaseless war can sap the strength of even the most formidable nation.

III. THE SPLINTERED STATES

The rulers of England, France, and Spain in the mid-sixteenth century came to thrones strengthened domestically and internationally. Their predecessors had centralized their governments, largely subdued the rivals to royal power, engaged in a huge expansion overseas, and brought a fair measure of prosperity and safety from lawlessness to their subjects. They had even begun to take over control of the individual from local lords. But in the European domains east of these three kingdoms, such developments took place fitfully and only within small territorial units such as city-states. Here the centrifugal forces retained the control they had enjoyed for centuries.

The Holy Roman Empire: Autonomous Princes

The Holy Roman Empire is a classic example of weak institutions preventing the emergence of a strong central government. Members of the leading family of Central Europe, the Hapsburgs, had been elected to the imperial throne since the thirteenth century, but they lacked the authority and machinery to halt the fragmentation of the lands they nominally ruled. In addition to about 2000 imperial knights, some of whom owned no more than four or five acres, there were 50 ecclesiastical and 30 secular princes, more than 100 counts, some 70 prelates, and 66 cities, all virtually independent politically though officially subordinate to the emperor.

The princes, who reigned over most of the area of the Holy Roman Empire, rarely had any trouble resisting the emperor's claims; their main concern was to increase their own power at the expense of their subjects, another prince, or the cities. The cities themselves also refused to remain subordinate to a central government. In 1500 fifty of them contained more than 2000 inhabitants—a sizable number for this time—and twenty had over 10,000. Their wealth was substantial, because many were situated along a densely traveled trade artery, the Rhine River, and many were also political powers. But their fierce independence meant that the emperor could rarely tap their manpower or wealth.

The only central institution alongside the emperor was the Diet, which consisted of three assemblies: representatives of the cities, the princes, and the electors (the seven princes who

elected each new emperor). Given this makeup, the Diet in effect became the instrument of the princes; with its legislation they secured their position against the cities and the lesser nobility within their own domains.

By the end of the fifteenth century, most of the princes had achieved considerable control over their own territories. Only in the southwest of the empire were they significantly restricted by representative assemblies led by the lesser nobility. The princes were thus enjoying a success that paralleled the accomplishments of the monarchs of England, France, and Spain except that the units were much smaller. Although the Hapsburgs tried to develop strong central authority, they exercised significant control only over their personal dominions, which in 1500 comprised Austria, the Low Countries, and Franche-Comté (Map 13.4). To the rulers of other states of the empire, they were feudal overlords in theory but powerless in practice.

Nevertheless the need for effective central institutions met with some response in the late fifteenth century, particularly in the west and southwest of the empire. In 1495, for example, a tribunal was established to settle disputes between local powers. Controlled and financed by the princes, the chief beneficiaries of its work, it made considerable headway toward ending the lawlessness that had marked the fifteenth century, an achievement similar to the restoration of order in France, Spain, and England at the same time. The tribunal's use of Roman law had a wide influence on legislation and justice throughout the empire, but again only to the advantage of the princes, who interpreted its endorsement of a leader's authority as referring only to themselves.

Further attempts at administrative reform had little effect, because ecclesiastical and secular princes reacted by tightening their hold on the multitude of territories that constituted the empire. The religious dissensions of the Reformation (see Chapter 14) worsened the rivalries, dividing the empire and making Charles V no more than the leader of one side in a conflict, incapable of asserting his authority over his opponents. Charles's many commitments elsewhere diverted him repeatedly, but even when he won decisive military victories over the princes, he could not break the long tradition of local independence.

Eastern Europe: Resurgent Nobles

In the late fifteenth century, the dominant force in Eastern and Central Europe was the Kingdom of Hungary, under the leadership of Matthias Corvinus (1458–1490). He was exactly in the mold of the other new monarchs of the day: he restrained the great nobles, expanded and centralized his administration, dramatically increased the yield of taxation, and established a standing army. The king's power thus grew spectacularly both at home and abroad. He gained Bohemia and some German and Austrian lands, and he made Vienna his capital in 1485.

Immediately after his death, however, royal authority collapsed. To gain Hapsburg recognition of his right to the throne, his successor gave up the conquests of Austrian and German territories and arranged dynastic marriages with the Hapsburgs. This retreat provided the nobles of Hungary with an issue over which to reassert their position. First they forced the king to dissolve the standing army by refusing him essential financial support. Then, following a major peasant revolt against increasing repression by landowners, they imposed serfdom on all peasants in 1514 at a meeting of the Hungarian Diet, the governing body, which was controlled by the aristocracy. In the course of the next 30 years, the country was overrun by the Ottoman Empire, whose system of rule—reliance on local powers who would give allegiance to Constantinople—strengthened the

nobility further at the expense of both the monarchy and the peasantry. By the middle of the sixteenth century, a revival of central authority had become impossible.

In Poland royal power began to decline in the 1490s, when the king turned to the lesser nobles to help him against the greater nobility. He issued a statute in 1496 that strengthened the lower aristocrats against those below them, the townsmen and the peasants. The latter virtually became serfs, for they were forbidden to buy land and were deprived of freedom of movement. In 1505 the national Diet, consisting only of nobles, was made the supreme body of the land, without whose consent no laws could be passed. Shortly thereafter the Diet established serfdom officially.

Royal and noble patronage produced a great cultural flowering in Poland in these decades, most famously represented by the astronomer Nicolaus Copernicus (see p. 562). Yet the monarchy was losing influence steadily, as was revealed by the failure of its attempts to found a standing army. At the end of Sigismund II's reign (1548–1572), his kingdom was the largest in Europe; but his death ended the Jagellon dynasty, which had ruled the country for centuries. The Diet immediately made sure that succession to the crown, which technically had always been elective and in the hands of the nobles, would now depend entirely on their approval. Thus the aristocracy confirmed both its own dominance and the ineffectiveness of royal authority.

The Hungarian and Polish patterns were repeated throughout Eastern Europe. By the early sixteenth century, serfdom had been officially imposed in all the territories east of the Elbe River. In the West at the same time, labor shortages caused by the plagues of the fourteenth and fifteenth centuries had brought a permanent end to this kind of subjection. Peasants who were needed to work the land became scarce, and since estates were relatively small, desperate landowners, competing with one another for labor, had to offer the remaining serfs freedom in exchange for services. In the East much of the territory was newly settled and divided into very large holdings. Here the lords could achieve economies of scale and make do with fewer laborers per acre; consequently, they did not feel the need to make concessions. Moreover, these great landowners also held the keys to political power, and hence they could combine influence in the government with economic pressure to subjugate the lowest levels of society.

The political and social processes at work in Eastern and Central Europe thus contrasted strongly with developments in England, France, and Spain in this period. Nevertheless, although the trend was toward fragmentation in the East, one class, the aristocracy, did share the vigor and organizational ability that in the West was apparent primarily in the policies of kings. To that extent, therefore, the sense of renewed vitality in Europe during these years was also apparent beyond the borders of the new monarchies. The critical difference lay in the leaders of the revival. When kings were in command, their states gained strength and status; when the nobles dominated, countries lost ground in the fierce competition of international affairs.

Italy: Independent City-States

The cultural and economic leader of Europe, Italy, had developed a unique political structure. In the fifteenth century the five major states—Naples, the Papal States, Milan, Florence, and Venice—had established a balance among themselves that was preserved without serious disruption for 40 years after the Treaty of Lodi in 1454.

This long period of peace was finally broken in 1494, when Milan asked Charles VIII of France to help protect it against Florence and Naples. Thus began the Italian wars, which

soon revealed that these relatively small territories were totally incapable of resisting the force that a new political organization, the national monarchy, could bring to bear.

Venice and Florence had long been regarded by Europeans as model republics—reincarnations of Classical city-states and centers of freedom governed with the consent of their citizens. In truth Venice was controlled by a small merchant oligarchy and Florence by the Medici family, but the image was still widely accepted. Moreover the Italians were regarded as masters not only of politics but also of culture and of manners.

It was a considerable shock to Europe therefore when the Italian states crumbled before the onslaught of French forces and then of the Spaniards and the Hapsburgs. Charles VIII drove the Medicis out of Florence in 1494 and established a new republic, but in 1512 Ferdinand of Aragon engineered their return, and eventually the Hapsburgs set up the Medici family as hereditary dukes. Ferdinand had annexed Naples in 1504, and Emperor Charles V ultimately took over Milan. The fighting finally ended in 1559 with the Hapsburgs in control; they would dominate the Italian peninsula for the next century. Only Venice and the Papal States remained independent, the former somewhat battered by a series of defeats and the latter the one gainer from the Italian wars. Julius II (1503–1513), known as the Warrior Pope, carved out a new papal territory in central and eastern Italy by force of arms.

The critical lesson of this disastrous sequence of events was that the small political unit could not survive in an age when governments were consolidating their authority in large kingdoms. No matter how brilliant and sophisticated, a compact urban state could not withstand such superior force. Italy's cultural and economic prominence took a long time to fade, but by the mid-sixteenth century its political independence had disappeared, not to return for 300 years.

IV. THE NEW STATECRAFT

At the same time as European political life grew more elaborate and complex, innovations appeared in the relations among states and the perspectives of political observers. Rulers had achieved levels of military and economic strength and a freedom of action that required equivalent transformations in the techniques of diplomacy. And theorists and historians who witnessed these changes began to see politics in a different light.

International Relations

The Italian states of the fifteenth century, in their intensive machinations and competition, developed various new ways of pursuing foreign policy. During the Italian wars these techniques spread throughout Europe and caused a revolution in diplomacy. Any state hoping to play a prominent role in international affairs worked under a serious disadvantage if it did not adopt the new methods.

The essential innovation was the resident ambassador. Previously rulers had dispatched ambassadors only for specific missions, such as arranging an alliance, declaring war, or delivering a message, but from the sixteenth century on, important states maintained their representatives in every major capital city or court continuously. The permanent ambassador could keep his home government informed of the latest local and international developments and could also move without delay to protect his sovereign's interests.

As states established embassies, procedures and organization became more sophisticated: a primitive system of immunities evolved, formal protocol developed, and embassy officials were assigned different levels of responsibility and importance. Considerable advances were still to come, but by the mid-sixteenth century the outlines of the new diplomacy were already visible—yet another reflection of the growing powers and ambitions of central governments.

The great dividing line between older arrangements and the new diplomacy was the Italian wars, the first Europe-wide crisis of modern times. Rulers as distant as the English King Henry VIII and the Ottoman Sultan Suleiman II were drawn into the conflict between the Hapsburgs and the Valois, and gradually all states recognized that it was in the interests of everyone to accept a system in which no one power dominated the rest. In later years this interdependence, this prevention of excessive aggression, was to be known as the balance of power, yet by the mid-sixteenth century the glimmerings of the idea were already affecting alliances and peace treaties. The lesson again came from the Italians, who on a smaller scale had tried to create a balance among the leading states of the peninsula with the Treaty of Lodi.

For Charles V, always on the defensive and an instinctive peacemaker, such orderliness had much to recommend it. But Francis I considered the Hapsburgs far too powerful, and he pursued his ambitions in Italy with all the means at his disposal, undeterred by repeated defeats. In 1535 he shocked Europe by concluding a treaty with the Muslim Suleiman, the Hapsburgs' most formidable enemy. And the sultan even paid the papacy a pension to help it pursue its own opposition to Charles V. Thus common political interests brought religious opponents together.

In military affairs the new monarchs took similar initiatives. A recent historian has called the period of Charles V's reign "more decisive for the evolution of the art of war" than any thereafter until the late eighteenth century. During this time the crossbow was finally superseded, armies combined artillery with infantry and cavalry, the division emerged as the basic military unit, city wall bastion fortification was devised, and the siege became the essential tactic of warfare. Logistics were now as important as any other military art, and strategists laid out careful systems of supply and

Hans Holbein's *The Ambassadors* shows the worldliness that was expected of diplomats (many of whom were also soldiers) in the sixteenth century. The two men are surrounded by symbols of the skills, knowledge, and refinement their job required—geography, mathematics, literature, and music. But despite this emphasis on material concerns, Holbein reminds us (in the optically distorted skull across the bottom of the painting) that death and spiritual needs cannot be forgotten. (Photo: National Gallery, London)

command. An amazing feature of this military revolution was that it advanced uniformly throughout Europe. No ruler could afford to be left behind in the deadly race.

Contemporary Appraisals: Machiavelli and Guicciardini

Political commentators soon began to seek theoretical explanations for the new authority and aggressiveness of rulers and the collapse of the Italian city-states. Turning from arguments based on divine will or contractual law, they looked to pragmatism, opportunism, and effective government as an end in itself.

The earliest full expression of these views came from the Italians, the pioneers of the methods and attitudes that were revolutionizing politics. When all military efforts proved futile in face of the superior forces of France and Spain, they naturally wanted to find out why. The most disturbing answer was given by an experienced diplomat, Niccolò Machiavelli, who was thrown out of his job when the Medicis took control of Florence in 1512. With a bitter pen he immediately set about analyzing exactly how power operated.

The result, *The Prince,* is one of the few radically original books in history. To move from his predecessors to Machiavelli is to enter a world that even the immediate Italian background does not foreshadow. Roman jurists talking of kings as the source of law and writers asserting that a monarch was not subordinate to the pope were still thinking in legalistic or moral terms. Machiavelli swept away all these conventions. If he came out of any tradition, it was the Renaissance fascination with method that had produced manuals on cooking, dancing, fencing, and manners. But he wrote about the methods of a subject never previously approached: power.

Machiavelli showed not why power does or should exist, but how it works. In the form of advice to a prince and without reference to divine, legal, or natural justification, the book explains what a ruler needs to do to win and maintain complete control over his subjects. Machiavelli did not deny the force of religion or law; what concerned him was how they ought to be *used* in the tactics of governing— religion for molding unity and contentment, and devotion to law for building the ruler's reputation as a fair-minded man. *The Prince* outlines the particular methods of a conqueror, legitimate heir, or usurper as well as the proper ways to deal with insurrection and the many other problems that a ruler is likely to encounter. Fear and respect are the bases of his authority, and he must exercise care at all times not to relax his control over potential troublemakers or over his image among his people.

Very few contemporaries of Machiavelli dared accept his view of politics. To men of the sixteenth century and long thereafter, "Machiavellianism" was synonymous with evil and cunning. Secular and pragmatic considerations might be gaining prominence, but Europe was not yet ready to abandon its reverence for law, divine providence, and natural morality.

The change in the perspective on power became noticeable in historical writings too. Machiavelli's other masterpiece, the *Discourses,* developed a cyclical theory of every government moving inexorably from tyranny to democracy and back again. His conclusion, drawn particularly from a study of Roman history, is that healthy government can be preserved only by the active participation of all citizens in the life of the state. He attributed the Italians' defeat to the fact that his countrymen relied on mercenary troops and abandoned their civic responsibilities. The vigor of the Roman Republic depended on its citizen army.

Another Italian, Francesco Guicciardini, writing in the 1530s, saw the root of the problem as the lack of unity in Italy. His great work, a *History of Italy,* rose above the particularism of previous narratives, which had dealt with events in only one city-state or region. Guicciardini's comparative analysis of the Italian states led him to conclude that government should be left in the hands of an intelligent ruler. There are no basic principles at work in history; experience, flexibility, and the ability to meet a situation on its own terms make for good government.

Guicciardini was the first major historian to rely heavily on original documents rather than secondhand accounts. If the conclusions he reached from his study of the sources seem dauntingly cynical—he attributed even less to underlying historical forces than did Machiavelli—the reasons for his pessimism are not far to seek. The actions of kings and princes in the early sixteenth century hardly gave much room for optimism, and shrewd observers like Machiavelli and Guicciardini must have found it difficult to avoid pessimism about public events. These writers were exposing the atmosphere of the times, capturing in print the obsession with power and pragmatism that propelled Europe's newly powerful rulers as they extended their ever growing authority both at home and abroad.

Beginning in the late fifteenth century, the rulers of England, France, and Spain consolidated their realms into strong polities with power centralized under their own command. These new monarchs, as historians have called them, extended their authority at home by undermining their traditional domestic rivals, the nobility and the Church, and pursued aggressive dynastic ambitions abroad. The Holy Roman Empire, Eastern Europe, and Italy did not experience this development. Instead local powers—cities, nobles, and princes—remained autonomous, preventing their countries from marshaling their resources and organizing themselves like the new monarchies. Ironically, though the Italian city-states were too small to retain their independence, their politicians were teaching the rest of Europe new methods of conducting international relations; and their political analysts and historians, perceiving the trends in statecraft before anyone else, broke new ground in their analysis of how power works and why states rise and fall.

Parallel to the political developments were remarkable economic advances and an expansion to other continents that reflected the vigor of a newly confident age. Europe's population was increasing, its prices were rising, and its trade was multiplying—all unmistakable signs of a healthy society. Yet the social consequences were not always benevolent, for the revival had paradoxical results. Social mobility did increase, but so did poverty. Strong central governments restored order, but they also provoked resentment. And rapid change by its very nature caused considerable bewilderment, producing signs of disquiet in the culture of the age. Of all the causes of tension, however, none equaled in impact the most shattering disruption of the sixteenth century, an upheaval that brought an end to more than 1000 years of Western Christian unity—the Reformation.

RECOMMENDED READING

Sources

*Guicciardini, Francesco. *The History of Italy and Other Selected Writings.* Cecil Grayson (tr.). 1964.
*Machiavelli, Niccolò. *The Prince and The Discourses.* Luigi Ricci (tr.). 1950.

Studies

Boxer, Charles R. *The Portuguese Seaborne Empire.* 1970. An excellent overview of the rise and structure of the Portuguese empire.
Cipolla, Carlo M. *Guns, Sails, and Empires: Technological Innovation and the Early Phases of European Expansion 1400–1700.* 1965. This is a lively study of the reasons that expansion succeeded, with particular emphasis on weaponry.
*Crosby, Alfred W. *The Columbian Exchange: Biological and Cultural Consequences of 1492.* 1972. A fascinating study of plants, diseases, and other exchanges between the Old World and the New.
*Elliott, J. H. *Imperial Spain, 1469–1716.* 1964. The best introduction to Spanish history in this period, covering mainly political and economic developments.

*Elton, Geoffrey R. *The Tudor Revolution in Government.* 1959. An important study of how government worked, and how its operations were expanded, during the reign of Henry VIII.
*Hale, J. R. *Machiavelli and Renaissance Italy.* 1963. The clearest and most straightforwardly written short account of Machiavelli and his times.
Knecht, R. J. *Francis I.* 1982. A thorough study of the longest of the reigns of a new monarch in France.
*Mattingly, Garrett. *Renaissance Diplomacy.* 1971. An elegant account of the changes that began in international relations during the fifteenth century.
*Parry, John H. *The Age of Reconnaissance.* 1963. The most complete history of Europe's expansion through 1620.
*Rice, Eugene F., Jr. *The Foundations of Early Modern Europe, 1460–1559.* 1970. One of the best short surveys of the period, with three pages of suggested readings.
Scarisbrick, J. J. *Henry VIII.* 1968. A detailed but vivid biography of one of the most forceful of the new monarchs.

---

* Available in paperback.

Chapter 14

❧

Reformations
in Religion
1500–1570

To the sixteenth-century European, the most momentous revolution of the time was not the growth of royal power, the rise of prices, or the discovery of new lands overseas but the movement that destroyed the West's religious unity: the Reformation. Two sides began to form, to be called Catholic and Protestant, each resolutely convinced of its own righteousness and the other's error, and their confrontation inspired wars for more than a century.

The new ideas of the religious thinkers Martin Luther, Ulrich Zwingli, John Calvin, and their successors stimulated a radical rethinking of traditional views of God, man, and society. At issue in the Reformation was the balance between the role of the Church and the piety of the individual in the answer to the fundamental question of Christian history: How can sinful humans gain salvation? The traditional answer was that the Church was the essential intermediary through which man could be saved. This laid the stress on community, on outward participation in rituals, and particularly on the seven sacraments, the principal channels of grace. But there was another answer that had been advocated by distinguished Church fathers such as St. Augustine: that man could be saved by his faith in God and love of him. This view emphasized the inward and personal and focused on God as the source of grace.

The two traditions were not incompatible; for centuries they had coexisted without difficulty, and elements of each would be retained by both Protestants and Catholics after the Reformation. Indeed, one of the problems theologians faced around 1500 was the absence of precise definition in many areas of doctrine. It was often difficult to tell where orthodoxy ended and heresy began. This indeterminacy might have been an asset had it reflected a commitment to flexibility and comprehensiveness by the leaders of the Church. In fact, however, as the papacy and the Church had grown in power and importance during the Central Middle Ages, official attitudes had shifted decisively toward the outward, sacramental, institutional view and away from the inward and personal approach. The main purpose of the Reformation was to reverse this trend. What was not clear at the outset was whether the change would be accomplished by reform from within or by a revolution and schism in the Church.

I. DISSENT AND PIETY

Dissatisfaction with the Church was evident at all levels of society in the early sixteenth century. Increasing numbers of deeply pious people were finding the Church's growing emphasis on ritual and standardized practices unhelpful in their personal quest for salvation. Their religious grievances were the root of the ferment; once the Reformation had begun, however, political, economic, and social issues influenced its course.

Sources of Malaise

The spiritual authority of the papacy had been declining for more than two centuries. During the 70 years of the Babylonian captivity, when the pontiffs had lived in Avignon, they had no longer seemed to be symbols of the universal Church but rather captives of the French monarchs. Far more demoralizing, the Great Schism that followed had threatened to undermine the unity of Western Christendom, as two and then three pretenders each claimed to be the true pope. The Council of Constance had closed this breach by 1418 but had also encouraged the conciliar movement. This attempt to subordinate papal power to the authority of Church councils ultimately failed, but it was yet another direct challenge to the pope's supremacy. Only the refusal of secular rulers to back the reform movements that arose around 1400—in particular, the efforts of John Wycliffe and John Huss and their followers—prevented a major split like the Reformation 100 years before it actually occurred.

The papacy had also lost spiritual influence because of its secularization. Increasingly popes were conducting themselves like Italian princes. With skillful diplomacy and even military action, they had consolidated their control over the papal lands in the peninsula. They had surrounded themselves with an elaborate court and become patrons of the arts, taking over for a time the cultural leadership of Europe. But this concern with political power and grandeur had eclipsed religious duties to the point that popes used their spiritual powers to raise funds for their secular activities. The fiscal measures developed at Avignon, which furnished the papacy with income from appointments to Church offices and from dispensations and indulgences, had enlarged revenues but led to widespread abuses. High ecclesiastical offices could be bought and sold, and men (usually sons of nobles) were attracted to them by the opportunities they provided for wealth and power, not by a religious vocation.

Abuses were widespread at lower levels in the Church as well. Some prelates held several offices at a time and could not give adequate attention to any of them. The ignorance and moral laxity of the parish and monastic clergy also aroused antagonism. The lower clerical orders, particularly the ordinary parish priests, were little better off than the peasants among whom they lived, and many of them used indulgences as a fund-raising device—granting the remission of some of the temporal punishment for sin to anyone who made a donation to the Church. Many laymen found this practice a shocking attempt to sell divine grace.

These abuses provoked two major responses: anticlericalism (hostility to the clergy) and a call for reform within the Church. Both reactions were symptomatic of a broader quest for genuine piety that was running throughout European society by the early 1500s.

The deepest source of discontent with the Church was its failure to meet spiritual needs. The institution had grown more formal, its doctrines supported by an elaborate system of canon law and theology and its services filled with pomp and ceremony. Increasing importance was being attached to the sacraments, the role of the priest, and the doctrine that salvation could be achieved only if faith was accompanied by good works—fasting, charity, abstinence, and similar acts of self-denial.

The laity sought a more personal piety than the official devotions provided. Observation of Church rituals meant little, they felt, unless the believer could cultivate an interior sense of the love and presence of God. They looked for nourishment, therefore, to those, like the mystics, who emphasized religious individualism. Rejecting the theological subtleties of Scholasticism, they sought divine guidance in the Bible and the writings of the early Church fathers, especially St. Augustine. Lay religious fraternities dedicated to private devotions and charitable works proliferated in the cities, especially in Germany and Italy. The most widespread of

1460–1560/TIMELINE

Social and Economic History	Cultural and Intellectual History

1460

1484 Botticelli's *Birth of Venus* painted

1486 *Hammer of Witches* published, marking start of rising persecution of witches

1487 Voyage of Dias around Africa

1492 Discovery of America by Columbus
Expulsion of Jews from Spain

1495–1498 Leonardo da Vinci's *Last Supper* painted

1487 Voyage of Dias around Africa

1501–1504 Michelangelo's *David* sculpted

1509 Erasmus's *Praise of Folly* published
1513 Machiavelli's *Prince* written
1516 More's *Utopia* published
1516 Castiglione's *Book of the Courtier* written
1517 Luther's 95 theses
1518 Titian's *Bacchanal* painted

1519 Magellan's voyage around the world begins

1533 Loyola completes *The Spiritual Exercises*
1534 Publication of Luther's German translation of the Bible
1536 First edition of Calvin's *Institutes*
1543 Publication of Copernicus's *Revolutions of the Heavenly Bodies*

1545 Discovery at Potosí, in present-day Bolivia, of largest silver mine in the New World

1545–1563 Council of Trent

1556 Spaniard, Azpilcueta, first explains that inflation is caused by the influx of silver to Europe

1556–1559 Clothes painted over Michelangelo's nudes in the Sistine Chapel

1560

them in Germany, the Brotherhood of the Eleven Thousand Virgins, consisted of laymen who gathered together, usually in a church, to sing hymns. In the mid-fifteenth century, more than 100 such groups had been established in Hamburg, a city of slightly more than 10,000 inhabitants. Churchmen, unhappy about a development over which they had no control, had tried to suppress them but to no avail. Itinerant preachers still roamed Central Europe in considerable numbers, urging direct and sometimes mystical communication between believers and God, free from ritual and complex doctrine. To the vast crowds they drew, they seemed to echo the words of St. Augustine: "God and the soul I want to recognize, nothing else."

The most spectacular outburst of popular piety around 1500 occurred in seemingly materialist Florence, which embraced Girolamo Savonarola, a zealous Dominican who wanted to banish the irreligion and materialism he saw everywhere about him. The climax of his influence came in 1496, when he arranged a tremendous bonfire, in which the Florentines burned cosmetics, light literature, dice, and other such frivolities. But Savonarola's attempts at internal reform eventually brought him into conflict with the papacy. At that point the Church intervened, and eventually he was executed for heresy.

The widespread search for a more intense devotional life was a sign of spiritual vitality. Had the hierarchy responded by adapting religious teachings and practices to meet this need, the Church might have been spared the upheavals of the Reformation. Instead churchmen gave little encouragement to ecclesiastical reform and the evangelization of the laity. They reacted with vigor only when they detected a clear threat to their authority—when for example they condemned the teachings of John Wycliffe and John Huss as heretical. Only in Spain was there a deliberate attempt to eradicate abuses and encourage religious fervor, and

there the leadership in the effort came not from Rome but from the head of the Spanish Church, Cardinal Francisco Ximenes de Cisneros. When the papacy finally did attempt to revitalize the Church in the mid-sixteenth century, the revolt of the reformers was already under way.

Piety and Protest in Literature and Art

Popular piety received unexpected assistance from technology. The invention of the printing press made reading material available to a much broader segment of the population and new ideas traveled with unprecedented speed (see Map A-18 in the Cartographic Essay and the table on p. 491). Perhaps a third of the professional and upper classes—townspeople, the educated, and the nobility—could read, but books reached a much wider audience. Throughout Europe, peddlers began to carry printed materials in their packs, selling them in country towns in all regions. Here they could be bought by a local person for reading out loud at a gathering of villagers. These evening readings to a group of people who would never have had access to written literature in the days of manuscripts became an important means of spreading new ideas.

Some publishers took advantage of this new market by printing almanacs filled with homely advice about the weather and nature that were written specifically for simple rural folk. And translated Bibles made Scripture available to ordinary people in a language that, for the first time, they could understand. For the reformers, therefore, books were a powerful weapon, but they were used by both sides in the religious conflict and revealed the general interest in spiritual matters. Devotional tracts, lives of the saints, and the Bible itself were the most popular titles—often running to editions of around 1000 copies.

THE SPREAD OF PRINTING THROUGH 1500
Number of Towns in Which a Printing Press Was Established for the First Time, by Period and Country

Period	German-Speaking Areas	Italian-Speaking Areas	French-Speaking Areas	Spain	England	Netherlands	Other	Total
Before 1471:	8	4	1	1	—	—	—	14
1471–1480:	22	36	9	6	3	12	5	93
1481–1490:	17	13	21	12	—	5	4	72
1491–1500:	9	5	11	6	—	2	8	41
Total by 1500:	56	58	42	25	3	19	17	220

Adapted from Lucien Febvre and Henri-Jean Martin, *The Coming of the Book: The Impact of Printing 1450–1800*, translated by David Gerard, London, NLB, 1976, pp. 178–179 and 184–185.

(*Note:* Printing did not spread to other towns in England because the government, to ensure control over printers, ordered that they work only in London and at Oxford and Cambridge universities.)

Printing may thus have lessened the laity's dependence on the clergy; whereas traditionally the priest had read and interpreted the Scriptures for his congregation, now many could consult their own copy. By 1522 eighteen translations of the Bible had been published. Some 14,000 copies had been printed in German alone, enough to make it easy to buy in most German-speaking regions.

Many books were profusely illustrated, and thus accessible to the illiterate as well. Perhaps the most famous was the German Sebastian Brant's *Ship of Fools* (1494), a long satire in verse describing life as a voyage. The poem dissects each passenger—the beggar, the friar, and so on—lampooning his lack of true faith or morality.

The most gifted satirist of the age, however, was François Rabelais, a humanist and an incisive critic of the clergy and morality of his day. He was a monk (as well as a doctor), but he was deeply unhappy that traditional religious practices had diverged so far from the ideals of Jesus. Rabelais is most famous for his earthy bawdiness, but again and again he returned to clerical targets. His *Gargantua* and *Pantagruel* (1533 and 1535) contain numerous sardonic passages:

"Don't [monks] pray to God for us?" "They do nothing of the kind," said Gargantua. "All they do is keep the whole neighborhood awake by jangling their bells. . . . They mumble over a lot of legends and psalms, which they don't in the least understand; and they say a great many paternosters . . . without thinking or caring about what they are saying. And all that I call a mockery of God, not prayer."

Scurrilous broadsides no less stinging in tone became very popular during the Reformation. These were single sheets, often containing vicious attacks on religious opponents and usually illustrated by cartoons with obscene imagery. These propaganda pieces were the product of partisan hostility, but their broader significance should not be ignored. Even the most lowly of hack writers could share with a serious author like Rabelais a common sense of outrage at indifference in high places and a dismay with the spiritual malaise of the time.

This concern with spiritual and religious themes, so evident in European literature, also permeated the work of northern artists in the late fifteenth and early sixteenth centuries (see Plate 18). The gruesome vision of Hieronymus Bosch, for example, depicts the fears and dangers his contemporaries felt threatening them. He put on canvas the demons, the temptations, the terrible punishments for sin that people considered as real as their tangible surroundings (see Plate 21). Bosch's younger contemporary Mathias Grünewald conveyed the same mixture of terror and devotion. Like Bosch, he painted a frightening *Temptation of St. Anthony* showing the travails of the saint who steadfastly resisted horrible attacks by the devil. These artists explored the darker side of faith, taking their inspiration from the fear of damnation and the hope for salvation—the first seen in the devils, the second in the redeeming Christ.

The supreme innovation of the finest northern artist of this period, Albrecht Dürer, was not in painting but in the art of the woodcut. Developed in the mid-fourteenth century, the technique of cutting a picture into wood so that it could be inked and reproduced grew in importance with the invention of printing. Until touched by the genius of Dürer, however, it remained a stiff and primitive art form. His hand transformed it into a subtle, versatile means of expression, a superb vehicle for the religious themes he portrayed.

The depth of piety conveyed by these artists reflected the temper of Europe (see, for example, the religious meaning put even into a secular painting like Holbein's *The Ambassadors,* reproduced on p. 483). In art and literature as in lay organizations and the continuing popularity of itinerant preachers, people showed their concern over individual spiritual values and their dissatisfaction with a Church that was not meeting their needs. But no segment of society expressed the strivings and yearnings of the age more eloquently than the northern humanists.

II. THE NORTHERN HUMANISTS

The salient features of the humanist movement in Italy—its theory of education, its emphasis on eloquence, its reverence for the ancients, and

its endorsement of active participation in affairs of state—began to win wide acceptance north of the Alps in the late 1400s. But the northerners added a significant religious dimension to the movement by devoting considerable attention to early Christian literature—the Bible and the writings of the Church fathers.

Christian Humanism

The first major center of northern Humanism was the University of Heidelberg, but by the end of the fifteenth century the influence of the movement was almost universal. As it grew, there was a quickening of activity in the world of letters and thought that paralleled the new energy in economic life, politics, and overseas enterprise. The ease of communication created by the printing press helped accelerate the exchange of ideas, for by 1500 there was at least one press in every city of any size along the Rhine River from Basel to Leiden (see Map A-18 in the Cartographic Essay).

The driving force behind northern Humanism came to be a determination to probe early Christianity for the light it could throw on the origins of current religious belief. But this scholarly pursuit soon produced a conflict that arrayed humanist intellectuals against more traditional scholars.

At issue was the danger inherent in the study of Jewish writings. On one side were those who considered Hebrew works pernicious and wanted them condemned; on the other was Johann Reuchlin, a humanist and brilliant Hebraist, who advocated research that would illuminate the parent faith of Christianity. The controversy inspired scores of polemical pamphlets. The most famous, the *Letters of Obscure Men* (1515 and 1517), a stinging defense of Reuchlin that ridiculed his opponents, was the creation of a group of aggressive young humanists; one of them, Ulrich von Hutten, was to be among Luther's most ardent supporters. Thus northern Humanism's broad ex-

Grünewald's *Temptation of St. Anthony* bears witness to the terrifying impact of the supernatural on the thought of northern artists.
(Photo: Lauros-Giraudon)

amination of religious issues helped create the atmosphere in which Luther's much more serious criticisms could flourish.

This new direction was especially noticeable in the work of the leading French humanist of the period, Jacques Lefèvre d'Étaples, who was one of the most important biblical scholars of his day. In his commentary on St. Paul (1512), he applied the humanist principle of seeking the straightforward, clear meaning of the text and in this way built a powerful case for a return to the simple godliness of early Christianity and for the primacy of biblical authority. The revival of interest in the apostle St. Paul was a major step on the road to Reformation, and it is notable that a number of Lefèvre's comments on Paul anticipated Luther's pronouncements.

Christian Humanism, as modern scholars call the phase of the movement represented by men like Reuchlin and Lefèvre, retained an interest in Classical authors and continued to utilize the methods of the Italian humanists—analysis of ancient texts, language, and style. But its purpose was different: to answer questions about the message of Jesus and the apostles so as to offer contemporaries a guide to true piety and morality. This was a deeply religious undertaking, and it dominated the writings of the most famous Christian humanists, one English and one Dutch.

Thomas More and Erasmus

Sir Thomas More (1478–1535), a lawyer and statesman, was the central figure of English Humanism. His reputation as a writer rests primarily on a brief work, *Utopia*, published in Latin in 1516, which describes an ideal society on an imaginary island. In it More condemned war, poverty, intolerance, and other evils of his day and defined the general principles of morality that should underlie human society.

The first book of *Utopia* asks whether a man of learning should withdraw from the world to avoid the corruptions of politics, or actively participate in affairs of state so as to guide his fellow men. The Italian civic humanists had established commitment to public responsibilities as an essential part of the humanist movement. More reopened the question from the standpoint of religious as well as ethical values and answered with a warning against evading public duties, even though rulers rarely heed the advice they are given.

The second and more famous book of *Utopia* describes the ideal commonwealth itself. In political and social organization, it is a carefully regulated, almost monastic community that has succeeded in abolishing private property—together with greed and pride—and has achieved true morality. The Utopians are non-Christian, and More implies that a society based on Christian principles can attain even greater good. Well-designed institutions, education, and discipline are his answer to the fall of man: weak human nature can be led to virtuousness only if severely curbed.

Deeply devout, and firmly against dissent, More entered public life as a member of Parliament in 1504. He rose high in government service, succeeding—against his will—to the lord chancellorship on Wolsey's fall in 1529. He gave his life (and eventually became a saint) for remaining loyal to the pope and refusing to recognize Henry VIII as head of the English Church. His last words revealed his unflinching adherence to the Christian principles he pursued throughout his life: "I die the King's good servant, but God's first."

The supreme representative of Christian Humanism was the Dutchman Desiderius Erasmus (1466?–1536). Erasmus early acquired a taste for ancient writers, and he determined to devote himself to Classical studies. For the greater part of his life, he wandered through Europe, writing, visiting friends, occasionally working for important patrons. He always retained his independence, however, for unlike More, his answer to the question of whether a scholar should enter public life was that he should avoid the compromises he would have to make in the service of a ruler.

Erasmus became so famous for his learning and his literary skills that he dominated the world of letters in Europe. Constantly consulted by scholars and admirers, he wrote magnificently composed letters that reflected every aspect of the culture of his time. The English humanists, particularly More, were among his closest friends, and it was during his first visit to England, in 1499, that his interests were turned away from purely literary matters toward the theological writings that became the main focus of his scholarship.

Erasmus's most famous book was *The Praise of Folly* (1509), inspired by the already popular *Ship of Fools,* but a subtler work with a deeper moral commitment. Some of it is gay, light-hearted banter that pokes fun at the author himself, his friends, and the follies of everyday life, suggesting that a little folly is essential to human existence. At the same time, the book points out that Christianity itself is a kind of folly, a belief in "things not seen." And in other passages Erasmus launches sharply satirical attacks against monks, the pope, meaningless ceremonies, and the many lapses from what he perceived to be the true Christian spirit.

At the heart of Erasmus's work was the message that he called the "philosophy of Christ." He believed that the life of Jesus himself and especially the teachings in the Sermon on the Mount should be the model for Christian piety and morality. For ceremonies and rigid discipline he had only censure: too often they served as substitutes for genuine spiritual concerns. People lit thousands of candles for Mary but cared little about the humility she is supposed to inspire. They forgot that what counts is the spirit of religious devotion, not the form. By simply following the precepts of Jesus, a Christian could lead a life guided by sincere faith. Because of his insistence on ethical behavior, Erasmus could admire a truly moral man even if he was a pagan. "I could almost say 'Pray for me, St. Socrates!'" he once wrote.

Erasmus believed that the Church had lost sight of its original mission. In the course of 15 centuries, traditions and practices had developed that obscured the intentions of its founder, and the only way purity could be restored was by studying the Scriptures and the writings of the early Church fathers. Here the tools of the humanists became vitally important, because they enabled scholars to understand the meaning and intention of an ancient manuscript. Practicing what he preached, Erasmus spent 10 years preparing a new edition of the Greek text of the New Testament so as to correct errors in the Latin Vulgate, which was the standard version, and revised it repeatedly for another 20 years.

But the calm, scholarly, and tolerant moderation Erasmus prized was soon left behind by events. The rising fanaticism of the reformers and their opponents destroyed the effort he had led to cure the ills of the Church from within. Despite its surface plausibility, the famous saying, "Erasmus laid the egg that Luther hatched," misses the fundamental difference between the two men: Erasmus, a classic nonrevolutionary, wanted a revival of purer faith, but *within* the traditional structure of the Church.

The final irony of Erasmus's career was that he inspired reformers in both camps and yet in the end was rejected by both. He was condemned by Catholics as heretical and by leaders of the Reformation as halfhearted. In an age of confrontation, it was impossible to keep a middle course, and Erasmus found himself swept aside by revolutionary forces that he himself had helped build but that Luther unleashed.

III. THE LUTHERAN REFORMATION

That the first religious conflict should have erupted in the Holy Roman Empire is not surprising. Here popular piety had been noticeably strong, as evidenced by the waves of Rhineland mysticism and the lay religious movements. In addition the chief local authorities in many areas were ecclesiastical princes, usually aristocratic bishops such as the ruler of the important city of Cologne on the Rhine. As a result no strong intermediaries like the rulers of En-

gland, France, and Spain stood between the papacy and the people, and the popes regarded the empire as their surest source of revenue. This situation may help explain why a determined reformer, Martin Luther, won such swift and widespread support; but the reasons he made his stand must be sought in the personal development of a highly sensitive, energetic, and troubled man.

Martin Luther

Martin Luther (1483–1546) was born into a simple worker family in Saxony in central Germany. The household was dominated by the father, whose powerful presence some modern commentators have seen reflected in his son's vision of an omnipotent God. The boy received a good education and decided to become a lawyer, a profession that would have given him many opportunities for advancement. But in his early twenties, shortly after starting his legal studies, he had an experience that changed his life. Crossing a field during a thunderstorm, he was thrown to the ground by a bolt of lightning, and in his terror he cried to St. Anne, the mother of Mary, that he would enter a monastery.

Although the decision may well have been that sudden, it is clear that there was more to Luther's complete change of direction than this one incident, however traumatic. He was obviously a man obsessed with his own sinfulness, and he joined an Augustinian monastery in the hope that a penitential life would help him overcome his sense of guilt. Once in the order he pursued every possible opportunity to earn worthiness in the sight of God. He overlooked no possible discipline or act of contrition or self-denial, and for added merit he endured austerities such as self-flagellation that went far beyond normal requirements. To no avail: at his first mass after his ordination, in 1507, he was so terrified at the prospect of a sinner like himself transforming the wafer and wine into the body and blood of Christ that he almost failed to complete the ritual.

Fortunately for Luther his superiors took more notice of his intellectual gifts than of his self-doubts and in 1508 assigned him to the faculty of a new university in Wittenberg, the capital of Saxony. It was from his scholarship, which was superb, and especially from his study of the Bible, that he was able at last to draw comfort and spiritual peace.

A second episode that probably took place when he was in his mid-thirties marked another crucial turning point in Luther's life. Until "the experience in the tower," as it is usually called, he could see no way that he, a despicable mortal, could receive anything but the fiercest punishments from a God of absolute justice. Now, however, he suddenly understood that he had only to rely on God's mercy, a quality as great as his justice. He later described the experience in these words:

> I greatly longed to understand Paul's Epistle to the Romans, and nothing stood in the way but that one expression, "the justice of God," because I took it to mean that justice whereby God is just and deals justly in punishing the unjust. My situation was that, although an impeccable monk, I stood before God as a sinner troubled in conscience, and I had no confidence that my merit would assuage him. . . . Night and day I pondered until I saw the connection between the justice of God and the statement [Romans 1:17] that "The just shall live by his faith." Then I grasped that the justice of God is that righteousness by which through grace and sheer mercy God justifies us through faith. Thereupon I felt myself to be reborn and to have gone through open doors into paradise.[1]

The many advances in Luther's thinking thereafter came ultimately from this insight: that justification—expiation of sin and attainment of righteousness through a gift of grace—is achieved by faith alone.

The Indulgence Controversy

In 1517 an event occurred that was ultimately to lead Luther to an irrevocable break with the Church. In the spring a Dominican friar, Johann Tetzel, began to sell indulgences a few miles from Wittenberg as part of a huge fundraising effort to pay for the new Church of St. Peter in Rome. Originally an indulgence had been granted to a person who was unable to go on a crusade and who gave sufficient money to permit a poor crusader to reach the Holy Land. The indulgence itself released a sinner from a certain period of punishment in purgatory before going to heaven, and was justified doctrinally as a sort of credit that could be drawn from the treasury of merit built up by Jesus and the saints. But the doctrine had not been defined exactly, and clerics had been taking advantage of this vagueness to sell indulgences indiscriminately. Tetzel, an expert salesman, was offering complete releases from purgatory without bothering to mention the repentance demanded of everyone as the condition for forgiveness of sin.

The people of Wittenberg were soon flocking to Tetzel to buy this easy guarantee of salvation. For Luther, a man groping toward an evangelical solution of his own doubts, it was unforgivable that people should be deprived of their hard-earned money for spurious, worthless promises. On October 31, 1517, he nailed to the door of the university church in Wittenberg 95 theses, or statements, on indulgences that he offered to debate with experts in Christian doctrine.

This was no revolutionary document. It merely described what Luther believed to be correct teachings on indulgences: that the pope could remit only the penalties that he himself or canon law imposed, that therefore the promise of a general release was damnable, and that every true believer shared in the benefits of the

---

[1] Quoted in Roland Bainton, *Here I Stand: A Life of Martin Luther* (1955), pp. 49–50.

Church whether or not he or she obtained letters of pardon. Within a few weeks the story was all over the empire that a monk had challenged the sale of indulgences. The proceeds of Tetzel's mission began to drop off, and the Dominicans, rallying to the defense of their brother, launched an attack against this presumptuous Augustinian.[2]

The controversy soon drew attention from Rome. At first Pope Leo X regarded the affair as merely a monks' quarrel. But in time Luther's responses to the Dominicans' attacks began to deviate radically from Church doctrine, and by 1520 he had gone so far as to challenge the authority of the papacy itself in three pamphlets outlining his fundamental position.

In *An Address to the Christian Nobility of the German Nation,* Luther made a frankly patriotic appeal to his countrymen to reject the foreign pope's authority. The Church, he said, consisted of all Christians, including the laity; hence the nobles were as much its governors as the clergy, and they had the responsibility to remedy its defects. Indeed, Emperor Charles V had an obligation to call a council to end the abuses. *The Babylonian Captivity,* the most radical of the three works, attacked the system of the seven sacraments, the basis of the Church's power.[3] In *The Liberty of the Christian Man,* a less polemical work, Luther explained his doctrine of faith and justification, stressing that he did not reject good works but that only the faith of the individual believer could bring salvation from an all-powerful, just, and merciful God.

There could no longer be any doubt that Luther was embracing heresy, and in 1520 Leo X issued a bull excommunicating him. Luther publicly tossed the document into a bonfire, defending his action by calling the pope an Antichrist. In 1521 Charles V, theoretically the papacy's secular arm, responded by summoning the celebrated monk to offer his defense against the papal decree at a Diet of the Empire at Worms, a city on the Rhine. The journey across Germany was a triumphant procession for Luther, who had evoked widespread sympathy. Appearing before the magnificent assembly dressed in his monk's robe, he offered a striking contrast to the display of imperial and princely grandeur. First in German and then in Latin, he made the famous declaration that closed the last door behind him: "I cannot and will not recant anything, since it is unsafe and wrong to go against my conscience. Here I stand. I cannot do otherwise. God help me. Amen." On the following day the emperor gave his reply: "A single friar who goes counter to all Christianity for a thousand years must be wrong."

Charles added legality to the papal bull by issuing an imperial edict calling for Luther's arrest and the burning of his works. At this point, however, the independent power of the German princes and their resentment of foreign ecclesiastical interference came to the reformer's aid. Elector Frederick III of Saxony, who had never met Luther and who was never to break with the Catholic Church, nonetheless determined to protect the rebel who lived in his territory. He had him taken to the Wartburg castle, one of his strongholds, and here Luther remained for almost a year, safe from the hands of his enemies.

Lutheran Doctrine and Practice

While at the Wartburg Luther, together with his friend Philipp Melanchthon, developed the doctrines of Lutheranism and shaped them into the independent set of beliefs that formed the background for most of the subsequent variations of Protestant Christianity.

---

[2] The Dominicans, long-time rivals of the Augustinians, were the traditional upholders of orthodoxy and prominent in the Inquisition. Luther liked to refer to them by using an old joke that split their Latin name into *Domini canes,* "dogs of the Lord."

[3] The seven sacraments are baptism, confirmation, matrimony, the eucharist, ordination, penance, and extreme unction. Apart from some special exceptions, these ceremonies are considered by Catholics to require the attendance of a priest, because his presence (and hence the mediation of the Church) is believed to be essential to the proper administration of the sacrament.

It is important to realize, however, that some of these positions had roots in the nominalist theology taught at Luther's old monastery. Two of the teachings in particular left a lasting impression on Luther and later reformers. First, in opposition to Aquinas and the thirteenth-century attempts to unite reason and faith, the nominalists stressed the primacy of faith, the inadequacy of reason, and the unknowableness of God. Second, as a natural corollary to his mystery, they emphasized the overwhelming power and majesty of God. Both of these beliefs were to reappear frequently in the reformers' writings. Their importance was hardly surprising, for Nominalism was by far the most influential philosophical and theological movement of the fourteenth and fifteenth centuries.

This influence is apparent in the two fundamental assertions that lay at the heart of Luther's teachings. First, faith alone—not good works, nor the receiving of the sacraments—justifies the believer in the eyes of God and wins redemption. People themselves are helpless and unworthy sinners who can do nothing to cooperate in their own salvation; God bestows faith on those he chooses to save. Second, the Bible is the sole source of religious authority. It alone carries the word of God, and Christians must reject all other supposed channels of divine inspiration: tradition, commentaries, or the pronouncements of popes and councils.

These two doctrines had important implications. According to Luther all people are equally capable of understanding God's word as expressed in the Bible and can gain salvation without the help of intermediaries; they do not need a priest endowed with special powers or an interceding church. Luther thus saw God's chosen faithful as a "priesthood of all believers," a concept totally foreign to Catholics, who insisted on the distinction between clergy and laity. The distinction disappeared in Luther's doctrines, because all the faithful now shared the responsibilities formerly reserved for the priests.

True to his reliance on biblical authority, Luther denied the efficacy of five of the Catholics' sacraments. Only baptism and the eucharist are mentioned in Scripture, therefore they alone can be the means by which God distributes grace. Moreover the ceremony of the eucharist was now called communion (literally "sharing") to emphasize that all worshipers, including the officiating clergyman, were equal. Confession was abolished, which reduced the priest's importance yet again, and the last sign of his distinctiveness was removed by allowing him the right to marry.

The new teachings on the sacraments transformed the mass, the ceremony that surrounds the eucharist, or Lord's Supper. According to Catholic dogma, when the priest raises the host during the mass and recites the words *Hoc est corpus meum* ("This is my body"), the sacrifice of Jesus on the cross is reenacted. The wafer and the wine retain their outward appearance, their "accidents," but their substance is transformed into the body and blood of Christ—in other words, transubstantiation takes place.

Luther asserted that the wafer and wine retain their substance as well as their accidents and undergo *con*substantiation at the moment the priest says "This is my body." The real presence of Christ and the natural substance *coexist* within the wafer and wine. Nothing suddenly happens, no miraculous moment occurs; the believer is simply made aware of the real presence of God, who is everywhere at all times. Again, it is the faith of the individual, not the ceremony itself, that counts.

Luther reduced the mystery of the Lord's Supper further by allowing the congregation to partake of the wine, which was reserved for the priest in the Catholic ceremony—a change that also undermined the position of the priest. The liturgy in general was simplified—by abolishing processions, incense, votive candles, and the like—to make it more approachable for ordinary people, and services were conducted in the vernacular.

Given the priest's reduced stature, it was

vital to make God's word more readily accessible to all worshipers. To this end Luther began the gigantic task of translating the Bible. He was to complete the work in 1534, creating a text that is a milestone in the history of the German language. Families could now read Scripture on their own, and Protestantism in fact stimulated rising literacy among women as well as men. With his Bible finished, Luther's new faith was complete, for its doctrines had been laid out in the Augsburg Confession of 1530. Although he was to live until 1546, henceforth the progress of the revolution he had launched would rely on outside forces: its popular appeal and the actions of political leaders.

It is usually said that Lutheranism spread from above, advancing only when princes and rulers helped it along. Although this view has some basis, it does not adequately explain the growth of the movement. The response to Luther's stand was immediate and widespread. Even before the Diet of Worms, heretical preachers were drawing audiences in many parts of the Holy Roman Empire, and in 1521 there were waves of image smashing, reports of priests marrying, and efforts to reform and simplify the sacraments.

Soon there were services following Luther's teachings throughout the empire and neighboring countries. Broadsides and pamphlets fresh from the printing presses were disseminating the news of the reformer's message with breathtaking speed, stimulating an immediate response from thousands who saw the opportunity to renew their faith (see Map A-17 in the Cartographic Essay).

As long as his own doctrines were adhered to, Luther was naturally delighted to see his teachings spread. But from the start people were drawing inferences that he could not tolerate. Early in 1522, for example, three men from the nearby town of Zwickau appeared in Wittenberg claiming to be prophets who enjoyed direct communication with God. Their ideas were both radical and, in Luther's eyes, damnable. When he returned from the Wartburg, therefore, he preached eight sermons to expose their errors—a futile effort, because the reform movement was now too dispersed to control. Capitalizing on mass discontent, radical preachers incited disturbances in the name of faith, and it was only a matter of time before social as well as religious protest exploded.

Disorders in the Name of Religion

The first trouble came in the summer of 1522, when fighting broke out between a number of princes of the empire and a group of imperial knights. The knights occupied a precarious position in the social hierarchy. Usually their holdings consisted of little more than a single castle, but they owed official allegiance to no one but the emperor himself, and inevitably they came to resent the growing power of cities and territorial rulers.

Posing as the true representatives of the imperial system—that is, as loyal supporters of the emperor's authority in contrast to the cities and princes, who wanted to be independent—and pointing to Lutheranism as further justification, the knights launched an attack on one of the leading ecclesiastical rulers, the archbishop of Trier. The onslaught was crushed within a year, but it was now easy for the Lutherans' opponents to suggest that the new religious teachings undermined law and order.

The banner of the new faith rose over popular revolts as well. A peasant uprising began in Swabia in 1524 and quickly engulfed the southern and central parts of the empire. Citing Luther's inspiration, the peasants published a list of 12 demands the next year. However, 10 of their grievances concerned social, not religious, injustices: they wanted an end to serfdom, tithes, and the restrictions and burdens imposed by their overlords, including prohibitions on hunting and fishing, excessive rents and services, and unlawful punishments. In religious matters they demanded the right to choose their own pastors and insisted that only Scripture could determine the justice of their cause.

Luther sympathized with the last two claims, and at first he considered the peasants' demands reasonable. But when it became apparent that they were challenging all authority, he ignored the oppressions they had suffered and wrote a vicious pamphlet, *Against the Rapacious and Murdering Peasants,* calling on the nobility to cut them down without mercy so as to restore peace. A few months later the rebels were defeated in battle, and thereafter Luther threw his support unreservedly on the side of the princes and the established political and social order. He also grew more virulent in his attacks on Catholics and Jews.

This is not to say that such tactics were needed to maintain popular support for Lutheranism; the advance of the movement still depended on its appeal to the ordinary believer. Nonetheless, after the mid-1520s popular enthusiasm alone would not have sufficed; Lutheranism could not have stood up to Catholic opposition had it not been defended by powerful princes in the empire and kings in Scandinavia.

One of the reasons the new set of beliefs could attract a number of princes was its conservatism. Any person who accepted the doctrines of justification by faith alone and Scripture as the sole authority could be accepted as a Lutheran. Consequently the new congregations could retain much from the old religion: most of the liturgy, the sacred music, and, particularly important, a structured church that, though less hierarchic, was still organized so as to provide order and authority.

Some rulers were swept up by the emotions that moved their subjects, but others were moved by more material interests. Since ecclesiastical property was abolished when reform was introduced, princes could confiscate the rich and extensive holdings of monasteries and churches in their domains. Furthermore, they now had added reason for flaunting their independence from Emperor Charles V, an unwavering upholder of orthodoxy. It was risky to adopt this policy, for Charles could strip a prince of his title. On the other side, a prince loyal to Catholicism could blackmail the pope into offering him almost as many riches as he could win by confiscation. Nevertheless, the appeal of the new faith eventually tipped the balance for enough princes to create a formidable party capable of resisting Charles's power. Gathered together at the imperial Diet of Speyer in 1529, they signed a declaration "protesting" the Diet's decree that no further religious innovations were to be introduced in the empire, and thereafter they were known as Protestants. The following year, at another imperial Diet, the Lutheran princes announced their support of the Augsburg Confession, a statement of the doctrines of the reformed faith drawn up by Melanchthon and approved by Luther; it is still the official creed of the Lutheran Church. Charles V now realized that military force would be needed to crush the heresy, and in the face of this threat, the Lutherans formed a defensive league in 1531 at the small Saxon town of Schmalkalden. Throughout the 1530s this alliance consolidated Protestant gains, brought new princes into the cause, and in general amassed sufficient strength to deter Charles from immediate action.

The reform party became so solidly established that it negotiated with the pope—on equal terms—about the possibility of reconciliation, but the talks collapsed, and the chances for a reunification of Christendom evaporated. Yet not until 1546, the year of Luther's death, was open battle finally joined. Then, in a brief war, Charles won a crushing victory. But matters had advanced too far for the entire movement to collapse merely because of a single defeat on the battlefield. The new faith had gained acceptance among a large part of the

German people, particularly in the north and the east, farthest away from the center of imperial power. Some of the great cities of the south, such as Nuremberg, which had been centers of Humanism, had also come over to the Lutheran side. By the 1550s Lutheranism had captured perhaps half the population of the Empire.

The Catholic princes also played a part in assuring the survival of the new faith. Fearful of Charles V's new power, they refused to cooperate in his attempt to establish his authority throughout the empire, and he had to rely on Spanish troops, who further alienated him from his subjects. The Protestants rallied, and in 1555 the imperial Diet at Augsburg drew up a compromise settlement that exposed the decline of the emperor's power. Henceforth each ruler was allowed to determine the religion of his territory, Lutheran or Catholic, without outside interference. Religious uniformity was at an end, and the future of Lutheranism was secure.

The influence that this first Protestant Church was to exert on all of European life was immense. The equality of believers in the eyes of God was to inspire revolutionary changes in thought and society: it promoted antimonarchical constitutional theories, the acceptance of economic life as worthy, and the undermining of the hierarchic view of the universe. But the most immediate effect of the new faith was on religious life itself: before the century was out, the dissent led by Luther created a multitude of sects and a ferment of ideas without precedent in the history of Europe.

IV. THE GROWTH OF PROTESTANTISM

Hardly had Luther made his stand in 1517 when heresy in many different forms suddenly appeared. It was as if no more was needed than one opening shot before a volley of discontent broke out—a testimony to the deep and widespread striving for individual piety of the times. As new ideas proliferated, it seemed that the fragmentation of the reform movement might lead to chaotic disunity. But the work of John Calvin gave the Reformation the organization that its further advance required.

Zwingli

Less than two years after Luther posted his 95 theses, another reformer defied the Church in the Swiss city of Zurich: Ulrich Zwingli (1484–1531). A priest, a learned humanist, and a disciple of Erasmus's, Zwingli began to develop a system of doctrine between 1519 and 1522 that was quite similar to Luther's. Like the Saxon reformer, he based his ideas entirely on Scripture, excluding all nonbiblical authorities. He rejected the role of the Church as mediator between the believer and God, the celibacy of the clergy, and the belief in purgatory after death. However, Zwingli was less concerned than Luther to demonstrate man's inadequacy. Instead he sought chiefly to simplify religious belief and practice, freeing them from complexity and ceremony. To this end he asserted that none of the sacraments was a channel of grace; they were merely signs of grace already given. Baptism does not regenerate the recipient, and communion is no more than a memorial and thanksgiving for the grace bestowed by God, who is present only symbolically—not in actuality, as Luther believed.

Despite his obvious debt to Luther, Zwingli's divergences were significant. When he met Luther in 1529, hoping to iron out differences in order to present a united front, their inability to agree on a doctrine of communion kept them apart. Zwingli had founded a new form of Protestantism, more thoroughly dependent on the individual believer and more devoid of mystery and ritual than anything Luther could accept.

Taking a line of argument closer to Sir Thomas More's than Luther's, Zwingli held that man is innately good but needs constant correction to lead a godly life. Since he recognized no distinction between secular and religious authority, he established a tribunal of clergymen and magistrates to enforce discipline among the faithful. It supervised all moral questions, from compulsory church attendance to the public behavior of amorous couples. The court could excommunicate flagrant transgressors, and it maintained constant surveillance—through a network of informers—to keep the faithful on paths of godliness.

Because Zwingli considered it vital for discipline that the faithful should receive a continuing education, he also founded a theological school and authorized a new translation of the Bible. He revealed a similar intent when he established the practice of lengthy sermons at each service. Worship was stripped bare, as were the churches, and preaching began to assume tremendous importance as a means of instructing the believer and strengthening his or her faith. Zwingli also revived the ancient Christian practice of public confession—yet another reinforcement of discipline.

Zwingli's ideas spread rapidly in the Swiss Confederation, helped by the virtual autonomy each canton enjoyed. By 1529 six cantons had accepted Zwinglianism. As a result two camps formed in the country, and a war broke out in 1531 in which Zwingli himself was killed. Thereafter Switzerland remained split between Catholics and reformers. Zwinglianism as such never grew into a major religion, but it had a considerable effect on subsequent Protestantism, particularly Calvinism.

The Radicals

Both Luther and Zwingli wanted to retain church authority, and therefore insisted that infant baptism was the moment of entry into the church, even though this had no biblical sanc-

tion. Some radical reformers, however, extending Luther's logic, believed that as in biblical times baptism should be administered only to mature adults who could make a conscious choice for Christ, not to infants who were incapable of understanding that they were receiving grace. Soon they were contemptuously called Anabaptists ("rebaptizers") by their enemies. The term is often used to describe all radicals, though in fact it applied only to one conspicuous group.

Diversity was inevitable among these extremists, who refused to recognize church organization, rejected priests, and gave individual belief free rein, sometimes to the point of recognizing only personal communication with God and disregarding Scripture. Many groups of like-minded radicals formed sects—voluntary associations of adult believers (rarely more than 100 or so)—in an effort to achieve complete separation from the world and avoid compromising their ideals. They wanted to set an example for others by adhering fervently to the truth as they saw it, regardless of the consequences.

Some sects established little utopian communities, holding everything in common, including property and wives. Others, direct descendants of the mystics, disdained all worldly things and lived only for the supreme ecstasy of a trance in which they made direct contact with God himself. Many, believing in the imminent coming of the Messiah, prepared themselves for the Day of Judgment and warned of the approaching Armageddon.

Such divergence in the name of a personal search for God was intolerable to Luther, Zwingli, and later to Calvin, each of whom believed that his doctrines were the only means of salvation. Once the major branches of Protestantism were firmly entrenched, they became as deeply committed as the Catholic Church to the status quo and to their hierarchies and traditions. The established reformers thus regarded the radicals' refusal to conform as an unmistakable sign of damnation; Heinrich Bullinger, Zwingli's successor, put it bluntly when he wrote that individual interpretation of the Bible allowed each man to carve his own path to hell. Indeed, Lutherans, Zwinglians, and Calvinists alike saw it as their duty to persecute these people who refused salvation.

The assault began in the mid-1520s and soon spread through most of Europe. The imperial Diet in 1529 called for the death penalty against all Anabaptists, and most members of a group of more than 30 Anabaptist leaders who met to discuss their ideas in 1533 eventually met a violent death. Finally, in the northwest German city of Münster, a particularly fiery sect known as the Melchiorites provoked a reaction that signaled doom even for the more moderate dissenters.

The Melchiorites had managed to gain considerable influence over both the ordinary workers of Münster and the craft guilds. Early in 1534 they gained political control of the city and began to establish their "heavenly Jerusalem" on earth. They burned all books except the Bible, abolished private property, introduced polygamy, and in an atmosphere of abandon and chaos dug in to await the coming of the Messiah.

Here was a sufficient threat to society to force Protestants and Catholics into an alliance, and they captured the city and brutally massacred the Melchiorites. Thereafter the radicals were savagely persecuted throughout the empire. To survive, many fled first to Poland, then to the Low Countries and England, and eventually to the New World.

John Calvin and His Church

The one systematizing force among the varied Protestant movements in the 1530s was the creation of a second-generation reformer, John Calvin (1509–1564). Born in Noyon, a small town in northern France, he studied both law and the humanities at the University of Paris. In his early twenties he apparently had a blind-

ing spiritual experience that he later called his "sudden conversion," an event about which he would say almost nothing else. Yet from that moment on all his energy was devoted to religious activity.

In November 1533 Calvin was indicted for heresy, and after more than a year in hiding, he took refuge in the Swiss city of Basel. There in 1536 he published a little treatise, *Institutes of the Christian Religion,* outlining the principles of a new system of belief. He would revise and expand the *Institutes* for the remainder of his life, and it was to become the basis of the most vigorous branch of Protestantism in the sixteenth century.

Later in 1536 Calvin settled in Geneva, where, except for a brief period, he was to remain until his death. The citizens of this prosperous market center had just overthrown their prince, a bishop. In achieving their independence they had allied with other Swiss cities—notably Bern, a recent convert to Zwinglianism. Rebels who had just freed themselves with the help of heretics from an ecclesiastical overlord would obviously be receptive to new religious teachings.

Outwardly Calvinism seemed to have much in common with Lutheranism. Both emphasized people's sinfulness, lack of free will, and helplessness; both rejected good works as a means of salvation; both accepted only two sacraments, baptism and communion; both regarded all positions in life as equally worthy in the sight of God; both strongly upheld established political and social authority; and both leaned heavily on St. Paul and St. Augustine in their views of faith, people's weakness, and God's omnipotence. But the emphases in Calvinism were very different.

Luther's belief in justification by faith alone assumed that God can predestine a person to be saved but rejected the idea that damnation can also be preordained. Calvin's faith was much sterner, however, for it recognized no such distinction: if people are damned, they should praise God's justice because their sins

This sixteenth-century caricature of John Calvin ridicules the stern religious leader.
(Photo: Gripsholm Castle, Sweden)

certainly merit such a judgment; if people are saved, they should praise God's mercy because their salvation is not a result of their own good deeds. Either way the outcome is predestined, and nothing can be done to affect their fate. It is up to God alone to justify a person; he then perseveres in his mercy despite the person's sins; and finally he decides whether to receive the sinner into the small band of saints, or elect, whom he wishes to save. Calvin's was a grim but powerful answer to the age-old Christian question: How can sinful human beings gain salvation?

Calvin believed that the life one leads on earth is no indication of one's fate. He did suggest that someone who has been justified by God is likely to be upright and moral, but such behavior is not necessarily a sign of salvation. However, because we have to try to please God at all times, we should make every effort to lead the kind of life that will be worthy of one of the elect.

Calvin therefore developed a strict moral code for the true believer that banned frivolous activities like dancing in favor of constant self-examination, austerity, and sober study of the Bible. To help the faithful observe such regulation, he reestablished public confessions, as Zwingli had, and required daily preaching. He made services starkly simple: stripped of ornaments, they concentrated on uplifting sermons and the celebration of communion. His doctrine of communion occupied a middle ground between Luther's and Zwingli's. He rejected Zwingli's interpretation, saying instead that Christ's body and blood were actually and not just symbolically present. But unlike Luther, he held that they were present only in spirit and were consumed only spiritually, by faith.

In order to supervise the morals of the faithful more closely, Calvin gave his church a strict hierarchical structure. It was controlled by deacons and lay elders, who could function even in the hostile territories where many Calvinists found themselves. A body of lay elders called the consistory served as the chief ecclesiastical authority. They enforced discipline and had the power of excommunication, though they always worked together with the secular magistrates, who imposed the actual punishments for failures in religious duties.

Calvin's genius produced a cohesiveness and organization achieved by no other Protestant church. The *Institutes* spelled out every point of faith and practice in detail—an enormous advantage for his followers at a time when new religious doctrines were still fluid. A believer's duties and obligations were absolutely clear, as was his or her position in the very carefully organized hierarchy of the church. In France, for example, there was a cell in each town, a local synod (or council) in each area, a provincial synod in each province, and a national synod at the top of the pyramid.

Tight discipline controlled the entire system, with the result that Calvinists felt themselves to be setting an example that all the world would eventually have to follow. They were part of a very privileged group, not necessarily the elect but at least possessors of the true faith. Thus they could be authoritarians when in power, yet also holy rebels when a minority. After all, since they were freed of responsibility for their own salvation, they were acting self-lessly at all times. Like the children of Israel, they had a mission to live out God's word on earth, and this sense of destiny was to be one of Calvinism's greatest strengths.

Preachers from Geneva traveled through Europe to win adherents and organize the faith-ful wherever they could. In 1559 the city opened a university for the purpose of training them, because Calvin regarded education as an essential means of instilling faith. From Geneva flowed a stream of pamphlets and books, which strengthened the faith of all believers and made sure that none who wished to learn would lack the opportunity.

By 1564, when Calvin died, his church was well established: more than a million adherents in France, where they were called Huguenots; the Palatinate converted; Scotland won; and considerable groups of followers in England, the Low Countries, and Hungary. Despite its severity, Calvin's coherent and comprehensive body of doctrine proved to have wide and pow-erful appeal in an age of piety that yearned for clear answers.

V. THE CATHOLIC REVIVAL

Those with Protestant sympathies usually refer to the Catholic revival that started in the 1530s as the Counter Reformation, implying that ac-tion came only as a result of criticisms by Lu-ther and others. Catholic historians call it the Catholic Reformation, implying that the move-ment began within the Church and was not merely a reaction to Protestantism. There is justification for both views. Certainly the pa-pacy was aware of its loss of control over mil-lions of Christians, but a great deal of the effort to put the Catholic Church's house in order was a result of deep faith and a determination to purify the institution for its own sake.

Crisis and Reform in the Church

There could be no doubt that a revival within the Catholic Church was badly needed. The first half of the sixteenth century was the lowest point in its history, and by the 1560s few ob-servers could have expected it ever to recover. Much of Europe had been lost and even in areas still loyal the papacy was able to exercise little control. The French Church, for example, had a well-established tradition of autonomy, which since 1516 had given Francis I and his successors the right to make ecclesiastical ap-pointments. In Spain, too, the monarchy re-tained its independence and even had its own Inquisition. In the Holy Roman Empire, those states that had rejected Protestantism gave the pope no more than token allegiance.

Moreover there was still no comprehensive definition of Catholic doctrine on justification, salvation, and the sacraments. Worse yet, the Church's leadership was far from effective. Al-though one pope, Leo X, had attempted to correct notorious abuses such as simony in the early sixteenth century, Rome simply did not have the spiritual authority to make reform a vital force in the Catholic Church.

The situation changed with the pope elected in 1534: Paul III, a man not renowned for saint-liness himself, but a genius at making the right decisions for the Church. By the end of his reign, in 1549, the Catholic revival was well under way.

The heart of Paul's strategy was his deter-mination to assert papal responsibility throughout the Church. Realizing that uncertainties in Catholic doctrine could be resolved only by a reexamination of traditional theology, he decided within a few months of taking office to call a Church council for that purpose, despite the danger of rekindling the conciliar movement. It took 10 years to overcome resistance to the idea, but in the meantime Paul relentlessly attacked abuses throughout the Church, disregarding both vested interests and tradition. He aimed his campaign at all levels of the hierarchy, undeterred by powerful bishops and cardinals long used to a lax and corrupt regime. And he also founded a Roman Inquisition, part of a growing commitment to persecution as a means of destroying dissent.

Paul realized that in the long run the revival of Catholicism would depend on whether his successors maintained the effort. Within a few years therefore he made a series of appointments to the College of Cardinals, which elected the popes, that transformed it into possibly the most illustrious group that has ever held that honor at one time. Many were famous for their piety, others for their learning. They came from all over Europe, united by their devotion to the Church and their resolve to see it once again command the admiration and reverence it deserved. The result of this farsighted policy was to be a succession of popes through the early seventeenth century who would fully restore the atmosphere of spirituality and morality that had long been missing from the papacy.

The Council of Trent

The ecumenical, or general, council called by Paul finally assembled at Trent, a northern Italian city, in 1545, and met irregularly until the delegates managed to complete their work in 1563. The council's history was one of stormy battles between various national factions. The non-Italians pressed for decentralization; the Italians, closely tied to the papacy, advocated a consolidation of power. Because the Italians were a large majority of the delegates, time after time the authority of the pope's office was confirmed and reinforced. The threat of a revival of conciliarism never materialized.

In keeping with Paul's instructions, the Council of Trent gave most of its time to the basic issue of doctrine, devoting little attention to the problem of reform. Almost all its decisions drew on the interpretations put forward by Thomas Aquinas, who now became the central theologian of the Catholic Church. The one major subject left unsettled was a definition of the extent of papal authority on matters of faith and morals.[4]

Trent's most important decrees affirmed the truth of precisely those teachings the Protestants had rejected. Catholicism from then on would be committed primarily to the outward, sacramental heritage of Christianity. In this view the Bible is not the exclusive authority—tradition also holds a place in establishing the true faith. Human will is free; good works as well as faith are means of salvation; all seven sacraments are channels of grace; and Christ's sacrifice is reenacted in every mass. The Council of Trent endorsed the special position of the priest and insisted that God be worshiped with appropriately elaborate ceremonies and rites.

These were the principal decisions at Trent, but hundreds of minor matters also had to be settled. Thus for the first time the priest's presence was declared to be essential at the sacrament of marriage, a further reinforcement of his importance. The Vulgate, the Latin translation of the Bible prepared chiefly by St. Jerome, was decreed to be a holy text, which rebutted humanists and other scholars who had found mistranslations of the Greek and Hebrew versions. And in direct contrast to the Protestants, gorgeous ritual was heavily stressed, which encouraged artists to beautify church buildings and ceremonies.

---

[4] Not until 1870, at the council known as Vatican I, was this matter settled by the assertion of the dogma of papal infallibility.

What the council was doing was adjusting the Church to the world. Many ordinary people, troubled by the stern self-denial and predestination taught by most Protestant churches and sects, were delighted to embrace the traditional faith, now infused with new vigor, for the council had not hesitated to deal with morality and discipline as thoroughly as with belief. In fact, it had given its approval to the Inquisition and the "Index of Forbidden Books," which informed all Catholics of works with heretical content that they were not allowed to read.[5]

The Aftermath of Trent

The new atmosphere of spiritual dedication swept through the Catholic Church, inspiring thinkers and artists throughout Europe to lend their talents to the cause. In many ways Baroque art was to be the genre of the Counter Reformation: painters, architects, and musicians caught up by the new moral fervor in Catholicism expressed their faith in brilliant and dramatic portrayals of religious subjects and in churches that were designed to dazzle the observer in a way that most Protestants could not allow.

This outpouring was of course far more than a reflection of the decisions of a few hundred prelates assembled in a council. It was also one of many indicators of the new vigor of Catholicism. Spain experienced a great flowering of mysticism, whose most famous representative was St. Teresa, one of the many women whom the Church encouraged to express their piety, found new religious orders, and set an example of devoted spirituality. In France the new generation of Church leaders who appeared in the late sixteenth century were

---

[5] The Index became a major weapon, used particularly effectively against borderline cases such as Erasmus. Later distinguished entries in the list included Michel de Montaigne, René Descartes, and Edward Gibbon. In the twentieth century, though, considerable relaxation has been allowed.

distinguished for their austerity, learning, and observance of their duties. The inheritors of the traditional Scholastic philosophy multiplied, and in the late sixteenth and early seventeenth centuries they were to become influential throughout Europe.

The most conspicuous examples of this new energy, however, were the popes themselves. Paul III's successors used their personal authority and pontifical resources not to adorn their palaces but to continue the enormous cleansing operation within the Church and to lead the counterattack against Protestantism. If a king or prince refused to help, they would try to persuade one of his leading subjects to organize the struggle (for example, the Guise family in France or the dukes of Bavaria in the empire). Their diplomats and agents were everywhere, ceaselessly urging the faithful to stamp out Protestantism wherever it was found. And the pontiffs insisted on strict morality in order to set the best possible example: one pope even ordered clothes painted on the nudes in Michelangelo's *Day of Judgment* in the Sistine Chapel.

With the leaders of the Church thus bent on reform, the restoration of the faith and the reconquest of lost souls could proceed with maximum effect. And they had at their disposal an order established by Ignatius Loyola in 1540 specifically for these purposes: the Society of Jesus.

Ignatius Loyola: The Making of a Reformer

The third of the great religious innovators of the sixteenth century, after Luther and Calvin, was Ignatius Loyola (1491–1556), but unlike his predecessors he sought to reform the Catholic Church from within.

Loyola was the son of a Basque nobleman, raised in the chivalric and fiercely religious atmosphere of Spain, and he was often at the court of Ferdinand of Aragon. In his teens he entered the army, but when he was 30 a leg wound ended his career. While convalescing he was deeply impressed by a number of popular lives of the saints he read, and soon his religious interests began to take shape in chivalric and military terms. He visualized Mary as his lady, the inspiration of a Christian quest in which the forces of God and the devil fought in mighty battle. This was a faith seen from the perspective of the knight, and though the direct parallel lessened as his thought developed, it left an unmistakable stamp on all his future work.

In 1522 Loyola gave up his knightly garb and swore to become a pilgrim. He retired to a monastery for 10 months to absolve himself of the guilt of a sinful life and to prepare spiritually for a journey to the Holy Land. At the monastery he had a momentous experience that, like Luther's and Calvin's, dominated the rest of his life. According to tradition it was a vision lasting eight days, during which he first saw in detail the outline of a book, the *Spiritual Exercises,* and a new religious order, the Society of Jesus.

The first version of the *Spiritual Exercises* certainly dated from this period, but like Calvin's *Institutes,* it was to be revised thoroughly many times. The book deals not with doctrines or theology but with the discipline and training necessary for a God-fearing life. Believers must undertake four weeks of contemplation and self-examination, culminating in a feeling of union with God in which they surrender their minds and wills to Christ. If successful, they are then ready to submit completely to the call of God and the Church and to pursue the commands they receive without question.

The manual was the heart of the organization of the Society of Jesus, and it gave those who followed its precepts a dedication and determination that made them seem like the Church's answer to the Calvinists. But while the end might be similar to Luther's and Calvin's—the personal attainment of grace—the

method, the emphasis on individual effort and concentration, could not have been more different. For the *Spiritual Exercises* prepared the believer's inward condition for grace through a tremendous act of will, and its severity relied on the belief that the will is free and that good works are efficacious.

During the 16 years after he left the monastery Ignatius led a life of poverty and study. Though lame, he traveled to Jerusalem and back barefoot in 1523–1524, and two years later he found his way to the University of Alcalá,

Loyola quickly became one of the major heroes of the Catholic revival. Within less than 60 years of his death (1556), he was to become a saint of the Church. This engraving, made in 1621, shows him as the saint he was in fact to be proclaimed the following year. St. Teresa also became a saint in 1622, but that was only *40 years after her death.*
(Photo: New York Public Library/Picture Collection)

where he attracted his first disciples, three fellow students. Suspected by the Inquisition, the little band walked to Paris, where they were joined by six more disciples. Ignatius now decided to return to the Holy Land, but the companions found themselves unable to travel beyond Venice because of war. Instead they preached in the streets, visited the poor and the sick, urged all who would listen to rededicate themselves to piety and faith, and in 1537 achieved ordination as priests. Their activities were beginning to take definite shape, and so they decided to seek the pope's blessing for their work. They saw Paul III in 1538, and two years later, despite opposition and suspicion at the Vatican, the pope gave his approval to a plan Ignatius had drawn up for a new religious order that would owe allegiance only to the papacy.

The Jesuits

The Society, or Company, of Jesus had four principal functions: preaching, hearing confessions, teaching, and founding and maintaining missions. The first two were the Jesuits' means of strengthening the beliefs of individual Catholics or converting heretics. The third became one of their most effective weapons. Loyola, much influenced by the Christian humanists he had encountered, was convinced of the tremendous power of education. The Jesuits therefore set about organizing the best schools in Europe, an endeavor in which they succeeded so well that some Protestants sent their children to the Society's schools despite the certainty that the pupils would become committed Catholics. The instructors followed humanist principles and taught the latest ideas, including for a while the most recent advances in science. The Jesuits' final activity, missionary work, brought them their most spectacular successes among both non-Christians and Protestants.

A number of qualities combined to make the Jesuits extraordinarily effective in winning

CHRONOLOGY OF THE REFORMATION AND COUNTER REFORMATION

1517: Luther's protest begins.
1521: Diet of Worms: Luther condemned by Emperor Charles V.
1524–1525: Peasants' Revolt in Germany.
Zurich adopts Zwingli's Reformation.
1531: Protestant League of Schmalkalden formed in Germany.
Death of Zwingli.
Henry VIII proclaims himself head of the Church of England.
1534: Paul III becomes pope.
Anabaptists take over the city of Münster in Germany.
1536: Calvin comes to Geneva; first edition of his *Institutes*.
1540: Pope Paul III approves the Jesuit Order.
1541: Calvin settles in Geneva permanently.
1545: Council of Trent begins.
1546: Death of Luther.
1553–1558: Mary restores Catholicism in England.
1556: Death of Loyola.
1559: First Index of Forbidden Books published.
Elizabeth reestablishes Anglican Church.
Execution of Protestants after Inquisition trials in Spain.
1564: Publication of the Decrees of the Council of Trent.
Death of Calvin.

converts and turning Catholics into militant activists. First, they had a remarkable knowledge of Scripture and traditional teachings and were usually more than a match for any serious opponent. In addition they were carefully selected and received a superb training that fashioned them into brilliant preachers and excellent educators. Their discipline, determination, and awareness of the contemporary world allowed them to make clever use of their fearsome reputation. They had no equal in the forcefulness with which they advanced the aims of the Council of Trent and the papacy.

It is not inappropriate to regard the Jesuits as the striking arm of the Counter Reformation; indeed, their organization was to some extent modeled on the medieval military orders. A Jesuit at a royal court was often the chief in-

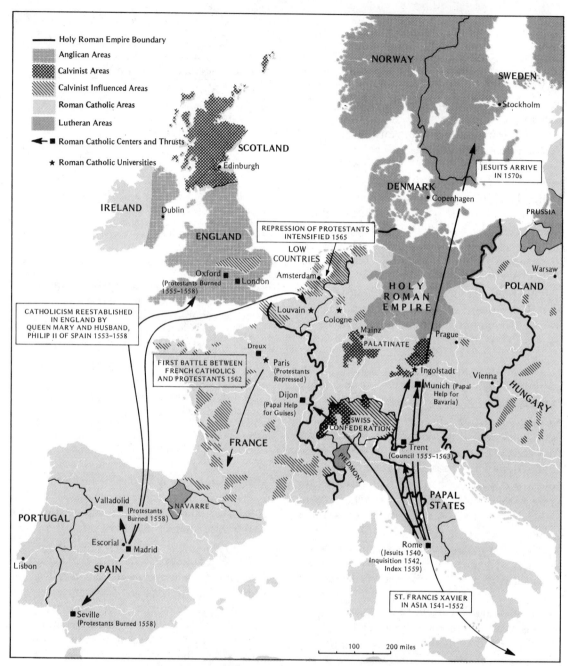

MAP 14.1. RELIGIOUS TENSIONS 1560

This map indicates not only the territories adhering to the major religions in 1560 but also the sources of religious conflict during the succeeding decades. From Rome came the Jesuits and also papal help for the Bavarians in the empire and the Guise family in France; from Spain a broad onslaught against Protestantism; and in England and France the struggles were both domestic and international.

Text within the map:

Holy Roman Empire Boundary
Anglican Areas
Calvinist Areas
Calvinist Influenced Areas
Roman Catholic Areas
Lutheran Areas
◄ ■ Roman Catholic Centers and Thrusts
★ Roman Catholic Universities

NORWAY
SWEDEN
• Stockholm
DENMARK
• Copenhagen
PRUSSIA
JESUITS ARRIVE IN 1570s
SCOTLAND
• Edinburgh
IRELAND
Dublin •
ENGLAND
REPRESSION OF PROTESTANTS INTENSIFIED 1565
LOW COUNTRIES
Amsterdam •
WARSAW
POLAND
Oxford ■ (Protestants Burned 1555–1558)
■ London
Louvain ★
Cologne ★
HOLY ROMAN EMPIRE
Mainz •
PALATINATE
Prague •
CATHOLICISM REESTABLISHED IN ENGLAND BY QUEEN MARY AND HUSBAND, PHILIP II OF SPAIN 1553–1558
Dreux ★
Paris ★ (Protestants Repressed)
Ingolstadt ★
Vienna •
HUNGARY
FIRST BATTLE BETWEEN FRENCH CATHOLICS AND PROTESTANTS 1562
Munich ■ (Papal Help for Bavaria)
Dijon ■ (Papal Help for Guises)
FRANCE
SWISS CONFEDERATION
Trent ■ (Council 1555–1563)
PIEDMONT
PAPAL STATES
Valladolid ■ (Protestants Burned 1558)
NAVARRE
PORTUGAL
Escorial • ■ Madrid
SPAIN
Rome ■ (Jesuits 1540, Inquisition 1542, Index 1559)
Lisbon •
ST. FRANCIS XAVIER IN ASIA 1541–1552
■ Seville (Protestants Burned 1558)

100   200 miles

spiration for a ruler's militant support of the faith, and in many areas the Society was the main conqueror of heresy. Yet it must be noted that in this age of cruel persecution, the Jesuits always opposed execution for heresy; they far preferred to win a convert than to kill a heretic. Their presence was soon felt all over the world—as early as the 1540s, one of Loyola's first disciples, Francis Xavier, was conducting a mission to Japan. (See Map 14.1 for the areas where the Jesuits and other Catholic forces concentrated their efforts.) Despite many enmities (some of them richly deserved), their unswerving devotion to Catholicism was a major reason for the revival of the Roman Church.

One of the saddest spectacles in history is the diversion of the wish for a purer, simpler religion, freed from abuses and material concerns, into fanaticism and bloodletting in the late sixteenth century. What had started as a desire to improve religious practice and belief within existing institutions soon became, in Luther's hands, a determination to start anew. Inevitably the ideas of those who broke with Rome became increasingly radical, and when they received the organization provided by Calvin, they had extraordinary success in winning new adherents.

Within the Catholic Church, meanwhile, a reform movement begun by Pope Paul III in the 1530s raised that institution's moral stature and gave it the organization and aggressive force to meet its opponents on equal terms. Spearheaded by the Jesuits, Catholic reformers made many gains and ensured that Protestantism would not engulf the Continent.

But it was not enough for either side to remedy religious deficiencies and abuses. Each had to launch a fanatical and unrelenting attack on the enemy religion. In this atmosphere of hatred and violence, voices of moderation such as Erasmus's were ignored, and pleas for toleration went unheard for there was a rare ferocity to the conflicts that now racked European civilization.

As the religious upheavals multiplied, the sources of hostility broadened, and revolutionary thought and action erupted on many other levels of society. Subjects challenged their governments; writers and artists expressed deep discontents. Lacerated by vicious warfare, Europe entered one of its most tormented centuries.

RECOMMENDED READING

Sources

*Calvin, John. *On God and Political Duty*. J. T. McNeill (ed.). 1950.

*Erasmus, Desiderius. *Essential Works of Erasmus*. W. T. H. Jackson (ed.). 1965.

Loyola, Ignatius. *The Spiritual Exercises of St. Ignatius*. R. W. Gleason (ed.). 1964.

*Luther, Martin. *Martin Luther: Selections from His Writings*. John Dillenberger (ed.). 1961.

Studies

*Bainton, Roland H. *Here I Stand: A Life of Martin Luther*. 1955. The standard biography in English, with many quotations from Luther's writings.

*Cohn, Norman. *The Pursuit of the Millennium: Revolutionary Messianism in Medieval and Reformation Europe and Its Bearing on Modern Totalitarian Movements*. 1961. A study of radical and extreme religious movements which indicates the kind of popular piety that existed in Europe during the medieval and Reformation periods.

*Davis, Natalie Zemon. *Society and Culture in Early Modern France*. 1975. A collection of essays about popular beliefs and attitudes, particularly on religious matters, during the sixteenth century.

*Dickens, A. G. *The Counter Reformation*. 1969. A clear and thorough introduction to the subject, handsomely illustrated.

*Huizinga, Johan. *Erasmus and the Age of Reformation*. 1957. A warm and sympathetic biography, beautifully written.

Koenigsberger, H. G., and G. L. Mosse. *Europe in the Sixteenth Century*. 1968. The best overall introduction to the period—compact, well written, and equipped with useful bibliographical notes.

Moeller, Bernd. *Imperial Cities and the Reformation*. H. C. E. Midelfort and M. U. Edwards (trs.). 1972. Three stimulating essays about the special role of cities in establishing the Reformation in Germany.

Scribner, Bob, and Benecke, Gerhard (eds.). *The German Peasant War of 1525—New Viewpoints*. 1979. A stimulating set of essays about the social upheaval that accompanied the Reformation.

*Weber, Max. *The Protestant Ethic and the Spirit of Capitalism*. Talcott Parsons (tr.). 1958. Originally published in 1904 and 1905, this study of the way in which the Reformation helped create the modern world has become a classic and has influenced much of the historical thinking about the Reformation.

* Available in paperback.

THE IMAGE
OF HUMANITY

In Renaissance Art

It has been said of the Renaissance that there are as many ways of defining it as there are branches of historic study and that the one point of agreement among experts is that the new era began when people realized they were no longer living in the Middle Ages. The Renaissance, in other words, was the first period in history to be aware of its own existence. Not only did it coin a name for itself—Renaissance means "rebirth"—but also for its predecessor, the "thousand years of darkness," which it thought followed upon the fall of ancient civilization. Both names have stuck, although today we no longer regard the Middle Ages as dark and are less sure what the Renaissance was a rebirth of.

To those who first thought in these terms—a tiny minority even among the educated in fourteenth-century Italy—"rebirth" meant the revival of the classics, the language and literature of ancient Greece and Rome; in the course of the next hundred years, however, the concept came to embrace the entire range of cultural life, including the visual arts. From this the Italian humanists distilled a new philosophy of man designed to reconcile what seemed to them two equal sources of authority: Christian revelation and the wisdom of the ancients. Its basis is still the biblical account of the creation by the Lord "in our image and likeness," but the emphasis is now on freedom of will rather than dependence on God. Thus Gianozzo Manetti, in his treatise "On the Dignity and Excellence of Man," proclaims him not only the most beautiful and perfect of all creatures but a second creator: "After that first, new and rude creation of the world [by God], everything seems to have been discovered, constructed and completed by us . . . all homes, all towns, all cities, finally all buildings in the world which certainly are so many and of such a nature that they ought rather to be regarded as the works of angels than of men. . . . Ours are the paintings, ours the sculptures, ours the arts, ours the sciences. . . ." Is it any wonder, Manetti asks, that "the first inventors of the various arts were worshiped as gods by the early peoples"?[1] In Pico della Mirandola's oration on the same theme, the Lord speaks to the newly created Adam as follows: "The nature of all other beings is limited . . . within the bounds of laws prescribed by Us. You, constrained by no limits, in accordance with your own free will . . . shall ordain for yourself the limits of your nature. . . . We made you neither of heaven nor of earth, neither mortal nor immortal, so that with freedom of choice . . . you may fashion yourself in whatever shape you prefer. You shall have the power to degenerate into the lower forms of life, which are brutish. You shall have the power . . . to be reborn into the higher forms, which are divine."[2] The humanists, then, saw man as endowed by God with gifts that make him the master of his own fate.

If Pico's exalted vision of human potential seems to anticipate Michelangelo (see Plate 24), Manetti's celebration of human beings as the active and self-confident shapers of their world, with special pride in his achievements in the

visual arts, suggests the new poise of Donatello (see Plate 17) and the clarity
and order of Masaccio (see Plate 19). Scientific perspective, the means by
which Masaccio achieved these qualities, was far more than a technical accomplishment; it permitted the painter, for the first time in the history of art, to
define, exactly and measurably, the individual's relation to spatial setting
within the picture and at the same time to treat the fictitious painted space as
an extension of the real space of our sense experience. This new structuring of
space also demanded a more precise knowledge of the structure of the human
body. The skeleton in Masaccio's mural, unlike those in earlier art, is anatomi-
cally correct, and in the figure of Christ we sense the same interest in the body
as an organic entity. Compared to older, less consistent methods of creating
pictorial space, such as that used by Jan van Eyck (see Plate 18), scientific
perspective is something of a paradox: subjective and impersonal at the same
time. Its system, based on a central vanishing point that corresponds to the
eye of a single beholder, expresses the individualism of the new era. It was
this individualism that made portraiture, neglected since the fall of the Roman
Empire, once more a major concern of painters and sculptors (see the kneeling
donors in Plate 19 as well as Plates 20 and 28–30). On the other hand, the
effectiveness of scientific perspective depends on mathematical rules that
leave little scope for personal interpretation. Perspective boasts of setting a
standard of objective truth and thus allies the artist with the scientist. To
Leonardo da Vinci, who was both, "seeing" was equivalent to "knowing." The
ultimate result of this alliance was to be the invention of photography in the
early nineteenth century, which to the painters of the time seemed at first a
threat, then a liberation that permitted them to abandon the Renaissance goal
of truth to nature.

"Truth to nature," however, could be interpreted in radically different ways
even by Renaissance artists. Comparing the paintings by Bellini and Botticelli
(Plates 22 and 23), we realize how little the two pictures have in common,
although both were painted in the 1480s. Bellini's view of nature, despite its
abundance of detail, is as firmly structured as the architecture in Masaccio's
"Trinity," and the individual's place in it is defined with equal precision. What
we see here is the familiar nature of everyday experience transfigured by the
saint's ecstasy. Botticelli's picture, in contrast, looks as flat and patterned as a
playing card. It bears out Leonardo's remark that Botticelli "paints very dull
landscapes." What concerns Botticelli is the individual's relation not to nature
but to an ideal of formal perfection embodied in the art of antiquity and reflecting man's desire, in Pico's words, "to be reborn into the higher forms,
which are divine." His goal is nature perfected rather than nature observed;
and since, according to Pico's God, such perfectibility is vouchsafed only to
man, the rest of the natural world holds little interest. This unconcern with
objective truth is still more evident in Parmigianino (see Plate 26) and in

Bronzino (see Plate 28). The problem of reconciling ideal and real nature haunted artists and critics for centuries to come.

The conflict of ideal and reality in art, like the humanists' new view of mankind, originated in Italy. But whereas Humanism found a ready response north of the Alps and profoundly influenced the religious Reformation, Italian Renaissance art did not become a model for the rest of Europe until the sixteenth century, and even then its authority was far from absolute. Jan van Eyck, Masaccio's contemporary, was an equally great innovator in his way, yet he perceived the visible world in terms of light and color rather than of its underlying structure (compare Plates 18 and 19). He founded a tradition so powerful that Altdorfer (see Plate 31), painting a century later, still owes more to Jan van Eyck than to any Italian source, despite the classical subject of the picture. Other Northerners, such as the remarkable Dutch painter Hieronymus Bosch (see Plate 21), mirror the conflict between the medieval and Renaissance concepts of man in their pessimistic visions of a sinful humanity remote from any hope of redemption. When, soon after 1500, Northern artists began to visit Italy in order to study classical antiquity and the "classic" masters of their own day, the new image of man they came to know tended to remain an alien element in their own work, like quotations in an unfamiliar language. Pieter Bruegel, the greatest Northern painter of the second half of the century, acknowledges the humanist vision in an oddly backhanded way; his "Land of Cockaigne" (Plate 32) is a sermon on the dignity of man, but in reverse, by showing the fate of those who fail to heed it. It was not until 1600 that the heritage of Italian Renaissance art was fully shared by the rest of Europe.

---

[1] Charles Trinkaus, *In Our Image and Likeness: Humanity and Divinity in Italian Humanist Thought* (1970), vol. I, p. 247.

[2] *The Renaissance Philosophy of Man,* edited by Ernst Cassirer et al. (1948), p. 225.

Among the founding fathers of Renaissance art, it was Donatello who first formed the new image of man demanded by the new era. His *Annunciation* in Plate 17 shows more strikingly than any of his other works why the Renaissance proclaimed itself the rebirth of antiquity, for nowhere else does he approach the classic Greek ideal of human beauty as closely as he does here. The two figures are carved in high relief rather than in the round, but they move with such complete ease and freedom that they seem in no way constrained by their architectural setting; and their response to each other—the reverential greeting of the angel, the Virgin's gentle gesture of surprise—is equally well-balanced and natural. For the first time in a thousand years, body and spirit seem to be in complete harmony. The contrast with the Romanesque *Annunciation* in Plate 12, done three centuries earlier, could hardly be more striking.

How Donatello achieved this is little short of miraculous. Although he was an ardent admirer of ancient sculpture, he knew it only from late and inferior examples. Yet he perceived in them, with the clairvoyance of genius, the underlying ideal of classical perfection and recreated it in his own work. The framework, too, bespeaks the rebirth of antiquity: its forms derive from the ornamental vocabulary of ancient Greece and Rome, although Donatello's way of combining them is uniquely his own.

Plate 17. Donatello, THE ANNUNCIATION
ca. 1430–1435, limestone,
height of niche 7'2"
Santa Croce, Florence

The revolutionary change that took place in northern European painting about 1420 becomes strikingly evident if we compare Jan van Eyck's panel in Plate 18 with the *April* miniature in Plate 16. Suddenly the bright fairytale world of the International Gothic style has given way to an art that brings us face to face with visible reality in all its richness and depth, as if the picture surface had been turned into a window. The difference between the two is technical as well as artistic: the miniature is painted in tempera (pigments mixed with diluted egg yolk) and the panel is an early instance of the use of oils. Tempera is thin, opaque, and quick-drying; oil viscous and slow-drying. Unlike tempera, oil permits the smooth blending of tones on the picture surface, and its body may vary from translucent colored glazes to thick layers of creamy, saturated paint. Jan van Eyck knew how to exploit the greater flexibility of the new medium to full effect. Yet the panel contains a contradiction: the lovely Virgin is far too big for the architecture. Only if we recognize this mistake and its hidden purpose can we understand the subtlety of Jan van Eyck's art. Realism to him did not limit the symbolic meaning of his pictures, but rather it actually enhanced it. In this panel, the church building stands for the Church and so does the

Plate 18. Jan van Eyck
THE VIRGIN AND CHILD IN THE CHURCH
ca. 1425—1430, oil on wood, height 12"
Staatliche Museen Preussischer
Kulturbesitz, Gemäldegalerie, Berlin (West)

Virgin; therefore, the interior is just tall enough to hold her. For final proof we need only look at the altar in the background, attended not by priests but by angels.

In Masaccio's mural in Plate 19, the surface is also treated as a window. Here, however, everything is lifesize, and the painted space seems a direct continuation of the actual space surrounding the beholder. This has been achieved by means of scientific perspective, one of the great discoveries of the Italian Early Renaissance, which is a system of projecting three-dimensional shapes onto a flat surface, analogous to the way the camera lens projects them onto a piece of film. Masaccio's entire composition embodies his faith in rational order and clarity. The figures are as massive as Giotto's and as fully articulated and self-sufficient as Donatello's; the architecture resembles the classically inspired framework of Donatello's *Annunciation* rather than the Gothic interior of Jan van Eyck's panel. Like the latter, Masaccio's mural was done for a private patron; he and his wife are kneeling in prayer just outside the sacred precinct. The step on which they kneel coincides with the beholder's eye level. It is also the dividing line between time and eternity: above it, salvation; below it, a skeleton to remind us of the brevity of life on earth.

Plate 19. Masaccio
THE HOLY TRINITY WITH
THE VIRGIN AND ST. JOHN
*ca. 1425, wall painting,
height 21'10"
Santa Maria Novella, Florence*

The exploration of visible reality in fifteenth-century painting has its counterpart in the daring sea voyages beyond the limits of the known world that culminated in the discovery of America. The Portuguese led the way in these ventures. It was they who explored the west coast of Africa and opened the sea route to India; they who first circumnavigated the globe. What was the impulse behind their journeys? A quest for riches and power, surely, but also a quest for knowledge, and, equally important, a sense of religious duty, as attested by Nuño Gonçalves' panel in Plate 20. Here St. Vincent displays to the reverently kneeling king a Gospel text concerning the Apostles' mission among the infidels, and in so doing appoints him their spiritual heir. The older man with hands folded in prayer is the king's uncle, Prince Henry the Navigator, the earliest royal sponsor of voyages of discovery. Gonçalves must have learned his art in close contact with the great Flemish realists, such as Jan van Eyck. Although a less subtle painter than Van Eyck, he was a portraitist of exceptional power who has left us an unforgettable record of the rulers of Portugal.

Plate 20. Nuño Gonçalves
SAINT VINCENT COMMANDING KING
AFFONSO V OF PORTUGAL TO SPREAD
THE CHRISTIAN FAITH IN AFRICA
1471—1481, oil on panel,
height 6'9½"
National Museum of Ancient Art, Lisbon

The Dutchman Hieronymus Bosch was a pioneer of another sort, venturing farther into the unexplored regions of man's imagination than any artist before him. His vision of Hell in Plate 21 is a nightmare world of burning cities and icy rivers where sinners are punished by being surfeited with the vices they had enjoyed on earth. Thus, in the center of our panel, a huge stomach houses a devilish inn; below it, musical instruments are engines of torture (secular music was "the food of love" and hence a sinful pleasure); and in the lower right-hand corner, a sow embraces a man who is vainly trying to escape. The interpretation of Bosch's pictures has proved extremely difficult, but enough is known about them to assure us that he intended every detail to have a precise didactic meaning, however strange his imagery may seem today. He was haunted—indeed mesmerized—by the power of evil to corrupt mankind; its counterweight, the promise of redemption, is barely hinted at in his work. This state of mind reflects the conflict between the other-worldly goals of traditional Christianity and an ever greater openness to the attractions of life on earth, a crisis of conscience that was to erupt soon in the Reformation.

Plate 21. Hieronymus Bosch
HELL WING (*from the triptych,*
THE GARDEN OF EARTHLY DELIGHTS)
ca. 1500, oil on wood panel, height 7'2½"
Prado Museum, Madrid

The work of the great Flemish realists was known and admired in fifteenth-century Italy. Although it had little immediate effect in Florence, birthplace of the Early Renaissance, it left a lasting imprint on Venice. Before long, the use of oils and an emphasis on light and color became hallmarks of Venetian Renaissance painting. Venetian masters, such as Giovanni Bellini, also raised landscape to a new level of importance. In Plate 22,

St. Francis is so small compared to the setting that he seems almost incidental, yet his mystic rapture before the beauty of nature sets our own response to the glorious view that is spread out before us. He has left his wooden clogs behind and stands barefoot, thus indicating that the ground is hallowed by the presence of the Lord. The soft, glowing colors, the warm late-afternoon sunlight, the tender regard for every detail, recall the art of Jan van Eyck. Unlike the Northerners, however, Giovanni Bellini knows how to define the beholder's relationship to the space within the picture; the rock formations of the foreground are clear and firm, like architecture rendered by the rules of scientific perspective.

In Florence, meanwhile, the revival of antiquity kindled a new interest in the pagan deities, who now began to appear once more in their original form. The Venus in Botticelli's famous painting in Plate 23 is modeled on a classical statue of the goddess. Could such a subject be justified in a Christian civilization? How did artist and patron escape the charge of being neo-pagans? Part of the answer to these questions is provided by the Neo-Platonic philosophers of the time. They believed that the life of the universe, including that of mankind, was linked to God by a spiritual circuit continuously ascending and descending so that all revelation, whether from the Bible, Plato, or classical myths, was one. Thus they could invoke the celestial Venus interchangeably with the Virgin Mary as a source of divine love. Once we understand this quasi-religious meaning of Botticelli's picture, we may find it less strange that the figures look so ethereal. They are embodiments of poetic and philosophical ideas rather than creatures of flesh and blood—exquisitely beautiful but accessible only to a select and highly educated circle of initiates.

Plate 23. Sandro Botticelli
THE BIRTH OF VENUS
ca. 1480, oil on canvas, height 69"
Uffizi Gallery, Florence

Plate 24.
Michelangelo, THE CREATION OF ADAM *(detail of the Sistine Ceiling), 1508–1512, wall painting*
Sistine Chapel, Vatican

The early sixteenth century— the High Renaissance—has been called the age of genius, for it was the time that formed the concept of artistic genius. Until then, even the greatest of artists were mere makers; now they were creators, set apart from ordinary people by divine inspiration. No less exalted term would fit men such as Leonardo da Vinci, who was both artist and scientist yet full of mystery like a magician, or Michelangelo, who was driven by a truly superhuman ambition. Their works immediately became classics, equal in authority to the most renowned works of the an-

cients, and their spell persists even today. This is certainly true of Michelangelo's masterpiece, the Sistine Ceiling, which had so vast an impact that it changed the course of Western art for several centuries to come. In this huge expanse of vaulted surface with its hundreds of figures, Michelangelo proclaimed a new ideal image of men and women: heroic, nude, and beautiful as the gods and goddesses of Greece but, unlike them, troubled by inner conflicts and unfulfilled yearnings. Thus Adam, in Plate 24, reaches out for contact with the Divine (characteristically, Michelangelo does not

Plate 25.
Titian, BACCHANAL, *ca. 1518, oil on canvas, height 69"*
Prado Museum, Madrid

show the physical making of Adam's body); at the same time, however, his glance meets that of Eve, who nestles yet unborn in the shelter of the Lord's left arm. No other artist ever achieved so dramatic a juxtaposition of Man and God.

Some of the figures in Titian's *Bacchanal* in Plate 25 have the muscular build, the animation, the complex poses of Michelangelo's (the influence of the Sistine Ceiling had reached Venice within a few years after its completion), but they form part of a very different world: a richly sensuous, untroubled pagan paradise, inspired by classical poetry. Titian clearly owes a good deal to Giovanni Bellini as well (compare Plate 22), although his brushwork is broader and more fluid, his colors deeper, and the play of sunlight and shadow more dramatic. These figures, unlike those in Botticelli's *Birth of Venus,* are full-blooded human beings who bring antiquity back to life with all the vigor and immediacy we could demand. If Titian lacks the heroic vision of Michelangelo, his works have a vitality whose direct appeal has hardly been dimmed by the passage of time.

Plate 26. Parmigianino
THE MADONNA WITH THE LONG NECK
ca. 1535, oil on wood panel, height 7'1"
Uffizi Gallery, Florence

In its twin centers, Florence and Rome, the High Renaissance lasted barely two decades, ending with the death of Leonardo in 1519 and that of Raphael in 1520. Michelangelo, it is true, lived until 1564, but his later work no longer had the radiant energy and assurance of the Sistine Ceiling. The next generation of artists reacted to the classic style of their great predecessors in strange and unexpected ways. Some, such as Parmigianino, pursued an ideal of unearthly grace; the long-limbed, languid figures in the *Madonna with the Long Neck* in Plate 26 have a formal perfection that defies any comparison with actual human beings. Characteristically, the meaning of the picture is so intricate that it went unrecognized until very recently. The crystal vessel displayed by the angel on the far left symbolizes the Virgin's purity; its surface, however, reflects a cross (now barely visible), and the Infant Christ, who has seen it, is frightened by this prophecy of his future suffering, while Mary, not yet aware of it, smiles at him tenderly.

The forms in Rosso's *Descent from the Cross* in Plate 27 are as

jagged and angular as Parmigianino's are smooth and sinuous. The
entire composition seems filled with
unbearable anguish whether we look
at the latticework of figures engaged
in lowering the body of Christ to
the ground or at the frozen grief of
those at the foot of the cross. The
colors, too, appear to be deliberately
off-key, designed to reinforce the
harsh expressiveness of the artist's
style. How are we to understand this
deliberate rejection of balance and
rationality? By High Renaissance
standards, the frantic Rosso and the
elegant Parmigianino are equally
anticlassical. The new trend they
represent, known as Mannerism, has
been explained as a symptom of the
spiritual crisis brought about by the
Reformation. It can be viewed
equally, however, as a response to
the perfection of High Renaissance
art, which had assumed an authority
greater even than nature and thus
had established style as an ultimate
value, an end in itself. Be that as it
may, Mannerism was to dominate
much of Italian as well as Northern
art from the 1520s to the end of the
century.

Plate 27. Rosso Fiorentino
THE DESCENT FROM THE CROSS
1521, oil on wood panel, height 11'
Pinacoteca Comunale, Volterra

Plate 28.
Agnolo Bronzino
ELEANORA OF TOLEDO AND HER SON GIOVANNI DE' MEDICI
ca. 1550, oil on canvas, height 38″
Uffizi Gallery, Florence

The elegant phase of Mannerism appealed particularly to aristocratic patrons and produced splendid portraits like that of Eleanora, the wife of Cosimo I de'Medici, by Cosimo's court painter Bronzino. The sitter in Plate 28 appears as the member of an exalted social caste rather than as an individual personality. Congealed into immobility behind the barrier of her lavishly ornate costume, Eleanora seems more akin to Parmigianino's Madonna (compare Plate 26) than to ordinary flesh and blood. Her masklike features betray no hint of inner life; she permits us to admire her, but under no circumstances would she deign to acknowledge our presence.

The ideal type underlying portraits of this kind reflects a development that was to reach its climax a hundred years later: the absolute monarchy, with all strands of state power gathered in the hands of the sovereign. El Greco's portrait in Plate 29 is based on an altogether different scale of values. The last and greatest of Mannerists, El Greco was born on the Greek island of

Crete. As a youth, he acquired the rich heritage of Venetian painting (he worked under Titian for a while), went to Rome, and finally settled in the Spanish town of Toledo. Spain had long been the home of the Counter-Reformation, and El Greco's mature work was decisively shaped by the spiritual climate of that movement. Unlike Bronzino, whose portrait of Eleanora conveys a sense of awed distance between artist and sitter, El Greco was on intimate terms with Paravicino, a scholar and poet who has left us several sonnets in praise of El Greco's genius. The contrast between the two pictures could hardly be more striking: Bronzino's forms are rigidly immobile, while El Greco's every brush stroke communicates a quivering movement; Eleanora's coldness is matched by Paravicino's emotional ardor. His frail, expressive hands and the pallid face, with its sensitive mouth and burning eyes, project an ideal image of the saints of the Counter-Reformation—mystics and intellectuals at the same time.

Plate 29.
El Greco
FRAY FELIX HORTENSIO PARAVICINO
ca. 1605, oil on canvas, height 44½"
Museum of Fine Arts, Boston

Plate 30. Hans Holbein the Younger, HENRY VIII
1540, oil on wood panel, height 32½"
National Gallery of Ancient Art, Rome

When the young German painter Albrecht Dürer visited Venice in 1495, two experiences made an indelible impresson on him: the high esteem accorded to Italian artists, and the clarity and rationality of Italian art. In his own work, Dürer spread the gospel of the Italian Renaissance with an almost religious zeal. However, the flowering of the Northern Renaissance which he had helped to bring about was as brief as the High Renaissance in Italy. By the mid-1520s, Germany and her neighbors were in the grip of the Reformation crisis; and since Protestantism opposed religious imagery, artists found themselves deprived of their principal task. The career of Holbein, Germany's greatest artist after Dürer, is characteristic of the times. When the city of Basel went Protestant he was saved by his gift for portraiture: he emigrated to England and became court painter to Henry VIII. His picture of the king in Plate 30 has the immobile pose, the air of unapproachability, and the emphasis on costume and jewelry familiar to us from Bronzino's court portraits (compare Plate 28). Its rigid frontality and physical bulk create an overpowering sensation of the king's ruthless, commanding presence. Here, we realize, stands not only the temporal sovereign, but also the creator and head of the Church of England.

Other northern artists tried their hand at subjects from classical antiquity, although more often than not they drew them from literary rather than from visual sources. Nothing could be less classical than Altdorfer's picture in Plate 31 of the battle in which Alexander defeated Darius, with its ant-like mass of sixteenth-century soldiers spread over an Alpine valley. In fact, the only classical element is the inscribed tablet in the sky, which enables us to identify the subject. The painting might well show some contemporary battle except for the spectacular sky, where we see the sun triumphantly breaking through the clouds and defeating the moon. This celestial drama, obviously correlated with the human contest below, raises the scene to the cosmic level.

Plate 31. Albrecht Altdorfer, THE BATTLE OF ISSUS
1529, oil on wood panel, height 62"
Alte Pinakothek, Munich

Plate 32.
Pieter Bruegel the Elder, THE LAND OF COCKAIGNE
1567, oil on wood panel, height 20½"
Alte Pinakothek, Munich

Although the Netherlands suffered more than any other country in the struggle between Protestants and Catholics, it was Dutch painters who led the field in developing new secular themes to replace the traditional religious subjects. The greatest of them, Pieter Bruegel, explored landscape, peasant life, and moral allegory. *The Land of Cockaigne* in Plate 32 is a fool's paradise, based on a folk tale, where tables are always laden with tasty dishes, houses have roofs made of pies, and pigs and chickens run about roasted to a turn. To reach it, one must eat his way through a mountain of gruel (see the upper right-hand corner). The lesson Bruegel teaches here is a philosophical comment on human nature; the men under the tree are not sinners in the grip of evil like those in Bosch's Hell (compare Plate 21), they are simply not wise enough to know what is best for them. By becoming slaves to their stomachs, they relinquish all ambition for the sake of a kind of animal happiness—the knight has dropped his lance, the farmer his flail, the scholar his books. "Beware of the fool's paradise," the artist seems to say; "it is more dangerous than hell because people *like* going there." And the impressive composition, in the shape of a great wheel turned on its side, shows that he must have thought the subject serious and important.

Chapter 15

A Century of
War and Revolt
1560–1660

In the wake of the rapid and bewildering changes of the early sixteenth century—the dislocations caused by the activities of the new monarchs, the rises in population and prices, the overseas discoveries, and the Reformation—Europe entered a period of fierce upheaval. It was difficult to come to terms with such radical alterations in so many elements of society: the increasing interference in local affairs by bureaucrats from distant capitals, the sudden soaring of food costs, or the questioning of hallowed authorities like the pope. Many people, often led by nobles who saw their power dwindling, revolted against their monarchs. The poor launched hopeless rebellions against their social superiors. And the two religious camps struggled relentlessly to destroy each other. From Scotland to Russia, the events of the century following the Reformation, from about 1560 to 1660, were dominated by warfare.

The pivot of the conflict was the Hapsburg family, which ruled most of southern and central Europe. Until the 1590s its chief representative was Philip II, king of Spain, whose ambitions and worldwide commitments lay at the center of 40 years of international disputes. Then, after a short respite, the Thirty Years' War began and involved large areas of Europe in the bloodiest fighting the Continent had ever seen. Domestic tensions, peasant revolts, and civil wars added to the perpetual upheaval. The constant military activity had widespread effects on politics, economy, society, and thought. The fighting was in fact a crucial element in the long and painful process whereby Europeans came to terms with the revolutions that had begun about 1500. Almost imperceptibly, fundamental economic, political, social, and religious changes took root, and troubled Europeans managed to come to terms with their altered circumstances. At last, in the mid-seventeenth century, the long struggle seemed to ease as conflict shifted to different issues. But by the time the long adjustment finally ended, countless lives had been sacrificed and endless suffering had been caused. Few, if any, centuries of European history have been so powerfully shaped by warfare until our own. The military revolution of the period, the international conflicts through which that revolution was worked out, and the domestic upheavals that followed—these were the dominant themes of a violent and complex age.

I. WARFARE

Western Europe was the scene of almost constant fighting during the late sixteenth century and the succeeding era of the Thirty Years' War. Warfare was so widespread between 1600 and 1650 that no country was immune to the effects of the mounting brutality.

The Military Revolution

Dramatic changes took place in the way battles were fought and armies were organized between the early 1500s and the middle of the seventeenth century. Gunpowder, which had been used occasionally and to little effect since the fourteenth century, now came to occupy a central place in warfare. The result was not only the creation of a new type of industry, cannon and gun manufacture, but also a transformation of tactics. Individual castles could no longer be defended against explosives; even towns had to build heavy and elaborate fortifications if they were to resist the new fire power. Sieges became complicated, expensive operations, whose purpose was to bring explosives right up to a town wall so that it could be blown up. This required an intricate system of trenches, because walls were built in star shapes so as to multiply angles of fire and make any approach dangerous (see illustration below). Although both attack and defense thus became increasingly costly, sieges remained essential to the strategy of warfare until the eighteenth century.

(top) **A view of the siege of Magdeburg during the Thirty Years' War. Cannon are pouring fire into the city. Star-shaped bastions are visible in the lower right and at the far left.**
(Photo: New York Public Library/Picture Collection)

(left) **A typical system of trenches approaching a bastion.**
(Photo: The Granger Collection)

1560–1660/TIMELINE

International and Military History	Political History
1560	
	1562–1598 Civil wars in France
1571 Battle of Lepanto	
1572 Beginning of Dutch revolt against Spain	1572 Massacre of St. Bartholomew
	1584 Assassination of William of Orange
1588 Spanish Armada	
	1598 Edict of Nantes
	Death of Philip II
	1603 Death of Elizabeth I; start of Stuart dynasty
1609–1621 Truce between Spanish and Dutch	
	1610 Assassination of Henry IV
	1611 Gustavus Adolphus King of Sweden
1618–1648 Thirty Years' War	
	1619 Ferdinand II Holy Roman Emperor
	1621–1641 Olivares chief minister of Spain
	1624–1642 Richelieu chief minister of France
1630 Sweden enters Thirty Years' War	1629 Petition of Right
1631 Battle of Breitenfeld	1632 Death of Gustavus Adolphus
1635 France declares war on Spain	
	1640–1660 Revolts and political upheavals throughout Europe
	1642 Civil War in England
1648 Treaties of Westphalia	1648 Fronde in France
	1649 Execution of Charles I
1655–1660 War in the Baltic	
1659 Treaty of the Pyrenees	
1660	1660 Charles II returns to England

Thirty Years' War *(bracket spanning 1618–1648)*

In open battles, the effects of gunpowder were equally expensive. The new tactics that appeared around 1500, perfected by the Spaniards, relied on massed ranks of infantry, organized in huge squares, that made the traditional cavalry charge obsolete. Interspersed with the gunners were soldiers carrying pikes. They fended off horses or opposing infantry while the men with guns tried to mow the enemy down. The squares with the best discipline usually won, and for over a century after the reign of Ferdinand of Aragon, the Spaniards had the best army in Europe. Each square had about 3000 troops, and to maintain enough squares at full strength to fight all of Spain's battles required an army numbering approximately 40,000. The cost of keeping that many men clothed, fed, and housed, let alone equipped and paid, was enormous. But worse was to come: new tactics emerged in the early seventeenth century that required even more soldiers.

Since nobody could outdo the Spaniards at their own methods, a different approach was developed by their rivals. The first advance was made by Maurice of Nassau, who led the Dutch revolt against Spain from the 1580s. He relied not on sheer weight and power, but on flexibility and mobility. Then one of the geniuses of the history of warfare, Gustavus Adolphus, king of Sweden, found a way to achieve mobility without losing power. His main invention was the salvo—instead of having his musketeers fire one row at a time, like the Spaniards, he had them all fire at once. What he lost in continuity of shot he gained in a fearsome blast that, if properly timed, could shatter enemy ranks. Huge, slow-moving squares were simply no match for smaller, faster units that riddled them with salvos that were well-coordinated. To add to his fire power, Gustavus had his engineers devise a light, movable cannon that could be brought into action wherever it was most needed on a battlefield.

These changes brought about a further increase in the size of armies, because the more units, the better they could be placed on the battlefield. Although the Spanish army hardly grew between 1560 and 1640, remaining at 40,000 to 60,000 men, the Swedes had 150,000, including mercenaries, by 1632; and at the end of the century, Louis XIV considered a force of 400,000 essential to maintain his dominant position in Europe.[1]

This growth had far-reaching consequences. Rulers knew the risks of relying on mercenary troops, who might change sides for a raise in pay, and Gustavus introduced conscription in the late 1620s. At least half his army consisted of his own subjects, who were easier to control. Because it also made sense not to disband such huge forces each autumn, when the campaigning season ended, the armies were kept permanently ready.

The need to maintain so many soldiers the year round caused a rapid expansion of supporting administrative personnel. Taxation mushroomed. All levels of society felt the impact but especially the lower classes, who paid the bulk of the taxes and provided most of the recruits. To encourage enlistment rulers made military service as attractive as possible—not a difficult task at a time when regular meals, clothing, housing, and wages were not always easy to come by. Social distinctions were reduced; an able young man could rise high in the officer corps, though the top ranks were still reserved for nobles. Even the lower echelons were given important responsibilities because the new system of small, flexible units required that junior officers, who were sometimes in command of only 50 men, be given considerable initiative. The decline of the cavalry, which had always been an aristocratic pre-

---

[1] An excellent analysis of the military revolution and its implications can be found in Michael Howard, *War in European History* (1976), Chapters 2–4.

serve, similarly reduced social differentiation.

Life in the army also changed. Maneuverability demanded tighter discipline, which was achieved by the introduction of drilling and combat training. The order of command was clarified, and many ranks familiar today—major, colonel, and the various levels of general—appeared in the seventeenth century. The distinctions were reinforced by uniforms, which became standard equipment. These developments created a sense of corporate spirit among military officers, an international phenomenon that was to occupy an important place in European society for three centuries.

As Gustavus himself put it, war nourishes itself. With ever larger armies, stimulated by national ambitions and governments in search of wider powers, it was inevitable that the devastations of warfare would proliferate. Gustavus himself enunciated the strategy of devastation—an opponent can be brought to his knees, he said, only if his strength is totally destroyed. Such conclusions clearly reflected the appalling slaughter of the era that has come to be known as the age of religious warfare.

The Wars of Religion

Although many other issues were involved in the wars that plagued Europe from the 1560s to the 1650s, religion was the burning motivation, the one that inspired fanatical devotion and the most vicious hatred. A deep conviction that heresy was dangerous to man and hateful to God made Protestants and Catholics treat one another callously and cruelly. Even the dead were not spared; corpses were sometimes mutilated to emphasize how dreadful their sins had been in their lifetimes. This was the bitter emotion that blended in with political and other ambitions to give Europe a century of almost ceaseless war.

Spain's Catholic Crusade

During the second half of the sixteenth century, the conflict was ignited by the leader of the Catholics, Philip II of Spain (1556–1598), the most powerful monarch in Europe. He ruled the Iberian peninsula, much of Italy, the Netherlands, and a huge overseas empire, but his main obsessions were the two enemies of his church, the Muslims and the Protestants.

Against the Muslims in the Mediterranean, Philip's successful campaigns seemed to justify the financial strains they caused. In particular, his naval victory at Lepanto, off the coast of Greece, in 1571 made him a Christian hero at the same time as it rid the western Mediterranean of Muslim interference. But elsewhere he found little but frustration. He tried to prevent a Protestant, Henry IV, from succeeding to the French crown, and after he failed he continued to back the losing side in France's civil wars even though Henry converted to Catholicism.

Philip's policy toward England was similarly ineffective. After the Protestant Queen Elizabeth I came to the throne in 1558, he remained uneasily cordial toward her for about 10 years. But relations deteriorated as England's sailors and explorers tried to take some of the wealth of Philip's New World possessions for themselves. Worse, in 1585 Elizabeth began to help the Protestant Dutch in their rebellion against Spain.

Philip decided to end all these troubles with one mighty blow: in 1588 he sent a mammoth fleet—the Armada—to the Low Countries to pick up a Spanish army, invade England, and crush his Protestant enemies. By this time, however, English seamen were among the best in the world; and their ships, which had greater maneuverability and fire power than the Spaniards', made up in tactical superiority what they lacked in size. After several skirmishes with the Armada, they set fire to a few vessels with loaded cannon aboard and sent them drifting toward the Spanish ships, anchored off Calais.

The Spaniards had to raise anchor in a hurry, and some of the fleet was lost. The next day the remaining ships retreated up the North Sea. The only way home was around Ireland, and wind, storms, and the pursuing English ensured that less than half the fleet reached Spain safely. This shattering reversal was comparable in scale and unexpectedness only to Xerxes' disaster at Salamis more than 2000 years earlier.

The defeat was a major setback to Philip's foreign policies. Though he improved the defense of the Spanish empire, English raids multiplied in a tremendous wave of privateering in the 1590s, and his possessions were under almost constant attack thereafter. Enemies to the bitter end, both Elizabeth and Philip died before peace came in 1604.

The Dutch Revolt

Philip's most serious reversal was the revolt of the provinces he had inherited from his father in the Netherlands. Here his single-mindedness provoked a determined reaction that grew into a successful struggle for independence, the first major effort in Western Europe to resist the new authority of a monarchy.

The original focus of opposition was Phil-

This engraving was published to arouse horror at Spanish atrocities during the Dutch revolt. As the caption indicates, after the Spanish troops (on the right) captured the city of Haarlem, there was a great bloodbath (*ein gross bliut batt*). Blessed by priests, the Haarlemites are decapitated or hung, and then tossed in a river so that the city is cleansed of them. The caption states that even women and children were not spared.
(Photo: New York Public Library/Picture Collection)

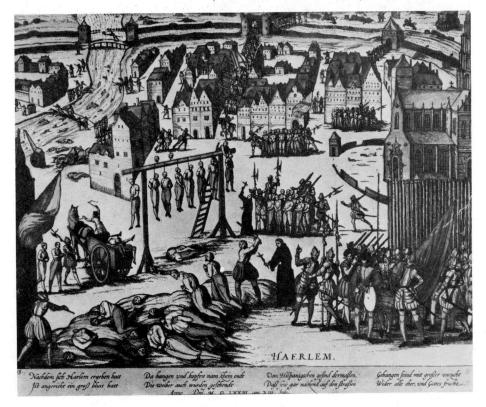

HAERLEM.

_{Nachdem sich Haerlem ergeben hatt   Da hangen vnd köpfen nam kleen ende   Von Hispanischen gesind dermassen   Gefangen seind mit grosser vnzucht}
_{Jst angericht ein groß bluit batt   Die weiber auch wurden geschendee   Daß sie gar nackend auf den strassen   Wider alle eher, vnd Gottes fruchc}
_{Anno Dni. M. D. LXXIII. am XII. Iuly.}

This detail from Brueghel's *Massacre of the Innocents* shows the brutality of Spanish soldiers toward the local population. The darkest figure, at the center of the detachment of cavalry, has been identified as the duke of Alva.
(Photo: Kunsthistorisches Museum, Vienna)

ip's reorganization of the ecclesiastical structure so as to gain control over the country's Catholic Church, a change that deprived the aristocracy of important patronage. The billeting of troops meanwhile aroused the resentment of ordinary citizens. Using this situation, the nobles, led by William of Orange, threatened mass disorder, but Philip kept up the pressure: he put the Inquisition to work against heretics, and summoned the Jesuits to combat religious unorthodoxy. These moves had a disastrous effect because they further undermined local autonomy and threatened the Protestants of the country.

Philip's interference in religion provoked violence in 1566: Protestant mobs assaulted Catholics and sacked Catholic churches. He therefore tightened the pressure, appointing as governor the ruthless duke of Alva, whose Spanish troops were used to suppress heresy and treason. Protestants were hanged in public, small rebel bands were mercilessly decimated, and two nobles who had been guilty of nothing worse than demanding that Philip change his policy were executed.

The reaction of one observer, the great painter Pieter Brueghel, was a searing indictment of the persecution. (For Brueghel's more general critique of human folly, see Plate 32.) When he painted a famous biblical subject, the *Massacre of the Innocents,* he set the scene in a village in the Netherlands during the harshest season, winter. His own countrymen were the victims, and the murderers were Spanish soldiers, watched over by the sinister figure of the duke of Alva.

Organized revolt broke out in 1572, when a small group of Dutch seamen flying the flag of William of Orange seized the fishing village of Brill, on the North Sea. The success of these "sea beggars," as the Spaniards called them, stimulated uprisings in towns throughout the Low Countries. The banner of William of Orange became the symbol of resistance, and under his leadership full-scale rebellion gathered momentum.

After the sea beggars' capture of Brill, the Spaniards advanced into the province of Holland, but they were stopped in 1574 by the opening of the dikes when they were only 25 miles from Amsterdam.[2] Following two more years of fighting, Philip's troops mutinied and rioted in Antwerp. In reaction, 16 out of 17 provinces united behind William to drive out the Spaniards. The next year, however, the 10 southern provinces again gave their allegiance to Philip in return for a number of compromises, especially with their nobility.

In 1579 the remaining seven formed the United Provinces (Map 15.1). Despite the assassination of William in 1584, they managed to hang on, for various reasons: they could always open the dikes; Philip was often diverted by other wars, and in any case never placed total confidence in his commanders; and the Calvinists, though still a minority, became the heart of the resistance with their determination to establish freedom for their religion as well as their country. William was succeeded by Maurice of Nassau, his son, a brilliant military commander who won a series of victories in the 1590s. The Spaniards could make no progress and agreed to a 12-year truce in 1609,

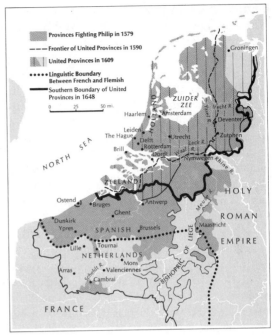

MAP 15.1.
THE NETHERLANDS 1579–1609

The 17 provinces making up the Netherlands, or the Low Countries, were detached from the Holy Roman Empire when Charles V abdicated in 1556. As the map indicates, their subsequent division into two states was determined not by the linguistic difference between French-speaking people of the south and Dutch-speaking people of the north, but rather by geography. The great river systems at the mouth of the Rhine eventually proved to be the barrier beyond which the Spaniards could not penetrate.

but final recognition of the independence of the United Provinces did not come until the Peace of Westphalia, in 1648, after 27 more years of fighting. The new state, bound together by religious, economic, and military ties, demonstrated the occasional positive effects of warfare in this period: it could unite a people and give them the means to achieve dignity and full autonomy.

---

[2] Most areas of the provinces of Holland and Zeeland lay below sea level and were protected by dikes. Defenders could flood them at very short notice by opening sluices in the seawalls. The forewarned population would take to boats, and the enemy soldiers, caught unawares, would have to beat a hasty retreat.

Civil War in France

The warfare that religion inspired had no such redeeming effects in France. By the 1550s Calvinism was widespread among the peasants and poorer middle classes in the southern and southwestern section of the country, and its leaders had virtually created a small, semi-independent state. To meet this threat, a great noble family, the Guises, assumed the leadership of a Catholic party, and in response the Bourbons, another noble family, championed the Calvinists, about a twelfth of the population. Their struggle with the majority split France apart.

It was ominous that in 1559, the year that Henry II, France's last strong king for a generation, died, the Protestant Huguenots organized their first national synod, an indication of impressive strength. During the next 30 years, a period when factional disputes among the nobles and religious passions overwhelmed the country, the throne was occupied by Henry's three ineffectual sons. The power behind the crown was Henry's widow, Catherine de Medici (see the accompanying genealogical table), who tried desperately to preserve royal authority. But she was often helpless because the religious conflict intensified the factional struggle for power between the Catholic Guises and the Protestant Bourbons, both of whom were closely related to the monarchy and hoped eventually to inherit the throne.

The fighting started in 1562, and lasted for 36 years, interrupted only by short-lived peace agreements. Catherine first turned to the Catholics for help but later switched to the Calvinists. When they became too powerful at court, she changed sides again, and she probably gave tacit approval to a massacre in Paris on St. Bartholomew's Day, August 24, 1572, which destroyed the Calvinist leadership. Henry of Navarre, a Bourbon, was the only major figure who escaped. When Catherine switched again and made peace with the Calvinists in 1576, the Guises, in desperation, formed the Catholic

League, which for several years virtually ran the government. In 1584 the league made an alliance with Philip II to destroy heresy in France and deny the Bourbon Henry's legal right to inherit the throne.

The defeat of the Armada proved to be the turning point in France's civil war. The duke of Guise lost his principal support, Spain; and Henry III, who had been a pawn of the league, ordered Guise's assassination and threw in his lot with the Bourbons. Within a few months he in turn was assassinated, and Henry of Navarre inherited the throne.

Henry IV (1589–1610) had few advantages as he began the reassertion of royal authority. The Calvinists and Catholics had formed almost independent governments, controlling large sections of France. The Catholic League was in command of the east, including the capital, Paris; the Calvinists dominated the south and southwest, remote from the central government. In addition the royal administration was in a sorry state, for power had returned to the crown's oldest rivals, the great nobles, who were now unchallenged in their domains.

Yet largely because of the assassination of the duke of Guise, Henry IV survived and recovered. The duke had been a forceful leader, a serious contender for the throne. He was succeeded by his brother, who had agreed to support a Spanish candidate for the crown. The prospect of a foreign ruler, the loss of a charismatic leader, and war weariness destroyed much of the support for the Catholic League, which finally collapsed as a result of revolts in eastern France against the Guises in the 1590s. The uprisings, founded on a demand for peace, increased in frequency and intensity after Henry IV renounced Protestantism in 1593 to win acceptance by his Catholic subjects. The following year Henry had himself officially crowned, and all of France declared its allegiance to the monarchy so as to join in the effort of repelling the Spanish invader.

When Spain finally withdrew and signed a

THE KINGS OF FRANCE IN THE SIXTEENTH CENTURY

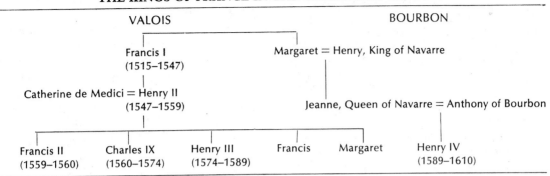

peace in 1598, the fighting came to an end. To complete the reconciliation, Henry issued (also in 1598) the Edict of Nantes, which granted toleration to the Huguenots. Although it did not create complete religious liberty, the edict made Calvinism legal, protected the rights of the minority, and opened public office to Protestants.

But the effects of decades of strife could not be brushed aside. A basic change in political thought, for example, was an inevitable response to the civil wars, because a number of theorists felt obliged to reassess the relationship between a king and his subjects.

The Huguenots were the first to justify resistance to a monarch. Seizing on a vague passage in Calvin's writings about the sanctity of conscience and ignoring his endorsement of obedience to authority, they asserted that when a king goes against God's wishes and disturbs the faith, he breaks his contract with his people, thus making revolt permissible. Catholics took up a similar argument when they were fighting the king. The Jesuits developed the idea of a contract between ruler and ruled and found excellent biblical support for the overthrow of a tyrant (for example, pharaoh) who turned against true religion.

These extreme positions soon lost appeal when order was restored, however, and a group whose views had previously gone unheeded gained the ascendancy: the politiques.

Although most were Catholics their main premise was that peace, security, and national unity were far more important than the claims of rival churches. Representing the forces of nationalism and central authority, the politiques were the heralds of a more stable future.

Their most famous representative, Jean Bodin, made his case by examining the basic structure of the state, and his analysis influenced political theorists for centuries. His principal work is *The Six Books of the Republic* (1576), in which he tried to define the nature and the limits of authority. By aiming for a balance between power and restraint, Bodin was seeking a principle for restoring stability in an age of shattering upheaval. But in the process he also exposed the paradox that has been the primary focus of political theory ever since: control versus freedom, the need for authority and yet the equal need for individual rights.

The Thirty Years' War

In the Holy Roman Empire fierce religious antagonisms were particularly dangerous because the empire lacked a central authority and unifying institutions. Small-scale fighting broke out repeatedly after the 1550s, always inspired by religion. And though in most of Western Europe the first two decades of the seventeenth century were a time of relative peace, which

CHRONOLOGY OF AN AGE OF CRISIS, 1618–1660

1618: Revolt in Bohemia, beginning of Thirty Years' War.

1621: Resumption of war between Spanish and Dutch.

1629: Edict of Restitution: High point of Hapsburg power.

1630: Sweden enters war against Hapsburgs.

1635: France declares war on Hapsburgs.

1639: Scots invade England.

1640: Revolts in Catalonia and Portugal against Spanish government.

1642: Civil War in England.

1647: Revolts in Sicily and Naples against Spanish government.

1648: Peace of Westphalia ending Thirty Years' War.

Outbreak of Fronde in France.

Coup by nobles in Denmark.

Revolt of Ukraine against Poland.

Riots in Russian cities.

1650: Constitutional crisis in Sweden.

Confrontation between William of Orange and Amsterdam in Netherlands.

1652: End of Catalan revolt.

1653: End of Fronde.

1655: War in Baltic region.

1659: Peace of the Pyrenees between France and Spain.

1660: End of English Revolution.

Treaties ending war in Baltic.

---

seemed to signal a decline of confessional conflict, in the empire the stage was being set for the bloodiest of all the wars fired by religion.

Known as the Thirty Years' War, this ferocious series of encounters began in the Kingdom of Bohemia in 1618 and continued until 1648. The principal battleground, the empire, was ravaged by the fighting, and eventually every major ruler of Europe became involved in the struggle. Political ambitions soon began to replace religious motives as the prime concern of the combatants, but the devastation continued to spread until international relations seemed to be sinking into total chaos. The chief victims were of course the Germans, who, like the Italians in the sixteenth century, found themselves at the mercy of well-organized states that used another country as the arena for settling their quarrels.

The immediate problem was typical of the situation in the empire. In 1609 Emperor Rudolf II promised toleration for Protestants in Bohemia, one of his own domains. When his cousin Ferdinand, a pious Catholic, succeeded to the Bohemian throne in 1617, he refused to honor Rudolf's promise, and the Bohemians rebelled. Since the crown was technically elective, they declared Ferdinand deposed, replacing him with the leading Calvinist of the empire, Frederick II of the Palatinate. Frederick accepted the crown, an act of defiance whose only possible outcome was war between the two religious camps.

For more than a decade, little went wrong for the Hapsburgs. Ferdinand became emperor (1619–1637), and the powerful Catholic Maximilian of Bavaria put his army at the emperor's disposal. Within a year the imperial troops won a stunning victory over the Bohemians at the Battle of the White Mountain. Leading rebels were executed or exiled, and Ferdinand II confiscated all of Frederick's lands. Half was given to Maximilian as a reward for his army, and the remainder was offered to the Spaniards, who occupied it as a valuable base for their struggle with the Dutch. It seemed as though the Catholic and imperial cause had triumphed. But in 1621 the truce between the Spaniards and the Dutch expired, hostilities reopened in the Netherlands, and religious warfare resumed in Germany (see Map 15.2).

Map 15.2 reveals both the extent and the fluctuations of fighting in Europe from the outbreak of the Thirty Years' War to the end of the Civil War in England. The principal battles are listed to give a more precise indication of the timing and location of major encounters. A look at the route followed by Spain's troops as they marched to the Netherlands, always staying close to friendly Catholic territories, will pinpoint the vital importance of the Valtellina, a vulnerable pass through the Alps that they had to cross.

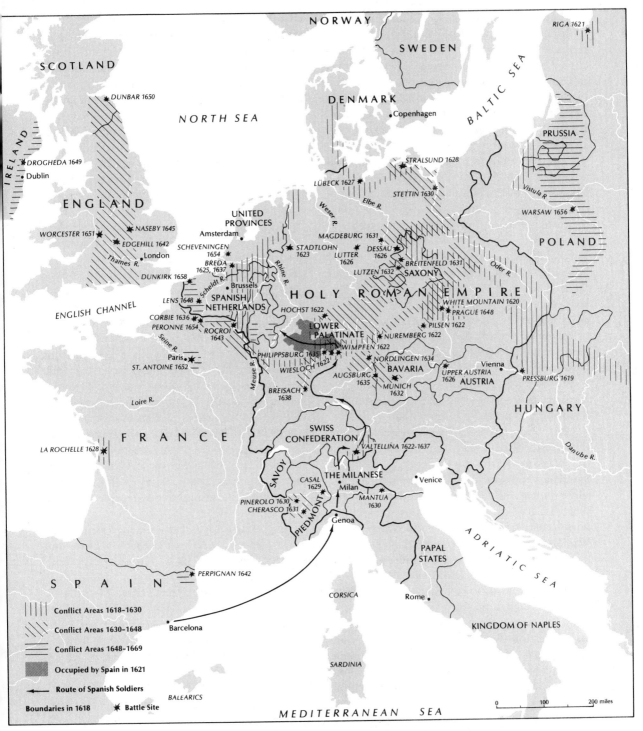

MAP 15.2. AREAS OF FIGHTING 1618–1660

Until 1630, however, the Protestants could do little in the face of the armies of the Hapsburgs and Bavaria. In 1622 the Spaniards occupied the Valtellina, a Swiss valley that was the best route for their troops traveling to the Netherlands. And in the empire all attempts by Protestants to help Frederick were beaten back. By 1630 Hapsburg power, bolstered by the creation of a new army, had reached its height.

The man who put together the new imperial army was Albrecht von Wallenstein, a minor Bohemian nobleman and a remarkable opportunist who had become one of the richest men in the empire. In 1624 Wallenstein, realizing that the emperor's great weakness was that he lacked his own army, offered to raise a force if he could billet it and raise its supplies among the population in whatever area it happened to be stationed. Ferdinand agreed, and by 1627 his army had begun to conquer the northern region of the empire, the last major center of Protestant strength. To emphasize his supremacy, Ferdinand issued the Edict of Restitution in 1629, ordering the restoration to Catholics of all the territories they had lost to Protestants— mainly in the northern empire—since 1552.

But these successes were more apparent than real because it was only the extreme disorganization of the empire that permitted a mercenary captain like Wallenstein to achieve such immense power. Once the princes realized their danger, they united against the Hapsburgs; and the forced contributions exacted by Wallenstein's army strengthened their determination to curb this growing menace to their independence. At an electoral diet in 1630, they made Ferdinand dismiss his general by threatening to keep his son from the imperial succession. The emperor's submission proved fatal to his cause, for Sweden and France were now preparing to unleash new aggressions against the Hapsburgs, and Wallenstein was the one military leader who might have been able to beat back the onslaught.

The year 1630 marked the beginning of a change in fortune and also a drift toward the more political aims that now came to dominate the war. Although France was a Catholic country, it was ready to ally with Protestants and attack other Catholics because of its fear of Hapsburg power on its eastern border. In the spring France attacked the duke of Savoy, a Hapsburg ally, and occupied his lands. The following year France, together with Saxony, signed an alliance with Gustavus Adolphus of Protestant Sweden, who feared that the Hapsburgs were threatening Swedish territory around the Baltic Sea, and who was alarmed at Ferdinand's treatment of Protestants. In July 1630 he had crossed the Baltic, and now at the head of a Swedish-Saxon army, he destroyed the imperial force at Breitenfeld in one of the few decisive battles of the war.

Ferdinand hastily recalled Wallenstein, whose troops finally met the Swedes in battle at Lützen in 1632. Although Gustavus's soldiers won the day, he himself was killed, and his death saved the Hapsburg dynasty from total destruction. Nothing, however, could restore Ferdinand's former position. The emperor was forced to turn against Wallenstein once more; a few months later he had him assassinated. The removal of the great general marked the end of an era, for he was the last leader in more than two centuries capable of establishing unified authority throughout what is now Germany.

Encouraged by Gustavus's success, the empire's princes began to raise new armies, and by 1635 Ferdinand had to make peace with them at the Treaty of Prague. In return for their promise of assistance in driving out the Swedes, Ferdinand agreed to suspend the Edict of Restitution and to grant amnesty to all but Frederick of the Palatinate and a few Bohemian rebels. Ferdinand was renouncing most of his ambitions, and it seemed that peace might return to the battle-scarred land.

But the French could not let matters rest. In 1635 they finally declared war on Ferdinand

and occupied the Valtellina. For the next 13 years, the French and Swedes rained unmitigated disaster on Germany. Peace negotiations began in 1641, but not until 1648 did the combatants agree to lay down arms and sign the treaties of Westphalia. Even thereafter the war between France and Spain, pursued mainly in the Spanish Netherlands, continued for another 11 years; and hostilities around the Baltic among Sweden, Denmark, Poland, and Russia, which had started in 1611, did not end until 1661.

The wars killed off more than a third of Germany's population. They caused serious economic dislocations, because a number of princes—already in serious financial straits—sharply debased their coinage. Their action worsened the continent-wide trade depression that had begun around 1620 and had brought the great sixteenth-century boom to an end, causing the first drop in prices since 1500. Few contemporaries perceived the connection between war and economic troubles, but nobody could ignore the interminable drain on men and resources or the widespread effects of the conflict on the life of the time.

The Peace of Westphalia

By the 1630s it was already becoming apparent that the fighting was getting out of hand, and that it would not be easy to bring the conflicts to an end. There had never been such widespread or devastating warfare; in the view of many diplomats, the settlement had to be far more decisive and of far greater scope than any negotiated before. And they were right. When at last the treaties were signed, after seven years of negotiation in the German province of Westphalia, a landmark in international relations was passed—remarkable not only because an anarchic situation was brought under control, but because a new system for dealing with wars was created.

The most important innovation was the gathering at the peace conference of all the participants in the Thirty Years' War, rather than the usual practice of bringing only two or three belligerents together. The presence of ambassadors from Bavaria, Brandenburg, Denmark, France, the Holy Roman Empire, Saxony, Spain, Sweden, Switzerland, and the United Provinces made possible, for the first time in European history, a series of all-embracing treaties that dealt with nearly every major international issue at one stroke. Although the Franco-Spanish and the Baltic wars continued for more than 10 years, the Peace of Westphalia in 1648 became the first comprehensive rearrangement of the map of Europe in modern history (Map 15.3).

The principal beneficiaries were France and Sweden, the chief aggressors during the last decade of the war. France made important gains on its northeastern frontier, notably the provinces of Alsace and Lorraine; and Sweden obtained extensive territories in the Holy Roman Empire, among them Western Pomerania, Bremen, and Verden. The main loser was the House of Hapsburg, since both the United Provinces and the Swiss Confederation were recognized as independent states and the German princes, who agreed not to join an alliance against the emperor, were otherwise given almost complete independence.

However, the princes' autonomy was not officially established until 1657, when they elected as emperor Leopold I, the head of the House of Hapsburg, in return for two promises. First, Leopold would give no help to his cousins, the rulers of Spain; and second, the empire would be a *Fürstenstaat,* a prince's state, in which each ruler would be completely free from imperial interference. This freedom permitted the rise of Brandenburg-Prussia and the growth of absolutism within the major principalities. In addition the Hapsburgs' capitulation prepared the way for their reorientation toward the east along the Danube River—the begin-

MAP 15.3. TERRITORIAL CHANGES 1648–1661

This map shows the territorial changes that took place after the Thirty Years' War. The treaties of Westphalia (1648) and the Pyrenees (1659) arranged the principal transfers, but the settlements in the Baltic were not confirmed until the treaties of Copenhagen, Oliva (both 1660), and Kardis (1661).

nings of the Austro-Hungarian Empire.

For more than a century the settlement reached at Westphalia was regarded as the basis for all international negotiations. The Treaty of the Pyrenees in 1659, ending the war between France and Spain, and the treaties of Copenhagen and Oliva in 1660 and Kardis in 1661, ending the Baltic struggles, were considered only to have rounded out the agreements made at Westphalia. Even major new accords, such as the one that ended yet another series of wars in 1713, were viewed primarily as adjustments of the decisions of 1648.

In practice of course multinational conferences were no more effective than brief, limited negotiations as means of reducing international tensions. Wars continued to break out with monotonous frequency, and armies grew in size and skill. But diplomats did believe that the total situation was under better control and that the anarchy of the Thirty Years' War had been replaced by something more stable and more clearly defined.

Confidence was reinforced as it became clear after 1648 that armies were trying to improve discipline and avoid the excesses of the previous 30 years. The treatment of civilians became more orderly, and on the battlefield the casualty rate went from as high as one death per three soldiers in the 1630s down to one death in seven at worst, or one in 20 at best, during the early 1700s. As religious passions declined, combat became less vicious, and the aims of warfare changed significantly.

The most obvious differences after the Peace of Westphalia were that France replaced Spain as the Continent's dominant power, and that northern countries—especially England and the Netherlands—took over economic leadership from the Mediterranean, where it had been centered for 2000 years. But behind this outward shift a more fundamental transformation was taking place. What had become apparent in the later stages of the Thirty Years' War was that Europe's states were interested in

fighting only for economic, territorial, or political advantages. Dynastic aims were still important—and were to remain so for centuries—but supranational goals like a religious cause could no longer determine a state's foreign policy.

The Thirty Years' War was the last major conflict in which two religious camps organized their forces as blocs. After 1648 such connections gave way to more purely national interests. Despite the universal wish for peace, Pope Innocent X, furious at the Catholics' compromises, denounced the treaties of Westphalia, but his voice went unheard. The declining influence of ideology meant that men would henceforth pursue the glory of their nation or ruler—not the advantage of their faith. This shift marked the final stage of a process that had long been under way: the emergence of the state as the basic unit and object of loyalty in Western civilization.

If the new aims of foreign policies, such as economic advantage, could not yet arouse the same passions as religion, they nevertheless revealed that commitment to one's country, and an interest in the way it was run, was becoming important throughout Europe. Indeed, at the very time that tensions were lessening in international affairs, they reached a new height in the internal affairs of a number of countries. Just as the mid-seventeenth century witnessed the most intense phase and also the settlement of the difficulties among states, so too did it mark the climax and the resolution of an era of upheaval and revolt within states.

II. REVOLTS

The warfare of the century from the 1560s to the 1660s affected the relations between rulers and their subjects no less than relations between countries. The additional taxes and bureaucrats required by the military created burdens that provoked the resistance to governments that was a major feature of the century. By the time the conflicts died away, after a particularly acute outburst in the mid-seventeenth century, they had helped create the national political structures that endured until the age of the French Revolution.

England

The one attempt at a radical transformation of politics and society—a revolution—occurred in England. Compared to its neighbors, England seemed relatively calm during the second half of the sixteenth century and the early years of the seventeenth. But tensions were rising that were to produce the most far-reaching upheaval of the age.

Elizabeth I

The tranquillity of the period from the 1560s to the 1630s had several causes. With only occasional fighting to support, and that largely at sea, England was far less affected by war than the Continental states. Furthermore the people were already united by such common bonds as a national Reformation and the institution of Parliament, so the crown did not experience the severe challenges that plagued royal authority in contemporary Spain and France. And the monarch also happened to be extraordinarily adept at the task of calming discontent.

Elizabeth I (1558–1603) has been an appealing figure to every generation because she combined shrewd hardheadedness and a sense of the possible with a disarming appearance of frailty. Her qualities are easily appreciated: her dedication to the task of government; her astute choice of advisers; her civilizing influence at court, where she encouraged chivalric notions and patronage of the arts, tempering the rougher manners of earlier times; her careful and usually successful handling of political

Elizabeth I was strongly aware of the power of propaganda, and she used it to foster a dazzling public image. Legends about her arose in literature. And in art she had herself portrayed in the most elaborate finery imaginable. Here, she is every inch the queen, with her magnificent dress and pet ermine—a pose of strict formality.

(Photo: Courtauld Institute of Art)

problems; and her ability to feel the mood of her people, to catch their spirit, to inspire their unquestioning enthusiasm.

Her concern for loyalty made Elizabeth reluctant to break openly with those who opposed her, but this sometimes led to an unfortunate indecisiveness, notably where the succession was concerned. Her refusal to marry caused serious uncertainties, and it was only because of the shrewd planning of Elizabeth's chief minister, Robert Cecil, that a crisis was avoided when she died in 1603 without naming a successor. Thanks to Cecil's diplomacy, the king of Scotland, James Stuart, succeeded without incident. Similar dangers arose from Elizabeth's reluctance to act firmly against England's remaining Catholics. Although most were loyal, a few plotted against her, hoping that if she died, Mary Queen of Scots, a Catholic, would come to the throne. Mary had been driven out of Scotland by the country's Calvinist nobles and was a prisoner in England. Not until Elizabeth grudgingly agreed to execute her (in 1587), and to deal more severely with Catholic plots, did this threat subside.

The advisers Elizabeth appointed to the Privy Council, the chief government body, were essential to her success. They distilled the flow of administrative business and worked closely with the queen, but they also represented different views. Some advocated caution, inaction, and discretion in international affairs, whereas others favored an aggressive foreign policy. Elizabeth showed great skill in balancing the contrasting viewpoints and her adroit maneuvering assured her of her ministers' loyalty at all times.

Even more important than her approval of a policy was the patronage she could offer. Because the government's powers and hence its need for officials had grown rapidly since the 1530s, dozens of new posts were being created for the crown to bestow. Whoever was the queen's favorite therefore had the best chance of nominating a successful candidate for a vacancy in the bureaucracy. But as a result of the patronage system, a swarm of parasites descended on London, hopeful of advancement. Many Englishmen viewed this development with distaste, and after Elizabeth's death it be-

came the cause of serious cleavage between crown and subjects.

Economic and Social Change

Another force with dangerous implications for the future was the result of rapidly shifting patterns in English society. With new methods of warfare, nobles no longer had a vital military role to play. Moreover they were losing their preeminence in government; nearly all the chief ministers were new men in national life, and the House of Commons was becoming at least the equal of the House of Lords in Parliament. The nobles were also not benefiting as much from England's rising prosperity as were other sections of society. Thus they were losing their hold over the power, wealth, and government of the country.

The gentry, the new group that joined them at the head of society, ranged from people considered great men in a parish or other small locality to courtiers considered great men throughout the land. There were never more than 60 nobles during Elizabeth's reign, but the gentry may have numbered close to 20,000 by the time she died.

The majority of the gentry was doing well economically, primarily from the purchase of land that the crown had confiscated when the monasteries were dissolved, in the 1530s. It also benefited from spiraling food prices and rising rents. Many profited too from crown offices; a number became involved in industrial activity; and hundreds invested in new overseas trading and colonial ventures. The gentry's participation in commerce made them unique among the landed classes of Europe, whose members were traditionally contemptuous of business affairs, and it testified to the enterprise and vigor of these Englishmen. Long important in local administration, they wanted their views respected by government, and they flocked to the House of Commons, for they regarded Parliament as the place to express their views. Their ambitions were to pose a serious threat to the monarchy, especially when linked with the effects of rapid economic change.

In the 1550s, stimulated by the general boom in trade and by the help of leading courtiers who recognized the importance of opening new markets, England's merchants began to transform its economic situation. During the next half-century, they started commerce with Russia, the Baltic and Mediterranean lands, the Levant, and East Asia. Although cloth remained the dominant export until the middle of the seventeenth century, it was joined by a growing trade in the reexport of overseas goods, such as Newfoundland fish, which were distributed throughout Europe.

Early attempts at colonization were not successful, with the exception of those in Ireland; but vital experience was gained, and the financial rewards were sometimes considerable. Within England, moreover, there was significant industrial development. The mining and manufacture of a whole variety of commodities, from alum to wire, grew at a rapid pace, and shipbuilding became a major industry. The production of coal alone increased fourteen-fold between 1540 and 1680, creating many new fortunes and an expertise in industrial and commercial techniques that took England far ahead of its neighbors.

The most revealing evidence of England's new position was the founding of nearly 50 companies devoted to overseas exploration, commerce, or colonization between 1600 and 1630. The more successful ones laid the foundations for the British Empire. In India, the Caribbean islands, Bermuda, Virginia, Maryland, New England, and Canada, colonies were started that within a century were to become the most populous offshoots of any European nation.

The economic vigor and growth that ensued, apparent also in industrial and agricultural advances, gave the classes that benefited the most—the gentry and the merchants—a cohe-

sion and a sense of purpose that made it dangerous to oppose them when they felt their rights infringed. They increasingly regarded themselves as the leaders of the nation, second only to the nobility, whose importance was diminishing. They wanted respect for their wishes, and they bitterly resented the economic interference and political high-handedness of Elizabeth's successors.

What made the situation particularly dangerous was that many of the gentry were sympathetic to the Puritans. These religious reformers believed that the Protestant Anglican Church established by Elizabeth was still too close to Roman Catholicism, and they wanted further reductions in ritual and hierarchy. Elizabeth had refused, and although she had tried to avoid a confrontation, in the last years of her reign she had had to silence the most outspoken of her critics. As a result, the Puritans had become a disgruntled minority, ready to add their demands to those of the gentry (some of whom were themselves Puritans). By the 1630s, when the government tried to repress such religious dissent more vigorously, there were many Englishmen who felt that the monarchy was leading the country astray and was ignoring the wishes of its subjects. Leading parliamentarians in particular soon came to believe that only major changes could restore justice to England.

Parliament and the Law

The place where the gentry made their views known to the government was Parliament, the nation's supreme legislative body. Three-quarters of the lower chamber, the House of Commons, consisted of members of the gentry. These men were better educated than before; at the end of the sixteenth century, more than half of them had attended a university, and slightly less than half had legal training. Through the House of Commons, they were beginning to make a bid to influence the government, and since the Commons had to approve all taxation, these members had no compunction about using the power of the purse to promote their demands.

The monarchy was still the dominant force in the country when Elizabeth died in 1603, but Parliament's challenge to that supremacy was beginning to gather momentum. Although the queen had been known for her care with money, in the last 20 years of her reign her resources had been overtaxed by the war with Spain and an economic depression, Thus she bequeathed to her successor, James I, a huge debt—£400,000, the equal of a year's royal revenue—and the struggle to pay it off gave the Commons the leverage to expand their powers.

Trouble began to mount in 1604, at the first meeting of Parliament in the reign of James I (1603–1625). Puritans who still hoped to change the Anglican Church by legislation and gentry who wanted to extend their influence led the opposition to the king. They began to dominate proceedings, and through 1629 they engaged in a running battle with the monarchy. They blocked the union of England with Scotland that James sought. They drew up an "Apology" explaining his mistakes and his ignorance, as a Scotsman, of English traditions. And they wrung repeated concessions from him until in 1624 they gained the unprecedented right to discuss foreign policy.

The parliamentarians used the law as justification for their resistance to royal power. The basic legal system of the country was the common law—justice administered on the basis of precedents and parliamentary statutes, decided with the assistance of juries. This system stood in contrast to Roman law, prevalent on the Continent, where royal edicts could make law, and decisions were reached by judges without juries. Such practices existed in England only in a few royal courts of law, such as the Star Chamber. Proceedings here were popular, because they were quicker, and powerful men could not influence the decisions of the judges who were usually prominent men themselves. But a court like the Star Chamber, directly under crown influence, could easily come to be seen as an instrument of repression.

The common lawyers, whose leaders were also prominent in the House of Commons, resented the growth of this rival system, and they attacked royal courts in Parliament. Both James and his successor were accused of putting pressure on the judges to gain their ends—particularly after they won a series of famous cases involving a subject's right to criticize the monarch. Thus the crown could be portrayed as disregarding not only the desires of the people but the law itself. Technically the king had extensive rights, but when he exercised them without regard to Parliament's wishes, his actions began to take on the appearance of tyranny.

Rising Antagonisms

The confrontation in Parliament grew worse during the 1620s. In 1621 the House of Commons forced the king's lord chancellor, Francis Bacon, out of office for accepting bribes, and in reaction to their attacks, James had some of the members sent to prison. Under his son Charles I (1625–1649), the hostilities intensified. At the Parliament of 1628–1629, the crown faced an open challenge, whose climax was the Petition of Right, an appeal that has become a landmark in constitutional history. The petition demanded an end to imprisonment without cause shown, to taxation without the consent of Parliament, to martial law in peacetime, and to the billeting of troops among civilians. Charles agreed, in the hope of gaining much-needed subsidies, but then broke his word.

The issue was now clearly whether Parliament, as the representative of the nation, would hold an essential position in the government alongside the king. To stop further confrontation Charles ordered Parliament dissolved, but in a move of great daring, two members denied the king even this hallowed right by holding the speaker of the House in his chair while they passed a final angry resolution.

Resentful subjects were clearly on the brink of open defiance of their sovereign. Puritans, common lawyers, and disenchanted country gentry had captured the House of Commons, and Charles could avoid further trouble only by refusing to call another session of Parliament. This he managed to do for 11 years, all the while increasing the repression of Puritanism and resorting to extraordinary measures to raise revenues.

But the smooth sailing could not last long. The leaders of the Puritan and parliamentary opposition kept in touch after 1630, and they finally had the opportunity in 1639 to extract from the king the concessions they sought when the Calvinist Scots took up arms rather than accept the Anglican prayer book. Religious persecution had once again sparked military combat: the Scots invaded England, and Charles had to raise an army. To obtain the necessary funds, he turned to Parliament, which demanded that he first redress its grievances. When he resisted, civil war followed.

The English Civil War

The Parliament that met in 1640 was dominated by John Pym, a Puritan and a prominent critic of the monarch for nearly 20 years, who opened the session with a two-hour speech outlining the long-standing grievances against both church and government. Charles refused to change his policies and the Commons refused to grant a subsidy, and the king angrily dissolved the session. But there was no way to pay for an army without taxes. By the summer of 1640, the Scots occupied most of northern England, and Charles had no alternative but to summon a new Parliament. This one sat for 13 years, earning the appropriate name of the Long Parliament.

Pym was in complete control of Parliament for the first year. The House of Commons passed legislation abolishing the royal courts, such as the Star Chamber, and establishing the writ of habeas corpus (which prevented imprisonment without cause shown) as mandatory; it declared taxation without parliamentary consent illegal; and it ruled that Parliament had to meet at least once every three years, with the additional proviso that the current assembly could not be dissolved without its consent. Meanwhile, the Puritans were preparing to reform the church. Oliver Cromwell, one of the leading members of the House, demanded abolition of the Anglican Book of Common Prayer and strongly attacked the institution of episcopacy. The climactic vote came the next year, when the Commons passed their Grand Remonstrance, outlining for the king all the legislation they had put through and asking that bishops be deprived of their votes in the House of Lords.

This was the prelude to a more revolutionary assault on the structure of the Church, but significantly the Grand Remonstrance passed by only 11 votes. A moderate party was detaching itself from Pym, and the beginning of a royalist party was appearing. The nation's chief grievances had been redressed, and there was no longer a uniform desire for change. Still Charles misjudged the situation and tried to arrest five leaders of the opposition, including Pym, ostensibly for plotting treason with the Scots. But Parliament refused to order their arrest, and the citizens of London, now openly hostile to Charles, sheltered the five.

In June 1642 the king received the Commons' final demands: complete parliamentary control over the Church, the appointment of ministers and judges, and the army. This would have meant the abdication of all effective royal authority, and Charles refused. Gradually England began to split in two. By the late summer both sides had assembled armies, and the Civil War was under way.

The fascination of this great revolution that sought to transform English government and society has been endless. Much attention has been given to religion and politics, to the motives of Puritans and parliamentarians, and it is now clear that simple differentiations cannot be made. Half the parliamentarians joined the king; the Puritans were split; and many members of the gentry who were not part of either of these opposition groups fought against Charles.

What made so many people overcome their habitual loyalty to the monarchy? One interesting distinction is that the royalists in Parliament were considerably younger than their opponents; this suggests that it was long experience with the Stuarts and nostalgia for Elizabethan times that created dedicated revolutionaries. Another clear division was regional. The south and east of England were primarily antiroyalist while the north and west were mostly royalist. What this implied was that the more cosmopolitan areas, which were closer to the Continent and also the principal centers of Puritanism, were largely on Parliament's side. Frequently the decision was very much a personal matter: a great man would take his locality to one side because his old rival, the great man a few miles away, had chosen the other. Those who opposed the Church of England were unequivocally antiroyalist, but they were a minority in the country and hardly even a majority in the House of Commons. Like all revolutions, this one was animated by a small group of radicals (in this case Puritans) who alone kept the momentum going.

The Stuarts' long alienation of their subjects can account for the situation in 1640, when Charles could find no support anywhere, but by the end of 1641 many felt that the necessary remedies had been obtained. Thus apart from Puritanism—or to put it more generally, apart from opposition to the Church of England—the historian can point only to the influence of local circumstances to explain how two sides came into being in the summer of 1642.

The Course of Conflict

The first round of fighting was indecisive—a year of small successes on both sides. Then in 1643 the antiroyalists, supported by the Scottish army, gained the first military advantage. The alliance with the Scots was Pym's last accomplishment, because shortly thereafter he died, and the first major split in the antiroyalist ranks occurred.

Increasingly during the last months of Pym's life, a group known as the Independents urged that the Anglican Church be replaced by the congregational system, in which each local congregation, free of all central authority, would decide its own form of worship. The most important representative of the Independents in Parliament was Oliver Cromwell (1599–1658). Opposed to them were the Presbyterians, who wanted to establish a strictly organized Calvinist system, much like the one that had been created in Scotland, in which local congregations were subject to centralized authority, although laymen did participate in church government. Since both the Scots, whose alliance was vital in the war, and a majority of the members of the Commons were Presbyterians,[3] Cromwell agreed to give way, but only for the moment. In addition to the religious issue, there was also a quarrel over the goals of the war because the antiroyalists were unsure whether they ought to attempt to defeat Charles completely. This dispute crossed religious lines, though on the whole the Independents were more determined to force him into total submission, and in the end they had their way.

Meanwhile the fighting continued. Hoping to create a more potent military force, Cromwell persuaded the House of Commons early in 1645 to create a completely reorganized

---

[3] This was a majority of a depleted House, however, because a few dozen royalists had departed from the Commons during 1641, especially after the Grand Remonstrance, and they never returned.

This contemporary Dutch engraving of the execution of Charles I shows the scaffold in front of the Banqueting House in Whitehall—a building that still can be seen in London. On the far right of the scaffold, the executioner displays the severed head for the crowd.
(Photo: The Granger Collection)

army, the New Model Army, to bring the war to an end under his command. Whipped to fervor by sermons, prayers, and the singing of psalms, the New Model Army became unbeatable. At the Battle of Naseby in June, it won a major victory over the royalists and a year later Charles surrendered.

The next two years were chaotic. The Presbyterians and Independents quarreled over what to do with the king, and finally the Civil War resumed. This time the Presbyterians and Scots backed Charles against the Independents. But even with this alliance the royalist forces were no match for the New Model Army; Cromwell soon defeated his opponents and captured the king.

At the same time, in 1647, the Independents abolished the House of Lords and removed all Presbyterians from the House of Commons, leaving behind a "rump" of less than 100 men, about a fifth of the original membership of the Long Parliament. The Rump Parliament tried to negotiate with Charles but discovered that he continued to plot a return to power. With Cromwell's approval the Commons decided that their monarch, untrustworthy and a troublemaker, would have to die. A trial without

legality was held, and though many of the participants refused to sign the death warrant, the "holy, anointed" king was executed by his subjects in January 1649, to the horror of all Europe and most of England.

England Under Cromwell: The Interregnum

Oliver Cromwell was now master of England. The republic established after Charles's execution—during what is known as the interregnum, or period between kings' reigns—was officially ruled by the Rump Parliament, but a Council of State led by Cromwell controlled policy, with the backing of the army. Military activity was far from over because first an Irish rebellion had to be crushed—and it was, brutally—and then the Scots fought for Charles II, the executed monarch's son, until they were defeated in 1651.

At home Cromwell had to contend with a ferment of political and social ideas. One group, known as the Levellers, demanded the vote for nearly all adult males and parliamentary elections every other year. The men of property among the Puritans, notably Cromwell himself, were disturbed by the political egalitarianism implied by these proposals and insisted that only men with an "interest" in England—that is, land—should be qualified to vote.[4]

Even more radical were the Diggers, a communistic sect that sought to implement the spirit of primitive Christianity by abolishing personal property; the Society of Friends, which stressed personal inspiration as the source of faith and all action; and the Fifth Monarchists, a messianic group who believed that the "saints"—themselves—should rule because the Day of Judgment was at hand. Men of great ability contributed to the fantastic flood of pamphlets and suggestions that poured forth in these years—the poet John Milton, Cromwell's secretary, was one of the most prominent pamphleteers—and their ideas inspired many future revolutionaries. But at the time they merely put Cromwell on the defensive, forcing him to maintain control at all costs.

Cromwell himself—as an Independent among the Puritans, a staunch parliamentarian, and a country gentleman—fought for two overriding causes: religious freedom (except for Anglicanism and Catholicism) and constitutional government. But neither came within his grasp, and he grew increasingly unhappy at the Rump's refusal to enact reforms. When the assembly tried to perpetuate itself, he dissolved it in 1653 (the final end of the Long Parliament).

During the remaining five years of his life, Cromwell tried desperately to lay down a new constitutional structure for his government. He always hoped that Parliament itself would establish the perfect political system for England. In fact, though, the three Parliaments he called

during these five years seemed to have no inclination to undertake such reforms. Cromwell refused on principle to influence proceedings—except to dismiss the assembly when he felt a selfish faction was seeking its own ends—but in so acting he ignored the realities of politics and left his ideals unfulfilled.

Cromwell was driven by noble aspirations, but he adhered to them so intensely that he could make few compromises. Finally, when he felt he had no recourse since nobody else was as high-minded as he was, he created a blatant military dictatorship, because the alternatives seemed worse. From 1653 on he was called lord protector and ruled through 11 major generals, each responsible for a different district of England and supported by a tax on royalist estates. To quell dissent he banned newspapers, and to prevent disorder he took such measures as enlisting innkeepers as government spies.

Cromwell always remained a reluctant revolutionary; he hated power and sought only limited ends. Some revolutionaries, like Lenin, have a good idea of where they would like to be carried by events; others, like Cromwell, move painfully, hesitantly, and uncertainly to the extremes they finally reach. It was because he sought England's benefit so urgently and because he considered the nation too precious to abandon to irreligion or tyranny that he remained determinedly in command to the end of his life.

Those final years, however, were filled with plots led by Levellers, royalists, and other dissidents of every shade of belief. The court that gathered around the young Stuart heir, Charles II, who had been in exile on the Continent since 1648, was a breeding ground of conspiracy. Only a superb counterespionage system, organized by the head of Cromwell's postal services (who simply read the mails), enabled him to quench all the plots.

Gradually more traditional forms reappeared. The Parliament of 1656 offered Crom-

[4] It should be recalled that voting rights were still tightly restricted; parliamentary elections by no means assured every Englishman a voice in government. In a town only the freemen (a small group, rarely more than about 20 percent of the population) and in the country only owners of land worth at least 40 shillings in rent a year (considerably less than 10 percent of all landowners) were entitled to vote.

well the crown, and though he refused, he took the title of "His Highness" and ensured that the succession would go to his son. Cromwell was monarch in all but name, yet only he assured stability. After he died his quiet, retiring son Richard proved no match for the scheming generals of the army. To bring an end to the chaos, General George Monck, the commander of a well-disciplined force in Scotland, marched south, assumed control, invited Charles II home from exile, and thus in May of 1660 brought the interregnum to an end.

The Results of the Revolution

Cromwell's chief success had been in foreign policy: he had strengthened the navy, captured Jamaica, gained Dunkirk, and in general reasserted England's importance in international affairs. But at home only the actions taken during the first months of the Long Parliament, in 1640 and 1641—the abolition of leading royal courts, the prohibition of taxation without parliamentary consent, and the establishment of the writ of habeas corpus—persisted beyond the interregnum. Otherwise everything seemed much the same as before: bishops and lords were reinstated; religious dissent was again repressed; Parliament was called and dissolved by the monarch; and though many old feudal rights were annulled, the king got a set annual income in their place. But the tone and balance of political relations had changed for good.

The long-term political and social changes seem minor by comparison with the French and Russian revolutions. And yet they had altered the structure of government and society significantly. Henceforth the gentry could no longer be denied a decisive voice in politics. In essence this had been their revolution, and they had succeeded. When in the 1680s a king again tried to impose his wishes on the country without reference to Parliament, there was no need for another major upheaval. A quiet, bloodless coup reaffirmed the new role of the gentry and Parliament (see p. 620).

Thus a new settlement was reached after a long period of growing unease and open conflict. The English could now enjoy untroubled a system of rule that with only gradual modification was to remain in force for some two centuries.

France

Before 1789, the civil wars of the sixteenth century were the closest France came to a revolutionary situation, but the tensions did not disappear when Henry IV brought the fighting to an end. Although the monarchy managed to extend its powers over the next 50 years, resistance continued until a final violent confrontation between the central government and its opponents in the 1640s and 1650s ended in victory for the crown.

Henry IV

Henry IV began the process of strengthening royal power as soon as the civil wars were over. During the remaining years of his reign, from 1598 to 1610, opposition was muted, and he was able to establish his authority in a variety of ways. He mollified the traditional landed aristocracy, known as the nobility of the sword, by giving its leaders places on the chief executive body, the Council of Affairs, and then, when he felt strong enough, by shunting them off to their country estates with large financial settlements that were little better than bribes.

The principal bureaucrats, known as the nobility of the robe, required more careful treatment. They were a formidable group, in control of the country's administration, and led by great officeholding dynasties that were highly suspicious of newcomers. Henry did not try to undermine their position, but he made sure to turn their interests to his benefit. Since all crown offices had to be bought, he used the system both to raise revenues and to confirm the bureaucrats in their loyalty to the king. His tactics involved not only an acceleration in the sales of offices, but also the invention of a new device, an annual fee known as the *paulette*. Regular payments of the *paulette* ensured that an officeholder's job would remain in his family when he died. This not only increased royal profits (by the end of Henry's reign, receipts from the sales accounted for one-twelfth of crown revenues), but also reduced the flow of newcomers and thus strengthened the commitment of existing officeholders to the status quo, that is, to the crown.

By 1610 Henry had succeeded in imposing his will throughout France to a degree that would have been unimaginable in 1598. His treasury was solvent, neither great nobles nor Huguenots gave him trouble, and he was secure enough to plan an invasion of the Holy Roman Empire to extend his power even further. He was assassinated as he was about to leave Paris to join his army, but he had already brought about a quite extraordinary revival of royal authority.

Economic Affairs

In economic affairs the religious wars had taken a toll that was not so quickly remedied. In the 1550s a most fruitful alliance in trading ventures had developed between merchants and nobles. Significant advances had been made overseas, where the French had begun to encroach on the Portuguese monopoly of slaves, gold, and ivory in West Africa. Great ports such as Bordeaux and Marseilles and trade centers such as Lyons had enjoyed unprecedented prosperity. France possessed more fertile agricultural land than any other country of Europe, and its manufactured goods, notably clothes, had been sought throughout the Continent.

The civil war had changed this rosy situation. Trade had suffered heavily, particularly in the once-bustling coastal areas along the Channel. The overseas effort had come to a halt, and the French had soon been replaced by the Dutch and the English as the principal challengers to the Spanish and Portuguese empires. Taxes had mounted, and a large part of the burden had fallen on the merchants in the form of heavy customs dues. Naturally they abandoned commerce as soon as they could afford to enter the nobility and gain a tax exemption by buying a royal office. The result was that capital was diverted from trade to unproductive expenditures, and by the end of the century the nobility had developed a lofty contempt for commerce. French trade did not recover its vitality for more than 100 years. Agriculture had suffered less, but uprisings of peasants, the main victims of the tax system, occurred almost annually in some part of France from the 1590s until the 1670s.

Although the restoration of political stability ended the worst economic disruptions, Henry could do little about the fundamental problems that faced the merchants and the peasants. Nevertheless, once the process of centralization started, the assumption developed that the government was also responsible for the health of economic affairs. This view was justified by a theory known as mercantilism that became an essential ingredient of absolutism, the belief that the king had absolute power in his realm.

Mercantilism was more a set of attitudes than a systematic economic theory. Its basic premise—an erroneous one—was that the world contained a fixed amount of wealth and that each nation could enrich itself only at the expense of others. To some thinkers this meant hoarding as much bullion (gold and silver) as possible; to others it required a favorable balance of trade—more exports than imports. All mercantilists, however, agreed that state regulation was necessary for the welfare of a country. A strong, centralized government was the only power that could encourage native industries, control production, set quality standards, allocate resources, establish tariffs, and take other measures to promote prosperity and improve trade. Thus mercantilism was as much a political as an economic viewpoint and fitted in perfectly with Henry's restoration of royal power.

Mercantilism's principal advocate was Henry's friend and chief minister, the duke of Sully. Sully was concerned that France be self-sufficient agriculturally, in food and drink. But above all he felt that only a strong monarchy could guide the country to prosperity and order. What is significant is that the mercantilists also approved of war. They were men of their times in believing that successful aggression was essential to a country's growth. Linkage warfare with strong government and even economics reflected the assumptions of the age.

The Regency and Richelieu

Unrest reappeared when Henry's death left the throne to his nine-year-old son, Louis XIII (1610–1643). The widowed queen, Marie de Medici, serving as regent, dismissed her husband's ministers and changed his aggressive foreign policy into friendship with the Hapsburgs. The Calvinists feared for their safety, and their stronghold, the southwest, came close to open revolt. The nobles too began to reassert themselves, infuriated because Marie, an Italian, took advice from her fellow countrymen and not from the aristocrats of the kingdom. Led by the prince of Condé, a cousin of Henry IV, they demanded an investigation of the Council of Regency and particularly of its financial dealings. In the face of these mounting troubles, Marie summoned the Estates General in 1614.

This was the last meeting of the Estates General for 175 years, until the eve of the French Revolution, and its failings demonstrated that the monarchy was the only institution around which the nation could be united. The session revealed only the impotence of those who wished to oppose the throne, and Marie put the issue beyond doubt by declaring her son to be of age and the regency dissolved. There was now nothing left to investigate, for the Estates General could only offer advice to a king; it had no legislative powers. The remaining aristocratic dissidents were silenced by large bribes, which consumed the entire treasure left by Henry IV, and the Calvinists were partially appeased by guarantees that their status would not be changed.

For a decade after the crisis, the court lacked the energetic direction that was needed to continue the consolidation of power begun by Henry IV. But in 1624 one of Marie's favorites, Armand du Plessis de Richelieu, a churchman who rose to the cardinalate through her favor, took control of the government. For the next 18 years, there was once more an ambitious and determined head of the central administration.

Many forces pressed on the monarchy as it concentrated its power, and it was Richelieu's great achievement that he kept them in balance. The strongest group was the bureaucracy, whose ranks had been swollen by the sale of office. Richelieu was a classic example of the great ministers of the seventeenth century in that he always paid close attention to the wishes of the bureaucrats and could then face the monarchy as the head of a vast army of indispensable royal servants. He also tried to reduce the independence of the traditional nobility by integrating them into the regime and giving them posts as diplomats, soldiers, and officials. Many remained resentful of the growing bureaucracy, but some did take prominent positions in the government.

And the Huguenots still stirred uneasily. Since the death of Henry IV, they had feared new repression and had engaged in sporadic fighting with the monarchy. The conflict reached a new intensity in the mid-1620s, and the royal army embarked on a systematic destruction of their military power in their stronghold, the southwest, capturing their chief bastion, the port of La Rochelle, in 1628. Richelieu then imposed strict terms. Most of the guarantees established by the Edict of Nantes

For all his considerable power, his aspirations to grandeur, and his shrewd political ambitions, Cardinal Richelieu always saw himself as a churchman. In his portraits, therefore, he could never appear in the rich clothes of a king or an aristocrat. Yet in some ways his simple church robes, adorned only by a cross, make him appear no less grand or potent.
(Photo: New York Public Library/Picture Collection)

peared. The sale of office was allowed to break all bounds: by 1633 it accounted for approximately one-half of royal revenues. Ten years later more than three-quarters of the crown's direct taxation was needed to pay the salaries of the officeholders. It was a vicious circle, and the only solution was to increase ordinary taxes, which fell most heavily on the lower classes.

As the burden of taxation mounted, Richelieu had to improve the government's control over the realm to obtain the revenue he needed. He increased the power of the *intendants,* the government's chief agents in the localities, and established them as the principal representatives of the monarchy in each province of France— a counterpoise to the traditionally dominant nobility. The *intendants* recruited for the army, arranged billeting, supervised the raising of taxes, and enforced the king's decrees. They soon came to be hated figures because the rising taxes were creating constant unrest.

In almost every year of the seventeenth century, but with greatest intensity from the 1620s to the 1670s, there was a peasant uprising in some area of France, and the main grievance was taxation. But there were other issues too, notably a dislike for the growth of the central government. The peasants were frequently led by local notables who resented the widening powers of the monarchy because the increase in taxes and the rise of the *intendants* threatened their own jurisdiction.

Thus, when Richelieu decided to ignore domestic problems and concentrate on foreign ambitions, he took a major gamble. It almost failed in 1636: troops sent to quell a peasant uprising left a serious gap in France's eastern defenses, allowing Spanish troops to invade to within 100 miles of Paris. But disaster was avoided, the French went on to increasing military success, and when Richelieu died in 1642, it appeared that the twin ambitions of absolutism at home and preeminence abroad were close to realization.

were abolished, and though the Huguenots were allowed freedom of worship, they no longer were permitted local independence, which might threaten the unity of the state.

Richelieu also hoped to reduce administrative expenses, but when money was needed for aggression abroad, the good intentions disap-

Yet it was clear that the costs of France's foreign policy during the early seventeenth century intensified its domestic problems. Those who resented the growing power of the central government were waiting only for the right moment to reassert themselves. But the centralization was so successful that when the moment came, in a series of revolts known as the Fronde, there was no major effort to reshape the social order or to reorganize the state into a new political system. The Fronde was certainly a strident clash between opposing forces, but it took place within the traditional political and social forms. The principal expressions of discontent came from the upper levels of society: the nobles, townsmen, and members of the regional courts and legislatures known as Parlements. Only occasionally were these groups joined by peasants, who had bitter grievances against taxation and royal officials, and only for a brief while in the city of Bordeaux was there a foretaste of the sweeping revolution that was eventually to overtake France in 1789.

The Fronde

The death of Louis XIII, in 1643, followed by a regency because Louis XIV was only five years old, provided the opportunity for those who wanted to hold back the rise of absolutism. The immediate issues strikingly resembled those of Louis XIII's own minority, under the regency of Marie de Medici. Louis XIII's widow, Anne of Austria, took over the government and placed all the power in the hands of the Italian-born Cardinal Giulio Mazarin, a protégé of Richelieu's who symbolized the influence of foreigners and the Catholic Church that both nobles and parlementaires disliked. Moreover, Mazarin used his position to amass a huge fortune. He was therefore a perfect target for the expression of a deep-seated resentment: anger at the encroachment of central government on local authority.

Early in 1648 Mazarin sought to gain a respite from the monarch's perennial financial trouble by withholding payment of the salaries of some royal officials for four years. In response the members of various administrative and legal institutions in Paris, including the Parlement, drew up a charter of demands. They wanted the office of *intendant* abolished, no new offices created, power of approval over the raising of taxes, and enactment of a habeas corpus law. The last two demands reflected what the English Parliament was seeking at this very time, but the first two were long-standing French grievances, intensified by the officials' fear for their class identity and authority in the face of royal power, and by general opposition to newly created officials and taxes.

Mazarin reacted by arresting the Paris Parlement's leaders, thus sparking a popular rebellion in the city that forced him and the royal family to flee from the capital—an experience the young Louis XIV never forgot. In the spring of 1649, Mazarin promised to redress the parlementaires' grievances, and he was allowed to return to Paris. But the trouble was far from over; during that summer uprisings spread throughout France, particularly among peasants and in the old Huguenot stronghold, the southwest.

The most turbulent developments took place in the city of Bordeaux, where the parlementaires lost control and minor artisans and lawyers, furious at the taxes imposed by the crown and eager to revenge themselves on the less-burdened upper orders of society, took over the municipal government. Peasants and street mobs roamed the city, directing their hostility as much at the rich and powerful as at the representatives of the king.

From Mazarin's point of view, however, a more direct threat was posed by two generals who had turned against the government: Henri de Turenne and Louis II of Bourbon, prince of Condé, who had won a series of brilliant military victories in the 1640s and paved the way for France's gains at Westphalia in 1648. Condé was particularly dangerous because he was the head of the greatest noble family in France, and many aristocrats followed his lead. Their aims had not changed much since the days of the Guises 80 years before: they wanted Mazarin removed, their local powers restored, and a more influential position at court. Some nobles made brief alliances with the regional parlementaires, but each group wanted power for itself, and thus they soon drew apart.

Capitalizing on the disillusionment that soon resulted from the perpetual unrest, Mazarin began to reassert the position of the monarchy. Turenne was simply bought over; military force and the threat to use it subdued Paris and most of the rural rebels; Condé, losing support, fled to Spain; and the vulnerable regency was brought to an end by the declaration that Louis was of age in 1652. When Bordeaux finally fell to royal troops the next year, the Fronde was virtually over. Although peasants continued their occasional regional uprisings for many years to come, no other element in French society seriously challenged the crown as the basis for order in the realm.

Mazarin's remaining years in power, until his death in 1661, were relatively free of trouble. In foreign affairs he brought the war with Spain to a triumphant conclusion at the Treaty of the Pyrenees in 1659. At home the nobles had now been weakened as never before; the royal administration, centered on the *intendants,* faced no significant resistance; and the Parlements subsided into quiescence, their demands all rejected when Louis was declared of age. This outcome was very different from the situation across the Channel in 1661, but just as surely as England, France had found a stable solution for long-standing conflicts.

Spain

For Spain the upheavals of the mid-seventeenth century were little short of disastrous. Until they erupted, it was the most powerful state in Europe; when they were over, it had lost its preeminence and was on its way to becoming a second-class power. Yet the seeds of Spain's difficulties—primarily administrative and financial—were already visible in the sixteenth century.

Stresses in the Reign of Philip II (1556–1598)

Philip's chief problem was the lack of unity in his diverse domains. From his father he inherited the Low Countries, Naples, Sardinia, Sicily, and Spain and its New World territories. In 1580 Portugal and its possessions also came under his rule.

To hold this sprawling empire together, Philip developed an elaborate bureaucracy. But he was an obsessively suspicious man, and he therefore determined to maintain close control over the administrative structure by keeping in touch with every decision. As a result proceedings were agonizingly slow and inefficient in both important and trivial matters. The effect on military affairs was crippling; commanders in the field were often paralyzed, waiting for orders from home before taking action. Moreover the bureaucracy was run by Castilian nobles, who were resented as outsiders in other regions of the empire.

The standing army also caused the king problems. Although the military gave the throne potent support, it was the regime's single largest expense. The cost was readily undertaken since the logistic and administrative needs of the army stimulated the growth of bureaucracy and government authority. But the populace was less appreciative of these outlays, particularly when, to meet some of the expense and to emphasize the might of the crown, soldiers were lodged in the homes of ordinary citizens without recompense. This aroused bitter resentment, especially in the Low Countries, where the Spanish troops were regarded as foreigners.

Within the Iberian peninsula, however, Philip was able to overcome the resentment by using religious belief to arouse his subjects' loyalty. Spaniards regarded their country as the bastion of Catholicism, and Philip's devoutness reflected their mood perfectly. He persecuted heresy, encouraged the Inquisition, and allowed his intolerance to affect even the great flowering of Spanish mysticism, led by St. Teresa. Neither the king nor the ecclesiastical hierarchy could feel comfortable about the mystics because such extremes of personal faith seemed to weaken the position of the Catholic Church. Nonetheless Philip's emphasis on the nation's faith powerfully stimulated Spain's political cohesion, which was promoted rather than hindered by the military activity and persecution on behalf of the Church.

Economic Problems

In other areas, notably the economy, there was little Philip could do to relieve the strains of constant warfare. Spain was a rich country in Philip's reign, but the most profitable activities were monopolized by limited groups, often foreigners. Because royal policy valued administrative convenience above social benefit, the city of Seville was arbitrarily given control over commerce with the New World so as to simplify supervision of this enormous source of income. Other lucrative pursuits, such as wool and wine production, were dominated by a small coterie of insiders who made large profits but needed little manpower. And the pasturage rights throughout Castile that the crown granted sheep breeders removed vast areas of land from use by growers of foodstuffs. The only important economic activity whose income spread beyond a restricted circle was the prosperous Mediterranean trade. This commerce, centered in Barcélona, brought wealth to much of Aragon.

The profits made by non-Spaniards were the most obvious example of the limited domestic benefit of Spain's vast wealth. Most of the American treasure was sent abroad to repay German and Italian bankers whose loans kept Philip's troops in the field. Apart from Seville the cities that gained most from the new wealth were Genoa and Antwerp. And the Genoese mercantile community, with long experience in international finance, dominated Seville's economic life and played a crucial role in financing Philip's campaigns. Antwerp, always important as the meeting place for traders from the Mediterranean and the north, now gained prominence as the focus of Spanish activity in the Low Countries.

Thus even though the influx of silver into Spain continued to rise (it quadrupled between the 1550s and 1590s), the money was not profitably invested within the country. Drastically overextended in foreign commitments, the king declared himself bankrupt three times during his reign. His misguided policies, especially his continuing military involvements, were causing a slow economic deterioration.

Spain's futile struggles with the Dutch and later with the French proved to be the final blows in a succession of multiplying difficulties—economic, political, and military. For a while it seemed that the problems might be overcome because there was peace during the reign of Philip's son, Philip III (1598–1621), following a truce with the Dutch in 1609. But in fact Philip's government was incompetent and corrupt, capable neither of dealing with the serious consequences of generations of excessive war spending nor of broadening the country's limited list of exports beyond wool and wine. Moreover, when the flow of treasure from the New World began to dwindle after 1600, the crown was deprived of a major source of income that it was unable to replace (see accompanying table). The decline was caused partly by a growing use of precious metals in the New World colonies but, more important, by a demographic disaster that overtook the Indians who worked as laborers and miners. Disease, overwork, and a drastic fall in the birth rate reduced their numbers with incredible

**IMPORTS OF TREASURE TO SPAIN
FROM THE NEW WORLD, 1601–1660**

Decade	Total Value★
1601–1610	66,970,000
1611–1620	65,568,000
1621–1630	62,358,000
1631–1640	40,110,000
1641–1650	30,641,000
1651–1660	12,785,000

★In ducats

Adapted from J. H. Elliott, *Imperial Spain 1469–1716,*
New York, 1964, p. 175.

speed. In Mexico and northern Guatemala alone, there had been approximately 25 million natives when the Spaniards first arrived in 1519. By the 1650s there were only 1.5 million.

In the meantime tax returns at home were shrinking, and at best they never covered expenses. The most significant factor in this decrease was a drop in the population of Castile and Aragon from 10 million in 1600 to 6 million in 1700. No other country in Europe suffered a demographic reversal of this proportion during the seventeenth century. In addition, though the wine and wool industries continued to prosper, their spectacular growth had come to a halt by the early seventeenth century, and no other important industries took their place. Worse still, Spain had to rely increasingly on the importation of expensive foodstuffs to feed its people.

It was under these conditions that Spain resumed large-scale fighting under Philip IV (1621–1665), first reopening hostilities against the Dutch in 1621 and then starting an escalating involvement in the Thirty Years' War. With its dwindling resources the burdens now became too much to bear. Through the 1620s a brilliant general, Ambrogio di Spinola, maintained the Spaniards' tradition of military victory, but his death, in 1630, removed their last able commander. The effort to continue the government's commitment to war during the

subsequent decades despite totally inadequate financial means was to bring the greatest state in Europe to its knees.

Revolt and Secession

The final crisis was brought about by the policies of Philip IV's chief minister, the count of Olivares. His aim was to unite the kingdom, to "Castilianize" Spain. He wanted all the territories to bear equally the burden of maintaining their country's dominant position in the world. Laws would be uniform, expenses would be apportioned equitably among the provinces, and each province would receive its fair share of the nation's gains. Although Castile would no longer dominate, it would also not have to provide the bulk of the taxes and army.

Olivares's program was called the Union of Arms, and though it seemed eminently reasonable, its implementation caused a series of revolts in the 1640s that split Spain apart. The reason was quite simple. For more than a century, Castile had controlled the other provinces, which had felt increasingly that local independence was being undermined by a centralized regime. The Union of Arms was regarded as the last straw because it added new substance to this long-standing grievance. Moreover Olivares undertook his plan at a time when Spain's military and economic fortunes were noticeably in decline. France had declared war on the Hapsburgs in 1635, and thereafter Spain's position had deteriorated. The funds to support an army were becoming harder to raise, and in desperation Olivares pressed more vigorously for the Union of Arms. But all he accomplished was to provoke crippling revolts against the Castilians in Catalonia, Portugal, Naples, and Sicily.

The precipitant was France's invasion of Catalonia in 1639. Thinking that the Catalans would not refuse to share some of the effort of repelling the invaders from their own territory,

Olivares ordered the troops fighting the French to be billeted in Catalonia. But instead of strengthening the government, the order provided the people with the issue that finally goaded them into open defiance in 1640.

Olivares tried to meet the revolt by asking the Portuguese to help subdue the Catalans, but this attempt to bind together the components of the Spanish empire only aroused further defiance. By the next year both Catalonia and Portugal declared themselves independent republics and placed themselves under French protection. Plots began to appear against Olivares, and Philip dismissed the one minister who had understood Spain's problems but who, in trying to solve them, had made them worse.

The Catalonian rebellion continued for another 11 years, and it was thwarted in the end only because the peasants and town mobs transformed the resistance to the central government into an attack on the privileged and wealthy classes in the province. At this point the Catalan nobility abandoned the cause and joined the government side. About the same time the Fronde forced the withdrawal of French troops. Thus when the last major holdout, Barcelona, fell to a royal army in 1652, the Catalan nobles returned with their rights and privileges guaranteed, and the revolt was over.

The Portuguese, on the other hand, though not officially granted independence from Spain until 1668, were fully capable of defending their autonomy and even invaded Castile in the 1640s. Their revolt against the central government never became tinged with the social unrest that undermined the Catalans' unity. Portugal's nobles maintained their authority throughout the struggle and dominated the government thereafter.

The revolts in Sicily and Naples, aimed at the Castilians who ruled and taxed both provinces, took place in 1647. In Naples the unrest soon developed into a tremendous mob uprising, led by a local fisherman. The poor turned against all the representatives of government and wealth they could find, and chaos ensued until their leader was killed. The violence in Sicily by contrast was more exclusively the result of soaring taxes and was directed almost entirely against government representatives. Severe countermeasures were taken in both Naples and Sicily, and within a few months the government regained control.

Spain had experienced a period of great cultural brilliance during Philip IV's reign, but even this died away as grim times descended on the country. Overextension in foreign war, financial and economic shortcomings at home, and the excessive reliance on Castile had all helped sap the nation's strength. The revolts during the 1640s were the result of decades of growing resentment at the monarch's inability to solve these basic, pressing problems; but the domestic unrest finally brought Spain's international ambitions and thus the worst of its difficulties to an end. Like England and France, Spain found a new way of life in the 1660s. It was to be a stable, second-level state, heavily agricultural, and run by its nobility.

The United Provinces

Although the United Provinces remained locked in a struggle for survival against Spain until 1648, and in various ways became a unique state, the Dutch did not escape the domestic tensions of the seventeenth century. Despite the remarkable fluidity of their society, they too went through a period of confrontation in the mid-seventeenth century that determined the structure of their government for over a century.

The Structure of the United Provinces

The United Provinces became a unique state for a number of reasons. Other republics existed in Europe, but they were controlled by small oligarchies; the Dutch, who had a long tradition of a strong representative assembly, the Estates General, created a nation in which many citizens participated in their own government through elected delegates. Although powerful merchants and a few aristocrats close to the House of Orange did create a small elite, the ordinary citizenry, participating in politics and united by a common cause, reduced the social differentiation prevalent elsewhere in Europe. The resulting openness and homogeneity colored the two most remarkable features of the United Provinces: economic mastery and cultural brilliance.

The most striking accomplishment of the Dutch was their rise to supremacy in the world of commerce. Amsterdam displaced Antwerp (and Genoa) as the Continent's financial capital and gained control of the trade of the world's richest markets. And in 1609 the Bank of Amsterdam was established, the first semiofficial financial institution of its kind in modern history; it made a vital contribution to the country's economy by offering the lowest interest rates in Europe. This encouraged native industries, such as shipbuilding, as well as overseas ventures, such as the East India Company, which needed substantial investments. In addition, the Dutch rapidly emerged as the cheapest shippers in international trade. As a result, by the middle of the seventeenth century they had become the chief carriers of European trade.

The openness of Dutch society permitted the freest exchange of ideas of the time. An official church, the Reformed Church, was established, but no religious groups were forbidden as long as they worshiped in private. The new state therefore gave refuge to believers of all kinds, whether extreme Protestant radicals or Catholics who wore their faith lightly, and the city of Amsterdam became the center of a brilliant Jewish community. This freedom attracted some of the greatest minds in Europe,

and fostered remarkable artistic creativity. Patrons were easy to find among the wealthy merchants, and Dutch painting in the seventeenth century is one of the glories of Western culture (see pp. 584–585 and Plates 39–41). Yet it was not the result of the taste or sensibility of a few patrons and geniuses but an outpouring from many directions; and it was not the climax of a long tradition but a sudden outburst whose greatest expressions appeared in the first generation. The energy that produced the wealth and creativity reflected the pride of a tiny nation that was winning its independence.

Domestic Tensions

From the earliest days of the revolt against Spain, there had been a basic split within the United Provinces. The two provinces of Holland and Zeeland dominated the Estates General because they supplied a majority of its taxes. Their representatives formed a mercantile party, which advocated peace abroad so that their trade could flourish unhampered, government by the Estates General so that they could make their power felt, and religious toleration. In opposition to the mercantile interest was a party centered on the House of Orange, which sought to boost that family's leadership of the Dutch. This party stood for war to strengthen a popular national leader, centralized power for the House of Orange, and (after William died) strict Calvinism.

The differences between the two factions came to a head in 1618, when Maurice of Nassau used the religious issue as a pretext for executing his chief opponent, Jan van Oldenbarneveldt, the principal representative of the province of Holland. Oldenbarneveldt opposed the resumption of war with Spain when the truce of 1609 expired in 1621, and his removal left Maurice in full control of the country. The mercantile party had been defeated, and war could resume in 1621.

For more than 20 years, the House of Or-

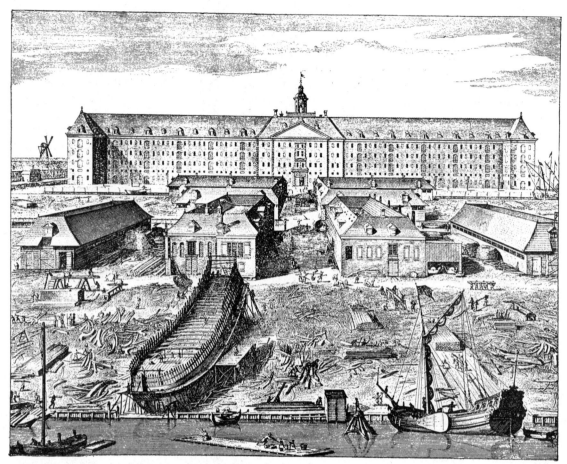

The Dutch became the best shipbuilders in Europe in the seventeenth century; the efficiency of their ships, which could be manned by fewer sailors than those of other countries, was a major reason for their successes in trade and commerce.
(Photo: The Granger Collection)

ange remained in command, unassailable because it led the army in time of war. Not until 1648, when the family was headed by a new leader, William II, could its opponents reassert themselves and sign the treaty of Westphalia that officially recognized the independence of the United Provinces. It then seemed that the mercantile party had gained the upper hand. But the outcome remained in the balance (there was even the threat of a siege of Amsterdam by troops loyal to the House of Orange) until William II suddenly died in 1650, leaving as his successor a posthumously born son, William III.

With serious opposition removed, the mercantile interest could now assume full power, and Jan De Witt, the representative of the province of Holland, took over the running of the government in 1653. De Witt's aims were to leave as much authority as possible in the hands of the provinces, particularly Holland; to weaken the executive in this way and prevent a revival of the fortunes of the House of Orange; to pursue trading advantage; and to maintain peace so that the economic supremacy of the Dutch would not be endangered. For nearly 20 years, he guided the country in its golden age. But in 1672 French armies overran the southern provinces, and De Witt, with his mercantile inclinations, lacked the military instinct to fight a dangerous enemy. The Dutch at once turned to the family that had led them to independence; a mob murdered De Witt; and the House of Orange, under William III, resumed the centralization that henceforth was to characterize the political structure of the United Provinces. The country had not experienced a mid-century upheaval as severe as those of its neighbors, but it had nevertheless been forced to endure unrest and violence before the form of its government was securely established.

Sweden

The Swedes, too, reached basic decisions in the mid-seventeenth century about political relations in the administration of the state. Violence was avoided, but tensions had to be resolved nonetheless.

The Achievement of Gustavus Adolphus

In the early 1600s Sweden, a Lutheran country of a million people which had gained its independence from Denmark less than a century earlier, was one of the backwaters of Europe. A feudal nobility dominated the countryside and sought to control the government, a barter economy made money almost unknown, and both trade and towns were virtually nonexistent. Moreover the Swedes found themselves in a running battle with the Danes, whose well-organized, well-armed, and prosperous monarchy dominated the Baltic Sea. Sweden, by contrast, lacked a capital, central institutions, and government machinery. The task of ruling was thus entirely dependent on the king and a few courtiers; officials were appointed only to deal with specific problems as they arose.

Gustavus Adolphus (1611–1632) transformed this situation. At the start of his reign, he faced a war that was to involve all the states in the area—his own, Denmark, Poland, and Russia—in a struggle to control the lands around the Baltic. Without his nobles' help, however, Gustavus could not raise an army. He therefore arranged an alliance with the nobles and gave them dominant positions in a newly organized bureaucracy. By winning their support he not only staffed an administrative machine but organized an army, thus equipping himself both to govern and to fight.

During the two decades of his reign, Gustavus engaged in a remarkable series of conquests abroad. By 1629 he controlled the coastline of the eastern Baltic, making Sweden the most powerful state in the area. He then entered the Thirty Years' War, advancing victoriously through the Holy Roman Empire until his death, in 1632, during the showdown battle with Wallenstein (see pp. 526–527). Although without their general the Swedes could do little more than hang on to the gains they had made, they remained for a century a force to be reckoned with in international affairs.

The system of government that Gustavus and his chief adviser, Axel Oxenstierna, established in 1611 was to be the envy of other countries until the twentieth century. At the heart of the system were five administrative departments,[5] each led by a nobleman, with the most important—the Chancellery—run by Oxenstierna, who supervised diplomacy and internal affairs. Gradually an administrative center emerged in Stockholm where, under Oxenstierna's capable leadership, the bureaucracy proved that it could run the nation, supply the army, and implement policy even during the last 12 years of Gustavus's reign, when

---

[5] They were the Chancellery, the Ministry of Justice, the Treasury, the Department of War, and the Department of the Navy.

the king himself was almost always abroad. During his absence Oxenstierna took charge, though executive power was officially vested in the Rad, an assembly of nobles.

Another major institution, the Riksdag, consisted of representatives of four estates: the nobility, the clergy, the townspeople, and (unique in Europe) the peasants. Although officially it was the highest legislative authority in the land, real power was retained by the nobles and the crown. For centuries the Riksdag functioned as no more than a sounding board that gave the appearance of popular approval to royal and aristocratic rule, which by the 1630s was already operating with an efficiency unparalleled on the Continent.

A major cause of Sweden's amazing rise was the development of the domestic economy. Early in Gustavus's reign new discoveries made possible the mining of huge deposits of copper, an important metal for cannon and coin manufacture, and the Swedes gained a virtual monopoly of copper mining in Europe. The crown maximized its profits by taking over the mines itself. To avoid dependence on one commodity, the government also encouraged iron mining. Foreign experts were brought in, and the discovery of a new smelting process made Swedish iron highly prized. At the same time, the country's traditional tar and timber exports were stepped up, and a fleet was built. By 1700 Stockholm had become an important trading and financial center, growing in the course of the century from fewer than 5000 to more than 50,000 inhabitants—a phenomenal rise and further evidence of the general northward shift of European economic activity.

The Role of the Nobles

The one source of tension amidst this remarkable progress was the position of the aristocrats. They had been Gustavus's partners and after he died they tightened their control over the government and society.

Between 1611 and 1652 nobles more than doubled the proportion of land they owned in Sweden, and increased sixfold their holdings in Finland, which Sweden ruled. Much of this growth was at the expense of the crown, which granted away or sold its lands to help its war efforts abroad. Both peasants and townspeople viewed these developments with alarm. Peasants always fared much worse under nobles than as direct tenants of the king because the great landowners sought the maximum possible return from their possessions. And the towns felt that their place in national affairs was being destroyed by an excessively powerful aristocracy. Both groups were frightened when the Danish nobles took advantage of the death of their country's strong king, in 1648, to gain control of government.[6] Two years later the showdown came in Sweden.

The ruler of Sweden was Gustavus's daughter Christina, an able but erratic young queen who usually allowed Oxenstierna to run the government. In the late 1640s she was becoming increasingly hopeful that she could abdicate her throne, become a Catholic, and leave Sweden—an ambition she fulfilled in 1654. She wanted her cousin Charles recognized as her successor, but the aristocracy threatened to create a nobles' republic if she abdicated. The queen therefore summoned the Riksdag, Sweden's representative assembly, in 1650, and taking advantage of the grievances of townspeople and peasants, she encouraged the three lower estates to mount a campaign against the aristocracy. Believing that they might now gain a new importance in national affairs, the townspeople and peasants demanded the return of nobles' lands to the crown, freedom of speech, and real power in the Riksdag so that the lower estates could outvote the nobles. Under this pressure the nobility gave way and recognized

---

[6] In 1660 the Danish king engineered a countercoup that firmly established absolutism in that country. Denmark was thus yet another state whose political structure was settled for a long time to come during this period.

the future Charles X Gustavus as successor to the throne—a good choice, because Charles was an able soldier who consolidated Gustavus Adolphus's gains and confirmed Sweden's mastery of northern Europe.

But the confrontation of 1650 proved to be short-lived. Once Christina had won the argument over her successor, she removed her support from the Riksdag and rejected the demands of the lower estates. Only gradually did power shift away from the great nobles toward a broader elite of lesser nobles and bureaucrats (see pp. 623–624).

Eastern Europe

The major powers of Eastern Europe, the Ottoman Empire, Poland, and Russia, were as affected by warfare as their western neighbors. And in Poland and Russia there were also upheavals in the mid-seventeenth century that helped determine these states' future political development.

The Ottoman Empire

In the Ottoman Empire central control was highly effective by the early 1500s. The first signs of a decline of strength at the center began to appear after the death of Suleiman, in 1566. Harem intrigues, corruption at court, and the loosening of military discipline became increasingly serious from the late sixteenth century onward. Yet the Ottomans remained an object of fear and hostility throughout the West—their constant wars with the Hapsburgs devastated Hungary, where most of the fighting took place, and in the eastern Mediterranean they remained a formidable force, though the English and Dutch were coming to play a dominant role in the area after 1600.

The Turkish rulers had unparalleled powers. A crack army of more than 25,000 men stood ready to serve the sultan at all times, and within his domains his supremacy was unquestioned. He was both spiritual and temporal head of his empire, completely free to appoint all officers, issue laws, and raise taxes. But these powers, geared to military conquest and extending over enormous territories, never became a focus of cohesion among the disparate races of the Balkans and the Middle East who were ruled from Constantinople, because the sultan left authority in the hands of local nobles and princes as long as his ultimate sovereignty was recognized. Whenever questions of loyalty arose (as they did sporadically in the Balkans), they revealed that the authority of the central government rested on its military might. That was more than enough, though, to prevent any serious challenges to the power of the Ottomans until they began to lose ground to the Hapsburgs in the eighteenth century.

Poland

The largest kingdom in Europe, Poland, was as disorganized as the Holy Roman Empire. The king could exercise control over his personal lands but elsewhere the country was entirely in the hands of powerful nobles, who from 1572 onward confirmed their independence by ensuring that the monarchy would be strictly elective. The Diet, an assembly of nobles, was required to meet at least once every two years, and without the approval of this body no policy could be enforced.

In Poland as elsewhere, religion was a major issue during the second half of the sixteenth century. Sigismund III (1587–1632), with the help of some members of the aristocracy and the Jesuits, crushed Protestantism. But not all the nobles favored Roman Catholicism; some belonged to the Greek Orthodox Church. Attempts were made to unite the Roman Catholics with the Greek Orthodox, and one group, known as the Uniate Church, agreed to acknowledge papal supremacy while retaining traditional Greek rites. When the Jesuits tried to increase their influence, however, the adherents of the Orthodox and Uniate churches formed a coalition for common defense that split the country into two religious camps.

Although Poland was constantly at war, Sigismund and his successors were never able to use the military situation to overcome the fragmentation of political authority and create a strong central government. Instead, the religious divisions and the power of local nobles became increasingly serious problems until, in the mid-seventeenth century, the Poles, like so many Europeans, faced a major internal clash.

The crisis arose in the Ukraine, the borderland in the southeast of Poland that had long been occupied by the soldier-farmers known as Cossacks. Like their Russian counterparts, these Cossacks were allowed considerable independence because of their importance in protecting the countryside against turbulent neighbors to the south and east. Firm adherents of the Greek Orthodox Church, they became increasingly annoyed at the government for encouraging Catholicism. Finally in 1648 they rebelled, took control of the eastern Ukraine, and in 1654 offered their allegiance to the Greek Orthodox tsar of Russia.

The Polish monarchy was much too weak to combat the revolt, and the nobility had little wish to undertake a long assault on this frontier region. Thus the Ukraine was lost—yet another casualty of the upheavals of the age—though internally Poland continued much as before, a country dominated by a small yet powerful aristocracy. Once again, the storms that swept political life had been succeeded by a sense of settlement.

Russia

The power of the central authority in Russia was already apparent in the reign of Ivan IV (1547–1584)—called the Terrible—who used his considerable military strength both at home and in conquests that extended Muscovite rule

The most violent and feared of the tsars, Ivan IV was even nicknamed "The Terrible." Yet his portrait gives little hint of his reputation. Instead, it draws on the great tradition of the Russian icon—a flat, formal, and idealized depiction—to create an impression of solemn piety.
(Photo: Nationalmuseum, Copenhagen)

along the length of the Volga River to the southeast.

Ivan was restricted by fewer political limitations than any other ruler in Europe. Russia was still feudal; her peasants were serfs, and her great lords, known as boyars, controlled local areas but had little say in national affairs. Jealous of their regional powers, Ivan launched a vicious campaign against the boyars and enormously increased the areas of Russia under his direct control. He enlarged his bureaucracy to meet the new administrative tasks created by his conquests, but the authority of the central government was now a divisive rather than a unifying force, discredited and hated because it had grown by military might.

The reaction came after Ivan's death, when the country entered a 30-year period that would later be called the Time of Troubles. Ivan's son Feodor, the last of the Rurik dynasty, which had ruled since the ninth century, lacked his father's vigor and could not prevent the boyars from reasserting their power. From 1591 onward he virtually handed over control of the government to his brother-in-law, Boris Godunov, whom the boyars regarded as an upstart. When Feodor died in 1598 Boris became tsar and major revolts soon broke out.

For 15 years the country was in chaos as peasants, townspeople, and petty nobles joined in various coalitions against the government and the boyars. The final confrontation took place when the leading boyars supported a Polish claimant to the throne, and a popular army, led by townspeople and lesser nobles who had been excluded from political authority by the higher nobility, drove the Polish claimant from Moscow. In his place a national assembly, consisting of nobles and townspeople, elected as tsar a grandnephew of Ivan the Terrible, Mikhail Feodorovich (1613–1645), founder of the Romanov dynasty.

The central government emerged from these disruptions with its powers essentially unimpaired. The boyars had been unable to weaken the tsar's ability to take firm military measures against his opponents, and under Mikhail they returned to docile inaction. They now depended on the throne for their control over local areas, and many had to serve the tsar in order to retain their estates. During the half-century after the Time of Troubles, the monarchy organized its administration systematically, codified Russia's laws, and continued the extension of its authority by the use or threat of armed force.

But the potential for domestic upheaval was not entirely removed, and indeed it was during this half-century that the groundwork was laid for new turmoil as the boyars gradually closed the last loopholes in the system of serfdom. Previously an escaped serf who remained uncaptured for a certain number of years was automatically liberated, but in 1646 the boyars persuaded Tsar Alexis (1645–1676) to abolish the limit. Now serfs remained in their status for life—hopeless fugitives even if they did escape their masters.

The result was constant agrarian unrest, met by harsh repression, which inspired even more violent uprisings. The disturbances were fed by increasing financial demands on both serfs and townspeople from the central government and local lords, and in 1648 the boiling point was reached. A major riot broke out in Moscow, the tsar was forced to hand over to the rebels a number of his financial administrators, and by the end of the year almost every large city in Russia had experienced serious disorders, quelled only by the intervention of royal troops. This year of upheaval, as fierce in Russia as in England and France, marked the beginning of a period of more than two decades when the lower classes made a major effort, for the last time in centuries, to restrain the growing power of the central government and the landowners.

The popular discontent intensified in the 1650s and 1660s, and finally in 1668 the major revolt that had long been brewing exploded in the southern provinces of Russia, led by a Cossack, Stenka Razin, who terrorized the area and launched a fleet that caused chaos on the Caspian Sea. In 1670 Razin led two expeditions up the Volga River, capturing a succession of towns and handing them over to mob rule. His very approach incited peasants to violence, for his troops included thousands of escaped serfs who hoped to bring liberty to all who were oppressed. There was open advocacy of what amounted to class war: the poor against the rich, the weak against the powerful. Eventually royal troops shattered the poorly equipped army; and though a number of marauding bands continued to harass the inhabitants of central Russia for years, the major threat was ended in 1671, when Razin was executed in Moscow.

Compounding Russia's troubles was serious dissension within the national Greek Orthodox Church. The dispute arose over the decision of the patriarch of Moscow, the head of the Russian Church, to correct the traditional liturgical books of the faith, which contained errors introduced by copyists over the centuries. A group calling itself the Old Believers, refusing to change usages hallowed by custom, objected to the revision and broke away from the estab-

lished church. The schism was accompanied by violence, which forced the patriarch and his followers to become entirely dependent on the secular power to maintain their authority. This reliance on the state undermined the clergy's spiritual leadership and helped the monarchy on its way to assuming complete control over all facets of Russian society.

Having overcome two potential threats to his authority—peasant unrest in areas far from Moscow and the rivalry within the church—Alexis began to feel strong enough in his last years to pay less heed to the boyars. It was clear that a determined ruler could once again make the tsar the dominant figure in Russian society, and in the late seventeenth century Peter the Great was to be that ruler.

Throughout Europe in the mid-seventeenth century long-standing tensions that had just passed through an especially virulent phase were resolved, and a period of relative stability began that was to last for over a century. In international affairs a vicious circle of brutality was broken as a degree of restraint was imposed on the anarchy of warfare. Within Europe's states, the resistance to central governments, usually the result of regional loyalties, traditional aristocratic independence, or resentment at soaring taxes, was effectively brought to an end. Whatever the outcomes—and they ranged from England's parliamentary system to France's absolutism—each country's political situation now settled into accepted forms, just as warmaking and diplomacy did after Westphalia.

Because the disturbances had been so widespread, historians have called the mid-seventeenth century an age of "general crisis." It is a rather vague term, but it does convey the flavor of a period when upheaval was common, reached crisis proportions, and then subsided. The sense of settlement in the 1660s contrasted sharply with the turmoil of the preceding decades. To the extent that the crisis was general, however, one would expect it to be reflected not merely in politics but in thought, art, and society. And indeed, the mid-seventeenth century was the time when, for example, the ideas of the scientific revolution became, after much doubt, an essential part of European civilization. One must not push the connections too far, because simple parallels distort the complexities of the period; nevertheless, the progression from turbulence to calm in politics was not without its analogies in the cultural and social developments of the sixteenth and seventeenth centuries.

RECOMMENDED READING

Sources

*Franklin, Julian H. (tr. and ed.). *Constitutionalism and Resistance in the Sixteenth Century: Three Treatises by Hotman, Beza, & Mornay.* 1969. Three of the most radical tracts of the period, each justifying rebellion.

Studies

*Aston, Trevor (ed.). *Crisis in Europe 1560–1660: Essays from Past and Present.* 1965. This is a collection of those essays in which the "general crisis" interpretation was initially put forward and discussed.

*Elliott, J. H. *Richelieu and Olivares.* 1984. A comparative study of the two statesmen who dominated Europe in the 1620s and 1630s, this book analyzes the nature of political authority at a time when governments were gaining new powers.

*Forster, Robert, and Jack P. Greene (eds.). *Preconditions of Revolution in Early Modern Europe.* 1972. An excellent series of essays on resistance to central governments, and its causes, in a number of European countries.

Hellie, Richard. *Enserfment and Military Change in Muscovy.* 1971. This study shows the links between military affairs and social change in Russia during the early modern period.

Howell, Roger. *Cromwell.* 1977. The clearest and most reliable short biography of the revolutionary leader.

Koenigsberger, H. G. *Estates and Revolutions: Essays in Early Modern European History.* 1971. A most useful set of articles, primarily on political history; of particular interest is a fascinating comparison of the revolutionary parties in France and the Netherlands.

*Mattingly, Garrett. *The Armada.* 1959. This beautifully written book, which was a best seller when it first appeared, is a gripping account of a major international crisis.

Moote, A. Lloyd. *The Revolt of the Judges: The Parlement of Paris and the Fronde 1643–1652.* 1971. This is the most detailed account of the causes of the Fronde and its failures.

*Neale, J. E. *Queen Elizabeth I: A Biography.* 1934. A lucid and affectionate account of the reign by its most distinguished twentieth-century historian.

*Pagès, Georges. *The Thirty Years' War: 1618–1648.* 1971. The most straightforward history of a highly complex period.

*Parker, Geoffrey. *Europe in Crisis 1598–1648.* 1979. A good recent survey of the period with an up-to-date bibliography.

*_____. *The Dutch Revolt.* 1977. This brief book gives a good introduction to the revolt of the Netherlands and the nature of Dutch society in the seventeenth century.

Pierson, Peter. *Philip II of Spain.* 1975. A clear and lively biography of the dominant figure of the second half of the sixteenth century.

*Rabb, Theodore K. *The Struggle for Stability in Early Modern Europe.* 1975. An assessment of the "crisis" interpretation, including extensive bibliographic references.

Roberts, Michael. *Gustavus Adolphus and the Rise of Sweden.* 1973. This is the best biography of the Swedish king, emphasizing especially his military and administrative achievements.

Salmon, J. H. M. *Society in Crisis: France in the Sixteenth Century.* A clearly written overview, focusing mainly on the religious wars and Henry IV.

*Shaw, Howard. *The Levellers.* 1968. This brief introduction to the ideas and activities of the most famous radical group in the English revolution is accompanied by extracts from their writings.

Stone, Lawrence. *The Causes of the English Revolution, 1529–1642.* 1972. A short but comprehensive assessment of the reasons for the outbreak of the seventeenth century's most far-reaching revolution.

Tapié, V. L. *France in the Age of Louis XIII and Richelieu.* D. McN. Lockie (tr. and ed.). 1974. The standard history of the 20-year period when the basic development of French absolutism took place.

---

* Available in paperback.

EXPERIENCES OF DAILY LIFE

The Soldier

Following the invention of gunpowder, long sieges became the most common form of military activity. They demanded increasing numbers of soldiers, and thus life in the army became an experience familiar to millions of Europeans in the 1600s.

It all started with recruitment. Some men genuinely wanted to join up. They had heard stories of adventure, booty, and comradeship. They were terribly poor, and were looking at least for food and clothing. Or they hoped to escape difficult times, problems with neighbors, or an unhappy marriage. The story of one such runaway soldier, a Frenchman named

Hendrik Goltzius. Soldier Marching to the Left. (National Gallery of Art, Rosenwald Collection)

Martin Guerre, whose wife lived with an impostor claiming to be Martin for many years, has recently been made into a film. But in most cases the "volunteers" did not want to go. They had heard as many stories of hardship, exhaustion, and danger as of excitement or glory. Unfortunately for them, recruiting officers had quotas, and villages had to provide the numbers demanded of them. Community pressure, bribery, drunkenness, and even outright kidnaping helped fill the ranks. When honest men could not be made to go, the authorities turned to criminals. Queen Elizabeth I of England, for example, emptied a prison in London to reinforce a besieged town.

Joining an army did not necessarily mean cutting oneself off from friends or family. Men from a particular area enlisted together, and in some cases wives came along. There were dozens of jobs to do aside from fighting, because soldiers needed cooks, laundresses, peddlers, and many other tradespeople. An entire family could fight together, with a child helping as a powder boy with an artillery unit. It has been estimated that an army in the field might need five people for every soldier. The large majority of the troops, though, were on their own. For companionship they looked to camp followers or the women of the town they were occupying. Few barracks had been built, and therefore, unless they were on the march or out in the open on a battlefield, they were housed with ordinary citizens. Since soldiers were almost never given their wages on time—delays could be as long as a year or more—they rarely could pay for their food and housing. Local civilians therefore had to supply their needs, or risk the thievery that was universal. It was no wonder that the approach of an army was a terrifying event.

Officially, there were severe penalties for misbehavior—imprisonment, flogging, or execution for crimes like desertion. Yet discipline, though harsh, was only occasionally enforced, because men were needed for combat, and it was easy for them to slip away from any army. Troops had their own law and courts, but their purpose was to maintain an effective fighting force. Thus, when there were disputes with civilians, it was difficult to get a judgment against a soldier. On the whole, the law was more relaxed in the military, even though the authority of superiors was more direct and continuous.

An ordinary soldier could rise to be a sergeant, but almost never an officer, for the higher ranks were filled by aristocrats and other leaders of the larger society. In these upper levels, there were many opportunities for corruption: officers were paid to raise troops, for instance, but often listed phantom recruits and kept their wages. For these crimes, too, punishment could be severe but was rarely imposed.

The relatively light legal restrictions did not mean that military life was easy. Soldiers were usually filthy, often wet, and nearly always uncomfortable. A garrison might be able to settle into a town in reasonable conditions for a long stretch, but if it was besieged it became hungry, fearful, and vulnerable. Days spent on the march could also be grim: slow, exhausting, and uncertain. Real danger was not common, though it was intense for the brief period of a battle, and occasionally during a siege. Even a simple wound could be fatal, though, because medicine was generally appalling. Yet the most persistent discomfort the soldier faced was boredom. Sieges dragged on for months, and even the hard labor of digging trenches or dragging cannon must have been a relief from the tedium of waiting and waiting. There were traditional recreations—drink, gambling, and the brawls common among soldiers. But the life was rarely easy, and although they sometimes drifted in and out of armies for years, joining new companies whenever better deals were offered, most military men had few regrets when they returned to civilian life.

One character in a play of the time called his service in the army "a nightmare." It was probably a more accurate description than the stories of heroism that were standard fare in the writings of the time. Bravery did occur, but for the average soldier the romantic view of the military as a promoter of adventure, courage, and easy living had little connection to the realities of his world.

Chapter 16

Culture and Society in the Age of the Scientific Revolution 1540–1660

The sense of upheaval and then crisis followed by a settling down in European politics and international relations from the mid-sixteenth to the mid-seventeenth century is also visible in other areas of life. Indeed it is remarkable how well cultural and social patterns reflect the progression from uncertainty to stable resolution. Here, too, the doubts of more than a century, from the days of the Reformation, the discovery of new worlds, and the beginnings of the scientific revolution, were gradually overcome.

Not only the clearest but also the most important development along these lines was the scientific revolution. Starting with tentative and disturbing questions about the theories of ancient authorities, whose views had been accepted for centuries, scientists eventually created a completely new way of looking at nature and a new way of thinking and arguing about physical problems. Their successes were remarkable, and they became very influential, because the certainty and orderliness of their results appealed to a Europe that was seeking relief from uncertainty.

The central event in the confrontation between the old and the new was the trial and condemnation by the Roman Inquisition of one of the greatest of the seventeenth-century scientists, Galileo. But in the next generation the ideas he represented triumphed, as part of a renewed sense of settlement that descended on European society. Stability was visible throughout intellectual life: in literature as well as in art, in painting as well as in poetry. Where the Mannerist painters and the writers of the late sixteenth century emphasized doubts, upheaval, and insecurity, their successors in the Baroque period gave themselves up to enormous ambitions, but the artists after the mid-seventeenth century increasingly stressed calm, restraint, and order. It was the exact equivalent to the resolution of tension one could see elsewhere in society.

Although for ordinary men and women these high intellectual movements had little meaning, their lives were changed in a similar direction as central governments gained considerable control over them, severely reducing the restlessness and rebelliousness that had been prevalent since the early sixteenth century. Even the inhabitants of country villages found that they were no longer as isolated and self-contained as they had once been. One of the most obvious symptoms of their unease, the tremendous outburst of witch hunting during this period, was curbed from above. And when religion no longer caused disruptions throughout Europe, the common people lost a major occasion for self-expression and violence. In general, with the powers of repression growing and their traditional local independence—and their wages—declining, ordinary people took an unavoidable part in the universal quieting down that characterized Western society in the late seventeenth century.

I. THE SCIENTIFIC REVOLUTION

To contemporaries the wars and crises of the sixteenth and seventeenth centuries seemed to dominate their lives. To us it is clear that European civilization was affected no less deeply in this period by the quiet revolution in ideas about nature that was the work of a handful of scholars and experimenters, known at the time as natural philosophers, but to us as scientists.

Origins of the Scientific Revolution

The study of nature by Europeans took its point of departure from the ancient Greeks whose interests shaped subsequent work until the sixteenth century—Aristotle in physics, Ptolemy in astronomy, and Galen in medicine. The most dramatic advances during the scientific revolution came in the fields the Greeks had pioneered, and were to some extent caused by increasing evidence that their theories required highly complicated and perplexing adjustments in order to cover all the facts. For instance, Aristotle's belief that all objects in their natural state are at rest created a number of problems, such as explaining why an arrow kept on flying after leaving a bow; while grappling with this question, some fourteenth-century scientists came up with a new explanation, the belief that a moving body possessed impetus, which kept the motion going until it died out. Similarly, observations revealed that Ptolemy's picture of the heavens, in which all motion was circular around a central earth, could not account easily for the peculiar motion of some planets, which at times seemed to be moving backward. Moreover, Galen's theories, often based on mistaken anatomical information, were shown by dissections to be inadequate.

Still, it is not likely philosophers would have abandoned their cherished theories—they far preferred making adjustments than beginning anew—if it had not been for various other influences at work in the fifteenth and sixteenth centuries. First was the humanists' rediscovery of the work of a number of ancient scientists, which showed that Classical writers themselves had not all agreed with the theories of Aristotle or Ptolemy. One particularly important rediscovery was Archimedes, whose studies of dynamics were an important inspiration for new ideas in physics.

A second influence was an increasing interest in what we now dismiss as "magic," but which at the time was regarded as a serious intellectual enterprise. There were various sides to magical inquiry. Alchemy was the belief that by mixing substances and using secret formulae the nature of matter could be understood. A related interest was the theory of atomism, the idea that all matter was made up of tiny particles, whose composition could be changed—again a theory newly recovered from ancient writers. One of the most famous sixteenth-century alchemists, Paracelsus, was also a proponent of new medical theories, notably the belief that diseases were separate entities with lives of their own. Another favorite study was astrology, which claimed that natural phenomena became understandable and predictable if planetary movements were properly interpreted. A similar easy key to the mysteries of nature was promised by Hermeticism, a school of thought that asserted that all of knowledge had once been given to man, that it was contained in some obscure writings, and that with the right approach and intelligence, a complete insight into the structure of the universe could be achieved.

What linked all this magic was the conviction that the world could be understood and that the answers to traditional questions consisted of simple, comprehensive keys to nature. The theories of Neoplatonism, which became

1560–1660/TIMELINE

Social and Economic History	Cultural and Intellectual History

1560

		1564	Michelangelo dies
		1572	Montaigne begins writing his *Essays*
1575	Second of seven bankruptcies of Spanish monarchy between 1557 and 1653	1576	Bodin's *Six Books of the Republic;* Titian dies
1580–1650	Most intense period of witch hunts and trials	1582	Gregorian calendar
1598–1610	Sully chief minister of France, first to apply mercantilism to government policy	1598	Bernini born
1600	English East India Company founded		
1602	Dutch East India Company founded		
1606	Founding of Virginia, first permanent English colony in North America	1606	Rembrandt born
1609	Bank of Amsterdam established	1607	Monteverdi's *Orfeo*
		1616	Shakespeare and Cervantes die
1619	Start of European-wide depression; end of sixteenth-century boom		
1628	Spanish treasure fleet from America captured by Dutch	1627	Kepler's *Rudolfine Tables* and Bacon's *New Atlantis*
		1632	Galileo's *Dialogue on the Two Great World Systems*
		1636	Corneille's *Le Cid*
		1637	Descartes's *Discourse on Method*
		1640	Rubens dies
1646	Final establishment of serfdom in Russia		
		1651	Hobbes's *Leviathan*
		1660	Royal Society of London founded

1660

very influential during the Renaissance, supported this conviction, as did some of the mystical beliefs that attracted attention in the fifteenth and sixteenth centuries. One of the latter, derived from a system of Jewish thought known as cabala, suggested that the key to the universe might consist of magical arrangements of numbers. For all its irrational elements, it was precisely this longing for new, simple solutions to ancient problems that made natural philosophers capable, for the first time, of discarding the honored theories they had inherited from antiquity, trying different ones, paying greater attention to mathematics, and eventually creating an intellectual revolution.

Two other influences deserve mention. The first was Europe's long fascination with technological invention. The architects, navigators, engineers, and weapons experts of the Renaissance were important pioneers of the belief in measurement and careful observation. For example, at the Arsenal in Venice, where huge cannon were moved and devices invented for handling great weights, Galileo got ideas and made experiments that helped his study of dynamics. A related interest was followed by the anatomists at the nearby university of Padua who created a school famous for its work in dissections and its direct investigations of nature; many of the leading figures of the scientific revolution received their training in methods of experiment and observation at Padua. It was not too surprising, therefore, that the period of the scientific revolution was marked by the invention of important new instruments which often made the discoveries possible: the telescope, the thermometer, the barometer, the vacuum pump, and the microscope. These instruments encouraged the development of a scientific approach that was entirely new in the seventeenth century—it did not go back to the ancients, to the practitioners of magic, or to the engineers. It was pioneered by Francis Bacon and consisted of the belief that in order to make Nature reveal her secrets, she had to be

made to do things she did not do normally: in Bacon's phrase, one had to "twist the lion's tail." What this meant was that one did not simply observe phenomena that occurred normally in nature—for instance, the apparent bending of a stick when placed in a glass of water—but created conditions that were *not* normal. With the telescope one could perceive secrets hidden to the naked eye; with the vacuum pump one could begin to understand the properties of air.

The influences that combined to create the scientific revolution were many. Yet there is no doubt that the heart of the change lay in purely intellectual breakthroughs. A small group of brilliant men, grappling with ancient problems of physics, astronomy, and anatomy—motion, heavenly phenomena, and the structure of the body—came up with persuasive discoveries that changed Western thought forever.

The First Breakthroughs

The earliest advances were in astronomy and anatomy. By coincidence, both were contained in books published in 1543, which was also the year when the first printed edition of Archimedes appeared. *The Structure of the Human Body,* by Andreas Vesalius, a member of the Padua faculty, pointed out errors in the work of Galen, the chief medical authority for over a thousand years. Vesalius himself did not always follow strictly the findings of dissections. Like Galen, he showed the liver as having five lobes, which is true of some animals but not of humans, though in a corner of the picture he also showed a small two-lobed liver, perhaps to indicate that he knew what the human one really looked like. His precise descriptions opened a new era of careful observation and experimentation in studies of the body.

On the Revolutions of the Heavenly Bodies, by Nicolaus Copernicus, a Polish cleric who had studied at Padua, had far greater consequences.

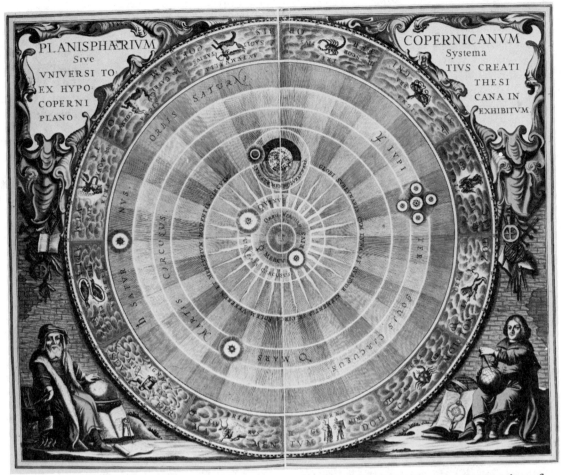

An engraving of Copernicus's conception of the universe shows the sun rather than the earth at the center, the spheres to which planets were attached, and the moons of Jupiter discovered by Galileo.
(Photo: British Museum)

A first-rate mathematician, he felt that the calculations of planetary movements under Ptolemy's system had grown too complex. In Ptolemaic astronomy, the planets and the sun, attached to transparent, crystalline spheres, revolved around the earth. All motion was circular, and observed irregularities were accounted for by epicycles—movement around small spheres that were attached to the larger spheres and which themselves revolved. Much influenced by Neoplatonic and related ideas, Copernicus believed that a simpler picture would reflect more accurately the true structure of the universe. In good Neoplatonic fashion,

he argued that the sun, as the most splendid of celestial bodies, ought rightfully to be at the center of an orderly and harmonious universe.

Copernicus's system was in fact no simpler than Ptolemy's—the spheres and epicycles were just as complex—and he had no way of proving that his theory was correct. But he was such a fine mathematician that his successors had to use his calculations even if they rejected his assumptions. He thus became part of intellectual discussion, drawn upon when Pope Gregory XIII decided to reform the calendar in 1582. The Julian calendar, in use since Roman times, counted century years as leap years, thus adding extra days that caused Easter—whose date is determined by the position of the sun—to drift further and further away from its normal occurrence in late March. The reform produced

the Gregorian calendar, which we still use—ten days were simply dropped, and since then three out of every four century years have not been leap years (1900 had no February 29, but 2000 will have one). The need for calendar reform had been one of the motives for Copernicus's studies, which proved useful even though his theories remained controversial.

What developed during the half-century following the publication of his *Revolutions* was a growing sense of uncertainty. The greatest astronomer of the period, Tycho Brahe, made the most remarkable observations of the heavens before the telescope, plotting the paths of the moon and planets every night for decades.

Kepler, surrounded by the instruments of the astrologer and the astronomer, discussing his work with his patron, the emperor Rudolf II. (Photo: New York Public Library/Picture Collection)

But the only theory he could come up with was an uneasy compromise between the Ptolemaic and Copernican systems. It was a disciple of his, the German Johannes Kepler, who made the first major advance on the work of Copernicus and who helped resolve the uncertainties that had arisen in the field of astronomy.

Kepler

Like Copernicus, Kepler believed that only the language of mathematics could describe the movements of the heavens. He was a famous astrologer and an advocate of the latest magical ideas, but he was also convinced instinctively that Copernicus was right. He threw himself into the task of confirming the sun-centered (heliocentric) theory, and as a result of his study of Brahe's observations, he discovered three laws of planetary motion (published in 1609 and 1619) that opened a new era in astronomy.

The first law states that the orbits of the planets are ellipses, with the sun invariably at one focus of the ellipse. This was an enormous break with the past, for the assumption that circular motion is the most perfect and natural motion had been an essential part of the study of nature since Aristotle. Even Galileo was unable to reject this assumption, but Kepler followed wherever his data and his mathematics took him. The second law states that if a hypothetical line is drawn from the sun to the planet, equal areas will be swept by that line in equal times. What this means is that the planet moves faster—that is, it has to cover more of the orbit in a given period—when it is closer to the sun than when it is farther away (see the figure above). This was a blow to the traditional view that all heavenly motion is steady and unchanging.

The third law enters an entirely different area, describing not the motion of an individual planet, as do the first two, but a relationship among the movements of all planets. It states

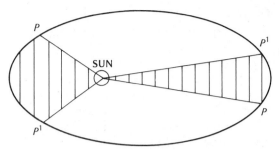

KEPLER'S SECOND LAW

P and *P*¹ are any two points on the orbit between which the planet passes in equal time. The area described by Sun—*P*—*P*¹—Sun is always equal.

that the square of the ratio of the *time* it takes any two planets to complete their orbits equals the cube of the ratio of these planets' average *distance* from the sun. This third law was Kepler's most elegant and subtle discovery, a worthy monument to his mathematical skills. However, it had little direct impact on the study of astronomy until Sir Isaac Newton used it late in the century as the foundation for his construction of a new system of the heavens.

Kepler's last major achievement was the publication in 1627 of the *Rudolfine Tables*, named after his patron, Emperor Rudolf II. The tables combined Brahe's observations of planetary positions with Kepler's theories of planetary motion and made it possible to predict celestial movements far more accurately, to the great benefit of navigators as well as astronomers. They demonstrated that Copernicus's and Kepler's discoveries had a practical value, and it became increasingly difficult to ignore or doubt the new findings. Adherents of Ptolemaic cosmology continued to hold firm for decades, but among serious observers of the heavens they were a rapidly dwindling group after the 1620s. A theory that at the beginning of Kepler's career had been uncertain at best had been transformed by the end of his life into a plausible explanation of planetary motion.

Galileo

A contemporary of Kepler's, the Italian Galileo Galilei, took the breakthrough a stage further when he became the first to perceive the connection between planetary motion and motion on earth. His studies revealed the importance to astronomy not only of observation and mathematics but also of physics. Moreover he was the first to bring the new understanding of the universe to the attention of a wider public. Galileo's concern with technique, argument, and evidence marks him as one of the first scientists recognizable as such to modern eyes.

The study of motion inspired Galileo's most fundamental scientific contributions. When he began his investigations, the Aristotelian view that a body is naturally at rest and needs to be pushed constantly to keep moving dominated the study of dynamics. Kepler, for example, believed that some steady force emanating from the sun maintains the planets' motion. Galileo broke with this tradition, developing instead a new type of physical explanation that was perfected by Newton half a century later.

Unlike Kepler, who was concerned with the strictly limited phenomena of planetary movements, Galileo wanted to uncover the principles of all motion. His observations were prolific. At the Arsenal in Venice, he watched the techniques workmen used to lift huge weights; adapting a Dutch lensmaker's invention, he built himself a primitive telescope to study the heavens; and he devised seemingly mundane experiments, employing anything from pendulums to little balls rolling down inclined planes, to test his theories. Moving from observations to abstraction, Galileo arrived at a wholly new way of understanding motion: the principle of inertia.

This breakthrough could not have been made on the basis of observation alone. For the discovery of inertia depended on mathematical imagination, the ability to conceive of a situation that cannot be demonstrated to the senses because it cannot be created experimentally: the motion of a perfectly smooth ball across a perfectly smooth plane, free of any outside forces, such as friction. Galileo's conclusion was that "Any velocity once imparted to a moving body will be rigidly maintained as long as external causes of acceleration and retardation are removed. . . . If the velocity is uniform, it will not be diminished or slackened, much less destroyed."

This insight completely undermined the Aristotelian view. Physics could never be the same again, because Galileo demonstrated that only mathematical language could describe the underlying principles of nature.

The most celebrated impact of Galileo's work was on astronomy. He first became famous when in 1610 he published his discoveries that Jupiter has satellites and the moon has mountains. Both these revelations were further blows to traditional beliefs, which held that the earth is changing and imperfect while the heavens are immutable and unblemished. Now, however, it seemed that other planets had moons, just like the earth, and that these moons might have the same rough surface as the earth.

This was startling enough, but Galileo also sought a complete change in the methods of discovery, believing, unlike his predecessors, that the principles he had uncovered in terrestrial physics could also be used to explain phenomena in the heavens. His purposes became apparent when he calculated the height of the mountains on the moon by using the geometric techniques of surveyors, when he described the moon's secondary light—seen while it is a crescent—as a reflection of sunlight from the earth, and when he explained the movement of sunspots by referring to the principles of motion that he had found on earth. In all cases Galileo was treating his own planet simply as one part of a uniform universe. Every physical law, he was saying, is equally applicable on earth and in the heavens, including the laws of motion. As early as 1597 Galileo had told Kepler that some of his discoveries in physics could be explained only if the earth were moving, and during the next thirty years he became the most famous advocate of Copernicanism in Europe.

Galileo conveyed his arguments with devastating logic. Citing Aristotle's principle that the simplest explanation is the best explanation, Galileo asked why it was necessary to keep the entire universe revolving around the earth when all the motions could be explained by the rotation of only one planet, the earth. When academic and religious critics pointed out that the moon looks smooth, that we would feel the earth moving, or that the Bible says Joshua made the sun stand still, he reacted with scorn to their inability to understand that his observations and proofs carried more weight than their traditional beliefs. And in response to religious objections, he asserted that "in discussions of physical problems we ought to begin not from the authority of scriptural passages, but from sense experience and necessary demonstrations."

For all the brilliance of his arguments, Galileo was now on dangerous ground. Although traditionally the Catholic Church had not concerned itself with the theories used in investigations of nature, in the early seventeenth century the situation was changing. Now deep in the struggle with Protestantism, the Church was responding to the increased challenge to its authority by seeking to control any potentially questionable views held by its followers. Moreover, Galileo's biting sarcasm toward others in the field had antagonized Jesuit and Dominican astronomers. These two orders were the chief upholders of orthodoxy in the Church in this period, and it was they who referred Galileo's views to the Inquisition and then guided the attack on Copernicanism and its most brilliant proponent.

In 1616 the Inquisition forbade Galileo, within certain limits, to teach the heretical doctrine that the earth moves. When one of his friends was elected pope in 1623, however, Galileo thought he would be safe in writing a ma-

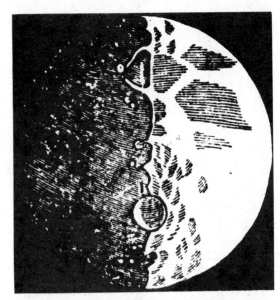

This sketch of the moon's surface appeared in Galileo's *Starry Messenger* (1610). It shows what he had observed through the telescope and had interpreted as proof that the moon had a rugged surface because the lighted areas within the dark section had to be mountains. These caught the light of the setting sun longer than surrounding lower terrain and revealed, for example, a large cavity in the lower center of the sketch.
(Photo: New York Public Library/Picture Collection)

jor work on astronomy, as long as he remained within the limits set in 1616. The result was Galileo's masterpiece, the *Dialogue on the Two Great World Systems,* published in 1632 (with the approval, probably accidental, of the Inquisition). A marvelously witty, elegant book, the *Dialogue* is one of the few monuments in the history of science that the lay person can read with pleasure. And so it was intended. Galileo wrote it in Italian, not the Latin that had always been used for scholarly works, because he wanted it to reach the widest possible audience.

In April 1633 he was brought before the

Inquisition for having defied the order not to teach Copernicanism. To establish their case, his accusers resorted to a forged document that suggested the 1616 limits were stricter than they really had been. In a trial that has caused controversy ever since, the aged astronomer, under threat of torture, abjured the "errors and heresies" of believing that the earth moved. Legend has it that as he left the hall, he murmured, *"Eppur si muove!"* ("And yet it does move!") and he certainly was not docile for the remainder of his life even though he was under perpetual house arrest and progressively lost his eyesight. He had his principal work on physics, the *Two New Sciences,* published in tolerant Holland in 1638, while many of his letters ridiculed his opponents.

Galileo's condemnation discouraged further scientific activity by his countrymen. Italy had been the leader of the new discipline, but now her supremacy rapidly passed northward, to the English, Dutch, and French. Yet this only showed that the rise of science, once begun, could not be halted for long. By the late 1630s no self-respecting astronomer could deny that Galileo's findings and his *Dialogue,* added to Kepler's laws and the *Rudolfine Tables,* had established the correctness of the Copernican theory beyond reasonable doubt.

In a progression of events remarkably similar to the movement from upheaval to resolution that was taking place in politics at this very time (see Chapter 15), scientists started out by causing tremendous bewilderment and doubt, but had ended up by creating a new kind of certainty that had far-reaching influence. And this was true not only in physics and astronomy, but also in anatomy. For with Vesalius there had begun a period in the study of the human body when many questions were raised but few answers were found. Finally, though, in 1628, another genius of the scientific revolution, the English doctor William Harvey, provided a new and more certain understanding of anatomy when he identified the function of the heart and proved that the blood circulated.

Scientific Method: A New Epistemology

Both Copernicus and Galileo stressed that their discoveries rested on a way of thinking that had an independent value, and they refused to allow traditional considerations, such as the promptings of common sense or the assumptions of theology, to interfere with their conclusions. What the scientists were moving toward was a new epistemology, a new theory of how to obtain and verify knowledge. They stressed experience, reason, and doubt, rejecting all unsubstantiated authority, and they developed a revolutionary definition of what could be accepted as a true description of physical reality.

The process the scientists followed after they formulated a hypothesis consisted, in their view, of three parts: first, observations; second, a generalization induced from the observations; and third, tests of the generalization by experiments whose outcome could be predicted by the generalization. A generalization remained valid only as long as it was not contradicted by the experiments specifically designed to test it. The scientist used no data except the results of strict observation, and scientific reasoning was confined to the perception of the laws, principles, or patterns that emerged from the observations. Since measurement was the key to the data, the observations had a numerical, not a subjective, value, and the language of science naturally came to be mathematics.

Perhaps the most famous example of the method was the series of experiments Galileo conducted with inclined planes. His original hypothesis was that all objects fall at the same speed and that the difference we see between the time it takes for a stone and a feather to fall is the result only of friction and air resistance (a hypothesis recently confirmed by astronauts on the moon). He first showed that acceleration is a function of time, a proposition that he proved geometrically and then demonstrated by rolling a ball down a plane, noting the time required to make the descent: "We [then] rolled the ball only one-quarter the length of the [plane]; and having measured the time of its descent, we found it precisely one-half of the former [descent]." He repeated such experiments a hundred times, and always the ratio of the distances was a square of the ratio of the times. From this basic regularity he proceeded to a proof, similarly resting on both geometry and experiment, that regardless of the angle of a descent, the average speed of the descent, and the speed of the body when it reaches the bottom, will always be the same if the vertical height of the descent remains the same.

This was a classic application of the new scientific method. Mathematics, in this case geometry, allowed Galileo to measure and describe natural phenomena. Carefully controlled experiments then verified conclusions that might seem contrary to common sense. And the progression—hypothesis, observation, generalization, and tests, conducted in the language of mathematics—provided him with a logical structure that could be defeated only on its own terms. Nothing was accepted as given. It was a self-contained mode of demonstration whose conclusions could be rejected solely if disproved by identical procedures.

Scientists in fact rarely reach conclusions in the exact way this idealized scheme suggests. Galileo's perfectly smooth balls and planes, for instance, did not exist, but Galileo understood the relevant physical theory so well that he knew what would have happened if one had rolled across the other, and he used this "experiment" to demonstrate the principle of inertia. In other words, experiments as well as hypotheses can occur in the mind; the essence of scientific method still remains a special way of looking at and understanding nature.

The Wider Influence of Scientific Thought

The principles of scientific inquiry received attention throughout the intellectual community only gradually; it took time for the power of the scientists' method to be recognized. For decades, as Galileo found out, even investigators of nature continued to use what he would have considered irrelevant criteria, such as the teachings of the Bible, in judging scientific work. If acceptance of the new method was to spread, then the literate public would have to be educated in the techniques being employed. This growing understanding was eventually achieved by midcentury as much through the efforts of ardent propagandizers as through the writings of the great innovators themselves.

Francis Bacon

Although not an important scientist himself, Francis Bacon was the greatest of these propagandists, and he inspired an entire generation with his vision of what the discipline could accomplish for mankind. His description of an ideal society in the *New Atlantis,* published in 1627, the year after his death, was the most famous of a series of seventeenth-century descendants of Sir Thomas More's *Utopia,* all of which placed the constant and fruitful advance of science at the center of their schemes. *New Atlantis* is a vision of science as the savior of the human race. It predicts a time when those doing research at the highest levels will be regarded as the most important people in the state and will work on a vast government-supported project to gather all known facts about the physical universe. By a process of gradual induction, this information will lead to universal laws that in turn will enable people to improve their lot on earth.

Bacon's view of research as a collective enterprise whose aim is the discovery of practical benefits for all made a powerful impact on a number of later scientists, particularly the founders of the English Royal Society. Many cited him as the chief inspiration for their work. Moreover Bacon advocated a total overhaul of the traditional educational curriculum: an end to the study of venerated philosophers and more attention to practical concerns. By the mid-seventeenth century, his ideas had entered the mainstream of European thought, an acceptance that testified to the broadening interest in science and its protagonists.

René Descartes

The French philosopher René Descartes made the first concentrated attempt to apply the new methods of science to theories of knowledge, and in so doing he laid the foundations for modern philosophy. The impulse behind his work was his realization that for all the importance of observation and experiment, people can be deceived by their senses. In order to find some solid truth, therefore, he decided to apply the principle of doubt—the refusal to accept any authority without strict verification—to all knowledge. He began his investigations with the assumption that he could know unquestionably only one thing: he was doubting. This allowed him to proceed to the observation, "I think, therefore I am," because the very act of doubting proved he was thinking, and thinking in turn demonstrated his existence.

The cardinal point of his philosophy was contained in the statement that whatever is clearly and distinctly thought must be true. This was a conclusion drawn from the proof of his own existence, and it enabled him to construct a proof of God's existence. We cannot fail to realize that we are imperfect, he argued, and we must therefore have an idea of perfection against which we may be measured. If we have a clear idea of what perfection is, then it must exist; hence there must be a God.

The proof may not seem entirely convincing to modern readers, particularly since one suspects that a major reason for its prominence was the desire to show that the principle of doubt did not contradict religious belief. Nevertheless the argument is a good illustration of Descartes's assertion that the activity of the mind is the vital element in the search for truth.

The portrait of René Descartes by the Dutch painter Frans Hals shows the austere thinker who fit well into the sober atmosphere of Amsterdam. Descartes spent a number of years in the United Provinces, where the exchange of ideas was much freer than in his native France.
(Photo: Hubert Joesse/EPI, Inc.)

The title he gave his great work, *Discourse on the Method of Rightly Conducting the Reason and Seeking Truth in the Sciences* (1637), is thus entirely appropriate.[1] Thought is a pure and unmistakable guide, and only by reliance on its operations can people hope to advance their understanding of the world.

Descartes developed this view into a fundamental proposition about the nature of the

[1] Like Galileo's *Dialogue*, Descartes's *Discourse* was written in a vernacular language. It thus had a much more popular audience than a Latin book would have received, though after a few years it was translated into Latin so that scholars from all European countries could read it.

world and of knowledge—a proposition that philosophers have been wrestling with ever since. He stated that there is an essential dichotomy between thought and extension (tangible objects) or, put another way, between spirit and matter. Various writers, including Bacon and Galileo, had insisted that science, the study of nature, is an undertaking separate from and unaffected by faith or theology, the study of God. But Descartes turned this distinction into a far-reaching principle, dividing not only science from faith but even the reality of the world from our perception of that reality. There is a difference, in other words, between a chair and our understanding of that chair in our minds.

So insistent was he that matter and spirit remain distinct that he undertook a careful examination of human anatomy to discover the seat of the soul. He had to find a part of the body that had no physical function whatsoever, because only there could the soul, a thing of spirit, reside. His candidate was the tiny pineal gland, which did absolutely nothing, according to the medicine of the day; modern investigations still have not discovered the function of the hormone it secretes.

The emphasis Descartes placed on the operations of the mind gave a new direction to epistemological discussions. A hypothesis gained credibility not so much from external proofs as from the logical tightness of the arguments used to support it. The decisive test was how lucid and irrefutable a statement appeared to be to the thinking mind, not whether it could be demonstrated by experiments. Descartes thus applied what he considered to be the methods of science to all knowledge. Not only the phenomena of nature but all truth had to be investigated according to what he regarded as the strict principles of the scientist.

Descartes's own contributions to the research of his day were theoretical rather than experimental. In physics he was the first to perceive the distinction between mass and weight, and in mathematics he was the first to apply algebraic notations and methods to geometry, thus founding analytic geometry. He was, without question, a prime mover of the revolution in Western thought during the seventeenth century. His emphasis on the principle of doubt irrevocably undermined such traditional assumptions as the belief in the hierarchical organization of the universe. Possibly he put too much trust in the powers of the mind, but he did lay down strict logical rules that philosophy—and in fact any speculation about man or his world—had to follow. And the European intellectual community accepted this approach with enthusiasm. The admiration he inspired indicated how completely the methods he advocated had captured his contemporaries' imagination.

Thomas Hobbes

A notable example of the borrowings inspired by the scientists was the work of Thomas Hobbes, who used their method to make an extraordinarily original contribution to political theory.

A story has it that Hobbes once picked up a copy of Euclid's *Elements* and opened the book in the middle. The theorem on that page seemed totally without foundation, but it rested on a proof in the preceding theorem. Working his way backward, he discovered himself finally having to accept no more than the proposition that the shortest distance between two points is a straight line. He thereupon resolved to use the same approach in analyzing political behavior. The story is probably apocryphal because as a young man Hobbes was secretary to Francis Bacon, who doubtless gave him his first taste of scientific work. Nevertheless it does capture the essence of Hobbes's approach, for he did begin his masterpiece, *Leviathan* (published in 1651), with a few limited premises about human nature from which he rigorously deduced major conclusions about political forms.

Hobbes's premises, drawn from his observation of the strife-ridden Europe of his day, were stark and uncompromising. People, he asserted, are selfish and ambitious; consequently, unless they are restrained, they fight a perpetual war with their fellows. The weak are more cunning and the strong more stupid. Given these unsavory characteristics, the state of nature—which precedes the existence of society—is a state of war, in which life is "nasty, brutish, and short." Hobbes's conclusion was that the only way to restrain this instinctive aggressiveness is to erect an absolute and sovereign power that will maintain peace. Everyone should submit to the sovereign because the alternative is the anarchy of the state of nature. The moment of submission is the moment of the birth of orderly society.

In a startling innovation Hobbes suggested that the transition from nature to society is accomplished by a contract that is implicitly accepted by all who wish to end the chaos. They agree among themselves to submit to the sovereign; thus the sovereign is not a party to the contract and is not limited in any way. A government that is totally free to do whatever it wishes is best equipped to keep the peace. However tyrannous, this solution is always better than the turmoil it has replaced.

Both contemporaries and later writers were strongly influenced by Hobbes, not only because his logic was compelling but also because he seemed so much like a scientist. From his observations of people, he had induced general propositions about human behavior, and from these he had deduced certain political lessons that were verified by European politics. Moreover he had applied a mechanistic view to people more thoroughly than ever before, reducing all that human beings do to simple appetites and aversions.

In doing so he contributed to the popularity of the mechanistic view of the universe, a theory derived in part from the materialistic implications of Descartes's philosophy. In its simplest form mechanism holds that the entire universe, including human beings, can be regarded as a complicated machine and thus subject to strict physical principles. The arm is like a lever, the elbow like a hinge, and so on. Even an emotion is no more than a simple response to a definable stimulus.

But this approach also aroused hostility. Although they were deeply affected by his ideas, most of Hobbes's successors denounced him as godless, immoral, cynical, and unfeeling. These were charges that could be leveled at all practitioners of science, but for a long time they were not raised, largely because the scientists dealt with areas that seemed to have nothing to do with human behavior.

Blaise Pascal

At midcentury only one important voice still protested against the new science. It belonged to a young Frenchman, Blaise Pascal, one of the most brilliant mathematicians and experimenters of the time. Before his death at the age of thirty-nine, in 1662, Pascal's investigations of probability in games of chance led him to the theorem that still bears his name, and his research in conic sections helped lay the foundations for integral calculus. He also discovered barometric pressure and invented a versatile calculating machine.

In his late twenties, however, Pascal became increasingly dissatisfied with scientific research, and he began to wonder whether his life was being properly spent. His doubts were reinforced by frequent visits to his sister, a nun at the Abbey of Port-Royal, where he came into contact with a new spiritual movement within Catholicism known as Jansenism.

The movement took its name from Cornelis Jansen, a bishop who had written a book suggesting that the Catholic Church had forgotten the teachings of its greatest father, St. Augustine. Jansen insisted that man was not free to determine his own fate, that salvation was entirely in the hands of an all-powerful God, and that unswerving faith was the only path to salvation. These doctrines sounded ominously like Protestant teachings, and during the years after Jansen's death, the Catholic Church and especially the Jesuits, who placed great emphasis on freedom of will, made various attempts to suppress his beliefs.

Jansenism was not a particularly popular movement at the time, and its adherents consisted of little more than the immediate circle of a prominent family of magistrates, the Arnaulds, one of whom was the head of Port-Royal. But Pascal was profoundly impressed by the piety, asceticism, and spirituality at Port-Royal, and in November of 1654 he had a mystical experience that made him resolve to devote the rest of his life to the salvation of his soul. He wrote a series of devastating critiques of the Jesuits, accusing them of irresponsibility and, as he phrased it, of placing cushions under sinners' elbows.

During the few remaining years of his life, Pascal put on paper a collection of reflections—some only a few words long, some many pages—that were gathered together after his death and published as the *Pensées* (or "reflections"). These writings revealed not only the beliefs of a deeply religious man but also the anxieties of a scientist who feared the growing influence of science. He did not wish to put an end to research; he merely wanted people to realize that the truths uncovered by science were limited and not as important as the truths perceived by faith. In the words of one of his more memorable phrases, "The heart has its reasons that the mind cannot know."

Pascal was warning against the replacement of the traditional understanding of humanity and its destiny, gained through religious faith, with the conclusions reached by the methods of the scientists. The separation between the material and the spiritual would be fatal, he believed, because it would destroy the primacy and even the importance of the spiritual. Pascal's protest was unique, but the fact that it was raised at all indicates how high the status of the scientist and his method had risen by the 1650s. A scant quarter-century earlier, such a dramatic change in fortune would have been hard to predict, but now many intellectuals, seeing an opportunity of ending the uncertainties that had bedeviled their work for decades, eagerly adopted the new epistemology. Turmoil was once again giving way to assurance.

Science Institutionalized

There were many besides Bacon who realized that scientific work should be a common endeavor, pursued cooperatively by all its practitioners, and that information should be exchanged so that researchers might concentrate on different parts of a project instead of wasting time and energy following identical paths. The first major effort to apply this view was undertaken by the Lincean Academy,[2] founded under the patronage of a nobleman in Rome in 1603. Organizations of scientists had existed before, but this was the first group interested in all branches of science and in publishing the findings of its members. After the decline of research in Italy, however, the academy gradually lost its importance.

More fruitful beginnings were made in France, where in the first decades of the seventeenth century a friar named Marin Mersenne became the center of an international network of correspondents interested in scientific work. He increased the dissemination of news by also bringing scientists together for discussions or experiments. The meetings were sporadic, but out of them developed contacts that led to a more permanent organization of scientific activity.

[2] The academy was named after Linceus, reputedly the most keen-sighted of the legendary Argonauts of ancient times.

The first important steps toward establishing a permanent body in England were taken at Oxford during the Civil War when the revolutionaries captured the city and replaced many traditionalists at the university. A few of the newcomers formed what they called the Invisible College, a group that met to exchange information and discuss one another's work. What was important was the enterprise, not its results, for the group included only one first-class scientist: the young chemist Robert Boyle. In 1660 twelve members, including Boyle and the architect Sir Christopher Wren, formed an official organization, the Royal Society of London for Improving Natural Knowledge, with headquarters in the capital and a council to supervise its affairs. In 1662 it was granted a charter by Charles II.

The Royal Society's purposes were openly Baconian. Its aim for the first few years—until everyone realized it was impossible—was to gather all knowledge about nature, particularly whatever might be useful. For a long time the members continued to offer their services for the public good, helping in one instance to develop the science of social statistics ("political arithmetic" as it was called) for the government. Soon, however, it became clear that the society's principal function was to serve as a headquarters and clearing center for research. Its secretaries maintained an enormous correspondence, encouraging foreign scholars to transmit their discoveries to the society. And in 1665 the society began the regular publication of *Philosophical Transactions,* the first professional scientific journal.

As a stimulus to new discoveries, the Royal Society was without peer in seventeenth-century Europe. Imitators were soon to follow. In 1666 Louis XIV gave his blessing to the founding of the Royal Academy of Sciences, and similar organizations were established in Naples and Berlin by 1700. Membership in these societies was limited and highly prized, a symptom of the glamour that was beginning to attach itself to the new studies. By the 1660s there

could be no doubt that science, secure in royal patronage, had triumphed. Its practitioners were extravagantly admired, and throughout intellectual and high social circles, there was a feverish scramble to apply its methods and its mode of thought to almost every conceivable activity.

Descartes himself had applied the techniques of science to epistemology and more broadly to philosophy in general; Bacon and Hobbes had put them at the service of social and political thought. But the borrowings were not only at these exalted levels. Formal gardens were designed to exhibit the order, harmony, and reason that science had made the most prized qualities of the time. And the arts of fortification and warfare were affected by principles taken from the new investigations, such as accurate measurement.

As the scientists' activities grew in popularity, amateurs known as virtuosos began to proliferate. These were usually aristocrats who spent their time playing at science. Herbariums and small observatories were added to country estates, and parties would feature an evening of star gazing. Some virtuosos took their tasks quite seriously—an early Italian enthusiast, Prince Federigo Cesi, joined in the first investigations with a microscope, a study of bees; and one English country gentleman inundated the Royal Society with meticulous observations of local sand dunes. But by and large these frivolous scientists are interesting primarily because they reveal the awe and delight aroused by a new discipline that had revolutionized man's understanding of nature.

Science was also beginning to have an impact on the general populace. Among the most eagerly anticipated occasions in seventeenth-century Holland was the public anatomy lesson. The body of a criminal would be brought to an enormous hall, packed with students and a fascinated public. A famous surgeon would dissect the cadaver, announcing and displaying each organ as he removed it.

On the whole, the influence of the scientists

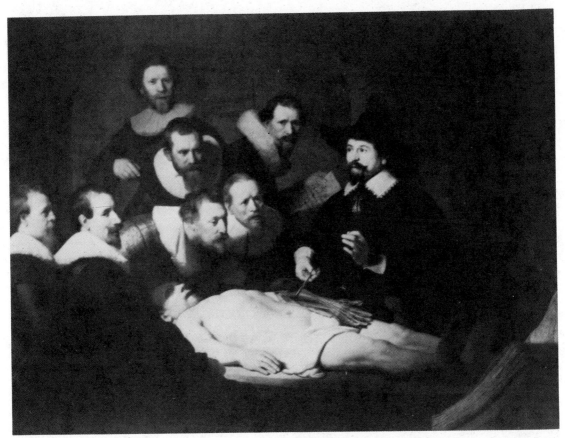

Among the many representations of the public anatomy lessons so popular in seventeenth-century Holland, the most famous is one of Rembrandt's greatest paintings, *The Anatomy Lesson of Dr. Nicolaas Tulp*.
(Photo: A. Dingjan)

on laypeople was not dependent on the technological improvements they inspired. By our standards much of what they did, even at the theoretical level, seems primitive at best. What this suggests is that the reverence for science and its methods developed not from a broad understanding of actual accomplishments or their potential consequences but from the fame of the spectacular discoveries that provided startlingly convincing solutions to centuries-old problems in astronomy, physics, and anatomy. Thus the disturbing implications of Hobbes's views, like the protests of Pascal, could be ignored, and the new discipline could be given unblemished admiration. The entire world was coming to be viewed through the scientist's eyes—a striking victory for a recently struggling member of the intellectual community—and the qualities of regularity and harmony associated with science began to appear in the work of playwrights and poets, artists and architects.

II. LITERATURE AND THE ARTS

Changes in culture were not as clear-cut as in politics or science, but certain parallels are evident. During the second half of the sixteenth century and into the 1610s, the tensions and uncertainties of the age were visible in the paintings of the Mannerists, and in the writings of Montaigne, Cervantes, and Shakespeare. Thereafter, two major styles dominated Europe: the Baroque, which consciously sought to arouse the emotions and achieve dramatic effects, and the Classical, which epitomized discipline, restraint, and sometimes decorum. Very gradually over the course of the seventeenth century, the emphasis moved from the values of the Baroque to those of the Classical. This shift in artistic aims bore a distinct resemblance to the sense of settlement that descended over other areas of European civilization at midcentury.

The Culture of the Late Sixteenth Century

One response to the upheavals of the sixteenth century was the attempt to escape reality, to challenge the serene view of the world. It was especially noticeable in the work of the great painters of the age.

The Mannerists

As early as the 1520s, a reaction had set in against the balance and serenity of the High Renaissance style. The artists involved in this movement, which lasted about eighty years, are generally called Mannerists. No specific characteristics united them, but they all wished to go beyond reality and to develop theatrical and disturbing qualities in their paintings (see Plate 27). They undermined perspective, distorted human figures, and devised unnatural colors and lighting to create startling effects. Even the great figures of the High Renaissance were affected by this orientation. Michelangelo, who lived until 1564, began to create tortured, agonized figures writhing in violent ac-

tion; Titian, who died in 1576, placed a shrieking Magdalene in his last painting, a subdued *Pietà*.

The movement was embodied, however, in Parmigianino, an Italian, and El Greco, a Greek living in Spain. Parmigianino's *Madonna of the Long Neck* (see Plate 26), named after its most salient feature, typifies his efforts to unsettle the viewer with tricks of perspective, odd postures, and an unbalanced composition. El Greco, a man whose compelling and almost mystic vision symbolized the uneasy age in which he lived, took these devices even further. His elongated human beings, cool colors, and eerie lighting make him one of the most distinctive painters in the history of art (see Plate 29).

Michel de Montaigne

The man who expressed the most vivid concern about the upheavals and uncertainties of his age was Michel de Montaigne, the greatest humanist and philosopher of the late sixteenth century. Born into the French petty nobility, he suffered a shock at the age of thirty—the death of his closest friend—that changed the course of his life. Obsessed by death, he began one of the most moving explorations in European intellectual history.

Determined to overcome his fears, Montaigne retired to a tower in his country home in order to "essay," or test, his innermost feelings by writing short pieces of prose even about subjects he did not fully comprehend. In the process he created a new literary form, the essay, and shaped the development of the French language. But his chief influence was philosophical: he has inspired the search for self-knowledge since his time, from René Descartes and Blaise Pascal to the Existentialists of the twentieth century.

In the 1570s Montaigne's anxieties led him to Skepticism, which appeared in full flower in his longest essay, "An Apology for Raymond

Sebond." Sebond was a Spanish theologian who tried to prove the truth of Christianity by the use of reason. Montaigne firmly rejected Sebond's belief in the power of the mind and emerged from this essay with the total uncertainty of the motto *"Que sais-je?"* ("What do I know?").

In his last years Montaigne struggled toward a more confident solution of his uncertainties, taking as his model the ancient saying, "Know thyself." By looking into one's own person, one can find answers and values that hold true at least for the individual: all truths and customs are relative, but by looking inward, one can be guided by one's own reflection of all humanity. Montaigne even came close to a morality without theology, because good and self-determination were more important to him than doctrine, and he saw everywhere religious people committing inhuman acts. People, he argued, can seek their own good and can achieve it by an effort of will. Trying to be an angel is wrong; being good is enough.

This process of self-discovery was a radical and totally secular individualism. It required a joyous acceptance of the world that finally gave Montaigne the optimistic answer to his anguish—though it was a unique, personal answer that gave comfort to few other people.

Cervantes and Shakespeare

In Spain the disillusionment that accompanied the decline of Europe's most powerful state was perfectly captured by Miguel de Cervantes (1547–1616). He was heir to a brilliant satirical and descriptive tradition that had already produced a classic literature in the sixteenth century in the writings of Erasmus and Rabelais. Cervantes saw the wide gap between the hopes and the realities of his day—in religion, in social institutions, in human behavior—and made the dichotomy the basis of the scathing social satire in his novel *Don Quixote.*

At one level Cervantes was ridiculing the excessive chivalry of the Spanish nobility in his portrayal of a knight who was ready to tilt at windmills, though he obviously admired the sincerity of his well-meaning hero and sympathized with him as a perennial loser. On another level the author brought to life the Europe of the time—the ordinary people and their hypocrisies and intolerances—with a liveliness rarely matched in literature. His view of that society, however, was far from cheery. "Justice, but not for my house," says Don Quixote as he experiences the foibles of mankind, particularly of those in authority. Cervantes avoided politics, but he was clearly directing many of his sharpest barbs at the brutality and disregard for human values that were characteristic of his fanatical times. What were Spain's repeated crusades accomplishing? Were Quixote's dreams as worthy as Sancho Panza's blunt and sensible pragmatism? These were not easy questions to answer, but they went to the heart of the dilemmas of the age. And in Spain's great enemy, England, another towering figure was grappling with similar problems.

For the English-speaking world, the most brilliant writer of this and all other periods was William Shakespeare, whose characters bring to life almost every conceivable mood—searing grief, airy romance, rousing nationalism, uproarious and farcical humor. Despite modest education he disclosed in his imagery a familiarity with subjects ranging from astronomy to seamanship, from alchemy to warfare. It is not surprising therefore that some have doubted that one man could have produced this amazing body of work.

Shakespeare started writing in the 1590s, when he was in his late twenties, and continued until his death, in 1616. During most of this time, he was also involved with a theatrical company, and he often had to produce plays on very short notice. He thus had the best of all possible tests as he gained mastery of theatrical techniques—audience reaction.

Shakespeare rose far above his setting to timeless statements about human behavior: love, hatred, violence, sin. Of particular interest to the historian, however, is what he tells us about attitudes that belong especially to his own era. For example the conservatism of his characters is quite clear. They believe firmly in the hierarchical structure of society, and throughout the long series of historical plays, events suggest that excessive ambition does not pay. The story begins with Richard II, a legitimate monarch who is overthrown by a usurper, with catastrophic results. Repeated disasters follow as England's history is taken through the War of the Roses to the restoration of order by the Tudors. Again and again legality and stability are shown as fundamental virtues—a natural reaction against turbulent times. Shakespeare's expressions of nationalism are particularly intense; when in *Richard II* the king's uncle, John of Gaunt, lies dying, he pours out his love for his country in words that have moved English people ever since:

> This royal throne of kings, this sceptered isle,
> This earth of majesty, this seat of Mars,
> This other Eden, demi-paradise, . . .
> This happy breed of men, this little world,
> This precious stone set in the silver sea, . . .
> This blessed plot, this earth, this realm, this England.
>
> [*Richard II,* act 2, scene 1]

The uncertainties of the day appear in many of the plays. In *Julius Caesar* the optimistic "There is a tide in the affairs of men, which, taken at the flood, leads on to fortune" celebrates vigor and decisiveness but also warns against missing opportunities. More unambiguously, the patriotism expressed by John of Gaunt and Henry V suggests the glory that is England's destiny. Yet Shakespeare's four most famous tragedies, *Hamlet, King Lear, Macbeth,* and *Othello,* end in disillusionment: the heroes

are ruined by irresoluteness, pride, ambition, or jealousy. He is reflecting the Elizabethans' interest in the fatal flaws that destroy great men and in dramas of revenge, but the plays demonstrate as well his deep understanding of human nature. For all the promise of the future, one cannot forget human weakness, the inevitability of decay, and the constant threat of disaster. The contrast appears with compelling clarity in a speech delivered by Hamlet:

> What a piece of work is man! How noble in reason! how infinite in faculties! in form and moving how express and admirable! in action how like an angel! in apprehension how like a god! the beauty of the world, the paragon of animals! And yet to me what is this quintessence of dust? Man delights not me.
>
> [*Hamlet,* act 2, scene 2]

Despite such pessimism, despite the deep sense of human inadequacy, the basic impression Shakespeare gives is of immense vigor, of a restlessness and confidence that recall the many achievements of the sixteenth century. Prospero, the hero of his last play, *The Tempest,* has often been seen as the symbol of the new magician-cum-scientist, and references to the discoveries overseas are abundant. Yet a sense of decay is never far absent. Repeatedly men seem utterly helpless, overtaken by events they cannot control. There is a striking lack of security in the world Shakespeare's people inhabit. Nothing remains constant or dependable, and everything that seems solid and reassuring, be it the love of a daughter or the crown of England, is challenged. In this atmosphere of ceaseless change, where all solid, safe landmarks disappear, Shakespeare forcefully conveys the tensions of his time.

The Baroque and Classicism

From around 1600 onward, new concerns began to gain prominence in the arts and literature. First, in the Baroque there was an attempt to drown uncertainty in a blaze of grandeur and drama. But gradually the aims of Classicism, which emphasized formality, balance, and restraint, came to dominate European culture.

The Baroque: Grandeur and Excitement

The word "Baroque" has been used to indicate ornateness, grandeur, and excess as well as all the traits, including the Classical, of seventeenth-century art. Historians have applied it to music, literature, politics, and even personality traits. Its usage here will be restricted to its most precise meaning: the characteristics of a style in the visual arts that emanated from Rome in the first half of the seventeenth century. Passion, drama, mystery, and awe are the qualities of the Baroque: the viewer must be involved, aroused, uplifted (see Plates 33 and 34). Insofar as these characteristics are reflected in other kinds of creative work, such as literature and music, it is reasonable to discuss the

The interior of the St. Andrea della Valle basilica was built in the late seventeenth century. It displays the elaborate yet gaudy splendor of the Baroque style, which was the signature of an age of royal absolutism and affluence. Among Roman edifices, the dome of this basilica is second in height only to St. Peter's. (Photo: Alinari/Scala/EPA, Inc.)

various examples together; but to regard all manifestations of dramatic splendor or grandiose extravagance as Baroque is to depart from the essentially visual meaning of the term.

The Baroque was closely associated with the Counter Reformation's emphasis on gorgeous display in Catholic ritual. The patronage given by leading church figures and the presence of art treasures accumulated over centuries made Rome a magnet for the major painters of the period. Elsewhere the Baroque flourished primarily at the leading Catholic courts of the seventeenth century, most notably the Hapsburg courts in Madrid, Prague, and Brussels, since the style expressed perfectly the pomp of seventeenth-century princes. Few periods have conveyed so strong a sense of grandeur, theatricality, and ornateness.

Peter Paul Rubens (1577–1640) was the principal ornament of the brilliant Hapsburg court at Brussels. His major themes typified the Baroque style: glorification of great rulers (see Plate 37) and exaltation of the ceremony and mystery of Catholicism. His secular paintings convey, by their powerful depiction of human bodies and vivid use of color, the enormous strength of his subjects; his religious works similarly overwhelm the viewer with the majesty and panoply of the church and excite the believer's piety by stressing the dramatic mysteries of the faith. Toward the end of his life Rubens's paintings became more lyrical, especially on mythological subjects, but he never lost his ability to generate strong emotions.

Other artists glorified rulers of the time through idealized portraiture. The greatest court painter of the age was Diego Velázquez, some twenty-two years Rubens's junior. His portraits of members of the Spanish court depict rulers and their surroundings in the stately atmosphere appropriate to the theme (see Plate 38). Yet occasionally Velázquez hinted at the weakness of an ineffective monarch in his rendering of the face, even though the basic pur-

pose of his work always remained the exaltation of royal power. And when he painted a celebration of a notable Hapsburg victory, *The Surrender of Breda,* he managed to suggest the sadness and emptiness as much as the glory of war.

Giovanni Lorenzo Bernini was to sculpture and architecture what Rubens was to painting, and like Rubens he was closely associated with the Counter Reformation. Pope Urban VIII commissioned him in 1629 to complete both the inside and the outer setting of St. Peter's, extending and elaborating Michelangelo's original architectural plan. For the interior Bernini designed a splendid papal throne that seems to float on clouds beneath a burst of sunlight, and for the exterior he created an enormous plaza, surrounded by a double colonnade, that is the largest and most imposing square in all Europe.

The glories of Baroque Rome owe much to the work of Bernini. The elaborate fountains he sculpted can be seen throughout the city; his busts of contemporary Roman leaders set the style for portraiture in marble or stone; and his dramatic religious works reflect the desire of the Counter Reformation popes to electrify the faithful. The sensual and overpowering altarpiece dedicated to the Spanish mystic St. Teresa makes a direct appeal to the emotions of the beholder that reveals the excitement of Baroque at its best (see Plate 35). And drama is also immediately apparent in his *David,* which shows the young warrior at his supreme moment, just after he has unleashed his slingshot at Goliath. Bernini emphasized the intense exertion and concentration of this moment as an expression of human vigor, and with a touch that was characteristic of the bravado of the times he gave the figure his own face.

Similar qualities can be seen in the architecture of the age. Ornate churches and palaces were built on a massive scale that paralleled exactly the concerns of painting and sculpture. And it is significant that the three most conspicuous centers of the Counter Reformation—

The contrasting postures of victory and defeat
are masterfully captured by Diego Velázquez
in *The Surrender of Breda*. The Dutch soldiers
droop their heads and lances, but the victorious Spaniards hardly show triumph, and the
gesture of the victorious general, Ambrogio
Spinola, is one of consolation and understanding.
(Photo: Prado Museum)

Rome, Munich, and Prague—were also major centers of Baroque architecture (see Map A-20 in the Cartographic Essay).[3]

The seventeenth century was significant, too, as a decisive time in the history of music. New instruments were developed, notably in the keyboard and string families, that enabled composers to create richer effects than had been possible before. Particularly in Italy, which in the sixteenth and seventeenth centuries was the chief center of new ideas in music (see Map 16.1), musicians began to explore the potential of a form that first emerged in these years: the opera. Drawing on the resources of the theater, painting, architecture, music, and the dance, an operatic production could achieve a panoply of splendors beyond the reach of any one of these arts on its own. The form was perfectly attuned to the courtly culture of the age, to the love of display among the princes of Europe, and to the Baroque determination to overwhelm one's audience.

The dominant figure in seventeenth-century music was the Italian Claudio Monteverdi, one of the most innovative composers of all time. He has been called with some justification the creator of both the operatic form and the orchestra. His masterpiece *Orfeo* (1607) was written for his patron, the duke of Mantua, whose court provided Monteverdi with the many skilled professionals needed to mount an opera, from scene painters to singers. The result was a tremendous success, and in the course of the next century, operas gained in richness and complexity, attracting composers, as well as audiences, in ever increasing numbers.

There was a similar extension of the range of instrumental music. The accompaniment to *Orfeo* was still scored primarily for plucked instruments like the lute, which (except for the harp) were soon to disappear from the orchestra, but in his later works Monteverdi began to

***David* by Bernini.**
(Photo: Alinari—Art Reference Bureau)

rely increasingly on bowed strings and woodwinds. He became much freer in his use of extended melodies and readier to introduce unexpected discords, which give his works a flavor decidedly different from the music of earlier composers and reasonably familiar to modern ears.

---

[3] A good survey of Baroque architecture can be found in Nikolaus Pevsner, *An Outline of European Architecture* (1943 and later editions), Chap. 6.

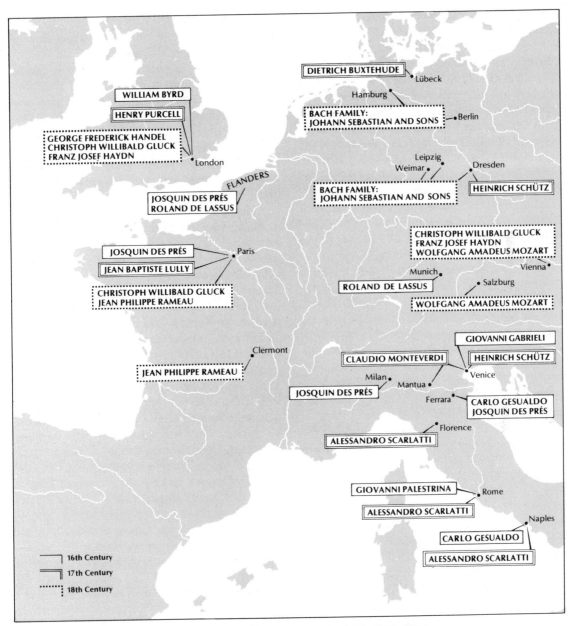

MAP 16.1. CENTERS OF MUSIC 1500–1800

This map indicates the shifting centers of new ideas in music from Flanders and Italy in the sixteenth century; to Italy in the seventeenth; and on to Germany, England, and France in the eighteenth.

Classicism: Grandeur and Restraint

Classicism, the second major style of the seventeenth century, attempted to recapture the aesthetic values of ancient Greece and Rome. What this usually meant in practice was an acceptance of the strict forms embodied in the works of antiquity. Like the Baroque, Classicism aimed for grandiose effects, but it achieved them through restraint and discipline, within the bounds of a formal structure. The gradual rise of the Classical style in the seventeenth century echoed the trend toward stabilization that was taking place in other areas of intellectual life and in politics.

The epitome of disciplined expression and conscious imitation of Classical antiquity is the work of Nicolas Poussin (1594–1665), a French artist who spent much of his career in Italy among the relics of Rome's glory. Poussin was no less interested than his contemporaries in momentous subjects and dramatic scenes, but the atmosphere in his canvases is always more subdued than in those of Velázquez or Rubens. The colors are muted, the figures are restrained, and the settings are serene. Peaceful landscapes, men and women in stately togas, and ruins of Classical buildings are consistent features of his work, even his religious paintings (see Plate 43).

In the United Provinces different forces were at work, but they too led to a style that was much more subdued than the powerful outpourings of Rubens and Velázquez. Two aspects of Dutch society had a particular influence: Protestantism and republicanism. The Reformed Church frowned on religious art and thus reduced the demand, both ceremonial and private, for paintings of biblical scenes. Religious works therefore tended to be expressions of personal faith, not glorifications of the church. The absence of a court meant that the chief patrons were sober merchants, who were far more interested in precise, dignified portraits than in ornate displays (see Plates 39 and 41). The result, notably in the work of the most powerful Dutch master, Rembrandt van Rijn, was an epic and compelling art whose beauty lies in its calmness and restraint.

Rembrandt explored an amazing range of themes, but his greatest paintings are his portraits. He was fascinated by human beings—their personalities, emotions, and self-revelations. Whether children or old people, simple servant girls or rich burghers, they are presented without elaboration or idealization; always the personality is allowed to speak for itself.

His most remarkable achievement in portraiture—and one of the most moving series of canvases in the history of art—is his depiction of the changes in his own face over his lifetime. The brash youth turns into the confident, successful, middle-aged man, one of the most sought-after painters in Holland. But in his late thirties the sorrows mounted: he lost his beloved wife, and commissions began to fall off. Sadness fills the eyes in these pictures. The last portraits move from despair to a final, quiet resignation as his sight slowly failed (see Plate 40). Taken together, these paintings bear comparison with Montaigne's essays as monuments to man's exploration of his own spirit—a searching appraisal that brings all who see it to a deeper understanding of human nature.

Rembrandt's large-scale, grandiose undertakings, like his smaller works, avoided startling effects. His many religious works, for example, are subdued and reverential in their approach, reflecting his own faith. The atmosphere differs sharply from the swirling passion conveyed by Rubens, who emphasized the drama of an event, whereas Rembrandt entered into the overwhelming emotions of the people present.

One could argue that Rembrandt cannot be fitted into either of the dominant styles of his time. Except for his powerful use of light, his work is far more introspective than most of the Baroque. On the other hand he did not adopt the forms of antiquity, as did Poussin and other

Classical painters. Yet like the advocates of Classicism, Rembrandt in his restraint seemed to anticipate the art of the next generation. After his death, in 1669, serenity, calm, and elegance became the watchwords of European painting (see p. 628). An age of repose and grace was succeeding a time of upheaval as surely in the arts as in other spheres of life.

By the middle of the seventeenth century, the formalism of the Classical style was also being extended to literature, especially drama. This change was most noticeable in France, but it soon moved through Western Europe, as leading critics demanded that new plays conform to the structure laid down by the ancients. In particular they wanted the three Classical unities observed: unity of place, which required that all scenes take place without change of location; unity of time, which demanded that the events in the play occur within a twenty-four hour period; and unity of action, which dictated simplicity and purity of plot.

The work of Pierre Corneille, the dominant figure in the French theater during the mid-century years, reflects the rise of Classicism. His early plays resemble rather complex Shakespearean drama, and even after he came in contact with the Classical tradition, his effervescent genius did not accept its rules easily. His masterpiece *Le Cid* (1636), based on the legends of a medieval Spanish hero, technically observed the three unities but only by compressing an entire tragic love affair, a military campaign, and multitudinous other events into one day. The play won immediate popular success, but the critics, urged on by Richelieu, an advocate of Classical drama, condemned Corneille for imperfect observance of the three unities. Thereafter he adhered to the Classical forms, though he was never entirely at ease with their restraints.

Passion was not absent from the strictly Classical play; the works of Jean Racine, the model Classical dramatist, portrayed some of the most intense emotion ever seen on the stage (see pp. 627, 628). But the exuberance of earlier drama, the enjoyment of life and of human nature, was disappearing. Only the figure of Molière was to retain these qualities, and even he respected the formalism of the Classical style (see pp. 629–630). Nobody summed up the values of Classicism better than Racine in his eulogy of Corneille:

> You know in what a condition the stage was when he began to write. . . . All the rules of art, and even those of decency and decorum, broken everywhere. . . . Corneille, after having for some time sought the right path and struggled against the bad taste of his day, inspired by extraordinary genius and helped by the study of the ancients, at last brought reason upon the stage.[4]

This was exactly the progression—from turbulence to calm—that was apparent throughout European culture in this period.

III. SOCIAL PATTERNS AND POPULAR CULTURE

It is difficult to draw analogies between, on the one hand, changes in the way ordinary people lived or in their customs and, on the other hand, the movement of ideas among a small, highly literate group of intellectual and artistic geniuses. There were points of contact and influence, to be sure. The magical interests of astrologers and alchemists were not far removed from the belief in hidden mysteries and spirits that influenced the inhabitants of every European village. In the late seventeenth century the first collections of folk tales were published, put together by writers who assumed

---

[4] Jean Racine, *Discours Prononcé à l'Académie Française à la Réception de M. de Corneille* (1685), in Paul Mesnard (ed.), *Oeuvres de J. Racine,* IV (1886), p. 366. Translation by Theodore K. Rabb.

that ancient wisdom was revealed in the sayings and stories of peasants. And ordinary men and women could not help but be affected by the attitudes and instructions imposed on them by their rulers. Nevertheless, one must not make the connections too close. Popular culture had roots of its own, determined by social and demographic forces, and if we see certain trends toward restraint and order that parallel what was happening in politics and literate culture, they must not be overdrawn.

Hierarchy and Rank in the Social Order

Seventeenth-century people occupied well-defined places in society. According to a common view, they formed links in the great chain of being, which, ascending by degrees, united all of creation with the angels and God. Humanity stood in the middle of the chain between animals and angels, and within its ranks there were also degrees, rising from the peasant through the well-to-do landowner or professional and the noble to the king. It was considered against the order of nature for someone to move to another level of society.

In fact, though, the people of the seventeenth century divided themselves into multiple groups and strata. Perhaps the clearest way to describe this structure is to liken society to a set of four ladders, each representing a distinct group: those on the land (about four-fifths of the population), those in the clergy, those in commerce (including artisans and shopkeepers), and those in the professions (mainly lawyers, doctors, and teachers). Within each ladder there was a sharply differentiated hierarchy, but most positions on each ladder had rough equivalents on the others. In almost every case, moreover, women were regarded as having a lower position than men. No abbess could take the same part in church government as an abbot; the few female artisans could not become prominent in a guild like their male

equivalents; and so forth. While all four ladders were parallel, they all had a separate coherence, and the landed ladder was clearly superior in that it rose higher and included the leaders of society, the courtiers and the great magnates.

Mobility and Privilege

The determinants of status in modern times—wealth, family background, and education—were viewed rather differently in the seventeenth century. Wealth was significant chiefly to merchants, education was important mainly among professionals, and background was vital primarily to the nobility. But in this period the significance of these three social indicators began to shift. Wealth grew increasingly respectable as ever-larger numbers of successful merchants bought their way into the nobility. Education was also becoming more highly prized; throughout Europe attendance at institutions of higher learning soared after 1550 because a smattering of knowledge was now considered to be a mark of gentility.[5] And background was being scrutinized ever more defensively (though to less effect) by old-line nobles, who were dismayed by the multiplication of "new" aristocrats.

The growing social importance of wealth and education indicates that mobility was possible despite the great chain of being. Thanks to the expansion of bureaucracies during the sixteenth and seventeenth centuries, it became easier to move to new levels, either by winning favor at court or by buying an office. High status conferred important privileges: great landowners could demand services and fees from their tenants; city freemen, nobles, and bureaucrats were often exempt from taxes; and courtiers controlled portions of the vast patronage that the government disbursed. This period witnessed the rise of some of the most successful self-made people in history, particularly

[5] See Lawrence Stone, "The Educational Revolution in England, 1560–1640," *Past & Present*, July 1964, pp. 41–80.

among the ministers who served the rulers of England and France.

Somewhat different patterns were emerging in Europe's colonies. From their earliest days, the overseas settlements had reflected their countries of origin. Both the Portuguese and the Dutch, for example, had concentrated almost exclusively on commerce. They had small populations and were incapable of occupying large areas; instead they established a network of trading posts linked by sea that were marked by some effort to live amicably amid the native populations. The French followed a similar practice for a different reason: because the home country was rich in land and prosperous, few of its inhabitants were willing to emigrate. The Spaniards and the English by contrast flocked to new settlements in search of gold, land, and religious freedom. They remained overseas, occupying vast territories, subduing the natives, and creating extensive political structures that were far more elaborate than the earlier commercial outposts.

The common problem of all the colonies was their vulnerability. They were exposed to attack from the local population and from rival colonizers, and they rarely had the defensive capability to feel completely secure. Under this pressure they often created societies imitative of but even more rigid than those of the countries they had left behind. Representatives of church and king dominated Portugal's settlements, and in her one major colony, Brazil, a few powerful landowners controlled society more tightly than they could in the homeland. Among the Dutch, as might be expected, the merchants took charge completely; and the French were subjected to strict supervision by the government—there was even an *intendant* for Canada. Spain's empire was also focused on the crown, and if its extent and remoteness permitted the emergence of a fairly independent society, great nobles and the church still stood at its head, as at home. And the English created a system in which landed gentry, such as the

plantation owners of Virginia, and thriving merchants remained the leading citizens, though independent-minded New England diverged significantly from this pattern, reflecting Puritanism's challenge to the traditional hierarchical view of social structure.

All the colonies, however, were distinguished from the mother countries by one institution that was vital to their economies but also degrading to its participants: slavery. The slaves posed yet another military threat to the settlers, thus reinforcing their inclination toward rigid social control.

It is important to realize that, both in Europe and in the colonies, the lower levels of society scarcely participated in the mobility caused by the growth of commerce and bureaucracy. Peasants throughout Europe were in fact entering a time of increasing difficulty at the end of the sixteenth century. Their taxes were rising rapidly, but the prices they could get for the food they grew were stabilizing. Moreover landowners were starting what has been called the "seigneurial reaction"—making additional demands on their tenants, raising rents, and taking as much as they could out of the land. The only escape was to cities or armies, both of which grew rapidly in the seventeenth century. A few lucky people improved their lot by such a move, but for the huge majority a life of poverty in cities caused even more misery and hunger than one on the land. Few were allowed to become apprentices, and day laborers were poorly paid and usually out of work. As for military careers, armies not only destroyed the well-being of the rural areas they passed through but were hardly less dangerous for their own troops. They were carriers of disease, frequently ill fed, and subject to constant hardship. For many, therefore, the only alternative to starvation was crime. In London in the seventeenth century, social events like dinners and outings took place during the daytime, because the streets were unsafe at night.

Demographic Patterns

During the last thirty years, a number of historians have developed a new technique called family reconstitution, which uses analyses of the records of births, marriages, and deaths in parish registers to re-create the patterns of seventeenth-century life.[6] Some of the contrasts they have revealed are startling. For example, in France illegitimacy appears to have accounted for only 1 percent of births in the countryside, about 4 or 5 percent in towns, and somewhat more in Paris. In England, however, illegitimacy accounted for 20 percent of births, and in some areas the rate reached 40 or 50 percent after 1700. In New England in the same period the proportion evidently rose from 10 to 50 percent. The view that contrasts the loose French with the proper English or repressed New Englanders is thus the reverse of the truth.

Once the babies were born, no more than 75 percent reached the age of one, only 50 percent survived to be twenty, and less than 10 percent lived to be sixty. This was a society dominated by those in their twenties and thirties, able to rise because their predecessors died earlier than they do in modern times. Since only one child in two reached adulthood, a couple had to produce four children merely to replace themselves.

The likelihood that they would be able to do so was not improved by the practice of marrying relatively late or the fact that women lost the capacity to bear children in their late thirties. The average age of marriage for men was around twenty-seven and for women close to twenty-five. On the average therefore a woman would have some twelve years in which to give birth to four children if the population was to be maintained. Because of lactation the mean interval between births was almost two and a half years, which meant that the average married couple was only just raising two adults. And in fact population levels were barely being maintained for most of the seventeenth century. There had been an enormous increase before 1600, and a slight rise was sustained thereafter, but the real resumption of growth did not come until the eighteenth century, though cities continued to grow throughout the 1600s (see Map 16.2).

The causes of the high mortality rate were simple but insuperable: famine, poor nutrition, disease, and war. The plague, erupting every few years from the fourteenth century on, swept away mainly the young and the old and it did not disappear until the 1720s. The upper classes, better fed and able to get away from plague centers, had a better chance for survival; but the odds were often equalized by their resort to dangerously incompetent doctors.

How and why the general population trend changed is impossible to know for certain. It is fairly clear that as early as the fifteenth century, the upper levels of society had begun limiting the size of their families in order to preserve their wealth—dowries for a daughter were expensive, and younger sons might not be able to live from family resources. Whether self-limitation was understood, let alone practiced, by other classes is difficult to say, though it is hard to offer an alternate explanation of the fact that the average gap between children sometimes rose to double the usual thirty months, particularly in troubled times. Late marriage for the upper classes was another means of controlling family size. For the lower levels of society, such postponement was a traditional economic defense: children had to work for their families until their parents' death allowed them to strike out for themselves.

Because of late marriages and low life expectancies, two married generations were rarely contemporary. Thus the extended family—more than one nuclear group of mother, father, and children living together—was extremely uncommon. Almost everyone who

---

[6] An excellent introduction to the work of the historical demographers is E. A. Wrigley, *Population and History* (1969).

MAP 16.2. CITIES OF EUROPE IN 1700

survived married, so there were few bachelors and spinsters, and usually each family could live on its own (see Plate 42).

These features and consequences of demographic behavior give a sense of the basic pat-terns of seventeenth-century society, but we still do not know why the population grew so markedly in the sixteenth century, so little in the seventeenth, and then again so rapidly in the eighteenth. One can but suggest that reper-

EUROPE'S POPULATION, 1600–1700, BY REGIONS

Region	1600★	1700	Percentage Change
Spain, Portugal, and Italy	23.6	22.7	−4
France, Switzerland, and Germany	35.0	36.2	+3
British Isles, Low Countries, and Scandinavia	12.0	16.1	+34
Total	70.6	75.0	+6

★All figures are in millions

Source: Jan de Vries, *The Economy of Europe in an Age of Crisis, 1600–1750*, Cambridge, 1976, p. 5.

cussions were felt from the political, economic, and social upheavals of the seventeenth century.

In only one area, the link between war and life expectancy, were the effects obvious. At the simplest level the Thirty Years' War alone caused the death of more than 5 million people. It also helped plunge Western Europe into a debilitating economic depression, which in turn decreased the means of relieving famine. These were mighty blows at the delicate balance that maintained population growth, and disasters of such magnitude could not easily be absorbed. The few regions that managed to avoid the worst effects were to become the leaders of Europe's economy (see table above).

If the seventeenth century was almost everywhere a time of stagnation or decline in population, a period of harsh weather and recurrent famines and plagues, it was so especially for the poorest members of society. The low life expectancy, the frequent deaths of children, and the struggle to survive were constant and desperate pressures. It is small wonder that their culture embraced beliefs in dark forces and rituals of violence and protest. Nor is it surprising that as governments extended their hold over their subjects, they reduced the autonomy of ordinary villagers and limited the extremes of popular self-expression.

Popular Culture

As is natural for people living close to the land and dependent for their livelihood on the kind-

ness of nature—good weather, health, fertility of soil—peasants in sixteenth- and seventeenth-century Europe assumed that outside forces controlled their destinies. Particular beliefs varied from place to place but there was general agreement that a mere human being could do little to assure his or her own well-being. The world was full of spirits and powers, and all one could do was to encourage the good, defend oneself as best one knew how against the evil, and hope that the good would win. Nothing that happened—the death of a calf, lightning striking a house, a toad jumping through a window into a home—was accidental. Everything had a purpose. Any unusual event was an omen, part of a larger plan, or the action of some unseen force.

To strengthen themselves against trouble, people used whatever help they could find. One device was to organize special processions and holidays to celebrate good times (such as harvests), to lament misfortunes, to complain about oppression, or to poke fun at scandalous behavior. These occasions, known as "rough music" in England and "charivari" in France, often used the theme of "the world turned upside down" to make their point. In the set pieces in a procession, a fool might be dressed up as a king, a woman might be shown beating her husband, or a tax collector might appear hanging from a tree. Whether ridiculing a cheating wife or lamenting the lack of bread, the community was expressing its solidarity in the face of difficulty or distasteful behavior through these rituals. It was a way of letting off steam and declaring public opinion.

The potential for violence was always present at such gatherings, especially when religious or social differences became entangled with other resentments. The viciousness of ordinary Protestants and Catholics toward one another—it was not uncommon for one side to mutilate the dead bodies of the other—revealed a frustration and aggressiveness that was not far below the surface. When food was scarce or new impositions had been ordered by their rulers, peasants and townspeople needed little excuse to show their anger openly. In many cases women took the lead, not only because they had firsthand experience of the difficulty of feeding a family but also because troops were more reluctant to attack them. This tradition was still alive in 1789, in the early days of the French Revolution, when a band made up primarily of women marched from Paris to the royal court at Versailles to demand bread.

There was a peasant uprising in one location or another in France every year during the century up to 1675. But ordinary people also had other outlets for their problems. Recognizing their powerlessness in face of outside forces, they resorted to their version of the magic that the literate were finding so fashionable at this very time. Where the rich patronized astrologers, paying fortunes for horoscopes and advice about how to live their lives, the peasants and the poor consulted popular almanacs or sought out "cunning men" and wise women for secret spells, potions, and similar remedies for their anxieties. Even religious ceremonies were thought of as being related to the rituals of the magical world, in which so-called "white" witches—the friendly kind—gave assistance when a ring was lost, when a new bride could not become pregnant, or when the butter would not form out of the milk.

For most Europeans, such support was all too necessary as they struggled with the unpredictability of nature. Misfortunes, they believed, could never be just plain bad luck; rather, there was intent behind everything that happened. Events were *willed*, and if they turned out badly, they must have been willed by the good witch's opposite, the evil witch. Such beliefs went back to the ancient world and for centuries had been the cause of mass scares and cruel persecutions of innocent victims—usually helpless old women, able to do nothing but mutter curses when taunted by neighbors, and easy targets if someone had to be blamed for unfortunate happenings.

In the sixteenth and seventeenth centuries, the hunt for witches intensified to levels never previously reached. This has been called the era of "the great witch craze," and for good reason. There were outbursts in every part of Europe, and tens of thousands of the accused were executed. The patterns varied—in some areas they were said to dance with the devil, in others to fly on broomsticks, in others to be possessed by evil spirits who could induce dreadful (and possibly psychosomatic) symptoms—but usually the punishment was the same: burning at the stake. And the hysteria was infectious. One accusation could trigger dozens more until entire regions were swept with fear and hatred. Political and religious authorities, who often encouraged witch hunts as expressions of piety or as means of stamping out disorder, found themselves unable to stop the flow once it started. It was the perfect symptom of an age of disruption, uncertainty, and upheaval.

By the middle of the seventeenth century, however, the wave was beginning to recede. The rulers of society came to realize how dangerous to authority the witchcraft campaigns could become, especially when accusations were turned against the rich and privileged classes. Increasingly, therefore, cases were not brought to trial, and when they were, lawyers and doctors (who approached the subject from a different point of view than the clergy) cast doubt on the validity of the testimony. Gradually, excesses were restrained and control was reestablished; by 1700 there was only a trickle of new incidents.

The decline reflected not only the more general quieting down of society but also the growing proportion of Europe's population that was living in cities. Here, less reliant on good weather or the luck of fertility, people could feel themselves more in control of their own fates. If there were unexpected fires, there were fire brigades; if a house nevertheless burned down, there might even be insurance—a new idea, just starting in the late seventeenth century. A notable shift in the world view of popular culture was under way, the inevitable result of basic changes in social organization.

Change in the Traditional Village

A number of forces were combining to transform the atmosphere of the traditional village. Over three-quarters of Europe's population still lived in these small communities, but their structure was not what it once had been. In the east peasants were being reduced to serfdom; in the west—our principal concern—familiar relationships and institutions were changing.

The essence of the traditional village had been its isolation. Cut off from frequent contact with the world beyond its immediate region, it had been self-sufficient and closely knit. Everyone knew everyone else, and mutual help was vital. There might be distinctions among

This woodcut, by the German artist Grien, shows the popular image of witches in early modern Europe. One carries a potion while flying on a goat. The others, including a ghastly hag, put together the ingredients for a magic potion in a jar inscribed with mystical symbols. The fact that witches were thought to be learned women who could understand magic was another reason they were feared by a Europe that expected women to be uneducated.
(Photo: Private Collection)

villagers—some more prosperous, others less so—but the sense of cohesiveness was powerful. It extended even to the main "outsiders" in the village, the priest and the lord. The priest was often indistinguishable from his parishioners: almost as poor and sometimes hardly more literate. He adapted to local customs and beliefs, frequently taking part in semipagan rituals so as to keep his authority with his flock. The lord could be exploitative and demanding, but he considered the village his livelihood, and he therefore kept in close touch with its affairs and did all he could to ensure its safety, orderliness, and well-being.

The first intrusion onto this scene was economic. As a result of the boom in agricultural prices during the sixteenth century, followed by the economic difficulties of the seventeenth, differences in the wealth of the villagers became more marked. The richer peasants began to set themselves apart from the poorer, and the feeling of unity began to break down. For hundreds of years, most villages had governed themselves through elected councils drawn from every part of the population. Toward the end of the seventeenth century, however, these councils started disappearing as the commitment to common interests declined.

Some of the other outside influences were more direct. In a few areas of Europe, especially in England and the Netherlands, the isolation of the villages was broken down by merchants who were experimenting with new ways of organizing labor. Traditionally, a village would raise sheep, shear them, and sell the wool at market to traders who would have it finished into cloth in towns. Now, aiming at greater efficiency, merchants were organizing production on a larger scale in a new industry that has been called the rural "putting-out" system or "cottage industry." What they were doing was buying up the raw wool in sheep-raising villages, distributing it to other villages that were now geared entirely to weaving and producing cloth, and then taking the finished material to

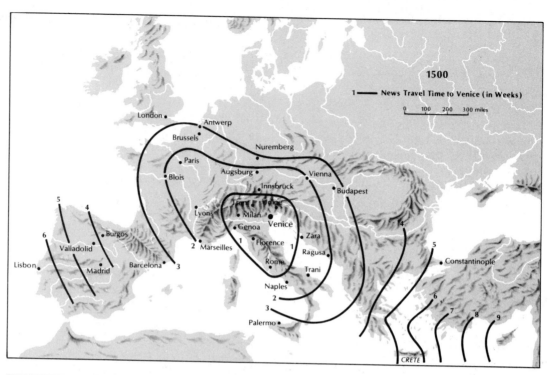

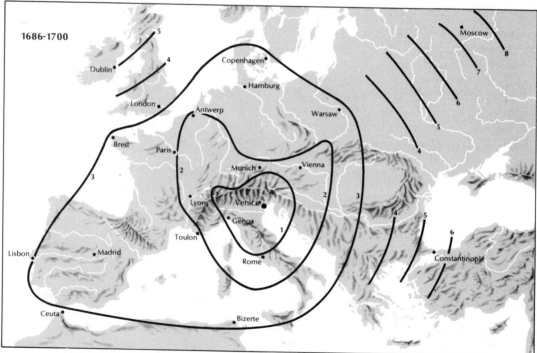

MAP 16.3. SPEED OF NEWS TRAVELING TO VENICE

market for sale. Entire areas came to be in the employ of merchants, dependent on them for materials and a livelihood. This created a new set of relationships, based on piecework rather than services, which again helped redirect the traditional patterns of life in the village, reducing independence and the ties of friendship and mutual help.

The isolation was also lessened as cities grew, not only because large urban centers needed ever wider regions to provide them with food and goods, but also because they attracted people who could not make ends meet in the countryside. Long-range communications became more common, especially as localities were linked into national market and trade networks, and immigrants in cities came to know fellow countrymen from distant villages (see Map 16.3).

Noneconomic forces, too, hastened the loss of autonomy. Over the course of the seventeenth century, nobles were looking more and more to central courts and capital cities, rather than to their local holdings, for position and power. Pursuing the seigneurial reaction, they treated the villages they dominated as sources of income and began to distance themselves from the inhabitants. Relations became impersonal where once they had been close. Charity, for example, was no longer thought to be the responsibility of neighbors: it was the duty of the church or the government.

The churches were taking on new roles, but these only had the effect of encouraging conformity. In Catholic countries the Counter Reformation produced better-educated priests who were trained to impose official doctrine instead of tolerating local customs. Among Protestants, ministers were similarly well educated and denounced traditional beliefs as idolatrous or superstitious. Regardless of church, the outside world was intruding yet again. Habits did not change overnight, but in the long run the villagers were being forced to accept new values and to abandon their old beliefs.

Another outside force was the growing presence of representatives of central government. In 1500 few villagers would have known what a servant of the king was, let alone have seen one. By 1700 they would all have had considerable experience with bureaucrats of one sort or another: tax collectors, recruiting officers, or distributors of food during famines. Villagers no longer lived on their own in a small corner of the land. They were a part of the territorial state, important resources that the national government had to control as well as protect if it was to increase its power. Institutions (such as charity) had to be uniform; order had to be maintained. With their autonomy fragmenting, the villages had no capacity to resist the integrating forces that were blending them into their nation states and subduing their eccentricities and traditions.

As Europeans entered the last decades of the seventeenth century, they had reason to feel that the upheavals and uncertain times they had gone through for more than one hundred years were behind them. An extraordinarily successful intellectual movement, the scientific revolution, had solved many ancient problems about nature. Artists and writers had developed a new confidence. And throughout society an atmosphere of orderliness was returning after over a century of change, disruption, and excesses like the witch craze. Religion had lost much of its power to arouse hatred and aggression; a calmer time seemed to be dawning, taking as its model the respect for reason that the scientists were encouraging.

The natural beneficiaries of these tendencies were the upper classes through-out Europe. Ordinary villagers may not have felt reconciled to the order being imposed upon them, but they proved unable to resist the forces—economic, political, and cultural—that were pressing them to conform. On the other hand, the sense of order was perfectly suited to the needs of aristocrats. They could now relax, confident that their power was secure. At dazzling princely courts, especially in France, they could enjoy the absence of turmoil and set their stamp on the culture of a new, less troubled age.

RECOMMENDED READING

Sources

*Drake, Stillman (tr. and ed.). *Discoveries and Opinions of Galileo*. 1957. The complete texts of some of Galileo's most important and readable works.

*Hall, Marie Boas (ed.). *Nature and Nature's Laws: Documents of the Scientific Revolution*. 1970. A good collection of documents by and about the pioneers of modern science.

Studies

*Butterfield, Herbert. *The Origins of Modern Science*. 1949. An elegantly written history of the scientific revolution that conveys its excitement.

*Debus, Allen G. *Man and Nature in the Renaissance*. 1978. A more up-to-date study than Butterfield's of the origins and course of the scientific revolution through 1650, with a good bibliography.

Frame, Donald M. *Montaigne: A Biography*. 1965. The best biography of this influential thinker.

*Geymonat, Ludovico. *Galileo Galilei*. Stillman Drake (tr.). 1965. A straightforward and clear biography.

*Ginzburg, Carlo. *The Cheese and the Worms: The Cosmos of a Sixteenth-Century Miller*. John and Anne Tedeschi (trs.). 1980. A remarkable account, focusing on the beliefs of a man who lived in a small northern Italian town, which brings to life the extraordinary variety of the popular culture of the time.

*Hibbard, Howard. *Bernini*. 1965. A graceful account of the life and work of the artist who was the epitome of the Baroque.

Kamen, Henry. *The Iron Century: Social Change in Europe 1550–1660*. 1971. This thorough, almost encyclopedic overview of the social history of the period also has a good bibliography.

*Krailsheimer, Alban. *Pascal*. 1980. The best brief biography, with good discussions of the life, the science, and the turn to religion.

*Kuhn, Thomas S. *The Structure of Scientific Revolutions*. 1962. A suggestive interpretation of the reasons the scientific revolution developed and took hold.

*Ladurie, Emmanuel Le Roy. *The Peasants of Languedoc*. John Day (tr.). 1966. A brilliant evocation of peasant life in France in the sixteenth and seventeenth centuries.

Maland, David. *Culture and Society in Seventeenth-Century France*. 1970. This survey of art, drama, and literature contains a good discussion of the rise of Classicism.

Palisca, Claude. *Baroque Music*. 1968. The best survey of this period in the history of music.

*Popkin, Richard H. *The History of Scepticism from Erasmus to Descartes*. 1964. Taking one strand in European thought as its subject, this lively study places both Montaigne and Descartes in a new perspective.

*Shearman, John. *Mannerism*. 1968. The best short introduction to a difficult artistic style.

Tapié, V. L. *The Age of Grandeur: Baroque Art and Architecture*. A. R. Williamson (tr.). 1960. Although concentrating primarily on France and Austria, this is the most comprehensive survey of this period in art.

*Thomas, Keith. *Religion and the Decline of Magic*. 1971. The most thorough account of popular culture yet published, this enormous book, while dealing mainly with England, treats at length such subjects as witchcraft, astrology, and ghosts in a most readable style.

White, Christopher. *Rembrandt and His World*. 1964. A brief but wide-ranging introduction to the artist's work and life.

———. *Rubens and His World*. 1968. As good on Rubens as the previous title is on Rembrandt.

*Available in paperback.

Chapter 17

The Triumph of Aristocrats and Kings 1660–1715

Ever since the time that effective central governments had coalesced in Europe in the Late Middle Ages, nobles and rulers had engaged in a running struggle for power. After the upheavals of the mid-seventeenth century, however, it became clear that central administrations—now highly complex and commanding large bureaucracies—would dominate political life. Yet no ruler could govern without the help of the aristocracy. Of the main orders, or estates, into which society was divided—aristocrats, clergy, townspeople, and peasants—only the aristocrats had the education, experience, and status essential for the running of a state.

The actual control they wielded over policy varied widely. In the absolutist realms they were most powerful in Austria, less so in France and Brandenburg-Prussia, and least in Russia. Moreover influence in the government was usually restricted to a small group; the class as a whole benefited only indirectly. But in England (where the ruling elite had been penetrated by members of the untitled gentry), the United Provinces, Sweden, and Poland, virtually no major decision could be executed without their approval. In effect, the aristocracy had taken possession of the administration of Europe's states and no longer had to compete with towns, representative assemblies, or the ruler himself for the fruits of power.

By the end of the seventeenth century, therefore, Europe's nobility was moving toward a new type of leadership. Historians have called this the domestication of the aristocracy, a process in which great lords who had once drawn their status primarily from the antiquity of their lineage or the extent of their lands gradually came to see service to the throne and royal favor as the best source of power.

To central administrations, eager to restore or confirm orderly government after over a century of disruptions, this alliance was more than welcome, and the rewards they bestowed—whether in patronage, privilege, or perquisites—were enormous. New power structures thus emerged in the age of Louis XIV, though the forms differed from country to country, and the fortunes of the lower classes fluctuated accordingly. Yet throughout Europe the quest for order was the underlying concern, a preoccupation that was already evident in the mid-seventeenth century and that pervaded not only political and social developments, but also thought and taste during the subsequent fifty years.

I. THE ABSOLUTE MONARCHIES

In countries that were ruled by absolutist monarchs—where all power was believed to emanate from the untrammeled person of the king—the center of society was the great court. Here the leaders of government assembled, and around them swirled the most envied social circles of the time. At the court of Louis XIV in particular, an atmosphere of ornate splendor arose that, though primarily intended to exalt the king, inevitably glorified the aristocracy too. No other ruler could match its scale and magnificence, but many tried to imitate its style.

Louis XIV at Versailles

In the view of Louis XIV (1643–1715), absolutism and the building of both the state and the government went hand in hand. But all three had to have a focus, preferably away from the turbulent city of Paris. To this end Louis, at a cost of half a year's royal income, transformed a small château his father had built at Versailles, 12 miles outside of Paris, into the largest building in Europe, surrounded by vast and elaborate formal gardens.

The splendor of the setting was designed to impress the world with the majesty of its principal occupant, and a complex ritual of daily ceremonies centered on the king gradually evolved. The name "Sun King" was another means of self-aggrandizement, symbolized by coins that showed the rays of the sun falling first on Louis and then by reflection onto his subjects, who thus owed life and warmth to their monarch. Versailles also provided an appropriate physical setting for the domestication of the nobility. Each year those who sought Louis's favor had to make an ostentatious appearance at court, and endless factions and plots swirled through the palace as courtiers jockeyed for position, competing for such privileges as handing the king his gloves in the morning.

Louis regarded all men as his servants, and they were kept constantly aware of their vulnerable status.

Conditions at Versailles were far from pleasant for these nobles. Crammed into tiny rooms, surrounded by the awful smells of an overcrowded palace without toilet facilities, and so cold that their drinking water froze at dinner parties, they continued to endure the discomforts in order to have access to the power only the court could bestow. In the end, the nobles found it easier to establish their prominence by obtaining offices and positions from the king than by resorting to their traditional unruliness. This domestication gave them a less dangerous route to influence, and it also provided Louis with the talents of able and loyal administrators. Moreover, he justified his supremacy with a new emphasis on an old political concept, the divine right of kings. This theory, which derived from the fact that kings were anointed with holy oil at their coronations, asserted that the monarch was God's representative on earth. He was therefore entitled to absolute power, because treason was also blasphemy. The main theorist at Versailles, Bishop Bossuet, called Louis God's lieutenant and argued that the Bible itself endorsed absolutism. Nothing happened at court that would have given anyone cause to think otherwise.

Government and Foreign Policy

Yet this system was not merely a device to satisfy one man's whim, for Louis was a gifted state builder. In creating or reorganizing government institutions to reflect his own wishes, he strengthened his authority at home and increased his ascendancy over his neighbors. In fact the most durable result of absolutism in seventeenth-century France was the state's winning of final control over three critical activities: the use of armed force, the formulation and execution of laws, and the collection and expenditure of revenue. These functions in turn

International and Military History	Political History
1660	
	1662 Crushing of rebellion in Konigsberg by Great Elector
1665–1667 War between England and the Netherlands	
1672–1678 War between France and the Netherlands	1672 Murder of Jan De Witt; takeover of Dutch government by William III
1675 Defeat of Swedes by Brandenburg-Prussia at battle of Fehrbellin	
	1678–1680 Exclusion Crisis in England
	1682 Peter the Great tsar of Russia
1683 Siege of Vienna	1683 Death of Colbert
	1685–1688 James II king of England
1688–1697 War between France and the League of Augsburg	1688–1689 Glorious Revolution in England
	1690 Bill of Rights and Act of Toleration in England
	1691 Death of Louvois
1697 Defeat of Turks by Hapsburgs at battle of Zenta	
1699 Treaty of Karlowitz: Hapsburgs gain territory in Balkans from Turks	
1700 Defeat of Russians by Swedes at battle of Narva	1700 Death of Charles II of Spain
	1701 Elector Frederick becomes "King in Prussia"
1702–1713 War of the Spanish Succession	1702 Death of William III
1704 Marlborough and Eugene defeat the French at the battle of Blenheim	1705 Death of Emperor Leopold I
1707 Union of England and Scotland	
1709 Defeat of Swedes by Russians at battle of Poltava	
1713–1714 Treaty of Utrecht	
	1715 Death of Louis XIV
20	1719 Death of Charles XII

Social and Economic History	Cultural and Intellectual History
—1660—	
1661–1665 Legislation restricting rights of religious dissenters in England	
1663 Beginning of English colonization of the Carolinas	
1664–1672 Major effort to stimulate French industry by Colbert	1665 First publication of the Royal Society's *Philosophical Transactions*
1665 Terrible outbreak of plague, especially in London	1666 Founding of the Royal Academy of Science in France
1667 Colbert imposes tariff on imports to France, aimed mainly at Dutch trade	1667 John Bunyan's *Pilgrim's Progress* and Milton's *Paradise Lost*
	1669 Death of Rembrandt
	1670 Molière's *Bourgeois Gentleman*
	1674 Boileau's *Poetic Art*
	1677 Racine's *Phèdre*
	1680 Death of Sir Peter Lely
1682 Policy of "Reversions" begun in Sweden by Charles XI	
1685 Revocation of the Edict of Nantes	
	1687 Newton's *Principia*
	1690 Locke's *Essay Concerning Human Understanding* and *Second Treatise of Civil Government*
1694 Founding of the Bank of England	1695 Death of Henry Purcell
	1700 Death of John Dryden
1703 St. Petersburg founded and building begins	
1709 Terrible famine throughout Europe	1710 Jonathan Swift's *Battle of the Books*
	1716 Death of Leibniz
1720 Collapse of South Seas Trading Company. "South Sea Bubble"	

depended on a centrally controlled bureaucracy responsive to royal orders and efficient enough to carry them out in distant provinces over the objections of local groups.

In its ideal form an absolute monarch's bureaucracy was insulated from outside pressure by the king's power to remove and transfer appointees. In the case of France, this involved creating new administrative officials—commissioners—to supersede some existing officers or magistrates who claimed their positions by virtue of property or other rights.[1] The process also required training programs, improved administrative methods, and the use of experts wherever possible. This approach was considered desirable both for the central bureaucracy in the capital and for the provincial offices.

At the head of this structure, Louis XIV was able to carry off successfully a responsibility that few monarchs had the talent to pursue: he served as his own first minister, actively and effectively overseeing administrative affairs. He thus filled two roles—as king in council and king in court. Louis the administrator coexisted with Louis the courtier, who cultivated the arts, hunted, and indulged in gargantuan banquets. In his view the two roles went together, and he held them in balance.

Among his numerous imitators, however, this was not always the case. Court life was the pleasanter, easier side of absolutism. It tended to consume an inordinate share of a state's resources and to become an end in itself. The display performed certain useful functions, of course; it stimulated luxury trades, supported cultural endeavors, and thus exercised a civilizing influence on the nobility of Europe. But beyond this it tended to be frivolous and wasteful, lending an undeserved prestige to the leisure pursuits of the upper classes, such as danc-

ing, card playing, and hunting, while sapping the energies of influential figures. Louis was one of the few who avoided sacrificing affairs of state to regal pomp.

Like court life, government policy under Louis XIV was tailored to the aim of state building. As he was to discover, there were limits to his absolutism; the resources and powers at his disposal were not endless. But until the last years of his reign, they served his many purposes extremely well. Moreover Louis had superb support at the highest levels of his administration—men whose viewpoints differed but whose skills were carefully blended by their ruler.

The king's two leading ministers were Jean Baptiste Colbert and the marquis of Louvois. Colbert was a financial wizard who had been raised to prominence by Mazarin and who regarded a mercantilist policy as the key to state building. He believed that the government should give priority to increasing France's wealth. This meant in turn that the chief danger to the country's well-being was the United Provinces, Europe's great trader state, and that royal resources should be poured into the navy, manufacturing, and shipping. By contrast Louvois, the son of a military administrator, consistently emphasized the army as the foundation of France's power. He believed that the country was threatened primarily by land—by the Holy Roman Empire on its flat, vulnerable northeast frontier—and thus that resources should be allocated to the army and to an extensive border fortification program.

Louis shifted back and forth between these considerations, but the basic tendencies of his policy can always be traced. In his early years he relied heavily on Colbert, who moved gradually toward war with the Dutch when all at-

---

[1] The *intendants,* who remained the chief provincial administrators, provided the model for the commissioners, because their success derived from dependence on royal approval. It should be noted that all bureaucrats were called officers, but those with judicial functions were known as magistrates.

The Palace of Versailles in 1668.
(Photo: Louvre)

Louis XIV (seated) is shown here in full regal splendor surrounded by three of his heirs. On his right is his eldest son, on his left is his eldest grandson, and, reaching out his hand, his eldest great-grandson, held by his governess. All three of these heirs died before Louis, and thus they never became kings of France.

(Photo: Wallace Collection, London)

tempts to undermine their control of French maritime trade failed. But the war, occupying most of the 1670s, was a failure, and so the pendulum swung toward Louvois. Adopting the marquis's aims, in the early 1680s Louis asserted his right to a succession of territories on France's northeast border. No one claim seemed important enough to provoke his neighbors to military action, especially since some of them were distracted by a growing Turkish threat from the East. Thus France was able to annex large segments of territory, ultimately extending her frontier to Strasbourg, on the Rhine (see Map 17.1). Finally, however, the

MAP 17.1. THE WARS OF LOUIS XIV

defensive League of Augsburg was formed against Louis, and another war broke out in 1688. This one too went badly for him, and when he decided to seek peace, Louvois fell from favor. In a move that surprised all of Europe, Louis then brought back to power a former foreign minister named Simon de Pomponne, who had always stood for peace and careful diplomacy. It was characteristic of the Sun King to use his servants this way—raising and discarding them according to their position on his policy of the moment. But even this balancing process broke down in the last two decades of his reign, when France became involved in a bitter, drawn-out war that brought famine, wretched poverty, and humiliation. Louis was seeking the succession to the Spanish throne for his family, and he was determined to pursue the fighting until he achieved his aim.

This final and ruinous enterprise revealed both the new power of France and her limits. By launching an all-out attempt to establish his own and his country's supremacy, Louis showed that he felt capable of taking on the whole of Europe; but by then he no longer had the economic and military base at home or the weak opposition abroad to assure success.

The strains had begun to appear in the 1690s, when shattering famines throughout France reduced both tax revenues and manpower at home, while enemies began to unite abroad. Louis had the most formidable army in Europe—400,000 men by the end of his reign—but both William III of the United Provinces and Leopold I of the Holy Roman Empire believed that he could be defeated by a combined assault. They worked persistently to this end, particularly after the Turkish threat to Leopold ended with the failure of the siege of Vienna, in 1683, and William gained the English throne six years later. The League of Augsburg, transformed into the Grand Alliance after William and other rulers joined it, fought a successful holding action against Louis's attempt to intervene across the Rhine, and the final showdown was precipitated when the Hapsburg king of Spain, Charles II, died without an heir.

There were various possible claimants to the throne, and Charles himself had changed his mind a number of times, but at his death his choice was Philip, Louis XIV's grandson (see the accompanying figure). Had Louis been willing to agree not to unite the thrones of France and Spain and to open the Spanish empire to foreign traders, Charles's wish might well have been respected by the rest of Europe. But Louis refused to compromise, insisting that there were no conditions to Charles's bequest. The rest of Europe disagreed and declared war on France so as to prevent Philip's unrestricted succession and the limitation of trade in the Spanish empire. Thus Louis found himself fighting virtually the entire Continent in the War of the Spanish Succession, not only at home but also overseas, in India, Canada, and the Caribbean.

Led by brilliant generals, the Englishman John Churchill, duke of Marlborough, and the Austrian Prince Eugène, the allies won a series of smashing victories. France's hardships were increased by a terrible famine in 1709. Yet the Sun King's hold over his subjects was unimpaired. Nobody rose in revolt against him; his policies were not seriously challenged; and despite military disaster he succeeded in keeping his nation's borders intact and the Spanish throne for his grandson (though he had to give up the possibility of union with France and the restrictions on trade in the Spanish empire) when peace treaties were signed at Utrecht in 1713 and 1714. In the end his great task of state building, both at home and abroad, had faced and withstood the severest of all tests: defeat on the battlefield.

Domestic Affairs

The assertion of royal supremacy at home was almost complete by the time Louis came to

THE SPANISH SUCCESSION, 1700

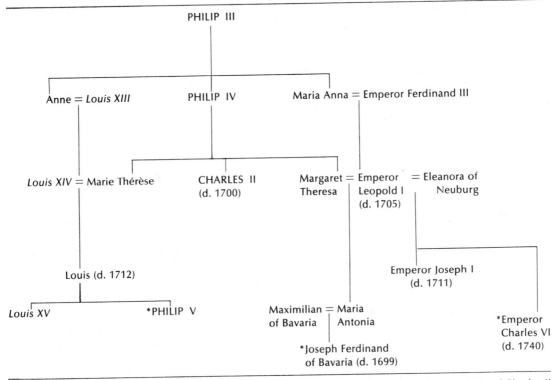

NAMES IN CAPITALS = Kings of Spain
Names in italics = Kings of France

*People designated at various times as heirs of Charles II

power, but he extended the principle of centralized control to religion and social institutions. Religion was a major area of activity because two groups, the Protestant Huguenots and the Catholic Jansenists, interfered with the spiritual and confessional uniformity that the king considered essential in the absolutist state.

Of the two the Huguenots were the more obviously unintegrated. Government pressures against them mounted after 1668, when their greatest adherent, the famous Marshal Turenne, converted to Catholicism. Finally in 1685 Louis revoked the century-old Edict of Nantes, thus forcing France's 1 million Protestants either to leave the country (four-fifths did) or to convert to Catholicism. This was a political rather than a religious act, taken for the sake of unity despite the economic consequences that followed the departure of a vigorous and productive minority.

Jansenism posed a more elusive problem. It had far fewer followers, though among them were some of the greatest figures in the land, such as the playwright Racine; and it was a movement within Catholicism. But the very fact that it challenged the official Church hierarchy and had been condemned by Rome made it a source of unrest and disorder. What was worse, it was beginning to gain support among the magistrate class—the royal officers in the Parlements, who had to register all royal edicts before they became law. The Parlement of Paris was the only governmental institution that offered Louis any real resistance during his reign.

The issues over which it caused trouble were usually religious, and the link between parlementaire independence and dislike for court frivolity on the one hand, and Jansenism on the other, gave Louis more than enough reason for displeasure. He razed the Jansenists' headquarters, the Abbey of Port-Royal, and then persuaded the pope to issue a bull condemning Jansenism. He was prevented from implementing the bull—over parlementaire opposition—only by his death, in 1715.

The drive toward uniformity that lay behind these actions was reflected in all aspects of domestic policy. Louis rapidly crushed what little parlementaire protest there was; an attempt by peasants in central France to resist the government was ruthlessly suppressed; Parisian publishers came under bureaucratic supervision; and the *intendants,* the government's chief provincial officers, were given increased authority, particularly in connection with the ever-growing needs of the army.

At the outset of his rule, Louis used the government's power to improve France's economy. In this he followed a pattern familiar from earlier monarchs' reigns: an initial burst of reform measures to cure the country's economic ills, which were gradually forgotten because foreign policy demanded instant funds. In the early years, under Colbert's ministry, major efforts were made to stimulate manufacturing, agriculture, and home and foreign trade. Some industries, notably those involving luxuries like the silk production of Lyons, received considerable help and owed their rise to prosperity to royal patronage. Colbert also tried, not entirely effectively, to reduce the crippling effects of France's countless internal tolls. These were usually nobles' perquisites, and they could multiply the cost of goods shipped any distance. The government divided the country into a number of districts, within which shipments were to be toll-free, but the system never removed the worst abuses. And finally, Louis made a concerted attempt to boost foreign trade, at first by financing new overseas trading companies and later by founding new port cities to strengthen maritime forces. He achieved notable success in the West Indies, which became a source of immense wealth.

Louis's overall accomplishments were remarkable, and France became the envy of Europe. Yet ever since the Sun King's reign, historians have recalled the ruination caused by famine and war during his last years and have contrasted his glittering court with the misery of French people at large. Particularly after the famines of the 1690s and 1709, many contemporaries remarked on the dreadful condition of peasants in various regions. Even at Versailles there was disenchantment, expressed not only by a shrewd critic like the duke of Saint-Simon, who looked on the emptiness of court life with disdain, but also by concerned men who had not previously found fault with Louis' policies. A notable example was the great fortifications expert Sébastien le Prestre, marquis of Vauban, who had made a vital contribution to the military successes of the reign (see Map 17.1). Late in life he called on the government to end its obsession with war because taxation was bringing the ordinary French person to a state of hopeless despair.

Such warnings of course went unheeded, but in recent years historians have questioned whether France was in fact so badly off. That there was hardship cannot be denied, but its extent and lasting effect are open to question for two reasons. First, the difficulties caused none of the uprisings that were the normal reaction in the countryside either to excesses on the part of the central government or to severe food shortages. Second, France's quick recovery and unprecedented economic and demographic growth in the years following 1715 could never have taken place if the country had been as shattered as the dramatic tales of catastrophe suggest.

Nonetheless the reign of Louis XIV can be regarded as the end of an era in the life of the lower classes. In the early eighteenth century, though there was still much suffering, the terrible subsistence crises, with their cycles of famine and plague, came to an end, largely because of government welfare policies; both manufacturing and agriculture entered a period of great prosperity; and cities enjoyed spectacular new growth. It is likely that the hand of the central government seemed heavier in 1715 than a hundred years before, but the small landowner and urban worker had been struggling with taxes for decades, whether the payee was king or noble. And the Counter Reformation Church, growing in strength since the Council of Trent, provided a measure of blessing, for it began to bring into local parishes better-educated and more dedicated priests who, as part of their new commitment to service, exerted themselves to calm the outbreaks of witchcraft and irrational fear that had swept the countryside for centuries. The fortunes of Jacques Bonhomme, the symbolic French everyman, had probably risen by 1715.

The improvement was also apparent in the mercantile class, which was about to enjoy a level of prosperity that outstripped even the sixteenth-century boom. Discontent at the government's interventions may have been felt by magistrates and parlementaires, who bewailed their lack of power, but these were voices in the wilderness. That there were strains nobody could deny, but on the whole the absolutist structure had achieved its ends—a united, prosperous, and powerful France.

The Hapsburgs at Vienna and Madrid

The pattern set at Versailles was repeated at the court of the Hapsburg Leopold I, the Holy Roman emperor (1658–1705). Heir to a reduced inheritance that gave him effective control over only Bohemia, Austria, and a small portion of Hungary, Leopold nonetheless maintained a magnificent establishment. His plans for a new palace, Schönbrunn, that was to have outshone Versailles were modified only because of a lack of funds. And his promotion of the court as the center of all political and social life turned Vienna into what it had never been before: a city for nobles as well as burghers.

Nevertheless, Leopold himself did not display the pretensions of the Sun King. He had been a younger son and had come to the throne only because of the death of his brother. An indecisive, retiring, deeply religious man, he had little fondness for the bravado Louis XIV enjoyed. He was a composer of no small talent, and his patronage laid the foundation for the great musical culture that was to be one of Vienna's chief glories. Whatever his inclinations, however, he found himself the holder of considerable royal authority: for more than a century, except during the Bohemian resistance of 1618 to 1621, the Hapsburg rulers had had few serious challenges to their power in their own domains. This was a tradition that Leopold felt obliged to continue, though unlike Louis XIV he relied on a small group of leading aristocrats to devise policy and run the administration.

The Thirty Years' War had revealed that the elected head of the Holy Roman Empire could no longer control the princes who nominally owed him allegiance, but within his own dominions he could maintain complete control with the cooperation of the aristocracy. The Privy Council, which in effect ran Leopold's domain, was filled largely with members of aristocratic families, and his chief advisers were always prominent nobles. But he did not switch about among representatives of various policies as Louis XIV did. Instead he carefully consulted each of his ministers and then, even when all of them agreed, came to decisions with agonizing slowness.

Unlike the other courts of Europe, Schönbrunn did not favor only native-born aristocrats. The leader of Austria's armies during the Turks' siege of Vienna in 1683 was Charles, duke of Lorraine, a prince whose duchy had long ago been taken over by the French. His predecessor as field marshal had been an Italian, and his successor was to be one of the most brilliant soldiers of the age, Prince Eugène of Savoy. None were members of the Austrian nobility until Leopold gave them titles within his own dominions, but they all fitted easily into the aristocratic circles that controlled the government and the army.

Prince Eugène was a spectacular symbol of the aristocracy's continuing dominance of European politics and society. A member of one of the most distinguished families on the Continent, he had been raised in France but found himself passed over when Louis XIV awarded army commissions, perhaps because he had been intended for the church. Yet he was determined to follow a military career and therefore volunteered to serve the Austrians in their long struggle with the Turks. His talents soon became evident: he was field marshal of Austria's troops by the time he was thirty. For the next forty years, though foreign-born, he was a decisive influence in Hapsburg affairs, the man primarily responsible for the transformation of Vienna's policies from defensive to aggressive.

Until the siege of 1683, Leopold's innate cautiousness kept Austria simply holding the line, both against Louis XIV and against the Turks. In the 1690s, however, he tried a bolder course at Eugène's urging and in the process laid the foundations for a new Hapsburg empire along the Danube River: Austria-Hungary (see Map 17.2). He helped create the coalition that defeated Louis in the 1700s, intervened in Italy so that his landlocked domains could gain an outlet to the sea, and began the long process of pushing the Turks out of the Balkans. Leopold did not live to see the advance more than started, but by the time of Eugène's death, the Austrians were within a hundred miles of the Black Sea.

However, the power of the aristocracy blocked the complete centralization of Leopold's dominions. Louis XIV supported his nobles after he had subdued their independent positions in the provinces; Leopold by contrast gave them influence in the government without first establishing genuine control over all his lands. The nobility did not cause him the troubles his predecessors had faced during the Thirty Years' War, but he had to limit his ambitions in territories outside of Austria. Moreover, as Austrians came increasingly to dominate the court, the nobles of Hungary and Bohemia reacted by clinging ever more stubbornly to local traditions and rights. Thus Leopold's was an absolutism under which the aristocracy retained far more autonomous power—and a far firmer base of local support, stimulated by regional loyalties—than was the case in France, despite the increased centralization achieved during his reign.

Madrid enjoyed none of the success of the Hapsburg court in Vienna. Its king, Charles II, was a sickly man, incapable of having children; and the War of the Spanish Succession seriously reduced the inheritance he left. Both the southern Netherlands and most of Italy passed to the Austrian Hapsburgs, and Spain's overseas possessions often paid little notice to the homeland.

The Spanish nobility was even more successful than the Austrian in turning the trappings of absolutism to its advantage. In 1650 the crown had been able to recapture Catalonia's loyalty only by granting the province's aristocracy considerable autonomy, and this pattern recurred throughout Spain's Continental holdings. Parasitic, unproductive nobles controlled the regime almost entirely for their own personal gain. The country had lapsed into economic and cultural stagnation, subservient to a group of powerful families, and reflecting its former glory only in a fairly respectable navy.

MAP 17.2. THE AUSTRIAN EMPIRE 1657–1718

The Hohenzollerns at Berlin

The one new power that emerged to prominence during the age of Louis XIV was Brandenburg-Prussia, and here again a close alliance was established between a powerful ruler and his nobles. Frederick William of Hohenzollern (1640–1688), known as the "great elector," was the ruler of scattered territories that stretched 700 miles from Cleves, on the Rhine, to a part of Prussia on the Baltic. (See Map 17.3.) Taking advantage of the uncertainties and hopes for a new order that followed the chaos of the Thirty Years' War, he made his territories the dominant principality in northern Germany and at the same time strengthened his power over his subjects. His first task was in foreign affairs,

because when he became elector most of his possessions were devastated by war, with troops swarming over them at will. Frederick William realized that by determination and intelligent planning, even a small prince could emerge from these disasters in a good position *if* he had an army. With some military force at his disposal, he could become a useful ally for the big powers, who could then help him against his neighbors, while at home he would have the strength to crush his opponents.

By 1648 Frederick William had 8,000 troops, and he was backed by both the Dutch and the French at Westphalia as a possible restraint on Sweden in northern Europe. Without having done much to earn new territory, he did very well in the peace settlement, and he then took brilliant advantage of the Baltic wars of the 1650s to confirm his gains by switching sides at crucial moments. In the process his army grew to 22,000 men, and he began to use it to impose his will on his own territories. The fact that the army was essential to all of Frederick William's successes—giving him status in Europe and power within his territories—was to influence much of Prussia's and thus also Germany's subsequent history.

The presence of the military, and its role in establishing the elector's supremacy, was apparent throughout Brandenburg-Prussia's society. In 1653 the Diet of Brandenburg met for the last time, sealing its own fate by giving Frederick William the right to raise taxes on his own authority, though previously he had had to obtain its consent. The War Chest, the office in charge of financing the army, took over the functions of a treasury department and collected government revenue even when the state was at peace. The execution of policy in the localities was placed under the supervision of war commissars, men who were originally responsible for military recruitment, billeting, and supply in each district of Brandenburg-Prussia, but who now became the principal agents of all government departments.

Apart from the representative assemblies, Frederick William faced substantial resistance only from the cities of his realm, which had long traditions of independence. Yet once again sheer intimidation swept opposition aside. The last determined effort to dispute his authority arose in the rich city of Königsberg, which allied with the Estates General of Prussia to refuse to pay taxes. But this resistance was brought to a swift conclusion in 1662, when Frederick William marched into the city with a few thousand troops. Similar pressure brought the towns of Cleves, on the Rhine, into submission after centuries of proud independence.

The nobles were major beneficiaries of this policy. It was in fact the alliance between the nobility and Frederick William that made it possible for the Diet, the cities, and the representative assemblies to be undermined. The leading families saw their best opportunities for the future in cooperation with the central government, and both within the various representative assemblies and in the localities, they worked for the establishment of absolutist powers—that is, for the removal of all restraints on the elector. The most significant indicator of their success was that by the end of the century, two tax rates had been devised, one for cities and one for the countryside, to the great advantage of the latter.

Not only did the nobles staff the upper levels of the elector's bureaucracy and army; they also won a new prosperity for themselves. Particularly in Prussia they used the reimposition of serfdom and their dominant political position to consolidate their land holdings into vast, highly profitable estates. This was a vital grain-producing area—often called the granary of Europe—and they made the most of its economic potential. To maximize their profits they eliminated the middleman by not only growing but also distributing their produce themselves. Efficiency became their hallmark, and their wealth was soon famous throughout the Holy Roman Empire. Known as Junkers, these Prussian entrepreneurs were probably the most successful group within the European aristocracy in their pursuit of both economic and political power.

Unlike Louis in France, however, Frederick William did not force his nobles to lead a life of social ostentation revolving around his person. The court at Berlin became a glittering focus of society only under his son, Elector Frederick III, who ruled from 1688. The great elector himself was more interested in organizing his administration, increasing tax returns, building up his army, and imposing his authority at home and abroad. He began the development of his capital, Berlin, into a major city and cultural center—he laid out the famous

This early eighteenth-century engraving of Berlin shows a skyline marked by the many new churches with which the kings were beautifying their capital. Yet the view also reminds us that, for all their rapid growth, eighteenth-century European cities (with the exception only of the three or four largest, which were surrounded by expanding suburbs) were still very close to the agriculture of the nearby countryside.
(Photo: New York Public Library/Picture Collection)

double avenue Unter den Linden, and he founded what was to become one of the finest libraries in the world, the Prussian State Library, in his palace—but this was never among his prime concerns. His son by contrast enjoyed the pomp of his princely status and set about encouraging the arts with enthusiasm.

Frederick III lacked only one attribute of royalty: a crown. He hungered for the distinction, and he gained it when Emperor Leopold I, who still retained the right to confer titles in the empire, needed Brandenburg's troops during the War of the Spanish Succession against

Louis XIV. Although none of Frederick's territories had been a kingdom previously, he was allowed to call himself "king in Prussia" (a technicality; the title soon became "king of Prussia"). At a splendid coronation in 1701, Elector Frederick III of Brandenburg was crowned King Frederick I, and thereafter the court, now regal, could feel itself to be on equal terms with the other monarchical settings of Europe.

Frederick undertook a determined campaign to improve the social and cultural atmosphere in his lands. He founded the noble Order of the Black Eagle to encourage aristocratic ambitions, and he made his palace a center of art and polite society to compete, he hoped, with Versailles. A major construction program in Berlin beautified the city with seven churches and a number of huge public buildings, making it an important center of Baroque architecture. Following English and French models, Frederick also created an Academy of Sciences in Berlin and persuaded the most famous German scientist and philosopher of the day, Gottfried Wilhelm von Leibniz, to become its first president. All these activities obtained generous support from state revenues, as did the universities of Brandenburg and Prussia. By the end of his reign, in 1713, Frederick could take considerable satisfaction from the transformation he had brought about. He had given his realm the prestige of a throne, the reputation derived from important artistic and intellectual activity, and the elegant manners of an aristocracy at the head of both social and political life.

Peter the Great at St. Petersburg

One of the reasons the new absolutist regimes of the late seventeenth and eighteenth centuries seemed so different from their predecessors was that many of them consciously created new settings for themselves. Versailles, Schönbrunn, and Berlin were all either new or totally transformed sites for royal courts. The palaces were far larger and grander and provided a more impressive backdrop than previous seats of government. But only one of the autocrats of the period went so far as to build an entirely new capital: Peter I of Russia, called the Great (1682–1725), who named the city St. Petersburg after his patron saint. Not surprisingly he was also the only man among his contemporaries to declare himself an emperor.

None of the monarchs of the period had Peter's terrifying energy or ruthless resolve. A man of fierce temper, he was determined to impose his will without regard for opposition, though his decisions were often made in anger and then blindly implemented. The supreme example of Peter's callousness was the torture of his own son, a quiet, retiring boy, who was killed by the inhumane treatment he received after trying to escape from his overbearing father.

Peter left no doubt about his intention to exercise absolute control in his realm. Of all the changes brought about in his reign, the most unprecedented was the destruction of ecclesiastical independence. When the patriarch of the Russian Church died in 1700, the tsar simply did not replace him. The government took over the monasteries, using their enormous income for its own purposes, and appointed a procurator (the first one was an army officer) to supervise all religious affairs. The church was in effect made a branch of government.

In the government itself Peter virtually ignored the Duma, the traditional advisory council, and concentrated on strengthening his bureaucracy. He carried out change after change. Few of them lasted any length of time, but their cumulative effect was the creation of an administrative complex many times larger than the one he had inherited. Copying Western models, especially the Swedish system, he set up carefully organized executive departments, some with specialized functions, such as finance, and others with responsibility for geographic areas, such as Siberia. The result was an elaborate but unified hierarchy of authority rising from local agents of the government through provincial officials up to the staffs and governors of eleven large administrative units and finally to the leaders of the regime in the capital. Peter's reign marked the beginning of the saturating bureaucratization that was to characterize Russia from that time on.

In the process the tsar laid the foundations for a two-class society that persisted until the twentieth century. Previously a number of ranks had existed within both the nobility and the peasantry, and a group in the middle, known as the *odnodvortsy* (roughly, "esquires"), were sometimes considered the lowest nobles

In the eighteenth century Peter the Great of Russia outstripped the grandeur of other monarchs of the period by erecting an entirely new city for his capital. St. Petersburg (now Leningrad) was built by forced labor of the peasants under Peter's orders; they are shown here laying the foundations for the city.
(Photo: Tass from Sovfoto)

and sometimes the highest peasants. Under Peter such mingling disappeared. All peasants were reduced to a uniform level, their equality emphasized by their universal liability to a new poll tax, military conscription, and forced public work, such as the building of St. Petersburg. Below them were the serfs, whose numbers were steadily increased by harsh legislation and who spread throughout the southern and western areas of Peter's dominions where previously they had been relatively unknown. The peasants possessed a few advantages over the serfs, but their living conditions were often equally dreadful.

At the same time Peter created a homogeneous class of nobles by substituting status within the bureaucracy for status within the traditional hierarchy of titles and ranks. In 1722 he issued a table of ranks that gave everyone his place according to the bureaucratic or military office that he held. Differentiations still existed under the new system, but they were no longer unbridgeable, as they had been when antiquity of family was decisive. The result was a more tightly controlled social order and greater uniformity than in France or Brandenburg-Prussia. By definition the Russian aristocracy was the bureaucracy and the bureaucracy the aristocracy.

But this was not a relatively voluntary alliance between nobles and government, such as existed in the West; in return for his support and his total subjection of the peasantry, Peter required the aristocrats to provide manpower for his rapidly expanding bureaucracy and officers for his growing army. When he began the construction of St. Petersburg, he also demanded that the leading families build splendid mansions in his new capital. In effect the tsar was offering privilege and wealth in exchange for what was virtual conscription into public service. Thus there was hardly any sense of partnership between aristocracy and throne—the tsar often had to use coercion to ensure that his wishes were followed.

On the other hand Peter did a good deal to build up the nobles' fortunes and their ability to control the countryside. As one recent interpreter of the tsar's policy put it, he wanted "the landowning nobility to be rich and powerful; but it must nonetheless be composed of his personal servants who were to use their wealth and power in his services."[2] It has been estimated that by 1710 he had put under the supervision of great landowners more than 40,000 peasant and serf households that had formerly been under the crown. And he was liberal in conferring new titles—some of them, such as count and baron, in imitation of German examples.

In creating an aristocratic society at his court, as in much else that he did, Peter mixed imitations of what he admired in the West with native developments. He forced the nobility to follow the ritual surrounding a Western throne; he founded an Academy of Sciences in 1725; and he encouraged the beginnings of a theater at court. Italian artists were imported, along with Dutch ship builders, German engineers, and Scandinavian colonels, not only to apply their skills, but also to teach them to the Russians. St. Petersburg, unquestionably the finest example of a city built in the Classical style of eighteenth-century architecture, is mainly the work of Italians, and the Academy of Sciences long depended on foreigners for whatever stature it had. But gradually the Russians took over their own institutions—military academies produced native officers, for example—and by the end of Peter's reign the nobles had no need of foreign experts to help run the government. Within little more than half a century, the Russian court would become the elegant, French-speaking gathering so penetratingly described in Tolstoy's *War and Peace*. Peter the Great had laid the foundations for the aristocratic society by which his people were to be ruled for 200 years.

---

[2] M. S. Anderson, *Peter the Great* (1969), p. 24.

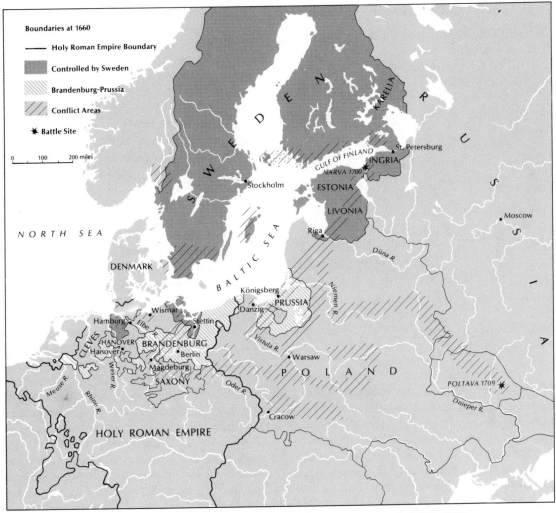

Boundaries at 1660

— Holy Roman Empire Boundary

Controlled by Sweden

Brandenburg-Prussia

Conflict Areas

★ Battle Site

0   100   200 miles

MAP 17.3. CONFLICT IN THE BALTIC AREA 1660–1721

The purpose of these radical internal changes was not only to consolidate the tsar's power at home but to extend it abroad. He established a huge standing army, more than 300,000 strong by the 1720s, and imported the latest military techniques from the West. One of Peter's most cherished projects, the creation of a navy, had limited success, but there could be no doubt that he transformed Russia's ca-

pacity for war and its status among European states. He extended Russia's frontier to the south and west, beginning the destruction of Sweden's empire at the battle of Poltava in 1709 and following this triumph by more than a decade of advance into Estonia, Lithuania, and Poland (see Map 17.3). By the time of his death Russia was the dominant power in the Baltic and a major influence in European affairs.

II. THE ANTI-ABSOLUTISTS

The absolutist regimes provided one model of political and social organization, but an alternative model, in most cases no less committed to uniformity and order, also flourished in the late seventeenth century: governments dominated by aristocrats or merchants. The contrast between the two was perceived by contemporary political theorists, especially opponents of absolutism, who compared France unfavorably with England. And yet the differences were often less sharp than such commentators suggested, primarily because the position of the aristocracy was similar throughout Europe. That there were genuine differences in social structure cannot be denied, but they were subtle and often below the surface.

The Triumph of the Gentry in England

To outward appearances Charles II (1660–1685) was restored to a throne not radically changed from the one on which his father had sat before the interregnum. He still summoned and dissolved Parliament, he made all appointments in the bureaucracy, and he signed every law. But the crown's effective power had changed drastically. Royal prerogative courts such as the Star Chamber had been abolished, thus lessening the king's control over judicial matters. He also could not interfere in parliamentary affairs: he could no longer arrest a member of Parliament and he could not create a new seat in the Commons. Even two ancient prerogatives, the king's right to dispense with an act of Parliament (give an exemption to a specific individual or group) and to suspend an act completely, crumbled when Charles tried to exercise them. And he could no longer raise money without parliamentary assent—instead, he was given a fixed annual income, financed by a tax on the favorite beverage of the English, beer.

The real control of the country's affairs had by this time passed to that large, somewhat amorphous group known as the gentry. Just above the gentry, and giving them some leadership, was a tiny group of aristocrats. In England, only 100 to 200 families held hereditary titles, such as duke or earl, that made them members of the peerage who sat in the House of Lords in Parliament. These nobles were important political figures, but most of the control of the country was in the hands of those just below them on the social scale—the gentry, whose representatives sat in the House of Commons. About 700 members of this class held baronetcies, which were inheritable knighthoods (but not considered peerages); and a few hundred more were knights, which meant that they could call themselves "sir" but could not pass the honor on to their heirs. Beyond these, in a country of some 5 million people, perhaps 15,000 to 20,000 other families were considered gentry, these being people of importance in the various localities throughout England.[3] This proportion, approximately 2 percent, was probably not significantly different from the percentage of the population that belonged to the nobility in most Continental states.

What set the gentry apart from the nobles of other countries was their ability to determine national policy. Whereas in France, Austria, Brandenburg-Prussia, and Russia aristocrats depended on the monarch for their power and were subservient to him, the English gentry regarded themselves as an independent force. Their status was hallowed by custom, upheld by law, and maintained by their representative assembly, the House of Commons, which was both the supreme legislative body in the land and the institution to which the executive government was ultimately responsible.

Not all the gentry took a continuing, active

---

[3] These totals are based on the estimates made by an early statistician, Gregory King, in 1696. His calculations were performed with remarkable accuracy, and they produced the oldest figures that historians still accept today.

interest in affairs of state, and no more than a few of their number sat in the roughly 500-member House of Commons. Even the Commons did not always exercise a constant influence over the government. All that was necessary was that the ministers of the king be prominent representatives of the gentry, whether lords or commoners, and that they be able to win the support of a majority of the members of the Commons. Policy was still set by the king and his ministers. But the Commons had to be persuaded that the policies were correct, for without parliamentary approval a minister could not long survive in office.

Despite occasional conflicts this structure worked relatively smoothly throughout

Charles II's reign. Most of the leading elements of society, for example, were united in enacting repressive legislation against dissenters, the descendants of the Puritans who still refused to join the official Anglican Church. But the gentry did have one fear: that Charles's brother, James, next in line for the succession and an open Catholic, might try to restore Catholicism in England. To prevent this they even managed

Court life under Charles II of England was similar to that of the absolute monarchs in that formal, elegant, aristocratic gatherings dominated the social scene. The occasion shown here is Charles and Queen Catherine dancing at The Hague.
(Photo: The Mansell Collection)

THE ENGLISH SUCCESSION FROM THE STUARTS TO THE HANOVERIANS

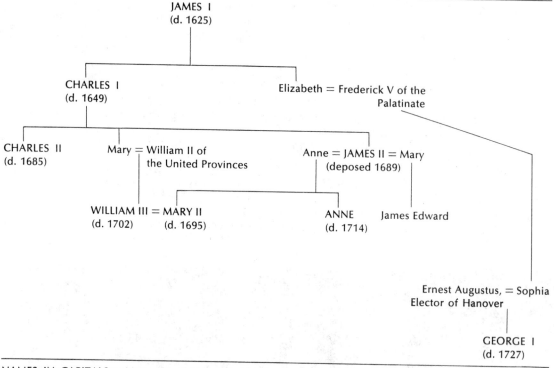

NAMES IN CAPITALS = Monarchs of England

to force Charles to exclude James from the throne for a few years, during a confrontation known as the Exclusion Crisis. But in the end the instinctive respect for legitimacy that was characteristic of the age, combined with some shrewd maneuvering by Charles, ensured that there would be no tampering with the succession.

Very quickly, however, the reign of James II turned into a disaster. Elated by his acceptance as king, James rashly attempted the very encouragement of Catholicism that the English had feared. This was a direct challenge to the gentry's newly won power, and in the fall of 1688, seven of their leaders—including members of some of the oldest families in the realm—invited the Protestant ruler of the United Provinces, William III, to invade the

country and take over the throne. Although William landed with an army half the size of the king's, James, uncertain of his support, decided not to risk battle and fled to exile in France.

The new king gained what little title he had to the crown through his wife, Mary (see the table above), and the couple were therefore proclaimed joint monarchs by Parliament early in 1689. The Dutch ruler had taken the throne primarily to bring England into his relentless struggles against Louis XIV, and he willingly accepted a settlement that confirmed the essential position of Parliament in the government of the country. A Bill of Rights was passed, settling the future succession to the throne, defining Parliament's powers, and establishing the basic civil rights of individuals; an Act of

Toleration put an end to all religious persecution, though members of the official Church of England were still the only people allowed to vote, sit in Parliament, hold a government office, or attend a university; and in 1694 a statute laid down that Parliament had to meet and new elections had to be held at least once every three years.

Despite the restrictions on his authority, William exercised strong command. He guided England into a new, aggressive foreign policy, picked the ministers favorable to his aims, and never let Parliament sit when he was out of the country to pursue the war or to attend to Dutch affairs. But unlike James, William recognized his limits. He tried to have the Bill of Rights reversed and a standing army established, but he gave up these attempts when they provoked major opposition. By and large, therefore, the gentry were content to let the king rule as he saw fit. For they had shown by their intervention in 1688 that ultimately they controlled the country.

Politics and Prosperity

The political system in England now reflected the social system: a small elite controlled both the country's policy and its institutions. This group was not monolithically united, however, as was apparent when a party system began to appear in Parliament during Charles II's reign. Its most concrete early manifestation was during the Exclusion Crisis, from 1678 to 1680, when the Whig party emerged in opposition to royal prerogatives and Catholicism. The Whigs were largely responsible for the passage of the exclusion legislation. Their rivals, the Tories, stood for the independence and authority of the crown and favored a ceremonial and traditional Anglicanism.

Because the Whigs were the prime force behind the removal of James II, they controlled the government for most of William III's reign. They naturally supported him in his campaigns against Louis XIV, since France harbored both James and his followers, the romantic but ill-fated Jacobites, who tried for decades to restore James's line to the throne. The Whigs were only too happy to give England what seemed her proper place in the restraining of France's ambitions. But on the whole this was a nonpartisan issue.

Where the sustained rivalry between the Tories and the Whigs was most evident was in their competition for voters. Because the qualification for voting—owning freehold land worth 40 shillings a year in rent—had become less restrictive as a result of inflation and was not to be increased until the late 1700s, this period witnessed the largest electorate in English history before the mid-nineteenth century. It has been estimated that almost 5 percent of the population, or more than 15 percent of the adult males, could vote.[4] Although results were usually determined by the influence of powerful local magnates, as they had been for centuries, fierce politicking took place in many constituencies. And in one election—that of 1700—it brought about a notable reversal: the Tories won by opposing further war, because for the previous three years France seemed to have been contained.

Within two years, however, and despite William's death, England was again at war with Louis XIV, and soon the Whigs were back in power. Not until 1710 did a resurgence of war weariness work in the Tories' favor. Queen Anne made peace with France at Utrecht in 1713, and it was only because the Tories made the mistake of negotiating with the Jacobites after Anne died the next year without heir that the Whigs regained power when the first Hanoverian, George I, came to the throne. They then entrenched themselves, and under the leadership of Robert Walpole, they began almost a century of political control.

[4] J. H. Plumb, "The Growth of the Electorate in England from 1600 to 1715," *Past and Present*, November 1969, pp. 90–116.

The system within which these maneuverings took place remained essentially unchanged until the nineteenth century, though it allowed considerable flexibility. The crown was still the dominant power: the monarch could dismiss ministers and could influence votes in the House of Commons through the patronage at the throne's disposal. But there were strict limits to royal power. Despite party struggles the gentry as a whole retained the upper hand. They were quiescent most of the time, but on major issues, such as war or peace, no government could survive without their support.

In this same period England was winning for itself unprecedented prosperity, and the foundations of its world power were being laid. During the reigns of the later Stuarts, the navy was built up and reorganized—largely under the direction of Samuel Pepys, the famous diarist—into the premier force on the sea, the decisive victor over France during the world-wide struggle of the early eighteenth century. In Charles II's time important new colonies were established, particularly along the North American seaboard, where the aristocracy provided the main impetus for the settlement of New Jersey and the Carolinas. The empire expanded steadily, so that when England and Scotland joined into one kingdom in 1707, the union created a Great Britain ready for its role as a world leader.

This growth was accompanied by a rapid economic advance both at home and in world trade. A notable achievement was the establishment of the Bank of England in 1694. The bank was given permission to raise money from the public and then lend it to the government at 8 percent interest. Within twelve days its founders raised more than a million pounds, demonstrating not only the financial security and stability of England's government but also the commitment of the elite to the country's political structure.

The success of the Bank of England, the rise of the navy, and the overseas expansion were not the only symptoms of England's mounting prosperity. London was becoming the financial capital of the world, and British merchants were gaining control over maritime trade from East Asia to North America. And perhaps most significantly, the benefits of this boom helped the lower levels of society.

There can be little doubt that with the possible exception of the Dutch, ordinary English people were better off than their equivalents elsewhere in Europe. Poverty was admittedly widespread, and London, rapidly approaching half a million in population, contained frightful slums and miserable, crime-ridden sections. Even the terrible fire of London in 1666 did little to wipe out the appalling living conditions because the city was rebuilt much as before, the only notable additions being a series of magnificent churches, including St. Paul's, designed by Christopher Wren. But the grim picture should not be overdrawn.

Compared to the sixteenth century, these years saw little starvation. The system of poor relief may often have been inhumane in forcing the unfortunate to work in horrifying workhouses, but it did provide them with the shelter and food that they had long lacked. After more than a century of crippling inflation the laborer could once again make a decent living, and artisans were meeting a growing demand for their work. Higher up in the social scale, more men had a say in the political process than ever before, and more could find opportunities for advancement in the rising economy of the period—in trade overseas, in the bureaucracy, or in the growing market for luxury goods. England had better roads than any other European country, lower taxes, a more impartial judicial system, and a freedom from government interference—especially since there was no standing army—that was unique for the times.

One thing is clear, however: these gains could not compare with those that the gentry had made. In fact many of the improvements, such as fairly administered justice and low taxes, were indirect results of what the upper classes had won for themselves. There is no question that the fruits of the seventeenth century's progress belonged in the first place to the gentry, now more surely than in previous centuries the dominant element in society.

Aristocracy in the United Provinces, Sweden, and Poland

In the Dutch republic the fall of Jan De Witt seemed to signal a move in the direction of absolutism rather than aristocratic control (see p. 549). William III, who took command of the government in 1672 and led the successful resistance to Louis XIV in a six-year war, was able to concentrate government in his own hands. Soon, however, the power of the merchant oligarchy and the provincial leadership in the Estates General reasserted itself. William did not want to sign a peace treaty with Louis when it became clear that the French invasion had failed. Like his forebears in the House of Orange, he wanted to take the war into the enemy's camp and reinforce his own authority by keeping the position of commander in chief in a time of war. But the Estates General, led by the province of Holland, brought the war to a conclusion.

A decade later it was only with the approval of the Estates General that William was able to seek the English throne and thus bring the two countries into limited union—limited because the representative assemblies, the effective governing powers of the two countries, remained separate. And when William died without an heir, the Dutch provinces' executive offices remained unfilled. His policies were continued by Antonius Heinsius, who now held the position of grand pensionary of Holland that Jan De Witt had once occupied. Heinsius had been a close friend of William's, but to all intents and purposes, policy was determined by the Estates General.

The representative assembly now had to preside over the decline of a great power. In finance and trade the Dutch were gradually overtaken by the English, while in the war against Louis XIV they had to support the crippling burden of maintaining a land force, only to hand command over to England. Within half a century Frederick II of Prussia was to call the republic "a dinghy boat trailing the English man-of-war."

The aristocrats of the United Provinces differed from the usual European pattern. Instead of ancient families and bureaucratic dynasties, they boasted merchants and mayors. The prominent citizens of the leading cities were the backbone of what can be called the Dutch upper classes. Moreover, social distinctions were less prominent than in any other country of Europe. The elite was composed of hard-working financiers and traders, richer and more powerful but not essentially more privileged or leisured than those farther down the social ladder. The situation discussed in much eighteenth-century literature and political writing—the special place given to nobles, often including some immunity from the law—was far less noticeable in the United Provinces. There was no glittering court with elegant trappings. Although in the United Provinces, as elsewhere, a small group controlled the country, it did so for largely economic ends and with a totally different style.

In Sweden the conditions of court life and political power more closely resembled those of Louis XIV's France, though the reigns of Charles XI and XII, the last half-century in which Sweden was still an imperial power, were marked by a continuing struggle between king and nobility. The nobles eventually established themselves as the dominant force, but not until they had gone through a long and sometimes bitter struggle with the monarch.

The chief issue was the policy of reversions, whereby Charles XI forced great lords to return huge tracts of land they had received as rewards for loyalty during the precarious years of Gustavus Adolphus and Christina (see p. 550). The aristocrats strongly opposed the policy, but the king had the bulk of the population on his side because the crown was always a more lenient landlord for peasant tenants. By clever maneuvering Charles not only had the reversion legislation passed by the Riksdag but also had himself proclaimed virtually an absolute monarch in 1682.

The remainder of his reign was spent consolidating the power of his government at home. He stayed out of war and strengthened both his administration and his finances. The great copper mines of Sweden gave out in the 1680s, and alternatives to this lucrative source of revenue had to be built up—primarily iron and timber products, such as cannon and tar. Tolls and taxes from captured territories helped sustain the empire, but it was clear that Charles's strength depended on his avoiding the strains of war.

His successor, Charles XII, had a different set of priorities. Harking back to the glorious days of Gustavus Adolphus, he wanted to cover Sweden in military glory. His ambitions and those of Peter I of Russia embroiled the Baltic in what came to be known as the Great Northern War. At first the fighting went Sweden's way, mainly because of a brilliant victory over the Russians at Narva in 1700, which immediately established Charles as one of the ablest commanders of his day. But then he decided—the first of a series of generals to do so—that he was capable of conquering Russia. His communications and logistics broke down, and at Poltava in 1709 his invading army was shattered. The dismemberment of the Swedish empire now began: by the time Charles was killed in battle nine years later, the Danes, Prussians, and Russians had begun to overrun Swedish possessions in Germany, Poland, and around the Gulf of Finland. (Map 17.3.) At a series of treaties signed from 1719 to 1721, the empire was parceled out, and Sweden reverted to roughly the territory she had had a century before.

Naturally the nobles took advantage of Charles XII's frequent absences to reassert their power. They ran Sweden while he was campaigning and forced his successor to accept a constitution that gave the Riksdag effective control over the country. The new structure was consciously modeled on England's political system, and the nobility came to occupy a position analogous to that of the English gentry—as the leaders of society and the controllers of politics. A splendid court arose, and Stockholm became one of the more elegant and cultured aristocratic centers in Europe.

Warsaw fared less well. In fact the strongest contrast to the French political and social model in the late seventeenth century was provided by Poland. There was no better object lesson to demonstrate what Louis XIV was preventing in France. The sheer chaos and disunity that plagued Poland until it ceased to exist as a state in the late eighteenth century were the direct result of continued dominance by the old landed aristocracy, which blocked all attempts to centralize the government.

There were highly capable kings of Poland in this period—notably John III, who achieved Europe-wide fame by relieving Vienna from the Turkish siege in 1683. These monarchs could quite easily gather an enthusiastic army to fight (and fight well) against Poland's many foes: Germans, Swedes, Russians, and Turks. But once a battle was over, the ruler was rarely in a position to exercise anything more than nominal leadership. Each king was elected by the assembly of nobles and had to agree not to interfere with the independence of the great lords, who were growing rich from serf labor on fertile lands. The crown had neither revenue nor bureaucracy to speak of, and so the country continued to resemble nothing so much as a feudal kingdom, where power remained in the localities.

If Poland seemed a nobleman's paradise, it

nonetheless produced no important cultural center like Berlin or Vienna. For that to happen some degree of central authority was necessary, a hub around which national life could revolve. Two cities in particular—London and Paris—occupied such a position, and therefore at the beginning of the eighteenth century, they became the heart of Europe's intellectual and artistic activity.

III. THE CULTURE OF THE AGE

The quest for regularity, order, and decorum which was the most notable feature of late-seventeenth-century culture contrasted strongly with the grandiose and dramatic strivings of the preceding age. The change in aesthetics offers striking evidence of the growing sense of settlement and calm in Europe after the crisis of midcentury. And it was paralleled by the emergence of new kinds of cultural institutions—formal, regulated, and controlled from above, unlike any that Europe had ever seen before.

The Academy and the Salon

A clear indication that the cultural atmosphere was becoming more ordered and restrained was the rise of academies and salons as mechanisms that organized intellectual life. The most carefully institutionalized setting was the official academy established under royal patronage to supervise cultural affairs. Such bodies were not entirely new—their pedigree went back to the Platonic academy, and there had been more immediate predecessors in sixteenth-century Italy—but their purpose, to set standards for artistic creations, was a departure from tradition.

France led the way in this development. The French Academy, founded by Richelieu in 1635, became the leading upholder of classical drama, while the Royal Academy of Painting and Sculpture, the Royal Academy of Architecture, and the Academy of Inscriptions and Literature, established over the next thirty-five years, performed equivalent functions in other fields. These bodies marked the beginning of a system that in France did not crumble until attacked by such nineteenth-century rebels as the Impressionists.

The cultural institutions that were founded elsewhere (mostly in Italy) during this period were less prestigious but no less reflective of cultural trends. The academies were intended to preserve and promote the standards that were considered essential to good art. Just as the Royal Society was regarded as an arbiter of scientific truth, a promoter of proper method, so too in art and literature academies would set the style.

The origins of the salon were diverse and its predecessors many. Artists have frequently united in coteries when they have shared a common outlook, and rich and noble patrons have often given them encouragement. The particular form that developed in seventeenth-century France was a small, intimate gathering that usually met in the drawing room, or salon, of an aristocrat's wife.

The crucial role that women played in setting taste and providing patronage in this period was unprecedented. There had been princesses and queens who had promoted art and learning; at Italian courts, educated duchesses and countesses had been essential to the creation of the refined culture of the Renaissance; but never had so large a group become so central in determining styles and reputations in the world of the arts. Some became remarkable literary figures themselves—a French princess was one of the finest letter writers of the age, and in England Aphra Behn was a noted playwright—but mainly they engaged in sharp and stimulating rivalries over influence and patronage.

At their salons, these ambitious and intelligent women tried to attract the most brilliant literary lights of the day. The artists for their part came in search of patronage and reputation, taking advantage of various social forces: the emergence of Paris as the cultural center of France, the clustering of the nobility in the capital as the nearby court grew in size and importance, and the pressures of a fiercely competitive society of women with money to spare. The would-be salon entrant had to make a mark rapidly, and wit, grace, and quick repartee were essential.

The salons stimulated the intimacy and elegance that were now preferred to the heroic ideals of the midcentury. They thus became the natural center and the perfect symbol of contemporary creative expression. An atmosphere of studied gentility was strongly apparent, even to outsiders, and it was well for a writer or painter not to offend the sensibilities of those who were the chief makers and breakers of reputations in the highly competitive world of letters and art.

The intellectual activities of most aristocrats revolved around both cultural centers, the court and the salon. At court they gathered in large, formal affairs to watch a play, a ballet, or an opera; in the salons they gathered in smaller, less formal groups, often including talented nonaristocrats, to discuss the latest gossip or cultural event. Even the enormous halls of a palace, hung with large canvases inherited from the past, contrasted with the frilly drawing rooms that served as salons, adorned with the small paintings that were the new fashion. In some ways the two were rival centers of activity, and a few prominent patronesses consciously sought to outdo a nearby prince.

Yet the contrasts should not be overdrawn. Most leading writers, musicians, and painters were equally at home in the two settings, for they needed the patronage of both; no artist could survive without nobles to commission works or pay salaries, and few were fortunate enough to have all their needs met by a single generous prince. Thus they turned to the multiple sources of support that the aristocracy, better educated than ever before and eager to outdo one another in patronage, were anxious to provide.

There was also a wider audience, of course, because salons were urban institutions, and the city offered theaters, opera houses, and publishers. Thus it was occasionally possible for an artist to achieve popular success without gaining aristocratic approval. But this was a hazardous way of making a living, and for this reason the salon, despite its regulation of taste and expression, was a vastly preferable target for most artists. As a result the qualities of harmony and order that were so appealing to the aristocracy came to dominate the aesthetics of the age.

Style and Taste

Discussions of literature and art developed a new emphasis on lightness and grace during the late seventeenth century. The most influential literary critic of the period, Nicolas Boileau, wrote a manual of style, *Poetic Art* (1674), that exalted craftsmanship over feeling. He insisted that the perfectly shaped poem was the ultimate ideal, and he valued obedience to rule as opposed to emotion or an exuberant, disordered vision. Not surprisingly his own literary output consisted of light satires, flawlessly executed but ephemeral.

Boileau's prescriptions gained a large following in France and in other countries as well. The leading English poet of the era, for example, John Dryden, gave his energies to writing hundreds of lines of graceful verse that were often scathing but almost never profound. The sharp end of his wit could sting, as can be seen in the following lines about the duke of Buckingham, a prominent politician known for his inconsistencies and dilettantism:

PHEDRE

&

HIPPOLYTE.

TRAGEDIE.

PAR Mʀ RACINE.

A PARIS,
Chez CLAUDE BARBIN, au Palais,
fur le Perron de la Sainte Chapelle.

M. DC. LXXVII.
AVEC PRIVILEGE DU ROY.

A man so various, that he seem'd to be
Not one, but all mankind's epitome.
Stiff in opinions, always in the wrong;
Was everything by starts, and nothing
   long;
But, in the course of one revolving moon,
Was chemist, fiddler, statesman, and buf-
   foon.
   Absalom and Achitophel, ll. 545–550

Dryden was greatly admired for writing in this vein because it was a time when the elite prized sardonic aloofness.

Jean Racine's plays appealed strongly to the aristocratic sensibilities of his age. He was regarded as the standard by which official taste could be measured and for many years was a major figure at the court of Louis XIV. The title page of *Phèdre*, one of his most enduring contributions to the French theater, is taken from the original 1677 edition.
(Photo: French Cultural Services)

Painters reflected these qualities only indirectly, but the change in their concerns was striking nonetheless. Gone were the vast canvases and towering themes of Rubens or Rembrandt. Instead, the leading figures of the decades around 1700 were flattering portraitists, like the Englishman Sir Peter Lely, or delicate genre painters, like the Frenchman Antoine Watteau (see Plate 44). Their canvases were smaller, and their subject matter rarely departed from placid landscapes or melancholic and idealized aristocratic scenes. The art of these exquisite painters epitomizes the new interest in grace, elegance, and repose.

That is not to say that emotion was totally absent from the creative work of the age. Stark passions were expressed in the operas of Henry Purcell and the prose of John Bunyan, both writing in this period. But the characteristic of their work that distinguishes them from the previous generation of artists is precisely their discipline—their anguish pours out of a framework of monumental self-restraint. And thus we are brought back to the theme that runs through the life of the time: the emphasis on order and regularity. It is particularly apparent in the work of the greatest court writer of the epoch, the French playwright Jean Racine.

By its nature Racine's art was not for the multitude. His concern was with tragedy, and he used the Classical drama to create a concentrated and sustained intensity of emotion that had not been achieved since the days of its ancient practitioners, Euripides and Sophocles. Severe discipline and yet overwhelming passion dominates his plays, which move to agonizing climaxes in superb, controlled language. Racine does not offer the appeal of recognizable human types; his characters are suffering men and women of unattainable nobility racked by impossible dilemmas that revolve around such perennial aristocratic preoccupations as honor and public duty. The heroine of *Phèdre* (1677), for example, falls in love with her stepson and

destroys him and herself as she wavers between love and honor. She wrestles with her dilemma in a series of solemn and carefully wrought but tormented speeches that give the play an almost unbearable emotional impact. There is none of the dramatic excitement—the rapid action, changes of pace, and flexible verse forms—of a Shakespearean play; instead, *Phèdre* focuses almost exclusively on the gripping human feelings that it so powerfully conveys.

Racine's appeal to the courtiers at Versailles was enormous. He explored the discipline and aristocratic bearing that, theoretically at least, the more thoughtful among them had adopted. They saw themselves on his stage, high-minded characters determined to act as social and political models. Racine thus portrayed an idealized court setting, guided by propriety and restraint, for all the world to see.

The tastes of the middle and lower strata of society are much harder to define, but there were a number of distinct ways in which they entertained themselves. Urban mercantile groups usually aped their superiors, though they were clearly more at home with the bawdiness of Restoration comedy or the scintillating wit of Molière than with Racine. They were also inclined to take part in creative activity themselves. Samuel Pepys, for example, remarked with satisfaction that his wife's painting efforts were coming along very nicely. And music, at least for the more educated urban dweller, was as much to be played as heard. In this respect the middle classes blended with the lower rather than the upper social levels, for singing was one of the great recreations of the ordinary man. Ballads were a major form of communication, and printers were quick to run off thousands of copies of a new song that was likely to catch on. Churches, moreover, gave congregations an institutionalized setting for creating and hearing music.

Among reading publics the nobility tended to read the Classics and philosophy while the

Molière's plays displayed a trenchant wit that was often aimed at the nobility. For this reason his works had a rather uneasy reception at court but were extremely popular with the Parisian middle class. Shown here is the acting company founded by Molière, La Troupe Royale, which was the prototype for the Comédie Française.
(Photo: French Cultural Services)

middle class read popular literature such as tales of travel, descriptions of rarities and wonders, and religious writings. The few literate members of the lower classes probably read religious works only; the rest had the Bible or a book like John Bunyan's *Pilgrim's Progress* (1667) read to them. Singing and an occasional troupe of traveling players performing the antics of standard characters like Harlequin and Columbine would have been their main recreation apart from the celebrations they themselves put on—feast day processions, "rough music," and the like (see Chapter 16).

In these interests, however, there was little reflection of the underlying concern for order so noticeable in court circles. Most people looked to music or a play for uplift or for a good time. And nowhere did they find these qualities more brilliantly represented than in the plays of the Frenchman Molière.

Molière (born Jean Baptiste Poquelin) learned his art in the same school that had taught Shakespeare half a century before: the traveling theatrical company, in which he was actor, manager, and director. After many years of touring the provinces, he came to Paris a master of his profession and founded a company, known as the Comédie Française, which soon became a national institution.

Molière followed the formal Classical style of his day, modeling his verse on that of the ancients and observing the conventions of time and place laid down so strictly by the French Academy. But his objectives could not have been more different from those of a Racine. For he never lost sight of the old tradition of farce and burlesque, which in his youth had still been the chief attraction wherever plays were performed. He used Classical style to create comedies with a serious undertone, a sustained concern with the follies of mankind. He ridiculed such types as the pretentious ladies of the salons, hypochondriacs, and the ignorant but aspiring *nouveaux riches*—these were captured forever in *The Bourgeois Gentleman* (1670), whose hero was delighted to discover that all his life he had been speaking prose.

The wit was unmatched, and soon Molière was winning highly favorable attention from Louis XIV himself. But occasionally the barbs came too close. The courtiers were offended when Molière had the nobles in one of his plays speak like ordinary people. And when in *Tartuffe* he ridiculed the hypocrisy that could lie behind ostentatiously displayed religious devotion, he roused powerful enemies in the Catholic Church. The play was banned, and a number of years passed before the playwright returned to the good graces of the monarch. But when *Tartuffe* reappeared in Paris, it was an instant success.

The contrast is revealing. Molière's sparkling dialogue and superb theatrical sense ensured his acceptance at court, but the welcome had its limits, set by standards of taste that the nobility considered unbreachable. In Paris he was always idolized, and for most French people he has remained unrivaled to this day. The difference, slight though it was, gave one of the first hints of the estrangement between court and country that was to build toward the explosion of the French Revolution during the next century. The aristocrats may have set the style, but they were to become increasingly insulated from the rest of society, which eventually was to find its own cultural models and heroes in the eighteenth century.

Science and Thought

The fascination inspired by the scientist and the widespread efforts to imitate scientific method in other fields were closely connected with the interest in order so characteristic of the age. The second half of the seventeenth century thus became the great age of the virtuosos, the hundreds of noblemen who dabbled in experiments and sought friendships with scientists. But it was less as participants than as eager admirers that the elite embraced science. In the eighteenth century for the first time statues were erected to honor the great discoverers. They were a new kind of hero, and they became the most widely acclaimed men of their age.

The late seventeenth and early eighteenth centuries witnessed in addition a raging controversy known as the Battle of the Books, a long dispute over the relative merits of the so-called Ancients and Moderns. In the end there could be little doubt that the advocates of the Moderns had won the dispute, largely because of the unprecedented advances in the understanding of nature during the previous century. The achievements in astronomy, physics, mathematics, and anatomy were being seen ever more frequently as a measure of human capabilities. And the qualities that the scientist seemed to represent—order, reason, and logic—corresponded with the aristocrats' aesthetic preferences in this period: balance, uniformity, and decorousness. It was only natural that the supreme scientist of the late seventeenth century, Isaac Newton, should become the idol not only of his own generation but of generations to come.

Isaac Newton

The culmination of the scientific revolution was reached in the work of Isaac Newton, who

This frontispiece from the 1710 edition of Jonathan Swift's long poem, *The Battle of the Books,* satirizes the controversy that broke out in the late seventeenth century over the relative superiority of ancient and modern writers.

made decisive contributions in the fields of mathematics, physics, astronomy, and optics and brought to a climax the progress that had been made by Copernicus, Kepler, Galileo, Descartes, and a host of other investigators. He united physics and astronomy in a single system to explain motion throughout the universe; he helped transform mathematics by the development of calculus; and he established some of the basic laws of modern physics.

Part of the explanation of his versatility lies in the workings of the scientific community at the time. Newton was a retiring man who got into fierce arguments with such prominent contemporaries as the English physicist Robert Hooke, who was studying gravity, and the German "universal man," Liebniz, who was working on calculus. Had it not been for his active participation in the Royal Society of London and the effort that was needed to demonstrate his views to the membership, Newton might never have pursued his researches to their conclusion. He disliked the give-and-take but felt forced in self-justification to prepare some of his most important papers for meetings of the society. There could be no better indication of how important it was that science had created its own institutions and its own competitiveness.

It was to refute another rival, the Cartesian approach to science, which was then much admired, that Newton wrote his masterpiece, *The Mathematical Principles of Natural Philosophy* (1687), usually referred to by the first word of its Latin title, the *Principia.* This was the last widely influential book in European history to be written in Latin, still the international language of scholarship, and useful to Newton because he was determined to have as many experts as possible see his refutation of Descartes's methods. In contrast to the Frenchman, who had placed such emphasis on the powers of the mind, on pure reason, he felt that mere hypotheses, constructions of logic and words, were not the tools of a true scientist. As he put it in a celebrated phrase, *"Hypotheses non fingo"* ("I do not posit hypotheses"), because everything he said was proved by experiment or by mathematics.

The most dramatic of his findings was the solution to the ancient problem of motion. He stated his system in three laws: first, in the absence of force, motion continues in a straight line; second, the rate of change of the motion is determined by the forces acting on it (for example friction); and third, action and reaction between two bodies are equal and opposite. To arrive at these laws, he defined the concepts of mass, inertia, and force in relation to velocity and acceleration as we know them today.

Newton extended these principles to the entire universe by demonstrating that his laws govern the motions of the moon and planets too. Using the concept of gravity, he provided the explanation of the movement of objects in space that is the foundation for current space travel. There is a balance, he said, between the earth's pull on the moon and the forward motion of the satellite, which would continue in a straight line were it not for the earth's gravity. Consequently the moon moves in an elliptical orbit in which neither gravity nor inertia gains control. The same pattern is followed by the planets around the sun. In one of his most elegant insights, Newton described the attraction mathematically in what is known as the inverse square law: gravitational force varies inversely as the square of the distance between the two bodies.[5] The resultant orbit has to be an ellipse, as Kepler had already discovered.

It was largely on the basis of the uniformity and the systematic impersonal forces Newton described that the view of the universe as a vast machine gained ground. According to this theory, all motion is a result of precise, unvarying, and demonstrable forces. There is a celestial mechanics just like the mechanics that operates on earth. It was not far from this view to the belief that God is a great watchmaker who started the marvelous mechanism going but intervenes only when something goes wrong and needs repair. Newton himself considered the creation of the force of gravity, which is not a *necessary* property of a body, as an indication of God's intervention in the assembling of the physical universe.

These general philosophical implications were as important as the specific discoveries in making Newton one of the idols of his own and the next centuries. Aristocrats, concerned with discipline and stability, could easily interpret the idea that a simple structure underlies all of nature as justification for the hierarchical patterns of government and society that were emerging. The educated applauded Newton's achievements, and the gentry made him one of their own—he was the first scientist to receive a knighthood in England. And only a few decades after the appearance of the *Principia*, Alexander Pope summed up the public feeling in a famous couplet:

> Nature and nature's law lay hid in night;
> God said, "Let Newton be!" and all was
>   light.

Although he also devoted a great deal of energy to mystical and numerological investigations (which he kept strictly separate from his science), Newton still managed to find the time to accomplish much else of immense scientific value. He was the main figure in late-seventeenth-century mathematics, particularly in the study of calculus, and his work on dynamics was a milestone on the subject. Another striking achievement, the lunar explanation of tidal action, was almost an aside in his masterpiece. The differences among various tides allowed him to calculate the mass of the moon—again almost in passing. Finally, his second major work, the *Opticks* (1704), presented an analysis that influenced the study of light for more than a century.

But it was the work on motion and the heavens that won Newton his reputation. So overpowering was his stature that in these fields

---

[5] In other words, the attraction increases much more rapidly than the distance closes. Stated as an equation, where G is the gravitational pull and D the distance between the two bodies, the law is $G \propto 1/D^2$.

the steady progress of 150 years came to a halt for more than half a century after the publication of the *Principia*. There was a general impression that somehow Newton had done it all, that no important problems remained. In large areas of physics and astronomy, no significant advances were made again until the late eighteenth century. There were other reasons for the slowdown—changing patterns in education, the influence of frivolous virtuosos, an inevitable lessening of momentum—but none was so powerful as the reverence for Newton. The professional was as overawed as the aristocrat in the presence of a man who became the intellectual symbol of his own and succeeding ages.

John Locke

The second idol of the late seventeenth and eighteenth centuries, John Locke, was not himself a scientist, but a major reason for his fame was the belief that he had applied a scientific approach to all of knowledge.

Locke also wrote to refute Descartes, whose dualism he rejected in favor of his own theory of knowledge. He believed that at birth man's mind is a *tabula rasa,* a clean slate; contradicting Descartes, he asserted that nothing is inborn or preordained. As a human being grows, he observes and experiences the world. Once he has gathered enough data through his senses, his mind begins to work on them. Then, with the help of his reason, he perceives patterns, discovering the order and harmony that permeate the universe. Locke was convinced that this underlying order exists and that every person, regardless of his individual experiences, must reach the same conclusions about its nature and structure.

This epistemology, elaborated in his *Essay Concerning Human Understanding,* published in 1690, was modeled directly on the example of the scientists. The *tabula rasa* is the counterpart of the principle of doubt, experience corresponds with experimentation, and reason plays the role of the process of generalization. Just as in science a single law appears again and again whatever experiments are performed, so in all knowledge any true principle is universal and will become apparent to every person even though individual lives are different.

Locke's thinking thus included a reverence for scientific method, a reliance on material phenomena and empiricism, and a belief in order. In all these respects, his outlook captured the interest of cultivated readers in the late seventeenth and eighteenth centuries, for he provided them with a theoretical model, built on a rejection of emotion and an elevation of reason, that allowed them to regard their mental equipment and functioning as scientific.

When Locke turned his attention to political thought, he caught the feeling of the times even more directly, because he put into systematic form the views of the English gentry and of many aristocrats throughout Europe. The *Second Treatise of Civil Government,* also published in 1690, was deeply influenced by Hobbes. From his great predecessor Locke took the notion of the state of nature as a state of war and the need for a contract among men to end the anarchy that precedes the establishment of human society. But his conclusions were decidedly different.

Employing the principles of the *Essay Concerning Human Understanding,* Locke asserted that the application of reason to the evidence of politics demonstrates the inalienability of the three rights of an individual: life, liberty, and property. Like Hobbes, he believed that there must be a sovereign power, but he argued that it has no power over these three natural rights of its subjects without their consent. Moreover this consent—for levying taxes, for example—must come from a representative assembly of men of property, such as the English Parliament.

The hero of eighteenth-century thought, John Locke, was almost as familiar from engravings as were warriors and kings. That a man of learning could achieve such fame was an indication of the importance of learning in this society. And the emphasis in the portrait is entirely on Locke's simplicity, intelligence, and straightforwardness—the marks of his work.
(Photo: New York Public Library/Picture Collection)

The affirmation of property as one of the three natural rights (it was changed to "the pursuit of happiness" in the more egalitarian American Declaration of Independence) is significant. Here Locke revealed himself as the spokesman of the gentry. Only people with a tangible stake in their country have any right to control its destiny, and that stake must be protected as surely as their life and liberty. The concept of liberty remained vague, but it was taken to imply the sorts of freedom, such as freedom from arbitrary arrest, that were outlined in the English Bill of Rights. All Hobbes allowed a man to do was protect his life. Locke permitted the overthrow of the sovereign power if it infringed on the subjects' rights—a course the English followed with James II and the Americans with George III.

Locke's intentions were admirable—he had a higher opinion of human nature than Hobbes, he admitted that truth was hard to find, and he tried, as Hobbes had not, to curb the potential for tyranny in sovereign power. His prime concern was to defend the individual against the state, a concern that has remained essential to liberal thought ever since. But it is important to realize that Locke's views served the elite better than the mass of society because of his emphasis on property. With Locke to reassure them, the upper classes imposed their preferences and control on eighteenth-century European civilization.

The situation of Europe's aristocracy had improved markedly by 1715. Half a century earlier, in the wake of a series of grave political and intellectual crises, the ancient power of the nobles, based on their local independence, had seemed radically weakened in the face of the bureaucratic state. But as the political structures of the various European countries settled into new and stable forms, it became clear that their cooperation was essential for the running of a state, and they adapted to this new role with remarkable skill. Under the absolute monarchs they became the allies and indispensable agents of government; in other countries they dominated events. In either case they came out of the transition with their power intact and even enhanced.

Thus regardless of the relative levels of order and uniformity the various regimes achieved and regardless of their degrees of absolutism, they were alike in their reliance on aristocrats. No government, however centralized, could function without the participation of the upper classes, and in most states—Peter I's Russia excepted—they took up their transformed role willingly. This new security of aristocratic power, both political and social, showed that the age-old conflict between princes and nobles had been resolved.

Moreover the qualities of order, discipline, and stability that the elite represented and that rulers sought were making themselves felt in culture as well as in society and politics. Changes in taste and even developments in science and philosophy were seen as reinforcing the aristocratic world view. The elaborately mannered life led by this newly invigorated ruling class reflected its confidence. And its remarkable society was to last for a glittering century until its frivolities and arrogance fell before a movement that demanded a better life not merely for the few but for all.

RECOMMENDED READING

Sources

*Locke, John. *An Essay Concerning Human Understanding.* A. D. Woozley (ed.). 1964. This study of the nature of the mind appeared at the same time as Locke's *Two Treatises of Government* and presents the philosophical basis of his political ideas.

Saint-Simon, Louis. *Historical Memoirs.* Lucy Norton (ed. and tr.). 2 vols. 1967 and 1968. Lively memoirs of the court at Versailles.

Studies

Adam, Antoine. *Grandeur and Illusion: French Literature and Society 1600–1715.* Herbert Tint (tr.). 1972. A clear and comprehensive survey of French literature and its social setting during the seventeenth century, with special attention to Classicism.

Baxter, S. B. *William III and the Defense of European Liberty, 1650–1702.* 1966. A solid and straightforward account of the career of the ruler of both England and the Netherlands.

*Carsten, F. L. *The Origins of Prussia.* 1954. The standard account of the background to the reign of the great elector, Frederick William, and the best short history of his accomplishments and the rise of the Junkers.

Chandler, David. *Marlborough as Military Commander.* 1973. A fluent and energetic narrative of military affairs, centered around the colorful career of a highly intelligent general.

Cranston, Maurice. *John Locke.* 1957. The best basic introduction to the man and his ideas. (See also MacPherson.)

*Goubert, Pierre. *Louis XIV and Twenty Million Frenchmen.* Anne Carter (tr.). 1970. This is not so much a history of the king's reign as a study of the nature of French society and politics during Louis's rule.

Hatton, R. N. *Charles XII of Sweden.* 1968. A thorough and well-written biography that does justice to a dramatic life.

*——. *Europe in the Age of Louis XIV.* 1969. A beautifully illustrated and vividly interpretive history of the period that Louis dominated.

*Hazard, Paul. *The European Mind, 1680–1715.* J. L. May (tr.). 1963. This stimulating interpretation of the intellectual change that took place around 1700 has become a classic work in the history of thought.

Lougee, Carolyn C. *Le Paradis des Femmes: Women, Salons, and Social Stratification in Seventeenth-Century France.* 1976. An interesting study of the place of women and the importance of salons in French high society.

*MacPherson, C. B. *The Political Theory of Possessive Individualism: Hobbes to Locke.* 1962. This provocative, Marxist-inspired study of the importance of property in English political thought views Locke's ideas in largely economic terms.

Manuel, Frank. *A Portrait of Isaac Newton.* 1968. Using psychoanalytic methods, this book shows Newton and the pressures he felt in a very different light from the usual analyses that pay tribute to genius.

*Plumb, J. H. *The Growth of Political Stability in England, 1675–1725.* 1969. A brief, lucid survey of the developments in English politics that helped create Britain's modern parliamentary democracy.

Rowen, Herbert H. *The King's State: Proprietary Dynasticism in Early Modern France.* 1980. A lucid study of the origins and elaboration of the theory by which Louis XIV ruled France.

Stoye, John. *The Siege of Vienna.* 1964. An exciting account of the last great threat to Christian Europe from the Turkish empire.

*Sumner, B. H. *Peter the Great and the Emergence of Russia*. 1950. This short but comprehensive book is the best introduction to Russian history in this period.

*Westfall, Richard S. *The Construction of Modern Science: Mechanisms and Mechanics*. 1971. The clearest account of the scientific developments of the sev-

enteenth century, and of Newton's climactic achievements, by a biographer of Newton.

*Wolf, J. B. *Louis XIV*. 1968. The standard biography, with particularly full discussions of political affairs.

*Available in paperback.

EXPERIENCES OF DAILY LIFE

The Peasant Household

Most peasant households in Western Europe practiced subsistence agriculture. Their foremost objective was to provide their own food. But this did not mean that the household produced only for itself, since it had to meet various external obligations as well: royal taxes, rents, seigneurial dues, the tithe to the local church, and interest on debts that invariably accumulated. In addition, even if this meant going hungry at certain times, the household had to set aside a portion of its crop as seed for next year's planting. Because traditional methods were relatively inefficient and yields so low, this seed could amount to one-fifth of the crop.

Every peasant household hoped to control enough land to ensure its subsistence and meet its obligations. Ideally it would own this land. But most peasants did not own enough land and were obliged to rent additional plots or enter into sharecropping arrangements. Peasants therefore hated to see the consolidation of small plots into large farms. For this meant that the small plots they could one day afford to buy or lease were becoming scarcer.

When the land that peasants owned and rented did not meet their needs, they employed various survival strategies. They could hire out as laborers on larger farms, or migrate for a

Peasants harvest their crops.   (The Bettmann Archive)

Landleute bei der Ernte. (Aus dem Bauernleben des XVII. Jahrh.)

638

Zeitgenössischer anonym. Stich.

few weeks to wine-growing areas to help with that harvest. They might practice a simple rural handicraft, or weave cloth for merchants on the "putting out" system. Some resorted to illegal means such as hunting game on restricted land, or smuggling salt or other taxable consumer goods. When all else failed they might be forced to take to the road temporarily as beggars.

In their precarious situation, peasants drew strength from their own community. Villages usually possessed common lands open to all their residents. Poorer peasants could forage for fuel, building materials, nuts and berries. Everyone could inexpensively graze whatever livestock they had. Since villagers generally planted the same crops at the same times, after the harvest livestock might be freed to roam over the arable fields and graze on the stubble.

A peasant holding was not a solitary enterprise, but depended on a partnership of husband and wife. Peasants in the eighteenth century married late—women averaged about 25 years of age, men 27. They waited until they had accumulated enough resources to establish their own household, including the bride's dowry. Later, if tragedy struck and a spouse died, the survivor would quickly remarry if that was at all possible.

Men looked for physical vigor and domestic skill in their prospective brides. "When a girl knows how to knead and bake bread, she is fit to wed," went a French proverb. In village rituals on the wedding day, the bride might be given a broom, a distaff, and a cooking pot, which she was expected to use economically and efficiently. "Whoever has an oversized frying pan, a fine sieve, and a spendthrift wife, stands exposed in the street," stated another proverb.

In peasant households the wife's domain was inside the cottage, where she looked after cooking, repair of clothing, and the like. She might spend her evenings spinning yarn. Wives were also responsible for the small vegetable gardens that peasant families often maintained, and for their precious hens and chickens. Vegetables, eggs, and an occasional chicken were rarely meant for the family's own consumption, however. They were sources of cash to help meet some of its obligations.

The husband's work was outside. He gathered the fuel, and if the household was fortunate enough to own cattle or draft animals, he was responsible for their care. His main tasks were in the fields: plowing the land, planting the fields, and nurturing the crops—two or three a year, depending on the system of crop rotation followed. The husband supervised the harvest, but everyone in the family lent a hand. He might wield the heavy sickle, while his wife followed with a scythe, and the children gathered the sheaves of grain.

There was scarcely such a luxury as privacy in a peasant household. Most cottages consisted of one poorly ventilated room or at most two, which sometimes had to be shared with farm animals. Nor could there be privacy from the ever-watchful eyes of the neighbors. Men were supposed to be the masters and "wear the pants" in their families, ("The hat must master the bonnet," ran a Breton proverb). If a husband let himself be dominated or henpecked by his wife, he could expect to be mocked. He might be jeeringly "serenaded" by his fellow villagers in a ceremony called a *charivari,* or even made to ride around on a donkey sitting backward. By the same token a husband who beat his wife was usually looked down on, notwithstanding proverbs that seemed to justify wife-beating ("From a donkey, a walnut, or a wife expect no good unless you've a stick in your hand").

When middle-class folklore collectors went out to the countryside in the nineteenth century, they were shocked not only by the material squalor of peasant life but also by the social behavior of peasants. When strolling around on a Sunday, for example, the husband might walk ahead of his wife. At home the wife spent mealtime on her feet serving the men, neither sitting nor eating herself. To observers from the city this seemed a form of male tyranny and boorishess, which indicated a lack of respect or affection for the wife. But was that necessarily the case? The wife considered it her duty to cook and serve a hot and hearty meal, and took pride in doing it well. By contrast, in bourgeois households servants were available to do such work, and cooking and serving were held in low esteem.

Index

Page numbers in *italics* refer to illustrations or maps.

Color Illustration Sources

About the Authors

Mortimer Chambers is Professor of History at the University of California at Los Angeles. He was a Rhodes scholar from 1949–1952 and received an M.A. from Wadham College, Oxford, in 1955 after obtaining his doctorate from Harvard University in 1954. He has taught at Harvard University (1954–1955) and the University of Chicago (1955–1958). He was Visiting Professor at the University of British Columbia in 1958 and the State University of New York at Buffalo in 1971. A specialist in Greek and Roman history, he is coauthor of *Aristotle's History of Athenian Democracy* (1962) and editor of a series of essays entitled *The Fall of Rome* (1963). He has contributed articles to the *American Historical Review* and *Classical Philosophy* as well as other journals.

Raymond Grew is Professor of History at the University of Michigan. He earned both his M.A. (1952) and Ph.D (1957) from Harvard University in the field of modern European history. He was a Fulbright Fellow to Italy (1954–1955), Guggenheim Fellow (1968–1969), Director of Studies at the Ecoles des Hautes Etudes en Sciences Sociales in Paris (1976), and a Fellow of the National Endowment for the Humanities (1979). In 1962 he received the Chester Higby Prize from the American Historical Association, and in 1963 the Italian government awarded him the Unita d'Italia Prize. He is an active member of the A.H.A., the Society for Italian Historical Studies, and the Society for French Historical Studies. He is the author of *A Sterner Plan for Italian Unity* (1963), edited *Crises of Development in Europe and the United States* (1978), and is presently the editor of *Comparative Studies in Society and History*. His articles and reviews have appeared in a number of European and American journals.

David Herlihy, Mary and Barnaby Keeney Professor of History at Brown University, is the author of several books on the economic and social history of the Middle Ages: *Pisa in the Early Renaissance, A Study of Urban Growth* (1958), *Medieval and Renaissance Pistoia, The Social History of an Italian Town* (1968), and *Medieval Culture and Society* (1968). He received his M.A. from the Catholic University of America in 1953 and his Ph.D. from Yale University in 1956. He is former president of both the American Catholic Historical Association and the Midwest Medieval Conference. He was a fellow of the Guggenheim Foundation (1962–1963), the American Council of Learned Societies (1966–1967), and the Center for Advanced Study in the Behavioral Sciences (1972–1973). His articles have appeared in *Speculum, Economic History Review,* and *Annales-Economies-Sociétiés-Civilisations.*

Theodore K. Rabb is Professor of History at Princeton University. A specialist in early modern European history, he received his B.A. degree from Oxford University (1958) and his Ph.D. from Princeton University (1961). He was a Guggenheim Fellow in 1970. He has taught at Harvard University, Stanford University, Northwestern University, Johns Hopkins University, and the State University of New York at Binghamton. He is co-founder and coeditor of the *Journal of Interdisciplinary History,* a member of the National Research Council, and a fellow of the Royal Historical Society. He is the author of *The Thirty Years' War* (1964) and *Enterprise and Empire* (1967), and coeditor of *Action and Conviction in Early Modern Europe* (1969). He has contributed articles to the *American Historical Review, Journal of Modern History, Commentary, Past & Present,* the *Economic History Review,* and other journals.

Isser Woloch is Professor of History at Columbia University. He received his Ph.D. (1965) from Princeton University in the field of eighteenth- and nineteenth-century European history. He has taught at Indiana University and at the University of California at Los Angeles where, in 1967, he received a Distinguished Teaching Citation. He has been a fellow of the A.C.L.S., the National Endowment for the Humanities, the Guggenheim Foundation, and the Institute for Advanced Study at Princeton. His publications include *Jacobin Legacy: The Democratic Movement Under the Directory* (1970), *The Peasantry in the Old Regime: Conditions and Protests* (1970), *The French Veteran from the Revolution to the Restoration* (1979), and *Eighteenth-Century Europe: Tradition and Progress, 1715–1789* (1982).

A Note on the Type

The text of this book has been set via computer-driven cathode-ray tube in a typeface named Bembo. The roman is a copy of a letter cut for the celebrated Venetian printer Aldus Manutius by Francesco Griffo, and first used in Cardinal Bembo's *De Aetna* of 1495—hence the name of the revival. Griffo's type is now generally recognized, thanks to the researches of Mr. Stanley Morison, to be the first of the old face group of types. The companion italic is an adaptation of the chancery script type designed by the Roman calligrapher and printer Lodovico degli Arrighi, called Vincentino, and used by him during the 1520s.

Composed by
Ruttle, Shaw & Wetherill, Inc.
Fort Washington, Pennsylvania

Printed and bound by
Rand McNally & Company
Taunton, Massachusetts

Inserts printed by
Universal Printing Co., Inc.

Text and cover design by Leon Bolognese